GW01157749

# Excavations 1999

# Excavations 1999:
# Summary accounts of archaeological excavations in Ireland

Edited by Isabel Bennett

Wordwell

Wordwell Ltd

First published in 2000
Wordwell Ltd
PO Box 69, Bray, Co. Wicklow
Copyright © The contributors

All rights reserved. No part of this book may be reprinted or reproduced or utilised in any electronic, mechanical or other means, now known or hereafter invented, including photocopying and recording, or otherwise without either the prior written consent of the publishers or a licence permitting restricted copying in Ireland issued by the Irish Copyright Licensing Agency Ltd, The Writers' Centre, 19 Parnell Square, Dublin 1.

ISBN 1-869857-461

British Library Cataloguing-in-Publication Data.
A catalogue record for this book is available from the British Library.

Typeset in Ireland by Wordwell Ltd
Origination by Impress

Cover design: Rachel Dunne

Copy editor: Aisling Flood

Printed by Brookfield Printing Company

# INTRODUCTION

By now those of you who are familiar with the *Excavations* bulletin will know about the phenomenal rise in the numbers of excavations that take place in the country each year, and 1999 is no exception. In 1987, when Clare Cotter compiled the bulletin for that year, there were 63 entries. In 1999 there were over 900. Indeed, in the past year alone the number issued has increased by 200. Can this go on? The indications for 2000 are that it will.

There was a very positive response to *Excavations 1998*, and especially to the index compiled by Eoin Bairéad, which many people have found very useful, not least myself. It will surely become a collector's item, and I wish to thank Eoin for all the work he put into it.

This year, once again, all thirty-two counties are represented, although some by very few sites (Carlow, Longford and Tyrone with two entries each, Fermanagh and Laois with three). In contrast, reflecting the road-development and building boom in the urban areas, there are 121 entries for Dublin and 102 for Louth. Kildare has the third-highest number, with 76 entries, beating Limerick (67) and Cork (53).

The compilation of the bulletin is now a year-long process, as so many excavations take place spread out over the whole year. Therefore I would be grateful if those who have directed excavations would send their summary entries to me shortly after the work has been completed, as this helps to speed up the production considerably.

## ACKNOWLEDGEMENTS

It is the editor's pleasure once again to thank all the people who helped make this publication possible. Thanks to the members of staff of the National Monuments and Historic Properties Service of *Dúchas*, especially to Chief Archaeologist David Sweetman, Edward Bourke, Tom Condit and the staff of the Excavation Licensing Section, who provided information on all licences issued in the Republic, and to Declan Hurl, of Built Heritage, EHS, who once again provided all the necessary initial information on the sites excavated in Northern Ireland.

I also thank the Heritage Council, which provided a grant some years ago for computer equipment, some of which is still giving Trojan service in carrying out this work.

*Agus, mar is gnáth, buíochas do Eoin, Áedán agus Seán Ó hÚallacháin.*

# Index of sites

| No. | Townland | County | Type | Excavator |
|---|---|---|---|---|
| 1. | Aghnahough | Antrim | Stone alignment | Eoin Halpin |
| 2. | Steeple, Antrim | Antrim | Ecclesiastical | Cormac McSparron |
| 3. | Toberdowney, Ballynure | Antrim | No archaeological significance | Alan Reilly |
| 4. | Ballyutoag | Antrim | Neolithic material | Cormac McSparron |
| 5. | Gordon Street, Belfast | Antrim | Urban post-medieval | Ruairí Ó Baoill |
| 6. | Waring Street, Belfast | Antrim | Urban post-medieval | Paul Logue |
| 7. | British | Antrim | No archaeological significance | Audrey Gahan |
| 8. | Irish Quarter West, Carrickfergus | Antrim | Urban post-medieval | Alan Reilly |
| 9. | 1–3 Joymount, Carrickfergus | Antrim | Town wall | Cia McConway |
| 10. | Joymount Manse, Carrickfergus | Antrim | Medieval ditch | Audrey Gahan |
| 11. | Crookedstone | Antrim | No archaeological significance | Norman Crothers |
| 12. | Drumakeely and Dundermot | Antrim | No archaeological significance | Cormac McSparron |
| 13. | Western Quay Wall, Glenarm | Antrim | No archaeological significance | Cia McConway |
| 14. | Larne (Port of) | Antrim | Mesolithic/Bronze Age | Cia McConway |
| 15. | Hightown Road, Mallusk, Phase 1A | Antrim | Early Bronze Age | Cia McConway |
| 16. | Ballyhenry, Newtownabbey | Antrim | Multi-period | Ciara McManus |
| 17. | Northern Counties Hotel, Main Street, Portrush | Antrim | No archaeological significance | Deirdre Murphy and Malachy Conway |
| 18. | Tullaghgarley | Antrim | Souterrain | Liam McQuillan and Chris Long |
| 19. | English Street, Armagh | Armagh | No archaeological significance | Eoin Halpin |
| 20. | Drumilly Bawn, Drumilly Demesne, Ballytyrone | Armagh | Walled garden | Alan Reilly |
| 21. | Navan Fort, Navan | Armagh | Iron Age enclosure | C.J. Lynn |
| 22. | Timakeel | Armagh | No archaeological significance | Cormac McSparron |
| 23. | Haughey's Fort, Tray | Armagh | Late Bronze Age enclosure | J.P. Mallory |
| 24. | Carlow | Carlow | Adjacent to rath | Cóilín Ó Drisceoil |
| 25. | Cox's Lane, Carlow | Carlow | Urban medieval | Christine Tarbett-Buckley |
| 26. | Leitir, Bailieborough | Cavan | Ringfort | Malachy Conway |
| 27. | 7 Farnham Street, Cavan | Cavan | No archaeological significance | Martin E. Byrne |
| 28. | Main Street/Gallows Hill (rear of), Cavan | Cavan | No archaeological significance | Martin E. Byrne |
| 29. | Cootehill Sewerage Improvement Scheme | Cavan | Monitoring | Judith Carroll |
| 30. | Cootehill | Cavan | Possible *fulacht fiadh* | Judith Carroll |
| 31. | Lislea | Cavan | Adjacent to ringfort site | Martin E. Byrne |
| 32. | Lismeen | Cavan | Proximity to rath | Rónán Swan |
| 33. | Ballycasey to Dromoland Road Scheme, N18/19 | Clare | Monitoring | Christine Grant |
| 34. | Ballycasey More, Site 44 | Clare | Field system | Thaddeus C. Breen |
| 35. | Ballyconneely | Clare | Middle/Late Bronze Age cemetery and ritual site | Christopher Read |
| 36. | Ballyduffbeg | Clare | No archaeological significance | Paul Stevens |
| 37. | Ballyhannan South | Clare | Vicinity of enclosure | Kenneth Wiggins |
| 38. | Cathair Mór, Ballylabban | Clare | Stone fort | Martin Fitzpatrick |
| 39. | Ballynacragga (Area 11) | Clare | No archaeological significance | Anne Connolly |
| 40. | Ballynacragga (Area 13) | Clare | No archaeological significance | Anne Connolly |
| 41. | Ballynacragga | Clare | No archaeological significance | Christopher Read |
| 42. | Ballynacragga (Area 17) | Clare | No archaeological significance | Anne Connolly |
| 43. | Ballynaliddy | Clare | No archaeological significance | Anne Connolly |
| 44. | Ballysheenbeg | Clare | No archaeological significance | Christine Grant |
| 45. | Bunratty West | Clare | No archaeological significance | Ken Hanley |

| | | | | |
|---|---|---|---|---|
| 46. | Carrigoran (Area 18) | Clare | Relict field system | Thaddeus C. Breen |
| 47. | Carrigoran, Area EX1 | Clare | Multi-phased | Fiona Reilly |
| 48. | Clonmoney West (Site M33) | Clare | Well and trackway | Carleton Jones |
| 49. | Cloonaherna | Clare | Stone-built enclosure | Damian Finn |
| 50. | Donmacfelim, Doolin | Clare | No archaeological significance | Christopher Read |
| 51. | Gortatogher | Clare | Enclosure (site of) | Ken Hanley |
| 52. | Gortnaboul | Clare | No archaeological significance | Ken Hanley |
| 53. | Gortnaboul | Clare | *Fulachta fiadh* | Ken Hanley |
| 54. | Killaloe Cathedral, Shantraud, Killaloe | Clare | Romanesque cathedral doorway | Celie O Rahilly |
| 55. | Kilquane/Ballylannidy | Clare | No archaeological significance | Richard Crumlish |
| 56. | Knocknaranhy | Clare | *Fulacht fiadh* | Fiona Rooney |
| 57. | Latoon South, Area 1 | Clare | Medieval occupation | Christine Grant |
| 58. | Lisdoonvarna Water Supply Scheme | Clare | *Fulachta fiadh* | Ken Hanley |
| 59. | Liskett | Clare | No archaeological significance | Christopher Read |
| 60. | Lismoher | Clare | No archaeological significance | Christine Grant |
| 61. | Dromoland Castle, Newmarket-on-Fergus | Clare | Adjacent to castle | Cóilín Ó Drisceoil |
| 62. | Parknabinnia | Clare | Court tomb | Carleton Jones |
| 63. | Parknabinnia | Clare | Wedge tomb | Ann Lynch |
| 64. | Main Street, Quin | Clare | Medieval settlement | Brian Hodkinson |
| 65. | Rosmadda West | Clare | Earthwork (environs of) | Ken Hanley |
| 66. | Smithstown Industrial Estate, Shannon | Clare | Earth and stone-built enclosure | Damian Finn |
| 67. | Sixmilebridge | Clare | No archaeological significance | Laurence Dunne |
| 68. | Sixmilebridge | Clare | No archaeological significance | Rose M. Cleary |
| 69. | Main Street, Sixmilebridge | Clare | Burnt spread/*fulacht fiadh*? | Ken Hanley |
| 70. | Tuamgraney | Clare | No archaeological significance | Fiona Reilly |
| 71. | Currane Hill, Ballineen | Cork | No archaeological significance | Emer Dennehy |
| 72. | Ballyhooly South | Cork | Close to earthwork | Eamonn Cotter |
| 73. | Ballymague | Cork | Ringfort | Sheila Lane |
| 74. | Ballynoe | Cork | Medieval church | Eamonn Cotter |
| 75. | Ballyrisode | Cork | Early Bronze Age copper mine | William O'Brien |
| 76. | MacSweeny Quay, Bandon | Cork | Urban | Eamonn Cotter |
| 77. | Banduff | Cork | Ringfort | Sheila Lane |
| 78. | *La Surveillante*, Bantry Bay | Cork | Historic shipwreck | Colin Breen |
| 79. | Castle Warren, Barnahely | Cork | Tower-house, bawn etc. | Mary O'Donnell |
| 80. | Brooklodge | Cork | Corn-drying kiln | Mark Clinton |
| 81. | Butlerstown Little | Cork | *Fulacht fiadh* | Tim Coughlan |
| 82. | Caheravart | Cork | Possible ringfort | Sheila Lane |
| 83. | Caherlag/Ballincollig | Cork | Monitoring | Tim Coughlan |
| 84. | Barryscourt Castle, Carrigtwohill | Cork | Late medieval castle | Dave Pollock |
| 85. | Castleview | Cork | *Fulacht fiadh* and stone-lined features | Margaret McCarthy |
| 86. | Corbally | Cork | Adjacent to ringfort | Jacinta Kiely |
| 87. | 3 Barrack Street, Cork | Cork | Urban medieval | Sheila Lane |
| 88. | 25–26 Barrack Street, Cork | Cork | Urban | Rose M. Cleary |
| 89. | St Fin Barre's Cathedral, Bishop's Street, Cork | Cork | Early ecclesiastical | Sheila Lane |
| 90. | Blackpool By-pass, Cork | Cork | Urban industrial | Catryn Power |
| 91. | Boreenmanna/Blackrock/Ballinlough/Centre Park Road, Cork | Cork | Urban | Máire Ní Loingsigh |
| 92. | Christ Church Lane/Hanover Street/Kift's Lane/Little Cross Street/St Augustine Street/St Patrick's Street/Emmet Place/Tuckey Street, Cork | Cork | Urban medieval and post-medieval | Catryn Power |

| | | | | |
|---|---|---|---|---|
| 93. | Half Moon Street, Cork | Cork | Urban medieval | Sheila Lane |
| 94. | Leitrim Street, Cork | Cork | Urban medieval | Sheila Lane |
| 95. | 23–24 Main Street North, Cork | Cork | Urban | Rose M. Cleary |
| 96. | City Car Park, Main Street South, Cork | Cork | Urban medieval | Maurice Hurley |
| 97. | 26 Main Street South, Cork | Cork | Urban medieval | Sheila Lane |
| 98. | Saint Mary's of the Isle, Cork | Cork | Urban medieval/industrial | Catryn Power |
| 99. | 114–115 Shandon Street, Cork | Cork | Urban | Rose M. Cleary |
| 100. | 13–14 Travers Street/ 12 Cove Street, Cork | Cork | Urban | Rose M. Cleary |
| 101. | Washington Street/ South Main Street/ Liberty Street, Cork | Cork | Urban | Mary O'Donnell |
| 102. | 15–16 Watercourse Road, Cork | Cork | Urban | Rose M. Cleary |
| 103. | Crumpane | Cork | Bronze Age copper mine | William O'Brien |
| 104. | Foildarrig | Cork | Vicinity of castle | Eamonn Cotter |
| 105. | Kilcoe Castle, Kilcoe | Cork | Tower-house | Jacinta Kiely |
| 106. | Killeens | Cork | *Fulacht fiadh* | Tim Coughlan |
| 107. | Catholic Walk Lower, Kinsale | Cork | Urban medieval | Sheila Lane |
| 108. | Church Square, Kinsale | Cork | Urban medieval | Sheila Lane |
| 109. | Church Square, Kinsale | Cork | Urban medieval | Sheila Lane |
| 110. | Market Lane, Kinsale | Cork | Urban medieval | Sheila Lane |
| 111. | Mill Hill, Kinsale | Cork | Urban medieval | Tony Cummins |
| 112. | The Ramparts, Kinsale | Cork | Urban medieval | Sheila Lane |
| 113. | Knockanenagark/ Tullig More | Cork | No archaeological significance | Mary O'Donnell |
| 114. | Blackrock Castle, Mahon | Cork | Tower-house | Sheila Lane |
| 115. | Meenane | Cork | *Fulacht fiadh* | Eamonn Cotter |
| 116. | Mitchellsfort | Cork | *Fulachta fiadh* | Eamonn Cotter |
| 117. | Monard | Cork | *Fulacht fiadh* | Tim Coughlan |
| 118. | Moneycusker | Cork | No archaeological significance | Eamonn Cotter |
| 119. | Fort Hill, Moneygurney | Cork | Ringfort | Meriel McClatchie |
| 120. | Rathpeacon | Cork | Site of standing stone | Tim Coughlan |
| 121. | Ringacoltig | Cork | Possible enclosure site | Martin E. Byrne |
| 122. | 16 South Main Street, (rear of) Youghal | Cork | No archaeological significance | Meriel McClatchie |
| 123. | 59 South Main Street/ Quay Lane, Youghal | Cork | Urban medieval | Paul Stevens |
| 124. | 34 The Diamond, Coleraine | Derry | Urban | Deirdre Murphy |
| 125. | St Mary's Dominican Priory, Hanover Place, Coleraine | Derry | Medieval priory and graveyard | Cia McConway |
| 126. | Kingsgate Street, Coleraine | Derry | Urban multi-period | Alan Reilly |
| 127. | River Bann, Coleraine | Derry | Underwater dock | Donal Boland |
| 128. | Bishop's Street Without, Derry | Derry | 17th-century urban | Paul Logue |
| 129. | Millennium Theatre, Derry | Derry | 17th-century city ramparts | Paul Logue |
| 130. | Magheramenagh | Derry | Souterrain, prehistoric house | Alan Reilly |
| 131. | Movanagher | Derry | 17th-century bawn and village | Audrey Horning |
| 132. | Quigley's Point, Carrowkeel | Donegal | No archaeological significance | Declan Moore |
| 133. | Carrowkeel | Donegal | No archaeological significance | Declan Moore |
| 134. | Clar–Barnesmore Road Realignment | Donegal | Monitoring | Declan Moore |
| 135. | Culdaff | Donegal | No archaeological significance | Richard Crumlish |
| 136. | Doonan/Mullins | Donegal | No archaeological significance | Donald Murphy |
| 137. | Eleven Ballyboes | Donegal | Souterrain | Richard Crumlish |
| 138. | Friarbush | Donegal | No archaeological significance | Declan Moore |
| 139. | Greencastle | Donegal | Adjacent to church | Dermot G. Moore |

| | | | | |
|---|---|---|---|---|
| 140. | Keadew Lower | Donegal | Drying kiln | Declan Moore |
| 141. | Magheracar | Donegal | Adjacent to church site | Christiaan Corlett |
| 142. | Tank Brea, Ramelton | Donegal | No archaeological significance | Eoin Halpin |
| 143. | The Quays, Ramelton | Donegal | Post-medieval | Declan Moore |
| 144. | Kilbarron | Donegal | No archaeological significance | Malachy Conway |
| 145. | Stranorlar/Ballybofey | Donegal | No archaeological significance | Fiona Rooney |
| 146. | Jordan's Castle, Ardglass | Down | Urban medieval | Mark Gardiner |
| 147. | Ballynahatty 5, Ballynahatty | Down | Late Neolithic ritual timber circle enclosure and settings | Barrie Hartwell |
| 148. | Drumadonnell | Down | Early Christian house | Cormac McSparron |
| 149. | Dunmore: 1 | Down | Burnt mounds | Audrey Gahan |
| 150. | Dunmore: 2 | Down | Possible Neolithic house | Audrey Gahan |
| 151. | Inch and Ballyrenan: 1 | Down | Multi-period landscape | Liam McQuillan |
| 152. | Mount Alexander, | Down | No archaeological significance | Alan Reilly |
| 153. | Nendrum, Mahee Island | Down | Early Christian tide mill | Norman Crothers and Tom McErlean |
| 154. | Mourne Conduit | Down | Monitoring | Audrey Gahan |
| 155. | Bagenal's Castle (McCann's Bakery), Newry | Down | Adjacent to tower-house | Dermot G. Moore |
| 156. | Bagenal's Castle, Newry | Down | Fortification | Liam McQuillan |
| 157. | River Road/Sugar Island, Newry | Down | Flood alleviation scheme | Dermot G. Moore |
| 158. | Newtownards | Down | Urban/intertidal monitoring | Alan Reilly |
| 159. | Mill Street/George's Hill, Balbriggan, Dublin | Dublin | Environs of 18th-century cotton mill | Daniel Leo Swan |
| 160. | Grange Abbey Church and House, Baldoyle | Dublin | Medieval grange and late 17th-century dwelling | Linzi Simpson |
| 161. | Ballough to Kilshane Gas Pipeline | Dublin | Various | Malachy Conway |
| 162. | Rosepark, Balrothery | Dublin | Enclsoures and associated landscape | Christine Baker and Rónán Swan |
| 163. | Rosepark, Balrothery | Dublin | Enclsoures and associated landscape | Christine Baker |
| 164. | St Peter's Church, Balrothery | Dublin | Site of medieval church and graveyard | Donald Murphy |
| 165. | Blanchardstown College, Business and Technology Park, Buzzardstown and Corduff, Blanchardstown | Dublin | No archaeological significance | Malachy Conway |
| 166. | Esso Centenary Service Station, Cabinteely | Dublin | Early Christian enclosed cemetery | Malachy Conway |
| 167. | Cabinteely | Dublin | Cemetery | Ken Hanley |
| 168. | Bank of Ireland, Old Bray Road, Cabinteely | Dublin | No archaeological significance | Malachy Conway |
| 169. | Cherrywood Science and Technology Park, Cherrywood | Dublin | Archaeological landscape | John Ó Néill |
| 170. | Kilcarberry Distribution Park, Nangor, Clondalkin | Dublin | Adjacent to monuments | Dermot Nelis |
| 171. | Old Mill Road/Nangor Road, Clondalkin | Dublin | Precinct of monastic site | Rosanne Meenan |
| 172. | Common | Dublin | Environs of possible ringfort and graveyard | Malachy Conway |
| 173. | 1–7 St Agnes Road, Crumlin | Dublin | Medieval church enclosure | Donald Murphy |
| 174. | 41–42 Barnhill Road (rear of), Dalkey | Dublin | Urban | Avril Purcell |
| 175. | Courtyard, St Patrick's Road, Dalkey | Dublin | No archaeological significance | Avril Purcell |
| 176. | Turvey Avenue, Donabate | Dublin | Medieval/post-medieval | Claire Walsh |
| 177. | All Hallows, Church Avenue, Drumcondra | Dublin | Post-medieval | Martin Reid |

| | | | | |
|---|---|---|---|---|
| 178. | 43–45 Abbey Street, Dublin | Dublin | Urban medieval, post-medieval | Helen Kehoe |
| 179. | 42–51 Benburb Street, Dublin | Dublin | Urban | Avril Purcell |
| 180. | 35–36 Bow Street, Dublin | Dublin | Urban | Claire Walsh |
| 181. | Napper Tandy public house, Bride Street, Dublin | Dublin | Urban | Dermot Nelis |
| 182. | Iveagh Trust, Bull Alley Street/Bride Street, Dublin | Dublin | Medieval activity | Audrey Gahan |
| 183. | St Mary's Abbey, 133a Capel Street/23 Mary Street Little, Dublin | Dublin | Site of medieval abbey | Rónán Swan |
| 184. | Carman's Hall, Dublin | Dublin | Medieval | Claire Walsh |
| 185. | Cecilia House, 3 Cecilia Street, Dublin | Dublin | Site of medieval friary, 18th-century music hall/theatre | Linzi Simpson |
| 186. | Christchurch Cathedral, Dublin | Dublin | Medieval cathedral | Linzi Simpson |
| 187. | Christchurch Cathedral, Dublin | Dublin | Medieval cathedral | Linzi Simpson |
| 188. | Christchurch Cathedral, Dublin | Dublin | Urban medieval | Helen Kehoe |
| 189. | College Street/Fleet Street/Westmoreland Street, Dublin | Dublin | Urban | Sylvia Desmond and Judith Carroll |
| 190. | 20–26 Conyngham Road, Dublin | Dublin | No archaeological significance | Nóra Bermingham |
| 191. | 2–4 Coppinger Row, Dublin | Dublin | Urban | Daniel Leo Swan |
| 192. | City Hall, Cork Hill, Dublin | Dublin | Medieval—town wall | Helen Kehoe |
| 193. | Cornmarket, Dublin | Dublin | Urban | Margaret Gowen |
| 194. | 1–5 Crampton Court (rear of 44 Essex Street East), Temple Bar, Dublin | Dublin | Urban | Helen Kehoe |
| 195. | 4 Dame Lane, Dublin | Dublin | Urban post-medieval | Helen Kehoe |
| 196. | Davis Place (off Francis Street), Dublin | Dublin | Urban | Helen Kehoe |
| 197. | Dawson Street, Dublin | Dublin | Urban post-medieval | Helen Kehoe |
| 198. | 33–35 Earl Street South, Dublin | Dublin | Urban post-medieval industrial | Rob Lynch |
| 199. | Essex Street West, Temple Bar, Dublin | Dublin | Urban | Linzi Simpson |
| 200. | 10 Fownes Street Upper, Dublin | Dublin | No archaeological significance | Audrey Gahan |
| 201. | Iveagh Market, Francis Street, Dublin | Dublin | Urban | Helen Kehoe |
| 202. | Iveagh Market, Francis Street, Dublin | Dublin | Urban medieval and post-medieval | Franc Myles |
| 203. | 47 Gardiner Street Upper, Dublin | Dublin | 18th-century urban | Erin Gibbons |
| 204. | 64–65 George's Street Great South, Dublin | Dublin | Urban | Helen Kehoe |
| 205. | 116 Grafton Street, Dublin | Dublin | Urban medieval/post-medieval | Helen Kehoe |
| 206. | 6–10 Hanbury Lane/Swan Alley, Dublin | Dublin | Urban medieval— floor-tile kiln, cemetery | Claire Walsh |
| 207. | 20–26 Hill Street/Grenville Street, Dublin | Dublin | No archaeological significance | Claire Walsh |
| 208. | Island Street/Bridgefoot Street, Dublin | Dublin | Urban post-medieval | Claire Walsh |
| 209. | James's Street, Dublin | Dublin | Urban | Margaret Gowen |
| 210. | 141–143 James's Street/Bow Lane, Dublin | Dublin | Medieval suburbs | Rosanne Meenan |
| 211. | 141–143 James's Street, Dublin | Dublin | Urban post-medieval | Rob Lynch |

| | | | | |
|---|---|---|---|---|
| 212. | Cardiac Unit, St James's Hospital, James's Street, Dublin | Dublin | 19th century | Rosanne Meenan |
| 213. | 189–194 King Street North, Dublin | Dublin | Urban, graveyard | Dermot Nelis |
| 214. | National Gallery of Ireland, Leinster Street, Dublin | Dublin | No archaeological significance | Alan Hayden |
| 215. | Longford Street Great/ Stephen Street Upper, Dublin | Dublin | Urban | Martin Reid |
| 216. | Department of Education, Marlborough Street, Dublin | Dublin | Urban post-medieval | Mary McMahon |
| 217. | Marrowbone Lane, Dublin | Dublin | No archaeological significance | Martin Reid |
| 218. | 28 Mary Street Little, Dublin | Dublin | Urban 18th/19th century | James Eogan |
| 219. | St Catherine's, Meath Street, Dublin | Dublin | Urban | Claire Walsh |
| 220. | Meeting House Lane/ 133a Capel Street, Dublin | Dublin | 19th-century street frontage | Christine Baker |
| 221. | Mercer Street/ Bow Lane East, Dublin | Dublin | Urban | Cia McConway |
| 222. | 31a–36 Ormond Quay Upper/Charles Street West, Dublin | Dublin | Urban post-medieval | Helen Kehoe |
| 223. | Oxmantown Lane, Dublin | Dublin | No archaeological significance | Dermot Nelis |
| 224. | 58–66 Parnell Street/ Moore Lane, Dublin | Dublin | Urban post-medieval | Edmond O'Donovan |
| 225. | Dublin Institute of Technology, Peter's Row, Dublin | Dublin | Urban | Avril Purcell |
| 226. | Adelaide Hospital Site, Peter Street/Wood Street, Dublin | Dublin | Urban medieval, post-medieval | Helen Kehoe |
| 227. | St Mary's Hospital, Phoenix Park, Dublin | Dublin | Within archaeological complex | Christiaan Corlett |
| 228. | Phoenix Park, Dublin | Dublin | No archaeological significance | Helen Kehoe |
| 229. | Marian Court, Queen Street, Dublin | Dublin | Urban | Rob Lynch |
| 230. | Trinity College, Dublin | Dublin | No archaeological significance | Helen Kehoe |
| 231. | Trinity College (Library extension site), Dublin | Dublin | Urban post-medieval | Helen Kehoe |
| 232. | 105–109 Weaver Street, The Coombe, Dublin | Dublin | Urban | Helen Kehoe |
| 233. | 13 Wellington Quay, Dublin | Dublin | Urban | Helen Kehoe |
| 234. | 34–5 Wellington Quay, Dublin | Dublin | Post-medieval | Claire Walsh |
| 235. | 44 Wellington Quay, Dublin | Dublin | Medieval/post-medieval | Helen Kehoe |
| 236. | 14–15 Werburgh Street, Dublin | Dublin | Viking/Anglo-Norman defences | Linzi Simpson |
| 237. | Hoey's Court, Werburg Street, Dublin | Dublin | Viking/Anglo-Norman defences | Linzi Simpson |
| 238. | Wolfe Tone Park, Dublin | Dublin | Post-medieval cemetery | Franc Myles |
| 239. | St Mary's Church, Wolfe Tone Street, Dublin | Dublin | Urban | Tim Coughlan |
| 240. | Proposed Dundrum Town Centre, Dundrum | Dublin | Industrial | Franc Myles |
| 241. | Holy Faith Convent, Cappagh Road, Finglas | Dublin | Urban medieval | Martin Reid |
| 242. | Meakstown, Finglas | Dublin | Post-medieval | Nóra Bermingham |
| 243. | Meakstown, Finglas | Dublin | Vicinity of 17th-century house | Daniel Leo Swan |
| 244. | St Patrick's Well, Mellowes Crescent, Finglas | Dublin | Possible Early Christian | Franc Myles |

| No. | Site | County | Description | Author |
|---|---|---|---|---|
| 245. | Convent of the Little Sisters of the Assumption, Patrickswell Place, Finglas | Dublin | No archaeological significance | Nóra Bermingham |
| 246. | Parkwest, Gallanstown | Dublin | Early Christian cemetery | Avril Purcell |
| 247. | 37 Park West Industrial Park, Gallanstown | Dublin | Close to cemetery | Donald Murphy |
| 248. | Gracedieu | Dublin | Early Christian cemetery | Malachy Conway |
| 249. | Jamestown | Dublin | Pale ditch | Niall Brady |
| 250. | 4–8 Bow Bridge, Kilmainham | Dublin | Urban 18th/19th century | James Eogan |
| 251. | 7–11 Mount Brown, Kilmainham | Dublin | Tanning pits | Erin Gibbons |
| 252. | Deputy Master's House, Royal Hospital, Kilmainham | Dublin | Urban | Sylvia Desmond |
| 253. | Kilshane | Dublin | Unenclosed cemetery | Malachy Conway |
| 254. | Killegar Road, Kiltiernan | Dublin | No archaeological significance | Sarah Cross |
| 255. | Castlefield Avenue, Knocklyon | Dublin | No archaeological significance | Thaddeus C. Breen |
| 256. | Lambay Island | Dublin | Neolithic axe production with associated activity | Gabriel Cooney |
| 257. | Shanganagh, Loughlinstown (Bray Road) | Dublin | Geophysical anomalies | Avril Purcell |
| 258. | Mount St Anne's Convent, Milltown | Dublin | No archaeological significance | Franc Myles |
| 259. | Cianlea, Moorestown | Dublin | No archaeological significance | Rónán Swan |
| 260. | Cruiserath, Mulhuddart | Dublin | 18th-century house and farmyard | Margaret Gowen |
| 261. | Rathfarnham Golf Club, Newtown | Dublin | Burnt mound, burnt spreads | Nóra Bermingham |
| 262. | Poppintree Park, Poppintree | Dublin | Site of well | Tim Coughlan |
| 263. | Robswall, Portmarnock | Dublin | Flint scatter | Malachy Conway |
| 264. | Robswall, Portmarnock | Dublin | Flint scatter | Ian W. Doyle |
| 265. | St Francis's Hospice, Raheny | Dublin | Site of windmill | Tim Coughlan |
| 266. | Irishtown Road/Dermot O'Hurley Avenue, Ringsend | Dublin | Urban | Avril Purcell |
| 267. | Coldwater Commons, Saggart | Dublin | Medieval | Claire Walsh |
| 268. | The Old Burial Ground, Saggart | Dublin | Possible Early Christian | Franc Myles |
| 269. | Newtown Link Road, St Margaret's | Dublin | Cultivation furrows | Claire Walsh |
| 270. | Sandymount Strand, Sandymount | Dublin | Underwater monitoring | Connie Kelleher |
| 271. | Phoenix Street North/ Stable Lane (Phase 1), Smithfield | Dublin | Urban medieval/post-medieval | Una Cosgrave |
| 272. | Smithfield | Dublin | Medieval and post-medieval water management | Audrey Gahan |
| 273. | 93–94 Manor Street, Stoneybatter | Dublin | No archaeological significance | Franc Myles |
| 274. | Bridge Street, Swords | Dublin | Quarry site | Eoin Halpin |
| 275. | Windmill Lands, River Ward, Swords | Dublin | Medieval burials | Karl Brady and Connie Kelleher |
| 276. | Kiltalown House, Tallaght | Dublin | Earthwork | Tadhg O'Keefe |
| 277. | Terenure College, Terenure | Dublin | Adjacent to Terenure Castle | Rónán Swan |
| 278. | Westereave | Dublin | Early Christian cemetery | Malachy Conway |
| 279. | Marble Arch Reservoir, Killesher | Fermanagh | Adjacent to souterrain and graveyard | Cóilín Ó Drisceoil |
| 280. | Molly Mountain, Molly | Fermanagh | Prehistoric | John Channing |
| 281. | Reyfad | Fermanagh | Post-medieval farm | Colm J. Donnelly and Eileen M. Murphy |

| | | | | |
|---|---|---|---|---|
| 282. | Ivymount House, Baunmore, Athenry | Galway | Adjacent to St Bridget's Church | Fiona Rooney |
| 283. | Chapel Lane, Athenry | Galway | Anglo-Norman town | Fiona Rooney |
| 284. | Court Lane, Athenry | Galway | Anglo-Norman town | Fiona Rooney |
| 285. | Cross Street, Athenry | Galway | Anglo-Norman town | Fiona Rooney |
| 286. | North Gate Street, Athenry | Galway | Urban | Martin Fitzpatrick |
| 287. | Creagh, Ballinasloe | Galway | Beside 18th-century church and possible medieval parish church | Deirdre Murphy |
| 288. | Parkmore, Ballinasloe | Galway | Rath/cashel | Donald Murphy |
| 289. | Dunmore | Galway | Urban medieval | Niall Gregory |
| 290. | Barrack Lane, Galway | Galway | Urban | Richard Crumlish |
| 291. | 33–34 Eyre Square, Galway | Galway | Urban post-medieval? | Anne Connolly |
| 292. | The Fairgreen, Galway | Galway | No archaeological significance | Anne Connolly |
| 293. | Custom House, Flood Street/ Courthouse Lane, Galway | Galway | Medieval castle, limekiln and building | Dominic Delany |
| 294. | Forster Street, Galway | Galway | Urban | Gerry Walsh |
| 295. | 9 Francis Street, Galway | Galway | Urban | Gerry Walsh |
| 296. | Lough Atalia Road/ Forster Street, Galway | Galway | Town (in vicinity of) | Dominic Delany |
| 297. | National University of Ireland, Galway, Newcastle, Galway | Galway | No archaeological significance | Anne Connolly |
| 298. | 26 Prospect Hill, Galway | Galway | Town | Dominic Delany |
| 299. | 6–7 Quay Lane, Galway | Galway | Town | Dominic Delany |
| 300. | 35 Shop Street, Galway | Galway | Urban | Fiona Rooney |
| 301. | Spanish Arch, Galway | Galway | Urban | Anne Connolly |
| 302. | Knockroe Hill, Gleenaveel | Galway | Cairns | Martin Fitzpatrick |
| 303. | George's Street, Gort | Galway | Urban medieval | Jacinta Kiely |
| 304. | Balrickard, Headford | Galway | Adjacent to castle | Richard Crumlish |
| 305. | High Island | Galway | Early Christian monastery | Georgina Scally |
| 306. | Mainistir Chiaráin, Inis Mór | Galway | Early Christian/medieval monastery | Sinéad Ní Ghabhláin |
| 307. | Kinalehin Friary, and Abbeyville | Galway | Earthworks | Tadhg O'Keefe |
| 308. | Kinalehin Friary, and Abbeyville | Galway | Earthworks | Tadhg O'Keefe |
| 309. | St Brendan's Church, Loughrea | Galway | Human remains | Martin Fitzpatrick |
| 310. | Oranmore Sewerage Scheme | Galway | Various | Jim Higgins |
| 311. | Oranmore, Site 28 | Galway | Stone-lined features | Leo Morahan |
| 312. | Oranmore, Site 27 | Galway | Bank | Leo Morahan |
| 313. | Oranmore, Site 17 | Galway | Kilns | Leo Morahan |
| 314. | Oranmore, Site 25 | Galway | No archaeological significance | Leo Morahan |
| 315. | Parkaloughan | Galway | No archaeological significance | Richard Crumlish |
| 316. | Townparks (1st Division), Tuam | Galway | Enclosure | Dominic Delany |
| 317. | Ardfert Community Centre, Ardfert | Kerry | Adjacent to ecclesiastical site | Isabel Bennett |
| 318. | New Road, Ballybunion | Kerry | Ringfort | Margaret McCarthy |
| 319. | Ballydwyer West | Kerry | Earthwork | Frank Coyne |
| 320. | Ballydwyer West II | Kerry | Enclosure | Frank Coyne |
| 321. | Ballymacthomas | Kerry | Enclosure (ringfort) | Frank Coyne |
| 322. | Ballynabooly | Kerry | Ringfort | Isabel Bennett |
| 323. | Ballywiheen | Kerry | Burial site | Margaret McCarthy |
| 324. | Bray Head (Valencia Island) | Kerry | Early medieval farm | Alan Hayden |
| 325. | Brosna–Knocknagoshel Regional Water Supply Scheme | Kerry | Monitoring | Emer Dennehy |
| 326. | Caherlehillian | Kerry | Early ecclesiastical enclosure | John Sheehan |
| 327. | Cappanacush East | Kerry | Adjacent to possible standing stone | Isabel Bennett |
| 328. | Cloghermore | Kerry | Ironworking areas | Frank Coyne |

| | | | | |
|---|---|---|---|---|
| 329. | Cloghermore Cave, Cloghermore | Kerry | Burials in cave | Michael Connolly |
| 330. | Emlagh West, Dingle | Kerry | Adjacent to ringfort, souterrains etc. | Isabel Bennett |
| 331. | Gortaneare | Kerry | Adjacent to (levelled) rath | Isabel Bennett |
| 332. | Loher | Kerry | No archaeological significance | Laurence Dunne |
| 333. | Aghadoe Heights Hotel (Parkavonear Townland), Aghadoe, Killarney | Kerry | Adjacent to early ecclesiastical site | Isabel Bennett |
| 334. | Carnegie Library, Market Street, Killorglin | Kerry | Burials | Laurence Dunne |
| 335. | Knockanish West | Kerry | No archaeological significance | Laurence Dunne |
| 336. | Magherabeg | Kerry | No archaeological significance | Isabel Bennett |
| 337. | Maglass East | Kerry | Earthwork | Frank Coyne |
| 338. | Rockfield | Kerry | Prehistoric burial/ritual | Tracy Collins |
| 339. | Castlemorris, Ballymullen Tralee | Kerry | Adjacent to tower-house | Laurence Dunne |
| 340. | Ballyvelly, Tralee | Kerry | Late Neolithic/Early Bronze Age | Emer Dennehy |
| 341. | Bunatalloon, Tralee | Kerry | Prehistoric pits | Jacinta Kiely |
| 342. | Bunatalloon, Tralee | Kerry | Prehistoric pit | Jacinta Kiely |
| 343. | Cloon, Tralee | Kerry | Test-trenches and monitoring | Jacinta Kiely |
| 344. | Dromthacker, Tralee | Kerry | Adjacent to ringfort | Rose M. Cleary |
| 345. | Dromthacker, Tralee | Kerry | Prehistoric pits | Jacinta Kiely |
| 346. | Killeen, Tralee | Kerry | Adjacent to 17th-century house | Jacinta Kiely |
| 347. | Knocknacuig, Tralee | Kerry | Monitoring | Jacinta Kiely |
| 348. | Market Place, Tralee | Kerry | Urban | Laurence Dunne |
| 349. | Monavalley, Tralee | Kerry | In vicinity of prehistoric burial activity | Frank Coyne |
| 350. | Cloch an Oighair (Carrigeendaniel), Mounthawk, Tralee | Kerry | No archaeological significance | Isabel Bennett |
| 351. | Athy–Stradbally (Co. Laois)–Portlaoise (Co. Laois) Gas Pipeline | Kildare | Monitoring | Breandán Ó Ríordáin |
| 352. | Convent Lane, Athy | Kildare | Urban | Claire Walsh |
| 353. | Garter Lane, Athy | Kildare | Urban medieval | Martin E. Byrne |
| 354. | Ballitore | Kildare | Medieval settlement | Hilary Opie |
| 355. | Plunkett Road, Ballymore Eustace | Kildare | No archaeological significance | Claire Walsh |
| 356. | Plunkett Road, Ballymore Eustace | Kildare | Medieval borough | Martin E. Byrne |
| 357. | North Cross, St John's, Ballymore Eustace | Kildare | High cross | Heather A. King |
| 358. | Ballysaxhills | Kildare | Area of burning | Daniel Leo Swan |
| 359. | Ballyvass | Kildare | *Fulacht fiadh* | Niall Gregory |
| 360. | Bishopslane Site 4 | Kildare | No archaeological significance | Rob Lynch |
| 361. | Broadleas Commons | Kildare | Environs of stone circle | Martin E. Byrne |
| 362. | Brownstown/Carnalway | Kildare | No archaeological significance | Finola O'Carroll |
| 363. | Church Road, Celbridge | Kildare | No archaeological significance | Franc Myles |
| 364. | 17 and 18 Main Street, Celbridge | Kildare | Urban | Sylvia Desmond |
| 365. | Churchtown South | Kildare | Deserted settlement site | Clare Mullins |
| 366. | Abbeylands, Clane | Kildare | Vicinity of Franciscan friary | Martin E. Byrne |
| 367. | Jones's Pub, Main Street, Clane | Kildare | No archaeological significance | Eoin Halpin |
| 368. | Moat Commons, Clane | Kildare | Vicinity of motte | Rosanne Meenan |
| 369. | Corbally | Kildare | Proximity to Neolithic settlement | Avril Purcell |
| 370. | Corbally | Kildare | Proximity to Neolithic settlement | Avril Purcell |

| | | | | |
|---|---|---|---|---|
| 371. | Curragh | Kildare | No archaeological significance | James Eogan |
| 372. | Curragh Camp, Curragh | Kildare | Environs of archaeological complex | Martin E. Byrne |
| 373. | 'The Race of the Black Pig', The Curragh | Kildare | Earthwork | Tadhg O'Keefe |
| 374. | Curragh/Pollardstown | Kildare | Black Pig's Race | Niall Brady |
| 375. | Curryhills I | Kildare | Fire-pit | Martin E. Byrne |
| 376. | Curryhills II | Kildare | No archaeological significance | Martin E. Byrne |
| 377. | Donaghmore | Kildare | No archaeological significance | Christine Baker |
| 378. | Easton | Kildare | No archaeological significance | Thaddeus C. Breen |
| 379. | Kilrathmurray, Enfield | Kildare | No archaeological significance | Christine Baker |
| 380. | Kilrathmurray, Enfield | Kildare | Non antiquity—animal pen? | Christine Baker and Rónán Swan |
| 381. | Glebe South (a) | Kildare | Environs of medieval borough | Martin E. Byrne |
| 382. | Glebe South (b) | Kildare | Environs of medieval borough | Martin E. Byrne |
| 383. | Graney East | Kildare | Adjacent to nunnery | Martin E. Byrne |
| 384. | Grangerosnolvan | Kildare | Burnt spread | Niall Gregory |
| 385. | Great Connel | Kildare | In vicinity of standing stone | Daniel Leo Swan |
| 386. | Kilcullen | Kildare | Monitoring | Breandán Ó Ríordáin |
| 387. | Kildare | Kildare | Urban medieval | Hilary Opie |
| 388. | Botharín na gCorp, Kildare | Kildare | No archaeological significance | Martin E. Byrne |
| 389. | Bride Street (rear of), Kildare | Kildare | Urban medieval | Martin E. Byrne |
| 390. | Bride Street, Kildare | Kildare | Urban medieval | Declan Moore |
| 391. | Medical Centre (rear of), Bride Street, Kildare | Kildare | Urban medieval | Martin E. Byrne |
| 392. | Bride Street/ Bangup Lane, Kildare | Kildare | Urban medieval | Clare Mullins |
| 393. | Kildare Credit Union, Bride Street, Kildare | Kildare | Urban | Frank Ryan |
| 394. | Round Tower House (rear of), Dublin Street, Kildare | Kildare | Urban medieval | Martin E. Byrne |
| 395. | Main Street, Kill | Kildare | Environs of medieval church | Martin E. Byrne |
| 396. | Killhill | Kildare | Enclosure | Clare Mullins |
| 397. | River Greese, Kilkea Lower and Grangerosnolvan Upper | Kildare | No archaeological significance | Niall Brady |
| 398. | Kilmeage | Kildare | Vicinity of church | Rosanne Meenan |
| 399. | Knockshough Glebe | Kildare | Monitoring | Breandán Ó Ríordáin |
| 400. | Leinster Lodge | Kildare | Hearth | Niall Gregory |
| 401. | Barn Hall, Leixlip | Kildare | In proximity to a bridge site | Donald Murphy |
| 402. | Mainham | Kildare | No archaeological significance | Anne Connolly |
| 403. | Maynooth | Kildare | Urban | Niall Brady |
| 404. | The Roost Bar, Leinster Street, Maynooth | Kildare | Urban | Eoghan Moore |
| 405. | Maynooth Castle, Maynooth | Kildare | Prehistoric and early medieval settlement and Anglo-Norman castle | Alan Hayden |
| 406. | Moone | Kildare | No archaeological significance | Christine Tarbett-Buckley |
| 407. | Moone Abbey, Moone | Kildare | Early Christian monastery | Miriam Clyne |
| 408. | Rivers Bothoge and Greese, Moone/Timolin/ Crookstown Upper | Kildare | Timber feature | Niall Brady |
| 409. | Moat Club, Abbey Street, Naas | Kildare | Adjacent to motte | Clare Mullins |
| 410. | Dublin Road, Naas | Kildare | Town wall | Martin E. Byrne |
| 411. | Friary Road, Naas | Kildare | Urban medieval | Clare Mullins |

| | | | | |
|---|---|---|---|---|
| 412. | Maudlins, Naas | Kildare | Unknown | Rosanne Meenan |
| 413. | Newbridge Road, Naas | Kildare | Possible medieval | Helen Kehoe |
| 414. | New Row (rear of)/ South Main Street, Naas | Kildare | Urban medieval | Martin E. Byrne |
| 415. | Tone's Public House, 1 North Main Street, Naas | Kildare | Urban | Eoghan Moore |
| 416. | 19 North Main Street, Naas | Kildare | Urban medieval | Clare Mullins |
| 417. | 19 North Main Street, Naas | Kildare | Urban medieval | Clare Mullins |
| 418. | St Mary's College, Naas | Kildare | Urban medieval | Martin E. Byrne |
| 419. | Prosperous–Robertstown Water Improvement Scheme | Kildare | Within zones of archaeological potential | Ian Russell and Donald Murphy |
| 420. | Mullatine, Rathangan | Kildare | Adjacent to urban medieval area | Martin E. Byrne |
| 421. | Timolin, Site 10 | Kildare | No archaeological significance | Thaddeus C. Breen |
| 422. | Timolin, Site 38 | Kildare | Scatter of medieval pottery | Thaddeus C. Breen |
| 423. | Timolin, Site 42 | Kildare | Earthwork | Thaddeus C. Breen |
| 424. | Timolin, Site 43 | Kildare | Bronze Age cemetery and medieval pottery scatter | Thaddeus C. Breen |
| 425. | Timolin | Kildare | Possible castle site | Martin E. Byrne |
| 426. | Baunlusk–Ballyconra Gas Pipeline | Kilkenny | Monitoring | Paul Stevens |
| 427. | Bonnetstown | Kilkenny | *Fulacht fiadh* | Paul Stevens |
| 428. | Tinnanamoona, Chapel Lane, Callan | Kilkenny | Urban medieval and post-medieval | Jo Moran |
| 429. | Mill Street, Callan | Kilkenny | Urban medieval | Jacinta Kiely |
| 430. | Castleblunden | Kilkenny | Flat cremation pit | Paul Stevens |
| 431. | Castleinch: 1 | Kilkenny | *Fulacht fiadh* | Paul Stevens |
| 432. | Arcon Mine (Galmoy), Castletown | Kilkenny | Proximity to *fulachta fiadh* and medieval castle | Tim Coughlan |
| 433. | Clonmantagh Castle, Clonmantagh Lower | Kilkenny | Settlement | Dominic Delany |
| 434. | Castletown, Galmoy | Kilkenny | 17th-century earthen fortification | Paul Stevens |
| 435. | St Mary's Church, Gowran | Kilkenny | Medieval church | Dave Pollock |
| 436. | Graiguenamanagh | Kilkenny | Urban medieval | Sheila Lane |
| 437. | Grange | Kilkenny | *Fulacht fiadh* | Paul Stevens |
| 438. | Granny and Aglish North | Kilkenny | Burnt spread | Mary Henry |
| 439. | Evan's Home, Barrack Lane, Kilkenny | Kilkenny | Urban medieval | Paul Stevens |
| 440. | 1 Greenhill, Kilkenny | Kilkenny | Urban medieval/post-medieval | Mary Henry |
| 441. | New Road, Greensbridge Kilkenny | Kilkenny | Urban | Cóilín Ó Drisceoil |
| 442. | Green Street, Kilkenny | Kilkenny | Urban medieval | Sheila Lane |
| 443. | Green Street, Kilkenny | Kilkenny | Urban medieval | Mary Henry |
| 444. | James's Street, Kilkenny | Kilkenny | Urban medieval | Christopher Read |
| 445. | Tynan's Bridge House, John's Bridge, Kilkenny | Kilkenny | No archaeological significance | Paul Stevens |
| 446. | Bridge House, 87–89 John Street Lower, Kilkenny | Kilkenny | Urban medieval | Paul Stevens |
| 447. | 24 John Street Upper, Kilkenny | Kilkenny | Urban post-medieval | Mary Henry |
| 448. | 1 The Parade, Kilkenny | Kilkenny | Urban | Sheila Lane |
| 449. | Kilkenny Castle, The Parade, Kilkenny | Kilkenny | 12th–19th-century castle | Ben Murtagh |

| 450. | Statham's Garage, Patrick Street, Kilkenny | Kilkenny | Urban medieval | Jacinta Kiely |
|---|---|---|---|---|
| 451. | 26 Patrick Street, Kilkenny | Kilkenny | Urban medieval | Jacinta Kiely |
| 452. | Burgermac, 20 Rose Inn Street, Kilkenny | Kilkenny | Urban | Dermot Nelis |
| 453. | St Canice's Place/ Vicar Street, Kilkenny | Kilkenny | No archaeological significance | Paul Stevens |
| 454. | St Francis's Abbey Brewery, Kilkenny | Kilkenny | Urban medieval | Edmond O'Donovan |
| 455. | River Breagagh at St Francis's Abbey Brewery, Kilkenny | Kilkenny | Urban | Margaret Gowen |
| 456. | River Breagagh at St Francis's Abbey (Smithwick's) Brewery, Kilkenny | Kilkenny | Urban medieval/riverbed | Paul Stevens |
| 457. | Moonhall | Kilkenny | Adjacent to archaeological complex | Cóilín Ó Drisceoil |
| 458. | Parksgrove: 1 | Kilkenny | Burnt mound and ironworking site | Paul Stevens |
| 459. | Parksgrove: 2 | Kilkenny | *Fulacht fiadh* | Paul Stevens |
| 460. | Parksgrove: 3 | Kilkenny | *Fulacht fiadh* | Paul Stevens |
| 461. | Kilmurry Castle, Sleiverue | Kilkenny | Late and post-medieval | Ben Murtagh |
| 462. | Mill Street, Thomastown | Kilkenny | Urban medieval/post-medieval | Mary Henry |
| 463. | The Quay, Thomastown | Kilkenny | No archaeological significance | Cathy Sheehan |
| 464. | Aghaboe Abbey, Aghaboe | Laois | Archaeological complex | Dominic Delany |
| 465. | Kilminchy | Laois | Possible site of castle | Finola O'Carroll |
| 466. | Jessop Street/ Coote Street, Portlaoise | Laois | Town | Dominic Delany |
| 467. | Aghavas | Leitrim | Medieval lacustrine habitation site | Victor Buckley and Aidan O'Sullivan |
| 468. | Garadice House, Ballinamore | Leitrim | 17th-century house | Donald Murphy |
| 469. | Bridge Street, Carrick-on-Shannon | Leitrim | Urban | Gerry Walsh |
| 470. | Main Street, Carrick-on-Shannon | Leitrim | Urban medieval/post-medieval | Mary Henry |
| 471. | Priest's Lane, Carrick-on-Shannon | Leitrim | Urban | Gerry Walsh |
| 472. | Fair Green, Manorhamilton | Leitrim | Adjacent to Manorhamilton Castle | Fiona Rooney |
| 473. | N20/N21 Road Improvement Scheme, Adare/Annacotty Contract 2 | Limerick | Monitoring | Damian Finn |
| 474. | Black Abbey, Adare | Limerick | Medieval monastery | Kenneth Wiggins |
| 475. | Main Street, Adare | Limerick | Urban medieval | Sarah McCutcheon |
| 476. | Ardanreagh | Limerick | Adjacent to possible rectangular enclosure | Celie O Rahilly |
| 477. | Attyflin, Site AR7 | Limerick | Medieval settlement | James Eogan |
| 478. | Attyflin | Limerick | Isolated trough | Mary Deevy |
| 479. | Attyflin | Limerick | *Fulacht fiadh* | Ciara MacManus |
| 480. | Ballinacurra (Hart)/ Ballinacurra (Weston)/ Rossbrien South/Rathbane/ Banemore | Limerick | Monitoring | Paul Stevens |
| 481. | Ballybronoge South | Limerick | Ring-ditch | James Eogan and Damian Finn |
| 482. | Ballyclogh | Limerick | Linear earthwork | Frank Coyne |
| 483. | Ballycummin | Limerick | *Fulachta fiadh* and 19th-century trackway | Noel Dunne |

| | | | | |
|---|---|---|---|---|
| 484. | Howmedica link road, Ballycummin | Limerick | Monitoring | Damian Finn |
| 485. | Ballygeale, Site 1 | Limerick | Settlement activity of unknown date | James Eogan and Sinclair Turrell |
| 486. | Ballygeale, Site 2 | Limerick | Undated field boundary and pits | James Eogan and Sinclair Turrell |
| 487. | Ballysimon II | Limerick | Watermill | Tracy Collins |
| 488. | Ballysimon IV | Limerick | No archaeological significance | Ken Hanley |
| 489. | Ballysimon | Limerick | Medieval enclosure (adjacent to church site) | Tony Cummins |
| 490. | Barnakyle | Limerick | *Fulacht fiadh* | Ciara MacManus |
| 491. | Bauranlicka | Limerick | No archaeological significance | Brian Hodkinson |
| 492. | Bohergeela | Limerick | No archaeological significance | Rose M. Cleary |
| 493. | Cahirguillamore, Bruff | Limerick | No archaeological significance | Una Cosgrave |
| 494. | Castlemungret | Limerick | Adjacent to monuments | Sarah McCutcheon |
| 495. | Castleroberts | Limerick | Vicinity of enclosure | Kenneth Wiggins |
| 496. | Cloghacloka | Limerick | Trough and adjacent pits | Mary Deevy |
| 497. | Cloghast | Limerick | Monitoring | Meriel McClatchie |
| 498. | Croom | Limerick | Ring-ditch | Fiona Rooney |
| 499. | Croom | Limerick | Enclosure | Martin Fitzpatrick |
| 500. | Derryknockane | Limerick | *Fulacht fiadh* | Ciara MacManus |
| 501. | Fanningstown | Limerick | Enclosure (ringfort) | Tracy Collins |
| 502. | Fanningstown | Limerick | Possible enclosure | Tracy Collins |
| 503. | Fanningstown | Limerick | Possible enclosure | Michael Connolly |
| 504. | Gorteen | Limerick | Possible corn-drying kiln | Ciara MacManus |
| 505. | Gorteen | Limerick | *Fulachta fiadh* and stone-lined well | Mary Deevy |
| 506. | Barrysfarm, Hospital | Limerick | Holy well (?) | Ken Hanley |
| 507. | Inchmore | Limerick | No archaeological significance | Ken Hanley |
| 508. | Kilgobbin | Limerick | Pits | Ciara MacManus |
| 509. | Abbey Farm, Kilmallock | Limerick | Historic town | Kenneth Wiggins |
| 510. | Shears Street, Kilmallock | Limerick | Urban medieval | Ken Hanley |
| 511. | Kilmallock | Limerick | Urban medieval/post-medieval | Cia McConway |
| 512. | Kilrodane | Limerick | No archaeological significance | Jacinta Kiely |
| 513. | Kilshane | Limerick | Adjacent to friary | Brian Hodkinson |
| 514. | Athlunkard Street/ Island Road (Site K.I.33), Limerick | Limerick | Part of historic town | Celie O Rahilly |
| 515. | Broad Street/George's Quay/ Abbey River, Limerick | Limerick | Urban medieval | Edmond O'Donovan |
| 516. | Charlotte's Quay, Limerick | Limerick | Urban medieval | Ken Hanley |
| 517. | Clancy's Strand, Limerick | Limerick | Environs of medieval mill | Edmond O'Donovan |
| 518. | 5–7 John's Gate, Limerick | Limerick | Part of historic town | Celie O Rahilly |
| 519. | Kilrush Church, Limerick | Limerick | Environs of Early Christian church | Edmond O'Donovan |
| 520. | 36–39 Nicholas Street/ 1–3 Peter Street (Site K.I.24), Limerick | Limerick | Part of historic town | Celie O Rahilly |
| 521. | Sir Harry's Mall, Limerick | Limerick | Urban medieval | Edmond O'Donovan |
| 522. | Sir Harry's Mall/ Long Lane/Fish Lane (Site K.I.16), Limerick | Limerick | Part of historic town | Celie O Rahilly |
| 523. | Thomond Gate, Limerick | Limerick | Urban post-medieval | Edmond O'Donovan |
| 524. | Cashel's Lane, Thomondgate, Limerick | Limerick | Part of historic town | Celie O Rahilly |
| 525. | Castle Demesne, Newcastle West | Limerick | Historic town | Rob Lynch |
| 526. | Old Abbey | Limerick | Adjacent to church and graveyard | Emer Dennehy |
| 527. | Ballycummin, Raheen | Limerick | Vicinity of enclosure | Kenneth Wiggins |

| No. | Site | County | Description | Author |
|---|---|---|---|---|
| 528. | Raheen | Limerick | No archaeological significance | Rose M. Cleary |
| 529. | Rathbane South | Limerick | Artificial platform and possible *fulacht fiadh* | Catherine McLoughlin and Emmet Stafford |
| 530. | Rathbane South | Limerick | *Fulacht fiadh* | Catherine McLoughlin |
| 531. | Rathbane South | Limerick | *Fulacht fiadh* | Catherine McLoughlin and Emmet Stafford |
| 532. | Rineroe | Limerick | Modern field drains | Mary Deevy |
| 533. | Rossbrien | Limerick | *Fulachta fiadh* | Mary Deevy |
| 534. | Rossbrien | Limerick | Possible *fulacht fiadh* | Catherine McLoughlin |
| 535. | Shanid Lower | Limerick | Adjacent to raised rath | Isabel Bennett |
| 536. | Towlerton | Limerick | Circular mound | Tracy Collins |
| 537. | Woodstown III | Limerick | Circular depression | Frank Coyne |
| 538. | Woodstown IV | Limerick | Circular mound | Frank Coyne |
| 539. | Main Street, Ballymahon | Longford | Adjacent to church and graveyard | Martin E. Byrne |
| 540. | Rathcronan, Granard | Longford | Town | Dominic Delany |
| 541. | Ardee Link Road | Louth | Monitoring | Matthew Seaver |
| 542. | 16–18 Castle Street, Ardee | Louth | No archaeological significance | Malachy Conway |
| 543. | O'Carroll Street/ Black Ridge/ Old Chapel Lane, Ardee | Louth | Urban medieval | Malachy Conway |
| 544. | Haggardstown, Blackrock | Louth | Various | Finola O'Carroll |
| 545. | Braganstown | Louth | *Fulacht fiadh* | Cóilín Ó Drisceoil |
| 546. | Broadlough 2, Ardee | Louth | Trough | Matthew Seaver |
| 547. | Broadlough | Louth | Pit, possibly part of *fulacht fiadh* | Carmel Duffy |
| 548. | Cappocksgreen | Louth | Burnt spread | Matthew Seaver |
| 549. | Carlingford town and environs | Louth | Urban | Dermot G. Moore |
| 550. | Castle Hill, Carlingford | Louth | Urban medieval | Donald Murphy |
| 551. | Castle Hill. Carlingford | Louth | Urban medieval | Rosanne Meenan |
| 552. | Castle Hill. Carlingford | Louth | Urban medieval | Deirdre Murphy |
| 553. | Church Lane, Carlingford | Louth | Medieval(?) burials | Cia McConway |
| 554. | Holy Trinity Heritage Centre, Carlingford | Louth | Post-medieval | Nóra Bermingham |
| 555. | Charleville | Louth | Pit | Cóilín Ó Drisceoil |
| 556. | Nuns Walk, Collon | Louth | Medieval borough | Donald Murphy |
| 557. | School Lane, Collon | Louth | Medieval borough | Donald Murphy |
| 558. | Dawsons Demesne | Louth | Medieval settlement/ possible site of friary | Finola O'Carroll |
| 559. | Dawsons Demesne | Louth | Irregular pit | Matthew Seaver |
| 560. | Carrick Road, Donaghmore | Louth | Possible site of graveyard/ church | Finola O'Carroll |
| 561. | 20 Bolton Square, Drogheda | Louth | Urban medieval | Deirdre Murphy |
| 562. | Bolton Street, Drogheda | Louth | Urban medieval | Deirdre Murphy |
| 563. | 1 Bolton Street/Square, Drogheda | Louth | Urban medieval | Ian Russell |
| 564. | The Gate Lodge, Sienna Convent, Chord Road, Drogheda | Louth | Medieval suburbs | Deirdre Murphy |
| 565. | 103/104 Duleek Street, Drogheda | Louth | Adjacent to town wall | Finola O'Carroll |
| 566. | Dyer Street, Drogheda | Louth | Urban medieval | Donald Murphy |
| 567. | Town Centre, Dyer Street, Drogheda | Louth | Urban medieval/post-medieval | Donald Murphy |
| 568. | Star and Crescent Centre, Fairgreen, Drogheda | Louth | Urban | Donald Murphy |
| 569. | Green Lanes, Drogheda | Louth | No archaeological significance | Malachy Conway |
| 570. | Horse Lane, Drogheda | Louth | Just outside medieval town | Deirdre Murphy |

| | | | | |
|---|---|---|---|---|
| 571. | John Street, Drogheda | Louth | Urban post-medieval tannery | Malachy Conway |
| 572. | 40 John Street, Drogheda | Louth | Urban medieval | Malachy Conway |
| 573. | John's Bridge, John's Street, Drogheda | Louth | Medieval town wall and 19th-century tannery | Avril Purcell |
| 574. | Former Drogheda Grammar School, Laurence's Street, Drogheda | Louth | Urban medieval | Deirdre Murphy |
| 575. | 23/24 Laurence Street, Drogheda | Louth | Urban medieval | Donald Murphy |
| 576. | Loughboy, Drogheda | Louth | Medieval monastic | Sarah Cross |
| 577. | 41 Magdalene Street Lower Drogheda | Louth | No archaeological significance | Malachy Conway |
| 578. | 49 Mary Street, Drogheda | Louth | Urban medieval | Donald Murphy |
| 579. | Millmount, Drogheda | Louth | Motte and 19th-century Martello tower | Donald Murphy |
| 580. | 2–3 Oulster Lane, Drogheda | Louth | Medieval town suburbs | Donald Murphy |
| 581. | 10 Palace Street/Francis Street, Drogheda | Louth | Urban medieval/post-medieval | Ian Russell |
| 582. | 11 Palace Street, Drogheda | Louth | No archaeological significance | Matthew Seaver |
| 583. | Scarlet Street, Drogheda | Louth | Urban medieval | Donald Murphy |
| 584. | Shop Street/Dyer Street, Drogheda | Louth | Urban | Tim Coughlan |
| 585. | 2–3 Mill Row, Trinity Street, Drogheda | Louth | Urban medieval | Donald Murphy |
| 586. | 9 West Street, Drogheda | Louth | Medieval town | Deirdre Murphy |
| 587. | 26 West Street, Drogheda | Louth | Urban medieval | Donald Murphy |
| 588. | Dromin | Louth | Adjacent to church/graveyard | Finola O'Carroll |
| 589. | Dromiskin | Louth | No archaeological significance | George Eogan |
| 590. | Dromiskin | Louth | Cemetery and possible trackways | Donald Murphy and Malachy Conway |
| 591. | Dromiskin | Louth | *Fulachta fiadh* | Donald Murphy |
| 592. | Drumleck | Louth | Pit | Cóilín Ó Drisceoil |
| 593. | Dundalk | Louth | No archaeological significance | Carmel Duffy |
| 594. | 35 Anne Street, Dundalk | Louth | No archaeological significance | Matthew Seaver |
| 595. | Castleblaney Road, Dundalk | Louth | Medieval borough | Donald Murphy |
| 596. | Castletown Road, Dundalk | Louth | Medieval cobbled road | Rob Lynch |
| 597. | 17/19 Chapel Street, Dundalk | Louth | Close to medieval friary | Deirdre Murphy |
| 598. | AIB Bank, 96 Clanbrassil Street, Dundalk | Louth | Post-medieval features | Rónán Swan |
| 599. | Demesne/Townparks, Dundalk | Louth | Urban medieval | Rob Lynch |
| 600. | Demesne/Townparks, Dundalk | Louth | Urban post-medieval | Rob Lynch |
| 601. | Dublin Road (Priorland/Marshes Lower), Dundalk | Louth | Cobbled road | Rob Lynch |
| 602. | Dublin Road (Priorland/Marshes Lower), Dundalk | Louth | Cobbled road | Rob Lynch |
| 603. | Dublin Street, Dundalk | Louth | Urban medieval | Deirdre Murphy |
| 604. | 3 Dublin Street, Dundalk | Louth | Urban post-medieval | Finola O'Carroll |
| 605. | 59 Dublin Street, Dundalk | Louth | Urban post-medieval | Finola O'Carroll |
| 606. | 80 Dublin Street, Dundalk | Louth | Urban | Matthew Seaver |
| 607. | Farrandreg, Dundalk | Louth | Souterrain | Rob Lynch |
| 608. | Linenhall Street, Dundalk | Louth | No archaeological significance | Malachy Conway |
| 609. | Xerox/ESB Electricity Sub-station, Mullagharlin, Dundalk | Louth | No archaeological significance | Dermot G. Moore |
| 610. | Mullagharlin/Haggardstown, Dundalk | Louth | Various | Catherine McLoughlin |
| 611. | 10 New Street, Dundalk | Louth | Urban | Cóilín Ó Drisceoil |

| | | | | |
|---|---|---|---|---|
| 612. | 87–88 Park Street (Townparks), Dundalk | Louth | No archaeological significance | Donald Murphy |
| 613. | Roden Place, Dundalk | Louth | Urban medieval | Donald Murphy |
| 614. | 5 Seatown, Dundalk | Louth | Medieval cemetery | Eoin Halpin |
| 615. | Tankardsrock, Dundalk | Louth | Archaeological landscape | Ian Russell |
| 616. | 16 Wynne's Terrace, Dundalk | Louth | Urban medieval | Donald Murphy |
| 617. | Dunleer | Louth | Urban | Rosanne Meenan |
| 618. | Dunleer | Louth | Vicinity of ecclesiastical enclosure | Cara Murray |
| 619. | Athclare Castle, Dunleer | Louth | Tower-house | Deirdre Murphy |
| 620. | Dromin Junction, Dunleer | Louth | Near possible earthwork | Donald Murphy |
| 621. | Main Street, Dunleer | Louth | Proximity to Early Christian monastic site | Donald Murphy |
| 622. | Main Street Upper, Dunleer | Louth | Possible early ecclesiastical/medieval | Daniel Leo Swan |
| 623. | Dunleer–Dundalk Motorway | Louth | *Fulachta fiadh*, pits, souterrain and rath | Cóilín Ó Drisceoil |
| 624. | Faughart Upper | Louth | Earthwork site (possible) | Donald Murphy |
| 625. | Harristown | Louth | *Fulacht fiadh* | Carmel Duffy |
| 626. | Marshes Upper | Louth | Adjacent to archaeological complex | Cóilín Ó Drisceoil |
| 627. | Monascreebe | Louth | Ringfort | Donald Murphy |
| 628. | River Boyne, Mornington | Louth | Boat of unknown date | Matthew Seaver |
| 629. | Newrath | Louth | *Fulacht fiadh* | Cóilín Ó Drisceoil |
| 630. | Newrath | Louth | Pit | Cóilín Ó Drisceoil |
| 631. | Phillipstown | Louth | Vicinity of holy well | Rosanne Meenan |
| 632. | Richardstown 1 | Louth | Isolated pit | Matthew Seaver |
| 633. | Richardstown 3 | Louth | Isolated pit | Matthew Seaver |
| 634. | Richardstown 4 | Louth | Subrectangular pit | Matthew Seaver |
| 635. | Richardstown 6 | Louth | Circular pit | Matthew Seaver |
| 636. | Richardstown | Louth | Burnt mound | Matthew Seaver |
| 637. | Richardstown | Louth | Archaeological complex | Emmet Byrnes |
| 638. | Sheetland Road, Termonfeckin | Louth | Anglo-Norman palace | Donald Murphy |
| 639. | Strand Road, Termonfeckin | Louth | Early Christian monastery | Donald Murphy |
| 640. | Knockabbey, Thomastown | Louth | Tower-house | Edmond O'Donovan |
| 641. | Chapel Lane, Tullyallen | Louth | Vicinity of church | Rosanne Meenan |
| 642. | Whiterath | Louth | Rath and souterrain | Cóilín Ó Drisceoil |
| 643. | Askillaun | Mayo | No archaeological significance | Gerry Walsh |
| 644. | Ballina Wastewater Treatment Plant, Belleek, Ballina | Mayo | No archaeological significance | Gerry Walsh |
| 645. | Abbey Street, Ballinrobe | Mayo | No archaeological significance | Richard Crumlish |
| 646. | Abbey Street, Ballinrobe | Mayo | No archaeological significance | Gerry Walsh |
| 647. | Ballinsmaula | Mayo | *Fulachta fiadh* | Joanna Nolan |
| 648. | Ballinsmaula | Mayo | Enclosure | Angela Wallace |
| 649. | Ballyglass | Mayo | No archaeological significance | Gretta Byrne |
| 650. | Barrack Street, Ballyhaunis | Mayo | Monitoring | Gerry Walsh |
| 651. | Caherduff | Mayo | No archaeological significance | Leo Morahan |
| 652. | Carrownlough | Mayo | No archaeological significance | Anne Connolly |
| 653. | Castlegar | Mayo | Ringfort | Suzanne Zajac |
| 654. | Castlegar | Mayo | Heat-fractured stone deposits | Paula King |
| 655. | Castlegar | Mayo | Mound | Paula King |
| 656. | Clare | Mayo | *Fulachta fiadh* | Joanna Nolan |
| 657. | Leedaun, Claremorris | Mayo | Adjacent to Bronze Age settlement site and levelled *fulacht fiadh* | Richard Gillespie |
| 658. | Dowagh West | Mayo | No archaeological significance | Richard Crumlish |
| 659. | Kilcashel Fort, Kilcashel | Mayo | Stone fort | Martin Fitzpatrick |
| 660. | Kiltullagh Hill, Kiltullagh | Mayo | See No. 769 below | |
| 661. | Knock North | Mayo | Adjacent to souterrain | Richard Gillespie |

| | | | | |
|---|---|---|---|---|
| 662. | Liscromwell | Mayo | No archaeological significance | Gerry Walsh |
| 663. | Lisduff/Clare/Castlegar/ Ballinsmaula/ Barneycarroll/ Ballynabrehon South | Mayo | Monitoring | Joanna Nolan |
| 664. | Mayo Parks, Mayo Abbey | Mayo | No archaeological significance | Gerry Walsh |
| 665. | Moyhastin | Mayo | No archaeological significance | Leo Morahan |
| 666. | Mucklagh | Mayo | Ringfort | Mary Henry |
| 667. | Rausakeera North | Mayo | No archaeological significance | Gerry Walsh |
| 668. | Robeen Graveyard, Robeen | Mayo | No archaeological significance | Gerry Walsh |
| 669. | Shrule | Mayo | No archaeological significance | Gerry Walsh |
| 670. | The Deserted Village, Slievemore (Achill Island) | Mayo | Multi-phase landscape | Theresa McDonald |
| 671. | Streamstown | Mayo | No archaeological significance | Gerry Walsh |
| 672. | Turin | Mayo | Tower-house | Richard Crumlish |
| 673. | Ballinavalley | Meath | Vicinity of archaeological complex | Rosanne Meenan |
| 674. | Bective, Site S | Meath | No archaeological significance | Carmel Duffy |
| 675. | Bective, Area 1 | Meath | No archaeological significance | Carmel Duffy |
| 676. | Bective Abbey | Meath | No archaeological significance | P. David Sweetman |
| 677. | Bellewstown | Meath | Mound, possible ring-ditch or barrow | Deirdre Murphy |
| 678. | Cabragh | Meath | No archaeological significance | Carmel Duffy |
| 679. | Colp West | Meath | Unknown | Donald Murphy |
| 680. | Cormeen | Meath | Proximity to fort | Deirdre Murphy |
| 681. | Larrix Street, Duleek | Meath | Early Christian monastic site | Deirdre Murphy |
| 682. | Dunmoe, N51 Road Re-alignment | Meath | Close to monastic complex and earthworks | Donald Murphy |
| 683. | Dunshaughlin | Meath | Vicinity of monastic enclosure | Rosanne Meenan |
| 684. | Main Street, Dunshaughlin | Meath | No archaeological significance | Rosanne Meenan |
| 685. | Ferganstown/Ballymackon | Meath | Cut features | Clare Mullins |
| 686. | Ferganstown/Ballymackon | Meath | Environs of 'Mound Site' | Clare Mullins |
| 687. | Ferganstown/Ballymackon | Meath | Souterrain | Ken Hanley |
| 688. | Gortloney | Meath | Castle site (possible) | Martin E. Byrne |
| 689. | Grange/Fidorfe/Kilrue | Meath | No archaeological significance | Finola O'Carroll |
| 690. | Priestown, Kilbride | Meath | Possible medieval settlement | Rosanne Meenan |
| 691. | Priestown, Kilbride | Meath | Adjacent to moat/ringfort | Finola O'Carroll |
| 692. | Killeen Castle, Killeen | Meath | Tower-house and medieval church | Rosanne Meenan |
| 693. | Knockharley | Meath | Holy well | Malachy Conway |
| 694. | Knowth | Meath | Multi-period | George Eogan |
| 695. | Ninch, Laytown | Meath | *Fulacht fiadh* | Eoin Halpin |
| 696. | Gun Hill, Lobinstown | Meath | Rectilinear earthwork | Ian Russell |
| 697. | Monknewtown | Meath | No archaeological significance | Christine Baker and Rónán Swan |
| 698. | Navan Sewerage Augmentation Scheme | Meath | Canal bridge | Ken Hanley |
| 699. | Navan Sewerage Scheme, Navan | Meath | No archaeological significance | Jacinta Kiely |
| 700. | Athlumney, Navan | Meath | Monitoring | Mark Clinton |
| 701. | IDA Business Park, Kilkarn, Athlumney, Navan | Meath | Souterrains | Carleton Jones |
| 702. | Moathill, Navan | Meath | Environs of motte and bailey | Malachy Conway |
| 703. | 22 Trimgate Street, Navan | Meath | Urban medieval | Rosanne Meenan |
| 704. | Navan–Trim Gas Pipeline | Meath | Monitoring | Margaret Gowen |
| 705. | Ninch/Laytown | Meath | Bronze Age enclosure, *fulacht* trough | Martin Reid |
| 706. | River Boyne, Oldbridge | Meath | No archaeological significance | Niall Brady |
| 707. | Pilltown/Painestown/ Kiltrough/Bey Beg/Bey More Platin/Caulstown/ | Meath | Monitoring | Mark Clinton |

| | | | | |
|---|---|---|---|---|
| | Carranstown/Commons (Duleek)/Newtown/Longford/ Downestown/Gillinstown/ Garballagh/Thomastown/ Sicily/Tuiterath/ Flemingstown/Kentstown/ Knockharley/Curraghtown/ Brownstown/Realtoge/ Staffordstown/Follistown/ Mooretown/Alexander Reid | | | |
| 708. | Randalstown | Meath | *Fulachta fiadh* | Donald Murphy |
| 709. | N4–N6 Kinnegad Link Road, Rossan | Meath | No archaeological significance | Dermot Nelis |
| 710. | Sarsfieldstown | Meath | Burials in a gravel mound | Mary Deevy |
| 711. | Stagrennan | Meath | Boyne dredging | Jane Whitaker |
| 712. | Tankardstown | Meath | Adjacent to ploughed-out ringfort | Finola O'Carroll |
| 713. | Castle Street, Trim | Meath | Environs of town wall | Clare Mullins |
| 714. | Dublin Road (Friaryland 3rd Division), Trim | Meath | Environs of castle | Rosanne Meenan |
| 715. | Haggard Street, Trim | Meath | Urban medieval | Clare Mullins |
| 716. | Haggard Street, Trim | Meath | No archaeological significance | Carmel Duffy |
| 717. | Kildalkey Road/ Athboy Road/ Haggard Street, Trim | Meath | Environs of town gate | Clare Mullins |
| 718. | Lackanash, Trim | Meath | Post-medieval | Rosanne Meenan |
| 719. | Maudlin/Commons, Trim | Meath | Adjacent to medieval town | Finola O'Carroll |
| 720. | Mill Street/High Street/ Haggard Street, Trim | Meath | Urban medieval | Clare Mullins |
| 721. | Trim Courthouse, Manorland, Trim | Meath | 19th-century courthouse and 13th-century Franciscan friary | Avril Purcell |
| 722. | Townspark South, Trim | Meath | Urban medieval | Rob Lynch |
| 723. | Cornapaste | Monaghan | Suspected brushwood surface | Donald Murphy |
| 724. | Cornapaste | Monaghan | Near Black Pig's Dyke | Donald Murphy |
| 725. | Mannan Castle, Donaghmoyne | Monaghan | Anglo-Norman motte, baileys and stone castle remains | Eoghan Moore |
| 726. | St Patrick's Churchyard, Donaghmoyne | Monaghan | Site of Early Christian church foundation | Eoghan Moore |
| 727. | Lisgall | Monaghan | Adjacent to rath | Cóilín Ó Drisceoil |
| 728. | Lissaraw | Monaghan | Environs of ringfort | Malachy Conway |
| 729. | The Diamond Centre, Monaghan | Monaghan | Urban | Eoghan Moore |
| 730. | The Diamond, Monaghan | Monaghan | Near Franciscan friary | Deirdre Murphy |
| 731. | 57 Dublin Street, Monaghan | Monaghan | Urban | Eoghan Moore |
| 732. | Busherstown | Offaly | Adjacent to earthwork | Brian Hodkinson |
| 733. | Cappancur | Offaly | Church and graveyard (vicinity of) | Dominic Delany |
| 734. | Casteltown Bog, Castlearmstrong | Offaly | Brushwood trackway | Ellen O'Carroll |
| 735. | Casteltown Bog, Castlearmstrong | Offaly | Brushwood togher | Ellen O'Carroll |
| 736. | Casteltown Bog, Castlearmstrong | Offaly | Brushwood togher | Ellen O'Carroll |
| 737. | Casteltown Bog, Castlearmstrong | Offaly | Brushwood togher | Ellen O'Carroll |
| 738. | Casteltown Bog, Castlearmstrong | Offaly | Brushwood toghers | Ellen O'Carroll |
| 739. | Casteltown Bog, Castlearmstrong | Offaly | Remains of brushwood togher | Ellen O'Carroll |
| 740. | Casteltown Bog, Castlearmstrong | Offaly | Remains of brushwood togher | Ellen O'Carroll |

| | | | | |
|---|---|---|---|---|
| 741. | Casteltown Bog, Castlearmstrong | Offaly | Linear plank togher | Ellen O'Carroll |
| 742. | Killaghintober Bog, Castlearmstrong | Offaly | Remains of linear trackway | Ellen O'Carroll |
| 743. | Killaghintober Bog, Castlearmstrong | Offaly | Remains of linear trackway | Ellen O'Carroll |
| 744. | Clonmacnoise | Offaly | Ecclesiastical | Donald Murphy |
| 745. | Clonmacnoise | Offaly | Early Christian ecclesiastical | Donald Murphy |
| 746. | Ballykilleen, Edenderry | Offaly | Monitoring | Martin Reid |
| 747. | Glasshouse | Offaly | 17th-century glasshouse | Jean Farrelly and Caimin O'Brien |
| 748. | Kilcormac or Frankford | Offaly | Mound (in vicinity of) | Dominic Delany |
| 749. | Killeigh | Offaly | Archaeological complex | Dominic Delany |
| 750. | Rathcobican | Offaly | Various | Dominic Delany |
| 751. | Tullamore/Ballycowan | Offaly | No archaeological significance | Rob Lynch |
| 752. | Killaghintober Bog, Tumbeagh | Offaly | Linear plank trackway | Ellen O'Carroll |
| 753. | Killaghintober Bog, Tumbeagh | Offaly | Remains of brushwood togher | Ellen O'Carroll |
| 754. | Tumbeagh Bog, Tumbeagh | Offaly | Dispersed brushwood togher | Ellen O'Carroll |
| 755. | Tumbeagh Bog, Tumbeagh | Offaly | Bushwood and hurdle togher | Ellen O'Carroll |
| 756. | Tumbeagh Bog, Tumbeagh and Killaghintober | Offaly | Togher | Jane Whitaker |
| 757. | Tumbeagh Bog | Offaly | Brushwood platform | Jane Whitaker |
| 758. | Tumbeagh Bog | Offaly | Togher | Jane Whitaker |
| 759. | Ardanaffrin | Roscommon | No archaeological significance | Jim Higgins |
| 760. | Ardcarn | Roscommon | No archaeological significance | Mary Henry |
| 761. | Ballyconboy | Roscommon | No archaeological significance | Fiona Rooney |
| 762. | Ballykilcline | Roscommon | Early 19th-century tenant village | Charles E. Orser |
| 763. | Ballypheasan | Roscommon | No archaeological significance | Dermot Nelis |
| 764. | Deerpark, Boyle | Roscommon | Burnt spread | Martin Fitzpatrick |
| 765. | Cloongownagh | Roscommon | Enclosure | Mary Henry |
| 766. | Derrane | Roscommon | Adjacent to earthwork | Richard Crumlish |
| 767 | Drum Heritage Centre, Drum | Roscommon | Adjacent to medieval site | Rónán Swan |
| 768. | Hughestown | Roscommon | *Fulacht fiadh* | Mary Henry |
| 769. | Kiltullagh Hill, Kiltullagh | Roscommon | Late Iron Age/Early Christian cemetery | R.A. Gregory and D.G. Coombs |
| 770. | Knockadoobrusna | Roscommon | Environs of archaeological complex | Declan Moore |
| 771. | Knockadoobrusna | Roscommon | Archaeological complex | Rónán Swan |
| 772. | Knockmurry | Roscommon | No archaeological significance | Gerry Walsh |
| 773. | Monksland Sewerage Scheme | Roscommon | Monitoring | Martin E. Byrne |
| 774. | Rockingham to Cortober | Roscommon | Monitoring | Mary Henry |
| 775. | Main Street, Roscommon | Roscommon | Urban | Donald Murphy |
| 776. | Main Street, Roscommon | Roscommon | Urban | Donald Murphy |
| 777. | Warren, or Drum | Roscommon | No archaeological significance | Anne Connolly |
| 778. | Gortalough, Ballinafad | Sligo | Adjacent to Ballinafad Castle and the Red Earl's Road | Martin A. Timoney |
| 779. | Ballincar | Sligo | No archaeological significance | Richard Crumlish |
| 780. | Ballincar | Sligo | Adjacent to ringfort | Richard Crumlish |
| 781. | Calteraun | Sligo | Adjacent to souterrain | Anne-Marie Lennon |
| 782. | Caltragh, Cummeen | Sligo | Enclosure | Eoin Halpin |
| 783. | Carrowhubbuck South | Sligo | No archaeological significance | Richard Crumlish |
| 784. | Innishfree House, Carrowmore | Sligo | Within passage tomb complex | Stefan Bergh |
| 785. | Carrownanty | Sligo | No archaeological significance | Anne Connolly |
| 786. | Cloonagleavragh | Sligo | No archaeological significance | Richard Crumlish |
| 787. | Collooney | Sligo | Infantry barrack, possible | Malachy Conway |
| 788. | Cregg | Sligo | Adjacent to rath | Eoin Halpin |

| No. | Site | County | Description | Author |
|---|---|---|---|---|
| 789. | Drumcliffe South/Drumcliffe North | Sligo | No archaeological significance | Richard Crumlish |
| 790. | Main Street (Carrowhubbuck South), Inishcrone | Sligo | Adjacent to enclosure/barrow? | Martin A. Timoney |
| 791. | Feall A'Mhuilinn, Inishmurray | Sligo | Horizontal mill | Jerry O'Sullivan |
| 792. | Laghta Patrick, Inishmurray | Sligo | Leacht | Jerry O'Sullivan |
| 793. | Relickoran, Inishmurray | Sligo | Cemetery | Jerry O'Sullivan |
| 794. | Teampull na mBan, Inishmurray | Sligo | Women's cemetery | Jerry O'Sullivan |
| 795. | Kilboglashy | Sligo | Shell midden | Richard Crumlish |
| 796. | Knocknarea Mountain | Sligo | Neolithic hut sites and bank | Stefan Bergh |
| 797. | Knocknarea Mountain | Sligo | Survey of prehistoric sites and stray finds | Stefan Bergh |
| 798. | Knocknarea Mountain | Sligo | Complex of Neolithic banks | Stefan Bergh |
| 799. | Knoxpark | Sligo | *Fulacht fiadh* | Cia McConway |
| 800. | Rathosey | Sligo | No archaeological significance | Gerry Walsh |
| 801. | Ardkeerin, Riverstown | Sligo | Adjacent to ringfort | Gerry Walsh |
| 802. | Sligo and Environs Water Supply Scheme | Sligo | No archaeological significance | Martin A. Timoney |
| 803. | Sligo and Environs Water Supply Scheme | Sligo | Urban | Anne-Marie Lennon |
| 804. | 6–7 Abbey Street, Sligo | Sligo | Urban medieval/post-medieval | Donald Murphy |
| 805. | 8 Abbey Street Lower, Sligo | Sligo | Medieval limekiln | Alan Hayden |
| 806. | Kempton Parade, Bridge Street, Sligo | Sligo | Urban | Eoin Halpin |
| 807. | Model Arts Centre, The Mall, Sligo | Sligo | Urban | Eoin Halpin |
| 808. | Town Hall, Sligo | Sligo | No archaeological significance | Eoin Halpin |
| 809. | West Gardens, Sligo | Sligo | No archaeological significance | Eoin Halpin |
| 810. | Methodist Church Hall, Wine Street, Sligo | Sligo | Urban | Martin A. Timoney |
| 811. | Sroove (Lough Gara) | Sligo | Crannog | Christina Fredengren |
| 812. | Strandhill | Sligo | No archaeological significance | Eoin Halpin |
| 813. | Ballysheehan Stud, Ballysheehan | Tipperary | Possible deserted medieval village | Avril Purcell |
| 814. | Ballytarsna Castle | Tipperary | Tower-house and bawn | Brian Hodkinson |
| 815. | Killemly, Cahir | Tipperary | Two enclosures | Mary Henry |
| 816. | Carrick-on-Suir | Tipperary | Urban | Florence M. Hurley |
| 817. | Mill Lane, Carrickbeg, Carrick-on-Suir | Tipperary | Urban | Florence M. Hurley |
| 818. | Bohermore, Cashel | Tipperary | Environs of medieval town | Emer Dennehy |
| 819. | Collier's Lane, Cashel | Tipperary | Urban medieval/post-medieval | Florence M. Hurley |
| 820. | Friar's Street, Cashel | Tipperary | Urban medieval | Niall Gregory |
| 821. | Lower Gate Street, Cashel | Tipperary | Urban medieval/post-medieval | Mary Henry |
| 822. | 100 Main Street, Cashel | Tipperary | Urban medieval | Dave Pollock |
| 823. | Little Island, Clonmel | Tipperary | Urban post-medieval | Edmond O'Donovan |
| 824. | 36–37 Parnell Street, Clonmel | Tipperary | Urban medieval and post-medieval | Jo Moran |
| 825. | Hearn's Hotel, Parnell Street, Clonmel | Tipperary | Urban medieval and post-medieval | Jo Moran |
| 826. | Suir Island, Clonmel | Tipperary | Urban | Avril Purcell |
| 827. | Rocklow Road, Fethard | Tipperary | Urban medieval and post-medieval | Jo Moran |
| 828. | 26 Killeenyarda, Holycross | Tipperary | Ringfort | Paul Stevens |
| 829. | 26 Killeenyarda, Holycross | Tipperary | Monitoring adjacent to ringfort | Stuart D. Elder |
| 830. | Kilfeakle | Tipperary | Medieval | Ken Hanley |
| 831. | Grantstown Castle, Kilfeakle | Tipperary | Tower-house | Claire Walsh |
| 832. | Newtown | Tipperary | Vicinity of watermill | Brian Hodkinson |
| 833. | Abbey Street, Roscrea | Tipperary | Adjacent to friary | Brian Hodkinson |
| 834. | Terryglass | Tipperary | Vicinity of castle | Brian Hodkinson |

| | | | | |
|---|---|---|---|---|
| 835. | The Munster Hotel, Cathedral Street, Thurles | Tipperary | Urban medieval | Paul Stevens |
| 836. | Crotty's Bakery, Friar Street, Thurles | Tipperary | Urban | Paul Stevens |
| 837. | Kickham Street, Thurles | Tipperary | Urban | Florence M. Hurley |
| 838. | 1–2 Parnell Street, Thurles | Tipperary | Urban | Paul Stevens |
| 839. | Tullahedy | Tipperary | Burnt mound complex and ditches, multi-period | Richard O'Brien |
| 840. | Lendrum's Bridge, | Tyrone | No archaeological significance | Cia McConway |
| 841. | Newtownstewart Castle, Newtownstewart | Tyrone | 17th-century castle and bawn/ Bronze Age segmented cist | Ruairí Ó Baoill |
| 842. | Croughateskin, Ballymacarbry | Waterford | Adjacent to church and graveyard | Joanna Wren |
| 843. | Buttery Lane, Dungarvan | Waterford | Post-medieval cottages | Dave Pollock |
| 844. | Carberrys Lane, Dungarvan | Waterford | Urban medieval/post-medieval | Dave Pollock |
| 845. | Church Street/ Parnell Street, Dungarvan | Waterford | Urban medieval/post medieval | Dave Pollock |
| 846. | Davitts Quay/ Old Market House, Dungarvan | Waterford | Urban post-medieval | Dave Pollock |
| 847. | Dungarvan Castle, Dungarvan | Waterford | Medieval and post-medieval castle | Dave Pollock |
| 848. | Kilmeaden | Waterford | No archaeological significance | Michael Moore |
| 849. | Waterford Main Drainage Scheme, Waterford | Waterford | Urban | Orla Scully |
| 850. | Bailey's New Street, Waterford | Waterford | Urban medieval, post-medieval | Orla Scully |
| 851. | Bailey's New Street, Waterford | Waterford | Urban | Mary O'Donnell |
| 852. | 17–18 Broad Street, Waterford | Waterford | Urban medieval and post-medieval | Jo Moran |
| 853. | 'Olympia Ballroom', Parnell Street, Waterford | Waterford | Urban | Maurice F. Hurley |
| 854. | Tanyard Arch, Waterford | Waterford | No archaeological significance | Audrey Gahan |
| 855. | Athlone Water Supply Scheme | Westmeath | Culverts | Martin E. Byrne |
| 856. | Athlone Westside Main Drainage Scheme | Westmeath | 19th-century fortifications | Martin E. Byrne |
| 857. | Northgate Street, Athlone | Westmeath | Town wall | Martin E. Byrne |
| 858. | Seán Costello Street, Athlone | Westmeath | Urban | Cóilín Ó Drisceoil |
| 859. | Carrick | Westmeath | Close to site of castle and house | Deirdre Murphy |
| 860. | Castletown Geoghegan | Westmeath | Medieval borough | Deirdre Murphy |
| 861. | Ballyhealy Road, Devlin | Westmeath | Souterrain | Deirdre Murphy |
| 862. | Farrancallin | Westmeath | No archaeological significance | Finola O'Carroll |
| 863. | Glasson | Westmeath | No archaeological significance | Niall Gregory |
| 864. | Tullamore Road, Kilbeggan | Westmeath | Town | Dominic Delany |
| 865. | Rattin, Kinnegad | Westmeath | No archaeological significance | Malachy Conway |
| 866. | Austin Friars Street, Mullingar | Westmeath | No archaeological significance | Matthew Seaver |
| 867. | Employment Exchange, Blackhall Street, Mullingar | Westmeath | Urban medieval | Martin E. Byrne |
| 868. | Church Avenue, Mullingar | Westmeath | Urban medieval | Clare Mullins |
| 869. | College Street, Mullingar | Westmeath | Urban | Rosanne Meenan |
| 870. | Friars Mill Road, Mullingar | Westmeath | Urban post-medieval | Matthew Seaver |
| 871. | Friars Mill Road, Mullingar | Westmeath | 19th-century graveyard | Donald Murphy |
| 872. | Lackan, Multyfarnham | Westmeath | Ringfort with souterrain | Sylvia Desmond |
| 873. | Newdown | Westmeath | Adjacent to earthworks | Jacinta Kiely |
| 874. | Brownswood | Wexford | Vicinity of *fulacht fiadh* | Cara Murray |
| 875. | Ferns Sewerage Scheme | Wexford | Multi-period | Frank Ryan |
| 876. | Castlelands, Ferns | Wexford | Pits | Claire Walsh |
| 877. | Ferns Lower, Ferns | Wexford | Ring-ditch | Frank Ryan |
| 878. | Ferns Upper, Ferns | Wexford | Proximity to Early Christian town | Avril Purcell |

| | | | | |
|---|---|---|---|---|
| 879. | Grange, Fethard | Wexford | Urban medieval | Jacinta Kiely |
| 880. | Glascarrig North | Wexford | Adjacent to monastery | Cóilín Ó Drisceoil |
| 881. | Mill Lands, Gorey | Wexford | No archaeological significance | Alan Hayden |
| 882. | Hook Lighthouse, Hook Head | Wexford | Medieval lighthouse | Alan Hayden |
| 883. | Mayglass | Wexford | Post-medieval house | Joanna Wren |
| 884. | Irishtown, New Ross | Wexford | Pits | E. Eoin Sullivan |
| 885. | Marshmeadows, New Ross | Wexford | Possible standing stone | Donald Murphy |
| 886. | Millbanks, Rosbercon, New Ross | Wexford | Adjacent to medieval suburb | Cóilín Ó Drisceoil |
| 887. | Rosslare Harbour Interim Drainage Scheme | Wexford | Monitoring/testing | Stuart D. Elder |
| 888. | Taghmon | Wexford | Ditch features | Clare Mullins |
| 889. | The Shambles, Church Lane, Wexford | Wexford | Urban | Cóilín Ó Drisceoil |
| 890. | The Faythe, Wexford | Wexford | No archaeological significance | Cathy Sheehan |
| 891. | Paul Quay/Crescent Quay, Wexford | Wexford | Urban | Tim Coughlan |
| 892. | Ballymaghroe | Wicklow | Adjacent to ecclesiastical enclosure | Frank Ryan |
| 893. | Mill Street, Baltinglass | Wicklow | Estate town | Martin E. Byrne |
| 894. | Burgage More | Wicklow | Environs of earthwork site | Martin E. Byrne |
| 895. | Wicklow Arms Public House, Delgany | Wicklow | Adjacent to medieval graveyard | Rónán Swan |
| 896. | Dunbur Lower | Wicklow | Monitoring | Ian W. Doyle |
| 897. | Market Square, Dunlavin | Wicklow | Urban medieval | Martin E. Byrne |
| 898. | Kilmacurragh | Wicklow | No archaeological significance | Martin Reid |
| 899. | Carysfort, Macreddin | Wicklow | Historic town | Malachy Conway |
| 900. | N11 Newtownmountkennedy/ Ballynabarney Road Improvement Scheme | Wicklow | Flint scatters | Martin E. Byrne |
| 901. | 'The Chestnuts', Church Hill, Wicklow | Wicklow | Adjacent to medieval church | James Eogan |
| 902. | 1 Church Street, Wicklow | Wicklow | Urban | Martin Reid |
| 903. | Church Street/ Wentworth Place, Wicklow | Wicklow | Urban | Dermot Nelis |

## ADDENDA

Reports of the following sites were received in press.

| | | | | |
|---|---|---|---|---|
| Ad1. | Dundalk Street, Carlingford | Louth | No archaeological significance | Cóilín Ó Drisceoil |
| Ad2. | Newtownbalregan, Castletown | Louth | No archaeological significance | Cóilín Ó Drisceoil |
| Ad3. | 74 Trinity Street, Drogheda | Louth | No archaeological significance | Cóilín Ó Drisceoil |
| Ad4. | Kilcarbry, Enniscorthy | Wexford | No archaeological significance | Cóilín Ó Drisceoil |

The following is a list of sites for which excavation licences were issued during 1999 but for which summaries were not received in time for publication.

## CLARE

**904. Ballynacragga, Area 7**
?
**98E0333**
*Billy Quinn, Archaeological Services Unit Ltd, Purcell House, Oranmore, Co. Galway.*

**905. Latoon South, Area 3**
?
**98E0332**
*Billy Quinn, Archaeological Services Unit Ltd, Purcell House, Oranmore, Co. Galway.*

**906. Main Street, Quin**
?
**99E0502**
*Billy Quinn, Archaeological Services Unit Ltd, Purcell House, Oranmore, Co. Galway.*

## DUBLIN

**907. Belinstown**
?
**99E0545**
*Patricia Lynch, 10 Ashford Place, Dublin 7.*

**908. Coldwinter**
?
**99E0548**
*Patricia Lynch, 10 Ashford Place, Dublin 7.*

**909. Lissenhall Great**
?
**99E0546**
*Patricia Lynch, 10 Ashford Place, Dublin 7.*

**910. Lissenhall Great (2)**
?
**99E0547**
*Patricia Lynch, 10 Ashford Place, Dublin 7.*

## GALWAY

**911. 47 Eyre Square, Galway**
Urban
**99E0403**
*Billy Quinn, Archaeological Services Unit Ltd, Purcell House, Oranmore, Co. Galway.*

**912. Oghil and Killeaney (Inis Mór)**
?
**99E0647**
*Billy Quinn, Archaeological Services Unit Ltd, Purcell House, Oranmore, Co. Galway.*

## KERRY

**913. Skellig Michael, Great Skellig**
Monastic site
**02453 06042**
**SMR 104A:001**
**95E0??? ext.**
*Edward Bourke, Dúchas The Heritage Service, 6 Ely Place Upper, Dublin 2.*

## KILDARE

**914. Ardscull, Athy**
?
**99E0170**
*John Tierney, Eachtra Archaeological Projects, Curragh, Ardmore, Co. Waterford.*

**915. Kilkea Lower**
?
**99E0587**
*Niall Gregory, 25 Westpark, Blessington, Co. Wicklow.*

## KILKENNY

**916. Dunmore Caves**
Viking artefacts
*Andrew Halpin, National Museum of Ireland, Kildare Street, Dublin 2.*

**917. Kilkenny Sewerage Scheme, Stage 4**
Urban
**97E0481**
*Patrick J.H. Neary, 12 Willow Close, Ardmore, Kilkenny.*

**918. 33 Patrick Street, Kilkenny**
Urban medieval
**98E0402**
*John Tierney, Eachtra Archaeological Projects, Curragh, Ardmore, Co. Waterford.*

**919. Patrick Street/Pudding Lane, Kilkenny**
Urban medieval
**97E0468**
*John Tierney, Eachtra Archaeological Projects, Curragh, Ardmore, Co. Waterford.*

**920. Piltown–Fiddown Road Improvement Scheme**
Monitoring
**99E0575**
*Patrick J.H. Neary, 12 Willow Close, Ardmore, Kilkenny.*

## LEITRIM

**921. Barrack Park, Lurganboy**
?
**99E0313**
*Billy Quinn, Archaeological Services Unit Ltd, Purcell House, Oranmore, Co. Galway.*

## LIMERICK

**922. Kilmallock**
Urban
**99E0215**
*Niall Gregory, 25 Westpark, Blessington, Co. Wicklow.*

## LOUTH

**923. Ballyvass–Ardee Gas Pipeline**
?
**99E0434**
*Niall Gregory, 25 Westpark, Blessington, Co. Wicklow.*

**926. Crumlin 1**
?
**98E0615**
*Patricia Lynch, 10 Ashford Place, Dublin 7.*

**927. Crumlin 2**
?
**99E0430**
*Patricia Lynch, 10 Ashford Place, Dublin 7.*

## MEATH

**929. Randalstown**
?
**98E0528**
*Niall Gregory, 25 Westpark, Blessington, Co. Wicklow.*

## OFFALY

**930. Church Street, Birr**
Urban
**99E0758**
*John Tierney, Eachtra Archaeological Projects, Curragh, Ardmore, Co. Waterford.*

## SLIGO

**931. Drumcliff**
**?98E0514**
*Cara Murray, 10 Martello Avenue, Dun Laoghaire, Co. Dublin.*

## TIPPERARY

**932. Cashel**
Urban
**99E0747**
*Niall Gregory, 25 Westpark, Blessington, Co. Wicklow.*

## WATERFORD

**933. N25 Road Realignment at Kilmacthomas**
Monitoring
**99E0623**
*Michael Tierney.*

## APPENDICES

*I.* Field-walking at Robswalls, Malahide, Co. Dublin.
*Avril Purcell, Margaret Gowen & Co. Ltd, 2 Killiney View, Albert Road Lower, Glenageary, Co. Dublin.*

*II.* The Louth Mask Regional Water Supply Scheme, Stage II, Contract 6, Ballinrobe–Claremorris–Ballindine.
*Gerry Walsh, Mayo County Council, Castlebar, Co. Mayo.*

## ANTRIM

### 1. AGHNAHOUGH
No archaeological significance
J23906680
Initial field survey along the line of a proposed aqueduct replacement revealed evidence of a linear setting of stones. As this feature lay within the scope of the cut for the aqueduct, a small test excavation (one trench measuring 3.5m x 1m) was carried out to identify the nature and extent of the feature. No further stones were found, but a very crude stone floor within the area confined by the stones suggested that it had functioned as a structure possibly associated with agricultural activity. Finds from the test excavation showed the feature to be late post-medieval in date.
*Eoin Halpin, ADS Ltd, Unit 48, Westlink Enterprise Centre, 30–50 Distillery Street, Belfast BT12 5BJ.*

### 2. STEEPLE, ANTRIM
Ecclesiastical
J15508795
Plans to extend service trenches in the vicinity of the round tower at Steeple townland in the north of Antrim town required initial archaeological investigation. Monitoring of the excavation of engineering test-pits was carried out. No archaeological finds or features were revealed.
*Cormac McSparron, NAC, Unit 6, Farset Enterprise Park, 638 Springfield Road, Belfast.*

### 3. TOBERDOWNEY, BALLYNURE
No archaeological significance
J31679359
SMR 45:16
Monitoring of a housing development took place here. The site is next to a medieval (or perhaps earlier—there is a 19th-century reference to a souterrain and to cashel-style walls being present) church and graveyard. There are references to a church at Ballynure from the early 14th century. The site was later occupied by a mill dam.

Mechanical topsoil-stripping was monitored before development. No pre-19th-century features or finds were noted. However, the outline of the edge of the millpond was uncovered.
*Alan Reilly, NAC, Unit 6, Farset Enterprise Park, 638 Springfield Road, Belfast.*

### 4. BALLYUTOAG
Neolithic material
J297804
At Ballyutoag townland, Co. Antrim, at Tarmac Quarry Products Ltd, Hightown Quarry, during monitoring of a quarry extension, a spread of western Neolithic pottery and struck flint was recorded at c. 270m OD. Although a team of archaeologists carried out further investigations in the area of the finds, no structures were found.
*Cormac McSparron, NAC, Unit 6, Farset Enterprise Park, 638 Springfield Road, Belfast.*

### 5. GORDON STREET, BELFAST
Urban post-medieval
J34107461
SMR 61:19
A rescue excavation was undertaken at a site on Gordon Street, Belfast, before the internal redevelopment of a mid-19th-century listed building. The site lies within the 17th-century core of Belfast.

Gordon Street was originally known as Buller's Row and is shown partially developed on Phillips's 1685 map of Belfast. The defended gate into Belfast, known as the Strand Gate, is thought to have occupied this location. Tanneries were common in the surrounding streets. The area was redeveloped by the fifth earl of Donegall in the years after 1757, following his accession.

The building within which the excavation took place occupies the corner of Gordon Street and Victoria Street. In earlier times it had been the Corn Exchange, constructed in 1851 by Thomas Jackson after the repeal of the Corn Laws in 1846. The building façade is listed.

Two trenches were opened at opposite sides of the development. The first uncovered 18th-century building foundations, founded in lough deposits, which had been both infilled and damaged as a result of modern building activity. Building remains included wall footings and plinths, mortared stone infilling away from the walls, wooden post-piles and a drain. The walls constituted part of the western and southern extent of a structure.

There was a maximum of 1.1m of stratigraphy encountered above the naturally occurring lough deposits. The lough deposits took the form of grey, silty sand, which occurred across the whole of the development site. It appears that the site lay within the Belfast Lough intertidal zone before land reclamation in this part of the town. Eighteenth-century artefacts were recovered from the foundation levels of the structure.

Excavation in Trench 2 produced no structural remains, with the stratigraphy consisting of a series of organic clay and silt dump deposits, sitting directly on top of the lough silts. The dump deposits contained artefacts dating to the 17th and 18th centuries, including fragments of pottery and clay pipes, and most likely represent both domestic and industrial rubbish.
*Ruairí Ó Baoill, Archaeological Excavation Unit, EHS, 5–33 Hill Street, Belfast BT1 2LA.*

### 6. WARING STREET, BELFAST
Urban post-medieval
J34087455
SMR 61:20
Assessment excavations were carried out on this site, which is within a zone of archaeological potential marking the commercial hub of the 17th-century town at Belfast, before urban development.

Two trenches were excavated close to the modern street frontage. The earliest stratum uncovered in Trench 1 was a sterile sand subsoil, overlain by a compact, grey, sandy clay. In the centre of the excavated area the grey sandy clay was cut by a brick-built structure. The earliest part of this structure was a foundation trench measuring 1.6m north–south by 0.8m, with a maximum depth of 0.2m. The primary fill of the cut was a north–south-running brick-built wall measuring 1.6m north–south by 0.37m, with a maximum height of 0.34m.

Above this, the cut was filled with a mix of loam

clay, brick fragments and mortar. A stick-pin, possibly medieval, was recovered from this fill. A further length of wall, running east–west, was uncovered at the southern limit of the north–south-orientated wall. The second wall was roughly jointed to the first, and no evidence was noted for tie-bricks. The exposed section of the second wall was 0.43m wide (north–south) and ran east for 0.88m before terminating. A third length of walling, the excavated dimensions of which were 0.36m wide (north–south) and 0.57m long, was exposed 1m east of this point. The bricks in the walls of this structure measured on average 0.22m x 0.1m x 0.05m and seem to be of 17th-century date.

The intervening space between the second and third walls, which measured 1m, almost certainly represents an external doorway opening onto Waring Street, suggesting that the line of the 17th-century street frontage does not differ significantly from the present one. The internal excavated limits of the structure measured 1.56m north–south by 1.9m. Within this area was a layer of compact, orange/brown clay. Five narrow linear features cut the upper surface of the clay. The features were all filled with a brown, organic loam and had a maximum depth of 0.05m. They have been interpreted as the remains of timber flooring.

The ceramic evidence, including Belfast delftware and saggar fragments, also seems to suggest a 17th-century date for the structure in Trench 1.

Trench 2 was positioned c. 5m east of Trench 1 and measured 2m by 1m. The earliest stratum uncovered was again the grey/yellow, sandy clay subsoil. A red brick wall cut into the subsoil close to the eastern limit of excavation. The wall was 1m long (north–south) and 0.46 wide and had a maximum height of 0.42m. This possible 17th-century wall may mark the eastern return wall of the same structure as that found in Trench 1. At the eastern limit of the excavation the early wall was disturbed by one, if not two, later walls and a gas main.

*Paul Logue, Archaeological Excavation Unit, EHS, 5–33 Hill Street, Belfast BT1 2LA.*

## 7. BRITISH
No archaeological significance
J14508080
Monitoring took place at this site, close to Aldergrove Airport, Co. Antrim, late in 1999. The site had been identified as a possible cropmark from aerial photographs. However, removal of topsoil to the depth of the proposed formation layer revealed nothing of archaeological significance. No further archaeological input was required.

*Audrey Gahan, ADS, Unit 48, Westlink Enterprise Centre, 30–50 Distillery Street, Belfast BT12 5BJ.*

## 8. IRISH QUARTER WEST, CARRICKFERGUS
Urban post-medieval
J41158734
Monitoring of a sheltered housing development took place at Irish Quarter West/Albert Road junction, Carrickfergus town, Co. Antrim. The site lay beyond the walls of the medieval and 17th-century town, outside the 'Irish Gate'. This area of the town was not occupied until the 17th century, according to surviving documentation. Previous excavations indicated a medieval pottery kiln in the area. Much of the road frontage where the 17th/18th-century houses were situated would have been destroyed in road-widening operations etc. The area monitored was open land before the 17th century and back gardens or yards thereafter.

Mechanical excavation of foundation trenches c. 2m deep and c. 0.6m wide was monitored. The area consisted of a series of dumps that were shallow at the seaward end and up to 2m deep inland. Some intermittent cobbling was noted in section. The areas close to the pavements were very disturbed.

The finds consisted overwhelmingly of 18th-century pottery, with lesser amounts of 17th-century and medieval examples.

*Alan Reilly, NAC, Unit 6, Farset Enterprise Park, 638 Springfield Road, Belfast.*

## 9. 1–3 JOYMOUNT, CARRICKFERGUS
Town wall
J414875
Monitoring was carried out at 1–3 Joymount, Carrickfergus, Co. Antrim. Cartographic evidence and excavations at the adjacent Ulster Bank suggested that the late 16th-century town wall would continue across the eastern end of the site. As anticipated, the town wall was uncovered during the excavation of the three main east–west ground-beams.

As investigated, the wall was constructed of stone and mortar, running at a slight angle north-north-west/south-south-east along the eastern edge of the site. The wall was up to 1.85m wide and consisted of heavily mortared basalt blocks of random-course construction. The facing-stones had been very roughly dressed, whereas the core was composed of undressed stone blocks. After recording, the wall was covered with several layers of a durable blue polyfoam and then with a thin layer of fine gravel. It was confirmed with the engineer that the town wall would not be bearing any of the load of the new development.

To the east of the wall, underlying post-medieval rubble, was natural beach sand, while to the west was some evidence of the robbing-out of the wall, with large, mortared basalt blocks strewn among the rubble.

To facilitate the piling rig, a mechanical excavator dug a small hole for each beam to soft ground. The piling rig cannot pile through stone, and, as the foundations closely followed the footprint of the original building, the incidence of hitting a stone wall was very high. Monitoring of these holes ensured that disturbance from ground level was kept to a minimum. Nothing of archaeological significance was noted in these holes—the soft ground encountered in the middle of the site, a potentially significant archaeological deposit, contained red brick fragments and late post-medieval pottery. The piles along the easternmost north–south wall cut through layers of natural sand below the post-medieval rubble build-up.

All other groundworks to facilitate drainage, gas and electricity ran tight against the cut ground-beams, within the upper rubble infill. Nothing of

archaeological significance was noted during this work.
*Cia McConway, ADS Ltd, Unit 48, Westlink Enterprise Centre, 30–50 Distillery Street, Belfast BT12 5BJ.*

### 10. JOYMOUNT MANSE, CARRICKFERGUS
Medieval ditch
J41938765

Licensed monitoring of strip foundations on the site of the proposed new Manse at Joymount, Carrickfergus, revealed evidence of a possible medieval ditch. The site lay just outside, to the north, of the 17th-century walled town of Carrickfergus.

A small excavation within the area of the development confirmed that a medieval ditch, which had been severely truncated in antiquity, extended across the site. On average, the U-shaped ditch was 5m wide where it cut subsoil, and it extended across the site for a distance of *c.* 13m, continuing beyond the limit of excavation to both the north and the east.

Pottery recovered from the basal fills was local 13th–14th-century material in association with Saintonge and Redcliffe ware, suggesting a late 13th–14th-century date for this fill. It has not been possible to associate the ditch with any known medieval structure in the area; however, it may form part of the medieval Carrickfergus town defences.
*Audrey Gahan, ADS Ltd, Unit 48, Westlink Enterprise Centre, 30–50 Distillery Street, Belfast BT12 5BJ.*

### 11. CROOKEDSTONE
No archaeological significance
J15618253
SMR 55:205

A machine-cut trench, 23m long by 2m wide and aligned approximately north–south, was excavated to subsoil to determine whether this was an archaeological or a natural feature. A band of mixed ploughsoil containing a high proportion of small to medium-sized stones and exhibiting clear signs of waterlogging was encountered 5m from the southern end of the trench at the approximate location of the cropmark. This band of stones had been laid down by plough action and does not represent archaeological activity. No archaeological features were observed, and no artefacts were recovered.
*Norman Crothers, Archaeological Excavation Unit, EHS, 5–33 Hill Street, Belfast BT1 2LA.*

### 12. DRUMAKEELY AND DUNDERMOT
No archaeological significance
D07071295

At Dundermot townland, Co. Antrim, monitoring was carried out before the building of a house. No archaeological finds or structures were revealed.
*Cormac McSparron, NAC, Unit 6, Farset Enterprise Park, 638 Springfield Road, Belfast.*

### 13. WESTERN QUAY WALL, GLENARM
No archaeological significance
D312154
SMR 29:6

Larne Borough Council proposes to refurbish the harbour at Glenarm, Co. Antrim. This work will initially involve the refurbishment and reconstruction of the existing harbour piers, the dredging of the refurbished harbour and finally the rebuilding of the Glenarm River quay walls, both east and west sides, from the Cloney Bridge to the sea.

The site is within an archaeologically highly sensitive area, within the immediate vicinity of Glenarm Friary, on a small promontory overlooking Glenarm Bay.

The area investigated consists of a thin strip of land 110m long, lying along the west bank of the river, to the east of St Patrick's Church of Ireland parish church.

Ten trenches were mechanically excavated, running east–west along the length of the western bank of the Glenarm River from Cloney Bridge to the end of the existing quay. Where possible, trenches were excavated to subsoil. This testing indicated that the present bank is of modern construction, 1.4m+ deep composed of compacted stone (predominantly shattered limestone), with flint nodules, red brick, 20th-century crockery, ceramic sewer pipe and tin cans.

No significant archaeological deposits were uncovered.
*Cia McConway, ADS Ltd, Unit 48, Westlink Enterprise Centre, 30–50 Distillery Street, Belfast BT12 5BJ.*

### 14. LARNE (PORT OF)
Mesolithic/Bronze Age
D414026

The Port of Larne authorities were planning to reduce the height of a parking area adjacent to the docks to facilitate freight traffic. This investigation was intended to assess the potential for archaeological survival within the development area.

The site encompasses an area 200m north–south by on average 100m east–west, standing *c.* 3.5m higher than the surrounding ground. The ground is currently under concrete, with the site being used as a storage area for haulage containers.

A site assessment carried out by Eoin Halpin in 1995 (*Excavations 1995*, 2) had noted the presence of a possible old ground surface in the north-western corner, but elsewhere this surface had appeared to have been scarped away during the construction of the storage area.

Owing to the number of developments that have taken place along the Curran Point area, the site represented one of the last possible raised beach areas within the immediate vicinity of Larne. A second assessment, concentrated in the north-west corner of the site, was carried out in December 1999, to evaluate the archaeological potential of both the old ground layer and what it had sealed.

Two trenches were investigated, in the north-western corner of the site. The stratigraphic sequence encountered in both was virtually identical, and it was generally uniform across each trench, although the western half of Trench 2 had concrete walls and floor slabs set deep below the concrete surface. Both trenches measured *c.* 11.5m east–west by 13.5m. Trench 1 incorporated the western 13m of the 1995 assessment Trench 1.

Immediately underlying the lowest layer of modern infill was an organic-smelling, 'soddy', black/dark grey/brown layer, which had been previously flagged as a possible old ground surface. Investigation concluded that it was indeed an old ground layer that extended across the eastern half of Trench 2 and most of Trench 1. It varied in depth across the trenches from 0.03m to 0.23m. Numerous struck flints, consistent with the Late Mesolithic heavy blade industry, and Neolithic flint scrapers were recovered, along with some post-medieval pottery, roof slate, metal and red brick fragments. The post-medieval finds were intrusive to the old ground surface and found just within its upper surface, having been mechanically pushed into the soft old ground deposit during the layering of the modern infilling.

Underlying the old ground surface and extending across the entire trench was a raised beach deposit, consisting of water-rolled pebbles and much struck flint within a loose, dark brown, sandy matrix. Excavation of one test-pit in the south-east corner of Trench 2 indicated that the raised beach material extended for at least 4m below the concrete surface, with large flakes and cores, indicative of the Late Mesolithic period, being recovered at this depth. The remaining raised beach material was left *in situ*.

In the south-eastern corner of Trench 1 a large pit was excavated cutting through this raised beach material. A large quantity of Late Bronze Age cooking ware was recovered from the fill, along with some struck flint. During the excavation of the test-pit in Trench 2, several features—small pits/post-holes—were recorded in the section faces, and it is presumed that these features also date to the Bronze Age and are associated with the pit excavated in Trench 1.

While the recovery of Late Mesolithic struck flints within the raised beach material was to be expected, the discovery of a large Bronze Age pit adds a new dimension to this area of Larne's prehistory. Further excavation will clarify the nature of this Bronze Age activity.

*Cia McConway, ADS Ltd, Unit 48, Westlink Enterprise Centre, 30–50 Distillery Street, Belfast BT12 5BJ.*

## 15. HIGHTOWN ROAD, MALLUSK, PHASE 1A
Early Bronze Age
J30008200
**SMR 56:41, 42 and 48**

Monitoring of topsoil-stripping was carried out before a large housing development. A desk-top survey had revealed that the development is within an archaeologically sensitive zone, with a man-made mound at Ballywonard td, the unlocated sites of a medieval chapel and a fortification at Ballyvaston, and an enclosure at Ballybought.

Although no evidence of these unlocated sites was found, a curving gully filled with a charcoal-rich soil and containing Early Bronze Age pottery and worked flint was encountered and excavated. The gully, when currently viewed in its isolation, indicates the presence of Early Bronze Age archaeological activity of a probable settlement nature. It is likely that, once stripping commences in the areas immediately adjacent to this phase, i.e. in Phases 2A and 2B, this feature will be better placed in a prehistoric landscape.

No other features of archaeological significance were found.

*Cia McConway, ADS Ltd, Unit 48, Westlink Enterprise Centre, 30–50 Distillery Street, Belfast BT12 5BJ.*

## 16. BALLYHENRY, NEWTOWNABBEY
Multi-period
J317848

The development of an industrial estate by the IDB necessitated this mitigation project, which is still ongoing; a summary will appear in *Excavations 2000*.

*Ciara MacManus, ADS, Unit 48, Westlink Enterprise Centre, 30–50 Distillery Street, Belfast BT12 5BJ.*

## 17. NORTHERN COUNTIES HOTEL, MAIN STREET, PORTRUSH
No archaeological significance
28566 44088
**SMR 2:18**

An assessment was carried out at the site of the former Northern Counties Hotel at Main Street, Portrush, Co. Antrim. The site is at the junction of Mark Street, Lower Mark Street and Main Street, an archaeologically sensitive area believed to be close to the site of an ecclesiastical enclosure. During excavation of a trench for a sewer in connection with the Northern Counties Hotel in the late 1800s, human bone was discovered, and in 1882 'regular' undisturbed interments were found during the laying of sewers through the principal streets of Portrush. This suggests that the burial-ground associated with the medieval church was quite extensive.

Two stages of assessment and monitoring were undertaken. Stage I was carried out by Deirdre Murphy on 3 August 1999, comprising two test-trenches (1–2) and monitoring of six test-pits (1–6), and Stage II monitoring of nine engineering test-pits (7–15) was undertaken by Malachy Conway on 19 November 1999.

Test-pit 1, in the north-west corner of the site, was orientated north-west/south-east and was 2.5m long, 1m wide and at maximum 1.4m deep (OD 11.158m). A red brick rubble layer containing stone and mortar, 0.45m deep, overlay a sterile, sandy layer. Bedrock was encountered at 1.4m.

Test-pit 2, orientated north–south along the northern site boundary, was 4.6m long, 1.3m wide and 1.5m deep. Red brick rubble and mortar 0.42m deep overlay a natural, sandy layer, with rock encountered 0.6m below the surface (OD 11.938m). An early modern east–west foundation wall was visible at a depth of 0.37m at the northern end.

Test-pit 3, excavated south of Test-pit 2, measured 3m² and 0.5m deep. Red brick rubble and mortar extended to a depth of 0.5m, at which point the natural rock was evident (OD 13.118m). Remains of a red brick manhole were present, quarried down to the bedrock. Eight metres south-east of the pit, bedrock was evident on the surface.

Test-pit 4, excavated along Main Street south-east of Test-pit 2, was 3.5m long, 1.6m wide and 1.5m deep. Red brick rubble, cement, tarmac and stone extended to a depth of 0.55m, below which a sterile, sandy layer was evident to a depth of 1.1m, at which point bedrock was exposed (OD 11.438m).

Test-pit 5, north-west of Test-pit 3, was 2m long, 1.4m wide and 0.55m deep. A concrete yard, 0.2m deep, overlay red brick rubble to a depth of 0.55m, where rock was encountered (OD 12.858m).

Test-pit 6, south of Test-pit 1, close to Mark Street, was 2m long, 1.2m wide and 1.1m deep. Red brick rubble and mortar 0.75m deep overlay a sterile, sandy layer. Bedrock was encountered at a depth of 1.1m (OD 13.098m). A north–south foundation wall of early modern date was evident 0.2m below the surface (OD 13.998m) at the west end of the pit.

Test-pit 7, excavated towards the south-west corner of the site in a south–north direction, was 2.5m long, 1m wide and 1.7m deep. Red brick rubble, stone and mortar 0.8m deep overlay a sterile, sandy layer. Bedrock lay below this layer at a depth of 1.7m+.

Test-pit 8, positioned in the south-west corner of the site, close to the gable wall of the adjoining property on Mark Street, and excavated in a south–north direction, was 3m long, 1m wide and 2m deep. A conglomerate concrete surface containing red brick fragments, stone, mortar and rubble extended to a depth of 0.8m. Below this a sterile, sandy layer extended to a depth of 1.7m. The natural bedrock lay at a depth of 1.7m+.

Test-pit 9, excavated along the western side of the site c. 20m north-west of Test-pit 8, was 3m long, 1m wide and 1.5m deep. Rubble overburden containing the remains of a red brick wall foundation parallel to the street extended to a depth of 0.9m. Below this a sterile, yellow, sandy layer extended to a depth of 1.5m. The natural rock lay at a depth of 1.5m+.

Test-pit 10, excavated at the north-west corner of the site c. 25m north-west of Test-pit 9, was 3m long, 1m wide and 0.4m deep. Rubble overburden mixed with dark brown loam extended to a depth of 0.4m, at which point the natural rock was encountered.

Test-pit 11, along the northern perimeter of the site c. 20m north-east of Test-pit 10, was 3m long, 1m wide and 0.9m deep. Rubble overburden mixed with dark brown loam extended to a depth of 0.9m, at which point the natural rock was encountered.

Test-pit 12, c. 10m north-east of Test-pit 10, was 2.5m long, 1m wide and 1.6m deep (OD 11.358m). Rubble overburden mixed with rubbish and dark brown loam extended to a depth of 1.6m, at which point the floor of a former swimming pool was encountered. Excavations ceased at this depth as the mechanical excavator could not break through this level.

Test-pit 13, excavated in a north-central section of the site, was 3m long, 1m wide and 1.5m deep (OD 11.258m). Rubble overburden extended to a depth of 0.7m, from where a sterile, yellow, sandy layer extended to a depth of 1.5m. Bedrock lay at a depth of 1.5m+.

Test-pit 14, in a west-central position, was 2m long, 1m wide and 0.8m deep (OD 10.558m). Rubble overburden mixed with dark brown loam extended to a depth of 0.8m, at which point the natural rock was encountered.

Test-pit 15 was excavated c. 8m north-east of Test-pit 7 and 8m south-west of a visible rock outcrop in the south-west area of the site. Removal of a very thin layer of rubble not over 0.1m deep revealed natural rock outcrop.

Trench 1 was 11.5m long, 1.4m wide and 0.7m deep. Rubble, brick fragments and sand extended to a depth of 0.5m, below which bedrock was evident. In some places the rock was as close as 0.3m to the surface.

Trench 2 was 30m long, 1.4m wide and 1m deep. A disturbed layer of mortar, red brick rubble and stone extended to a depth of 0.25m at the west end of the trench, below which lay orange boulder clay. Bedrock was encountered at 0.75m below surface. Further east the disturbed rubble layer extended to a depth of 0.6m, below which the boulder clay was evident. The bedrock was here exposed at a depth of 1m.

Although the site is in an archaeologically sensitive area, the environs of a medieval church and graveyard, both stages of testing and excavation of engineering test-pits failed to reveal any archaeological stratigraphy or finds. Clearly the site was stripped down to bedrock sometime in the past, perhaps for the construction of the former hotel. Foundation walls of early modern date encountered in Stage I, Test-pits 3 and 6, and Stage II, Test-pit 9, lay directly on the bedrock. The bedrock on the site appears to be stepped from north-east to south-west. Along Main Street the rock is below the surface; at the centre of the site it is visible on the surface; and further south-west along Mark Street the rock is visible in sections above present ground level. It is possible that the graveyard at one time extended onto this site, but, with the site being stripped to bedrock, any traces of the former burial-ground have been removed. It is also possible that the ecclesiastical remains and the burial-ground were located north-east of the present site and never actually extended this far.

*Deirdre Murphy and Malachy Conway, Archaeological Consultancy Services Ltd, 15 Trinity Street, Drogheda, Co. Louth.*

## 18. TULLAGHGARLEY
Souterrain
D095015
SMR 32:71

During the construction of a road at this site, near Ballymena, the remains of a souterrain had been exposed in a south-facing section. The remains were recorded, and the cleaning of other areas that had already been stripped was supervised. This cleaning was carried out using a machine with a toothless bucket.

The cut for a creep was revealed in the section face. This was c. 14m long, ranged from 0.6m to 1.7m deep and yielded sherds of souterrain ware. It ran from the east to the upstanding remains of a stone structure at the west. During cleaning it was discovered that this structure was the remains of a passage. The area beneath a lintel was cleared of debris, and the presence of voids beyond suggested that the passage continued further north and that substantial remains may be preserved beneath the ground surface.

Upon return to the site, the lintels of the souterrain were exposed, as well as a subcircular depression to the east, delimited by curving stone-lined cuts and arcs of stake-holes and containing sizeable quantities of souterrain ware.

*Liam McQuillan and Chris Long, ADS Ltd, Unit 48, Westlink Enterprise Centre, 30–50 Distillery Street, Belfast BT12 5BJ.*

# ARMAGH

### 19. ENGLISH STREET, ARMAGH
No archaeological significance
H87634524

An assessment was carried out on the site of the proposed new Ulster Bank at English Street, Armagh. Previous investigation had revealed evidence of material of archaeological significance in this area. However, construction of buildings on the site in the past had removed any material of archaeological importance that may have existed here. There was no further archaeological input required on the site.

*Eoin Halpin, ADS Ltd, Unit 48, Westlink Enterprise Centre, 30–50 Distillery Street, Belfast BT12 5BJ.*

### 20. DRUMILLY BAWN, DRUMILLY DEMESNE, BALLYTYRONE
Walled garden
H91145134
SMR 8:12

It was thought that the foundations of a 17th-century bawn, known from Plantation period documentation, may have been present on or under the site of the walled garden know as 'Drumilly Bawn'. The name was the only indication of any great antiquity. No bawn features were noted in the make-up of the present garden wall.

Excavation trenches, their position dictated by those of rare clearances in the forest, confirmed that the site was a late 18th-century walled garden, consisting of a tall inner wall, a ha-ha and a slip. No traces of earlier occupation were found.

*Alan Reilly, NAC, Unit 6, Farset Enterprise Park, 638 Springfield Road, Belfast.*

### 21. NAVAN FORT, NAVAN
Iron Age enclosure
H847452
SMR 12:12

In 1994 a geophysical survey in the interior of Navan Fort revealed the existence of a sharply defined circular anomaly 30m in diameter to the north of the area between Sites A and B. Site A was a ring-barrow, and Site B a large mound. Both were excavated in the 1960s (Waterman 1997). The anomaly appeared to be two narrow features, perhaps circular-plan trenches or slots rather than ditches. There was no sign of an entrance or internal features. Overlay of plans suggested that the feature, now designated 'Site C', joined or was cut by a triple ring-slot feature found under Site A.

In 1999 four trenches were laid out at widely spaced points on the perimeter of Site C. These showed that it consisted of two concentric slots *c.* 0.5m wide and 0.6m deep, spaced about 1m apart. The strong geophysical signature was clearly given by the considerable amount of burnt soil, with scraps of ash and charcoal in the upper fill. Where excavation continued deeper there was evidence for close-set posts in the base of the outer slot. However, the burnt material in the upper fill at all the points where the slots were exposed appeared to have been packed or have subsided into the trench and was unlike the remains of burnt vertical timbers. The looser material in the upper filling contained a significant admixture of bone fragments, some burnt to the degree of cremation. The 58 fragments were identified by Eileen Murphy as pig, cattle and sheep/goat.

A fifth test-trench was laid out *c.* 50m to the north-west to examine a linear geophysical anomaly running roughly parallel to the inner edge of the main enclosure ditch. A deep slot, packed with charcoal-rich soil and stones, was found on the expected line but stopped abruptly in the middle of the excavation trench.

One of the excavation trenches was laid out over the area of intersection between Site C and Site A, Phase A. This showed that Site C was earlier than the bank of Site A, but rabbit burrows had disturbed the burnt ashy layers underneath and it was not possible to determine the precise relationship between Site C and Phase A of Site A. This area will be reopened in a future season to examine deposits that survive below the disturbed zone.

One of the palisade slots, Z', running east from the 'northern enclosures' of the Site B excavation, was found in a small trial-trench. Its point of intersection with Site C was excavated. This showed that Site C clearly cut through Z', providing a valuable link back into the pre-mound stratigraphy recorded in the 1960s. Site C was later than a point in time around the middle of Site B, Phase 3 (ii–iii), around 150 BC. Four $^{14}$C determinations were carried out on charcoal collected from the filling of the inner and outer slots, two from each slot in different excavation trenches. All four dates lie within the range cal. 400 BC–AD 26. Site C is therefore a part of the Iron Age sequence of structures on the Navan Hill and may well also have been used for ceremonial purposes.

A further season of investigation is planned for 2000, when the excavation of three trenches begun in 1999 will be completed. The main thrust of the work will be to study in detail the deposits in the slots, in particular the evidence for infilling with burnt soil, the existence of structural timbers and the distribution of burnt and unburnt bone fragments in the slots. Traces of what may prove to be a third slot with much cleaner fill, between the two containing burnt material, were uncovered at the end of the 1999 season. These features will be fully explored. Another, detailed geophysical survey of Site A is planned in 2000 in the hope of identifying internal features such as pits or smaller structures, potential targets for further sampling excavation.

*Reference*
Waterman, D.M. 1997 *Excavations at Navan Fort 1961–71.* Belfast.

*C.J. Lynn, EHS, 5–33 Hill Street, Belfast BT1 2LA.*

### 22. TIMAKEEL
No archaeological significance
H96545546
SMR 9:2, 9:3 and 9:13

At Timakeel townland, Co. Armagh, monitoring was carried out before a small housing development, but no archaeological finds or features were recovered.

*Cormac McSparron, NAC, Unit 6, Farset Enterprise Park, 638 Springfield Road, Belfast.*

### 23. HAUGHEY'S FORT, TRAY
Late Bronze Age enclosure
H83514529
SMR 12:13

The excavations were undertaken over four weeks (28 June–23 July) as part of the excavations module taught by the School of Archaeology and Palaeoecology in The Queen's University of Belfast. The primary purpose of the 1999 excavation was to complete the excavation of the features associated with those that had been opened in 1998 (*Excavations 1998*, 3). Therefore, the work was aimed at finding the resumption of the inner ditch and further elucidating a series of arcs formed by several hundred stake-holes.

No traces of the suspected continuation of the inner ditch were discovered during the excavation. This indicates that the gap between the terminal previously discovered and its corresponding terminal must be at least 15m. This is an exceptionally wide gap, and consequently it may call into question the previous identification of the small segment as a portion of the inner ditch. It is possible, however, that such a wide gap does exist between the terminals.

The excavations in Trench 15 failed to intersect the outer ditch, even though a parallel trench offset by 20m did cross this feature. Clearly the results obtained through excavation to date have not been able to resolve the nature of the monument at this location. Total excavation might assist, but remote sensing may be a solution to this problem.

A further large number of stake-holes were identified within the area excavated in 1999. These stake-holes were found to penetrate the dark, charcoal-rich cultural layer that had been observed during all previous excavation. The 1999 season was the first occasion on which were found clear traces of the level from which these stake-holes were cut. This was achieved because the area investigated included a section where the overburden was of sufficient thickness to partially protect earlier ground surfaces. The stake-holes indicate a series of arcs that were centred on positions upslope from the putative line of the entrance.

During the 1998 season a large pit was excavated that contained a substantial quantity of Late Bronze Age pottery. The 1999 excavation revealed a second pit of even larger dimensions. The pit measured *c.* 2m in diameter and had a depth of *c.* 2.5m measured from the modern ground level, the largest single feature other than the ditches to be uncovered at Haughey's Fort. The basal deposits of this pit were waterlogged and contained a major concentration of Late Bronze Age pottery (at least two large vessels were present), a quantity of animal bones (preliminary analysis has identified bones from species including cattle, pig and red deer) and a variety of other organic material. The last included two timber posts, one of which had been worked and perforated, that were *c.* 1m long and were found upright against the side of the pit. The timber has been tentatively identified as willow, and the artefacts are currently under conservation. Seeds and insect remains were also present in the organic material that had survived in the base of the pit.

*J.P. Mallory, School of Archaeology and Palaeoecology, Queen's University, Belfast BT7 1NN.*

## CARLOW

### 24. CARLOW
Adjacent to rath
27358 17525
SMR 7:23
99E0058

Archaeological assessment of a housing development adjacent to a rath included the mechanical excavation of nine test-trenches. No archaeological materials were found.

*Cóilín Ó Drisceoil, 6 Riverview, Ardnore, Kilkenny.*

### 25. COX'S LANE, CARLOW
Urban medieval
S719773
SMR 7:18
99E0602

Assessment of the site adjoining Cox's Lane showed that it has the potential to contain evidence of the medieval settlement of Carlow town. The site is within the urban zone of archaeological potential. In addition, the development is adjacent to a listed building, 'Evergreen Lodge'. Further archaeological work was recommended before any development.

*Christine Tarbett-Buckley, c/o Valerie J. Keeley Ltd, 29–30 Duke Street, Athy, Co. Kildare.*

## CAVAN

### 26. LEITIR, BAILIEBOROUGH
Ringfort
26532 29837
SMR 28:34
99E0635

Monitoring of an extension to the rear of an existing dwelling at Leitir, Bailieborough, Co. Cavan, was undertaken on 9 November 1999. The bungalow (built some 30 years ago) is within the north-east corner of a ringfort. The fort consists of a raised circular area, internally 42m west-south-west/east-north-east by 47m north-north-east/south-south-east enclosed by an earthen bank identifiable only from the north-north-west, east and south-east, and a shallow ditch traceable from the south-west, north and north-north-east. The original entranceway can no longer be discerned, and present access to the site is via a tarmac road running through the earthwork at the south-east, extending around the interior of the site from the south-east, south, north-west and north, ending at the north-west corner of the dwelling.

Four foundation trenches were excavated to the rear of the existing dwelling on its north-eastern side. Trenches 1 and 2 were dug in the area of a proposed kitchen extension. Trenches 3 and 4 were dug at an angled corner of the rear of the building. All were excavated by mini-digger to a depth of 0.9m. In all cases, removal of the concrete surface of the yard revealed a thin layer of sandy gravel overlying yellow boulder clay.

No archaeological stratigraphy was revealed during the excavation. It is clear that the area immediately surrounding the existing dwelling had been reduced to boulder clay, possibly during its construction. The top of the enclosing bank is between 5m and 10m to the east of the excavated foundations, and its graded appearance suggests that some material has been redeposited along its inner face, probably to provide a bed for planting during the initial landscaping of the site.

*Malachy Conway, Archaeological Consultancy Services Ltd, 15 Trinity Street, Drogheda, Co. Louth.*

## 27. 7 FARNHAM STREET (REAR OF), CAVAN
No archaeological significance
241793 309401
99E0074

Trial-trenching was carried out at the site of a proposed housing complex on 27 February 1999. The work was undertaken in compliance with a condition attached to the grant of planning in respect of the proposed development and following a request from NMHPS, *Dúchas*. The area of development is within the zone of archaeological potential for Cavan, as defined by the OPW, Urban Archaeological Survey. Before the commencement of testing, a number of outbuilding and boundary walls were demolished to ground level and all ground slabs were removed.

Six trenches, ranging from 10m to 50m long, were excavated mechanically in order to determine the nature and extent of any possible archaeological structures or deposits within the area of development. No such features were revealed, and no material finds were recovered during the testing.

*Martin E. Byrne, 31 Millford, Athgarvan, Co. Kildare.*

## 28. MAIN STREET/GALLOWS HILL (REAR OF), CAVAN
No archaeological significance
241899 309349
99E0073

Trial-trenching was carried out at the site of a proposed cinema complex, incorporating office and retail units, on 20 February 1999. The work was undertaken in compliance with conditions attached to the grant of planning in respect of the proposed development. The development is within the zone of archaeological potential for Cavan, as defined by the OPW, Urban Archaeological Survey. The site is on the western slopes of Gallows Hill, with the greater part situated in a green-field setting and the reminder an existing surface carpark.

Seven trenches, ranging from 20m to 50m long, were excavated mechanically, with the sections cleaned by hand, in order to determine the nature and extent of any possible archaeological structures or deposits within the area of development. No such features were revealed, and no material finds were recovered during the testing.

*Martin E. Byrne, 31 Millford, Athgarvan, Co. Kildare.*

## 29. COOTEHILL SEWERAGE IMPROVEMENT SCHEME
Monitoring
99E0355

Monitoring of the Cootehill Sewerage Improvement Scheme took place from June to December 1999. Some works involving the opening of new areas are planned to resume in summer 2000. The scheme involved pipe-laying for 3–4m around the Plantation town of Cootehill, Co. Cavan.

During the initial assessment it was found that the scheme could have an indirect impact on a possible feature found during field-walking, while the river-crossing at Clement's Bridge, north along the Belturbet Road, was investigated before works took place here. No other features of archaeological interest were found during the assessment, except for some iron pumps along the road, for which preservation was recommended.

During monitoring, an archaeological feature (probably part of a *fulacht fiadh*) was found, and this was excavated in September 1999 (see No. 30 below).

*Judith Carroll, Pine Forest Art Centre, Pine Forest Road, Glencullen, Co. Dublin, and 13 Anglesea Street, Dublin 2.*

## 30. COOTEHILL
Possible *fulacht fiadh*
H59601443
99E0644

A possible *fulacht fiadh* was found during the construction of the Cootehill Sewerage Improvement Scheme, Cootehill, Co. Cavan. The site is *c.* 200m to the east of the town of Cootehill and was identified during monitoring of the topsoil-stripping of rough pasture fields before the excavation of the pipe-trench. These groundworks exposed a spread of charcoal and burnt stone overlying peat and organic clay. The site is on a north-west-facing hill slope at *c.* 89m above OD in a slight hollow on the hillside. Some 1.5m to the west of the burnt spread was a modern bottle dump. The underlying geology is greywacke, a poor-quality slate/shale, overlain in this area by a yellow, silty, slightly sandy clay derived from its weathering.

Once it was exposed by topsoil-stripping, further excavation of the site was undertaken. The area of burnt material identified within the pipeline corridor was subject to hand cleaning, which revealed that the spread extended eastward out of the pipeline corridor. After consultation with *Dúchas*, an area to the east of, and outside, the pipeline corridor was excavated by machine to determine the extent of the burnt deposit. A baulk, 0.8m wide, was left in place between the two areas.

Excavations showed that the layer of burnt stone and charcoal, F21, covered an area of *c.* 22m$^2$, of which about two-thirds lay in the pipeline corridor. Owing to the shallowness of the burnt contexts, topsoil-stripping had unfortunately removed a large proportion of them, leaving only isolated patches of burnt stone and charcoal within the pipe corridor. This spread sealed a shallow trough, F7, which had been cut into the underlying peat layer, Context 22, and contained abundant charcoal fragments, burnt stone and black-stained peat, F9. The stones within the fill and the associated charcoal spread were not of uniform size, most measured 0.05–0.1m in diameter and some were up to 0.35m, the larger stones being more common towards the base of the trough. The stones were almost exclusively fragments of local greywacke shale, with occasional quartz fragments. All of the burnt stone had undergone degradation due the heat and as a consequence was very friable.

The trough itself was roughly rectangular in plan and almost uniformly 0.8m wide, widening slightly at its western end to almost 0.9m, and 0.36m deep at its deepest. It was 1.75m long and oriented north-east/south-west. On the south-west side a series of large stones, F6, was encountered, lying against the inside edge of the trough in their final resting place after being tipped into it. The north-western edge of the trough was generally steeper than its opposite side, possibly owing to the protection offered by the dump of stones (F6). Adjacent to the south-east and north-west ends of the trough were shallow depressions.

Two post-holes, F12 and F15, were exposed to the north-east of the trough. The furthest, F12, lay 3.3m north-east of the trough, was circular in plan and measured 0.25m in diameter and 0.15m deep. Within the fill, F13, two stones, representing the remains of stone-post packing, survived. The second post-hole, F15, was 1.15m north-east of the trough, irregular in plan and infilled with burnt stone, charcoal and black-stained peat. It was 0.25–0.5m in diameter and 0.22m deep, and no packing stones or post-pipe were observed within the fill. No other cut features were observed during the excavations.

To the north-east of the trough the ground level had been raised by *c.* 0.1m and made more stable by the dumping of redeposited, yellow clay, F10. This material had been dumped directly onto F22, the peat layer cut for the construction of the trough.

There was no evidence for the location of the fire that had heated the stones. Excavation of the site and examination of the pipeline corridor found no areas of *in situ* burning or scorching to the peat outside or within the trough.

During excavation of the trough a curved piece of waterlogged timber 0.57m long, 0.12m wide and 0.09m thick was exposed. The relative thinness of the timber suggested that it may represent a disturbed piece of planking, incorporated within the fill of the trough, rather than a piece of branch or trunk. The timber was too fragile to be lifted whole. No *in situ* planking nor any structural element to the sides of the trough was present.

Samples from the fill of the trough are at present being identified before their submission for radiocarbon dating at Beta Analytic, Miami, USA. Samples were also taken from the earlier horizons of burnt stone and charcoal, F3 and F8, for radiocarbon dating.
*Judith Carroll, Pine Forest Art Centre, Pine Forest Road, Glencullen, Co. Dublin, and 13 Anglesea Street, Dublin 2.*

## 31. LISLEA
Adjacent to ringfort site
**263446 286180**
**SMR 39:58**
**99E0166**
A programme of archaeological trial-trenching was carried out at the site of a proposed dwelling-house at Lislea, Virginia, Co. Cavan, on 3 April 1999. The work was undertaken in compliance with a request for additional information in respect of the proposed construction of a single dwelling. The development is a minimum of 12m from a ringfort site that was extant in 1970 but has since been levelled, although there are some slight traces visible on the ground. A public road separates the development area from the ringfort site.

Five trenches, ranging from 11m to 70m long, were excavated mechanically in order to determine the nature and extent of any possible archaeological structures or deposits within the area of development. No such features were revealed, and no material finds were recovered during the testing.
*Martin E. Byrne, 31 Millford, Athgarvan, Co. Kildare.*

## 32. LISMEEN
Proximity to rath
**25425 29154**
**SMR 32:38**
**99E0277**
This mobile phone mast was to be erected 25m to the south-east of the rath. The area had already been significantly affected by groundworks associated with the adjacent waterworks. However, no archaeological features or remains were revealed during this monitoring programme. Thus it is concluded that no further archaeological work is necessary at this location.
*Rónán Swan, Arch-Tech Ltd, 32 Fitzwilliam Place, Dublin 2.*

# CLARE

## 33. BALLYCASEY TO DROMOLAND ROAD SCHEME, N18/19
Monitoring
**99E0350**
Several substantial archaeological sites were uncovered during monitoring of the N18/N19 Road Scheme, Ballycasey to Dromoland, Phase 1. These were:

Ballyconneely td (AR4A), a spread of burnt mound material;
Latoon South td (AR46), a prehistoric burial/industrial(?) site;
Ballyconneely td (AR47), a large ditched enclosure;
Ballyconneely td (AR48), a spread of burnt material and high concentration of animal bone;
Ballygirreen td (AR49), a small circular enclosure, possibly a dwelling;
Ballyconneely td (AR50), a linear ditch;
Ballyconneely td (AR52), a possible wetland site;
Ballyconneely td (AR53), two adjoining *fulachta fiadh*;
Ballyconneely td (AR61–AR62), a linear arrangement of four *fulachta fiadh*;
Ballyconneely td (AR63), a *fulacht fiadh*.

Several other potential sites (AR55, 56, 57, 58 and 60) are awaiting investigation. As this project is ongoing, further details will be given in the future.
*Christine Grant, c/o S. Schorman, Ballyalla, Ennis, Co. Clare.*

## 34. BALLYCASEY MORE, SITE 44
Field system
**142300 162950**
**99E0574**
The site was on the route of an access road

connected with the Newmarket-on-Fergus bypass. It was identified as a complex of earthworks during field-walking. It was an area surrounded on three sides by marsh, and a possible motte and bailey stand beside the affected area.

A preliminary investigation was carried out, consisting of four cuttings. The first two cuttings crossed linear earthworks. One was found to be a denuded bank with a V-sectioned fosse 1m deep running alongside it, now filled with stones. The other was found to be the base of a stone wall 1.2m thick.

The other two cuttings were to investigate a possible rectangular structure. A cutting through the 'interior' revealed a natural gravel surface with no sign of habitation. A narrow slit-trench through the north 'wall' showed it to be similar to the wall mentioned above, probably another field wall.

*Thaddeus C. Breen, 13 Wainsfort Crescent, Dublin 6W, for Valerie J. Keeley.*

## 35. BALLYCONNEELY
Middle/Late Bronze Age cemetery and ritual site
**97E0042**

Between 12 July 1999 and 7 April 2000 large-scale excavation and topsoil-stripping were carried out before the N18/19 Road Improvement Scheme. The site was originally tested by Christine Grant in 1997, with a number of potential archaeological features identified (*Excavations 1997*, 203). The original aim of the project was to investigate two known SMR sites that would be affected by the roadway construction. In the extreme north-west of the site was a standing stone (SMR 42:153), with a large archaeological complex (SMR 42:125) covering the remainder of the area. The archaeological complex consists of a number of early field boundaries and enclosures covering several acres, with only the easternmost portion being affected by the road. The original mandate was to excavate a 10m-by-10m area around the standing stone, culminating in its removal for later re-erection, and two smaller trenches through previously identified early field boundaries. The remainder of the area within the take of the road was to be stripped by machine.

Cutting A, 10m by 10m, was centred on the standing stone at the northern end of the site, which was previously investigated during the testing phase by Christine Grant in 1997 (*Excavations 1997*, 203). While a number of features cutting the subsoil had been identified, no datable material was retrieved. The recent excavation revealed several features including the foundation of a field boundary and related furrows. Sherds of 19th-century pottery were retrieved from the base of the boundary wall, indicating a likely late date for most, if not all, of the features. None of the other features or contexts contained any datable material.

The base of the standing stone and related stone kerbing was encased in concrete. It rested on loose stone and gravel, filling a shallow circular pit. While the stone was clearly re-erected in the recent past, it remains uncertain whether this was its original position. No dating evidence was retrieved from the cut below the stone. The stone certainly looks like a standing stone, and local legend tells that it was moved to this location in the 19th century from further up the Turret Hill to the north-east. This is in keeping with the dating of the other features revealed in the cutting, with the pit below the standing stone having been cut at the same level as the wall and furrows.

Cutting B, 8m by 2m, was made along the western edge of the site to investigate one of the early field boundaries previously identified. As in the earlier testing phase, no datable materiel was retrieved. The 'field boundary' consisted of loose, small to medium-sized stones piled atop a prominent, east–west-orientated ridge of bedrock. While this bedrock may have functioned as a boundary, the loose stones appeared more like field clearance than a concerted effort to build a wall.

Cutting C, 8m by 2m, was made in the extreme southern end of SMR 42:125 to investigate a noticeable north–south-orientated hump and also because this end of the site had not been previously investigated. At the northern limits of the cutting, a stone and gravel trackway was exposed, orientated north–south and resting atop a low linear mound of silty clay. The trackway and both of the layers above and below yielded moderate amounts of animal bone, some worked chert and flint, worked bone and small pieces of copper wire. Beneath the trackway's foundation layers, a number of pits cutting the subsoil were revealed. Two of these yielded small quantities of bone and charcoal.

Throughout the excavation the remainder of the site within the take of the road was stripped by machine. No further features or finds of an archaeological nature were revealed. Other previously identified field boundaries turned out to be similar to that investigated in Cutting B. The stripping was carried out down to the level of the subsoil where the extensive east–west seams of bedrock allowed.

As the trackway identified in Cutting C clearly extended southwards outside the established perimeter of the SMR site, yet still within the take of the road, an extension to it was opened. This measured 8m north–south by 6m and revealed the full extent of the trackway, with a total length of 8m. While curving slightly to the west, it continued to run roughly north–south. To the south of the trackway's extent a natural platform, partially obscured by a modern field wall and hedges, was evident and seemed the likely focus of the trackway. The platform is flat on top, *c.* 35m wide, with its southern end sloping sharply, with panoramic views to the west and south overlooking the Shannon/Fergus estuary.

In an attempt to include the platform within the scope of the investigation, it was decided to extend the soil-stripping south of the known limit of the site to include the area surrounding the extension to Cutting C, the platform and the area below it, effectively extending the limit of the site by 60m to the south.

During the initial phase of stripping the platform, a pit cutting the layer above natural was revealed *c.* 20m south-west of the trackway. The pit was filled with dark soil and charcoal, with the initial investigation revealing a ground stone axe lying directly beneath a large sherd of very coarse pottery. The axe is asymmetrical and highly polished. There

Ground stone axe found at Ballyconneely.

is some evidence of use at both ends, although overall the axe is in near-perfect condition. Of particular interest are two circular cupmarks on either face near the top. Each mark appears to have been finely pecked and purposefully sited slightly off line with the other. The pottery is black and very light and crumbly. It has evidence of a slight shoulder and the remains of a small portion of the rim. There is no evidence of decoration. A small quantity of cremated bone was also retrieved.

Owing to the presence of the trackway and the pit, the remainder of the area on the platform (c. 35m by 32m) was cleared by hand down to the archaeological levels. In excess of 600 features cutting the natural subsoil were excavated. These include post-holes, stake-holes, slot-trenches and pits of varying sizes. All were stratigraphically earlier than the trackway.

Most of the post-holes, stake-holes and slot-trenches were clustered in the north-east corner of the platform and indicate likely structural activity, with several possible structures and related pits. Patterns in the placement of these features are not readily discernible at this stage, but circular and oval shapes predominate. No related floors or occupational debris have been identified. There is no reasonable evidence to suggest that this complex of features was related to settlement activity, with the structures likely related in some fashion to the burials found immediately to the south.

The southern and central portions of the platform were dominated by pits of varying size. Most were filled with charcoal-enriched soil, with the larger pits containing considerable quantities of heat-fractured sandstone. The pits ranged in size from small, post-hole-sized cuts (c. 0.01m in diameter) to larger pits, 1m to 2m long. While there is some evidence of pits cutting each other, there is no clear indication of discrete phases of activity. In fact, of the several hundred cut features excavated, it is surprising how closely spaced they were, with so little interference.

Over seventy of the pits excavated yielded small quantities of cremated bone. The bone exhibits evidence of having been efficiently cremated and crushed into tiny pieces. In one case the bone was intentionally cut into small squares. Seven of the pits have yielded pottery of varying types but consistently in small amounts. Most appear to be similar to the Late Bronze Age coarseware found at Mooghaun Hillfort, which is less than three miles away. A few sherds are clearly of finer quality and may be earlier in date. The only other pit, besides that containing the axe, to yield finds other than pottery was a shallow cut between two seams of bedrock in the extreme north-east of the site. This pit yielded two polished bone pins and a tiny (<20mm), serrated, copper-alloy blade, possibly a mini-razor. While the cremated bone has yet to be identified as human, its presence in discrete pits, in consistently small quantities and in association with other burnt material, sherds of Middle to Late Bronze Age pottery and other intentionally deposited finds, may indicate that these pits represent token cremations dating to the Middle to Late Bronze Age.

An early experiment at sieving samples from these and some of the many other pits that did not yield evidence of cremated bone has indicated that some of the pits considered to be relatively sterile have minute quantities of cremated bone and charcoal in them. As post-excavation analysis has just begun, it is possible that upwards of another 100 burials will be identified.

Also within this cluster of pits, a small circular furnace was revealed. It yielded 3–4kg of dull grey slag, mostly in one conglomerate, with layers of large pieces of charcoal beneath. There is no evidence of iron oxide, and the initial feeling is that this is copper slag.

*Christopher Read, Northwest Archaeological Services, Cloonfad Cottage, Leitrim Village, Co. Roscommon, for Valerie J. Keeley Ltd.*

## 36. BALLYDUFFBEG
No archaeological significance
**12200 18025**
**99E0218**

An archaeological assessment was undertaken at Ballyduffbeg townland, near Inagh, as part of an environmental impact assessment for a proposed landfill site to be undertaken by Clare County Council. The assessment followed a report to *Dúchas*, by a local person, of a children's burial-ground on the site.

The reported site was a small clearing within a Coillte forest, containing a single upright boulder. The area was exhaustively archaeologically tested. No archaeological soils or deposits were uncovered in the assessment.

*Paul Stevens, Farney Bridge, Holycross, Co. Tipperary.*

## 37. BALLYHANNAN SOUTH
Vicinity of enclosure
R401734
SMR 42:15
99E0669

Groundwork associated with the construction of a dwelling-house near the south-western quadrant of a well-preserved drystone cashel was monitored in December 1999. The substratum comprised sterile gravel, grey/brown, silty clay and loose limestone. The stripping of topsoil and the cutting of foundation trenches revealed no trace of material or activity of archaeological origin.

*Kenneth Wiggins, 77 Vartry Close, Raheen, Co. Limerick.*

## 38. CATHAIR MÓR, BALLYLABBAN
Stone fort
99E0506

This project involved the excavation of the gatehouse of Cathair Mór stone fort, in the Burren, Co. Clare. The work was undertaken as part of a Dúchas plan to make the site more accessible to visitors. The entrance passage was partly blocked with rubble, and the stone lintel, which once spanned the doorway, had fallen across the entrance.

Cathair Mór stands on the east shoulder of a north-east/south-west-running valley, with higher ground to the east. The complex consists of a stone fort with an outer and inner wall, with evidence of stone structures in the interior. There is a second stone fort to the south-east of the site, while aerial photographs from the 1960s indicate the possible existence of a number of further structures that have since been destroyed or obscured from view by thick vegetation cover.

The work involved the manual excavation of one trench, which was orientated north–south, measured 11m x 10m and incorporated the gatehouse and its immediate environs. Removal of topsoil (C1) and rubble (C2) revealed the extent and shape of the gatehouse, which was found to consist of a rectangular structure with a splayed entrance passage and a small chamber on either side of the passage. Underlying C1 and C2 in both the interior and exterior of the gatehouse was bedrock, which in the exterior of the entrance was found at a level 0.5m below the level of the interior. This meant that on entering the fort one had to step up to the entrance passage. Underlying rubble in the entrance passage was a surface of stone and clay that formed the floor level of the passageway. In the west end of the passage, bedrock was used as the floor, but as the bedrock level was lower in the east it was necessary to use small stones and sandy clay to build up the floor. A spud stone, found immediately inside the doorway at this level, confirms that this was the original floor level of the gatehouse.

In the interior of the gatehouse a single small chamber was revealed on either side of the entrance passage. On the south side a dressed limestone block, 0.93m x 0.26m, marks the entrance to a small rectangular chamber. The entrance stone is 0.63m above ground level, and on its west side is a small rectangular spud stone (0.08m x 0.07m x 0.03m) that would have supported a doorway. On the opposite, north side of the entrance passage is a similar rectangular chamber. While no entrance stone survives, access is 0.56m above the level of the passage floor. It leads to an irregular-shaped chamber constructed of uncut limestone blocks with moderate mortar inclusions. The wall survives best in the north and west, where it is 1.07m high. Photographic records from the 1950s indicate a gabled roof; however, this is likely to have been a later feature. The floor level, like that in the chamber opposite, has been dug through for a depth of 0.9m.

On the exterior east and west sides of the gatehouse the removal of topsoil revealed bedrock that sloped downwards from south to north. While the exterior wall of the gatehouse ran flush with the wall of the fort in the interior, the gatehouse projected eastward beyond the fort wall. This projection of the gatehouse wall meant that in the north-west, where the bedrock level was low, a foundation was required to support the structure. This foundation consisted of small stones with frequent oyster shell and animal bone inclusions. This layer, which was 0.4–0.45m deep, was partially removed to reveal the inner facing wall of the fort. The removal of this rubble showed that the gatehouse structure was built on top of the existing cashel wall.

The archaeological excavations revealed that the gatehouse was a later addition to a pre-existing fort, and the present structure is most likely constructed on top of the original entrance.

Four artefacts were recovered during the excavations. Three of these were coins and the fourth was a fragment of a rotary quern. Two of the coins, an Irish halfpenny dated to 1932 and an American half-dollar dated to 1965, were recovered during the removal of rubble from the entrance passageway. The third coin, dating to the 1690s, was found in a crevice in the bedrock immediately east of the entrance. The rotary quern fragment was recovered from below the rubble and on top of bedrock in the south of the trench. Animal bone fragments and oyster shell remains were found in various layers, especially from the foundation of the gatehouse.

*Martin Fitzpatrick, Arch. Consultancy Ltd, Ballydavid South, Athenry, Co. Galway.*

## 39. BALLYNACRAGGA (AREA 11)
No archaeological significance
13792 16862
98E0334

Pre-development testing was carried out as part of the N18/N19 (Ballycasey to Dromoland) Road Improvement Scheme. Two trial-trenches were excavated to natural, and no archaeological features or deposits were encountered. Natural soils of silty clay and silty sand were excavated and found to be sterile and featureless.

*Anne Connolly, Archaeological Services Unit Ltd, Purcell House, Oranmore, Co. Galway, for Valerie J. Keeley Ltd.*

## 40. BALLYNACRAGGA (AREA 13)
No archaeological significance
98E0335

Archaeological monitoring of topsoil-stripping was carried out as part of the N18/N19 (Ballycasey to

Dromoland) Road Improvement Scheme in Area 13, Ballynacragga townland, Co. Clare. No archaeological features or deposits were encountered. Natural soils of silty clays and silty sands were excavated and were found to be sterile and featureless.
*Anne Connolly, Archaeological Services Unit Ltd, Purcell House, Oranmore, Co. Galway, for Valerie J. Keeley Ltd.*

### 41. BALLYNACRAGGA
No archaeological significance
**98E0335**
This small excavation was to investigate the area around a potential stone alignment that would be affected by the N18/19 Ballycasey to Dromoland Road Improvement Scheme. The site is *c.* 1 mile to the north of Newmarket-on-Fergus and had been identified as a possible stone alignment during the pre-planning stage. It consists of three stones orientated east–west and forming an almost straight line with a total length of 13m. Of the stones, only the westernmost, a large erratic-like boulder, appeared to be earthfast. The other two are flat, thin slabs of limestone.

Testing was completed by Anne Connolly in 1998 (*Excavations 1998*, 8), and although the findings were inconclusive it was recommended that full excavation be undertaken before road construction. However, the road's route was changed slightly, leaving only the westernmost of the three stones bordering upon the take of the road. Thus a small area, measuring 4m east–west by 9m north–south, was excavated. No archaeological materials or features were uncovered. Where the area excavated bordered the westernmost stone, there was no evidence that it rested within an artificial cut, and it was likely glacially deposited, being similar to the many erratics dotting the surrounding fields.
*Christopher Read, Northwest Archaeological Services, Cloonfad Cottage, Leitrim Village, Co. Roscommon, for Valerie J. Keeley Ltd.*

### 42. BALLYNACRAGGA (AREA 17)
No archaeological significance
**98E0336**
Archaeological monitoring of topsoil-stripping was carried out as part of the N18/N19 (Ballycasey to Dromoland) Road Improvement Scheme on Area 17, Ballynacragga townland. No archaeological features or deposits were encountered. There was much evidence at the site of modern disturbance. Natural soils of silty clay were excavated and found to be mainly featureless.
*Anne Connolly, Archaeological Services Unit Ltd, Purcell House, Oranmore, Co. Galway, for Valerie J. Keeley Ltd.*

### 43. BALLYNALIDDY
No archaeological significance
**12986 17703**
**99E0098**
Two foundation trenches were mechanically excavated along the line of a proposed development at Ballynaliddy, Ennis, Co. Clare. Nothing of archaeological significance was discovered.
*Anne Connolly, Archaeological Services Unit Ltd, Purcell House, Oranmore, Co. Galway.*

### 44. BALLYSHEENBEG
No archaeological significance
**168500 146190**
**99E0671**
Testing was carried out at this site before construction of a domestic dwelling. The site is close to a known monument, SMR 52:007–012. No archaeological material was uncovered.
*Christine Grant, c/o S. Schorman, Ballyalla, Ennis, Co. Clare.*

### 45. BUNRATTY WEST
No archaeological significance
**SMR 61:11**
**99E0664**
The site of a proposed conversion (into a guesthouse) and extension of a disused retail outlet at Bunratty West, Co. Clare, was tested in December 1999 as part of an archaeological impact statement. The development also required the extension of the existing carpark to the west. This 0.8-acre site impinged on the area of archaeological potential associated with the medieval borough of Bunratty. The site is *c.* 350m to the north-west of Bunratty Castle and immediately to the north of the bank and ditch, interpreted in recent trial excavations as 17th-century defensive earthworks (Bradley *et al.* 1991).

Nine test-trenches were opened within the main area of development. Trenches I–III were excavated under the proposed eastern extension to the existing building. These revealed a substantial (1.1m) amount of landfill overlying the natural subsoil.

Trenches IV–VII were opened under the proposed western extension. These also revealed *c.* 0.9–1m of modern landfill under the carpark surface. Below this was a flattened sod/topsoil horizon, which rested on undisturbed, light grey clay marl. A deeper examination in Trench V revealed a further 0.9m of soft, spongy peat below the grey marl.

Trenches VIII and IX were excavated to the west of the site, where it was proposed to extend the existing carpark. Stratigraphic evidence from Trench VIII suggested that the upper 0.55m in this general area had been imported during or after the construction of the carpark. Overall, no finds or features of archaeological significance were noted.
*Ken Hanley, 44 Eaton Heights, Cobh, Co. Cork.*

### 46. CARRIGORAN (AREA 18)
Relict field system
**13854 16778**
**SMR 51:1802**
**98E0337**
The site, west of Newmarket-on-Fergus, was originally identified during field-walking for the proposed N18/N19 Road Improvement Scheme. An initial investigation by Fiona Reilly took place in 1998 and confirmed that the remains of stone walls were present (*Excavations 1998*, 8).

The feature was the remains of a number of field walls in what is now a field 15ha in area and was formerly part of the deerpark of Carrigoran House. The field is used as cattle pasture. There are limestone outcrops at intervals.

Before excavation, the stone walls appeared as discontinuous linear features—small raised areas with some exposed stones. One complete field could be seen. It was approximately square, measuring 55m x 55m. Most of the walls had an orientation approximately parallel to, or perpendicular to, the line of the proposed road, and therefore of the site, but some ran diagonally, to follow the contours. Some of the walls appeared to mark the division between level land and the beginning of a slope.

Over much of their length the walls had been denuded, but the better-preserved sections were found to be quite consistent in form. The northernmost wall, Feature 1, was found to consist of a line of large stones (0.25–0.3m across) along the north-west face, behind which were some smaller stones, 0.1–0.2m across. Whereas the larger stones were blocks, roughly rectangular in shape, these smaller stones were round—not symmetrical like river stones but identical to the stones found locally in the natural subsoil. At the very base was a layer of still smaller stones (c. 0.1m across). The thickness of the feature at this point was 0.91m. In most of the walls the medium-sized stones were found on both sides of the central 'spine' rather than on one side only. Three examples were found of large, flat slabs of limestone placed on edge to form the centre part of the wall. One was resting on a similar slab, laid flat, and another rested on the layer of small stones that underlay the wall proper.

The few finds were mostly of recent date, and none was found in association with the walls. Some other features were found, including drains, shallow pits and a corn-drying kiln. The last was excavated by Billy Quinn.

*Thaddeus C. Breen, 13 Wainsfort Crescent, Dublin 6W, for Valerie J. Keeley.*

### 47. CARRIGORAN, AREA EX1
Multi-phased
**SMR 51:171**
**98E0338 and 98E0426**

This large, multi-phased site is to the north-east of Carrigoran Nursing Home in the townland of Carrigoran, west of Newmarket-on-Fergus, Co. Clare. It was identified as an area of archaeological potential by Celie O Rahilly during preliminary work for the N18/19 Road Improvement Scheme. She described it as a possible linear system in her report. It has since been included in the Sites and Monuments Record as a possible field system. The site lies on rough grazing land that slopes gently from the north-west to the south-east, with a marshy area and stream lying to the south and east. The stream feeds Lough Gash to the north-east.

A geophysical survey identified several areas of archaeological potential: areas of burning and a suggested barrow. It was recommended after the site was tested under two licences in 1998 (*Excavations 1998*, 8–9) that further investigation be made, under a single licence. This was carried out during 1999.

Initial excavation suggested that the site was the remains of a large, stone, oval enclosure with earlier post-hole activity in the north-western sector. As work proceeded, it became clear that the site was much more extensive than originally thought. It can be regarded as a multi-phased mini-landscape, c. 120m by 120m, with the remains of stone field walls, ditches and probable structures represented by post-holes. A possible *fulacht fiadh* was found in the marshy area in the south-east.

Unfortunately there is evidence of plough disturbance over most of the site; therefore many finds came from immediately below the sod. These included finds of diverse type and date, e.g. a polished stone axe and copper-alloy stick-pin. As work on the site is still in progress, the following is not a definitive phasing: Phase 1: post-hole and pit activity; Phase 2: ditch activity; Phase 3: limestone wall activity; Phase 4: limestone wall destruction; Phase 5: large drainage ditch; and Phase 6: ploughing.

*Phase 1*
Area A is in the north of the site and produced evidence of a structure 4.3m wide and orientated roughly north–south. It has been truncated at its northern end, so the remains are 3.4m long. It was constructed of posts c. 0.6m in diameter, with a double row of stakes inserted down the longitudinal centre of the structure. A possible fire-pit, 0.7m in diameter, was excavated 1.1m from the southern end of the structure. Other post-holes in the area suggest that the area was fenced. A definite date for the structure cannot be suggested, as no datable finds have yet been recovered from the post-holes, pits or fire-pit. An extended male inhumation, orientated roughly east–west, was uncovered to the north-west of the structure. No datable finds were buried with him.

Other areas also produced post-holes, pits and drainage channels. An extended female inhumation was discovered in the south of Area D. The two burials are c. 50m apart. It is not possible to comment further on them at this stage.

*Phase 2*
Area A produced evidence of field boundaries in the form of ditches. One of these had silted up, and another ditch had been cut, therefore reducing the size of the field. A bone comb fragment was found in the fill of the second trench, suggesting an Early Christian date for the silting up of the ditch.

*Phase 3*
This phase post-dates the ditch phase. It is represented by a wide, well-constructed limestone wall. This wall once enclosed a large area c. 60m north–south by 50m east–west and seems to have incorporated the bedrock outcrop to the north. There is also evidence of a wall running roughly south-west through the centre of the area. The wall survives in several places as a single course, with large facing-stones and medium-sized packing stones. The facing-stones have been extensively robbed in other areas; therefore only the smaller packing stones survive at the destruction level.

*Phase 4*
This was a limestone wall that had been destroyed and extensively robbed.

*Phase 5*
A large drainage ditch was cut through the south of

the site at a late stage in the site's history. It was c. 1.8m wide and 0.6m deep.

*Phase 6*
At some stage extensive ploughing occurred and disturbed the destruction level of the limestone walls. In some areas the sod was removed directly onto non-archaeological glacial material. This was probably due to the plough action.

*Fulacht fiadh*
The possible *fulacht fiadh* was 30m to the south-east of the main activity on site and consisted of a mound of burnt sandstone. A possible trough was cut into the marl below. An area of small to medium-sized compacted stones was found to the north-west of the mound. A flint blade was found on this surface, although it is not directly related to the *fulacht fiadh*.

Post-excavation work is now in progress; therefore it is not possible to discuss the site in more detail.
*Fiona Reilly, Wood Road, Cratloekeel, Co. Clare, for Valerie J. Keeley Ltd.*

## 48. CLONMONEY WEST (SITE M33)
Well and trackway
99E0617
The site consists of a well and a metalled trackway, situated on low-lying pasture/marsh. The object of the test excavation was to investigate the area immediately surrounding the well to determine whether it could be linked to the trackway, or any other features, or assigned a date. Excavations were carried out on 22–4 November 1999. One cutting and three trenches were excavated by hand.

Finds included a sheep metapodial, fragments of red brick, concrete slabs incorporated into the well, a horseshoe and an oyster shell.

Cutting 1 revealed concrete slabs incorporated into the well, indicating that it dates to the last few centuries. Trenches 2 and 3 revealed a metalled trackway extending to the west and east of the well. Broken bricks incorporated into the trackway indicate that it also dates to the last few centuries. Trench 4 showed that the track post-dates the well, though probably only by a short time.

As both the well and the track date to the last few centuries and the track points towards Clonmoney House (a 19th- or possibly 18th-century house), it seems almost certain that both features relate to the house. As the track continues to the west of the well, it may also relate to Ballycaseymore House, another 18th/19th-century house a short distance to the west.

The well and the track therefore are features arising from 18th- to 20th-century farming practices in the area. They were probably built by one of the larger landowners in the area, residing in either Clonmoney House or Ballycaseymore House.
*Carleton Jones, 63 Cregaun, Tobarteascain, Ennis, Co. Clare.*

## 49. CLOONAHERNA
No archaeological significance
14651 17487
SMR 35:99
99E0153
The proposed development at Cloonaherna, Craggaunowen, Co. Clare, adjacent to a stone-built enclosure, was subject to an archaeological condition in the planning permission. Monitoring was carried out on 8 April 1999.

The development consisted of the topsoil clearance for a dwelling-house, driveway, septic tank and percolation area. The digging of foundation trenches for the house was also monitored.

No archaeological material was discovered, disturbed or destroyed during this development.
*Damian Finn, Ballycurreen, Glounthaune, Cork.*

## 50. DONMACFELIM, DOOLIN
No archaeological significance
99E0676
The site is on high ground overlooking the village of Doolin and the Atlantic Ocean. It is within the bounds of SMR 8:57, listed as a field system, and is close to another site, SMR 8:109, described as an archaeological complex.

Three test-trenches were excavated by machine before the construction of a dwelling-house and septic tank. No archaeological materials or features were revealed.
*Christopher Read, Northwest Archaeological Services, Cloonfad Cottage, Leitrim Village, Co. Roscommon.*

## 51. GORTATOGHER
Enclosure (site of)
15942 16068
SMR 53:13
99E0024
On 8 January 1999 archaeological testing was carried out in the environs of an enclosure (site of), at Gortatogher, Co. Clare. This work was undertaken before the laying of a gas pipeline from Limerick to the village of Parteen and on through the townland of Gortatogher. The enclosure was partially indicated by hachures on the 1842 edition OS 6-inch map but does not appear on any of the subsequent OS editions.

A house had been built on the south-eastern end of the site, and the western end was destroyed, before 1842, by the construction of the Limerick–Broadford road. Field inspection failed to identify any traces of the enclosure.

A single test-trench was inserted on the eastern side of the road, in a north–south direction, following the line of the proposed pipeline. This trench was c. 15m long x 0.5m wide x 1.2m deep. No finds, features or deposits of archaeological significance were noted.
*Ken Hanley, 44 Eaton Heights, Cobh, Co. Cork.*

## 52. GORTNABOUL
No archaeological significance
R157926
99E0492
A series of limited archaeological tests was carried out in August 1999 on several small anomalies identified during the monitoring of a 10m-wide wayleave leading from the Ennistymon–Kilfenora road to a proposed new reservoir at Cahereamore. This work formed part of the Lisdoonvarna Water Supply Scheme.

Nothing of archaeological interest was uncovered.
*Ken Hanley, 44 Eaton Heights, Cobh, Co. Cork, for Sheila Lane & Associates.*

### 53. GORTNABOUL
*Fulachta fiadh*
R158926
99E0504

Three suspected *fulachta fiadh* were identified, in August 1999, during the archaeological monitoring of a 10m-wide wayleave, leading south from the Ennistymon–Kilfenora road to a proposed new reservoir at Cahereamore. This work formed part of the Lisdoonvarna Water Supply Scheme.

The mound of burnt stone at Site A measured *c.* 16m by 7m by 0.3–0.4m high and was almost fully exposed by the wayleave. The site contained a well-constructed wood-lined trough and two smaller pits. The trough measured 1.86m by 0.6m by 0.2–0.35m deep and had an estimated capacity of 394 litres. The trough pit was partially lined with small, inwardly angled stake-holes. This strongly suggested that it was covered by a light canopy or 'tent-like' structure. A solitary stake survived in the south-west corner of the trough. A series of wider, deeper stake-holes formed a fence line (windbreak?) to the west of the trough. A general scatter of smaller stake-holes was also identified.

There were four main phases of use at the site, representing an approximate total of 110 episodes of use, based on crude estimations of volume. Finds included a thumb scraper and an unworked flint flake. No animal bones were present. The possible windbreak and the apparent canopy cover over the trough itself point towards bathing/sweating as a primary function. Dating results are pending.

Only the outer edge of the (*c.* 12m by 9m by 0.4m high) burnt mound at Site B was exposed by the wayleave, and very little archaeological detail could be retrieved.

Site C was a localised, thin spread of heat-shattered stone, which continued north beyond the limit of the wayleave. Excavation failed to reveal any other features of archaeological significance.

The areas between Sites A and B and between Sites A and C were also examined. No features of archaeological significance were noted.

*Ken Hanley, 44 Eaton Heights, Cobh, Co. Cork, for Sheila Lane & Associates.*

### 54. KILLALOE CATHEDRAL, SHANTRAUD, KILLALOE
Romanesque cathedral doorway
17050 17280
SMR 45:33
99E0172

This work was carried out on behalf of the Killaloe Cathedral Restoration Project. The conservation of the Romanesque doorway involved the removal of the existing blocking wall and window, both modern insertions. Monitoring of the removal of the base of this was carried out in February 1999. Subsequently, further lowering of the ground was required in order to construct a foundation for a porch outside the doorway. This was carried out over two weeks in April 1999.

The area excavated was immediately south of the cathedral wall and the threshold of the doorway. It was defined to the west by the buttress wall abutting the wall of the cathedral and to the east by a low retaining(?) wall built at right angles to the cathedral, a width of 3m. The southern definition was 2m from the cathedral, later reduced to 1m in order to avoid the excavation of *in situ* burials.

The ground sloped gradually in the southern half of the site. In the northern half, near the cathedral wall, this was more pronounced, the result of a lowering of the ground some years ago in an attempt to reduce the damp. The area was excavated in two parts east and west of a central baulk, 0.75m wide.

Around the doorway the outer face of the cathedral wall had been rebuilt before the construction of the two walls (as these clearly abut the cathedral wall). The wall was 0.65m wide to the west of the ope and 0.7m wide to the east. Judging by the stonework and pointing, the wall had been rebuilt in at least two phases—presumably when the Romanesque doorway was put in and later when the window and infill wall were built. Included in the conservation of the doorway was the removal, on the east side, of the later pillar that replaced the inner order. A pencilled inscription on the render behind dated this replacement to 1892.

Two decorated slabs formed the threshold (OD 34.91m). The outer one was partly covered by the base of the blocking wall. Along its northern edge was a row of seven sockets (for a grill?) The inner orders of the doorway were positioned at the joint of the two slabs. To the east, the base overlapped the slab by 0.25m, to the west by 0.5m. Behind this jamb was a 0.05m gap, filled with stoppers, west of which was a rectangular cut block of sandstone (OD 35.075m). This was placed directly in line with the end of the threshold slab, at right angles to the cathedral wall. This block measured 0.31m of visible length north–south by 0.22m wide by 0.2m high. The base of the blocking wall overlay this block, and between the wall and the supporting masonry behind the jamb was a recess in which a 17th-century clay pipe was found. West of the block was a flat facing-stone that directly overlay the plinth stone of the cathedral wall. A similar block stone occurred on the east side of the doorway, 0.09m beyond the slab. It overlay the plinth of the cathedral wall and was covered with mortar.

The excavation ceased at the level of a row of eight slabs (OD 34.911–35.014m) aligned east–west and set at right angles to the threshold and the cathedral wall, below the level of the footing of all three walls and extending under the threshold. The westernmost four were larger, 1.52m long by a maximum of 0.6m wide, narrowing to 0.5m wide (from the threshold). At the eastern end were four smaller stones, some overlapping, 0.98m long and ranging in width from 0.44m to 0.28m. South of these was a layer of dark grey, loose soil and gravel under a band of coarser gravel and slates.

There was no evidence for the construction of the original cathedral wall. All features and deposits were related to the insertion of the Romanesque doorway, the threshold slabs and the two side-walls, the refacing of the cathedral wall and the associated ground disturbance to the south of the doorway. Beyond this were the fills of sand, slate etc., in which were burials presumably post-dating the insertion of the doorway. The purity of the gravel layer, particularly in the north-western corner, implies that once construction fill reached the level of the threshold the area was covered with other material that became the working surface, including the build-up of burnt layers. It may be that the pits, containing only large human bones, were dug on completion of the work to contain bones from disturbed burials.

The upper deposits of sand and slate debris may relate to reroofing activities: possibly the removal of ceramic tiles and their replacement with slates. Judging by the amount of human bone and the looseness of these deposits, they may well contain burials post-dating these works. The compacted surface and sod overlay both areas.

It seems that after the opening was made in the cathedral wall and the ground level was reduced, the footings for the side-walls and the row of slabs were laid. There was then what appears to be a levelling of the area with the placing of mortar, slates and gravel. This was followed by the footing for the refaced part of the cathedral wall, the placing of the threshold slabs, the insertion of the doorway orders and the refacing of the cathedral wall externally. The presence of the bulbous clay pipe bowl in the recess between this and the support for the inner order suggests a 17th-century date for this activity.

The two decorated threshold slabs were placed in opposing directions. The inner one was aligned west–east. It has been described in the Urban Archaeological Survey as an Early Christian cross-slab. The outer one, now fully exposed, seems likely to be another cross-slab and not a cross-shaft (Urban Survey). There was an incised equal-armed cross linked by a circle. Visible on either side of the slightly tapered shaft were two carved panels in different designs. The inner one consisted of a running pattern of six spirals with three juxtaposed foil-like motifs on one side, arranged alternately. On the other side was a running pattern of seven spirals with what looked like a projecting animal snout, also arranged on alternate sides. The end of this panel was terminated by the expanded base of the cross, consisting of an inscribed double line. As described above, there was a further 0.5m of the slab (covered by the sandstone block), but it cannot be determined whether this was also decorated.

The building sequence relating to the insertion of the doorway, coupled with the fact that the two stones were arranged head-to-toe, suggests that they were not in their original position but were specifically reused as the threshold for the inserted Romanesque doorway.

Outer threshold slab at Killaloe Cathedral, exposed.

*Reference*
Bradley, J. *et al. c.* 1988 Urban Archaeology Survey Part XV, County Clare. Unpublished report. OPW, Dublin.

*Celie O Rahilly, Limerick Corporation, City Hall, Limerick.*

### 55. KILQUANE/BALLYLANNIDY
No archaeological significance
13039 17719
SMR 33:65
99E0253

Pre-development testing was carried out on 29 May 1999 in response to a condition of planning for a development that consisted of the construction of five houses with ancillary services, as well as a variation of the site layout previously approved at Kilquane and Ballylannidy townlands, Co. Clare. The condition was included because the proposed development was adjacent to an enclosure.

The site lay in grassland just east of Woodstock Golf and Country Club, on a slight downslope from the enclosure to the north.

Three trial-trenches were excavated by machine, positioned to cover that area of the proposed development nearest the recorded monument. They were orientated east-north-east/west-south-west and were 20.2m long, 1–1.5m wide and 0.1–1.1m deep. The stratigraphy was the same in all three: topsoil above orange/brown natural subsoil and bedrock. The bedrock outcropped in places along the trench and was never more than 0.6m below the surface.

No artefacts were in evidence. The testing revealed undisturbed stratigraphy only.
*Richard Crumlish, Archaeological Services Unit Ltd, Purcell House, Oranmore, Co. Galway.*

### 56. KNOCKNARANHY
*Fulacht fiadh*
99E0449

This development is associated with the Lisdoonvarna Sewerage and Sewage Disposal Scheme and is funded by Clare County Council. An assessment of the scheme identified the remains of a possible archaeological site that measured *c.* 16m north–south by 7m, formed a U-shaped feature and lay along the proposed access route to the new treatment works site. It will be completely destroyed by the construction of the proposed roadway. Pre-development testing was carried out to ascertain the archaeological significance of the site.

Two trenches were manually excavated, Trench A in the north and Trench B in the south of the mound. Excavations in Trench B revealed only natural marl layers with no finds. However, in Trench A removal of the sod revealed a burnt stone layer. This ran in an east–west direction for 2.3m, sloping sharply on the east and west sides. The burnt layer was recorded, and it was recommended that full excavation be carried out on the site before any future developments. It is possible that this burnt layer represents a burnt mound or *fulacht fiadh*.
*Fiona Rooney, Arch. Consultancy Ltd, Ballydavid South, Athenry, Co. Galway.*

### 57. LATOON SOUTH, AREA 1
Medieval occupation
SMR 42:52
98E0338 ext.

This site was uncovered during archaeological monitoring before development on the N18–N19 road scheme, Co. Clare. It consisted of five areas of activity. The main concentration of activity was during the medieval period. The archaeological evidence consisted in the main of a series of post-holes and pits from a habitation site. Remains of a light 'flooring' of small stones were excavated on part of the site. The floor overlay a small drainage channel. This area of the site was subsequently covered by midden material, of stone, clay and animal bone.

Finds from the site include bone cylinders, fragments of a decorated bone comb, sherds of medieval pottery, bronze pins, fragments of rotary querns and a fragment of a decorated bone mount(?), with rivet hole. A large amount of animal bone was recovered from the site, a selection of which shows evidence of butchering.

*Christine Grant, c/o S. Schorman, Ballyalla, Ennis, Co. Clare.*

### 58. LISDOONVARNA WATER SUPPLY SCHEME
*Fulachta fiadh*
R111968
99E0199

The Lisdoonvarna Water Supply Scheme involves the insertion of water pipes across a 32km route between Ennistymon, Doolin and Lisdoonvarna, Co. Clare. The project had been ongoing for some time before an archaeological assessment was commissioned in early 1999. Monitoring commenced in April 1999. Most of the pipes followed existing road lines. In most cases the roads were cut into or built on top of natural subsoils. In several areas, especially along tertiary roads, the roads sealed substantial quantities of peat.

A *fulacht fiadh* was identified in the townland of Aughiska More, *c.* 2km to the south-west of Lisdoonvarna on the R478. A thin band of dark, heat-shattered stone was exposed within the pipe-trench, which was inserted along the southern side of the roadway. The burnt stone was sealed under *c.* 0.4–0.5m of road bedding and lay directly on top of natural subsoils. The spread, which was 20–100mm thick, was only identified in a localised area of *c.* 1–2m. Examination of the adjacent field identified a low (0.2–0.5m) kidney-shaped mound, which also appeared to contain heat-shattered stone. This feature may originally have measured *c.* 8m by 8.5m. The pipe-trench appeared to have clipped the southern tip of the stone spread.

The only significant off-road section of pipeline to be monitored involved the insertion of a 10m-wide wayleave, leading from the Ennistymon–Kilfenora road to a proposed new reservoir at Cahereamore td (R157926). Three *fulachta fiadh* were identified along the wayleave, near the Gortnaboul–Cahereamore townland boundary. These were excavated under a separate licence (see No. 53 above).

Monitoring of the water scheme is ongoing and is expected to conclude in April 2000.

*Ken Hanley, 44 Eaton Heights, Cobh, Co. Cork, for Sheila Lane & Associates.*

### 59. LISKETT
No archaeological significance
99E0694

This site is on the south-facing slope of a low hill, *c.* 2 miles outside Kilfenora, Co. Clare. A possible bivallate ringfort lies in an adjacent field to the north-west of the existing house. The proposed development involved the construction of an extension to the house and the excavation of a septic tank.

The area to be disturbed by the extension, septic tank and connecting pipes was stripped by machine down to the level of the subsoil. No archaeological materials or features were revealed.

*Christopher Read, Northwest Archaeological Services, Cloonfad Cottage, Leitrim Village, Co. Roscommon.*

### 60. LISMOHER
No archaeological significance
120651 196198
99E0338

Monitoring was carried out at this site during the construction of a domestic dwelling. It is close to a known monument, SMR 34:76. No archaeological material was uncovered.

*Christine Grant, c/o S. Schorman, Ballyalla, Ennis, Co. Clare.*

### 61. DROMOLAND CASTLE, NEWMARKET-ON-FERGUS
Adjacent to castle
138713 170484
99E0147

Assessment of an extension to a golf club-house adjacent to Dromoland Castle included the mechanical excavation of three test-trenches in the area of the development. No archaeological materials were found.

*Cóilín Ó Drisceoil, 6 Riverview, Ardnore, Kilkenny, for Mary Henry & Associates.*

### 62. PARKNABINNIA
Court tomb
98E0230

The 1999 field season ran for eight weeks from 5 July to 27 August. Trench A, begun in 1998, was finished in 1999. Trench C, a new trench encompassing the north-east quadrant of the site, was opened, and excavation was also begun on the first and second chambers.

The base has not yet been reached in either Chamber 1 or Chamber 2. Both contained a mixture of small to large stones with very dark brown/black silt loam between the stones. Bone was found throughout the stone and soil fill. Some of the bone appears to be *in situ* relatively high in the rubble fill of the chamber. In other words, some of the bone in the chambers may post-date some of the stones in the chambers.

Within a fairly homogeneous spread of human and animal bone in Chamber 1 were two discernible concentrations. In the north-east corner of Chamber 1 is an upright pillar-like stone that may have been a support for a corbelled roof. Near the base of this stone a group of long bones had been pushed down along the stone's edge. The second concentration is against the southern wall of Chamber 1, where a pile of disarticulated bone was topped with a partial skull.

Four large slabs were used to block the rear of the tomb off from Chamber 1. These stones leaned against the jamb stones that separate Chamber 1 from Chamber 2. A femur and a pelvis lay in apparent articulation on top of what may be a sill stone separating the two chambers. One of the slabs used for the blocking was wedged down on top of the femur, snapping it off near its proximal end.

A large amount of human and animal bone was recovered, most contained in the two chambers. Some of the human bone was cremated; a large amount was not. Most of the human bone appears to have been deposited in a disarticulated state. In two instances, however, a femur and a pelvis were close enough and aligned properly enough to suggest articulation.

Finds included a leaf-shaped arrowhead with a possible tang, a convex scraper, a chert blade, debitage, a possible sharpening stone, a bone 'bead' and pottery.
*Carleton Jones, 63 Cregaun, Tobarteascain, Ennis, Co. Clare.*

### 63. PARKNABINNIA
Wedge tomb
12608 19326
SMR 17:18012
99E0455

During a site inspection of the wedge tomb at the top of Roughan Hill in August 1999 Carleton Jones brought to this writer's attention fragments of human bone lying on the surface of the clay floor of the chamber. Nine fragments in all (including one tooth) were collected, in addition to a waste flake of cream-coloured flint, a tiny waste flake of chert and a small sherd of pottery. These have been deposited in the National Museum of Ireland, Kildare Street. As the chamber of this tomb is easily accessible, it was decided to cover the clay floor with large, flat stones that will help protect it from further visitor erosion.
*Ann Lynch, National Monuments and Historic Properties Service, Dúchas The Heritage Service, 6 Ely Place Upper, Dublin 2.*

### 64. MAIN STREET, QUIN
Medieval settlement
SMR 42:27
99E0146

Three parallel test-trenches were excavated on a proposed development site in the centre of Quin village. No stratified deposits were encountered. A linear feature cutting across two of the trenches is believed to be an old boundary ditch, which cut the present area in half. Further testing of the front part of the site, which is currently inaccessible, was recommended.
*Brian Hodkinson, Annaholty, Birdhill, Co. Tipperary.*

### 65. ROSMADDA WEST
Earthwork (environs of)
15942 16152
SMR 53:12
99E0023

On 7 January 1999 testing was carried out in the environs of a linear earthwork at Rosmadda West, Co. Clare, before the laying of a gas pipeline from Limerick to the village of Parteen and on through Rosmadda West. This site is on the western edge of the Limerick–Broadford road, on the approach to the Blackwater Bridge. It was not marked on either the 1st or the 2nd edition of the Ordnance Survey 6-inch maps but does appear on the 3rd edition as a linear earthwork.

Field inspection identified an earthen ridge, 18.2m long x 2–3m wide x 0.4m high. This ridge lay *c.* 8m in from the road line. The proposed pipeline crossed the zone of archaeological potential for the earthwork. A test-trench was inserted in order to ascertain the existence of associated archaeological activity.

No finds, features or deposits of archaeological interest were noted.
*Ken Hanley, 44 Eaton Heights, Cobh, Co. Cork.*

### 66. SMITHSTOWN INDUSTRIAL ESTATE, SHANNON
Earth- and stone-built enclosure
14099 16352
SMR 51:142

The construction of an office/production facility, carparking and associated site works at Smithstown Industrial Estate, Shannon, Co. Clare, was subject to an archaeological condition in the planning permission. Monitoring was carried out between 1 June and 26 August 1999.

The development consisted of the removal of topsoil from an area that was subject to the deposition of construction rubble over a period of several years to raise the ground level. The digging of foundation trenches and service trenches was also monitored.

No archaeological material was discovered, disturbed or destroyed by this development.
*Damian Finn, Ballycurreen, Glounthaune, Cork.*

### 67. SIXMILEBRIDGE
No archaeological significance
R476662
SMR 52:16
99E0118

The grant of planning permission for the construction of forty houses in Sixmilebridge was subject to two archaeological conditions, one of which stipulated monitoring of all ground disturbance. This was due to the site being partly within the town's zone of archaeological potential and also to the size of the development. The 5-acre development site is in the north-west of Sixmilebridge townland, just north of the town. It lies on undulating ground, which slopes dramatically from west to east towards the Owenagarney River and commands extensive views of the surrounding terrain. Sixmilebridge developed as an important medieval crossing-point of the Owenagarney River, which led to its growth as an important trading town.

Topsoil-stripping for raft foundations for the houses was monitored, in addition to roads and services. Topsoil was excavated by machine to a depth of between 0.1m and 0.5m. It was quite shallow in both the south-west and central area of the development site because of the high level of the underlying limestone bedrock. The underlying stratum was a light yellow/brown, silty clay subsoil, with occasional pockets of leached soil, indicating the occurrence of iron-panning.

A possible archaeological artefact was identified in a mound of rubble in the vicinity of the site entrance. A large, fractured sandstone was discovered with a centrally located circular hollow. This may represent the remains of a bullaun stone. It lay on ground recently disturbed to accommodate the erection of an ESB pole.

No stratigraphy of an archaeological nature was identified during the ground disturbance activities.
*Laurence Dunne, Eachtra Archaeological Projects, 3 Canal Place, Tralee, Co. Kerry.*

### 68. SIXMILEBRIDGE
No archaeological significance
Q470660
SMR 52:01601–03
99E0361

The development of townhouses within the historic town of Sixmilebridge necessitated an archaeological assessment. The village includes 18th-century industrial buildings fronting onto the main street and a late medieval bridge. The development site was itself used as a garden.

Test-trenching did not uncover any archaeological features or finds.
*Rose M. Cleary, Department of Archaeology, University College, Cork.*

### 69. MAIN STREET, SIXMILEBRIDGE
Burnt spread/*fulacht fiadh*?
99E0746

A large-scale development at the rear of Main Street, Sixmilebridge, Co. Clare, was tested in December 1999, as part of an archaeological impact statement. The 1.8-acre site leads south from Main Street along the western bank of the Owenagarney River. The front (northern) sixth of the site consists of a coalyard (still in use), while the rest consists of a relatively flat, poorly drained field.

Eight test-trenches were opened. Trench I led south from Main Street through the entrance into the coalyard. This revealed only modern building debris/landfill. It was not possible to test under the coalyard area because of access problems caused by existing structures and storage areas.

Trenches II–VIII were excavated to the south of the coalyard in the open green-field area of the site, which was subject to substantial flooding. These revealed a c. 0.2–0.85m depth of modern landfill on the northern half of the site. The original surface contained a relatively consistent, silty clay topsoil cover, which rested directly on the underlying natural, sandy subsoil. The only anomalies identified (apart from field drains) were three post-medieval cut features at the southern end of Trench VI and a spread of burnt stone in the western end of Trench IV.

The burnt spread was sealed under a 0.2–0.4m cover of clay topsoil and appeared as a spread of dark, heat-shattered stone c. 2.5m north–south x c. 4m x 0.08–0.1m deep, forming a slight arc. The burnt stone was indicative of a *fulacht fiadh*.

Further archaeological examination of the coalyard area and the burnt spread was recommended, as was some general monitoring.
*Ken Hanley, 44 Eaton Heights, Cobh, Co. Cork.*

### 70. TUAMGRANEY
No archaeological significance
99E0275

Testing was carried out in July 1999 at the site of a proposed dwelling and two septic tanks in Tuamgraney, Co. Clare. The second septic tank was to be built behind and to service an already existing house. It was noted from the Sites and Monuments Record that the area was rich in archaeological remains: Tuamgraney church, graveyard, tower-house and cross-slab and the site of a round tower were to the north of the proposed dwelling-house site. These sites are numbered CL028:05801–05 in the Sites and Monuments Record.

Six trenches were investigated by machine. Trenches 1 and 2 were in the area of the proposed septic tank and percolation area; Trenches 3 and 4 were in the area of the proposed house; and Trenches 5 and 6 were in the area of the proposed septic tank and percolation area of the existing house.

Nothing of archaeological significance was discovered during test-trenching. A large dump of wood waste material was found in the vicinity of the proposed dwelling. It may be that this material was dumped here in recent times from the sawmill that stood to the south (G. Daly, pers. comm.) and that it obscures the well marked on the 3rd edition OS map.
*Fiona Reilly, Wood Road, Cratloekeel, Co. Clare.*

## CORK

### 71. CURRANE HILL, BALLINEEN
No archaeological significance
1338 0502
99E0668

Testing was undertaken at Currane Hill, Co. Cork, before the grant of planning permission for the erection of a 30m-high radio communications tower. A single test-trench was excavated. The topsoil was present to an average depth of 0.25m; it was a black, sandy loam containing a high percentage of charcoal. The presence of the charcoal was due to the annual burning of scrub to enhance summer grazing. The underlying subsoil was a red/brown clay loam, with sandstone bedrock apparent.

No artefacts or stratigraphy of an archaeological nature were identified during the testing.
*Emer Dennehy, Eachtra Archaeological Projects, 3 Canal Place, Tralee, Co. Kerry.*

### 72. BALLYHOOLY SOUTH
Close to earthwork
17277 10151
SMR 26:200
99E0157

All groundworks associated with the construction of a bungalow were monitored, in compliance with a planning condition imposed because the site was close to a small earthwork enclosure.

No archaeological features were noted, but one small sherd of pottery was recovered. This has been identified by Rose M. Cleary as a rimsherd of Beaker period pottery.
*Eamonn Cotter, Ballynanelagh, Rathcormac, Co. Cork.*

## 73. BALLYMAGUE
Ringfort
15537 10628
SMR 25:7
99E0045

Planning permission was granted to build a dwelling-house on a site *c.* 30m to the west of a ringfort. The fosse survived to a depth of 0.25m to the south and west but had been backfilled to the north. Access to the house was to be by a roadway running to the north of the ringfort outside the backfilled fosse on this side.

Four test-trenches were opened in January 1999 along the line of the proposed road. No evidence for the fosse or other archaeological finds or features were noted.

*Sheila Lane, 1 Charlemont Heights, Coach Hill, Rochestown, Cork.*

## 74. BALLYNOE
Medieval church
19348 08964
SMR 46:03302
95E0260 ext.

A further phase of excavations was carried out at the medieval church of Ballynoe in March 1999, before conservation work on the church walls. The surviving ruins consist of the east end of the nave, an almost complete chancel and a vestry or sacristy extending northwards from the east end of the chancel. A small area was excavated within the north-east corner of the chancel (Area A), and another cutting was excavated in the field outside the church, immediately east of the vestry and chancel (Area B).

Area A measured 2.2m north–south x 1.3m east–west and was a continuation northwards of a cutting excavated in March 1996 in which the base of a mortared stone structure, presumably the altar, was uncovered (*Excavations 1996*, 10).

The present excavation uncovered the foundation course of an unmortared stone structure extending northwards from the altar to the north-east corner of the chancel. The position of this structure directly under a large aumbry at the north end of the east wall of the chancel suggests that the aumbry was a statue niche or a reliquary with a side altar underneath, perhaps dedicated to the patron saint of the church.

Beneath the stone base were two adjacent graves, both orientated east–west. Near their base the graves were divided by thin sandstone slabs set on edge. Because of their proximity to the north chancel wall, part of which is leaning inwards, neither of these graves was fully excavated for fear of further disturbing the wall foundations. It was clear, however, that neither contained a full skeleton, although some disarticulated human bone was found in each. A number of coffin nails were also found, as well as a tiny metal pin 12mm long. The latter may have been a shroud pin.

Area B was an L-shaped area excavated on the east side of the chancel and vestry, measuring a maximum of 6m north–south and 4.2m east–west. Rubble clearance around the area of a breach in the southern end of the east wall of the vestry revealed that this was formerly a doorway. Two surviving jamb stones displayed chamfered edges with tapered stop-chamfers suggesting a late 13th-century date.

Two layers of cobblestones uncovered outside the doorway and extending southwards from it represent two separate phases of deliberate raising of the ground level and the creation of a hard surface, and it is likely that they were laid down to create a pathway outside the door.

Beneath the cobblestones a series of post-holes extended north-eastwards from the junction of the chancel and vestry, suggesting the presence of a stout boundary fence. The area to the south of this boundary contained a dense concentration of human burials. Two of these were excavated, as they lay in an area where conservation work on the walls will be necessary, while the others were left undisturbed. Both were of children, one aged 8–10 years, the other aged 3–4 years. In both cases the skulls were supported by 'ear-muffs', flat stones set on edge on either side of the skull.

To the north of the boundary less ground disturbance and fewer burials were encountered. Directly outside the vestry doorway two fully extended supine burials were excavated, both orientated west–east. The most southerly lay in an earth-dug grave and was of an adolescent aged 15–19 years. The other skeleton lay in a cist grave, i.e. a grave lined with flat slabs set on edge and with covering slabs resting on the side slabs. This was the skeleton of a female in her twenties. Both burials had been disturbed by the digging of a trench parallel to the vestry wall, possibly in an attempt to consolidate the sagging foundations by packing stone underneath.

The burials and post-holes had been cut into the fill of a *c.* 2m-deep ditch, another section of which had been excavated in 1996. The ditch is likely to have been the enclosing element of an Early Christian site.

*Eamonn Cotter, Ballynanelagh, Rathcormac, Co. Cork.*

## 75. BALLYRISODE
Early Bronze Age copper mine
8339 2989
SMR 147:13
99E0409

This site is an isolated example of a Mount Gabriel-type copper mine, 10km south-west of the said mountain in the Mizen Peninsula, Co. Cork.

The mine consists of a single inclined opening at the base of a low outcrop exposure of sedimentary copper mineralisation. Directly outside the 3–4m-long chamber is a low mound formed by the dumping of waste rock during the mine operation. This spoil mound, measuring 13m by 7m, is bisected by a 1m-wide trench extending 13.5m out from the mine entrance. Antiquarian records reveal that the latter was dug in 1854, leading to the discovery of the mine chamber and a hoard of twelve polished stone axeheads therein (*Journal of the Royal Society of Antiquaries of Ireland* 1880, 341–2).

A sample excavation was carried out in August 1999 to examine the composition of the spoil mound and to recover charcoal samples for radiocarbon dating. Three cuttings were opened across the mound, at right angles to the 1854 trench. Excavation on the southern side revealed upcast sediment from these diggings, overlying a buried sod horizon and iron pan formation. This sealed early mine sediment comprising layers of crushed sandstone containing charcoal and stone hammer fragments. The last consist of broken cobbles from local beach sources, with a small number of haft-modified examples.

A charcoal sample from a basal spoil layer has been radiocarbon dated to 3400±30 BP (GrN-25066, courtesy Jan Lanting). The sample can be directly linked to fire-setting extraction, placing this short-lived mine operation within the Early Bronze Age, and by association the use of polished stone axeheads at this site.

*William O'Brien, Department of Archaeology, National University of Ireland, Galway.*

### 76. MACSWEENY QUAY, BANDON
Urban
14900 05497
99E0158

In compliance with a condition of planning permission, test-trenching was carried out before the construction of apartments and retail outlets. The site is on MacSweeny Quay and is within the line of the town walls of Bandon. Scale's map of Bandon in 1775 shows the area of the site to be occupied by formal gardens with no structure. The area seems likely to have remained undeveloped until Burlington (now MacSweeny) Quay was built in the early 19th century.

A cotton mill was constructed by the Scott family on the site in 1835. This had closed by 1840, and the site was acquired by the milling company J.P. Deasy & Sons, who established a provender mill on it in 1927. The site was periodically upgraded and expanded during the following decades and remained in use until recent times. A substantial portion of the original mill building survives, though now in ruins.

Test-trenching was carried out in April 1999. Two trenches, one 17m long and one 7m long, were excavated on the eastern side of the site in the areas least likely to have been disturbed by modern development. The stratigraphy in both trenches was very similar, but the depth varied. It consisted of a build-up of 0.4–0.9m depth of modern material (stone chippings etc.) lying on a *c.* 0.6m-deep layer of silty loam, which in turn lay on natural gravels. The silty loam layer contained several sherds of post-medieval and 18th/19th-century pottery. No archaeological features were noted.

*Eamonn Cotter, Ballynanelagh, Rathcormac, Co. Cork.*

### 77. BANDUFF
Ringfort
17042 07417
SMR 74:20
99E0113

Three test-trenches were opened here in March 1999. A ringfort ditch was identified in each of the trenches. A subsequent excavation was carried out that exposed the northern arc of the ringfort ditch and evidence of the levelled bank, with both internal and external stone facing. No features associated with the ringfort were found. All finds were 18th/19th-century in date and post-dated the ringfort, with the exception of a ring pin.

*Sheila Lane, 1 Charlemont Heights, Coach Hill, Rochestown, Cork.*

### 78. *LA SURVEILLANTE*, BANTRY BAY
Historic shipwreck
99E0244

The French 12-pounder frigate *La Surevillante* was lost in Bantry Bay in January 1797. It had been part of a failed invasion attempt of Ireland led by General Lazare La Hoche and supported by the United Irishmen and Wolfe Tone. The site, one mile north-east of Whiddy Island, was rediscovered in 1980 during seabed clearance operations following the oil terminal disaster in 1979. The wreck was the focus of an integrated marine archaeological project during the summer of 1999 funded by the Royal Irish Academy, *Dúchas* and the University of Ulster. This project involved a multi-disciplinary team from the University of Ulster, University College Cork and the National University of Ireland, Galway, and is part of the broader Bantry Bay Maritime Landscape Project.

A range of marine survey techniques was deployed on the wreck site, including marine geophysics, oceanographic sampling, geomorphological coring and underwater diver survey and excavation. These investigations have revealed that the site is one of the best-preserved historic wreck sites in Irish waters. *La Surveillante* lies in 32m of water at the upper end of the bay. A considerable portion of the hull survives, standing up to 4m off the seabed at the bow. Excavation and sub-bottom profiling have shown that the wreck lies on a gravel layer 1–2m beneath the bed sediments and is in a relatively stable condition. The structure and a huge range of associated artefactual material survive encased in copper sheathing. Thirteen cannon, a large central anchor, the remnants of a galley structure and an assortment of small arms, saddlery and rigging elements lie about the wreck.

Further non-invasive survey work is scheduled to take place on the wreck in the summer of 2000 with a view to the development of a comprehensive management plan for the site and the production of an associated research monograph.

*Colin Breen, Centre for Maritime Archaeology, University of Ulster, Coleraine, Belfast BT52 1SA.*

### 79. CASTLE WARREN, BARNAHELY
Tower-house, bawn etc.
SMR 87:5201
99E0279

The site at Castle Warren consists of a complex of medieval and post-medieval buildings around a courtyard and includes a tower-house and bawn of probable late 16th-century date and Castle Warren House, which dates to the 18th century. It is currently owned by the Industrial Development Authority, who wished to secure the site by erecting a chain-link fence with an access gate around the tower-house and bawn, at a distance of 10m from the boundary walls.

Five trenches were excavated by machine just inside the line of the fence before the digging of the foundation pits for the fence. No archaeological features relating to the later medieval occupation at the site were uncovered during excavation of the test-trenches or monitoring of the excavation of the foundation pits.

*Mary O'Donnell, Archaeological Services Unit, University College, Cork.*

## 80. BROOKLODGE
Corn-drying kiln
**W747764**
**99E0438**

This site was discovered during topsoil-stripping in the corridor being prepared for the Little Island to Ballincollig gas pipeline. The site is on the lower slopes of a ridge extending north-north-west/south-south-east. A stream lay 10m to the immediate east. Local information indicated that the kiln was immediately adjacent to the line of an old roadway.

Excavation established the presence of a complete structure consisting of a lintelled flue and an open-topped bowl; a stoke-hole and fire-pit were also uncovered.

The flue extended for 1.7m on a basically north-east/south-west axis. Its floor level maintained a relatively even profile. There were five lintels *in situ*, although these had been severely damaged by the weight of the heavy machinery. The height of the flue gradually increased from 0.45m to 0.6m; its width varied from 0.5m to 0.8m.

The bowl was almost circular with outwardly battered sides. Its diameter at the top varied from 1.62m to 1.52m, and diameter at floor level from 1.26m to 1.2m. The original height was 0.8m. In an unusual development, the flue and bowl were positioned in a P-shaped configuration.

The floor of the bowl was represented by a loosely set cobble layer. A deliberate arrangement of large rocks had been placed at its junction with the flue. These probably acted as a crude filter (after the fashion of a 'baffle stone') that prevented flying embers from entering the bowl.

*Mark Clinton for Margaret Gowen & Co. Ltd, 2 Killiney View, Albert Road Lower, Glenageary, Co. Dublin.*

## 81. BUTLERSTOWN LITTLE
*Fulacht fiadh*
**W075077**
**99E0437**

This site was exposed during monitoring of topsoil-stripping along the route of a Bord Gáis Éireann pipeline that extended from Caherlag to Ballincollig, Co. Cork. The site was initially identified as a large spread of blackened and fire-shattered stone immediately beneath the topsoil. Preliminary investigations appeared to confirm the presence of a trough beneath the burnt spread. There had been no evidence of the site before the plant works.

The spread extended north–south along the line of the pipeline for approximately 25m and up to 10m into the western side of the wayleave (presumably continuing for a similar distance outside the wayleave). Preliminary investigation of the site indicated the presence of a probable trough and hearth, and the excavation sought to expose these features fully, and any other features that were present beneath the spread.

The trough lay immediately inside the western boundary of the wayleave and took the form of an elongated oval pit that was orientated roughly east–west. The pit had maximum dimensions of 4.62m x 1.4m and was between 0.45m and 0.55m deep. The pit had been cut through a yellow/brown, loamy subsoil and was relatively straight-sided and flat-bottomed. The trough was stone-lined at the east and west ends, and the stones had been removed in antiquity from the sides. The stones had probably been originally sealed with clay, or possibly animal hide, in order to make them watertight.

The hearth lay at the east end of the trough and was roughly horseshoe-shaped, with the open end facing the trough. The edge of the hearth area was lined with small stones forming a kerb. The hearth covered an area 1.3m across the horns and 1.1m from front to back. There was no evidence that the hearth was floored, although the underlying subsoil was not badly scorched, indicating that it may originally have been floored.

Around the north-east side of the trough was evidence of a crudely laid stone surface. These stones were roughly set into the natural subsoil, and there was no evidence of this surface continuing on the other sides of the trough. There were no other features (post-holes etc.) associated with the surface.

The final feature recorded was a possible roasting pit to the south of the trough. This was a circular pit that cut through the southern edge of the trough pit. It could only have functioned as a roasting pit if the trough had been stone-lined on all sides, otherwise it would have flooded. It was contemporary with the trough, as the deposits filling both consisted of the same material.

*Tim Coughlan, Margaret Gowen & Co. Ltd, 2 Killiney View, Albert Road Lower, Glenageary, Co. Dublin.*

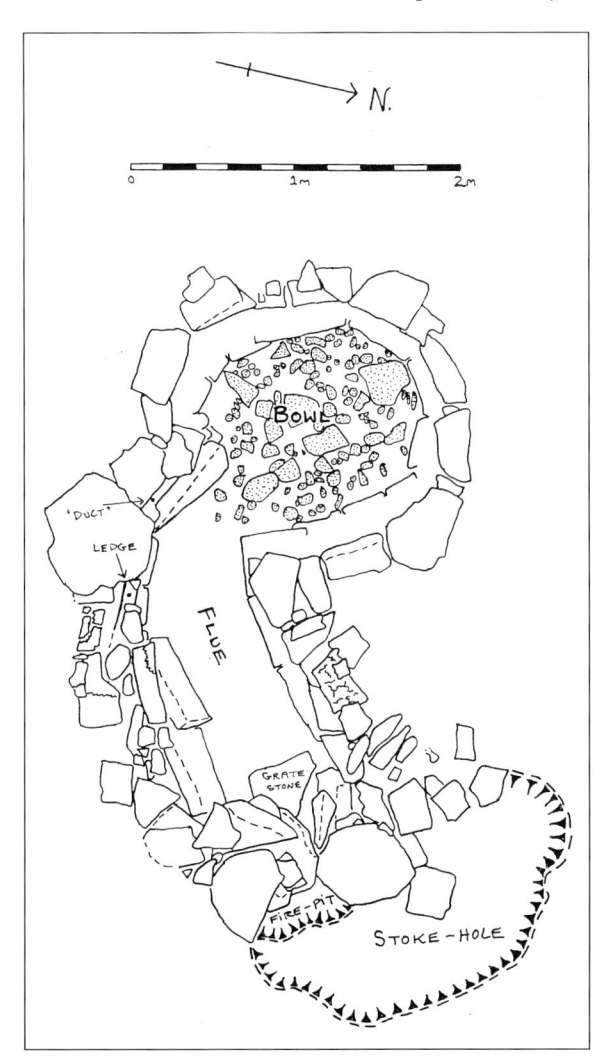

Plan of corn-drying kiln at Brooklodge.

### 82. CAHERAVART
Possible ringfort
06778 05108
SMR 102:12
99E0336

Four test-trenches were opened here in July 1999. The opening of Trench 4 established that an enclosing element existed on the south side of the site. Nothing of an archaeological nature was noted.
*Sheila Lane, 1 Charlemont Heights, Coach Hill, Rochestown, Cork.*

### 83. CAHERLAG/BALLINCOLLIG
Monitoring
**W059071 (Caherlag), W075073 (Ballincollig)**
99E0314

Monitoring of topsoil-stripping along the route of the Bord Gáis Éireann Caherlag to Ballincollig pipeline was carried out during the summer of 1999. The pipeline was 22.5km long and extended over undulating pastureland around the outskirts of Cork City. The wayleave of the pipeline was fenced off before any plant excavations took place along the route. This created a 20m-wide corridor, within which all works on the pipeline were contained.

Topsoil was stripped from a 15m-wide area within the corridor, with the remaining 5m being used for stockpiling the excavated topsoil. At intervals of approximately 100m, sections of the remaining 5m-wide area were also stripped to facilitate stockpiling of a sand mix that was used during the laying of the pipe. The trench for the pipe was 0.6m wide (on average) and was excavated to a depth of *c.* 2.5m.

During monitoring of the topsoil removal four sites were excavated—three *fulachta fiadh* and a corn-drying kiln—at Killeens, Monard, Butlerstown Little and Brooklodge (see Nos 80 and 81 above and 106 and 117 below) respectively. A number of other spreads of burnt material were recorded along the route of the pipeline, some of which may have been associated with features/sites that lay outside the wayleave, while others represented the remains of more recent activity.
*Tim Coughlan, Margaret Gowen & Co. Ltd, 2 Killiney View, Albert Road Lower, Glenageary, Co. Dublin.*

### 84. BARRYSCOURT CASTLE, CARRIGTWOHILL
Late medieval castle
1822 0725
96E0238

Another season of excavations at Barryscourt completed the investigation of more than half of the bawn area and cut a pair of trenches for drainpipes west of the tower-house. Part of the bawn area opened this season, in front of the tower-house door, would benefit from further investigation.

The tower-house and a second mortared stone building appear to have been built on a green-field site above a stream fed by a nearby spring. The tower-house occupied the corner position of an enclosure defined by a considerable bank and ditch on at least two sides and the ponded watercourse on another. Gun positions in the basement of the tower-house would have covered three sides; the fourth would have been covered from the second mortared building.

The second building overlooked two ponds, at different levels, and had a narrow controlled channel around its other two sides. A potential holding tank for fish has been identified a short distance upstream in the nearby watercourse.

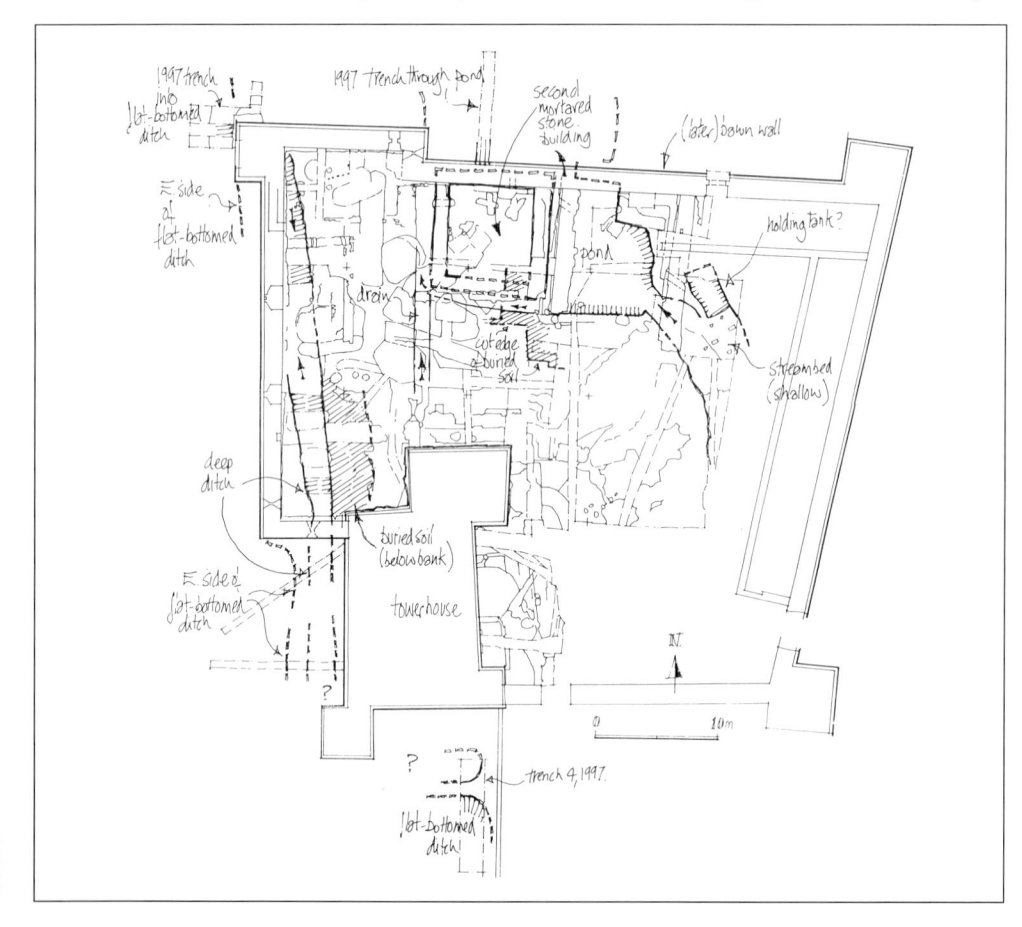

Ditches and ponds etc., early bawn, Barryscourt Castle.

At some stage (in the 16th century) the traditional enclosing bank and ditch were replaced with a string of ponds, but before the present bawn wall was built (in the later 1580s/1590s?) the waterworks were in ruins and the stream had reasserted its meandering course.

The stream was diverted (to its present location?) when the bawn was walled. The new enclosure was divided with an internal wall, restricting access to the north-west. A timber range, most of it one lofty storey over a half-cellar, was built into the corner, overlooking a terraced garden. The garden was probably not maintained for longer than 30 years and should have provided excellent information. However, truncation had generally removed the late 16th/early 17th-century ground level, and the surviving deeper features do not provide a clear design.

*Dave Pollock, ArchaeoGrafix, Church Lane, Stradbally, Co. Waterford.*

### 85. CASTLEVIEW
*Fulacht fiadh* and stone-lined features
**99E0462**

Excavations were undertaken at Castleview, Little Island, Co. Cork, over five weeks in August and September 1999. The monitoring of topsoil removal revealed four archaeological sites consisting of three stone-lined linear features (Sites 1–3) and a levelled *fulacht fiadh* (Site 4). This work was carried out before the construction of three factories, four business units and a landfill area, as part of the East Gate development project.

The *fulacht fiadh* had clearly been levelled before the present development was undertaken. There was no surface indication of its presence before topsoil removal, and it was not marked on any edition of the Ordnance Survey maps. A laneway had been built over the northern edge of the site, probably as part of the pre-existing farmlands, sometime between 1842 and 1935, on OS map evidence.

Topsoil removal revealed a large spread of burnt material consisting of charcoal and heat-shattered stones, which overlay several cut features. A modern land drain extended in a north–south direction through the burnt spread, and a curvilinear arc of stones to the south of the *fulacht fiadh* was also investigated. It became apparent on excavation that the arc of stones overlay a thick layer of grey clay that sealed the outer extremities of the burnt mound material. The land drain, the arc of stones and the layer of grey clay were relatively modern in date, as they all contained numerous fragments of modern glass.

The trough consisted of two adjoining circular pits (F16 and F18), which were revealed following removal of the burnt mound material. The fills were a black, charcoal-enriched, sandy silt with inclusions of heat-shattered stones (80%) and water. Both pits were circular in plan with a sharp break of slope at the top that graded towards a rounded base. F16 measured 1.45m x 1.45m and was 0.5m deep. The eastern edge of this pit was lined with a curved stone. F18 measured 2m x 1.92m and had a maximum depth of 0.25m. A small, slightly curving stone lined the western edge of the pit. The two circular troughs were divided by a large, flat stone oriented north–south between the two cuts.

To the south of F16 and F18 were three small stake-holes aligned along the same axis as the troughs. The fills were a black, loosely compacted, silty sand with occasional charcoal flecks. They measured *c*. 0.2m in diameter with depths of 0.2m to 0.31m. An intact wooden stake was recovered from one of the stake-holes and was 0.42m long.

A large waterlogged pit (F12) was found to the north of the trough, close to the limits of the site. The pit was subcircular in plan, measuring 1.5m x 1.4m and 0.35m deep. The fill resembled that of the trough, a black, silty sand with large quantities of heat-shattered stones. A shallower pit (F10) was exposed close to the northern edge of the trough. It was oval in plan and measured 0.29m x 0.24m and 0.26m deep. The fill was a black, silty sand with pebble inclusions and charcoal flecks. Two other pits, 0.16m deep, were excavated to the south of the trough. The fills were a black, sandy silt with occasional flecks of charcoal and large pebbles.

Sites 1–3 can be described as linear stone-lined features with fills consisting of charcoal-enriched deposits and red, oxidised soil resulting from intense burning. They were between 2.2m and 4.1m long and had an average width and depth of 0.65m and 0.52m respectively. A large quantity of charred cereal grain was recovered from Site 1, which seemed to indicate that this particular feature functioned as a cereal-drying kiln. No artefacts or bone material were found in the fills, despite an intensive programme of sieving. Large quantities of charcoal were recovered from all three features, and these, along with samples from the *fulacht fiadh*, have been submitted for radiocarbon dating.

*Margaret McCarthy, with Annette Quinn and Miriam Carroll, for Archaeological Services Unit, University College, Cork.*

### 86. CORBALLY
Adjacent to ringfort
**13618 03575**
**SMR 144:10**
**99E0463**

Test-trenches were excavated in the footprint of the foundations of a single house and septic tank to comply with a planning condition. The house site is to the immediate south of a ringfort. There is a local tradition of the interior of the ringfort being used as a burial-ground.

Trench 1 measured 13.5m north-west/south-east by 2m, and Trench 2 measured 10m north–south by 2m. The topsoil overlay a red/brown, sandy loam. No archaeological stratigraphy was recorded nor were artefacts recovered from the test-trenches.

*Jacinta Kiely, Eachtra Archaeological Projects, Clover Hill, Mallow, Co. Cork.*

### 87. 3 BARRACK STREET, CORK
Urban medieval
**16716 7177**
**SMR 74:122**
**99E0650**

One test-trench was opened here in November 1999. A sherd of medieval pottery in a layer of oyster shells was noted. A subsequent excavation exposed several medieval deposits overlying a timber floor or

walkway of 12th-century date. Finds included animal bone, medieval pottery and some metal slag.
*Sheila Lane, 1 Charlemont Heights, Coach Hill, Rochestown, Cork.*

### 88. 25–26 BARRACK STREET, CORK
Urban
W675715
SMR 74:122
99E0349

The site is within the zone of archaeological potential of the city. The test-trenches showed that the street-fronting houses had cellars, which intruded into the ground for a depth of 2m. Trial-trenching did not uncover any archaeological features or finds.
*Rose M. Cleary, Department of Archaeology, University College, Cork.*

### 89. ST FIN BARRE'S CATHEDRAL, BISHOP'S STREET, CORK
Early ecclesiastical
SMR 74:03802
99E0734

Three test-trenches were opened here in December 1999. All three contained redeposited material with human bone fragments and 18th/19th-century pottery. No archaeological levels were found.
*Sheila Lane, 1 Charlemont Heights, Coach Hill, Rochestown, Cork.*

### 90. BLACKPOOL BYPASS, CORK
Urban industrial
16700 07300
97E0457

Archaeological monitoring of the Blackpool Bypass was completed in March 1999. In early 1999 the foundations of a substantial limestone, sandstone and red brick building with an industrial stack were recorded in the former Hewitt's Watercourse Distillery. The building was marked as 'steam mills' on the Ordnance Survey 5-inch map of 1869; however, it was identified as 'the entrance to a multi-storey grain store and kiln drying complex' in the industrial archaeology survey carried out as part of this development. On the evidence of the roof construction of a surviving part of the building, it was dated to the late 18th century (Rynne 1999, 16–17).

The construction features of the main stack at Hewitt's Distillery (a landmark in the Blackpool Valley) were recorded and found to be comparable to other industrial stacks in the British Isles. The base of the stack measured 5.5m north–south by 5.2m and was built in the first part of the 19th century, while the upper levels were built in the 1870s. The stack was 28.9m high. The lower (and earlier) levels of the outer shell were of mortar-bonded, coursed red sandstone rubble, and the upper levels were constructed of brick. The outer shell was strengthened by the insertion of bars of cast iron within the masonry. The inside of the stack was lined with a layer of large Staffordshire firebricks. The average size of the firebricks was 0.46m by 0.28m by 0.14m. The firebricks in turn enclosed an unmortared, central, circular flue of wedge-shaped yellow bricks laid on their beds. The manufacturer of these bricks was J. & M. Craig, Kilmarnock. 'The original purpose of the stack was to create a draught for the boiler furnaces and to disperse the fumes created by this process' (Rynne 1999, 13). At the lower levels of the stack two flues were recorded.

Samples from two of the tanning pits excavated in 1998 (*Excavations 1998*, 17) were analysed by Meriel McClatchie (Archaeological Services Unit, UCC) for archaeobotanical remains. Both samples contained plant material preserved as a result of waterlogging. A range of plant species was present in the samples, providing evidence for foodstuffs and the surrounding environment. The samples also contained a wide range of other material, including coprolites, textile fragments, animal hair, mosses, insect remains and charred and waterlogged wood fragments. The plant material in the samples probably reflects the background environment around the pits. The weed seeds present are commonly found in medieval assemblages from Dublin and Waterford from contexts associated with disturbed and waste ground. The samples did not contain plant material, such as bark, that can be directly associated with the tanning process, but leather fragments and animal hair were recovered.

*Reference*
Rynne, C. 1999 An industrial archaeology survey of selected sites in the Watercourse Road Area, Cork City. Unpublished report carried out for Cork Corporation Planning Department.

*Catryn Power, Cork Corporation, City Hall, Cork.*

### 91. BOREENMANNA/BLACKROCK/BALLINLOUGH/ CENTRE PARK ROAD, CORK
Urban
17000 07110
99E0212

Excavation of service trenches for this phase of the Cork Main Drainage Scheme began on 5 May 1999 and is ongoing. It involves the laying of sewer pipes (maximum diameter 1.05m) and storm drainpipes (diameter 1.35m) in trenches varying in depth from 2m to 5m and the construction of associated chambers of a small pumphouse at Blackrock.

The areas affected by the scheme are in the south-east suburbs of Cork City, which were largely settled by the wealthy upper classes in the 18th and 19th centuries. Blackrock village was historically a harbour defended by the eponymous castle. There are two other castles in the vicinity, Dundanion and Mahon, indicating settlement in the medieval period. The strategic location of the settlement at the entry to the inner reaches of Cork harbour implies that Blackrock was important in historic, and perhaps in prehistoric, times. The placename Boreenmanna (*Bóithrín na Manach*, 'The Monks' Road') indicates a link with the graveyard at Churchyard Lane and with the reputed foundation of the Knights Hospitallers at Temple Hill.

The route of the drainage pipes under the late 18th-century 'Citadella lunatic asylum' (to the east of Victoria Avenue, between the Blackrock and Boreenmanna Roads) was thrust bored. This Georgian building is a recorded monument and was not interfered with by the engineering works.

Monitoring of excavation in the east section of the Boreenmanna Road recorded no features apart from a 19th-century road foundation and associated wall. Stratigraphy in the Centre Park Road area consisted of 19th- and 20th-century layers of reclaimed ground over a gravelly silt that did not yield any archaeological material. At Blackrock a wall and road associated with 19th-century improvements at the harbour were recorded. No archaeology was recorded in Ballinlough. The works in the above areas did not directly impinge on any recorded monuments.

Máire Ní Loingsigh, Cork Corporation, City Hall, Cork.

## 92. CHRISTCHURCH LANE/HANOVER STREET/KIFT'S LANE/LITTLE CROSS STREET/ST AUGUSTINE STREET/ST PATRICK'S STREET/EMMET PLACE/TUCKEY STREET, CORK

Urban medieval and post-medieval
W670720
96E0157

Archaeological monitoring of the Cork Main Drainage Scheme has been ongoing since May 1996. The streets monitored in 1999 that are within the medieval core of the city were St Augustine Street, Christchurch Lane, Hanover Street, Kift's Lane, Little Cross Street and Tuckey Street. Also monitored were Emmet Place and St Patrick's Street, which were developed when Cork expanded beyond the confines of the city wall from the 17th century onward. The trenches for the modern services were on average 1–1.5m wide, with a maximum depth of 2.3m.

*Christchurch Lane*
A limestone wall interpreted as part of Hopewell Castle (a tower on the medieval city wall) was discovered in Christchurch Lane. The line of this wall was curved. It was exposed for a length of 4.35m and a height of 1m. The wall corresponds with the 'site of Hopewell Castle' as marked on Ordnance Survey maps. Sherds of imported Minety-type and Ham Green B ware, as well as Cork-type ware from a sealed layer abutting the north face of this wall, substantiate a medieval date for its construction.

*Hanover Street*
Part of the western circuit of the medieval city wall was uncovered in Hanover Street. This limestone wall was orientated in a north-west/south-east direction and was exposed for a maximum length of 1.1m at its east (inner) face. The wall was 2.3m wide and was cut by a drain that was probably contemporary. The east face of the wall was constructed of at least eight courses of regular limestones and was 0.8m high. A 17th/18th-century drain obscured the west face of the wall.

Organic medieval layers in Hanover Street contained worked leather, Ham Green B ware and Saintonge green-glazed ware. These deposits occurred directly inside the city wall and also at the east end of the street, where they were associated with the scant remains of masonry and wooden structures. The deposits at the east end of the street were at levels that may correspond with excavations carried out by Rose Cleary in 1996 (*Excavations 1996*, 11, 96E0128) on the southern side of the street, near the junction with South Main Street.

A post-medieval wooden barrel was found cut into a medieval organic deposit directly inside the city wall. The barrel, which may have been used as a cistern and ultimately as a refuse pit, contained organic material including pieces of wood, lumps of mortar and brick, and a sherd of North Devon gravel-tempered ware. The bottom of the barrel was lined with powdered limestone/calcite. Plant fragments in the barrel have been identified as oat grains, which suggests that it had been used to carry cereal before it became a cistern.

*Kift's Lane*
A 19th-century brick culvert was recorded in the western part of this lane.

*Little Cross Street*
A medieval wall, orientated north–south, was exposed at the junction of Little Cross Street and Washington Street. The wall had a base batter, and its construction consisted of a face of coursed limestone and sandstone rubble with a clay-bonded rubble core. The minimum thickness of the wall was 0.5m, and it survived to a minimum height of 1.2m. The wall may have been part of a building, such as a house, on this street.

*St Augustine Street*
A portion of the medieval city wall, 1.13m long, was exposed in St Augustine Street. It follows the line of the city wall excavated by Joanna Wren in 1992 in Nos 81–83 Grand Parade (*Excavations 1992*, 8, and Wren 1995, 88–90). The wall uncovered in this season's excavation was on a north–south axis and was constructed of roughly squared limestones. It was 2.18m wide, and the exposed east face was 1.8m high. The wall had a rubble core of which the exposed upper surface was bonded with a coarse mortar. There was no evidence of bonding material on the east face. The west face of the wall was not exposed.

*St Patrick's Street and Emmet Place*
Archaeological stratigraphy in St Patrick's Street and Emmet Place consisted of layers of 18th- and 19th-century rubble that were used to reclaim the waterways that once ran along the course of these streets. Contemporary culverts were also recorded.

*Tuckey Street*
Vestiges of at least one or two medieval structures were uncovered in Tuckey Street. These remains included at least one possible sill-beam house (represented by three beams) associated with deposits of organic refuse containing wood, shells, worked leather and pottery. Silts from episodes of flooding from the River Lee were distributed between the organic layers. A row of collapsed wattling was associated with a line of posts and stakes at the same level as the sill-beam house. To the north of this wattling were remnants of a floor surface consisting of fine gravel with patches of pinkish-grey clay associated with silty, organic material.

A second line of posts was also uncovered within the medieval layers. These posts were in two parallel lines running for over 4m and ranged from 0.03m to 0.09m in diameter; their length was not fully exposed. They were part of a house wall or a fence and were associated with collapsed wattling. All of these features are probably related and may represent the remains of at least one wooden house and associated fencing. Similar findings were made at nearby Christchurch, where excavations were carried out in the 1970s (Cleary et al. 1997).

These wooden remains were all within organic layers and were probably contemporary, or were constructed within a short time frame. The pottery accompanying these deposits included Ham Green A and B, Redcliffe, Minety and Saintonge wares dating from the 12th–14th centuries. The medieval archaeology was present in the eastern part of Tuckey Street near the junction with the medieval main street.

A medieval roadway was seen above some organic levels in Tuckey Street. This road consisted of a layer of sandstone paving stones and an underlying foundation layer of stone rubble. This stone surface extended for 25m. The existence of the road indicated that the trenches for the services followed the east–west line of a medieval lane.

The city wall did not survive in the trenches excavated in Tuckey Street because the building of culverts in the 18th and 19th centuries had destroyed it.

A stone-lined pit dating to the post-medieval period contained gravel, red brick, mortar, animal bones, clay, silt, ash, charcoal and large amounts of post-medieval pottery, including an almost complete North Devon gravel-tempered ware pitcher. This stone-lined pit may have been used as a rubbish dump for a house on Tuckey Street. Other post-medieval features included a street surface (directly above the medieval road) and a wall of a dwelling with a wooden pile foundation.

*References*
Cleary, R.M., Hurley, M.F. and Shee Twohig, E. 1997 *Skiddy's Castle and Christchurch, Cork: Excavations 1974–77 by D.C. Twohig*. Cork.
Wren, J. 1995 The city wall at 81–83 Grand Parade, Cork. In M.F. Hurley, 'Excavations in Cork City: Kyrl's Quay/North Main Street and at Grand Parade (Part 1)', *Journal of the Cork Historical and Archaeological Society* **100**, 88–90.

*Catryn Power, Cork Corporation, City Hall, Cork.*

### 93. HALF MOON STREET, CORK
Urban medieval
16750 07202
SMR 74:57
99E0087

Two test-trenches were opened in February 1999. The presence of earthern and lead pipes in the trenches indicated that the subsurface levels had been previously disturbed. The content of the trenches confirmed this. Nothing of an archaeological nature was noted.
*Sheila Lane, 1 Charlemont Heights, Coach Hill, Rochestown, Cork.*

### 94. LEITRIM STREET, CORK
Urban medieval
16735 07237
SMR 74:03303
99E0247

Two test-trenches were opened here in May 1999. A general rubble fill overlay natural gravels. Nothing of an archaeological nature was noted.
*Sheila Lane, 1 Charlemont Heights, Coach Hill, Rochestown, Cork.*

### 95. 23–24 MAIN STREET NORTH, CORK
Urban
W672716
SMR 74:122
99E0532

The site is on the North Island within the core area of the walled Anglo-Norman town. The buildings on the site are scheduled for refurbishment, and the aim of the excavation was to establish whether any archaeological remains were within the depth of 0–0.04m below the modern floor level. This depth is the maximum required in order to lay a raft foundation to the rear (east) of the existing building and the depth required to install service trenches.

The excavation showed that modern fill underlay the present floor and extended to at least 0.4m below the present ground level.
*Rose M. Cleary, Department of Archaeology, University College, Cork.*

### 96. CITY CARPARK, MAIN STREET SOUTH, CORK
Urban medieval
16741 7151
SMR 74:122
99E0315

Cork Corporation is anxious to take the initiative to ensure that an adequately funded, adequately resourced and adequately scheduled excavation takes place on this site, which is regarded as of the utmost importance. It was felt that some precise information on the physical preservation of the site would highlight the issues. The developer, Kenny Homes Ltd, agreed to finance and facilitate the testing in conjunction with the services of Cork Corporation.

The site is potentially one of the most important archaeological sites in Cork City. The Viking settlement in Cork probably occurred in this area (Hurley 1998). Recent excavations by Mary O'Donnell at Tuckey Street have uncovered wooden structures of early 12th-century date at *c*. 4m below present ground level (*Excavations 1997*, 12, 97E0040). The structures occurred below a deep layer of estuarine silt, at a level at which previous excavations in Cork were suspended. At Hanover Street, houses of mid-12th-century date were excavated by Rose Cleary in 1996 within 2m of the modern surface (*Excavations 1996*, 11, 96E0128), and more than 2m of material remained unexcavated beneath that level. All of this points to the significance of the South Main Street area as an archaeological resource for Cork of comparable importance to sites at Arundel Square in Waterford and Fishamble Street, High Street, Essex Street etc. in Dublin.

The site was investigated on 28 and 29 June 1999.

Two trenches were excavated to pinpoint the location of the medieval city wall. A third trench was opened to investigate a stone structure lying close to the surface, in order to facilitate the positioning of a trial-bore.

In addition four trial-boreholes were inserted to determine the nature and depth of the archaeological stratigraphy and the underlying geological composition of the site.

The city wall is between 5.6m and 5.7m to the north of the present quay wall. This corresponds to the position as shown on the OS map of 1869. The area outside of the city wall is of limited archaeological importance as it is composed mostly of estuarine silt.

In this area the archaeological stratigraphy survives to c. 0.7m of the modern surface and continues to a depth of over 4m. Houses are likely to be represented by stone walls in the upper levels, overlying organic layers representing timber and wattle houses in the lower levels. Overall, preservation of organic material appears to be good.

The natural slope of the ground is from west to east (i.e. beneath the archaeological stratigraphy). The layers continue to c. 4.3m below the modern surface on the eastern side, but much of the stratigraphy in the eastern part of the site appears to be made up of fill and midden material.

*Reference*
Hurley, M.F. 1998 Viking Age towns: archaeological evidence from Waterford and Cork. In M.A. Monk and J. Sheehan (eds), *Early medieval Munster: archaeology, history and society*. Cork.

*Maurice Hurley, Planning Department, Cork Corporation, City Hall, Cork.*

## 97. 26 MAIN STREET SOUTH, CORK
Urban medieval
16718 07187
SMR 74:03401
99E0310

Two test-trenches were opened here in July 1999. Archaeological deposits of medieval date were identified. A suitable foundation design was drawn up to ensure the protection of these deposits.
*Sheila Lane, 1 Charlemont Heights, Coach Hill, Rochestown, Cork.*

## 98. SAINT MARY'S OF THE ISLE, CORK
Urban medieval/industrial
167000 071500
99E0353

Excavation of trenches for the laying of sewer pipes for the Cork Main Drainage Scheme was monitored by archaeologists from Cork Corporation. The work took place in the grounds of the Mercy convent of Saint Mary's of the Isle. The site is adjacent to a Dominican priory excavated in 1993 (*Excavations 1993*, 9–10, 93E0103, and Hurley and Sheehan 1995).

Part of a garden wall, which was 1m high, was excavated; it was discovered that its original purpose was as an 18th/19th-century quay wall on the south bank of a tributary of the River Lee. It was excavated to a height of 3m.

Eighteen walls and associated floorings, culverts and a drystone well were evident in the eastern part of the grounds. These were the remains of the 19th-century buildings of St Anne's Adoption Society, which had been demolished during the 1970s. This orphanage was founded in 1853. Some of the walls uncovered abutted the quay wall, and these represent the washrooms of the orphanage, while the walls excavated immediately to the south-west are the remains of the dormitories and refectory.

To the south-west of these 19th-century buildings part of a medieval stone structure was discovered. Three substantial walls form the western portion of a room that had a mortared floor; its remaining internal dimensions were 1.15m from east to west and 2.3m from north to south. These walls were built on wooden foundation piles. One of these walls extended from the building for a further 9.47m to the west and may be part of a mill-race that carried water to or from a waterwheel via this channel. Maps dating to the medieval period depict a mill in this vicinity.

*Reference*
Hurley, M.F. and Sheehan, C.M. 1995 *Excavations at the Dominican Priory, Saint Mary's of the Isle, Crosse's Green Cork*. Cork.

*Catryn Power, Cork Corporation, City Hall, Cork.*

## 99. 114–115 SHANDON STREET, CORK
Urban
W666725
SMR 74:122
99E0510

The site is within the zone of archaeological potential of the city and within an area that developed in the post-Famine period owing to industrial expansion on the north side of Cork. Trial-trenching uncovered no archaeological features or finds.
*Rose M. Cleary, Department of Archaeology, University College, Cork.*

## 100. 13–14 TRAVERS STREET/12 COVE STREET, CORK
Urban
W670717
SMR 74:122
99E0648

The development site is within the area that may be part of the Hiberno-Norse settlement in Cork. Topographical information from early charters has suggested[1] that the south bank of the south channel may have been part of the Hiberno-Norse settlement. The church of St Nicholas is on the site of an earlier church known as the church of St Sepulchre[2], which is associated with the Hiberno-Norse settlement in Cork.

Archaeological excavations on Cove Street[3] have established a medieval date for the use of the graveyard associated with St Sepulchre's/St Nicholas's church. Recent excavations by Sheila Lane on the north end of Barrack Street (see No. 87 above) have established medieval settlement on the south bank of the river. The probability is that the south bank was part of the Hiberno-Norse settlement, but it was definitely in use in the Anglo-Norman phase of the development of Cork City.

The development site is c. 40m north of the present St Nicholas's church, and the associated graveyard is almost adjacent to the west boundary of the site. Three test-trenches were excavated, two on the Travers Street end and one on the Cove Street end of the development site.

The excavation uncovered human bones that were concentrated in the north end of the test-trench in Cove Street and the west end of the trench in Travers Street. The Cove Street remains were c. 0.3m below the modern surface, and those in the Travers Street end were at a depth of 1.4m. They were disarticulated and may be the remains of disturbed burials. It is possible that further undisturbed burials lie below the present surface.

*Notes*
1. H.A. Jefferies, 'The history and topography of Viking Cork', *Journal of the Cork Historical and Archaeological Society* 90 (1985), 14–25. Jefferies places the settlement on the south bank of the river. J. Bradley and A. Halpin, 'The topographical development of Scandinavian and Anglo-Norman Cork', in P. O'Flanaghan and C.G. Buttimer (eds), *Cork: history and society* (Dublin 1993), 15–44. Bradley and Halpin suggest that the settlement was on the south island with a satellite settlement on the south bank of the river.
2. *Ibid.*, 21.
3. R.M. Cleary, 'Medieval graveyard and boundary wall at Cove Street, Cork', *Journal of the Cork Historical and Archaeological Society* 101 (1996), 94–111.

*Rose M. Cleary, Department of Archaeology, University College, Cork.*

### 101. WASHINGTON STREET/SOUTH MAIN STREET/LIBERTY STREET, CORK
Urban
99E0122

Monitoring was carried out intermittently from April to July 1999 during the excavation of slit-trenches by Esat Telecom on South Main Street, Washington Street and Grand Parade in Cork City. The trenches were designed to be as shallow as possible in order to avoid archaeological deposits. No archaeological stratigraphy was uncovered.
*Mary O'Donnell, Archaeological Services Unit, University College, Cork.*

### 102. 15–16 WATERCOURSE ROAD, CORK
Urban
W675721
SMR 74:122
99E0373

The site is within the zone of archaeological potential and within an area that developed in the post-Famine period owing to industrial expansion on the north side of Cork. Trial-trenching uncovered no archaeological features. Some iron slag was recovered from the base of one trench at a depth of 1m below ground level.
*Rose M. Cleary, Department of Archaeology, University College, Cork.*

### 103. CRUMPANE
Bronze Age copper mine
6671 5194
SMR 102:23
99E0410

This primitive copper mine is 2km north-east of the village of Eyeries at the western end of the Beara Peninsula, Co. Cork. The site consists of a series of three inclined openings at the base of a low rock face that exposes sedimentary copper mineralisation. The mines are flooded and partly infilled but have all the characteristics of Mount Gabriel-type operations. There are extensive deposits of mine spoil to the immediate south and north of these workings, with a thin cover of blanket bog growth in this area.

A sample excavation was carried out here in August 1999, primarily to recover charcoal samples for radiocarbon dating. Two $1m^2$ cuttings were excavated on the spoil deposits adjacent to the mine. Both test-pits produced a large number of stone hammers, consisting of broken beach cobbles with a number of haft-modified examples. Test-pit 1 revealed a 0.22–0.35m thickness of blanket peat, overlying a 0.37–0.46m-thick deposit of mine spoil. A charcoal sample from this broken rock sediment has been radiocarbon dated to 3200±30 BP (GrN-25063, courtesy Jan Lanting).

Test-pit 2 is 8m north of the mine entrance, on a low mound of eroding mine spoil. Removal of thin blanket peat growth exposed a 1.3–1.4m thickness of loose mine spoil. A charcoal sample from the upper part of this deposit has been radiocarbon dated to 3370±30 BP (GrN-25064), with a second charcoal result of 3370±30 BP (GrN-25065) from near the base.

These results confirm an Early to Middle Bronze Age date range for this copper-mining activity.
*William O'Brien, Department of Archaeology, National University of Ireland, Galway.*

### 104. FOILDARRIG
Vicinity of castle
06805 04617
SMR 115:21
99E0197

Test-trenching was carried out in May 1999 before housing construction, in compliance with a planning condition imposed because of the proximity of the development to the site of a castle that formerly stood in this area. No visible trace of the castle now survives, and its exact location is uncertain.

Three test-trenches, each c. 30m long, were opened across the area of the proposed development. Trench A ran east–west across the southern part of the site, Trench B ran parallel to it across the northern part of the site, and Trench C ran north–south, connecting A and B and extending c. 6m further north to the edge of a low-lying marshy area in the north-western corner of the site.

Topsoil varied from 0.2m to 0.7m deep and was deepest at the south-east corner of the site, where modern dumping had taken place. The topsoil lay directly on undisturbed natural subsoil and gravels.

Nothing of archaeological significance was noted.
*Eamonn Cotter, Ballynanelagh, Rathcormac, Co. Cork.*

## 105. KILCOE CASTLE, KILCOE
Tower-house
10192 03282
98E0133 ext.

Kilcoe Castle is on Mannin Island on the northern shore of Roaringwater Bay, Co. Cork. The main rectangular tower is conjoined to the east by a smaller tower. The owner of the castle is undertaking a programme of complete restoration. Eamon Cotter carried out an archaeological excavation within the area of and to the south of the main tower in 1998 (*Excavations 1998*, 20).

A test-trench was opened 15m to the west of the main tower. The trench measured 6.8m north–south by 9m east–west. Three wall lines were recorded within the area of the trench. The walls possibly form the western return of the northern and southern bawn walls. The northern wall, aligned east–west, was 7.8m long and 1.1m deep. It is broken at the western end by a doorway, the basal chamfered jamb stones of which were still *in situ*. The eastern side of a possible window embrasure was recorded 3.65m east of the doorway. The southern wall, aligned east–west, was recorded 6.6m to the south of the northern wall. It was 5.5m long and 1.1m deep. Two stone steps, keyed into the wall, were recorded 0.5m from the western end of the wall. A third wall was recorded in the western section of the trench. It measured 2.6m externally and was 0.7m deep. It may post-date the other two walls.

Area of excavation from east at Kilcoe Castle.

Two layers had accumulated under the sod overlying the bedrock within the area of the walls. The upper layer was on average 0.5m deep. A variety of cut stone fragments were recovered from this layer including five fragments of chamfered arch stones, an ogee window head, and chamfered door- and window-jambs. Both layers included animal bone, medieval pottery, oyster shells and fragments of roof slate.

Future work on site may shed light on the remainder of the circuit of the bawn wall.
*Jacinta Kiely, Eachtra Archaeological Projects, Clover Hill, Mallow, Co. Cork.*

## 106. KILLEENS
*Fulacht fiadh*
W636754
99E0503

The site was exposed during monitoring of topsoil-stripping along the route of a Bord Gáis Éireann pipeline that extended from Caherlag to Ballincollig, Co. Cork. The site was initially identified as a large spread of blackened and fire-shattered stone immediately beneath the topsoil. Preliminary investigations of the site appeared to confirm the location of a trough beneath the burnt spread. There had been no evidence of the site before the plant works.

The trough lay inside the southern boundary of the wayleave and took the form of a rectangular pit that was orientated north–south. The northern side of the pit had been removed by a relatively modern pit that appeared to have been dug by a mechanical digger. The trough pit would have had maximum dimensions of *c*. 3m by 1.8m and was 0.5m deep.

The trough was timber-lined. Only two small pieces of the side-walling survived. The first of these was at the south end where one small, badly decayed fragment of a vertical timber had collapsed slightly onto the floor of the trough. A similar, slightly larger piece of timber was found along the western edge. At the base of the trough were four relatively large planks that provided a floor to the trough. All four of these were orientated north–south. While the timbers were in fairly good condition, it was clear that they had badly decayed at the ends. The timber-lined trough would have measured *c*. 2.2m by 1.1m. The length of the trough has been estimated because of the disturbance at the northern end caused by the later pit. It was not clear from the evidence of the excavation to what height the walls of the trough would have stood.

Beneath and between the timbers at the base of the trough was a fine, grey sand. This appeared to have been a deliberately laid foundation for the timber floor. This deposit was a maximum of 0.01–0.02m thick. At the base of the trough, following the removal of the sand deposit, a cluster of four stake-holes became evident in the north-west corner. The stake-holes were in two sets of two and may have supported the vertical plank walls in this part of the trough.

Around the eastern edge of the trough was a roughly laid stone surface. The surface covered an area measuring 2.3m north–south by 1.3m east–west, but its northern extent had been cut by the later pit. The stones varied in size from 0.4m by 0.3m to just 0.06m by 0.04m. The stones were either loosely set into the underlying subsoil or just sitting directly on top of it.

There was no evidence of the hearth associated with this *fulacht fiadh*, and it must be assumed that this was removed by the later pit at the north of the trough.
*Tim Coughlan, Margaret Gowen & Co. Ltd, 2 Killiney View, Albert Road Lower, Glenageary, Co. Dublin.*

## 107. CATHOLIC WALK LOWER, KINSALE
Urban medieval
16466 05009
SMR 112:03401, 112:03402
99E0585

Two test-trenches were opened here in October 1999. Nothing of an archaeological nature was noted.
*Sheila Lane, 1 Charlemont Heights, Coach Hill, Rochestown, Cork.*

### 108. CHURCH SQUARE, KINSALE
Urban medieval
SMR 112:03401, 112:03402
16387 05048
99E0032

Two test-trenches were opened here in January 1999. Wet conditions in the trenches prevented a full archaeological assessment. Two further trenches were opened in April 1999. Nothing of an archaeological nature was noted.
*Sheila Lane, 1 Charlemont Heights, Coach Hill, Rochestown, Cork.*

### 109. CHURCH SQUARE, KINSALE
Urban medieval
16371 05053
SMR 112:003401
99E0367

During renovations in the rear yard of The Tap Tavern, a public house in Church Square in the centre of the medieval town of Kinsale, Co. Cork, a portion of an ogee-headed window was found in a well. The medieval church of St Mulltose stands on a cliff behind the public house. The window fragment was removed, recorded and returned to the church, where there is a matching window fragment. The well was recorded, and a licence was granted to monitor pipe-laying in the area.

Two pipe-trenches were opened to a depth of 0.7m, and rubble fill was noted in them. No archaeological finds or features were noted in the trenches. The yard has now been paved, and the well is open.
*Sheila Lane, 1 Charlemont Heights, Coach Hill, Rochestown, Cork.*

### 110. MARKET LANE, KINSALE
Urban medieval
16384 05051
SMR 112:03401, 112:03402
99E0156

Two test-trenches were opened here in April 1999. Nothing of an archaeological nature was noted.
*Sheila Lane, 1 Charlemont Heights, Coach Hill, Rochestown, Cork.*

### 111. MILL HILL, KINSALE
Urban medieval
16436 05065
99E0065

Pre-development testing in the form of trial-trenching was carried out before the proposed construction of a residential dwelling. The development site is on a terrace on the west side of Mill Hill and is within the probable line of the medieval town wall.

Two trenches were opened across the development area, and no archaeological features or finds were uncovered.
*Tony Cummins, Aegis Archaeology, 16 Avondale Court, Corbally, Limerick.*

### 112. THE RAMPARTS, KINSALE
Urban medieval
16399 05005
SMR 112:03401, 112:03402
99E0572

One test-trench was opened here in October 1999. Nothing of an archaeological nature was noted.
*Sheila Lane, 1 Charlemont Heights, Coach Hill, Rochestown, Cork.*

### 113. KNOCKANENAGARK/TULLIG MORE
No archaeological significance
14763 7678
99E0169

A 25-acre site in Knockanenagark and Tullig More townlands was acquired by Ducon Concrete Ltd of Kanturk, Co. Cork, for the extraction of sand and gravel. There are no known monuments on the land, but it is in an area containing many recorded archaeological sites, including sites within both Knockanenagark and Tullig More townlands, just south of the site itself.

Work was monitored over four weeks in April and May 1999. The topsoil was removed using a bulldozer. No archaeological features were observed during the work.
*Mary O'Donnell, Archaeological Services Unit, University College, Cork.*

### 114. BLACKROCK CASTLE, MAHON
Tower-house
17236 07202
SMR 74:52
99E0297

Three test-trenches were opened here in June 1999. Nothing of an archaeological nature was noted.
*Sheila Lane, 1 Charlemont Heights, Coach Hill, Rochestown, Cork.*

### 115. MEENANE
*Fulacht fiadh*
17716 08534
SMR 53:95
99E0705

The site lay on high, wet land *c.* 1km north-east of the village of Watergrasshill, Co. Cork, and was excavated before the construction of the Watergrasshill Bypass, a proposed new section of the N8 roadway. The excavation was funded by Cork County Council.

The site was an irregularly shaped mound of burnt, shattered stone measuring 15m north–south x 14m east–west at its maximum extent, with a maximum depth of *c.* 0.5m. A modern, stone-filled land drain ran north–south 2m to the west of the mound, and two similar drains extended northwards and eastwards from the north-east corner of the mound.

A trough and associated features were uncovered beneath the mound. The trough was rectangular and measured 2.1m east–west x 1.3m, with an average depth of 0.3m, giving it a capacity of *c.* 800 litres (176 gallons). It was filled with burnt, heat-shattered stones with some clay and silting.

The long axis of the trough was aligned with the slope of the ground, i.e. west–east. The higher ground immediately to the west of the trough had been worked so as to form a horseshoe-shaped shelf, with each terminal of the 'horseshoe' formed by an upright stone set in the subsoil at the north-west and south-west corners of the trough. To the west of the 'shelf' was an arc (1.2m long) of stones set on edge in the subsoil. The extent of fracturing of these stones and the two stones at the corners of the trough, as well as the burnt clay on the 'shelf', indicates that this was the hearth on which stones were heated before being deposited in the trough.

A setting of post-holes to the north and south of the trough suggests either a structure enclosing the west end of the trough to protect it from the elements or a structure forming part of the hearth. The size of the two largest post-holes, 0.3m in diameter x 0.38m deep and 0.4m in diameter x 0.34m deep, suggests a low, sturdy structure, something that would have been necessary to retain the fire on the hearth while the stones were heating.

A large pit, approximately oval, lay 1.6m to the east of the trough, downslope from it. The pit measured 2.9m north–south x 2.2m, with a maximum depth of 0.6m. The fill of the pit consisted mainly of grey/black silt layers with small amounts of burnt stone, suggesting that the pit lay open for a long period and silted up gradually. Its function is uncertain.

*Eamonn Cotter, Ballynanelagh, Rathcormac, Co. Cork.*

## 116. MITCHELLSFORT
*Fulachta fiadh*
17618 08311; 17620 08313; 17624 08315
SMR 53:09201–3
99E0673

These sites, in close proximity to each other c. 1.3km south of the village of Watergrasshill, Co. Cork, were excavated before the construction of the Watergrasshill Bypass, a proposed new section of the N8 roadway. The excavations were funded by Cork County Council.

The sites are on low-lying, boggy land that has been partially drained and reclaimed in recent years. Given their close proximity, all three were excavated under the same licence.

### Site A (53:09201)
Topsoil was removed from an area measuring 11m north–south by 12m, revealing an oval mound of heat-shattered stone measuring c. 3m north–south x 4m and 0.56m deep. In addition, there were two spreads of burnt stone extending to the north-east and west of the mound. In both of these spreads the stone was mixed with soil, suggesting that the mound had been disturbed by modern machinery. A modern land drain (0.2m deep) ran north–south across the west side of the cutting, c. 5m to the west of the mound. A second trench (c. 2m wide x 0.5m deep), running north-east/south-west across the south-east corner of the cutting, is also likely to be a drainage feature.

Two pits were uncovered cut into the underlying clay. One, at the north-east corner of the cutting, was slightly oval and measured 2m x 1.5m x 0.25m deep. It was set apart from the burnt mound, c. 2.5m away, but was filled with burnt stone, similar to the mound material, with some silting.

The second pit was 6m to the south-east, underneath the burnt mound. It was approximately rectangular, measuring 1.5m x 1.5m x 0.38m deep. It too was filled with material similar to that in the burnt mound, and a quantity of white clay was found in the southern half of the pit.

No definite evidence for lining was recovered in either of the pits, although the white clay found in the second one may represent collapsed clay lining. However, the high clay content of the natural subsoil in the area makes it quite impermeable so that, as was evident during the excavation, the pits retained water naturally, without any need for lining. No evidence for a hearth was uncovered.

### Site B (53:09202)
Site B was c. 15m north-east of the mound of Site A. It was an irregularly shaped mound of burnt, shattered stone measuring 3.5m east–west x 5.5m north–south at its maximum extent with an average depth of 0.5m. Around the north-west, west and south-west sides the edges of the mound extended under the red clay, indicating modern disturbance of the site.

Underneath the mound a pit was dug into the clay. The pit was oval and measured 2.3m east–west x 1.6m x 0.35m deep. It was filled with the same material as the burnt mound, with some silting and patches of white clay.

A second, smaller pit 3m to the north measured 1m east–west x 0.5m x 0.12m deep. It was filled with loamy soil with some burnt stone. Its function is unclear.

### Site C (53:09203)
Site C was 30m to the north-west of Site B. It was an approximately rectangular mound of burnt, shattered stone measuring 6m east–west x 4m with an average depth of only 0.2m. A modern field drain cut through the mound in a north–south direction. No definite archaeological features were uncovered, although near the north-east corner of the cutting what appeared to be one side of a feature cut into the subsoil was noted. The fill in this area consisted of inclusions of natural clay mixed with peat and naturally occurring gravel. This may have been the location of a trough that has suffered extensive disturbance during modern drainage work.

A trench 2.5m wide and 18m long was excavated in the area between Sites B and C. No archaeological features were present in this trench.

*Eamonn Cotter, Ballynanelagh, Rathcormac, Co. Cork.*

## 117. MONARD
*Fulacht fiadh*
W663767
99E0478

The site was exposed during monitoring of topsoil-stripping along the route of a Bord Gáis Éireann pipeline that extended from Caherlag to Ballincollig, Co. Cork. The site was initially identified as a large spread of blackened and fire-shattered stone immediately beneath the topsoil. Preliminary investigations appeared to confirm the location of a trough beneath the burnt spread. There had been no evidence of the site before the plant works.

The spread extended along the line of the pipeline for 15m and up to 10m into the wayleave. Only the trough and a possible hearth were identified during the excavation. The trough was roughly square, measuring 2.1m by 1.8m, and was orientated roughly east–west. It was fairly straight-sided, but its base sloped slightly to the north with a maximum depth of 0.65m. The base of the trough was filled with a 0.15–0.2m-deep deposit of grey silt mixed with heat-shattered stones. This was in turn sealed by 0.4m of heat-shattered stone in a loose, black/brown soil with charcoal flecks. There was no evidence of a lining for the trough.

Immediately to the east of the main area of the trough was a slightly shallower (0.25m), horseshoe-shaped cut that may have been the location of the hearth. The upper edge of the cut for the trough and this possible hearth cut were indistinguishable from one another, with the hearth area being an extension of the trough. The hearth covered an area 1.85m across the horns and 1.25m from front to back. A number of small stones set into the eastern face of the hearth cut may represent the remains of possible walling/kerbing. There was no evidence that the hearth was floored.

The location of the hearth to the east of the trough is suggested primarily because no other features were recorded during the excavation and this was therefore the most likely siting for the hearth.

*Tim Coughlan, Margaret Gowen & Co. Ltd, 2 Killiney View, Albert Road Lower, Glenageary, Co. Dublin.*

### 118. MONEYCUSKER
No archaeological significance
1302 06695
SMR 82:19
99E0672

In compliance with a condition of planning permission, test-trenching was carried out before the construction of a dwelling-house on 27 November 1999. The site lies in hilly countryside with frequent rock outcrops. Some low outcropping was visible in the area of the proposed construction. Local information indicated that quarrying had taken place on the site in recent times.

Two trenches, 18m and 17m, long were excavated across the site. Topsoil depth in the trenches varied from 0.15m to 0.5m. In sections of the trenches the thin topsoil lay directly on natural gravel and bedrock, while in other sections topsoil lay on undisturbed, orange, sandy clay subsoil.

With the exception of some sherds of modern pottery, no archaeological artefacts or features were noted.

*Eamonn Cotter, Ballynanelagh, Rathcormac, Co. Cork.*

### 119. FORT HILL, MONEYGURNEY
Ringfort
17200 06792
SMR 86:15
99E0374

Outline planning permission has been granted by Cork County Council for the construction of domestic dwellings at Fort Hill, Moneygurney td, Co. Cork. The outline permission required that an assessment be undertaken before development in order to determine the impact of the work on a levelled possible ringfort within the development site.

The possible ringfort is recorded on the 1842 edition of the 6-inch OS map. The cartographic evidence indicates that the site enclosed an area of *c.* 35m in diameter. The site is currently under grass, and there are no visible remains above ground. The land has been ploughed up to recent times, and the foundations for a road, Fort Hill East, were constructed across the ringfort *c.* fifteen years ago.

Four test-trenches were excavated in order to ascertain the perimeters of the ringfort. The excavation uncovered clear evidence for the upper fill of a ditch outside the now-levelled bank. The fill of the ditch lay directly beneath topsoil. The upper fill was a brown/grey, silty soil with some charcoal inclusions. The area outside the ditch was sterile.

Once the perimeter of the ringfort had been established, no further excavation was undertaken. Using the locations of the excavated perimeters of the ditch as a guide, the ringfort diameter has been established as 42m.

*Meriel McClatchie, Archaeological Services Unit, Department of Archaeology, University College, Cork.*

### 120. RATHPEACON
Site of standing stone
16442 07619
SMR 63:55
99E0352

Test-trenching was carried out in the vicinity of the site of a standing stone at Rathpeacon, Co. Cork. The site was close to the proposed route of the Caherlag to Ballincollig Bord Gáis Éireann pipeline. The standing stone had not been located, but the route of the pipeline ran within 10m of the site, according to the environmental impact statement prepared by Dominic Delaney.

Three test-tenches were opened by mechanical digger and then cleaned by hand before topsoil-stripping along the wayleave of the pipeline. The trenches were between 32m and 39m long. No archaeological remains were identified in the trenches or in the area of the wayleave after the stripping of topsoil for the pipeline.

*Tim Coughlan, Margaret Gowen & Co. Ltd, 2 Killiney View, Albert Road Lower, Glenageary, Co. Dublin.*

### 121. RINGACOLTIG
Possible enclosure site
17798 06679
SMR 87:9
99E0334

A possible enclosure site is marked on the 1st edition OS 6-inch map in an area of a proposed residential development site on the north-western outskirts of Cobh. The precise location, nature and extent of the site had not been determined because it had been levelled sometime in the mid–late 19th century and the area had been constantly ploughed over a long period of time. A geophysical survey was undertaken by GeoArc Ltd in the general area of the site in order to determine its extent, as well as to indicate whether any associated and/or additional features of archaeological interest might be discovered. It was believed that the enclosure may have been a ringfort with an external fosse and that this latter feature may still remain cut into the subsoil. However, no traces of the enclosure were found by the geophysical survey, although a number of subsurface anomalies were detected. It was suggested in the geophysical report that certain areas be subjected to investigation by intrusive excavation.

In addition, it was decided to excavate more trenches to verify the results and conclusions of the geophysical report, as well as to determine the nature of the anomalies.

Testing was carried out at the site on 10 and 11 July 1999. This consisted of the combination of machine- and hand-excavation of eight trenches. In general, it was found that the topsoil/ploughzone material was deepest to the west and south, which would be expected given the existing slope down to these areas. Furthermore, it was found that the ploughzone contained occasional metal items such as nuts, bolts and nails, which probably explain the 'dipolar anomalies' suggested by the geophysical report. In addition, the negative geophysical anomalies appear to have been caused by both a modern burning episode and the compaction and rutting formed by a track used by heavy vehicles and machinery. The positive geophysical anomalies all appear to have been caused by natural variations in the depth of both topsoil and subsoil.

None of the geophysical anomalies reflected features or deposits of archaeological interest or potential. In addition, no finds of archaeological or historical interest were recovered during the archaeological testing.

It is suggested that the site depicted on the map may have been a circular enclosure comprising only a bank. This bank was levelled, and all traces of the site were subsequently destroyed by constant ploughing.
*Martin E. Byrne, 31 Millford, Athgarvan, Co. Kildare.*

**122. 16 SOUTH MAIN STREET (REAR OF), YOUGHAL**
No archaeological significance
X095769
SMR 67:02901
99E0300

Two test-trenches were excavated at the site before an application for planning permission in order to establish whether archaeological stratigraphy existed in the development area. The site forms part of the back garden to 16 South Main Street and lies in the south-western corner of the Base Town, a medieval suburb of Youghal. The site is bounded on the south and west by the line of the town wall.

There were no traces of any archaeological remains uncovered in either test-trench. The nature of the stratigraphy suggests that the layers represent relatively modern dumps of material.
*Meriel McClatchie, Archaeological Services Unit, Department of Archaeology, University College, Cork.*

**123. 59 SOUTH MAIN STREET/QUAY LANE, YOUGHAL**
Urban medieval
210550 077900
SMR 67:29
98E0605

An archaeological assessment and engineering trial boring took place in March 1999 before development of a site at the northern end of the medieval Base Town, close to the Southgate occupied by the 18th-century clock tower (SMR 67:29/011). The site is bordered to the south by Quay Lane, which contains Cromwell's Arch, and the site of the Watergate (SMR 67:029/12) and the courthouse (SMR 67:45) to the east. The rear of the site was subject to a previous archaeological inspection by Catryn Power, in 1993, which revealed a depth of 0.46m of topsoil on top of masonry of potential medieval date.

Three linear test-trenches were opened across the site, which revealed archaeological deposits containing medieval pottery, at a depth of 0.4–0.6m to 2–2.55m below present ground level. This appeared to represent a deliberate ground raising to avoid high floodwater and was sealed to the front of the site by a possibly medieval clay floor. Waterlogged peat deposits were also noted from boreholes at a depth of 2m towards the rear of the site on top of estuarine mud, confirming the site's location across the medieval waterfront. Further work was recommended.
*Paul Stevens for Margaret Gowen & Co. Ltd, 2 Killiney View, Albert Road Lower, Glenageary, Co. Dublin.*

## DERRY/LONDONDERRY

**124. 34 THE DIAMOND, COLERAINE**
Urban
28485 43245
SMR 7:47, 7:90, 7:51, 7:19 (close to)

An assessment was carried out at the site of 'Tweedies', No. 34 The Diamond, Coleraine, Co. Londonderry, in September 1999. The proposed development involved the part refurbishment and part demolition of an existing building at The Diamond to provide two retail units. Groundworks involved the insertion of a number of reinforced concrete ground-beams in the southern part of the site, in the area of existing and infilled basements.

Six trenches were excavated in the area of the proposed development, and the excavation of the ground-beams was carried out under archaeological supervision.

Trench 1 was excavated east–west in the area of one of the ground-beams; it was 4.8m long and 1.18m wide and was excavated to a depth of 1m. A concrete floor extended to a depth of 0.1m and overlay a layer of rubble consisting of large stone, mortar and brick. This extended to a depth of 0.4m and lay above a dark brown, loamy garden soil that contained animal bone and red brick. This extended to a depth of 0.9m, at which point the natural, orange, gravelly clay was exposed. Excavation ceased at a depth of 1m. No features were evident, and no finds were recovered.

Trench 2, excavated along Bellhouse Lane in a north–south direction, was 8.5m long and 0.9m wide and was excavated to a depth of 0.7m. The floor of the basement was a mortar and stone layer and extended to a depth of 0.07m. This overlay a layer of crushed red brick that extended to a depth of 0.36m, which in turn overlay a light brown, sandy clay. This extended to a depth of 0.6m and directly overlay the natural gravel. No features were evident, and, apart from a few pieces of natural flint recovered from the bottom of the trench, no finds were recovered.

Trench 3 was excavated east–west parallel to Church Street in the area of an infilled basement; it was 4.5m long and 1.2m wide and was excavated to a maximum depth of 1.8m. The fill consisted entirely of stone and brick rubble that had obviously been used to backfill the basement. The excavation ceased at a depth of 1.8m owing to the rubble continually collapsing into the trench. No features were uncovered, and no finds were recovered.

Trench 4 was excavated north–south in the northern area of the site along the line of a demolished external wall in an area of proposed groundworks; it was 16m long and 1m wide and was excavated to a depth of 1.5m. A concrete floor extended to a depth of 0.1m, below which a brown, sandy layer was exposed. This sand was clearly a base for a pavement along Bellhouse Lane and extended to a depth of 0.18m, where it overlay a hardcore layer. This extended to a depth of 0.7m and overlay the natural gravel. No features or finds were uncovered.

Trench 5, excavated east–west in the northern area of the site perpendicular to Trench 4, was 6m long and 1m wide and was excavated to a depth of 1m. The concrete floor had already been removed, and a hardcore rubble layer was visible that extended to a depth of 0.4m. This overlay a thin layer of loose, grey gravel that contained animal bone, a sherd of medieval pottery, a sherd of post-medieval stoneware and some pieces of flint. With the exception of one butt-trimmed flake, all the pieces were natural. This layer overlay one of brown sand and gravel at a depth of 0.65m, which most likely represented the natural ground.

Trench 6 was excavated in a north–south direction near the centre of the site parallel to Trench 4; it was 12m long and 1m wide and was excavated to a depth of 1.2m. The concrete floor overlay a layer of hardcore rubble that extended to a depth of 0.4m. This overlay a layer of fine, loose gravel that extended to a depth of 1m and overlay the natural gravel. No features were evident, and no finds were recovered.

The monitoring of these trenches revealed no evidence of archaeological stratigraphy. The ground-beams were for the most part found within an infilled cellar, which consisted of a rubble fill above the natural gravel. The northern area of the site had not been disturbed by the construction of the cellars, and the natural gravel was exposed at an average depth of 0.7m below the surface. All groundworks are completed, and no further archaeological work is required at this site.

*Deirdre Murphy, Archaeological Consultancy Services Ltd, 43 Downshire Road, Newry, Co. Down.*

## 125. ST MARY'S DOMINICAN PRIORY, HANOVER PLACE, COLERAINE

Medieval priory and graveyard
C84663230

Excavations at the site of the priory took place over five months between November 1998 and May 1999, before a proposed major retail development.

Before the arrival of archaeologists on site, the mid-19th-century buildings fronting onto Hanover Place and Bridge Street had been demolished and the concrete slab, which had originally covered the workyard area for Stuart's garage and had extended across the entire southern half of the site, had been broken up. The slab and associated overburden were removed under archaeological supervision. Before the removal of these there were no visible remains of the priory, associated buildings or graveyard.

Extensive excavation across the site uncovered the footprint of the medieval Dominican priory and an associated burial-ground. The intensity of the post-medieval activity had effectively razed all medieval deposits to the extent that even the priory walls survived only as subsoil-cut features.

Historical documents record that the priory was founded in the mid-13th century and abandoned at the end of the 16th century during the continuing Dissolution of the Monasteries under Elizabeth I. Thereafter the priory and its land were granted to James Hamilton in 1605, who in turn gave the land to Thomas Phillips later that year. Phillips set about fortifying the monastic buildings and in 1609 claimed that he had almost finished constructing a fort, but by 1610 he had surrendered his lands to the Crown. The priory was converted into storehouses in 1612 and eventually fell into disrepair and was razed to the ground.

The earliest illustrations of the priory are in Carew's map of 1611 and later in Raven's map of 1622. Excavations have shown that the maps give quite a faithful representation of the priory, which was of typical Dominican architecture. As it survived, the priory consisted of a nave, a chancel and two transepts. The church formed the northern side of the cloister; the western side of the cloister ran parallel to Hanover Place and had been destroyed by basements. The maps show the western side of the cloister as being of two storeys. This is highly unusual but was perhaps necessitated by the natural slope of the ground. The eastern side of the cloister was a continuation of the line of the southern transept. Entrance to the priory was through a single doorway along the western side, presumably via a staircase.

The almost complete footprint of the priory had survived and was excavated as a series of subsoil-cut foundation walls and trenches. As all of the walls had been truncated at ground level, no architectural details such as window embrasures or doorways had survived. In its final phase the church had internal measurements of just over 32m east–west by almost 11m north–south. A columned aisle had been added along the north of the church, running east–west, making the north–south interior length ratio 1:3. A stone rood screen divided the chancel in the east from the nave in the west.

A number of burials were excavated in the church, most lying within the nave. A subdivided transept lay to the north of the church, but the southern transept had been removed by the later citadel wall and survived only as a series of infilled foundation trenches.

Two walls projected from the southern face of the southern church wall and were of identical construction. These walls have been identified as part of the cloister range. During the earlier part of the 17th century a citadel was constructed on the site. Its origins are obscure, although it would appear to have been constructed after 1625 and demolished in the 1660s, standing south of the priory cloisters and Phillips's house. Excavations uncovered a substantial, 2m-wide wall constructed from heavily mortared, roughly dressed blocks running along the southern area of the site. This wall ran east–west from Hanover Place, removing all evidence for the southern cloister arcade, and terminated in a north-eastern bastion. The wall was enclosed with a wide ditch that would have had the effect of creating a moated site. This wall has been identified as part of the citadel.

Over two hundred human skeletons were excavated, along with a quantity of disturbed, disarticulated remains. The burials were found both within the nave and chancel and to the east and south-east of the church. Males, females, children and babies were all represented, indicating that the burial-ground was not solely used by the Dominicans.

Excavations in the north-western corner of the site, along the junction of Hanover Place and Bridge Street, uncovered a wooden structure $c$. 5–6m long, which has been identified as part of a quay or jetty. The oak uprights were very substantial and had been fixed to a long vertical beam by wooden pegs. The timbers were sealed within an organic-smelling, plastic, grey riverine clay. Pottery recovered from this clay butting against the timbers has been dated to the early medieval period. A second line of uprights lay $c$. 1.5m to the south of the wooden timbers and may have facilitated the mooring of small boats. Small areas of wicker were also uncovered within the riverine clay, suggesting the location of fish traps—historical records inform us that the Dominicans had fishing rights on the Bann. The date of the pottery found in association with the timbers would suggest that the jetty is contemporary with the priory.

To the east of these timbers, upslope along Bridge Street, a linear feature had survived in a narrow strip of ground undisturbed by basements. This feature cut through subsoil and was filled with a friable, grey/brown, soily clay. As excavated, it had a maximum depth of 0.96m and width of 2.4m, although the full width could not be determined as it continued beneath present-day Bridge Street. The fill was free of any datable artefacts, although it can be assumed that it was part of the enclosing precinct ditch associated with the medieval priory.
*Cia McConway, ADS Ltd, Unit 48, Westlink Enterprise Centre, 30–50 Distillery Street, Belfast BT12 5BJ.*

### 126. KINGSGATE STREET, COLERAINE
Urban post-medieval
C85023240
SMR 7:91

Monitoring of the foundation trenches ($c$. 1.5m wide) of a retail building development at 1, 3 and 5 Kingsgate Street/2 and 4 Society Street, Coleraine, Co. Derry, was carried out. This exposed the surface of what was probably the fill of a large ditch on the eastern side of the site, which ran 5.5m east of and parallel to Society Street. An 18th-century jug handle was found in the upper part of the fill, but further investigation could not be carried out as the foundations only intruded on the surface of the fill. Only the western edge of the ditch was exposed—the eastern edge lay under a standing building. Cartographic evidence indicates that the cut and fill were a stretch of the early 17th-century town's defensive ditch. A maximum width of 8m of the ditch was noted. Historical records indicated that it was originally $c$. 12m wide.
*Alan Reilly, NAC, Unit 6, Farset Enterprise Park, 638 Springfield Road, Belfast.*

### 127. RIVER BANN, COLERAINE
Underwater dock
C845324

Management for Archaeology Underwater was contracted by DOE (NI) to carry out underwater archaeological investigations in the River Bann at Coleraine. The investigations were required to assess the threat to archaeological remains from the proposed construction of a footbridge on the northern side of the old bridge in Coleraine.

The site is directly to the north of Coleraine Bridge. It consists of two 6m$^2$ plots where the proposed footbridge piers would be installed. The centres of these piers are 7.7m from Coleraine Bridge. The river is bordered at this point by stone walling on the Waterside (west) and the metal piles of the Bannside Wharf to the east.

The investigations required a number of underwater strategies. The river was visually inspected by divers, noting the components of the riverbed and searching for archaeological features. Given the relatively unpolluted nature of the river and the small area involved, full coverage was possible even in low visibility. Divers carried out the inspection by laying a central north–south baseline and setting a grid around the area involved. They then carried out an open-water grid search. This involves the diver moving up and down the grid within a set number of lanes, the width of which depends on the visibility. The topography of the riverbed was also noted during the inspections, as any profound anomalies would require further investigation.

Limited probing into the riverbed was carried out during the inspection by the use of a 0.5m wooden rod. This is a quick method of locating any large objects buried in the sediment.

Metal-detection was carried out using Fisher metal-detectors. In a low-visibility environment this was an added tool in assessing the man-made content of the riverbed by non-intrusive means. Again, transects were followed within the grids and the frequency of hits was noted. Metal-detection is by definition only an indicator of metal items, but it does give a glimpse of the overall density of man-made material at the different locations. In addition, it hints at buried items that may be of archaeological value. Metal artefacts, notably a large collection of prehistoric items, have been recovered from the River Bann in the past. Where possible, divers identified these metal items, although a great deal were covered in sediment and would have required extensive excavation.

As a final testing method for archaeology, two test-trenches were excavated. These were positioned north–south along the central baseline, cutting right through the centre of the grid. The trenches were 0.5m wide and $c$. 0.4–1m deep and were excavated using a diver-operated water dredge. The pumped material was discharged onto a sieve on the surface for examination.

Among the finds were some coins, including three British halfpennies or pennies, two definitely from the reign of George III (1760–1820). The single piece of flint found showed signs of working in antiquity. It had a subtle bulb of percussion and some striking on the opposite face. It is a piece of debitage rather than a finished artefact.

*Donal Boland, Management for Archaeology Underwater Ltd, Arden Road, Tullamore, Co. Offaly.*

### 128. BISHOP'S STREET WITHOUT, DERRY
17th-century urban
C43211645
SMR 14:64

An excavation funded by Built Heritage, EHS, was undertaken on this site from 9 February to 14 May 1999. The excavation took place before housing construction within a zone of potential urban archaeology.

The site measured *c.* 90m x 35m, and extensive archaeological remains were uncovered during the excavation. In part, these remains provided evidence of at least two phases of extramural occupation outside Bishop's Gate during the 17th century. This evidence took the form of drainage gullies, rubbish pits, possible property boundaries and cobbled surfaces. Preliminary post-excavation work suggests that there was an early phase of occupation, dating to the first half of the 17th century, followed by secondary occupation during the later part of that century. No direct structural evidence of the actual 17th-century houses was recovered, as these were almost certainly removed during a phase of activity on site dated to the commencement of the Jacobite siege in 1688–9.

Further evidence of the siege was uncovered in the form of a north-west/south-east-orientated ditch fronting the destroyed earthwork ravelin before Bishop's Gate. The extant remains of a sally port 2.6m wide interrupted the ditch. A larger ditch, scarped from the sloping ground outside Double Bastion, was exposed to the north-west of the ravelin. This was a maximum of 9.8m wide and 2.8m deep. The larger ditch may have been part of an earthwork constructed to protect the flanks of the ravelin and Double Bastion during the siege of 1688–9. The excavation also recovered over 5000 artefacts of various types. These include pottery sherds of Irish, English and Continental origin, metal artefacts, bone artefacts, clay pipes and glass.

*Paul Logue, Archaeological Excavation Unit, EHS, 5–33 Hill Street, Belfast BT1 2LA.*

### 129. MILLENNIUM THEATRE, DERRY
17th-century city ramparts
C43631674
SMR 14:39

The 17th-century walls (SMR 14:33) surrounding the core of the modern City of Londonderry are one of Northern Ireland's most important historical monuments. The walled city was largely built between the years 1614 and 1619 as part of the wider Plantation of Ulster. The ground-plan of the city defences, envisaged as a strong wall with outer ditch, was trodden out in 1613, and the ditch is known to have been completed by 1616. The material excavated from the ditch and scarping activity was used to create an earthen rampart around the circuit of the defences. The wall was then built on and against the front of this rampart. When completed, the rampart, was said to have been 12ft thick within the city, with a 24ft-high, 6ft-thick wall on the outside. Certain encroachments were made on the walls in the vicinity of the Millennium Theatre site in the north-east of the city during the 18th century, and by 1853 most of the Water Bastion, which faced onto Foyle Street, had been removed. More recent times have seen the classification of the walls as a historic monument, and, under the guardianship of the Environment and Heritage Service, a major programme of repair and conservation has been undertaken.

The site lay in the north-east of the walled city at the proposed location for the Millennium Theatre Project. Initially, assessment excavations by Stephen Gilmore (*Excavations 1998*, 24–5) and a detailed paper search were undertaken on the site. These showed that any significant archaeology was restricted to the locality of known possible 17th/18th-century cellars (SMR 14:35). Accordingly, before the main construction began, these cellars were encased beneath a concrete raft to ensure their preservation.

During the main construction phase, however, the rear retaining wall of the city defences proved to be of too poor build to cope with the nearby disturbance. One 25m length of this wall became sufficiently weakened as to require major repair. The wall was constructed in the 19th century and has been slightly repaired on several occasions since then, making it of little or no archaeological significance. It was originally built to retain the remains of the city's 17th-century rampart. Therefore, any major repair work to the wall was likely to disturb potential archaeological deposits. The subsequent repair work was carried out under archaeological supervision after the completion of a two-week explorative rescue excavation.

Five trenches were excavated along the stretch of damaged walling, and evidence was recovered of the 17th-century earthen rampart. The excavation showed the rampart to have originally been 7–8m wide and 2–3m high. It contained potsherds of 17th-century date and sealed an old ground surface probably also dating to the 17th century, on the basis of an associated potsherd.

*Paul Logue, Archaeological Excavation Unit, EHS, 5–33 Hill Street, Belfast BT1 2LA.*

### 130. MAGHERAMENAGH
Souterrain, prehistoric house
C860389

This development site is in the extreme north-east of County Londonderry, on the southern outskirts of Portrush. The land, between 20m and 30m above sea level, sloped gradually downhill to the north. There was a gentle ridge to the east of the site, running north in the direction of Portrush and Ramore Head. The surrounding fields appeared to be quite fertile, with barley, wheat and root vegetables being grown.

The site is multi-period, dating to both the Neolithic and the Early Christian period. The archaeology uncovered included: pits near the souterrain; a fire-pit and associated post-holes; wall slots and associated features; a dump and burnt layers; post-holes below the dump layers; slots and pits to the west of the house; and a souterrain.

An area on the road to the north-east of Plot 82 produced concentrated patches of charcoal. The major concentration appeared to be a rectangular area of *c.* 8m x 5m, the long axis of which lay approximately east–west.

The eastern ends of Plots 83 and 84, on the south-east of a small hillock overlooking the eastern field boundary, produced post-holes or pits in two concentric arcs. There appeared to be at least 0.15–0.2m of archaeological strata remaining in the western area of the feature, similar in the east, and possible wall slots to the north and south. There was a possible hearth in the centre. The site was very rich in charcoal interleaved with burnt soil/clay. About 30 sherds of coarse, unglazed pottery and some struck flint were recovered during the preliminary clean-up of the area.

On the road to the north of the charcoal area, in Plots 90 and 91, was a semicircular or right-angled ditch, *c.* 2m wide. The ditch appeared to run approximately eastwards downhill. Possible stone-packed features ran at right angles to this ditch. This feature was untraceable closer than about 5m from the hedge.

A semicircular enclosure *c.* 5m in diameter appeared to lie in Plot 82, *c.* 5m to the south-west of the rectangular charcoal area.

The rectangular and circular buildings appeared to be Neolithic in date, evidenced by artefacts recovered in the vicinity, including coarse pottery (mostly undecorated) and crudely struck flint. The pottery appeared to be Western Neolithic or bucket-shaped pottery similar to Case's Killyhoyle ware. This may be a Neolithic or Early Bronze Age house. Further evidence for the presence of Neolithic people in the area came from the two polished axes found during topsoil-stripping.

It is harder to determine the date of the series of pits and post-holes in the vicinity of the western end of the souterrain. They surrounded its entrance and may have formed a structure over this to conceal or protect it.

The fire-pit was in the centre of the rectangular structure, or to the west of the central post-holes in the circular structure. It was very rich in charcoal. It was not possible to connect it stratigraphically with either of the major structures, but radiocarbon dating may resolve this. On the south-west edge of the fire-pit were two small stake-holes that appeared to be associated with it, possibly as supports for some sort of spit, along with a deeper post-hole to the other side.

Overlying the circular structure and the burnt material was the foundation trench of a rectangular structure. This appeared to be a rectangular building 8–10m long and 6m wide with an entrance on the south side

The dump or conflagration layers were composed of mixed sand and were carbon-rich. Because of their rectangular form and their being bounded by construction trenches, it is probable that a rectangular building burnt down in this location.

The post-holes form a circular structure 8–9m in diameter. In the centre of this arc was a group of post-holes that may have been used to hold up a roof. Several of the post-holes showed evidence of their posts having been replaced, probably as a result of decay. This structure was the oldest on its site and was later covered with layers of burnt material, either owing to the destruction of a later rectangular structure or as a result of an industrial process.

The curving gully to the west of the main site may be a defensive palisade trench enclosing the settlement. It may also have functioned as a windbreak.

A souterrain was discovered on a knoll in the northern part of the field. It was constructed by excavating a trench into the subsoil and utilising and modifying edges of rock outcrop within the subsoil. The trench was 2.4m wide on average and 1.4m deep. After completion, the passage was *c.* 1m wide and 1.2m deep. Most of the sides had drystone walling, denuded in places. Only the south end of the entrance area and the east end of the main passage were rock-cut and unlined. The former incorporated a rock-cut step that was still functional at the time of excavation. The drystone walling was variable in nature, from neat to fairly untidy. In general, large, bulky, subrectangular stones were used.

Although the roof did not survive, it is clear from the upper courses of the side-walls that corbelling was used.

The souterrain had a *c.* 12m-long, straight passage that ran from the corner of the right-angled turn side passage to the eastern rock-cut end of the main passage's elevated area. The right-angled turn at the west end formed a passage measuring 8m by 0.8m. At the other end it terminated at a point where two passages emerged at right angles to form a T-junction. They were both entered via very similar, deliberately constricted creeps, created by using large stones in the main passages side-walls to create a drystone-built aperture that was roughly central to each side passage. The creeps and side passages were directly opposite each other. The southern passages measured 5m by 1m. The northern passage was *c.* 4m long and of uncertain width.

The fill was generally uniform. It seems likely that the souterrain floor was debris-free until the destruction of the structure, which seems to have been deliberate and involved the removal of the upper stonework.

Souterrain ware was found on the floor of the southern side passage, as well as at the right-angled turn at the western end of the main passage. The sherds may have fallen in from surface occupation deposits when the souterrain was destroyed or may be *in situ*. Fragments of a bone comb were also found in the right-angled extension. Slag was also recovered. A substantial quantity of lithic material consisting of flakes, blades and scrapers, dating to the Neolithic or Early Bronze Age, was found in the souterrain, clearly in a derived context. This probably related to the activity at the prehistoric house sites to the south. Bone was also recovered, some of it burnt. There was a very small quantity of later material in the fill including medieval or post-medieval glazed pottery and a pipe stem. This may indicate that the souterrain remained open until the last few centuries.

No certain trace of a surface structure was found at Magheramenagh, but the presence of a rock-cut step at the western end hints that there may have been one in that area.

*Alan Reilly, NAC Ltd, Unit 6, Farset Enterprise Centre, Springfield Road, Belfast.*

### 131. MOVANAGHER
17th-century bawn and village
C92031589
SMR 19:3

Excavations at Movanagher, the site of a 17th-century Plantation bawn and village established by the Mercers Company of London and situated on the western banks of the Bann in County Londonderry, c. 2 miles north of the village of Kilrea, were carried out between May and August 1999. Funded by the Environment and Heritage Service of the Department of the Environment for Northern Ireland, co-sponsored by the Institute of Irish Studies at The Queen's University of Belfast, the research excavation was undertaken as part of a larger, transatlantic research endeavour entitled 'Comparative archaeology of 17th-century British expansion: Ulster and the Chesapeake'.

The excavation phase of the project concentrated on tracing the extent and location of the village that accompanied the bawn, constructed in around 1611 and abandoned following the 1641 Rebellion. A 1622 survey map by Thomas Raven shows the village as scattered through a heavily wooded landscape extending south and south-east of the 120ft-square masonry bawn. Although 75% of the bawn remains standing today, including a circular flanker, the presumed location of the village is greenfield, serving as pasture.

Through the experimental use of geophysical prospecting and the application of an area sampling strategy throughout the projected village location, several features of interest were uncovered. Although the site had been heavily plough damaged, activity areas and the location of at least two dwellings were discernible through artefact patterning in the disturbed layers. The most significant find was a vernacular Irish dwelling, distinguishable by a subrectangular pattern of post- and stake-holes. The structure measures c. 14ft by 20ft and features a central hearth. One half of the house appears to have had a swept dirt floor. Evidence for external cobbling and a fenced entry were unearthed on the south-eastern side of the structure.

The discovery is significant for Irish archaeology, where structures such as this are known only from the documentary record and have been presumed too ephemeral to be recovered archaeologically. The discovery of an Irish house that was adapted and occupied by English settlers represents another important step towards achieving a balanced understanding of the experiences of Ulster's 17th-century inhabitants, be they natives or newcomers.

The structure was also found close to its position relative to the bawn as depicted on the 1622 survey map, while the location of a timber-framed house was surmised from its postition on the same survey drawing and through concentrations of architectural and domestic artefacts in the ploughed layers. All substantial structural remains of this timber-framed house had been destroyed through agricultural activity.

As an exercise in historical archaeology, the Movanagher Village Project employed documentary as well as material sources within the framework of a larger research endeavour comparing Plantation-period Ulster with the 17th-century English colonisation of the Chesapeake region of North America. Although the landscapes and cultures of the two regions were dissimilar, English settlers employed similar solutions to settlement with very different and often disastrous results—results that have left an indelible mark on the archaeological record. While the political histories of colonisation and of plantation are well-documented, understandings of the daily experiences of those individuals caught up—willingly and unwillingly—in the process of enforced settlement are hazy at best.

Informed archaeological research on sites such as Movanagher plays a critical role in redressing this deficiency.

*Audrey Horning, Institute of Irish Studies, Queen's University, Belfast BT7 1NN.*

## DONEGAL

### 132. QUIGLEY'S POINT, CARROWKEEL
No archaeological significance
SMR 30:12
99E0679

Testing was carried out on the site of the proposed development of eleven houses, a roadway, a sewage treatment plant and related percolation area east of Quigley's Point in the vicinity of the site of a burial-ground at Carrowkeel td, Co. Donegal, at the north-east of the shore of Lough Foyle. The site is on a south-south-west-facing slope, at the base of which is a north-west/south–east-flowing stream.

Testing was carried out on 27 November 1999. Using a wide, toothless trenching bucket, twenty test-trenches were excavated.

The natural olive to yellow/brown subsoil was sealed by a series of deposits of silts, gravels and sands. These strata in turn underlay a deposit of small to medium-sized stones, widely undulating sod and topsoil.

Nothing of archaeological significance was noted.
*Declan Moore, 8 Yewland Green, Renmore, Galway.*

### 133. CARROWKEEL
No archaeological significance
SMR 30:13
99E0646

Testing was carried out on the site of the proposed development of a dwelling-house, driveway, septic tank and related percolation area in the vicinity of the site of a possible megalithic tomb at Carrowkeel, Co. Donegal, ¼ mile north of Quigley's Point and c. 500m north-east of the shore of Lough Foyle. The site is on low ground in an area of rich pasture.

Testing was carried out on 19 November 1999. Using a wide, toothless trenching bucket, nine test-trenches were excavated. The natural, stony subsoil was sealed by a series of narrow bands of silts, gravels and sands. These strata in turn underlay a deposit of small to medium-sized stones, sod and topsoil.

Nothing of archaeological significance was noted.
*Declan Moore, 8 Yewland Green, Renmore, Galway.*

### 134. CLAR–BARNESMORE ROAD REALIGNMENT
Monitoring
99E0167

Monitoring of construction works on the Clar–Barnesmore road realignment has resulted in the excavation of one site—see No. 140 below—a drying kiln. Monitoring is ongoing at the time of writing.
*Declan Moore, IAC, 8 Dungar Terrace, Dun Laoghaire, Co. Dublin.*

### 135. CULDAFF
No archaeological significance
2531 4489
SMR 5:12
99E0083

Pre-development testing was carried out on 23 February 1999 in response to a condition of planning for a house extension to the north-east of an existing building at the south-east end of Culdaff village, on the Inishowen peninsula, Co. Donegal. On arrival on site, it was discovered that the foundations for the proposed development had already been excavated but were still open. Culdaff is the site of an early ecclesiastical site founded by St Buadan. No extant remains survive; however, a small graveyard called 'Ardmore graveyard', a short distance west-north-west of the development, may be part of the ecclesiastical site. The buildings adjacent to the development were constructed during the 20th century.

Eleven foundation trenches were excavated by machine before this writer's arrival on site. They were 1.83–12.19m long, 0.9–1.4m wide and 1–1.4m deep. The stratigraphy revealed was the same over the entire area: topsoil mixed with fill, lying directly above bedrock. The bedrock was located at 0.9–1.4m below the surface. The only exception was the presence of the foundation of a recently demolished one-storey building in two of the trenches. This foundation was 0.3–0.4m wide and 0.5m thick.

The trenches revealed nothing of archaeological significance. The topsoil/fill contained large quantities of ashes, modern pottery sherds including whiteware, and modern bottles. This site consisted of a backyard/garden that had been backfilled over the past 60–70 years with modern rubbish.
*Richard Crumlish, Archaeological Services Unit Ltd, Purcell House, Oranmore, Co. Galway.*

### 136. DOONAN/MULLINS
No archaeological significance
19244 37898
99E0420

Monitoring of topsoil-stripping for a proposed hotel at Doonan and Mullins townlands, Co. Donegal, was carried out. The site is close to an earthen ringfort listed as site 1014 in the *Archaeological Survey of Donegal* and 93:12 in the *Record of monuments and places for County Donegal*.

The topsoil was stripped by mechanical excavator. The sod and topsoil came directly down onto the natural boulder clay at an average depth of 0.4m. The only feature exposed was an old sewerage pipe of red earthenware along the new road. Finds from the topsoil included black glass, blue and white tin-glazed earthenware, Willow Pattern pottery, some rimsherds of unglazed earthenware and some white delft ware. No further archaeological work was necessary at the site.
*Donald Murphy, Archaeological Consultancy Services Ltd, 15 Trinity Street, Drogheda, Co. Louth.*

### 137. ELEVEN BALLYBOES
Souterrain
2655 4411
99E0138

Pre-development testing was carried out between 22 and 24 March 1999 following a report of the discovery of a souterrain on a development site during clearance works at Eleven Ballyboes, Greencastle, Co. Donegal. The development consisted of the construction of a single dwelling-house and septic tank. The testing was carried out with the assistance of a mechanical digger and had two aims: to better define the location of the souterrain and to test those areas of the development site that would be further disturbed as proposed locations for water and sewerage services. The removal of a large spoilheap north-west of the dwelling was also monitored.

The site lay on a steep south-east-facing slope, less than one mile north-east of Greencastle village, with a panoramic view of Lough Foyle to the east and south.

The souterrain was 1.4–1.7m north-west of the north-west wall of the dwelling that was under construction. A section of the roof of the souterrain had collapsed close to its south-east end. This section was 2.7m long and 0.8–1.2m wide. It revealed a feature constructed of uncoursed rubble and capped by flat stone lintels, orientated north-west/south-east. The souterrain was accessible for a short distance to the north-west of the collapsed section before more collapse blocked access. No excavation was carried out at this location.

Seven trenches were excavated, four to the north-west of the dwelling under construction and three to the south-east. Two of the four trenches to the north-west of the development produced undisturbed natural stratigraphy, while the remaining two produced further evidence of the souterrain. Finds were one sherd of pottery (yet to be analysed) recovered from the souterrain interior, three flints from the topsoil, one of which was possibly worked, occasional fragments of bone and several tiny fragments of burnt bone.

The two sections of souterrain that were uncovered appeared to represent the main passage, orientated west-north-west/east-south-east, with the original exposed section being a chamber located south, off the passage.

Two of the three trenches excavated to the south-east of the development produced undisturbed natural stratigraphy, while the remaining trench contained backfill (recently dumped during construction of the dwelling) above undisturbed natural stratigraphy. The monitoring of the removal of a large spoilheap to the north-west of the development revealed topsoil only. No artefacts were recovered.

The test-trenches achieved their aim of better defining the extent of the souterrain. The test-trenching also cleared the area of the proposed sewerage service. Because a section of the souterrain was on the proposed line of the water main, it was recommended that the water main be repositioned along the north-east site boundary.
*Richard Crumlish, Archaeological Services Unit Ltd, Purcell House, Oranmore, Co. Galway.*

### 138. FRIARBUSH
No archaeological significance
**99E0505**

Testing was conducted on the site of a series of anomalous earthworks before the Clar–Barnesmore road realignment (see No. 134 above). The site lay on the north-west side of the Barnesmore Valley, north of the present N15, to the rear of Biddy O'Barnes's public house. It consisted of two low linear earthen banks at right angles to one another and a shallow ditch feature aligned roughly north–south.

Testing revealed a modern field ditch and related field clearance and spoil. No archaeological features of significance were observed. The natural, blue/grey subsoil was sealed by a yellowish-brown, silty clay, which was in turn sealed by a grey/brown, sandy gravel with frequent small stone and pebble inclusions.
*Declan Moore, IAC, 8 Dungar Terrace, Dun Laoghaire, Co. Dublin.*

### 139. GREENCASTLE
Adjacent to church

As part of the planning conditions for the proposed construction of six houses in Greencastle, Co. Donegal, by Donegal County Council, an area 65m by 30m was topsoil-stripped under archaeological supervision. Because the site is adjacent to a field containing the ruins of Templemoyle Church, it was possible that burial remains and other significant archaeological deposits would be encountered.

Topsoil immediately overlay the undisturbed, natural, orange/brown, slaty, gravelly subsoil, and it was clear that nothing of archaeological significance lay within the development area.
*Dermot G. Moore, ADS Ltd, Unit 48, Westlink Enterprise Centre, 30–50 Distillery Street, Belfast, BT12 5BJ.*

### 140. KEADEW LOWER
Drying kiln
**99E0379**

Excavation was carried out on the site of a drying kiln between 28 June and 3 July 1999, before the proposed Clar–Barnesmore road realignment.

Topsoil, sod and a single stone fill of the bowl were removed, exposing a kiln built into a natural ridge of peat. The kiln comprised a circular bowl with outwardly battered sides, built of randomly coursed, small to medium-sized, roughly rectangular stones with two courses of larger stones at the base, and an outwardly splayed, north-west/south-east-aligned flue, built of upright slabs and roofing lintels (only one of which survived). The bowl had been deliberately backfilled. A stone surface built on the peat ridge surrounded the kiln.

The feature had been extensively disturbed at the south-east end of the flue by construction works associated with the present N15 embankment and the earlier construction of the embankment for the railway to the south. It was not possible from the evidence gathered to arrive at a definite date for the kiln.
*Declan Moore, IAC, 8 Dungar Terrace, Dun Laoghaire, Co. Dublin.*

### 141. MAGHERACAR
Adjacent to church site
**18096 35799**
**99E0082**

As a condition of planning permission, archaeological testing was carried out before the construction of a bungalow because of its proximity to a recorded monument (SMR 109:2, ecclesiastical remains). Five trenches were excavated; however, no archaeological features were revealed. There are no longer any traces of the nearby church site, which is occupied by a modern bungalow (which in turn replaced a late 19th-century farmhouse), and, other than limited cartographic evidence, nothing is known about the site.

However, the site owner showed the writer a fragment of a small rotary quern, a stone basin and an architectural fragment with a pronounced ribbed moulding of a late 12th- or early 13th-century doorway, which can be compared to similar fragments from nearby Assaroe Abbey. These artefacts may be the only archaeological evidence for the recorded monument but were not affected by the development.
*Christiaan Corlett, 88 Heathervue, Greystones, Co. Wicklow.*

### 142. TANK BREA, RAMELTON
No archaeological significance
**C225210**
**99E0343**

The test excavations were positioned in order to assess the location and complexity of the remains of any archaeological deposits on the site of the proposed development. The site, which overlooks the Leanann River, slopes steeply downwards from south to north, and, although it was much overgrown along the margins, it was possible to excavate the two long trenches without difficulty. The third trench, however, was excavated running across the line of the slope from north-east upwards to south-west. The line of this trench was dictated by the fact that the general slope of the site was too great for the mechanical digger to track directly up the incline.

The results from all three trenches were similar, with topsoil directly covering a yellow/brown, compacted, sandy clay. The results suggested that nothing of archaeological significance survives on the site. In fact, the general steepness of the area may have mitigated against any occupation of this general area of Ramelton in the past.
*Eoin Halpin, ADS Ltd, Unit 48, Westlink Enterprise Centre, 30–50 Distillery Street, Belfast BT12 5BJ.*

### 143. THE QUAYS, RAMELTON
Post-medieval
**SMR 30:5**
**99E0636**

Monitoring was carried out of the excavation of lift shaft trenches and foundation trenches and general ground reduction to an existing mill building and bottle factory in the vicinity of the site of an earlier castle at The Quays, Ramelton, Co. Donegal, between 22 October and 9 November 1999.

The natural subsoil was sealed by a dark brown, silty clay that contained a number of sherds of post-medieval pottery and modern rubble with frequent red brick, slate, tiles etc. The uppermost strata are interpreted as representing redeposited archaeological layers/formation deposits for the building of the warehouse/mill buildings, and the deposits in Lift shaft 1 as material deposited to facilitate land reclamation or deeper excavations for the construction of the upstanding buildings.

*Declan Moore, 8 Yewland Green, Renmore, Galway.*

### 144. KILBARRON
No archaeological significance
**G848647**
**99E0544**

A pre-development assessment was undertaken on 19 October 1999 at five sites (Sites A–E) within Kilbarron townland, south of Rossnowlough. The sites lie to the north (C–E) and south (A–B) of a narrow laneway running west from the main Ballyshannon to Rossnowlough road. Two archaeological sites are close to the proposed development at Site A. A wedge tomb, SMR 107:2, lies at least 53m east, and an enclosure, SMR 107:1, marked as Carrickcullen on the 1900 OS map, lies on the opposite side of the laneway *c*. 40m to the north.

Three test-trenches were excavated by mechanical digger at each of the five proposed development plots. They ranged from 12m to 20m long, and all were 2m wide.

Site A contains the remains of a wedge tomb. Trenches 1 and 2 contained topsoil 0.3m deep over mottled, grey/brown clay subsoil with a high stone component. Trench 3 contained topsoil 0.4m deep over subsoil of mottled, orange/brown clay with numerous stones and boulders, with a rock outcrop 2m long at the northern end of the trench.

Site B lay within a field immediately east of Site A. Removal of dark brown topsoil 0.26m deep revealed mottled, orange/brown clay subsoil at either end of Trench 4, with a central spread (7m long) of grey/brown subsoil containing much stone. Trench 5 revealed topsoil 0.26m deep over mottled, orange/brown clay subsoil with intermittent spreads or outcrops of rock. Trench 6 comprised topsoil 0.3m deep over a thin layer of sandy, brown loam containing fist-sized stones, in turn over the mottled, orange/brown clay. A single sherd of 18th-century brownware was recovered from the loam interface deposit.

Site C was north-east of Area B within a field immediately north of the laneway and east of a small, abandoned and derelict farmyard. In Trench 7 topsoil removal to a depth of 0.32m revealed sterile, mottled, light brown, sandy subsoil, with numerous stones protruding, some flat and slab-like. Trench 8 lay on sloping ground. Removal of topsoil to a depth of 0.32m revealed mottled, orange/brown clay subsoil with intermittent spreads/outcrops of limestone. Trench 9 revealed topsoil 0.32m deep over mottled, orange/brown clay subsoil with intermittent spreads or outcrops of limestone.

Site D was just over 130m north-west of Site C at the end of an overgrown, stone-lined trackway. The field was very wet underfoot during assessment. In Trench 10 topsoil consisted of wet, brown, humic peat 0.3m deep lying over mottled, grey/brown limestone boulder clay with intermittent spreads of decayed stone. In Trench 11 a peaty topsoil 0.3m deep overlay mottled, grey/brown limestone boulder clay. In Trench 12 peaty topsoil 0.3m deep overlay alternate south-east to north-west bands of limestone outcrop and mottled, grey/orange-brown boulder clay.

Site E was just over 170m north of Site D at the end of an overgrown, stone-wall-lined trackway. The field consists of very rough and waterlogged ground. The field was characterised by numerous limestone outcrops including a vertical face along the southern field perimeter and the denuded remains of several north–south-aligned stone walls, mostly consisting of large limestone boulders. Trench 13 was not fully excavated owing to difficult ground conditions. Trench 14 was excavated across very uneven and wet ground. Removal of wet, dark brown, humic topsoil to a depth of 0.3m revealed mottled, orange/brown and grey boulder clay. In Trench 15 removal of wet, peaty topsoil to a depth of 0.3m revealed mottled, orange/brown and grey boulder clay.

No archaeological features or finds were uncovered during the assessment.

*Malachy Conway, Archaeological Consultancy Services Ltd, 15 Trinity Street, Drogheda, Co. Louth.*

### 145. STRANORLAR/BALLYBOFEY
No archaeological significance
**21420 39470**
**98E0203**

This project concerns the monitoring of the groundworks, by a mechanical excavator, associated with the Ballybofey/Stranorlar Sewerage Scheme. The scheme involved the construction of a new treatment works site and the laying of pipelines. It was carried out at different stages between April 1998 and April 1999.

The stratigraphy revealed during the monitoring indicated no evidence of features, deposits or artefacts of archaeological significance.

*Fiona Rooney, Arch. Consultancy Ltd, Ballydavid South, Athenry, Co. Galway.*

## DOWN

### 146. JORDAN'S CASTLE, ARDGLASS
Urban medieval
**J561371**
**SMR 45:20**

Excavations examined two areas either side of the trench dug in 1998 (*Excavations 1998*, 31), which had uncovered a substantial wall to the east of the tower-house. Trench C was intended to determine the western limit of the quarry found in the earlier work and to provide a section across it.

A floor of stone flags with a drain was found above the level of the quarry. The floor is provisionally identified as that of a byre and dated by associated pottery to the 17th or early 18th century. The southern wall of the byre was set against a more substantial wall identical in construction to that found in 1998 and almost certainly its counterpart.

It now appears that during the later medieval period a building was constructed next to the tower-house from stone extracted from a quarry dug inside the structure. Excavation sectioned the quarry to its full depth, and, although no artefacts were recovered, stone chippings and mortar in the backfill provide confirmation of its character.

A second trench (D) uncovered a street that gave access to the door of the tower-house from the harbour. It had a drain on one side and a single, deep post-hole that may have marked the position of a gate.

Mark Gardiner, Department of Archaeology, Queen's University, Belfast BT7 1NN.

## 147. BALLYNAHATTY 5, BALLYNAHATTY
Late Neolithic ritual timber circle enclosure and settings
**J326677**
**SMR 9:62**

Since 1990 there have been nine seasons of excavation on this extensive Late Neolithic ceremonial site, all generously supported by the EHS and The Queen's University of Belfast. The site, 100m by 70m in extent, sits on the top and northern slopes of a ridge overlooking the hengiform enclosure of the Giant's Ring and passage tomb, 100m to the south. By 1997 the inner enclosure complex (BNH6), a portion of the outer enclosure (BNH5) and the northern section of the annexe attached to the east end of BNH5 had been excavated. Five cremation burials with passage grave affinities were found in the entrance area. The entrance to the complex was through the annexe, and this was found at a point halfway down the façade on the eastern side. This showed as a simple gap, 2m across, but with a more complex setting of posts within it. A series of east–west post-holes seemed to define a corridor or entrance chamber between the façade of the annexe and BNH5. The entrance to BNH5 was identified but only excavated to just below the plough zone.

The dating evidence centred around 2700 Cal. BC with the exception of one date that indicated that there was occupation in the area of BNH6 about 1000 years earlier.

*1999–2000 excavation*
The excavation began on 2 August 1999 and lasted seven weeks; 103m$^2$ of new ground was opened in addition to work continuing on the 320m$^2$ open from previous seasons. A further week was taken in January 2000 to complete the excavation of the entrance to BNH5. The excavation concentrated on the central and southern parts of the annexe on the eastern side of BNH5 but also included the completion of excavation of the annexe façade north of the entrance. Some features were fully excavated, while others were surface-located by topsoil-stripping, cleaning and planning.

*The entrance structure*
Excavation started in the north section of the façade in 1996 and has been a particularly difficult task. A small baulk had been left towards the north end, and this was progressively trowelled down and recorded in 0.2m layers and along three section faces. The history of this feature seems to have been that a line of post-holes (*c.* 1.5m deep and at 1.4m intervals) was dug through an area of particularly mixed and contorted glacial till. These posts were later removed, and the post-moulds were filled with charcoal and stones. A second row of post-holes was then dug immediately to the east. These were massive (*c.* 2.4m in diameter and 2m deep) and so close together that they cut one another and removed most of the upper post-holes of the first phase. The moulds of the post-butts were visible at the base and were *c.* 1.4m in diameter. At least one of the posts probably had heart-rot. The posts, which were probably *c.* 6m high and spaced 0.1–0.2m apart, ran across the line of the ridge. A trench was later dug along the west side of the row, and the posts were pulled over and lifted out. This was then backfilled, and the post positions were marked by dumps of charcoal and stone. The façade post-holes therefore contained up to five different mixes of the original fill and two secondary fills. A third line of discrete posts was then constructed on the west side.

The sequence on the north side was only understood by work at the south end of the façade. Here no attempt was made to excavate in sections, but an area of 48m$^2$ was taken down in three levels to a depth of 1m. At this point two of the third set of post-holes could be seen to clip the secondary fill of the second set and are therefore later. The second line in turn could be seen to cut the last post-hole of the first row, confirming its primary position.

After a short entrance gap the post-holes of the first phase of the façade continued south beyond the annexe, heading directly down the slope of the ridge towards the passage tomb in the centre of the Giant's Ring. This was surface-traced in a series of shallow cuttings for 16m. One post-hole was fully excavated, but all showed a characteristic secondary fill of charcoal and stones. At one point the post-holes overlap, indicating that they were dug from the south to the north, possibly confirming the primacy of the passage tomb in the area.

Most work was in the area between the entrance, midway along the façade, and the gap in the outer enclosure (BNH5) due west of it. When this was combined with evidence from the 1992–7 excavations the full extent of the entrance chamber could be seen. It consisted of a square of post-holes (8m x 8m x *c.* 1.6m deep) with opposing gaps (1.6m across) midway along the east and west sides and in line with the entrance through the façade. Ten post-holes were fully excavated in the southern area, and three more on the north side. The line on the north side appears incomplete but is the result of the difficulty in identifying and fully excavating the features in previous seasons. Indeed one post-hole had been missed altogether, and the surface of another had been labelled as a hearth.

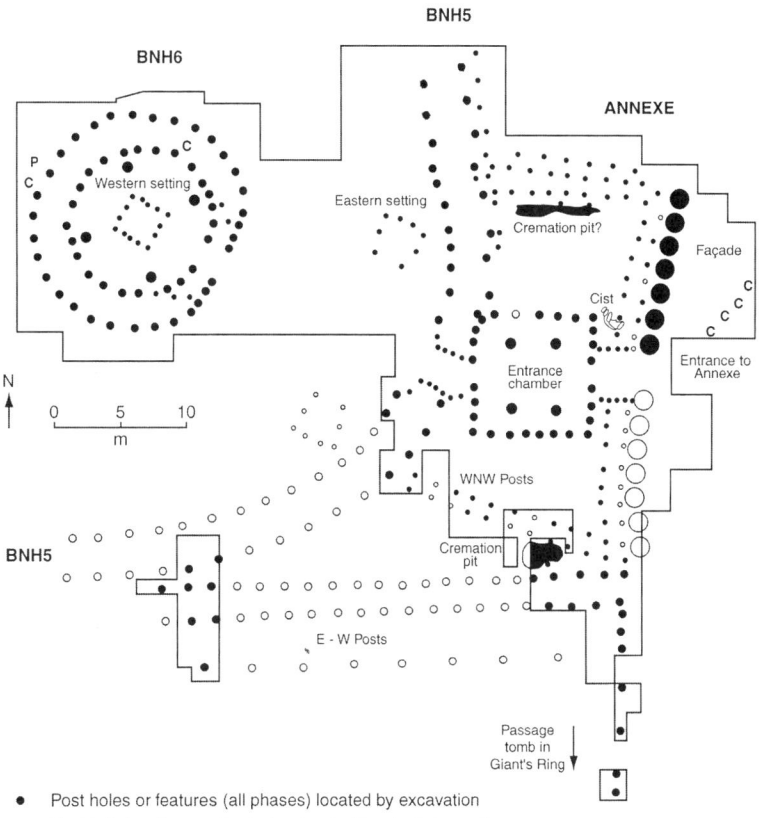

Site plan of Ballynahatty.

- Post holes or features (all phases) located by excavation
- Post hole locations estimated or located by air photography
— Limit of excavation
C Cremation
P Pit

Perhaps the most unfortunate aspect was the critical relationship of the chamber to BNH5. The north-west corner of the chamber overlapped with one of the post-holes of the outer enclosure, but, although this area was recognised as being more complicated in 1992, the presence of the annexe and its related structures was not known. The second post was regarded as a replacement, and the second post-hole was not recognised, so the chronological relationship was not recorded.

Within the chamber were four posts, two on either side of the entrance passage, reflecting the four posts within the inner enclosure BNH6. These posts were all $c.$ 1.8m deep and contained the typical secondary fill of charcoal and stone. The south-east post-hole also contained over 100 flint flakes in the upper part of the secondary fill. The four post-holes on the south side of the west end of the chamber all contained grooved ware in the primary fill. Grooved ware had previously been found in the primary fill of the post-holes on the north-east side and in the area of the annexe to the immediate north of the chamber.

There was evidence of a slot containing a line of three shallow posts connecting the east entrance of the chamber to the entrance in the façade. The easternmost post had been cut by the façade, possibly the secondary fill of the second phase, and therefore relates to the first or second line of façade posts. The chamber probably consisted of free-standing posts $c.$ 4.5m high.

The relationship between the chamber and BNH5 was finally established in January 2000. This was a specialised entrance structure that accommodated the change in the direction of the passageway from the east–west orientation of the annexe to the east-south-east/west-north-west of the final approach to the inner enclosure BNH6. This entrance structure was laid out on the same geometry as the eastern setting and was defined by two slots that contained posts similar to those at the east entrance of the chamber.

*The south side of the annexe*
At the southern end of the façade a complex of post-holes was resolved into at least two differently orientated rows.

A double line of post-holes ran in an east–west orientation from the south end of the façade due west to BNH5. They contained a secondary fill of charcoal and stones but were larger and of a different spacing than the post-holes of the north side of the annexe. A post-hole from the east end was fully excavated, and the west end was surface-located where it ran against the arc of BNH5. Also visible at this point was a third, amorphous feature that can probably be associated with a third row of post-holes, visible in aerial photographs, running parallel to and on the south side of the double row of post-holes. The north side of the annexe also had a third row of outer post-holes at a wider interval.

Another double row of post-holes, $c.$ 1.6m deep, articulated with the last two post-holes of the façade and ran in a west-north-west direction to BNH5. This was sampled in three places, with full excavation of five post-holes in the east and central zone and surface location at the west end. The last post-hole of this line cut a post-hole of the outer enclosure and is therefore later.

The east end of the east–west rows was accompanied by a charcoal-filled pit on its inner side (mirrored in a slighter way on the north side of the annexe), *c.* 0.6m deep. In character it was suggestive of a cremation pit. The charcoal was from a light wood source (e.g. brushwood) and contained flecks and small pieces of burnt bone. The bottom had been burnt, and lenses of burnt, sandy natural had, over time, collapsed from the sides into the charcoal, suggesting a series of fires. Only part of this feature was excavated, but wet sieving has produced large quantities of charred grain, some weed seeds and fragments of beads. The upper layers contained heat-cracked stones.

*Conclusion*
It has been established that the elaborate annexe is at least a three-phase structure. The first phase may be associated with the passage tomb complex at Ballynahatty, but the construction of the entrance chamber is certainly contemporary with or later than the grooved ware occupation. There may have been a major reorientation of the south side of the annexe early in the sequence, although this may have been part of the original concept. The posts of west-north-west orientation seem to delineate a clearly bounded cell on the south side of the entrance and are firmly attached and effectively perpendicular to the arc of BNH5. However, the line of the ridge would hide much of the west end of the west-north-west rows when viewed from the south. They are identical in character to the double line of post-holes that delimit the other cell on the north side of the entrance chamber.

The function of the east–west rows, which simply rest against the arc of the outer enclosure (BNH5) at the western end, seems to be purely cosmetic. These rows, which are double the length, crown the ridge to provide a false façade that would have dominated the important view from the south and made the BNH5 complex appear larger and even more impressive when viewed from the passage tomb in the Giant's Ring.
*Barrie Hartwell, School of Archaeology and Palaeoecology, Queen's University, Belfast BT7 1NN.*

## 148. DRUMADONNELL
Early Christian house
J24483917

At Drumadonnell townland, Co. Down, as part of the construction of a primary school, monitoring of topsoil-stripping revealed the existence of a small Early Christian house *c.* 7m in diameter. A central hearth, with a stone setting within it, was excavated, along with a subcircular setting of post-holes around it. A second hearth was found nearby, but it was not associated with any post-holes. There were no traces of an enclosure.

Finds included souterrain ware pottery and burnt bone. Soil samples from the excavation were processed by John Davidson of The Queen's University of Belfast. Burnt bone fragments as well as seeds and grains were recovered, mostly from the hearths and from a pit to the north of the rest of the archaeology. Analysis of the bone was carried out by Dr Eileen Murphy, and analysis of the seeds and grains by Dr Dave Weir. Most of the bone was too fragmentary to be identified, but cattle and sheep bone were present in the assemblage. The seed and grain assemblage was mostly composed of oats, barley and a much smaller amount of wheat. $^{14}$C testing of samples from the two hearths provided dates of AD 705 to 1005 and AD 680 to 980 calibrated at 2 sigma.
*Cormac McSparron, NAC, Unit 6, Farset Enterprise Park, 638 Springfield Road, Belfast.*

## 149. DUNMORE: 1
Burnt mounds
J368461

The construction of the Mournes' water pipeline has necessitated constant monitoring and occasional intervention, such as at the site of this burnt mound at the base of the east slope of Dunmore Mountain. Two burnt mound spreads had been identified, linked by an area of rough cobbling or platform. Excavation of only one, and part of the stone platform, was necessary, as the remainder could be preserved *in situ*.

The stone platform, or walkway, was found to be the earliest feature on the site. This was *c.* 5m wide and continued beyond the limit of excavation on both sides. A series of post-holes and small pits covered by the burnt mound material may relate to that phase of activity. The burnt mound consisted of layers of charcoal-rich soil containing large amounts of burnt and heat-shattered stone. It measured *c.* 10m east–west x 6m north–south and was crescent-shaped. A subsoil-cut trough was identified and found to be roughly U-shaped. This measured 2.4m x 1.6m and was 0.5m deep. The burnt mound appeared to relate to the final phase of activity on the site, and during the period of its use the stone walkway was added to.
*Audrey Gahan, ADS Ltd, Unit 48, Westlink Enterprise Centre, 30–50 Distillery Street, Belfast BT12 5BJ.*

## 150. DUNMORE: 2
Possible Neolithic house
J364460
**SMR 29:50**

This site, on the east slope of Dunmore Mountain, was identified during topsoil-stripping for the Aquarius Pipeline. It appeared as a subrectangular slot measuring *c.* 8m x 6m, with corner post-holes and four internal post-holes, all of which were subsoil-cut. Further post-holes were noted outside the feature, possibly representing an associated structure or structures. Pottery sherds recovered from the area of one of the post-holes suggest a Neolithic date for the feature, and it has been interpreted as the remains of a Neolithic house.

As the site is not under threat from the development, it was decided that no excavation would take place, and the site will be preserved *in situ*.
*Audrey Gahan, ADS Ltd, Unit 48, Westlink Enterprise Centre, 30–50 Distillery Street, Belfast BT12 5BJ.*

## 151. INCH AND BALLYRENAN: 1
Multi-period landscape
J46934579

The Phase 2 excavations on this site, following Phase

1 undertaken by Ciara MacManus in 1998 (*Excavations 1998*, 33–4), uncovered a high density of archaeological activity, ranging in date from the Neolithic to the medieval, in a flat field alongside the Inch Abbey Road.

A substantial linear ditch, containing 13th-century pottery sherds and measuring *c.* 3m wide and 1.5m deep, was uncovered in the north of the field. Ten metres south of this a stone-lined pit, 0.5m in diameter and 0.3m deep, and two associated parallel narrow slots, each *c.* 1m long, were investigated. The soil between the two slots showed signs of intense burning. No artefacts were recovered from any of these features.

Adjacent to this a three-phased subrectangular enclosure was uncovered. A narrow subrectangular gully (*c.* 0.5m wide and 0.3m deep), enclosing an area *c.* 14m x 13m, was cut by a larger gully up to 2m wide and 1m deep. This second gully enclosed a larger area of 23m x *c.* 18m, and its northern half was cut by a curvilinear gully *c.* 1m wide and 1m in maximum depth. In plan the gullies appeared to be concentric, the earlier being enclosed by the later. An Early Christian date was indicated by the recovery of souterrain ware from the middle phase gully, and the enclosures are suspected of having an agricultural function, because of the lack of occupation evidence in the interior. These gullies also cut a circular feature *c.* 15m in diameter. This consisted of at least one ring (but possibly two concentric rings) of possible post-holes. Cremated remains were recovered from two of the potential post-holes, and sherds of pottery found in association with the circular feature suggest a Neolithic date. This may indicate a ritual function, and the suggestion is that the feature represented the remains of a timber circle.

South-west of the circular structure two ring-ditches were uncovered. The larger of these was 5m in diameter and enclosed a cremation burial. The burial consisted of a circular pit into which a flat stone slab had been placed. A crude vessel of probable Bronze Age date containing cremated remains was placed on the stone slab. A further deposit of cremated remains was revealed adjacent to the vessel. Two similar, crude, cist-like burials were discovered to the south of this point.

Approximately 15m south of the Early Christian subrectangular features, evidence of a rath, 27m in diameter, was uncovered. An entrance was discovered in the west. To the south of the entrance the ditch contained souterrain ware and had maximum dimensions of 3m wide and 2m deep. This stepped up to a depth of 0.5m as it approached the entrance. The ditch to the north of the entrance was a maximum of 1m wide and 0.5m deep. No evidence of a bank or occupation was discovered internally. Although such evidence may have been removed during the construction of the road, it is possible that this rath was never finished and that the narrower ditch was a marker gully for the digging of the more substantial cut.

South of this feature, evidence of two Bronze Age hut circles was revealed. The more complete example was 8–9m in diameter. This had a narrow wall slot and internal post-holes to provide roof support. The entrance faced east and consisted of a porch-like feature of four post-holes.

*Liam McQuillan, ADS, Unit 48, Westlink Enterprise Centre, 30–50 Distillery Street, Belfast BT12 5BJ.*

## 152. MOUNT ALEXANDER
No archaeological significance
J46457045
**SMR 10:29**

Monitoring of the construction of a telecommunications mast close to a ringfort (SMR 10:29) took place. No finds or features were noted.

*Alan Reilly, NAC, Unit 6, Farset Enterprise Park, 638 Springfield Road, Belfast.*

## 153. NENDRUM, MAHEE ISLAND
Early Christian tide mill
J52626376
**SMR 17:5**

Since 1995 staff of the Centre for Maritime Archaeology, sponsored by the Environment and Heritage Service, have been carrying out an archaeological survey of the intertidal zone of Strangford Lough. The survey revealed sites of many periods from the Mesolithic up to the present relating to the submerged landscape, defence, communications and economic exploitation of the shore. Many of these sites, however, have little or no parallel, and excavation is required to decide the nature of the site and to which period it belongs. One such site was an area beside the ancient monastic settlement site of Nendrum on Mahee Island, marked 'pond' on the OS 1:2500 map. The excavation was undertaken in an attempt to determine the function and date of this 'pond' as part of an ongoing series of investigations within the Strangford Lough intertidal zone.

The excavation revealed that this was not a fishpond but a millpond for a horizontal mill of the Early Christian period. This site differs from most of other horizontal mills in that it is a tide mill, which uses the flow of the tide to fill the millpond and the water released from the millpond to drive the wheel when the tide has receded. Only one other tide mill of this period has so far been found in Ireland (at Little Island, Co. Cork). Three mills had been constructed on the site, with the linear stone wall representing the final phase.

The only visible evidence of the Phase 1 mill is the substantial drystone feature with two gaps aligned roughly north-west/south-east across the bay. Excavation revealed a revetment of vertical timbers with horizontal planking held in place by a series of wattle walls (three to date) and the badly disturbed remains of a wheelhouse, including a badly eroded wooden flume (left *in situ*), associated with this millpond bank. This mill has been dated by dendrochronology to AD 619.

No structural remains of the Phase 2 mill-house or wheelhouse survived, but excavation revealed evidence of its millpond walls. No date has so far been obtained for this phase of the complex. A large beam uncovered during the excavation was sampled for dating by dendrochronology, but a good match has not yet been found. It is proposed to take further samples from other timbers in an attempt to obtain a firm date for the second mill.

Phase 3 saw the mill replaced by a third mill

comprising a millpond on an east–west alignment, a large stone flume and a drystone-built wheelhouse. Drystone-built wheelhouses are not uncommon in Ireland, but the stone flume at the time of writing is unique. The flume had been constructed from two large sandstone blocks chiselled out and butt-jointed within the back wall of the wheelhouse. Immediately above the floor of the wheelhouse was a layer of silt containing souterrain ware, two bone pins, discarded timbers and the remains of wattle screens. Two millstones and three horizontal wheel paddles were also recovered from this layer. The lower millstone was complete and still retained the bush to allow the shaft to pass through to the upper stone. The upper millstone had been broken before deposition and was recovered in three fragments with a small portion missing. This mill has been dated by dendrochronology to late AD 788/early 789.

Most of the artefacts recovered from the excavation were wooden, ranging from small chips, pegs and wedges to substantial squared timbers up to 2.5m long. Among the larger pieces are a horizontal mill hub and shaft, a possible second hub, an oar/paddle, a possible second oar and several mill fittings. The remains of a lathe-turned wooden bowl were found in the silted-up flume of the third-phase mill. Flint artefacts and struck flakes, clearly residual, were scattered throughout the excavated area. Other small finds recovered were a bronze buckle, two possible whetstone fragments, iron-working slag, tuyère fragments and an amber bead. Animal bones and teeth were recovered from many of the deposition layers.

A second season is planned for early spring 2000.
*Norman Crothers, Archaeological Excavation Unit, EHS, 5–33 Hill Street, Belfast BT1 2LA, and Tom McErlean, Centre for Maritime Archaeology, University of Ulster, Coleraine.*

### 154. MOURNE CONDUIT
Monitoring
J36204825
The construction of the Mourne Conduit Replacement, Aquarius Pipeline, necessitated archaeological attendance to monitor the removal of topsoil. Work commenced in April 1999 and is ongoing. Several sites were identified during 1999, and, while engineering solutions allowed for most of the sites to be preserved *in situ*, it was necessary to excavate at one location during 1999 (see No. 149 above).
*Audrey Gahan for ADS Ltd, Windsor House, 11 Fairview Strand, Dublin 3.*

### 155. BAGENAL'S CASTLE (McCANN'S BAKERY), NEWRY
Adjacent to tower-house
J08732615
SMR 46:40
As part of the planning conditions for the proposed construction of a carpark at McCann's Bakery, a large area to the north and north-west of the present buildings was to be reduced to enable hardcore and services to be inserted. This involved the removal of large platforms of concrete overlying rubble landfill and was monitored under archaeological supervision.

Although the site lay within the area of the Cistercian monastery founded at Newry in 1153, nothing now remains of the monastic buildings. Records indicate that in 1552 the lands and buildings were granted to Sir Nicholas Bagenal, who built an elaborate tower-house on the site. This tower-house was presumed to have been demolished when the bakery was constructed in the 1830s, but a site visit in 1998 revealed that a substantial portion of the castle remained standing, albeit severely damaged in places, within the fabric of the bakery complex.

In total, an area of 1500m$^2$ was reduced by machine and concrete/rock-breaker. Nothing of archaeological significance was uncovered in the area monitored.
*Dermot G. Moore, ADS Ltd, Unit 48, Westlink Enterprise Centre, 30–50 Distillery Street, Belfast BT12 5BJ.*

### 156. BAGENAL'S CASTLE, NEWRY
Fortification
J08732615
SMR 46:40
During development at McCann's Bakery, Newry (see No. 155 above), the unauthorised removal of ten stanchions from an archaeologically sensitive area took place. The stanchions were situated just south and east of the castle, and it was decided to record the stratigraphy in the pits left after their removal. Unfortunately, several of the pits had been filled with rubble and spoil after the removal of the stanchions, and only nine of the ten were examined. The tenth pit could not be successfully located, without risking further damage to surviving underground remains. Once each pit had been cleared of debris, a section face was cleaned down and drawn.

Eleven walls were detailed in the sections, along with evidence for possible pre-tower-house activity. Of the walls examined, six were shown, by association with finds such as glass and red brick, to be quite late. Sherds of pottery recovered from one of the remaining five walls may indicate a medieval date. This feature had a north–south orientation. The other four walls were all constructed of stone but yielded no datable evidence. Samples of mortar were taken from all five walls.

A tumbled granite stone feature was found at the northern end of several of the stanchion holes but would require further examination to assess whether it represents the remains of a wall. When observed in plan, this tumbled material seems to run in a straight east–west orientation through several of the pits, and it is almost parallel to the south wall of the castle.

A post-hole, recorded in section beneath the south wall of the castle, may be indicative of pre-tower-house activity, but no associated features were revealed.
*Liam McQuillan, ADS, Unit 48, Westlink Enterprise Centre, 30–50 Distillery Street, Belfast BT12 5BJ.*

### 157. RIVER ROAD/SUGAR ISLAND, NEWRY
Flood alleviation scheme
J085266
As part of the flood alleviation scheme along the

Newry (Clanrye) River by DOE/Water Service, a new wall and trunk sewer line are being constructed along the eastern edge of the river. At present this work is being undertaken at two locations—River Road/Kilmorey Street at the southern end of the town and Sugar Island at the northern end.

The works are being monitored, but no significant archaeological material has as yet been uncovered.

*Dermot G. Moore, ADS Ltd, Unit 48, Westlink Enterprise Centre, 30–50 Distillery Street, Belfast BT12 5BJ.*

## 158. NEWTOWNARDS
Urban/intertidal monitoring
**J49407241**

Monitoring of the sea defences was carried out in various townlands in the parish of Newtownards, Co. Down. The remodelling of the sea defence bank and the creation of a new back drain took place. A set of archaeological mitigation measures was carried out. World War II structures were photographed. A section of the bank (dating from 1810 onwards) was observed and drawn. The excavation of the new back drain was monitored. One piece of worked oak (yet to be examined) was the only possible pre-19th-century archaeological artefact or feature noted during monitoring to date. Archive research unearthed a private map showing the pre-reclamation outline of part of the north of Strangford Lough.

*Alan Reilly, NAC, Unit 6, Farset Enterprise Park, 638 Springfield Road, Belfast.*

## DUBLIN

## 159. MILL STREET/GEORGE'S HILL, BALBRIGGAN
Environs of 18th-century cotton mill
**32028 26378**
**99E0727**

A historical assessment of an extensive area of open ground between Mill Street and George's Hill, Balbriggan, indicated industrial activity from the late 18th century onwards. This was centred around the Hamilton (later Gallen) cotton works, the main factory building of which is still in use. Inspection of the site following removal of a dense cover of vegetation revealed that most of the elements of the industrial complex depicted on the Ordnance Survey 1:2500 scale map for 1868, and its subsequent revisions, could be clearly identified on the ground. These elements included the millpond, feeder channel, two well-preserved sluice-gates, a spillway, weaving sheds and outbuildings.

This good state of preservation meant that a detailed record of the industrial heritage of the site could be made without recourse to extensive excavation, which was deemed necessary only where the record of activity on the site was unclear and where industrial features were not fully defined. The combined programme of testing and recording was designed to create a detailed record of existing elements of the industrial complex and to identify potentially unrecognised archaeological remains in the area.

Testing was undertaken on 14 and 15 December

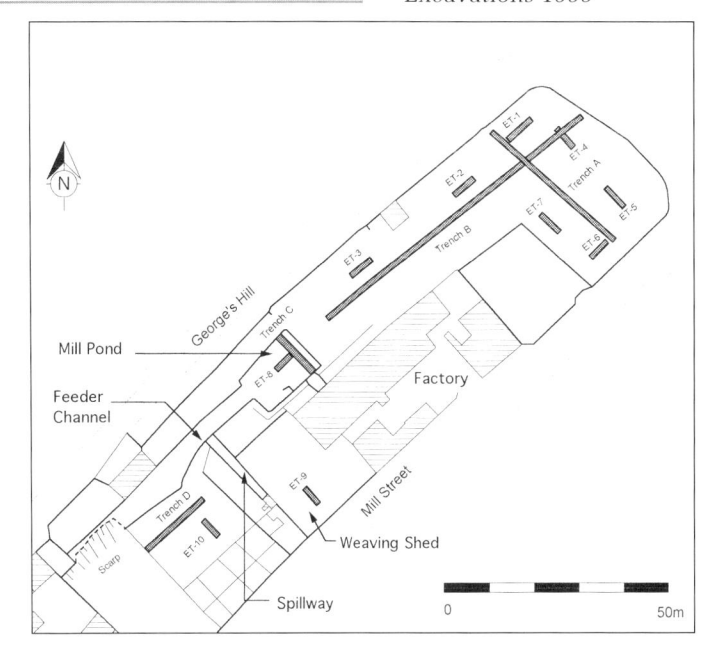

*Overall plan of site at Mill Street/George's Hill, Balbriggan.*

1999. Four trenches were opened, three of them in areas of the site where no structures or features had previously been identified. A number of waste pits and boundary features of 19th- and 20th-century date were noted. An area of *in situ* burning was identified at the base of the topsoil in Trench B to the north-west of the millpond, but no finds or structures were associated with it. Trench C was placed across the millpond in order to clarify its dimensions. This trench established that the deposits infilling the pond were on average only 0.5m thick and appeared to have been recently disturbed, with no clear stratigraphic sequence. The base of the millpond was formed by a roughly mortared surface with a dished profile, dipping to 0.75m below the lip of the sluice-gate at the centre.

Monitoring of ten engineering test-pits was undertaken on 13 December 1999, immediately before the testing programme. No features of archaeological interest were noted.

No structures or elements of the mill complex that had not already been identified from historical or cartographic sources were found on the site. In addition, no archaeological material was recovered during testing or monitoring that would suggest any substantial activity on the site before the late 18th century.

*Daniel Leo Swan, Arch-Tech Ltd, 32 Fitzwilliam Place, Dublin 2.*

## 160. GRANGE ABBEY CHURCH AND HOUSE, BALDOYLE
Medieval grange and late 17th-century dwelling
**O225405**
**SMR 15:70, 15:69**
**99E0321 and 99E0322**

In June and July 1999 a section of an M50 link road, 160m long, was monitored by the writer, and two areas were opened up for excavation. The corridor extended to the south of the extant Grange Abbey Church, a large stone church thought stylistically to date to the late 13th/early 14th century. This church and surrounding graveyard (no longer in use) originally formed part of the 'grange' of Baldoyle, a large, self-sufficient farm that belonged to the Priory of All Hallows (where Trinity College is now sited), in Dublin. Thus it was designed to exploit the lands given to the monastery by grateful benefactors in the Baldoyle–Donaghmede area and to provide fresh produce for the house in Dublin. After the Dissolution in the 16th century, a residence belonging to the Fitzsimon family is recorded at Grange, and this may be the residence depicted by Rocque in 1756. A house, known as 'Grange House', stood to the north of the road corridor and is possibly that depicted by Rocque, although Rocque's map shows the dwelling positioned slightly further south (SMR 15:69, south of Grange House). The house, yard and gardens were demolished in 1972, when the entire area became a large housing estate.

The excavation found scant remains of the medieval grange, as this area, to the south of the church, appears to have been substantially disturbed in the early 17th century. However, the remains of a stone wall over 1.1m wide were uncovered in section on the eastern side, and this may represent part of an eastern precinct wall. To the east the remains of a small stone 'water-house' were also found, which was dated to the mid- to late 17th century and was probably used to control water into a series of fishponds (marked on the Ordnance Survey map dated 1843). This structure was well built and tapped into a stone drain that extended through the entire site, allowing access to the water at that point. It was subsequently enlarged on the northern side by a red brick extension, sometime in the early to mid-18th century.

At the western end of the site the excavation exposed a series of pits that contained few finds but could be dated to the late 17th century. These appear to represent domestic refuse pits in an area that originally formed part of the pond complex. The most surprising and unexpected discovery, however, was in an area that was a pond until the demolition of Grange Abbey house in 1972. After the demolition the remains of the house were used to infill the pond and to build up the ground level. In one such dump of rubble a hoard of 41 gold sovereigns was found, some in almost mint condition. They ranged in date from 1817 to 1830 (George III and George IV), but the vast majority dated to between 1821 and 1825.

Linzi Simpson, Margaret Gowen & Co. Ltd, 2 Killiney View, Albert Road Lower, Glenageary, Co. Dublin.

## 161. BALLOUGH TO KILSHANE GAS PIPELINE
Various
**SMR 7:15, 11:84, 14:0490**
**99E0395**

Monitoring of topsoil removal for the construction of the northern section of the new NEP 3 gas pipeline was undertaken between April and September 1999. The pipeline will extend south from Ballough as far as Brownsbarn, Co. Dublin, reusing sections of the previously excavated NEP 1 and 2 pipelines (1983 and 1988). The first stage of this route saw monitoring of the pipeline excavation from Ballough to Kilshane. The remaining stages of pipeline construction south of Kilshane as far as Brownsbarn will be undertaken from summer 2000.

The pipeline corridor was stripped of topsoil running south from the Bord Gáis Éireann station at Ballough through Richardstown to Gracedieu. The excavation of this stretch of corridor revealed two archaeological sites in 1988, both of which were fully excavated before construction (*Excavations 1988*). Monitoring of this stretch in 1999 did not reveal further archaeological features, soils or finds.

The NEP 3 pipeline extended through two fields forming part of the Gracedieu archaeological complex, revealed during pipe-laying in 1988 (Margaret Gowen in *Excavations 1988*, 15–17) and subsequently defined by Dúchas The Heritage Service. The NEP 3 route deviated from the NEP 2 corridor, running parallel to it on the west, and passed through the western edge of the Gracedieu archaeological complex from the north-east to south-west. This route lay west of the site of the cemetery and enclosure ditches uncovered and partially excavated in 1988. Low-level aerial photography and subsequent geophysical surveying revealed a double enclosure around the burial area and a further ditched enclosure close to the road to the north. An archaeological assessment followed by excavation was undertaken at the site before the pipeline construction (see No. 248 below).

From Gracedieu the pipeline reused the original route of NEP 2, extending southwards through Dollardstown to Saucerstown. A *fulacht fiadh* site (SMR 7:33) in Brownstown townland was uncovered and fully excavated during construction of NEP 2. At several locations the NEP 3 route diverged from the original route. No features of archaeological interest were uncovered along this stretch of pipeline. Some surface finds comprising mainly brownwares and modern delft wares with occasional clay pipe stems were noted but were not found to be associated with any features of archaeological interest.

Between Saucerstown and Westereave the entire length of pipeline followed the route of the original pipeline NEP 2, crossing the location of two recorded archaeological sites, both discovered and excavated during pipe-laying in 1988. This included a small enclosure at Saucerstown (SMR 11:83, *Excavations 1988*, 17–18, report by Eoin Halpin) and an unenclosed cemetery at Westereave (SMR 11:84, *Excavations 1988*, 18, report by Margaret Gowen). Geophysical survey and an archaeological assessment undertaken at Westereave before construction works did not reveal any further archaeological features or finds (see No. 278 below).

From Westereave the pipeline was laid through Laurestown to Broghan, where monitoring did not reveal any archaeological features. However, a number of artefact scatters, comprising mainly brownwares, delft wares and clay pipe stems, were recorded in conjunction with flint nodules, representing dumped spreads of farmhouse waste, occasionally associated with field drains and former field boundaries. The pipeline passed within 60m of SMR 11:23, a ringfort/graveyard at Common. Nothing of archaeological interest was encountered.

From Broghan the pipeline extended to Kilshane, following the line of NEP 2 between the townlands of Kilshane and Broghan. The pipeline itself switched to 5m east of the original line, and the original wayleave was reused and slightly widened to the end of this stage of pipeline at the block valve at Kilshane. The cemetery site at Kilshane (SMR 14:0490) uncovered during the NEP 2 operation (Margaret Gowen in *Excavations 1988*, 17) lies *c.* 420m north-east of the block valve. The cemetery extends to the west of the former pipeline corridor and may extend into the adjacent field on that side. The eastern limit of the burial area was defined during excavation.

Geophysical survey was undertaken before an archaeological assessment of the site took place, providing a number of targets for testing. A single archaeological feature was revealed and excavated in a location east of the cemetery site and does not appear to be related to it (see No. 253 below).

No further archaeological features or burials were encountered during monitoring of the pipeline construction.

*Malachy Conway for Margaret Gowen & Co. Ltd, 2 Killiney View, Albert Road Lower, Glenageary, Co. Dublin.*

**162. ROSEPARK, BALROTHERY**
Enclosures and associated landscape
32020 26121
SMR 5:05708, 5:05707
99E0155

A two-week pre-development testing programme was undertaken on a 7.82-acre site in the vicinity of a holy well (SMR 5:05707) and in the area of a significant concentration of cropmarks (SMR 5:05708), with a standing stone (SMR 5:05702) in an adjacent field. Eight cuttings were opened by machine, five north–south and three east–west. A consistent stratigraphy was revealed in all the cuttings, with a thin top sod overlying the ploughsoil, a mid- to dark brown, silty clay with a moderate amount of small stone, which in turn overlay the natural deposits. There is variation in the depth of ploughsoil, which seems to be the product of tillage across the site, with the elevated areas of the site having a limited depth (maximum 0.4m) while the low-lying areas have a greater accumulation of ploughsoil.

Sixty-nine features were identified. The principle concentration is in the south-western area of the site, which is also elevated. This area is represented on an aerial photograph by two circular cropmarks. The testing revealed the presence of a series of ditches, which appear to follow the contours of the slope. Furrows are also discernible within this area, as are pits and other occupation features, e.g. areas of burning.

The features that appear to comprise the principal enclosure(s) are F2–7 in Cutting 1; F47, F54 and F55 in Cutting 6; and F65 in Cutting 7. This conclusion has been reached from an analysis of an aerial photograph and an examination of the character, extent and location of all features revealed in the testing. F2 and F4 were sectioned, while F54 and F65 are characterised by very significant breaks in slope.

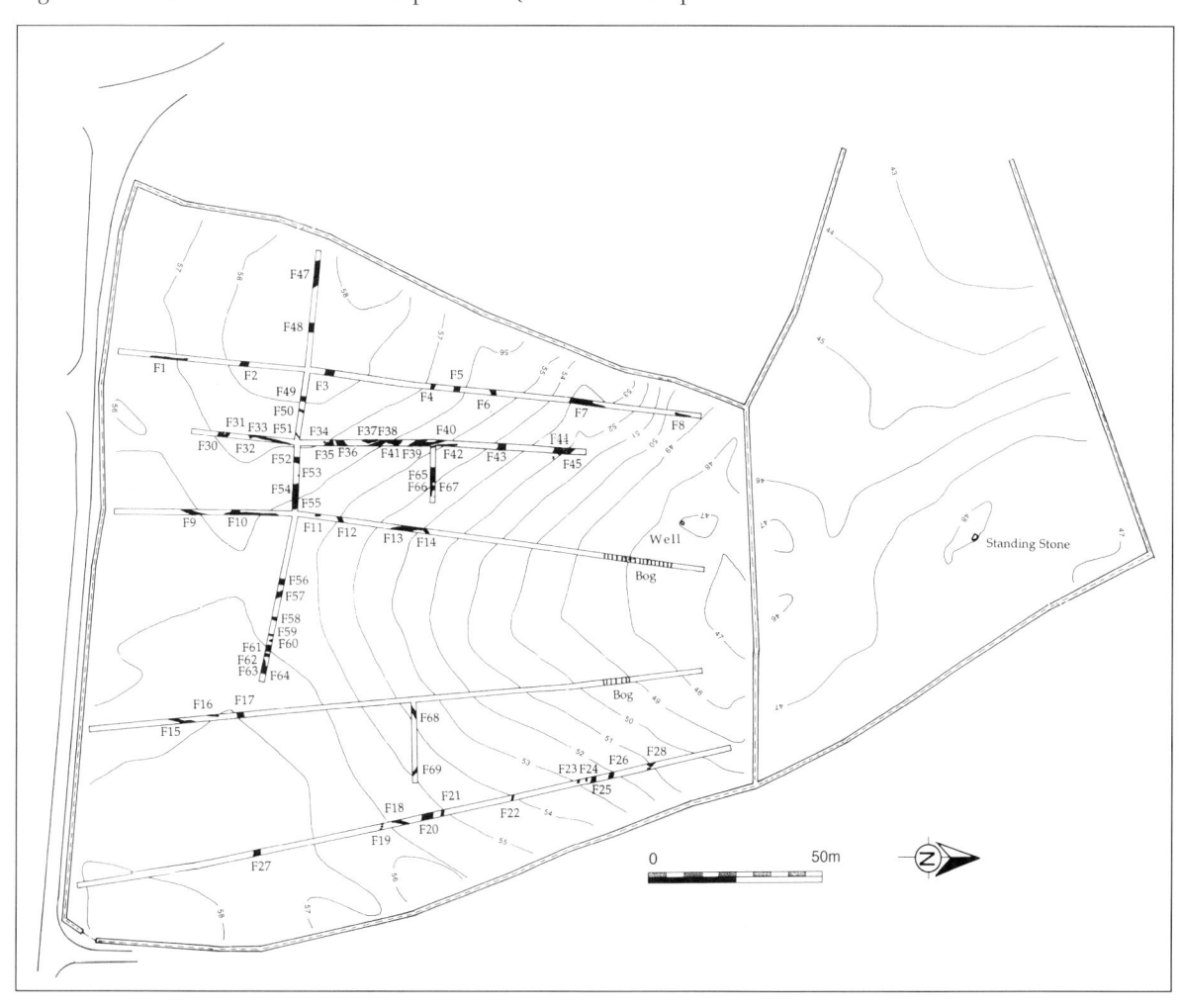

Plan of archaeological features at Rosepark, Balrothery.

A piece of worked flint and a piece of slag were recovered from F4. Fragments of bone and charcoal were recovered from F2 and F4.

The features throughout the rest of the site include furrows. Sections were cut through two of them. A section was also cut through a possible boundary feature that had evidence of a double ditch within it. Charcoal was recovered from these three features.

There appears to be a change in the axis of the cultivation furrows on the site, which is most apparent in Cutting 5, where F56–64 have a north–south axis, while in Cutting 4 F20–26 have an east–west axis. This change in axis may represent two separate patterns of land use.

The central area to the south-east of the holy well is the only part of the site lacking any discernible archaeological features. However, it is characterised by a small tract of bog. This central area also had some of the deepest deposits of ploughsoil.

The features identified appear to include the remains of partially destroyed enclosure(s) and evidence of a settlement landscape, including furrows, boundary features, areas of burning and the holy well. The landscape may represent a ringfort with its associated fields, enclosures and well.
*Christine Baker and Rónán Swan, Arch-Tech Ltd, 32 Fitzwilliam Place, Dublin 2.*

### 163. ROSEPARK, BALROTHERY
Enclosures and associated landscape
32020 26121
SMR 5:05708, 5:05707
99E0155 ext.

It was recommended that, should this development proceed in its proposed form, the entire area would need to be excavated. As a result of discussions with the National Monuments and Historic Properties Service and the developer, it was decided to proceed in a phased manner. Phase I was the south-western quadrant of the site, an area measuring a maximum of *c.* 95m east–west and 70m north–south, which encompassed *c.* 1.64 acres and rose from a level of 56m OD to the highest area of 58m OD. Soil-stripping took place over three-and-a-half weeks until groundworks were stopped at the request of the developer.

The topsoil varied in depth from a maximum of 1.3m along the southern field boundary to only 0.4m at the summit of the hill. It consisted of a mid- to dark brown, silty clay with moderate small stone inclusions and overlay a yellowish-orange, sandy natural. Most of the features were cut into natural subsoil.

A complex series of enclosures and associated occupation features (including two possible corn-drying kilns) was found, many of which had been previously indicated in the testing programme (No. 162 above).

The soil-stripping revealed clear evidence for multiple phases of concentric enclosing features in the exposed area, which seem to be replicated in the undisturbed portions of the site. Extensive evidence for occupation and associated activity has been identified across the site, concentrated on the hill crest. To date, only a portion of the inner enclosure has been exposed, and the enclosing ditches have been subject to very limited investigation. It is difficult to offer conclusive statements about the date of this site, but the presence of a small iron bill-hook of probable later first millennium AD date, together with the generally aceramic character of the finds, indicates that this is likely to be an enclosed settlement of the Early Christian period. Further, the large concentric enclosing features mark this site as being of a morphological type previously known only from aerial photography. The multiple phases of enclosures would also suggest that the site was occupied for some time. These conclusions indicate that this is a site of great archaeological importance, and any future works must take this into account.
*Christine Baker, Arch-Tech Ltd, 32 Fitzwilliam Place, Dublin 2.*

### 164. ST PETER'S CHURCH, BALROTHERY
Site of medieval church and graveyard
31991 26118
99E0026

A limited archaeological excavation was carried out at St Peter's Church, Balrothery, Co. Dublin, in January 1999. The proposed development consisted of the refurbishment of the church, part of which included the excavation of a drainage trench and manhole.

During the monitoring of the excavation of a new manhole, human remains were uncovered. Construction work was halted, and an area measuring 1.8m by 1.25m was archaeologically excavated. Three phases of burial were noted, the first phase consisting of a single individual who had evidently been inserted without prior knowledge of the location of earlier burials. This burial truncated the legs of an earlier burial. Phase 2 consisted of two burials, which were both interred above earlier burials without truncating them. This may suggest prior knowledge of the grave locations. Phase 3 consisted of three burials, all of which were placed in graves dug into the natural ground.

The total number of individuals present, including disarticulated remains, was twelve, and

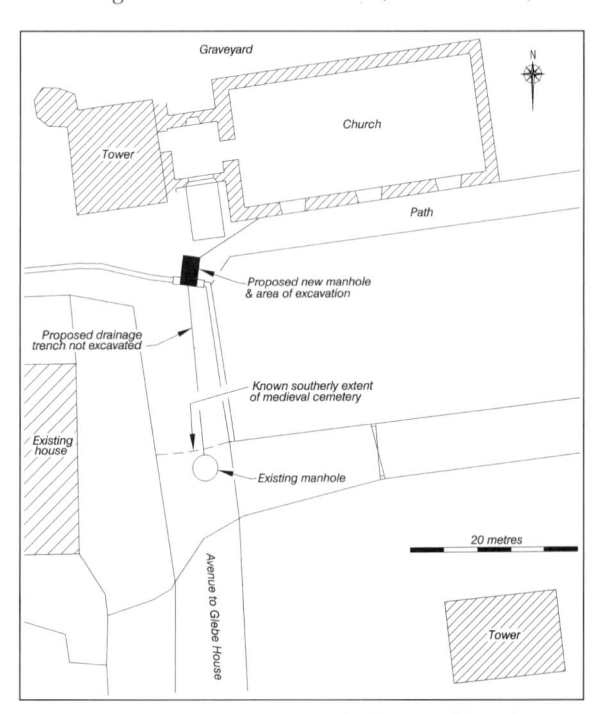

Location of excavated area at St Peter's Church, Balrothery.

they included three adult males, two adult females and seven juveniles. There was no evidence of coffin fittings within the graves, and it is probable that shrouds were used. Sherds of medieval pottery recovered from the burials of Phase 2 would suggest a 13th- to 14th-century date. Fragments of nails were also recovered from a clay loam layer with disarticulated human bone, above the *in situ* burials. These fragments may have been used as shroud pins, as has been suggested for some burials at St Peter's Church, Waterford.

A further trench excavated along the pipeline that leads from the new manhole to the existing manhole further south revealed more burials and indicated that the cemetery extended to at least this point. An alternative pumping mechanism was used for the pipeline rather than causing further disturbance to these burials.
*Donald Murphy, Archaeological Consultancy Services Ltd, 15 Trinity Street, Drogheda, Co. Louth.*

### 165. BLANCHARDSTOWN COLLEGE, BUSINESS AND TECHNOLOGY PARK, BUZZARDSTOWN AND CORDUFF, BLANCHARDSTOWN
No archaeological significance
99E0046
An assessment was undertaken at the site of a proposed College, Business and Technology Park at Blanchardstown, Co. Dublin. The site lies between Buzzardstown and Corduff, *c.* 2km north-west of Blanchardstown village and 2km north of the N3. The site comprises fifteen fields and is bounded by the Cruiserath and Ballycoolin roads to the north, a residential housing estate and public park (Lady's Well Park) to the south and Blanchardstown Road North to the east.

Four test-trenches were excavated at areas close to recorded monuments outside the proposed development site. Trenches 1 and 2 were excavated in Field 2 at the south-west corner of the site, close to Corduff mound (SMR 13:12) and Corduff House (SMR 13:25). Trenches 3 and 4 were excavated in Field 14 along the western edge of the proposed site, close to a church site in Buzzardstown (SMR 13:10) and a holy well site in the vicinity of Lady's Well Park to the south of Field 14.

Trenches 1 (east–west) and 2 (south-west/north-east) were 49m and 66m long respectively. Topsoil on average 0.3m deep was removed to reveal orange/brown clay loam 0.5m deep over grey boulder clay in both trenches. Trenches 3 (south-west/north-east) and 4 (north-west/south-east) were 69m and 44m long respectively. Removal of topsoil to a depth of 0.3m revealed a sandy clay loam on average 0.3m deep, which overlay gravelly clay subsoil. No deposits, features or finds of archaeological significance were encountered.
*Malachy Conway for Margaret Gowen & Co. Ltd, 2 Killiney View, Albert Road Lower, Glenageary, Co. Dublin.*

### 166. ESSO CENTENARY SERVICE STATION, CABINTEELY
Early Christian enclosed cemetery
SMR 26:119
98E0035 ext.
Monitoring during construction of the Centenary Service Station during January 1999, following the excavation of the site in 1998 (see *Excavations 1998*, 36–7), revealed a single adult inhumation burial along the eastern perimeter of the site. The burial, from Phase 6, was found *c.* 1m to the south of the northern site perimeter and lay in a supine position with head to the west and arms by its sides. No clear grave-cut could be discerned, and, while no finds were associated with the interment, a small quantity of disarticulated human bone was recovered from directly above the burial. The burial was removed for analysis and has been added to the corpus of 1153 recovered from the 1998 excavation. No further burials or finds were recovered during the remaining site works.
*Malachy Conway for Margaret Gowen & Co. Ltd, 2 Killiney View, Albert Road Lower, Glenageary, Co. Dublin.*

### 167. CABINTEELY
Cemetery
SMR 26:119
98E0582 ext.
The proposed addition of a front porch and rear extension to an existing dwelling at 'The Bungalow', Ards, Cabinteely, Co. Dublin, had been archaeologically tested in December 1998 (*Excavations 1998*, 35–6). The development was within the zone of archaeological potential of a recorded cemetery site. Some limited monitoring also took place under the porch area of the development on 22 May 1999. No features of archaeological significance were noted owing to extensive disturbance caused by the existing house services.
*Ken Hanley, 44 Eaton Heights, Cobh, Co. Cork.*

### 168. BANK OF IRELAND, OLD BRAY ROAD, CABINTEELY
No archaeological significance
99E0162
An assessment was carried out at the site of the Bank of Ireland Operations Centre, Old Bray Road, Cabinteely, Co. Dublin, on 27 April 1999 and involved the mechanical excavation of one test-trench across the footprint of the proposed development. The site is in Cabinteely village between the Old Bray Road (west) and the N11 dual carriageway (east) and lies *c.* 180m north of an enclosed cemetery at Mount Offaly (SMR 26:119), part of which was excavated during 1998 (*Excavations 1998*, 36–7, 98E0035).

One test-trench was excavated north–south through the central line of the proposed building on its southern side. The trench, 40m long and 1.3m wide, was positioned *c.* 35m south of the existing building and was excavated to the top of the natural subsoil deposits. The profile of the northern 15m of the trench revealed dark brown topsoil containing patterned ceramics of 19th–20th-century date and brownware of late 18th-century date, up to 0.6m deep. This overlay sterile, yellow clay loam containing numerous small stones. The southern 25m profile of the test-trench comprised dark brown topsoil with patterned ceramics of 19th–20th-century date 0.4m deep, over orange/brown clay loam containing numerous small stones 0.35m deep,

over sterile, brown clay containing decayed stones. No deposits, soils or finds of archaeological significance were revealed within the test-trench.
*Malachy Conway for Margaret Gowen & Co. Ltd, 2 Killiney View, Albert Road Lower, Glenageary, Co. Dublin.*

### 169. CHERRYWOOD SCIENCE AND TECHNOLOGY PARK, CHERRYWOOD
Archaeological landscape
32425 22322
98E0526, 99E0517, 99E0518, 99E0519, 99E0523

The Science and Technology Park at Cherrywood and Laughanstown is divided into a number of components, known as Park One, Park Two and the District Centre lands. A link road from the N11 to the proposed M50 motorway also goes through the Park. The works carried out to date are within the area of Science and Technology Park One.

Initially, geophysical analysis was carried out across most of the area, which was to be landscaped and developed during the construction of Park One. This work was undertaken by GeoArc Ltd and GSB Bradford and identified several potential archaeological features. Testing of these features revealed that many were simply geological variations in the subsoil and glacial till. Two of the sites, Sites 3 and 18, were identified during testing of the anomalies uncovered during the geophysical surveys. Most of the archaeological sites were identified during monitoring of ground disturbance works, carried out as part of the landscaping phase of the Park One development. In total, 21 locations were designated as archaeological sites for the purpose of recording during the on-site works. A number of these were subsequently dismissed as non-archaeological, although the site numbers were retained to avoid confusion.

After the initial testing and monitoring a number of sites were investigated and published in *Excavations 1998* (40–2). The locations around these sites were reassigned licence numbers this year to distinguish the separate landscape units that they represent. The areas were labelled A, B, C and D and are described as such below. All investigations in these areas are now complete.

A number of other features, including the remaining 19th-century agricultural fabric such as field walls, banks and drains, were recorded as part of the pre-development and monitoring works, as was a footbridge crossing over the old Harcourt Street–Shankill railway line, which was laid through the site in the 1850s and closed down in 1958.

The Park One area of the Science and Technology Park lay within lands belonging to the Domville estate, which took in much of Loughlinstown and the surrounding area. In 1179 Tully Church, which is immediately to the north-west of the development, was donated by a Hiberno-Norse family, the MacTorcaills, to Christchurch. It is likely that the lands on which the Science and Technology Park is being built were also under the control of the MacTorcaills.

The area comprises a reasonably discrete landscape unit, as it crosses two low hills (at 40m and 48m OD) separated by a glen and bordered by the Loughlinstown River to the south and the Shanaganagh River to the east. The confluence of the two rivers lay to the south-east of the development, from where the Shanaganagh River flows on out into Killiney Bay.

The area to the north was monitored by Ed O'Donovan during a previous development *(Excavations 1997*, 25, 97E0279), when a number of isolated cremations were uncovered. Tully Church and the Laughanstown wedge tomb are to the north-west and west of the development respectively. There are also portal tombs nearby at Ballybrack and Brennanstown.

In overall terms the area has now produced evidence for the use of the lands from the Neolithic onwards. The earlier evidence is mainly of settlement, primarily within the glen or on a terrace on an east-facing slope in the glen (Area B, Site 11). This includes Neolithic and Beaker material. From the Bronze Age we begin to get evidence of burial, associated with cordoned urns or unaccompanied, on top of the low hills. This continues into the Iron Age, when a ring-barrow (Area A, Site 4) and a larger barrow (Area C, Site 18) were constructed on both hills. To date, no evidence of Iron Age settlement has been identified within the glen. The use of the hilltops for burial continues into the Later Iron Age, when Site 18 was reused as an inhumation cemetery. A possible drying kiln and another structure (also within the enclosure) appear to be contemporary with this cemetery.

Sometime after the cemetery went out of use, and was no longer recognised as a burial-ground, the large enclosure was reused as a settlement site. A large rectangular building and then two smaller buildings were erected within the enclosure. The finds associated with this phase have strong Norse and Hiberno-Norse affinities.

The later evidence from the area is mainly agricultural, such as furrows, drains and field walls, although traces of the hut sites contemporary with the Loughlinstown Military Camp (1791–9) were also uncovered.

A summary of each area of the Science and Technology Park is given below.

*Area A (99E0517)*
Area A lay on top of a low hill overlooking the confluence of the Loughlinstown and Shanaganagh rivers and measured *c.* 40m (north–south) by 40m. The top of the hill was at around 40m OD. Three archaeological sites (Sites 4, 5 and 7) were identified in Area A during the monitoring phase. The first (Site 4) consisted of a late prehistoric, probably Iron Age, ring-barrow. The other two sites were single features in the vicinity of the ring-barrow. Site 7, at least, appears to be contemporary with the ring-barrow. These sites are summarised in *Excavations 1998*, 41, and no new features were uncovered during further monitoring this year.

*Area B (99E0518)*
Area B lay in a glen between Area A and another low hill to the west, overlooking the Loughlinstown River, and measured *c.* 100m (north–south) by 80m. The base of the glen was at about 33m OD, *c.* 7m lower than the top of the hill containing Area A, to the east, and *c.* 15m lower than the hill to the west

containing Areas C and D. The glen was between 30m and 50m wide with two fairly steep slopes on either side.

Four archaeological sites (Sites 2, 3, 8 and 11) were identified in Area B during the monitoring. A range of evidence was uncovered in this area, including *fulachta fiadh* (Sites 3, 8 and 11) and occupation material from the Neolithic (Sites 3 and 11) through to the Bronze Age (Sites 2 and 11). There was also evidence of later activity from two sites dating to the 1790s military camp (Sites 3 and 11). Sites 2, 3 and 8 were summarised in *Excavations 1998*, 40–2, and so only Site 11 is described below.

*Site 11: multi-period*
The earliest phases of Site 11 were cut into and below a soil level (F278) below a deposit of *fulacht fiadh*-firing debris (F215). The buried soil level was up to 0.15m deep in places. Some sherds of modified carinated bowls were uncovered from F278, along with a javelinhead, a leaf-shaped arrowhead, scrapers and knapping debris. A series of features was recorded within the subsoil below F278, including some stake-holes and four small cobbled surfaces.

A number of post- and stake-holes cut through F278 also appeared to substantially pre-date F215. Some of these features appeared to represent the remains of a subrectangular structure, 5m east–west by 3.5m. This survived mostly as a series of post- and stake-holes with two large post-holes at the south-east, possibly indicating an entrance. This interpretation is somewhat conjectural.

Another group of features was assigned a date immediately preceding the *fulacht fiadh* phase. These features included two possible hearths, a substantial pit and further possible structural remains. These probably date to the Bronze Age. The remains of two 3.5m-diameter circles of post-holes could be identified on the ground, with the two possible hearths at *c.* 1.5–2m outside of each. Again, the condition of the surviving remains makes this interpretation conjectural.

Ardmarks were also preserved beneath the main *fulacht fiadh* deposit (F215), which seem to represent activity associated with the initial ground-stripping for the construction/use of the *fulacht fiadh*.

The *fulacht fiadh* covered most of the area of the site and survived as an oval, unlined trough and a large spread of burnt stone and charcoal.

A series of furrows had been excavated through the burnt spread. A small number of sherds of medieval pottery (green-glazed local wares) probably dating to the 13th/14th century or later were recovered from the topsoil on the site and may be contemporary with the furrows. At the very least, the furrows pre-date the 1790s, and they may be substantially earlier.

The site was reoccupied during the military camp phase in the 1790s, with evidence of possible hut platforms and a cobbled area. A field bank from an 1812 land sale was built over the site, and a number of drains and pipes were also laid through the site in the 19th century and later.

*Area C (99E0523)*
Area C lay to the south-west of Area D and measured *c.* 60m north–south by 80m. Both areas lay on a low hill to the west of Area B, at around 47m OD. The southern end of the hill overlooks the Loughlinstown River. Two sites were identified during a geophysical survey and test-trenching in the area. The larger site (Site 18) was a 41m-diameter circular enclosure. This provided evidence of its use from the later prehistoric period through to the 11th/12th century. A small Early Bronze Age flat cemetery (Site 19) was found 20m east of the enclosure.

*Site 18: multi-period*

*Later prehistoric/Iron Age*
A 43m-diameter subcircular enclosure was identified on the site, *c.* 20m west of the earlier cremation cemetery (Site 19, below). The enclosure was defined by a continuous 2–3m-wide ditch, which was between 0.4m and 1.8m deep.

Cremations were identified at various depths within the ditch or even scattered along the sides, suggesting that the use of the enclosure as a burial site took place over an extended period of time. At the western side of the site, in two places, a setting of stones had been placed in the ditch and cremated bone placed on top of it. Two pits were also inserted into the silted-up ditch fill and covered over with a large boulder.

A small quantity of struck flint was recovered from the site, including a thumbnail scraper. Some blue glass beads, a bronze fragment, a bone pin and an iron pin from separate deposits of burnt bone suggest that the site was probably constructed in the Iron Age. Only one cremation was found intact in the centre of the site, and the fragments of burnt human bone in the grave fills of a later inhumation cemetery probably derive from cremation burials disturbed during the later interments.

It is unclear whether any of the post-holes in the centre of the site are associated with this phase.

*The inhumation cemetery*
In the later Iron Age (possibly the 6th and/or 7th century) the interior was reused as a cemetery. Thirty-eight burials were recovered, although around half were disarticulated or badly disturbed

Adult male and female burials were present, as were child burials. Most were laid in earth-dug graves orientated roughly east–west, with the head to the west. In the burials where the skull area survived intact, some 76% had the head protected by a number of stones. This generally took the form of a large stone placed on either side of the skull.

In two instances buckles, one a D-shaped belt-buckle, were found, as were a fragment of an iron pin and another iron fragment. These indicate at least some clothed burials; otherwise, grave-goods were absent. Animal bone was found in one or two graves, as was burnt bone, but this material may be intrusive. An iron spade shoe was uncovered from one of the grave fills, along with a second iron object.

*Early occupation phase*
In the period before the Norse occupation of the site two structures were built at the southern end, away from the burials on the site (although one burial, an

isolated, badly disturbed inhumation, lay between the two). The eastern structure appears to be some form of keyhole-shaped drying kiln. The western structure (Structure 4) was described by an oval setting of post-holes containing a sunken area. A bone pin/needle was recovered from the sunken area.

These two structures appear to represent some form of use of the site broadly contemporary with the inhumation cemetery.

Two parts of the ditch, at the east and west, were deliberately backfilled as entrances, possibly at this time. Some sherds of an unidentified type of coarse pottery were recovered from the eastern entrance. A single sherd of B ware has also been identified from topsoil finds on the site. Other finds that may date to this phase include some tiny bone comb fragments and a lignite bracelet.

*The Norse settlement*
At least two phases of Norse settlement were also present on the site. These were associated with a long house (Structure 1) and at least two later structures (Structures 2 and 3) and pits. A number of Norse artefacts were found in the fill of the ditch, including an amber bead, an 11th/12th-century bone comb and some ferrous artefacts that were paralleled in more secure Norse features. A three-pronged object and a number of knives were among the iron objects recovered from the ditch.

The earlier Norse phase saw the construction of a long house (Structure 1), 17.5m long and between 5.75m and 6.8m wide, which was roughly trapezoidal in outline. The entrance of a later house (Structure 2) overlay the north-eastern corner, and portions of the walls had been destroyed by 19th-century field drains.

The long house was followed by a more dispersed settlement consisting of two buildings (Structures 2 and 3), at either end of a north–south axis through the site. A large rectangular pit, west of the two structures, was also contemporary with this stage.

The northern structure (Structure 2) was an aisled house 8.15m by 5.4m with a single entrance, at the north. The outer walls were slightly bow-sided. There were pairs of opposing roof supports at either end of the building and a number of larger post-holes along the side-walls and internally, which must also have supported the roof. A number of finds were recovered from cobbling associated with the entranceway, including a ringed pin, bone comb fragments and other small metal finds.

The second structure (3) was rectangular and measured 9.4m by 5.3m. This survived as a rough setting of post-holes.

The large rectangular pit contained a bronze ringed pin, a three-pronged object, other fragmentary bronze and iron objects and a decorated whale bone plaque. Whale bone plaques are typically associated with wealthy Norse women and suggest Norse settlement here in the 9th/10th century.

*Site 19: cremation cemetery*
A small, unenclosed cremation cemetery was also identified beyond the eastern limits of the site. Two cremations contained some body and rimsherds of a cordoned urn (or urns) and are very much of a token nature; they date to the Early or Middle Bronze Age. The largest cremation contained no pottery but was inserted within a pit slightly larger than the actual cremation deposit. The pit containing the cremated bone was 0.7m in diameter and 0.27m deep.

*Area D (99E0519)*
Area D contained a single site (Site 21). This survived as a circular paved area that may represent the remains of some form of drying kiln. This site is medieval in date.

The paved area was 2.6m in diameter, and the paving itself was fairly irregular, although it was a generally a single course deep. The ground surface had been deliberately lowered by 0.2m for the paving to be put in place. A fragment of a millstone was used as part of the stone surface. Some of the other stones may also have been reused from elsewhere. Another stone had a concave depression on one side (a pivot stone?).

Some other small finds were recovered between the stones and the topsoil overlying the feature, including a small number of sherds of local cooking and glazed wares.

There was a small, 0.8m by 0.5m, rectangular area of paving attached to the main area, perhaps marking the location of a flue. There was a single post-hole at the opposite side to the 'flue'.

*John Ó Néill for Margaret Gowen & Co. Ltd, 2 Killiney View, Albert Road Lower, Glenageary, Co. Dublin.*

**170. KILCARBERRY DISTRIBUTION PARK, NANGOR, CLONDALKIN**
Adjacent to monuments
**SMR 17:37 (vicinity of)**
**98E0572**
Archaeological monitoring at this site was ongoing when the summaries published in *Excavations 1998* (42) were written. A further three days' monitoring was required in January 1999 to bring this project to completion.

The development is for the provision of roads, sewers, water mains and other ancillary infrastructural works to serve an Industrial Distribution Park. Because of the presence of recorded archaeological remains within the general landscape, *Dúchas* The Heritage Service recommended that archaeological monitoring be requested as a condition to any planning permission. Reference to the Sites and Monuments Record reveals the presence of a number of monuments within the general landscape, although there are no known archaeological sites within the proposed development area. A 15th-century tower-house (SMR 17:34), recorded on the Down Survey of c. 1655, is 600m north of the development site. Nangor Castle (SMR 17:37), a castle incorporated into a 19th-century mansion, is 500m east of the development area. All buildings on the site have now been demolished, however, leaving no surface trace of the earlier building. The site of Kilbride Castle (SMR 21:4) is 600m south of the proposed development, although again no visible surface remains are present. An unplastered wall is extant, but it does not contain any cut stone, although it was probably constructed using material from the castle. Slightly to the south-east of this are a church and graveyard (SMR 21:00501), a ringfort (21:00502) and earthworks (21:00503). The church is in ruins and stands in a circular raised graveyard at the edge of a broad-bottomed valley. It is possible that this is the site of an early ecclesiastical enclosure.

Monitoring has failed to reveal any archaeological features on the site, with the exception of one 1m-wide north–south modern field drain. Finds have been restricted to the north-west corner of the site, but these include only several small sherds of post-medieval pottery, along with several sherds of modern pottery, all recovered from the topsoil.

Removal of topsoil has revealed naturally deposited limestone bedrock across the site, with occasionally a *c.* 0.5m-thick natural layer of friable, mid-grey, fine, silty clay with moderate stone inclusions, 30–70mm, evenly distributed, sealing the bedrock layer and sealed by topsoil.

*Dermot Nelis, IAC Ltd, 8 Dungar Terrace, Dun Laoghaire, Co. Dublin.*

### 171. OLD MILL ROAD/NANGOR ROAD, CLONDALKIN
Precinct of monastic site
O068315
98E0343 ext.

A condition of the planning permission required a site assessment before development. The site is within the zone of archaeological potential of Clondalkin as defined by the Urban Survey of County Dublin, carried out by the Archaeological Survey of Ireland.

Clondalkin was an early ecclesiastical site, founded by St Mochua in the 7th century and was plundered by the Vikings in 833 (Gwynn and Hadcock 1988, 31). There is evidence that the Vikings built a settlement nearby in the 9th century—the name of the nearby townland of Raheen is the only surviving possible evidence for this fort (Bradley, 215). The area was granted as a manor to the See of Dublin by Hugh de Lacy, and there is also evidence that the village had borough status. By the 17th century the village seems to have shrunk (Bradley, 216).

It is likely that the monastic site was enclosed by a circular feature such as a ditch or a bank and ditch. The line of this ditch may be preserved in the street pattern formed by Orchard Lane and Main Street to the east of the round tower. It was considered possible that the development site is within the line of the ditch at its western limit.

The site is on the side of a cul-de-sac and is bordered on the south-west by a millpond and sluice. It was covered with building rubble that appeared to be dumped some time ago, as vegetation covered it. The development comprised three blocks at the back of the site, close to the boundary fence.

A mill stood on the site in the 19th century and was demolished sometime in the 20th century.

Six trenches tested the development site. The area closest to the millpond was avoided as the developer was afraid that trenching would undermine the bank enclosing the pond, resulting in flooding of the site. The trenches revealed evidence for major dumping of building rubble, possibly from the demolition of the mill-house here and/or brought in from elsewhere. The rubble contained brick and stone. Two stone shores crossed the site from the south-west towards the north-east. They were cut into the lower layers of rubble fill and were sealed by the upper levels. A deposit of grey silt in Trench 4 was interpreted as the remains of a possible pond or water-filled feature that was reclaimed when the building rubble was deposited.

There was no evidence for archaeological material in the test-trenches.

*References*
Bradley, J. *Urban Survey of Co. Dublin*, 215.
Gwynn, A. and Hadcock, R.N. 1988 *Medieval religious houses: Ireland*. Dublin.

*Rosanne Meenan, Roestown, Drumree, Co. Meath.*

### 172. COMMON
Environs of possible ringfort and graveyard
31239 24583
SMR 11:23
99E0693

An assessment was carried out at the site of proposed residential dwellings at Common, Co. Dublin, in the barony of Nethercross. The greenfield site consists of an irregularly shaped field with pronounced north–south undulations, currently under pasture, lying on the west side of the Oldbawn Road, east and south-east of which is St Margaret's Golf and Country Club, in Skephubble townland. The site of a possible ringfort and graveyard, shown on the 1837 1st edition OS map, is in the south-east corner of the field, now occupied by a modern bungalow. Local tradition describes this area as 'Kit's Green, the site of an old fort or buying place', although the townland name 'Common' is most likely derived from the Norman-French *comun,* which denotes public land. Archaeological monitoring of a Bord Gáis reinforcement pipeline (see No. 161 above) along the east side of the Oldbawn Road during September 1999 did not reveal any archaeological features or finds.

The assessment was undertaken on 30 November 1999 under recommendation from *Dúchas* before a planning application and focused on the area closest to the site of the ringfort/graveyard. The south-eastern edge of the proposed development is *c.* 34m west of the hedge surrounding the dwelling now built on the ringfort site, and the proposed access road into the site from the Oldbawn Road is *c.* 15m south of a delineated dwelling in the north-east corner of the field. Excavation of three test-trenches was undertaken with the aid of a mechanical excavator.

Trench 1 was positioned north-east/south-west along the eastern side of the proposed development site. It measured 106m by 1.2m. Dark brown topsoil on average 0.25m deep overlay grey/brown, gravelly clay subsoil across the southern 60m stretch of the trench and orange/brown clay over the remainder. The change in the underlying subsoil reflects a gradual decrease in slope from south to north.

Trench 2 was parallel to Trench 1, 38m to the

west. It measured 100m by 1.2m and in profile revealed dark brown topsoil on average 0.25m deep overlying grey/brown, gravelly clay 0.35m deep and orange/brown clay 0.3m deep, the latter confined to the northern 30m stretch of the trench. As with the Trench 1 sequence, the change in the underlying subsoil reflects a gradual decrease in ground level from south to north.

Trench 3 was perpendicular (west–east) to the north end of Trench 2. It was excavated in interrupted fashion, comprising four trenches measuring 10m by 1.2m and set c. 10m apart. The purpose of these trenches was to test the site of the proposed access road into the site from the Oldbawn Road. Dark brown topsoil 0.3–0.4m deep overlay orange/brown clay at least 0.2m deep, in turn over very gravelly, orange/brown clay.

The assessment did not reveal any soils, features or finds of archaeological significance. Dúchas The Heritage Service recommended archaeological monitoring of all groundworks across the western margin of the proposed development site.

*Malachy Conway, Archaeological Consultancy Services Ltd, 15 Trinity Street, Drogheda, Co. Louth.*

### 173. 1–7 ST AGNES ROAD, CRUMLIN
Medieval church enclosure
31198 23198
99E0305

A limited excavation of a proposed residential development was carried out at 1–7 St Agnes Road, Crumlin, Dublin, in July 1999. Previous testing of the site by Archaeological Projects Ltd (*Excavations 1998*, 43, 98E0362) revealed a ditch feature traversing the site from east to west. The ditch possibly represents an outer enclosing element around the medieval churchyard to the north of the present development site. The proposed development involves the construction of twelve houses, two of which would impinge on the enclosing ditch.

Two areas measuring 10m by 8.5m and 10m by 7.5m were excavated in the area of the ditch to be affected by the development. Both areas revealed consistent stratigraphy over the northern part of the site, and natural boulder clay was encountered at 0.7m below present ground level. It would appear that the ground above the natural soil had been disturbed in post-medieval to modern times, and the only surviving archaeological deposits were cut into the subsoil. These consist of the ditch and cultivation furrows in the area south of the ditch. The fill of the ditch was fairly consistent in the two areas examined, with a natural, grey silting of the ditch near the bottom followed by a stony, brown clay of late medieval date. The ditch almost certainly represents an enclosing element around the medieval church site and was purposely infilled in the later medieval period. The present graveyard wall may be indicative of an inner circular enclosure. The cultivation furrows uncovered during previous testing at this site are probably late medieval in date and occur outside the enclosing ditch of the medieval church.

*Donald Murphy, Archaeological Consultancy Services Ltd, 15 Trinity Street, Drogheda, Co. Louth.*

### 174. 41–42 BARNHILL ROAD (REAR OF), DALKEY
Urban
O263269
99E0060

Two test-trenches were excavated on the site and revealed very similar deposits. Dark brown, humic, rich garden soil, containing a large amount of modern rubbish and tree roots, was found to directly overlie light yellow/brown clay subsoil. No archaeological features or finds were revealed on the site.

*Avril Purcell, Margaret Gowen & Co. Ltd, 2 Killiney View, Albert Road Lower, Glenageary, Co. Dublin.*

### 175. COURTYARD, ST PATRICK'S ROAD, DALKEY
No archaeological significance
O265269
99E0102

Two test-trenches were opened on the site. Both revealed similar deposits: 18th- and 19th-century material sitting above stony, yellow/brown subsoil. The site was of no archaeological significance.

*Avril Purcell, Margaret Gowen & Co. Ltd, 2 Killiney View, Albert Road Lower, Glenageary, Co. Dublin.*

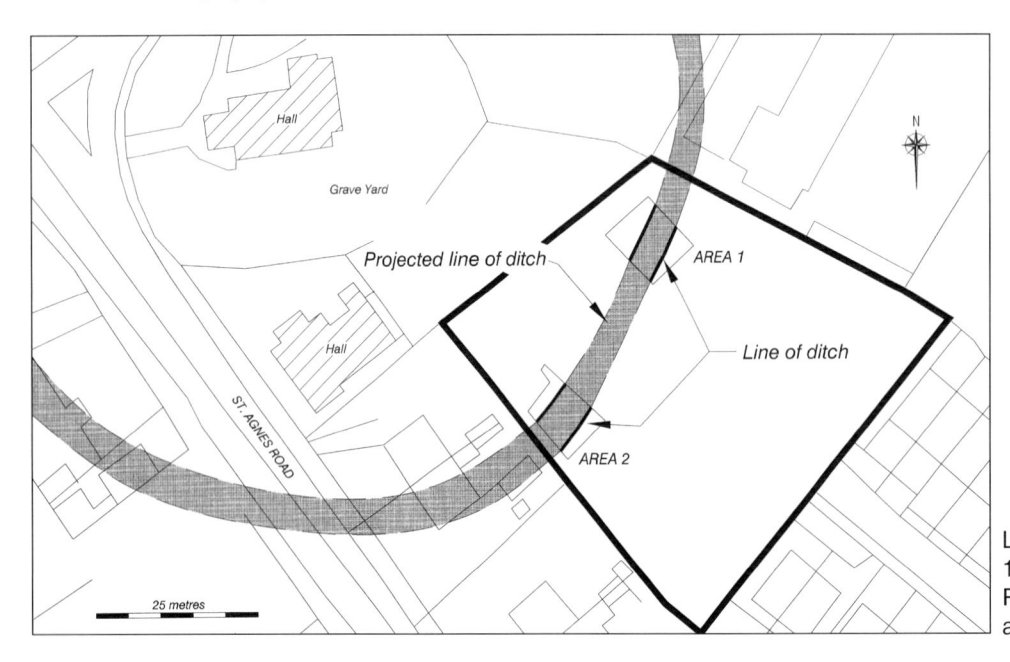

Line of ditch at 1–7 St Agnes Road, uncovered and projected.

### 176. TURVEY AVENUE, DONABATE
Medieval/post-medieval
O228499
SMR 12:5 (adjacent to)
99E0690

Test excavation was undertaken at a site at Turvey Avenue, Donabate, Co. Dublin, on 25 November 1999. Fingal County Council intends to widen the footpath on the south side of Turvey Avenue, which will entail the scarping of the existing slope to an estimated depth of 0.6m below present ground level. The works to be carried out are adjacent to the medieval church of St Patrick.

The fields to the north of the church of St Patrick slope steeply to Turvey Avenue. There is a considerable drop (c. 0.75m) to the existing footpath along Turvey Avenue, resulting from soil build-up along the field boundary. This may represent a plough lynchet. It was noted that a greater build-up of soil occurred at the eastern end of the field, i.e. closest to the tower and church, than elsewhere. The ground is currently in grazing.

Five trenches were excavated by mechanical excavator. A considerable amount of activity, ranging in date from probably the medieval period to the 19th–early 20th century, was represented in the test-trenches.

The trenches excavated revealed a thick (max. 1.35m) depth of ploughsoil, of probable medieval date. No cultivation furrows or ridges were evident in the soil, and there was no apparent stratification, except that of the upper humic sod level. Finds of recent date were not recovered from the ploughsoil, except where it was evident that a pit (Trench 4) cut into it. No finds of medieval pottery were made from the ploughsoil, but a coin, identified by Michael Kenny as a 'Patrick' dating to 1564, was recovered.

Pits containing food debris, bone and shell were uncovered in Trench 1. While these may relate to the cottages present on the north side of Turvey Avenue, there is a strong possibility that they are late medieval in date.

Finds of more recent date were recovered from the upper black loam.
*Claire Walsh, Archaeological Projects Ltd, 25A Eaton Square, Terenure, Dublin 6W.*

### 177. ALL HALLOWS, CHURCH AVENUE, DRUMCONDRA
Post-medieval
3164 2371
97E0383

Two areas of investigation were cleared on this site, which fronts onto Church Street, Drumcondra, and adjoins the graveyard at the west side of the medieval parish church of All Hallows. One was to further expose a ditch feature identified in an original site assessment by Paul Logue in 1997 (*Excavations 1997*, 30). This was found to be a natural low point rather than a ditch. Nevertheless, after a small quantity of medieval pottery was found in a layer that abutted the north wall of the site, the whole of this wall was exposed to foundation level and an elevation of this stone foundation was drawn. It was concluded that the medieval pottery was redeposited along with later ceramics and that the wall was post-medieval in date.
*Martin Reid, 37 Errigal Road, Drimnagh, Dublin 12, for ADS Ltd.*

### 178. 43–45 ABBEY STREET, DUBLIN
Urban medieval, post-medieval
99E0177

Two test-trenches were mechanically excavated at an existing basement level 2.2m below present street level. There was an overall uniformity of stratigraphy throughout the site, consisting of a rubble infill layer that overlay the 18th-century black, organic refuse material. This deposit was revealed mainly in the western side of the site for a depth of c. 0.4m and included 18th-century ceramics, clay pipe stem and shell.

A small, cellar-like feature adjacent to the western boundary wall of the site appeared to form part of an original 18th-century basement.

No other archaeological features or deposits were revealed during the monitoring of the underpinning or general excavation of the site area.
*Helen Kehoe, c/o Margaret Gowen & Co. Ltd, 2 Killiney View, Albert Road Lower, Glenageary, Co. Dublin.*

### 179. 42–51 BENBURB STREET, DUBLIN
Urban
O142345
99E0413

Six test-trenches were opened on the site, all of which were extremely deep. Substantial deposits of gravel and cobbles were revealed, above which was 18th- and 19th-century material. No features or finds of archaeological significance were revealed on this site; however, further work is to be undertaken.
*Avril Purcell, Margaret Gowen & Co. Ltd, 2 Killiney View, Albert Road Lower, Glenageary, Co. Dublin.*

### 180. 35–36 BOW STREET, DUBLIN
Urban
O145342
96E0371

The assessment was undertaken as an addition to site assessment initially carried out in 1996. To date, no deposits shown to be earlier than the 17th century have been uncovered at Church Street/North King Street, and none was encountered on this site in the test-trench.
*Claire Walsh, Archaeological Projects Ltd, 25A Eaton Square, Terenure, Dublin 6W.*

### 181. NAPPER TANDY PUBLIC HOUSE, BRIDE STREET, DUBLIN
Urban
31529 13375
SMR 18:02073 (vicinity of)
99E0075

The development site, designed for apartment accommodation, is in an area of archaeological and historical importance. It is very close to two medieval ecclesiastical sites, that of St Bride's (SMR 18:02073) and the Norman church of St Michael le Pole (18:02082). As St Bride's (Brigid's) Church (from which Bride Street takes its name) is of pre-Norman origin, it is to be presumed that Bride Street itself is likely to be pre-Norman.

The site is also c. 100m outside the walled medieval town of Dublin and is on the junction of two medieval streets. It has been suggested by Andy Halpin, who carried out work here in 1992

(*Excavations 1992*, 17–18, 92E0054), that suburban settlement spread along the Bride Street axis during the 13th century, if not earlier. At the southern end of Bride Street, which is furthest away from the main focus of medieval settlement in Dublin, is the palace of St Sepulchre, residence of the archbishops of Dublin from the late 12th century onwards. Further evidence of the archaeological importance of the area is provided by the recording of a number of finds from 'opposite the church' in Bride Street, which include an Early Bronze Age halberd, a sword, a spearhead and a shield-boss, which probably derive from a Viking burial, along with another iron spearhead, eight bronze pins apparently found with a human skull, and a bronze seal, which is probably medieval in date.

Speed's map of 1610 records buildings on the very northern corner of Bride Street, opposite St Bride's Church, i.e. in the same spot as the development site. A number of archaeological programmes have been undertaken in the immediate vicinity of the development site. In 1993, immediately south of the site, Judith Carroll undertook archaeological trial-trenching (*Excavations 1993*, 15, 93E0028) and recorded substantial deposits of rubble with brick and mortar, interpreted as the result of cellaring on the site. Halpin (see above), along the eastern side of Bride Street, recorded undisturbed boulder clay, where not truncated by 18th/19th-century foundations, occurring over the site at a depth between 1.5m and 1.7m below present ground level. Immediately over boulder clay in many parts of the site was a layer of brown, garden-type soil, between 0.4m and 1.5m thick and with an occasional amount of ceramic material of 13th/14th-century date. An excavation was undertaken by Mary McMahon in 1993 (*Excavations 1993*, 15, 93E0153) in an area *c*. 25m south of the present site, in the vicinity of one of the test-trenches opened during Halpin's trenching (see above), where a charcoal spread was recorded on what was interpreted as natural boulder clay. The excavation confirmed the presence of archaeological activity from within the general area of the development site. As part of the present programme, two test-trenches were mechanically excavated. Trench 1 measured 15m east–west x 1.5m and was excavated in the western and middle parts of the site. Because of road-widening, the present street frontages are set back considerably from the medieval frontages, although some medieval and post-medieval cultural deposits would still be expected along this part of the proposed site. Trench 2 measured 8m north–south by 1.5m and was excavated in the eastern end of the site.

Both trenches revealed activity associated with post-medieval cellars and modern infill material. The earliest phase of activity revealed in Trench 1 related to three *in situ* north–south post-medieval walls. These were sealed by two layers containing red brick deposited when the cellars went out of use. A cellar for the public house was excavated in the western part of the site, and this was infilled by material containing beer kegs from when the bar went out of use.

There was a friable, mid-green, silty clay with occasional animal bone inclusions at the eastern end of Trench 1. This layer also contained frequent red brick evenly distributed with plastic bag material. It is suggested that this layer represents the deposition in the modern period of a disturbed archaeological horizon and represents relict remains of cultural activity from the Bride Street area.

Trench 2 revealed post-medieval remains associated with cellars previously recorded on the site. As with Trench 1, there was evidence for modern infilling of the site having caused disturbance to previously *in situ* archaeological deposits.
*Dermot Nelis, IAC Ltd, 8 Dungar Terrace, Dun Laoghaire, Co. Dublin.*

### 182. IVEAGH TRUST, BULL ALLEY STREET/BRIDE STREET, DUBLIN
Medieval activity
3152 2337
98E0218 ext.

A small pre-development excavation was carried out during February and March 1999 within the main courtyard of the Iveagh Trust buildings. Previous assessment here by James Eogan had shown that deposits of medieval date were present (*Excavations 1998*, 45, 98E0218).

The excavation, which measured a maximum of 8m x 5m, revealed evidence of a medieval gully, possibly for drainage, as well as several pits and random post-holes also of medieval date. Naturally occurring subsoil was found to slope to the south and east. A substantial amount of estuarine material was found banked up against the subsoil.

Although only generalisations can be made because of the size of the excavation, it was assumed that the estuarine deposits were flood material from the River Poddle, part of which it is thought ran close to the site. The raised area of naturally occurring subsoil may represent a small headland within the Poddle flood-plain.

Pottery dating primarily to the 13th century was found, consisting of wares of native, English and French manufacture, as well as the remains of two stick-pins.
*Audrey Gahan for ADS Ltd, Windsor House, 11 Fairview Strand, Dublin 3.*

### 183. ST MARY'S ABBEY, 133A CAPEL STREET/23 MARY STREET LITTLE, DUBLIN
Site of medieval abbey
3152 2345
99E0080

Testing was undertaken at this site. The developers proposed to keep their ground disturbance to a minimum, and thus only a limited area was required to be tested, in the area of the proposed lift shaft.

Two cuttings were mechanically excavated to the underlying natural. It was clear that the site had been extensively disturbed by cellarage, and thus the proposed development was unlikely to have a major impact on any potential archaeological remains. No features of archaeologial significance were recovered.
*Rónán Swan, Arch-Tech Ltd, 32 Fitzwilliam Place, Dublin 2.*

### 184. CARMAN'S HALL, DUBLIN
Medieval
O1485033650
98E0254 ext.

Phase 2 test-trenching was carried out on 24 May

1999 at a development site at Carman's Hall/Ash Street/Garden Lane, Dublin 8 (see *Excavations 1998*, 46–7, for Phase 1). The results of the trenching confirmed the presence of a deposit of 'garden soil' of medieval date across the entire site. The medieval soil, which overlay subsoil, was overlain by a post-medieval soil layer and the demolition levels of recent buildings. The conditions imposed in 1998 were stipulated for archaeological monitoring in 1999, with the addition of a requirement to search the medieval and post-medieval garden soils with a metal-detector. This was done under licence 99R0002.

Clearance of the western part of the site was undertaken over two weeks in June–July 1999, during a spell of dry weather. Consequently, ground conditions were good for the retrieval of finds and the observation of features. No features of medieval date occurred over this side of the site. The medieval soil F103 was uniform in appearance and depth across the western part of the site.

Fragments of medieval pottery, mostly very small and abraded, and a single nail were recovered from the soil. No finds were recovered using the metal-detector. This may be due to the nature of the soil, where the iron was very poorly preserved, and also to the form of deposition of the medieval artefacts. Animal bone and shell throughout the soil was also extremely fragmented, occurring as splinters rather than the larger bones that are commonly recovered from medieval cesspits. It seems unlikely that metal artefacts are present in any significant numbers in this soil. A thicker band of darker, post-medieval soil overlay the medieval layer.

*Claire Walsh, Archaeological Projects Ltd, 25A Eaton Square, Terenure, Dublin 6W.*

### 185. CECILIA HOUSE, 3 CECILIA STREET, DUBLIN
Site of medieval friary, 18th-century music hall/theatre
O157342
98E00155

Cecilia House is within the site of a 13th-century Augustinian friary where previous archaeological excavations have found parts of the eastern (Nos 4–5 Cecilia Street, *Excavations 1996*, 20–1, 96E0003) and western (No. 1 Cecilia Street, *Excavations 1997*, 35–3, 97E0005, by Malachy Conway) friary precinct wall, as well as part of the cemetery on the southern side (at the Green Building, Crow Street, *Excavations 1993*, 29, 93E0139, by Martin Reid).

After the dissolution of the friary the buildings were converted into mansions, one of which was known as the 'Crow's Nest'. In 1731 a music hall was in the centre of the site under discussion and measured 10m east–west by 20m north–south. The music hall site was subsequently converted into the 'Crow Street Theatre', established in 1757 as a rival to the famous Smock Alley Theatre, which lay further west at Essex Street West. The music hall was comprehensively demolished at this date, and the site was expanded on the east and west by the addition of the adjoining plots. A wider, landlocked site to the north (7a Fownes Street Upper), stretching from Temple Lane in the west to Fownes Street Upper in the east (behind the houses fronting onto Temple Bar), was also purchased at this date, and the main theatre was built there, orientated east–west. Cecilia House formed the main entrance into this theatre, with subsidiary entrances on the east (Temple Lane) and west side (Fownes Street Upper).

The Crow Street theatre underwent many substantial rebuilding programmes throughout the late 18th century, but by 1820 it was closed. In 1836 the building was bought by the Apothecaries for use as their hall but was subsequently sold in 1852 to the Catholic University, which rebuilt the northern end of the building in 1898 for use as its medical school. In 1930 the building was converted into offices.

The assessment found no traces of the medieval friary as, although Cecilia House (until recently) had only two small irregular cellars, it originally must have had extensive cellars, almost 3m deep. However, the assessment and building appraisal established that the building was composed of three distinct buildings, each constructed within pre-existing early 18th-century east and west boundary walls. All of the buildings vary in height and have independent roof structures. The central section appears to be the earliest (theatre phase: after 1757), followed by an extension, at both the south and north side. The south extension is of brick (the present façade of Cecilia House) and can be related to the theatre phase, possibly dating to 1777 when the main entrance to the theatre was 'improved'. The addition on the northern side is more difficult to date, as the walls found suggest that there were at least three building periods at this side, from the late 18th century onwards.

The assessment revealed a substantial stone wall, thought to date to *c.* 1600, which was probably related to the mansion phase, possibly part of the Crow's Nest. In addition, the original northern boundary wall, which formed the northern wall of the music hall, was also found. In the present development the internal walls of Cecilia House have been removed to facilitate the new development; however, a section of the music hall wall will be on display, as will the main walls.

*Linzi Simpson, Margaret Gowen & Co. Ltd, 2 Killiney View, Albert Road Lower, Glenageary, Co. Dublin.*

### 186. CHRISTCHURCH CATHEDRAL, DUBLIN
Medieval cathedral
O152340
98E0606

The site is on the north side of the Cathedral in an area known as the 'north yard', bounded by John's Lane on the north and the North Transept on the west. A trial-pit, against the medieval north wall of the cathedral, revealed the foundations of the wall, below the refacing carried out by Street in the 19th century (between 1871 and 1878). In addition, at 1.05m below the ground level a mortared mass, medieval in date, was found, which may represent either a medieval wall or a building/construction level.

In the north-west corner of the yard the remains of a small post-medieval manhole/cellar, which probably date to the 18th century, were found during monitoring. This stone-built chamber (with some brick) was filled with rubble deposits and measured internally 1m north–south by 1.8m and 1.1m deep. It had an entrance in the west wall and a possible ope in the east wall but no formal floor level *in situ*. At the base of the chamber a substantial French drain was found, which originally exited northwards through an opening in the precinct wall but had been replaced by a ceramic pipe. This was probably the work of Street, as a similar pipe was found in the concrete floor of the crypt. After the ceramic pipe was inserted the chamber was backfilled.

The proposed floor level of the new development was raised to accommodate the chamber, which was then carefully backfilled.

*Linzi Simpson, Margaret Gowen & Co. Ltd, 2 Killiney View, Albert Road Lower, Glenageary, Co. Dublin.*

### 187. CHRISTCHURCH CATHEDRAL, DUBLIN
Medieval cathedral
O152340
99E0091

An assessment was carried out in the medieval crypts of Christchurch Cathedral, Dublin, in February 1999, before proposed removal and replacement of the existing concrete floor. Only three small test-pits were excavated, to assess the depth of the concrete laid down by Street during the extensive renovations in the 19th century (1871–7). The assessment revealed, however, that there were no deep archaeological levels within the crypts. The crypt walls and piers stand directly on boulder clay in shallow foundation trenches.

However, during monitoring works by Helen Kehoe it was established that one of the pier bases sat directly on an earlier, unidentified stone structure. Along the east side of the crypts a thin organic deposit sat directly on boulder clay, and a small pit, which contained animal bones, was also found. Three small post-holes were also revealed in the central area. One of the test-pits was positioned along a drop in the floor level and a change in the pier base type, which was thought to mark a division in the date of the crypts, when the western end of the nave was extended in the mid-13th century. However, no original west wall was found.

At the extreme western end the remains of what may represent an earlier wall foundation were revealed, orientated north–south and bordered by an internal laneway on the eastern side. This laneway may mark the maintenance of a public route through the crypts of the cathedral after the nave was extended over the original line of Winetavern Street in 1234. Although no definitive evidence of burials *in situ* was revealed during the assessment, fragments of bone, which were probably human, suggested that there may have been surviving burials in the crypts; this was subsequently confirmed by Helen Kehoe during monitoring of the works.

The proposal to remove the entire crypt floor was subsequently dropped, and the ducting and other services were placed within the thickness of the existing concrete.

*Linzi Simpson, Margaret Gowen & Co. Ltd, 2 Killiney View, Albert Road Lower, Glenageary, Co. Dublin.*

### 188. CHRISTCHURCH CATHEDRAL, DUBLIN
Urban medieval
99E0539

As part of redevelopment works to open up the 12th-century crypts to the public, a series of service trenches was excavated in the existing 19th-century concrete floor in the crypt of Christchurch Cathedral. During the monitoring, stone wall remains and some skeletal material were exposed in two of the trenches (Trenches 1 and 2).

After consultation with the relevant authorities it was agreed to open an additional two trenches in the vicinity of the wall features to establish their nature and extent.

Trench 1, orientated east–west, extended the full length of the crypt and was 0.4m wide and 0.25m deep. At the eastern end the depth of rubble/concrete was 0.4m, with boulder clay revealed at the western end. A small area of one-coursed mortared stone revealed in the eastern half of the trench may represent the foundations of a wall; however, this could not be firmly established from the extant remains. It appeared to date to the Anglo-Norman period as two small sherds of medieval pottery were recovered from the trench during trowelling. The mortar used in the wall feature was similar to that in the present building.

At the western end of the trench, *in situ* skeletal material was exposed, consisting of two femurs orientated east–west.

Trench 2 was orientated north–south to facilitate air-handling ducts. It was 1.4m wide by 0.3m deep. During the initial hand-excavation of this trench, stone remains were exposed, revealing a two-phase stone wall structure lying beneath the present late 12th/13th-century cathedral. The walls appear to represent the north-west corner of a masonry structure, which was reused as a foundation for a pier in the Anglo-Norman period.

The first phase consists of a west wall orientated north–south, 2.6m long and standing two courses high. The top of the north wall of this structure was also exposed, orientated east–west, 4.6m long and 0.4m wide. The full width of the wall could not be ascertained as the base of the crypt pillar was built directly on top. Both walls were bonded by a distinctive, off-white mortar.

The second phase consisted of a second clay-bonded wall built up against the Phase 1 north and west walls. The precise extent and function of this wall could not be established conclusively owing to excavation limitation. It was 0.5m wide and was built of large limestone blocks, one course high, cut into boulder clay. There is a slight curve to the east. At the southern end of Trench 2 some badly decomposed skeletal remains were revealed. They appeared to be the remains of adult lower leg bones orientated east–west.

The earlier remains were comprehensively demolished on the western side and sealed with a hard, redeposited boulder clay. On the eastern side a section of wall was remortared and reused, forming part of the foundation base for the existing crypt pier. The location of the existing pier base obscures the line of the walls, and consequently their nature and extent could not be established fully. However, the stone remains pre-date the present structure, which dates to the 12th/13th century. No finds were recovered associated with the recording of the wall remains; however, two sherds were recovered in a disturbed context at the northern end of the trench, which may suggest that the walls date to the pre-Norman period. All features revealed remain *in situ*, with a section of the wall features permanently visible.

At the western end of the cathedral the last bay at the southern end had not been concreted over in the 19th century, as all of the remaining crypt floor had been. A beaten slate/mortared floor was revealed in this bay, measuring 2.6m east–west (at its widest) by 5m north–south. A layer of modern sand 0.06m deep covered the surface, which, owing to water seepage, was badly degraded. This floor surface may represent the original crypt floor level or, alternatively, may be a pathway surface associated with a passageway thought to have extended north–south in this area of the crypt.

*Helen Kehoe, c/o Margaret Gowen & Co. Ltd, 2 Killiney View, Albert Road Lower, Glenageary, Co. Dublin.*

### 189. COLLEGE STREET/FLEET STREET/WESTMORELAND STREET, DUBLIN
Urban

**96E0276 ext.**

Monitoring of this large site commenced in November 1998, with full archaeological excavation taking place during the early part of 1999. The finding, during the 1860s, of a tiled medieval pavement, possibly *in situ*, underneath the present AIB bank, which fronts onto College Street, indicated that this large site may house an important ecclesiastical foundation (J. Carroll, *Excavations 1997*, 38). The proximity of the site to Trinity College (itself the location of a medieval ecclesiastical foundation), the site of the Viking stone at the junction of D'Olier Street and Townsend Street, and the River Liffey, suggested that archaeological remains may be found.

Monitoring of the site, which measured 1500m$^2$, and the archaeological excavations revealed that the site had been reclaimed in the 17th century and lay on a deep gravel bank. The western side of the site, fronting onto Westmoreland Street, revealed a channel of what may have been the River Steine or a tributary of this river, now culverted. Several large wooden stakes, including one fine piece of oak timber, squared and with dowels and a mortice-and-tenon joint, were found to the east of the riverbank. These wooden stakes were embedded in the gravel bank, suggesting that they may have been used as mooring posts when the River Steine flowed through the site and when the area would have frequently been flooded by the River Liffey, which in the medieval period ran along the present Fleet Street, before the reclamation of the land.

A row of seven structures dating from the 18th century was revealed, fronting onto Westmoreland Street. These houses had been erected at the time of the Wide Streets Commission. The partial remains of several structures fronting onto College Street and Fleet Street were also revealed. These also dated to the 18th century. Several wells and ice pits were revealed to the rear of the houses. One rather enigmatic feature, a large circular brick structure measuring 3.2m east–west by 3m, with a height of 2.6m, was revealed to the rear of one of these houses. The bricks of this structure exhibited a considerable amount of calcium carbonate residue, indicating that it may have been used to hold water.

At the northern end of the site, fronting onto Fleet Street, a square wooden trough was revealed. This box, 0.88m x 0.88m with a depth of 0.4m, contained a quantity of fabric; it was deliberately placed within a cut in the river silt and held in place by small stakes. The box was sealed by a green marl, making it somewhat waterproof.

Most of the artefacts and finds date from the post-medieval period, with a high concentration of post-medieval pottery, leather scraps and what appear to be dress-making pins. However, a small quantity of medieval finds were retrieved, concentrated mainly in the southern portion of the site. A fine late medieval spoon, a rowel spur and two merchant's tokens dating from the 1600s were recovered. A small quantity of medieval pottery including some fragments of line-impressed floor tiles was also discovered in the southern portion of the site. The eastern portion of the site had housed the College Street Divisional Police Office during the 19th century, which extended the width of the site onto Fleet Street. A very fine granite lintel bearing the word 'POLICE' was recovered from this portion of the site.

There was no evidence of any structures before the 18th century, although two fine brick culverts, one found below a structure that fronted onto Fleet Street and one found during test-trenching under the bank, may date to the earlier part of the 18th century. Further work will take place during 2000 under the AIB bank.

*Sylvia Desmond and Judith Carroll, Judith Carroll & Co. Ltd, Pine Forest Art Centre, Pine Forest Road, Glencullen, Co. Dublin, and 13 Anglesea Street, Dublin 2.*

### 190. 20–26 CONYNGHAM ROAD, DUBLIN
No archaeological significance

**31324 23442**

**99E0594**

The proposed construction of two apartment blocks on the site of 20–26 Conyngham Road, Dublin 8, was subject to an archaeological testing condition. The site is on the north bank of the River Liffey, opposite the site of a Viking cemetery discovered on the river's south bank in the mid-1800s.

There were no known areas of archaeological significance on the site, and an examination of 18th- and 19th-century cartographic sources showed that before the construction of a series of domestic dwellings and gardens in the late 19th century the site was an open meadow with light tree cover.

The site covered an area *c*. 50m x 50m. Six test-trenches were mechanically excavated to natural. The trenches were 4–12m long, 2m wide and 0.9–3.8m deep. Testing revealed a series of dump layers, containing rubble, ash, charcoal, mortar, red brick and sherds of crockery. This material had been deposited to facilitate the construction of a terrace of houses in the late 19th century, only recently demolished before the new development.

There were no indications that the site had been occupied before the late 19th century. It may be that construction of the houses destroyed any evidence for earlier occupation. As nothing of archaeological significance was uncovered, it was recommended that no further archaeological work was required on this site.

*Nóra Bermingham, ADS Ltd, Windsor House, 11 Fairview Strand, Dublin 3.*

### 191. 2–4 COPPINGER ROW, DUBLIN
Urban
3159 2337
99E0285

Monitoring commenced on the site at Nos 2–4 Coppinger Row on 8 July 1999 before an apartment development and continued until 19 August 1999. The site is opposite the southern wall of the Powerscourt Townhouse Centre, one plot to the west of the intersection of Clarendon Street and Coppinger Row and one plot to the east of the Dublin City Assembly House (now housing the Civic Museum).

The site would have been *c.* 150m to the north-east of the pre-Norse ecclesiastical enclosure that surrounds the church of St Peter del Hulle, St Stephen's Hospital and the Whitefriars Monastery. From cartographic and historical sources the area appears to have been open ground until the late 17th century, with the earliest depiction of Coppinger Row (then Coppinger Lane) being on Charles Brooking's map of Dublin, produced in 1728. Howard Clarke's conjectural superimposition of John Speed's map of 1610 onto the present Dublin streetscape places the course of the River Steine as running through Nos 2–4 Coppinger Row, dividing the lots of Clarendon Street from those of William Street.

Monitoring was carried out in two phases: (1) monitoring of the boring of 33 pile-holes of 300mm diameter and (2) monitoring of the mechanical excavation of pits for pile caps, lift shaft and crane base, and trenches for ground-beams and services. No archaeological material that could be identified as pre-18th century was uncovered during the monitoring programme. This supports the picture of a late 17th/early 18th-century origin for this part of the city. It should, however, be noted that the site had been cellared over 70% of its area and disturbed by drains from the 18th century onwards, greatly reducing the chances of finding any potential evidence of earlier activity.

The monitoring programme produced evidence for three cellars, each 4.5m wide and *c.* 9m long, apparently internally subdivided and cut deeply into natural subsoil. The main cellar walls were composed of coursed rubble stone, 0.5m thick, while internal subdivisions were much thinner and generally composed of brick. The westernmost cellar extends under the street for *c.* 1m, with a half-arched brick roof accessed through two brick-detailed doorways. While the two eastern cellars may have similar features, these were not identified during the monitoring. The presence of a blocked-up entrance in the northern wall of the middle cellar certainly suggests that this is the case. The western cellar appears to have had access from the rear yard area, where the partially destroyed western corner of a probable doorway was identified.

The current development did not disturb the cellars as far as their bases, except in the pile-holes themselves, but those levels that were exposed had a clear stratigraphy: a lower layer of dark silt and woody material at least 0.75m thick underlay a loose infill of rubble dominated by red brick up to 1.5m thick. This suggests that the cellars were disused and had been accumulating debris for some time before

Plan of site at 2–4 Coppinger Row.

the demolition of the overlying buildings, from which the upper layer of rubble is derived.

The three cellars fit well with the position of Nos 2–4 of the late 18th-century terrace that stood along the south side of Coppinger Row until their dereliction and demolition in the mid-1960s. An open space identified at the south of the site also agrees with this interpretation, and while the 1906 Ordnance Survey 1:1000 map shows an outhouse in each of the three plots, the fact that the 1901 census does not record their presence strongly suggests that they are outside toilets.

An uncellared area at the east of the site, between the east wall of the cellar identified as belonging to No. 2 Coppinger Row and the wall of the present No. 45 Clarendon Street, was occupied by No. 1 Coppinger Row as shown on the 1936 OS 1:1250 map. This building should not be confused with the present No. 1 Coppinger Row, which is part of the Nos 45–46 Clarendon Street building. A number of features survived in the area beneath this building, including a narrow trench and a partially destroyed stone-lined pit at the southern end, probably a well. It is significant that this area of the site is shown as open ground on John Rocque's map of 1757.

From the absence of any clearly riverine deposits on the site, it must be concluded that the River Steine did not flow through this part of Coppinger Row as had been previously suggested by the depiction on Speed's map of 1610. However, the identification of a probable well of unknown date at the south-east of the site may be of interest in discussions of the hydrology of this part of the post-medieval city. Given the east-facing slope visible across the site, it may be suggested that the course of the Steine actually ran some distance to the east.
*Daniel Leo Swan, Arch-Tech Ltd, 32 Fitzwilliam Place, Dublin 2.*

## 192. CITY HALL, CORK HILL, DUBLIN
Medieval—town wall
34 16
98E0576

The City Hall was built originally as the Royal Exchange by the merchants of Dublin to the design of architect Thomas Cooley. Construction commenced in August 1767 and was completed in 1779. The Royal Exchange was subject to major alterations in 1851, when it was taken over by Dublin Corporation in order to create new offices. The last major structural alteration carried out on the City Hall to date was in 1926, when the woodwork supporting the dome was found to be badly affected by dry rot.

During the excavation for a proposed lift shaft, a blackstone wall emerged at 2.1m down from present street level (or 1.8m from first-floor level, 6.23m OD). This portion of blackstone wall extended north–south for 2.45m, and a width of 1.1m was exposed, co-linear with the north-eastern structural wall of the City Hall. The southern end of the wall had been demolished during the construction of a deep service trench; its northern end extended into the north section face.

This portion of wall remains appears to form part of the town wall that enclosed medieval Dublin. The condition of the wall was good, comprising faced regular blackstones 0.3m x 0.3m, with thinner, long slabs between them, all bonded by a yellow/white, gritty mortar.

The material excavated out for the service ducts and the overall ground reduction was uniform throughout, consisting of a brown, shell-concentrated clay with some 18th-century inclusions. It would appear that the ground had been built up to create a building surface for the construction of the Royal Exchange in 1769. This clay layer was at least 3.8m deep, as verified during the excavation for the lift ram.

The original floor level of the vaulted basement was 6.413m OD (i.e. with present street level). This floor level was reduced by 0.65m all over the basement area. The material was uniform throughout, consisting of a redeposited, brown clay infill with shell concentrations, animal bone, clay pipe stem, black- and creamware sherds and one 18th-century wig curler. A broken vertex of human skull was retrieved from the fill thrown down over an old manhole trench, at a depth of 1.8m from the existing basement level. There were no significant changes in the overall stratigraphy of the deposits excavated out for the insertion of ducts and services.

The section of blackstone wall co-linear with the internal east wall of City Hall appeared to extend onwards into its northern section, following the geographical position of the eastern side of the town wall, which extended towards present-day Parliament Street up to the now-demolished Dames Gate entrance.
*Helen Kehoe, 11 Norseman Place, Stonybatter, Dublin 7.*

## 193. CORNMARKET, DUBLIN
Urban
O082419
99E0239

This site is bounded by St Augustine Street and 14–17 Cornmarket, Dublin 8, and required assessment for the purposes of a planning submission; the site is crossed by the western side of the medieval town ditch on the north side of Cornmarket.

The appraisal reviewed the evidence for the Anglo-Norman extramural town ditch on this western side of the medieval city, adjacent to its principle gate. It assessed the results of three excavations on sites at Bridge Street Upper, the west side of St Augustine Street and Bertram Court. It also included the excavation of test-pits on the site.

The development site is immediately outside the western line of the medieval town wall, straddling the western limit of the medieval town ditch. Clarke's map of medieval Dublin shows the ditch running through the bank building on the proposed development site. One of the most potent indications of the ditch's presence is the position of the structural fault that occurs within the extended bank building (one building is founded on relatively soft ditch material, the other on harder boulder clay). Test-pits opened within the basement of the bank revealed the uppermost, dumped, late 17th-century deposits of the ditch.

St Augustine Street appears to define the extent of the medieval ecclesiastical complex that developed to the west of the proposed development site. There was a concern before the investigation of this site that a cemetery revealed on its western side might extend eastwards. However, this was found not to be the case.

Test-pits opened on the western side of the site revealed no accumulated archaeological deposits of any sort, and the only below-ground remains in this area are the foundations of early 18th-century houses.

Speed's map of 1610 suggests that the northern side of Cornmarket was developed with street-front buildings at that time. Rocque's map of 1756 reveals that the development site had five properties fronting onto Cornmarket and a further two or three fronting onto St Augustine Street. Map-based research and a study of the fabric of Nos 16 and 17 revealed that the development of Cornmarket at the time of the Wide Streets Commission removed the street-front houses recorded by Rocque. However, the below-ground fabric of the demolished basements along the St Augustine Street frontage may be early 18th-century in date.

The development has been designed to retain the bank building (over the ditch) and to use piles in order to retain the foundation layout of the 18th-century structures in situ.
Margaret Gowen, Margaret Gowen & Co. Ltd, 2 Killiney View, Albert Road Lower, Glenageary, Co. Dublin.

### 194. 1–5 CRAMPTON COURT (REAR OF 44 ESSEX STREET EAST), TEMPLE BAR, DUBLIN
Urban
99E0427

A new addition to the rear of the existing List 2 building at No. 44 Essex Street East necessitated archaeological evaluation of a series of five pits excavated by mini-digger, c. $1m^2/1.5m^2$. The pits comprised mainly rubble infill. Apart from some evidence for the deposition of reclamation material, which included shell and bone, there was no other evidence for significant archaeological features.
Helen Kehoe, c/o Margaret Gowen & Co. Ltd, 2 Killiney View, Albert Road Lower, Glenageary, Co. Dublin.

### 195. 4 DAME LANE, DUBLIN
Urban post-medieval
99E0357

Before the redevelopment of the site an archaeological assessment involved the excavation of four trenches opened by mechanical excavator. The total footprint of the existing building to be redeveloped is 18m by 7m. Number 4 Dame Lane is situated parallel to Dame Street, on its southern side. Dame Street derives its name from a dam built across the Poddle to provide water-power for milling.

From the evidence of the test-trenches the site area appeared to have been filled with 18th-century blackstone/red brick basements. The infill within and outside of these basement remains was post-medieval, and excavation for the building went down to the natural clay.

There was no evidence for any significant archaeological soils or features. Two ceramic plate remains were of 19th-century date.
Helen Kehoe, c/o Margaret Gowen & Co. Ltd, 2 Killiney View, Albert Road Lower, Glenageary, Co. Dublin.

### 196. DAVIS PLACE (OFF FRANCIS STREET), DUBLIN
Urban
99E00452

A second phase of archaeological assessment was carried out at Davis Place, Dublin 8, in August 1999. Davis Place is off Thomas Davis Street South, which runs between Francis Street (west) and John Dillon Street (east). The site is within the city ward of St Nicholas Without. A preliminary assessment was undertaken by Malachy Conway before a planning submission in the vacant garden area on the north side of the site in January 1997 (Excavations 1997, 40, 96E0374), from which 'nothing of archaeological significance was revealed in this small area of investigation'.

According to Clarke's Map of Dublin, c. AD 840–1540, the site is just outside the medieval walled town of Dublin and is on or close to the site of St Francis's Abbey, founded in 1233.

Two trenches were opened, and human remains were found at two locations in both. The remains consisted of both articulated and disarticulated material and were not associated with medieval soils or structures from within the boundaries of the trenches. The finds retrieved from the soil deposit, from which the bone emerged, were post-medieval.

It would appear that some remains were redeposited or disturbed at an earlier date, as the position of the human remains just underneath the rubble infill conveyed the impression of earlier disturbance. An example was the disarticulated bones of the young adult found in Trench 1, with much of the skeletal remains, including the skull, missing.
Helen Kehoe, c/o Margaret Gowen & Co. Ltd, 2 Killiney View, Albert Road Lower, Glenageary, Co. Dublin.

### 197. DAWSON STREET, DUBLIN
Urban post-medieval
99E0663

The proposed development for the vacant site south of the Mansion House comprises a five-storey over basement office building. Excavation for the development necessitated ground reduction of 3m from present ground level. Two trenches were opened by mechanical excavator, one extending north–south at the west end of the site, the second east–west.

Two post-medieval, yellow brick, stone-capped drains, which appeared to be built on yellow, natural clay and extended east–west, were found in both trenches. One of the drains appeared to have been constructed on top of three sheets of timber 0.06m thick laid side by side. There were no other associated finds or features.
Helen Kehoe, c/o Margaret Gowen & Co. Ltd, 2 Killiney View, Albert Road Lower, Glenageary, Co. Dublin.

### 198. 33–35 EARL STREET SOUTH, DUBLIN
Urban post-medieval industrial
3146 2337 (vicinity of)
SMR 18:02051
99E0021

An archaeological assessment of a proposed development by the Eastern Health Board to the rear of the City Dispensary at 33–35 South Earl Street was requested by the City Archaeologist. The development is to the south of the site of The Abbey of St Thomas the Martyr and within the zone of archaeological potential as identified in the survey of medieval Dublin. The proposed development involved the construction of a single-storey extension to the existing clinic. Two trenches were excavated on the site in February 1999.

Trench 1 was orientated east–west along the north side of the site and contained a number of archaeological features and deposits that suggested two main phases of activity in this part of the site. Phase 1 was a small, circular, red brick furnace, which was filled with ash and iron slag. Another component of this complex was a north–south-orientated red brick drain 0.6m west of the furnace. Further west lay the remains of a curving, east–west-orientated internal wall. The occupation layers C9, C21 and C24 contained a high level of ash and cinder inclusions. Phase 2 consisted of the accumulation of several deposits of dumped clay and rubble over the abandoned features associated with Phase 1.

Trench 2 was 0.5m east of Trench 1 and orientated north–south. The features within Trench 2 mirrored those recorded in Trench 1. Phase 1 was an occupation deposit rich in cinders and ash. This was sealed by the remains of a degraded stone surface associated with a small rectangular furnace that had been inserted into a massive red brick wall. The furnace was in turn sealed by several further occupation layers. This suggested that the industrial activity was occurred over a prolonged period of time. As in Trench 1, Phase 2 consisted of the deposition of several layers of mixed clay and rubble over the remains of Phase 1.

In summary, Phase 1 represented the remains of a 17th–18th-century smelting or metalworking workshop to the rear of the property fronting onto South Earl Street, while Phase 2 consisted of modern episodes of dumping over the site following the abandonment of the workshop.

Subsequent monitoring of the foundation trenches revealed several walls associated with the industrial complex.
*Rob Lynch, IAC Ltd, 8 Dungar Terrace, Dun Laoghaire, Co. Dublin.*

### 199. ESSEX STREET WEST, TEMPLE BAR, DUBLIN
Urban
O155341
96E0245

In May 1999, excavations were carried out for services at Temple Bar West, including Essex Street West and the new north–south street. As the services were designed to lie above the archaeological level, no archaeological levels were exposed.
*Linzi Simpson, Margaret Gowen & Co. Ltd, 2 Killiney View, Albert Road Lower, Glenageary, Co. Dublin.*

### 200. 10 FOWNES STREET UPPER, DUBLIN
No archaeological significance
1572 3418
98E0378 ext.

Five trenches were monitored before development. Activity on the site in the past, namely the construction of basements during the post-medieval period, had removed any significant archaeological remains that may have existed in the area. Nothing of archaeological significance was identified.
*Audrey Gahan for ADS Ltd, Windsor House, 11 Fairview Strand, Dublin 3.*

### 201. IVEAGH MARKET, FRANCIS STREET, DUBLIN
Urban
34 14
99E0184

The site, just outside and to the west of Dublin's medieval town wall and ditch, is bounded by Lamb Alley to the east, Francis Street to the west and Dean Swift Square to the south. This area is thought to have been laid out in the 13th century, with medieval settlement along Francis Street. The redevelopment of the Iveagh Market and the development of a site at Nos 22–27 Francis Street are being carried out as an integrated project; however, two separate planning applications were made for the sites.

Two engineering test-pit trenches were opened in the former clothes market area on the east side of the building. One trench extended east–west, the other north–south. In each case no archaeological deposits of a sensitive nature were revealed. Early, pre-market red brick basements filled with loose rubble were emptied, the floor slab broken and the underlying soil exposed in places. In all instances it was low-grade, silty clay with very sparse inclusions of charcoal and no other obvious finds. Some of the backfill contained significant amounts of clay pipe stems and bowls.

Because of the location of the site within the town ditch, further archaeological investigation was recommended. This work was carried out by Franc Myles (see No. 202 below).
*Helen Kehoe, c/o Margaret Gowen & Co. Ltd, 2 Killiney View, Albert Road Lower, Glenageary, Co. Dublin.*

### 202. IVEAGH MARKET, FRANCIS STREET, DUBLIN
Urban medieval and post-medieval
99E0261

Five weeks of survey and excavation was undertaken in the dry goods section of the Iveagh Market ,following the exposure of limestone and brick foundations and cobbled surfaces during clearance work. The market was constructed c. 1900, on the site of a disused brewery. It would appear that before the market's construction the buildings were demolished into their basement spaces and the ground was then levelled and slabbed. The site is to be redeveloped as a market in a joint venture between Dublin Corporation and a private developer.

As the overburden and demolition debris had been removed, it was initially difficult to establish stratigraphical relationships between the structures uncovered. The exposed structures were planned at 1:20 and transferred into AutoCAD. This was transferred onto the current Ordnance Survey plan. The structures were then interpreted on the basis of overlays of the 1836 preliminary manuscript edition of the Ordnance Survey and John Rocque's 1756 *An exact survey of the city and suburbs of Dublin*.

While most of the structures can now be identified as belonging to Sweetman's Brewery, which occupied the site from 1791 until its take-over by Guinness in the 1890s, four structures fronting Francis Street were identified as being the lower ground floors of 'Dutch Billys', gable-fronted buildings that were the dominant building type in the Liberties from the late 1600s. The buildings survived in an extended form of those depicted on Rocque's map, and they appear to have been serviced by sewers that pre-dated their primary phases. The buildings occupied wider plots than those occupied by cobbled yards extending behind the houses to the east. This would indicate that the yards relate to earlier street-front structures that were removed when the 'Dutch Billys' were built. John Speed's *Dubline* shows buildings on either side of Francis Street in 1610, and it is possible that the cobbled surfaces relate to these structures.

The large buildings depicted on Rocque's map, between the backyards of the 'Dutch Billys' and the line of the medieval city wall, were not evident and were possibly included by Rocque to fill an empty space. Twenty-four samples of bonding mortar and lime render were collected from the buildings and structures identified and will be analysed for composition as part of this phase of recording.

Eight test-trenches were excavated in order to determine the level of natural subsoil and to investigate the depth of the cast-iron columns supporting the market roof. These identified two areas where medieval deposits had not been truncated by later occupation. Two layers of cultivated medieval garden soil were evident in the one surviving earthen section along the northern boundary of the site. This material may be associated with the medieval fair green that was situated to the north of the market. A second area of garden soil in the south-eastern corner of the site sealed refuse pits that contained locally produced medieval pottery. Several areas of subsidence along the southern boundary of the site suggest the possible presence of large pits pre-dating the surviving structures.

Further excavation will take place in the wet market, the site of the medieval city ditch, in 2000.
*Franc Myles for Margaret Gowen & Co. Ltd, 2 Killiney View, Albert Road Lower, Glenageary, Co. Dublin.*

### 203. 47 GARDINER STREET UPPER, DUBLIN
18th-century urban
31577 23577
**SMR 18:23**
**99E0530**

Testing was undertaken on the rear yard of 47 Upper Gardiner Street, Dublin 1, on 27 and 28 September 1999. The yard abuts two service lanes that lead into Dorset Lane, which acts as a rear access to the rear yards of a row of Georgian buildings at the north-west end of Gardiner Street Upper.

A trench was opened mechanically across the length of the site for a distance of 26m south-west/north-east, to an average width and depth of 1m. The excavation trench was widened to cover a 1.6m$^2$ area in the south-west corner because of the presence of an unidentified structure. It was excavated to a depth of 1.6m, at which point natural, undisturbed soil was identified. A bricked and vaulted structure was partly exposed in the cutting. It abutted the boundary wall to the south, of the same depth as the structure. A narrow drainage channel was present at the base of the boundary wall. It is probable that the bricked and vaulted structure was constructed to conceal a water drainage channel that traversed the rear yard. A similar feature may be present in the yard of the adjoining plot. The roof of the vaulted chamber only partly survived. Finds from the backfill within the chamber suggest that the vaulted roof collapsed or was deliberately broken through in the past 40 years.

No further exploration of the chamber was undertaken because of the danger of undermining a poorly built extension to the building. However, enough of the structure was exposed to give a reasonable interpretation of its date and function. It would be useful to know whether other rear yards in adjoining buildings had such elaborate chambers to cover drainage channels, as this would give an interesting insight into rear yard/garden layouts of the Georgian period in the area.

Traces of the foundation of a brown brick building that formerly housed a woodwork shop were identified, surviving to a depth of 0.4m. The average depth of natural soil within the trench was 1m. The upper surface was made up of 0.2m of concrete. Fragments of yellow and red brick and mortar in garden soil made up the stratigraphy of the remaining 0.8m. No horizons earlier than the 18th century were present.
*Erin Gibbons, 45 Daniel Street, Dublin 8, for Arch-Tech Ltd.*

View from the east of early cobbled surfaces, with later 'Dutch Billy' behind, at the Iveagh Market, Francis Street.

### 204. 64–65 GEORGE'S STREET GREAT SOUTH, DUBLIN

Urban
99E0537

The present building is to be refurbished. As part of these works, it is proposed to reduce the depth of the existing basement level by 0.4m.

Six trenches were excavated by machine in the area of proposed ground reduction. The stratigraphy of all the trenches was generally uniform throughout the site footprint. An earthenware service pipe extended the length of the site and was encountered in Trenches C, E, and F. There was no evidence for archaeological structures or features within the trenches opened. Two sherds of post-medieval pottery and a clay pipe stem were recovered in Trench C.

Redeposited late infill and the ceramic pipe insertion east–west through the site indicated extensive late intrusion. Sandy natural was revealed at 2m on average throughout the site.

*Helen Kehoe, c/o Margaret Gowen & Co. Ltd, 2 Killiney View, Albert Road Lower, Glenageary, Co. Dublin.*

### 205. 116 GRAFTON STREET, DUBLIN

Urban medieval/post-medieval
99E0048

Two test-trenches were opened by hand to the rear of the basement of the existing building. The development involves the change of use of a List 2 building from commercial to residential. The basement slab may be replaced but will not be lowered.

There was no evidence for any archaeological features or soils. The existing concrete floor appears to have been laid directly on yellow natural, 0.5m of which was excavated out to determine precisely the nature of the boulder clay. There were no finds.

*Helen Kehoe, c/o Margaret Gowen & Co. Ltd, 2 Killiney View, Albert Road Lower, Glenageary, Co. Dublin.*

### 206. 6–10 HANBURY LANE/SWAN ALLEY, DUBLIN

Urban medieval—floor-tile kiln, cemetery
O342142
98E0199

Excavation took place over three weeks in February 1999 on a large development site on the eastern border of the abbey of St Thomas the Martyr, founded in 1177. The site had been previously tested (*Excavations 1998*, 50). The current excavation was suspended by *Dúchas* when it was discovered that the site had been used as a cemetery in the 13th century.

A short length of clay-bonded walling, dated to the 14th century, was uncovered towards the western site boundary. A well-laid cobbled surface, representing a yard level or a pathway, lay to the west of the wall. The wall, though slight, may be the eastern precinct wall of the abbey. Excavation concentrated on the north-eastern part of the site, where an extensive layer of grey soil dating to the late medieval period was removed. This soil contained numerous floor tiles, which derived from a floor-tile kiln that probably lies at the northern part of the centre of the site. A small pit, filled with floor tiles, wasters and fired clay impressed with tiles, which is part of the kiln furniture, was excavated. The tiles parallel the *in situ* pavements of the abbey church at Meath Market, South Earl Street (*Excavations 1997*, 53–4, 96E0357), and two-colour, line-impressed tiles and line-impressed mosaic, with many variants and new types, are present.

The level of production of the tiles cut through several burials, and it appears that the entire area to the east of the abbey precinct had been used as a graveyard in the 13th century. Seventeen burials were excavated, and many more graves were noted. The burials are all in simple, earth-cut graves. The low density of burials may indicate the use of this ground on the edges of the abbey as an informal burial-ground for a short time. The formal graveyard of the monks is likely to lie to the west of the site at Hanbury Lane, where graves, as yet unexcavated but defined by stones and markers, have been noted.

*Claire Walsh, Archaeological Projects Ltd, 25A Eaton Square, Terenure, Dublin 6W.*

### 207. 20–26 HILL STREET/GRENVILLE STREET, DUBLIN

No archaeological significance
O162348
99E0612

The site is a rectangular block on the corner of Grenville Street and Hill Street. Much of the site had been in use as a carpark for some period, while buildings of fairly recent construction occupied the frontage along Grenville Street. The development will involve the construction of a basement carpark.

No archaeological deposits have been recorded from sites in the vicinity. None were encountered in the trenches mechanically excavated on this site.

*Claire Walsh, Archaeological Projects Ltd, 25A Eaton Square, Terenure, Dublin 6W.*

### 208. ISLAND STREET/BRIDGEFOOT STREET, DUBLIN

Urban, post-medieval
O145356
98E0358 ext.

Test excavation of two areas off Island Street and Bridgefoot Street, Dublin, was carried out on 2 and 3 November 1999. Provisional assessment had been undertaken by Daire O'Rourke (*Excavations 1998*, 45–6); however, the level of subsoil had not been determined in several of the test-trenches, and further areas had become available for testing. This report extends the earlier test report and confirms the findings of that assessment. All trenches were dug by an Atlas 1604 machine, using a toothed bucket.

Thick deposits of organic silt, with a depth averaging 2.4m and up to 2.7m, occur over the entire Site D and over Site A with the exception of the Bridgefoot Street frontage. The silts mainly date from the late 17th–18th century, although some residual medieval material may be present. The lower deposit of brown sod/silt, uncovered in all trenches where subsoil was reached, appears to represent a natural soil, probably formed from periodic inundation—a water meadow.

The noxious black silts indicate fairly low-grade (and rapid) dumping, and finds do not appear to be concentrated in their lower levels. Their very organic nature suggests that in part they represent the clearance of cesspits and stabling around the city.

Concentrations of more interesting material, sugar cone vessels and clay pipe debris, were evident towards the upper levels of the deposits. These upper levels contain cinders and crushed brick and are less organic in nature. Later industrial material, a stone-footed chimney structure and clay pipe kiln debris, is significant.

A culverted stream, which is probably the Limerick watercourse, runs through the site. It extends east–west and then appears to turn northwards, continuing east towards the Liffey inlet. The culvert is probably 18th-century in date. Further work on the site is required.

*Claire Walsh, Archaeological Projects Ltd, 25A Eaton Square, Terenure, Dublin 6W.*

### 209. JAMES'S STREET, DUBLIN
Urban
O138338
99E0660

This licence refers to a preliminary archaeological appraisal of a proposed residential development site, currently comprising eight properties, at 126–133 James's Street, Dublin 8. The site is on the northern side of the street and extends to within two properties on the corner of Steeven's Lane. At the north the site is bounded by a portion of the Guinness brewery complex, and on the east it extends as far as the boundary wall of St James's churchyard. This church was a medieval foundation. The façades of Nos 131–133 are to be retained within the proposed development, along with the interior of No. 132, which is a List 2 building in the Dublin City Development Plan, 1999. Elsewhere, the proposed development seeks to provide an extensive basement for carparking as part of a proposed residential scheme.

This assessment, based on just three test-trenches owing to restricted access and standing buildings on the site, was conducted in order to address the potential archaeological issues for the proposed basement that forms part of the scheme. The trenches were opened on the only accessible portions of the site, in the areas known as Nash's Court (1st edition OS) and Lamb's Court. Many of the buildings, outbuildings and yards within the site are currently in use, and the one vacant site on the street-front portion of the proposed development area could not be examined for safety reasons.

It was understood by all concerned that a further, more detailed phase of archaeological investigation is necessary, but this can only be undertaken when access to a far greater portion of the site is gained.

The results provided the basis for an evaluation of the archaeological potential of the site and the scope of further archaeological requirements. They suggested that there may be very limited areas of the site that possess archaeological deposits *in situ* (only one area, which has never seen development or building, on the north-east of the site revealed a very thin organic deposit, which was interpreted as old ground level). The results also suggested that the primary phase of building development on the site in the late 17th/early 18th century, as depicted by Rocque, had been very largely replaced above ground, and possibly below ground also, by later, 19th-century development.

*Margaret Gowen, Margaret Gowen & Co. Ltd, 2 Killiney View, Albert Road Lower, Glenageary, Co. Dublin.*

### 210. 141–143 JAMES'S STREET/BOW LANE, DUBLIN
Medieval suburbs
O138338
99E0144

A condition of the planning permission required a site assessment before the development, which comprised apartments with a retail element fronting onto James's Street and three townhouses on the frontage on Bow Lane along the north of the site. There is a considerable slope in ground level from James's Street down to Bow Lane to the north.

The test-trenches were laid out to test the street frontage, the Bow Lane frontage and an area of the slope.

The east–west trench along the street frontage was pulled first. It was started at the east end, 2.6m west of the wall of the adjoining building, 2.6m in from the line of the original footpath and to a depth of 1.4m. A layer, 0.4m deep, of compacted, dark grey clay was exposed. This overlay soft, slightly sandy, dark brown clay with very little stone.

*In situ* human long bones were exposed at 1.1m below street level in the bottom of the trench and in the section face along the south side of the trench. Other long bones and rib bones were recovered from the loose material, as were pelvis bone and vertebrae. Skull material was not observed, and it is possible that the digger had not moved sufficiently to the west to disturb skull material. These were located in the plot corresponding to 142 James's Street.

The test-trenching was abandoned at this stage. Rob Lynch of IAC Ltd undertook the full excavation of the site (see No. 211 below).

*Rosanne Meenan, Roestown, Drumree, Co. Meath.*

### 211. 141–143 JAMES'S STREET, DUBLIN
Urban post-medieval
31408 18878
99E0144

Between April and May 1999 a number of fieldwork programmes including test-trenching, excavation and monitoring were undertaken at 141–143 James's Street, Dublin, following a planning application to develop an apartment complex with a carpark at basement level, retail units fronting onto James's Street and three townhouses fronting onto Bow Street. The archaeological deposits were concentrated between the surviving foundations of two 18th-century structures, Nos 141 and 142 James's Street.

Test-trenching at 141–143 James's Street was initially undertaken by Rosanne Meenan (see No. 210 above). One trench was excavated, which revealed the *in situ* remains of at least one individual at a depth of 1m below present ground level. At this point the trench was covered, and the rest of the proposed trenches were left unexcavated. The licence holder was no longer available to carry out the remainder of the trial-trenching, and the developer appointed the writer to complete the assessment of the site.

Test-trenching was completed between 15 and 17 April 1999. Two new trenches were opened. Trench 2 was 8m long and was orientated north–south. It ran perpendicular to and bisected the existing trench opened by Ms Meenan (Trench 1). Trench 3 was orientated north-east/south-west and ran for 12m along the northern end of the site. In addition to these trenches, the existing trench (Trench 1), orientated east–west, was extended westward for 5m.

Trench 3, to the north of the site, contained no evidence of archaeological material and consisted of, on average, 0.65m of modern rubble overlying boulder clay.

The excavation of the two trenches to the south of the site revealed four extended inhumations within a roughly square grave pit measuring 2.2m x 2.2m and several other archaeological features including 0.9m of dumped post-medieval deposits overlying the natural boulder clay. Some of the dumped clay also contained fragments of what appeared to be human skull, which suggested the presence of further inhumations on the site.

The site was visited by the City Archaeologist, who recommended that a small-scale excavation take place in the area surrounding the identified grave pit.

This excavation was undertaken between 26 April and 12 May 1999. It revealed two phases of post-medieval industrial activity, several dumped deposits of medieval clays and an isolated burial, which brought the total number of inhumations on the site to six. The site was divided into two areas, east (No. 141) and west (No. 142).

Phase 1 of activity on the site consisted of a shallow irregular pit in the eastern half of the site, which was medieval in date. This was sealed by 0.2–0.3m of dumped clays dating to the medieval period (Phase 2). The medieval deposits were also concentrated in the eastern half of the site.

Phase 3 was the truncated remains of a post-medieval industrial complex that was confined to the western half of the site. This consisted of a small oval pit containing lumps of iron slag, which was surrounded by a small area of metalling. Immediately to the north of the pit lay an east–west-orientated drain; 1m to the west lay a north–south-orientated line of five stake-holes, 5m long, which presumably acted as some form of fence, screening the pit and its associated activity from the surrounding area. Phase 3 occurred over the highly truncated remains of a layer of introduced clay that probably functioned as some form of flooring level.

Following the abandonment of this industrial area, the site was used as a burial-ground. Six articulated skeletons were recovered from the site. Five young males (17–30 years) were recovered from a single grave pit measuring 2m x 2m, in the south-eastern corner of the site. A further single inhumation, a female, was discovered in the north-western part of the site.

The disarticulated remains of at least a further four individuals, including those of a young child, were recovered from a number of dumped deposits across the site, suggesting the presence of more graves in the area. However, no further *in situ* human remains were recovered during subsequent monitoring.

The next significant phase of activity across the site was the construction of the 18th-century properties. A cobbled laneway and associated furnace were recorded in the western half of No. 142.

The removal of the remainder of the rubble across the site and of the natural geology was monitored on 19 May 1999. No further archaeological features or deposits were observed.

*Rob Lynch, IAC Ltd, 8 Dungar Terrace, Dun Laoghaire, Co. Dublin.*

### 212. CARDIAC UNIT, ST JAMES'S HOSPITAL, JAMES'S STREET, DUBLIN
19th century
O136334
98E0560

Six trenches tested the location of the new cardiac building for the hospital, at the south side of the James's Hospital campus. All six showed evidence for dumping of 19th-century material, some of which was domestic rubbish, that probably derived from the workhouse and hospital. There was also some building rubble.

The site is close to the Grand Canal, and there is some evidence that there was an overflow pool for the canal at the approximate location of the proposed building. The nature of the underlying grey silt was consistent with the presence of such a pool.

Archaeological material underlying the material mentioned above was not observed.

*Rosanne Meenan, Roestown, Drumree, Co. Meath.*

### 213. 189–194 KING STREET NORTH, DUBLIN
Urban, graveyard
31513 23465
SMR 18:20
98E0088

Before a planning application was lodged by Dublin Corporation to construct a community centre on the site, three test-trenching programmes were conducted by Daire O'Rourke in this area (*Excavations 1997*, 37, 97E0086, and *Excavations 1998*, 52). Results indicated that the site had been a burial-ground. Fully articulated *in situ* human skeletal material was found in all of the trenches. Articulated skeletal material was found directly below a layer of rubble and overburden, between *c.* 0.7m and *c.* 2.2m below present ground level. Within the rubble layer was a large quantity of disarticulated human remains.

The site is on the southern side of the eastern end of North King Street and extends along Halston Street and Green Street. Known originally as Abbey Green, 1558 is the first recorded usage of the name. The monastic buildings of St Mary's occupied an area bounded by Capel Street on the east, by East Arran Street on the west, by Little Mary Street on the north, and by the street called St Mary's Abbey on the south. The wall surrounding St Mary's Abbey was encircled by a stream of water diverted into small rivulets. The river Bradogue ran on the west side, from which a branch appears to have entered the grounds on the north side at about the present

North King Street.

In 1213 the citizens of Dublin granted that 'The monks are to maintain their green place which is opposite their outside gate, as a common pasture'. According to Speed's map, this would fix the location at approximately the area of Green Street. The Abbey Green, as it was known c. 1568, and as the Little Green c. 1727, seems to have been part of the land granted by the city in 1213.

In the early 18th century, land on the northern end of the Green was put aside for the building of a church, and the decision was taken to cover in the River Bradogue. On Rocque's map of 1756 Green Street is called Little Green and the portion granted for the church is walled in. The present street pattern had been established, and the medieval market place had moved northwards to the site of what is now St Michan's Park.

In the 18th and 19th century the area comprised Newgate prison, completed in 1781 (a scaffold was located there); Sessions House, now Green Street Courthouse, completed 1797; City Marshalsea, prison for the poorest class of debtor, completed 1804; Sheriff's prison, completed 1794; and the residence of the Governor of Newgate. From the 1780s onwards Newgate became the main gallows for the city. The convicted felons were hanged high up against a prison wall. Green Street proved to be a popular venue for the hangings as it was in a thriving populated area. In general the bodies were left hanging for a number of hours before they were handed over to surgeons for anatomical dissection.

Excavation began on the site on 13 September 1999 and is ongoing at the time of writing (spring 2000). To date, c. 430 articulated human skeletons along with c. 120 disarticulated human remains have been excavated and recorded. All articulated skeletal material has been found cut into post-medieval layers containing frequent amounts of red brick, glass and post-medieval pottery. No archaeological material earlier than the post-medieval period has been recorded.

Outstanding excavation is focused on an area measuring 15m east–west x 4m in the very north-west corner of the site.
*Dermot Nelis, IAC Ltd, 8 Dungar Terrace, Dun Laoghaire, Co. Dublin.*

### 214. NATIONAL GALLERY OF IRELAND, LEINSTER STREET, DUBLIN
No archaeological significance
O165336
99E0201

Assessment trenches were mechanically excavated in May and June 1999. These showed, as was suggested by cartographic evidence, that the site was first developed for housing in the 18th century.
*Alan Hayden, Archaeological Projects Ltd, 25A Eaton Square, Terenure, Dublin 6W.*

### 215. LONGFORD STREET GREAT/STEPHEN STREET UPPER, DUBLIN
Urban
O157335
97E0094

An area measuring c. 12m east–west x 9m was excavated in the north-east corner of this site, where the remains of twenty articulated inhumations were identified. These were part of a medieval burial horizon that was delimited to the west by the stone foundations of a medieval boundary wall c. 1.2m wide. Medieval pottery and line-impressed floor tiles were recovered from the clearance work—from later cellars where residual materials dating to the medieval phase had been dumped. The wall and cemetery have been provisionally identified as belonging to the medieval parish church of St Peter, as illustrated on John Speed's map of Dublin dating to 1610.
*Martin Reid, 37 Errigal Road, Drimnagh, Dublin 12.*

### 216. DEPARTMENT OF EDUCATION, MARLBOROUGH STREET, DUBLIN
Urban post-medieval
31613 23451
99E0097

Planning permission was granted for the erection of office buildings with basements and underground carparking. An assessment was required before the development, and a number of trial-trenches were excavated. Test-pits dug for engineering purposes were also monitored. Subsequently, a condition that monitoring of all subsurface clearance to the naturally occurring gravels should take place was included in the planning permission.

Evidence of activity on the north-east bank of the River Liffey is scarce before the 18th century. A reference to a possible Viking grave and a stray find of a decorated medieval ring brooch are all that are known from the vicinity. There is little evidence from Speed's map of 1610 that the north-eastern neighbourhood had undergone any urban development, the site probably being mud-flats at this time. Charles Brooking's map shows that considerable reclamation had taken place along both banks of the Liffey by 1728, and Great Marlborough Street is shown running between Great Britain Street and Abbey Street. In 1740 Tyrone House, now a listed building on the development site, was designed by Richard Cassels for Marcus Beresford, viscount (later earl) of Tyrone. By 1837 Tyrone House was just one of a complex of buildings called the National Model Schools. This complex was further added to during the latter half of the 19th century and again at the beginning of the 20th century. Some of these buildings were demolished to facilitate the new development.

There was no evidence from either the trial-trenches or the test-pits for any activity earlier than the 18th century, and, other than garden clays, no structures were found associated with this period. Basements of the 19th-century buildings had occupied a large proportion of the site, and these overlay natural gravels. In the remainder of the site garden-type clays with a mix of modern pottery sherds, including some blackware sherds of possible 18th-century date, occurred at c. 0.6–1m below present ground level and overlay the gravels. The shaft of a stone-lined well, which appeared to be associated with the 19th-century building development on the site, was revealed. Approximately 1m of the shaft was removed by machine before it was noticed, but the remainder of

the well was left *in situ*.
*Mary McMahon, 77 Brian Road, Marino, Dublin 3.*

### 217. MARROWBONE LANE, DUBLIN
No archaeological significance
020328
99E0501

The records of Dublin Corporation's City Archaeologist showed that no previous investigations had taken place on Marrowbone Lane, and as this was a large Corporation site it was decided to have an assessment carried out.

Three test-trenches excavated across the site exposed the concrete foundations of the recently demolished buildings and no materials of archaeological significance.
*Martin Reid, 37 Errigal Road, Drimnagh, Dublin 12.*

### 218. 28 MARY STREET LITTLE, DUBLIN
Urban 18th/19th century
315316 234481
99E0628

The site is a small yard to the rear of a three-storey over basement red brick building; the proposed development is an extension to the existing premises fronting onto Mary Street Little. It is within the original precinct of the Cistercian monastery of St Mary's Abbey. The proposed extension will occupy the entire site and is built on pad foundations. The hand-excavation of the 0.65m-deep pits for these pads was monitored.

No remains of archaeological significance were uncovered. A layer of rubble fill was found under the concrete surface of the yard; this material is most likely to be contemporary with the construction of the existing building. A similar layer was found during monitoring by Deirdre Murphy to the rear of 25–26 Mary Street Little in 1997 (*Excavations 1997*, 47). No further archaeological work will take place before development on this site.
*James Eogan, ADS Ltd, Windsor House, 11 Fairview Strand, Dublin 3.*

### 219. ST CATHERINE'S, MEATH STREET, DUBLIN
Urban
O147333
99E0457

The site is outside the precinct of St Thomas's Abbey, in lands between the abbey and the city. Much of this ground was probably pasture and dumping ground during the medieval period. Meath Street is of 17th-century date, and St Catherine's church is a late 18th-century foundation, although the present structure dates to the mid-19th century. The large building to the south of the church, which is undergoing some renovation and extension, dates to this period. It has large cellars, which extend eastwards beyond the east wall of the return.

Foundations for the extension were excavated to a depth of *c*. 2.8m. Subsoil was encountered at a depth of 2.7m. The intervening ground was extensively disturbed in the 19th century, when the existing building on the site was constructed. No archaeological deposits were encountered.
*Claire Walsh, Archaeological Projects Ltd, 25A Eaton Square, Terenure, Dublin 6W.*

### 220. MEETING HOUSE LANE/133A CAPEL STREET, DUBLIN
19th-century street frontage
3152 2345
SMR 18:02048
99E0080 ext.

Monitoring was undertaken here as a sewerage pipe was laid from an area of previous archaeological testing to an area previously monitored. A 28m north–south trench, 0.6m wide, was cut to an average depth of 1.6m. Two walls (F1 and F2) and two drains were identified. F2 consisted of undressed mortared stone and red brick and extended intermittently for *c*. 9m. The nature and position of F2 suggest that it may represent the west face of Meeting House Lane. The old street frontage is uneven, as evidenced on the 1838 plan by Drew, which is mirrored in the unevenness of recovery in the west section face of the service trench. It is probable that the walls identified represent construction along the frontage of that area in the 18th/19th century.
*Christine Baker, Arch-Tech Ltd, 32 Fitzwilliam Place, Dublin 2.*

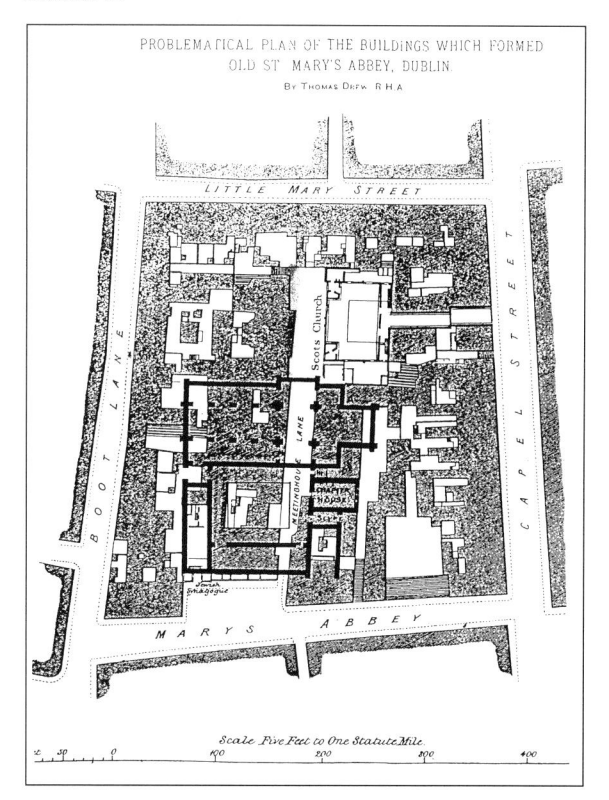

19th-century street frontage at Meeting House Lane/133A Capel Street, taken from 'Problematical Plan of the Buildings which formed Old St. Mary's Abbey', Drew 1886.

### 221. MERCER STREET/BOW LANE EAST, DUBLIN
Urban
O155340
99E0354

A site assessment was carried out in a temporary carpark at the corner of Mercer Street Lower and Bow Lane East, Dublin. Investigations showed that the site had been extensively built up with 0.5–1m depth of modern, red brick rubble infill. This in turn generally overlay a varying depth of post-medieval garden soils and clays. Along the western area of the site, i.e. fronting onto Digges Lane, post-medieval basements and rubble infill extended to a depth of 2.3m below ground level onto subsoil.

Elsewhere, however, a substantial depth of compact, charcoal-flecked, light brown/ochre clays was uncovered underlying the post-medieval soils and clays and overlying the subsoil. While some post-medieval pottery was recovered from the upper level of this clay, a few sherds of medieval pottery were recovered from the lower level. This clay was uncovered at a depth of 0.8–1m along the southern and eastern areas of the site and at 1.3–1.6m in the centre of the site. This clay represents a medieval horizon across the site, similar to that found during excavations at Digges Lane in 1996 (*Excavations 1996*, 23, 96E0006), with some post-medieval contamination.
*Cia McConway, ADS Ltd, Unit 48, Westlink Enterprise Centre, 30–50 Distillery Street, Belfast BT12 5BJ.*

### 222. 31A–36 ORMOND QUAY UPPER/CHARLES STREET WEST, DUBLIN
Urban post-medieval
O3515
99E0126

This assessment, carried out on behalf of Dublin Corporation, was to be included as pre-planning additional information before the development of the site. The area is currently used as a carpark. The site is outside the medieval walled town of Dublin but, by the completion of Brooking's map of 1728, this area north of the Liffey appears to have been well established and was in use as a thriving marketplace since 1682.

Four trenches were opened for assessment purposes. The initial 2m of late building material was extremely loose and tended towards 'shelving', which made the examination of the lower levels quite difficult. The lowest levels in all trenches consisted of natural, orange/brown gravels.

Two pieces of cut timbers and wooden post remains retrieved from the gravels and grey silt respectively appeared to be indiscriminately scattered throughout the gravel only at the junction of Trench A and Trench B. There did not appear to be any new 'break' marks on the timbers. The timbers were only 30mm thick and were radially cut, suggesting a 'planking' function, possibly a pathway. The wooden posts found strewn in the silt appear to be associated with the timber remains. The relatively small radius of the posts suggests a lightweight function. Three post-medieval sherds of North Devon ware (two gravel-tempered and one Sgraffito sherd) were retrieved from the silt/gravel deposits.

Trenches C and D did not produce any material of an archaeological nature.
*Helen Kehoe, 11 Norseman Place, Stonybatter, Dublin 7.*

### 223. OXMANTOWN LANE, DUBLIN
No archaeological significance
SMR 18:020310 and 18:020185 (vicinity of)
99E0494

The development site was within a zone of archaeological interest as outlined for Dublin in the Sites and Monuments Record. The name Oxmantown comes from Ostmantown, a place where the Anglo-Normans compulsorily resettled the Vikings living in the city. A Viking settlement stretched north of the River Liffey to King Street and Smithfield. In 1635, together with College Green and St Stephen's Green, the area of Oxmantown Green was to be 'kept for the use of the citizens to walke and take the open air by reason this cittie is at present growing very populous'. In the second half of the 17th century the area was becoming popular, with the building of King's Hospital, an open-air market and fashionable houses.

The monitoring of three 8-inch piles was carried out on 1 and 2 September 1999. Monitoring failed to reveal the presence of archaeological material and showed *c.* 1m of made ground sealing natural geology.
*Dermot Nelis, IAC Ltd, 8 Dungar Terrace, Dun Laoghaire, Co. Dublin.*

### 224. 58–66 PARNELL STREET/MOORE LANE, DUBLIN
Urban post-medieval
O15903490
98E0357

The test excavation uncovered a number of house walls from buildings that originally fronted onto O'Rahilly Parade, Moore Street and Parnell Street. The street front at O'Rahilly Parade and Moore Street has remained constant since the 18th century; however, Parnell Street has been significantly widened, and the 18th-century street front is now under the present street.

The basement foundations and cellars found in Trenches 3, 6 and 7 all belonged to buildings constructed in the 18th and 19th century that fronted onto O'Rahilly Parade and Moore Street. It is clear from the early cartographic sources that buildings were present on some portions of the site by the middle of the 18th century. The foundations revealed in Trenches 2 and 8 adjacent to Parnell Street were substantially later and dated from the 20th century.

The deposits in the centre of the site consist of accumulations of 18th- and 19th-century rubbish deposited at the rear of the street-front properties. The china and delph identified in the trenches were contemporary with the buildings on the site, consisting largely of Willow Pattern painted vessels (19th century), although a single sherd of an early 18th-century mug was identified in Trench 6.

No medieval archaeological deposits were recorded in any of the test-trenches. No trace of any medieval structures (such as St Mary's Abbey precinct wall) was identified on the development site.
*Edmond O'Donovan, Margaret Gowen & Co. Ltd, 2 Killiney View, Albert Road Lower, Glenageary, Co. Dublin.*

### 225. DUBLIN INSTITUTE OF TECHNOLOGY, PETER'S ROW, DUBLIN
Urban
O156335
99E0272

Test-trenches were opened on this site in 1991 by Margaret Gowen before the initial construction of the Dublin Institute of Technology building (*Excavations 1991*, 11). No features or finds of archaeological significance were revealed at that time.

Four additional trenches were opened on the western, undeveloped portion of the site in 1999.

The trenches revealed a substantial depth of rubble that appears to relate to the demolition of the Old Jacob's Biscuit Factory, which formally stood on the site. Subsoil was revealed below this rubble, except in one trench, where the top of a sewer (probably relating to the factory) was revealed.

No features or finds of archaeological significance were revealed in these trenches.
*Avril Purcell, Margaret Gowen & Co. Ltd, 2 Killiney View, Albert Road Lower, Glenageary, Co. Dublin.*

### 226. ADELAIDE HOSPITAL SITE, PETER STREET/WOOD STREET, DUBLIN
Urban medieval, post-medieval
99E0043

This site was tested in two phases. Phase 1 was carried out in advance of planning permission before the demolition of extant buildings at the site, and Phase 2 was completed on grant of planning permission following building demolition. The site is outside the medieval walled town of Dublin, to the south of the River Poddle, and west of the suspected site of the medieval, Carmelite St Mary's Priory.

Seven trenches were mechanically excavated as part of Phase 1. No evidence of a significant archaeological nature was revealed during the first phase of testing. Two cesspits and two associated pottery sherds retrieved from them were post-medieval in date.

An additional six trenches were opened during Phase 2 of the assessment within the footprint of the demolished buildings. Each of the buildings had a basement that was built on natural, yellow clay. There was no evidence for any archaeological features within the trenches opened. It appeared that the excavation for the basements had removed all material down to natural clay, and therefore any possible *in situ* archaeology is likely to have been lost at this stage.
*Helen Kehoe, c/o Margaret Gowen & Co. Ltd, 2 Killiney View, Albert Road Lower, Glenageary, Co. Dublin.*

### 227. ST MARY'S HOSPITAL, PHOENIX PARK, DUBLIN
Within archaeological complex
31087 23475
99E0435

Testing was carried out in fulfilment of planning permission for alterations to buildings at St Mary's Hospital, as the development is within an area of archaeological potential of a recorded monument (SMR 18:7). Six test-trenches were excavated; however, no features of archaeological interest were revealed. Much of the ground had been disturbed during the construction of the modern buildings at the site, as well as during the construction of the nearby chapel and garden grounds attached to the hospital, which was formerly a military school, established by the Hibernian Society in 1768.
*Christiaan Corlett for Arch-Tech Ltd, 32 Fitzwilliam Place, Dublin 2.*

### 228. PHOENIX PARK, DUBLIN
No archaeological significance
36 12
99E0206

It is intended to extend the grounds of Dublin Zoo northwards by 30 acres (doubling its present size), incorporating part of the lands in the vicinity of Áras an Uachtaráin.

The principle works for the redevelopment of the lands consisted of excavation for foundation and animal enclosure trenches, and drainage/service trenches.

A two-phase series of test-trenching was carried out across the site; no evidence for any significant archaeological remains was encountered during testing. There were some remains of small stone drains and some late, glazed, patterned plate sherds in several trenches. A 1940s-built brick culvert, which connects the lake in the present zoo grounds with the lake in the newly developed area, and its *in situ* sluice mechanism were retained within the new development.
*Helen Kehoe, 11 Norseman Place, Stonybatter, Dublin 7.*

### 229. MARIAN COURT, QUEEN STREET, DUBLIN
Urban
99E0271

Test-trenching was carried out on 22 June 1999. Four test-trenches were excavated within the carparking area to the east of Marian Court Flats, Queen Street, Dublin 7. The proposed development involved the amalgamation of 28 existing one-bedroom ground-floor units into 14 two-bedroom units and the construction of a corner shop at the junction of Queen Street and Blackhall Street. The area of Queen Street/Blackhall Street is within the zone of archaeological potential for medieval Dublin, as defined by the Urban Archaeological Survey. Queen Street was laid out in the mid-17th century. The church and graveyard of St Paul are to the north-west of the site. The graveyard is still in use.

The test-trenches revealed that no significant archaeological deposits or features were present on site. That stratigraphy exposed consisted of 18th–19th-century dumped material and backfilled cellars.
*Rob Lynch, IAC Ltd, 8 Dungar Terrace, Dun Laoghaire, Co. Dublin.*

### 230. TRINITY COLLEGE, DUBLIN
No archaeological significance
98E0435

Service trenches were opened for one week to facilitate the insertion of new water pipes. No material of an archaeological nature was found.
*Helen Kehoe, c/o Margaret Gowen & Co. Ltd, 2 Killiney View, Albert Road Lower, Glenageary, Co. Dublin.*

### 231. TRINITY COLLEGE (LIBRARY EXTENSION SITE), DUBLIN
Urban post-medieval
98E0361

Initial site works before the building of an extension to the Berkeley Library revealed a pit filled with animal and human bone remains. Subsequent archaeological excavation revealed post-medieval boundary walls, the foundations of a blackstone square building and the remains of a well with an associated blackstone/slate drain feature. Pit F6 was almost in the centre of the site. This pit was densely filled with human and animal bones (including camel). The human bones displayed evidence for anatomical dissection, with the high proportion of femurs and skulls from the pit showing both lateral and longitudinal anatomical cut/sawmarks.

Further excavation/monitoring revealed two 18th-century boundary walls, with more anatomical remains placed in a series of piles in shallow trenches against the base of the walls, generally in groups of two or three individuals. The remains consisted of both adults and children. Two more shallow pits were revealed, one against each boundary wall, F7 and F32. These pits were shallower than F6 and less densely packed with human remains. It is estimated that the remains of over 250 individuals were excavated out of the pits and from along the boundary walls.

The F7 boundary wall extended north–south and was built of regular blackstone blocks. Its state of preservation was good at the northern end, with substantial demolition and collapse towards the southern end. It was only along its western side that human bones were recovered. This wall, shown on an 1864 map of Trinity, appears to be the boundary wall dividing what was known then as the Fellows' Garden from the area known as College Park.

The F32 boundary wall remains extended north–south from the Nassau Street boundary wall to the south-east corner of the Arts Block building. It was in a poor state of preservation and was built of a combination of blackstone and red brick. The human remains were recovered against the eastern face of the wall. However, the lower blackstone base courses of this wall are likely to be contemporary with the F7 wall, with the red brick addition built on at a later date. The two walls demarcated a strip of land dividing Fellows' Garden from College Park, which was known as the 'Physick Garden'.

The foundation remains of an almost square structure, F19, emerged west of the F7 wall. It appeared to be built of regular blackstone on the natural gravel, and the remains of a red brick floor were evident at its southern end. There appear to be two phases to this building, but its function is still unclear. It has been suggested that it was a 'well house', as the partial remains of an 18th-century well lay immediately south of the structure. However, recent research suggests that it may have been built as a detached extension to the Anatomy House, which existed at a location north of the structure until its demolition in 1820. Reference to repairs to a 'Bath-house' in the vicinity of the Anatomy House in 1815 suggests a strong possibility that this F19 feature is the remains of this building.

The blackstone/slate drain was built in the 18th century after the construction of the well. It extended south from the well at a slight curve towards the Nassau Street boundary wall.

The finds associated with the excavation/monitoring are all 18th–19th-century in date. They consisted mainly of ceramic and glass, bottles, post-medieval pottery sherds, copper wiring and a small metal canula used in dissection.

*Helen Kehoe, c/o Margaret Gowen & Co. Ltd, 2 Killiney View, Albert Road Lower, Glenageary, Co. Dublin.*

### 232. 105–109 WEAVER STREET, THE COOMBE, DUBLIN
Urban
**99E0560**

Testing was carried out in advance of proposed development and before a planning application. It is proposed to demolish the existing Massey Funeral Home, which fronts onto The Coombe, and the garage to the rear of the site. The derelict, listed Widow's House, which forms part of the site, is to be refurbished.

Three trenches were mechanically excavated in the carpark. The stratigraphy was generally uniform throughout the trenches, with less than 1m of late rubble infill noted in each. The remaining trench profile comprised loose, garden-type soils.

Trench B produced four medieval pottery sherds from 1m depth of a compact, grey deposit, which did not reveal any associated archaeological structures/features. Natural, yellow clay was revealed on average at 2m.

There was no evidence for significant archaeological material; however, there was a notable absence of deep rubble infill deposits. Additional testing will be required should planning permission be granted.

*Helen Kehoe, c/o Margaret Gowen & Co. Ltd, 2 Killiney View, Albert Road Lower, Glenageary, Co. Dublin.*

### 233. 13 WELLINGTON QUAY, DUBLIN
Urban
**99E0194**

The area proposed for redevelopment measured 5.6m x 8m. Ground reduction for foundation trenches to a depth of 3.8m from present street level was monitored.

Wellington Quay extends along the south bank of the Liffey from Crampton Quay at Asdill's Row to Grattan Bridge. In 1621 a quay was built downstream of Grattan Bridge to facilitate the new custom premises.

There was no evidence for significant archaeological features. Reclamation material revealed some 19th-century pottery sherds and clay pipe fragments.

*Helen Kehoe, c/o Margaret Gowen & Co. Ltd, 2 Killiney View, Albert Road Lower, Glenageary, Co. Dublin.*

### 234. 34–35 WELLINGTON QUAY, DUBLIN
Post-medieval
**O158342**
**99E0101**

Test excavation of this site uncovered deposits of post-medieval date. The site was monitored during construction work. No finds of significance were made.

*Claire Walsh, Archaeological Projects Ltd, 25A Eaton Square, Terenure, Dublin 6W.*

### 235. 44 WELLINGTON QUAY, DUBLIN
Medieval/post-medieval
**99E0090**

An assessment of this site was carried out before development. One trench extending north–south was opened by mechanical excavator. It was 9.5m long and 0.75m wide. It contained rubble infill to a depth of 3.7m. At 3.7m reclamation material was revealed, with oyster shell, animal bone and leather inclusions. This deposit of soft, brown/black, pungent material was consistent with the nature of the reclamation material. Limited excavation through this layer was carried out at its extreme northern and southern ends for 0.8m. In both locations it consisted solely of reclamation fill. One small body sherd of medieval ware (Dublin type 003) was retrieved from the southern section of the reclamation material.

A cement and red brick wall extended down the northern section face for 2m.

*Helen Kehoe, c/o Margaret Gowen & Co. Ltd, 2 Killiney View, Albert Road Lower, Glenageary, Co. Dublin.*

### 236. 14–15 WERBURGH STREET, DUBLIN
Viking/Anglo-Norman defences
O152337
99E0651

The assessment at 14–15 Werburgh Street (on the south of the entrance to Jury's carpark) found a sequence of defences on the southern side of the town, dating from the 10th century onwards. The earliest of these was part of an artificial clay embankment also found by Alan Hayden in a previous investigation to the immediate east (*Excavations 1994*, 31, 94E0025). In that assessment a series of sections through the bank was excavated, establishing it to have survived to 0.9m high by *c.* 5m wide. In the assessment under discussion a hard, green clay, interpreted as the top of the bank, was exposed at 2m below present ground level.

The remains of two city walls, orientated east–west, were also exposed, one on top of the other. The lower wall was tentatively identified as the Viking wall (dated to *c.* 1100 in Wood Quay), which was demolished at some date and reused as a foundation for a second, replacement wall, presumably dated to the Anglo-Norman period (after 1170). The earlier wall was cut into the clay bank and was built of limestone block; it had a small offset on the northern side. The wall was 1.7m wide and survived to 0.8m high, mortared with a light yellow, gritty mortar. It was comprehensively demolished when the second wall was built, and the facing-stones, on the southern side, were robbed out, presumably for reuse in the new wall.

The second, Anglo-Norman wall sat directly on the first but was narrower, 1.1m wide. Thus, although the second wall was flush with the Viking wall on the northern side, on the southern side the earlier wall projected out for almost 0.6m. There was some evidence, however (in the form of hand-made brick), that the southern side of the Anglo-Norman wall was refaced in the 17th century, resulting in a reduction in the width of the wall at that date. The Anglo-Norman wall was also bound with a yellow, gritty mortar, but surprisingly the lower three courses of a surviving stretch of 18th-century boundary wall, 2.4m long, were found to incorporate part of the city wall to a height of *c.* 0.45m.

Further investigations are expected to take place on the site in the near future.

*Linzi Simpson, Margaret Gowen & Co. Ltd, 2 Killiney View, Albert Road Lower, Glenageary, Co. Dublin.*

### 237. HOEY'S COURT, WERBURGH STREET, DUBLIN
Viking/Anglo-Norman defences
O15338
99E0228

The site is within the medieval town, along the known line of the earthwork defences and bordered by an extant section of city wall on the southern side (along Ship Street Little). However, the assessment was not completed, and no medieval deposits were exposed. Initial investigations revealed the complete section of a red brick culvert, orientated north–south, which lies at 3.3m below present ground level and is thought to feed into the active Poddle culvert to the immediate south, outside the site. This culvert extends beneath an extant cellar (see below).

The assessment also found the partial remains of a cellar, the top of which lies 0.3m below ground level. A section of the brick roof, measuring 2.55m north–south by 3.2m, was also exposed, as well as a section of the northern wall. This wall was of limestone and had an entrance on the eastern side that was internally 1.2m wide by 1.4m high and was edged in brick. The cellar appears to have been backfilled with cinder/soil deposits but survives relatively intact.

*Linzi Simpson, Margaret Gowen & Co. Ltd, 2 Killiney View, Albert Road Lower, Glenageary, Co. Dublin.*

### 238. WOLFE TONE PARK, DUBLIN
Post-medieval cemetery
99E0726

Seven test-trenches were opened in December 1999 and January 2000 in order to find the level of human burials in the graveyard attached to St Mary's Church. The church was built between 1697 and 1702, and the earliest burials would appear to date from 1709.

The trenches confirmed previous results obtained by Helen Kehoe where disarticulated human remains were recorded at between 0.45m and 0.9m below the present ground level. In addition, several horizontal grave slabs were exposed and their levels recorded. One bore the inscription:
This Stone burial place
Belongeth to James Elliott U his
Posterity 1784.

*Franc Myles, Margaret Gowen & Co. Ltd, 2 Killiney View, Albert Road Lower, Glenageary, Co. Dublin.*

### 239. ST MARY'S CHURCH, WOLFE TONE STREET, DUBLIN
Urban
O155344
98E0236 ext.

An initial assessment of the site was carried out in May 1998 (*Excavations 1998*, 55; an incorrect licence number is given in that report). At that time a number of articulated and disarticulated human skeletal remains were identified in the six underground crypts associated with the church. A subsequent excavation was carried out in September 1998 to record and remove these remains. A number of test-pits excavated on the north and north-west sides of the church grounds did not reveal any archaeological deposits.

An additional assessment was carried out in

December 1998 to the south of the church, in the area between the church and Wolfe Tone Park (originally the graveyard associated with the church). A number of articulated and disarticulated human remains were identified in this area. The subsequent excavation of deposits to facilitate the construction of two fire escapes from basement level in this area was monitored. This work was carried out in May–June 1999.

A total of 25 full skeletons and 7 partial skeletons were identified and removed during the excavations in these two areas at the south of St Mary's Church, with a maximum of four levels of burials identified. The results of the excavation confirmed the evidence produced in the earlier assessment—that the graveyard extended right up against the south wall of the church. All of the remains were orientated east–west, with the exception of eight burials in lead coffins within a small walled chamber, which were orientated north–south owing to the size of the chamber (see below).

The excavation also produced evidence to suggest that the construction of the stepped entrances to the four underground crypts, accessed from outside the south wall of the church (Crypts 2, 3, 4 and 6), may not be contemporary with the construction of the main structure of the church. This was seen in the entrance to Crypt 4, at the Jervis Street side of the church, where *in situ* human remains were identified beneath the steps. It is unlikely that there were any burials in the graveyard before the completion of the church. The presence of a section of a broken, dressed window mullion in the wall of these steps would also suggest that the steps were built during a period of restoration of the original church structure.

A small chamber, which contained eight skeletons in lead coffins, built between the entrance to Crypt 4 and the Jervis Street boundary wall, was also not contemporary with the church and was probably a later construction than the crypt entrance. The coffins in the chamber were possibly reinterred here from one of the underground crypts. The north–south alignment of the coffins may also indicate reinterment, as all of the other burials followed the traditional Christian west–east orientation. It is possible that the other three burials found in lead coffins outside the chamber were also reinterred.

A large quantity of loose, broken and disarticulated bone was recovered from all areas of excavation and at all levels. It is clear from this, and from the fragmentary and disturbed nature of many of the excavated remains, that little care or regard was given to *in situ* remains when graves were being opened/reopened for burials.

All of the skeletal remains were removed from the church in caskets, by Nicholls Funeral Directors, shortly after their excavation. The remains were brought to Glasnevin Crematorium, and the ashes were then returned to the Church Representative Body.

A further additional assessment was carried out before planning permission to record the nature of archaeological deposits, if any, in the area of the south-west corner of the church grounds, between the church and Wolfe Tone Park, which took place on 19 June 1999. This area was previously unavailable for testing. The assessment was based on the excavation of a single test-trench, opened by mechanical digger.

The test-trench produced no evidence of human skeletal material, indicating that the graveyard to St Mary's Church did not extend into the south-west corner of the present church grounds.

A north–south culvert identified in the south-west of the test-trench appeared to be a substantial structure, although it was only partially exposed during the assessment. Its function is unknown, and it is not clear whether it is associated with the church or the graveyard.

*Tim Coughlan, Margaret Gowen & Co. Ltd, 2 Killiney View, Albert Road Lower, Glenageary, Co. Dublin.*

### 240. PROPOSED DUNDRUM TOWN CENTRE, DUNDRUM
Industrial
SMR 22:100
99E0089

Testing was carried out before the development of the proposed Dundrum Town Centre. Three trenches were opened underneath the overflow dam of a millpond (Area A), at a point along a mill-race (Area B) and at a point along the River Slang (Area C), in order to test for the possible survival of archaeological deposits relating to milling in the area. One trench was mechanically opened with a concrete-breaker and a 1.5m back bucket, and a second with a 600mm bucket on a mini-digger; a third trench was excavated by hand. All three trenches were reduced to natural subsoil and/or bedrock.

The site consists of 22 acres contained by the Ballinteer Road to the north, the Sandyford Road to the east, the proposed Wyckham Bypass to the south and the proposed Dundrum Main Street Bypass to the west. The River Slang forms the north-western boundary of the site for approximately one-third of the site's length, before transecting the site and dividing it in half. The central section of the river flows through a deep gully before turning sharply north and entering a wider valley. This section of the site is overlooked by Dundrum Castle on the ridge to the west and has itself an SMR designation, owing to the possibility of the archaeological survival of medieval milling activity along the riverbank.

The area to the south of the river was once occupied by the grounds of Rockmount House, an early 19th-century residence that was demolished in the 1980s. Its walled garden and a portion of its farmyard wall still survive. The southernmost area is now occupied by the grounds of Crazy Prices, while the remainder is waste ground. The north-western sector of the site is occupied by the grounds of the mill-house (which has a List 2 designation on the Dun Laoghaire–Rathdown Development Plan). This consists of the mill-house itself; an 18th-century residence with Victorian alterations, its garden and orchard; a mill-race leading from the River Slang to a large millpond to the rear of mill-house; and an area of upcast to the south of the pond, which is grassed over. The water in the pond was held by an overflow dam consisting of a large granite wall. The level of water in the mill-race and pond was controlled at this point and additionally by a sluice system along the mill-race, which appears to have been blocked relatively recently, draining the pond in the process.

Area A is that area along the eastern bank of the River Slang occupied by the Pye buildings and the access yard. Trench 1 was opened in the yard to the east of the Pye buildings, at a point directly below the overflow dam of the millpond, adjacent to a cut feature that may have originally housed the wheel pit. The earliest cartographic evidence for this specific location dates from 1760, in John Rocque's 'Map of the County of Dublin', which would appear to depict a building in the approximate position of the mill-house, linked by a drafter's line to a building on the riverbank. This building's position in relation to Dundrum Castle on the ridge on the opposite side of the river would place it quite close to that building in the Pye complex immediately to the west of Trench 1.

A trench was mechanically excavated, 14.6m long and 1.5m wide, $c.$ 10m west of the overflow dam and parallel to it. This area is directly to the west of a small building on a raised platform that was demolished recently. It was opened at this point in order to assess the extent and antiquity of the tail-race and to see whether any earlier evidence of milling had survived.

At either end of the trench, decayed granite bedrock lay just underneath the concrete surface. Firmer, undisturbed bedrock lay 0.3m underneath the decayed material. At a point 1.6m north of the southern end, the bedrock was cut to accommodate two 16-inch pipes in a trench extending to the south-west. The cut was filled with loose rubble. The pipes would appear to connect with the channel running from the area that possibly housed the wheel pit and are typical of drainage pipes used from the early part of the 20th century onwards. The pipes rested on decayed granite at $c.$ 1.2m below the surface of the concrete.

From $c.$ 3.2m north of the southern end of the trench, a surface of cinder bricks extended from the edge of the pipe cut. This surface extended from a straight edge north of the pipe cut, and it is likely that the pipes were accessible from it. It extended 6.2m to the north, terminating at a straight edge. The bricks were wire-cut and were laid on a 0.04m bed of fine lime mortar that in turn overlay a layer of black silt. The silt layer was between 0.07m and 0.15m thick, overlying undisturbed bedrock and truncated to the south by the pipe-trench. It extended for $c.$ 6.2m to the north, where it was truncated by the cut for a brick culvert. There were no inclusions in the silt.

A brick culvert of 2ft 8in diameter occupied the remaining 5.4m of the trench. The culvert ran towards the north-west, and its apex was just below the surface of the concrete. It was constructed from a trench cutting through the bedrock, the brickwork rising from granite sides, and filled with brown silt and cinders. The base of the culvert was 1.55m below the surface of the concrete. It appeared to run from a cast-iron pipe extending out from the overflow dam and possibly connects with the tail-race as depicted on the 2nd edition of the Ordnance Survey.

The trench appears to have exposed no features earlier than the mid-19th century, although the respective functions of the culvert and the twin pipes are difficult to extrapolate without more evidence relating to the workings of the ironworks, the laundry and the millpond, which are all evident on various editions of the Ordnance Survey. While the ironworks presumably used the reserves of water held by the overflow dam both as a coolant and to drive the machinery, it is unlikely that the laundry used the silty water of the millpond for washing clothes, although it may have been used to drive primitive tumblers. It would seem probable therefore that the brick culvert relates to functions carried out by the ironworks and that the double pipes may have utilised a previously cut channel through the bedrock to supply the laundry. On the basis of the above evidence, it is likely that if any archaeological evidence of milling in the area survives, it will be found along the riverbank underneath the Pye buildings.

Area B is the area along either side of the mill-race, which flows to the north from its junction with the River Slang, before curving to the west and forming the millpond to the rear of mill-house. Although the water supply has been cut off, the mill-race has not completely drained off into the pond and remains full but stagnant for most of its length. The area west of the race and south of the pond is mostly clear of trees. Its contours indicate that it is composed of the upcast from the millpond, and the plot is referred to as 'waste from millpond' in the records of the Valuations Office. A steep slope to the south of this area runs down to the river, while a wooded slope runs down on the western side to a concrete retaining wall in the Pye precinct. Trench 2 was opened across the mill-race to test for evidence that this feature pre-dates the first cartographic evidence.

The mill-race and pond first appear on Duncan's map of 1821, albeit in a different form to that depicted in subsequent editions of the Ordnance Survey. Although the race as represented here comes off the River Slang at approximately the correct position, as has been stated above, it continues to flow north of a cigar-shaped pond, continuing under the Ballinteer Road before finally rejoining the Slang at a point north of the Catholic church. Despite the eventual destination of Duncan's mill-race, an examination of the frequent meanders of the surrounding watercourses on his map would suggest that he took a fanciful notion of hydrography, which cannot be relied upon for exactness. There is, however, enough there to suggest that an arrangement of mill-race and pond was in existence by 1821.

Trench 2 was opened at either side of the mill-race 2m to the south of the sluice at the head of the millpond. It was excavated to a width of 2m with a 600mm mini-digger bucket in three sections: Trench 2a to the east of the mill-race; Trench 2b through the channel itself; and Trench 2c on the west side of the mill-race. The individual trenches were co-linear and extended for 12.2m.

Trench 2a extended for 4.4m eastwards of the mill-race. The stratigraphy encountered was a slight bank of upcast extending for 2.2m, overlying an old soil horizon and 1.1m of mid-brown, sandy loam. This overlay a very hard, compact, grey silt with frequent granite stones through the matrix, first evident in the western end of the trench at c. 1.6m below the surface. This layer sloped upwards gradually to the east, levelling out at the end of the trench at c. 0.6m below the topsoil. The silting became more ephemeral before disappearing at c. 2m east of the baulk. This overlay compact boulder clay. Undisturbed bedrock was not encountered in a 3.5m test-pit excavated at the eastern end of the trench.

Trench 2b attempted to determine the nature of the bottom of the mill-race by dredging across the channel and holding the water back with the spoil. The mill-race at this point is 3.75m wide. The banks of the mill-race are lined for most of its length with squared-off granite blocks, which have been inserted into the upcast. The bottom of the mill-race does not seem to be so lined, although several granite blocks were dredged up by the bucket. The mill-race appears to have a depth of 1.8m in the centre (where the silting gave way to more solid material), the sides rising steeply forming a wide V-shape. The silt and mud taken from the channel contained 20th-century refuse.

Trench 2c extended for 4m westwards of the mill-race. A 0.3m baulk was maintained at the eastern end, where the stones lining the mill-race were particularly well set, forming a higher bank than that on the opposite side. Solid bedrock was encountered at 2.1m west of the channel, 0.4m below the sod surface, which extended back the length of the trench.

The area between the bedrock and the baulk was excavated by hand to a depth of 1.2m below the sod surface. It was found that the bedrock had been deliberately cut at an almost vertical slope, presumably to create a channel for the mill-race. An examination of the sections revealed that a deposit of soft, grey silt overlay the cut in the bedrock but was itself sealed by the topsoil and the upcast bank running alongside the mill-race.

The silting at either side of the mill-race, which is sealed by the upcast on both sides, would indicate that the present channel is a secondary one. The distance between the cut in the bedrock and the equivalent level of the silting in Trench 2a is c. 7m, which may indicate that either Duncan's map was accurate in depicting a stream at this point or an earlier mill-race had at some point burst its banks, which were later reinforced with the granite blocks.

Area C is that area at either side of the River Slang between its junction with the mill-race and the sharp turn to the north, 115m downstream. The area is heavily overgrown with trees and bushes, and access is consequently difficult. A steep slope of over 3m, which is vertical in places, delineates the southern extent of this area, forming a gorge. The slope across the river to the north is less marked, although the ground rises rather sharply in the area of the millpond upcast. The river, flowing from east to west, drops several metres in its passage through the area, falling over four small weirs. They are not shown on the 1907 Ordnance Survey revision and would appear to be relatively modern. Concrete work is visible in places, although it is unclear whether this is primary or repair.

The banks of the river have been deliberately constructed with large granite boulders that survive well on the southern side. The retaining walls appear to be of drystone construction, but test excavation has indicated the presence of a lime-mortar bonding agent. A formalised pathway also seems to have existed along the southern bank of the stream and is possibly that shown on the 2nd edition of the Ordnance Survey (1869). This also depicts a relative lack of vegetation in the area, suggesting that the trees here today were planted in the 1860s or afterwards to create an afforested riverside walk, presumably for the enjoyment of the occupants of Rock Mount House.

A trench was opened by hand on the southern riverbank, primarily in order to test for earlier milling activity in the area but also to investigate the nature of the riverbank itself. It was 1m wide and 6m long, extending north–south from the riverbank to a near-vertical rock face.

The wall along the southern bank of the river stood to a height of 1.2m from the silt at the bottom, and its upper course protruded from the topsoil. It was constructed of large granite blocks and was roughly coursed.

On removal of a thin layer of topsoil, a layer of rough cobbling was exposed in the centre of the trench. This was composed of roughly laid sub-angular granite stones, with an average diameter of less than 0.2m. A spread of lime mortar ran along the length of the wall and extended outwards to the south for 0.1m. The cobbling lay on a layer of mid–light brown, sandy loam, which contained more granite chippings at the southern end of the trench. Here, at its greatest depth, the layer was 0.2m deep. At the northern end the layer was disturbed by the riverbank wall. The granite bedrock underlies the loam and chippings at c. 0.3m below the upper level of the topsoil.

The pathway and retaining riverbank wall would both appear to be Victorian garden features, and no evidence of earlier features was recorded.

*Franc Myles for Margaret Gowen & Co. Ltd, 2 Killiney View, Albert Road Lower, Glenageary, Co. Dublin.*

### 241. HOLY FAITH CONVENT, CAPPAGH ROAD, FINGLAS
Urban medieval
O129388
95E0100

Following assessments carried out at this site by Eoin Halpin in 1995 (*Excavations 1995*, 24–5) and 1997 (*Excavations 1997*, 56–7) and by Una Cosgrove (*op. cit.*), it was proposed by the Dublin Corporation archaeologist, Daire O'Rourke, that further areas be cleared before development works at the site. This took place on 29 October 1999; however, owing to concern about site security, further investigation was postponed until 2000.

*Martin Reid, 37 Errigal Road, Drimnagh, Dublin 12, for ADS Ltd.*

### 242. MEAKSTOWN, FINGLAS
Post-medieval
99E0351

Pre-development test excavation was undertaken in Meakstown, Finglas, Co. Dublin, in July 1999. The site, then in pasture, is to be the focus of a housing development. In its north-east corner is the site of a suspected enclosure, as well as a late 16th-century brick mansion, SMR 14:20. At present this part of the development area is occupied by farm buildings. All test excavation took place external to these farm buildings in the adjoining field, c. 300m x 150m.

Sixteen test-trenches placed in relation to the proposed housing construction footprint were excavated and recorded. All were 2m wide and ranged from 7m to 20m long.

Five trenches placed immediate to the farm buildings revealed that this area had formerly been a natural hollow built up using red brick rubble and general modern infill material and extended over an area of c. 70m north–south by 40m east–west. Nothing of archaeological significance was uncovered in these trenches.

Approximately 70m to the south of the existing farm buildings two east–west trenches (Nos 7 and 8) were opened, in which short stretches of two limestone block and red brick walls were uncovered. In Trench 7 the wall was oriented north–south and was c. 0.6m wide and at least 0.4m deep. Sherds of post-medieval pottery were also recovered from this trench. In Trench 8 the second wall was visible for 3.6m of its length and was up to 0.5m deep. It was oriented east–west. The walls may represent buildings ancillary to the brick mansion referred to in the SMR or other late farm buildings.

The remaining trenches placed in the centre and the north-western parts of the development area revealed topsoil overlying natural. A further two trenches opened across a subsurface linear feature extending from the southern field boundary to the western field edge proved the feature to be a former field boundary of relatively recent origin.

On the basis of the presence of the two walls in the south-eastern part of the development area, it was recommended that all further groundworks be subject to archaeological monitoring.

*Nóra Bermingham for IAC Ltd, 8 Dungar Terrace, Dun Laoghaire, Co. Dublin.*

### 243. MEAKSTOWN, FINGLAS
Vicinity of 17th-century house
31360 24075
SMR 14:20
99E0351 ext.

Testing was undertaken at Meakstown, Finglas, on 23 and 24 September 1999, before a proposed residential development. A previous programme of testing under the same licence was carried out by Nóra Bermingham (No. 242 above)

The testing was undertaken to determine the impact that the proposed residential development would have on the recorded monument SMR 14:20, identified in the Record of Monuments and Places as a 'dwelling site'. This is marked on the archaeological constraint map as being in the north-east corner of Module G of the proposed development, which is currently occupied by an extensive series of farm buildings. This location is based on the 1st edition of the Ordnance Survey 6-inch map (1838), which places the legend 'Site of Castle' directly to the south of the roadside farm buildings still visible today, almost exactly in the centre of the present farmyard. This identification is consistent with the OS Name Book for Santry parish, which states: 'the offices and out-houses now stand on the site of Castle which formerly fronted the road'.

Adams (1881, 492) makes the connection between the Ordnance Survey site and the Meakstown property of Sir James Ware (1594–1666), noted scholar, antiquarian and Auditor-General of Ireland. The Civil Survey (1654–6) describes Ware's Meakstown holdings in some detail: 'There is upon ye premises a dwelling house of Brick with other office houses therto belonging—as a barne & a stable. Also an orchard and Garden Plott Valu'd by ye Jury at 300 *li*.' Together with 140 acres of land, the Meakstown house constituted the most valuable of Ware's Dublin properties, granted to him in 1638. Unfortunately the Down Survey does not depict Meakstown townland, and thus it is not possible precisely to identify the site of what must have been a substantial brick house.

The earlier programme of archaeological testing did not produce conclusive evidence for this house. However, the immediate area of the farm buildings, the area of greatest archaeological potential, was not part of the proposed development at that time and thus was not included in the testing programme.

Three trenches were opened mechanically, in open areas of the farm, as the buildings were still in use for wintering cattle. Two trenches were placed within the concreted yard, the third in the field immediately to the south of the main barn. Within the northern portion of farmyard a number of drains were identified, as well as spreads of red brick rubble and the disturbed remains of a slight brick wall. The southern portion of the farmyard was built on a depth of made ground, composed of a mixture of clays, gravels, stones, mortar and red brick. To the south of the farmyard, the third trench also identified a considerable depth of made ground, up to 2m thick, overlying a buried sod layer. Beneath this old sod layer a number of features were noted. The foundations of three mortared walls were identified running roughly north–south across the line of the trench, as well as a probable silted-up agricultural drainage ditch. Extending for 10m to the west of the ditch, a compacted mantling of small stones overlain by a layer of red brick and mortar rubble suggests an attempt to provide a stable surface, possibly for a laneway or yard. None of the available cartographic sources indicates either a track or a building in this location.

The testing programme did not conclusively identify the site as the location of the destroyed castle noted in the Name Books and depicted on the 1st edition 6-inch map of 1838. However, the presence of significant quantities of brick and rubble, as well as a number of wall foundations and rough surfaces, suggests considerable activity on the site before its present use as a farmyard. As virtually all the farm buildings shown on the 1838 map are still extant, and none is built predominantly of brick, it must be concluded that these remains relate to an earlier phase of building. As there are no such structures depicted on Rocque's map for 1758, it is possible that the remains are of buildings either already destroyed before this date or, alternatively, constructed and subsequently destroyed between 1758 and 1838.

There is considerable historical evidence for a substantial house and outbuildings belonging to Sir James Ware existing in this immediate area from 1638, and probably constructed somewhat earlier, and thus there is a strong possibility that the remains noted relate to this period. The identification on the OS map of this location as the site of a castle would, according to this interpretation, be seen to refer to the site of a house of the early 17th century.

*Reference*
Adams, B.W. 1881 Antiquarian notes on the parishes of Santry and Clogher. *Journal of the Royal Society of Antiquaries of Ireland* **15**.

*Daniel Leo Swan, Arch-Tech Ltd, 32 Fitzwilliam Place, Dublin 2.*

### 244. ST PATRICK'S WELL, MELLOWES CRESCENT, FINGLAS
Possible Early Christian
30128 22393
SMR 14:06602
99E0196

The monitoring of several foundation trenches on a small sheltered housing development adjacent to St Patrick's Well was undertaken over two days in July 1999. The developer was the City Architect's Department of Dublin Corporation, which funded the work. Initial inspection of the site suggested that the area had been artificially raised over the years to a point where the surface was at least 0.65m above the level of the well.

Although the origins of the well are unknown, the local association with St Patrick would suggest an Early Christian foundation. The well is several hundred metres to the north-west of the medieval St Canice's church and outside the projected extent of the ecclesiastical boundary. It is within the zone of archaeological interest as outlined in the current Dublin City Development Plan.

St Patrick's Well in its present form dates to 1982, when a local committee constructed a canopied housing for it of concrete blocks incorporating a statue of the national patron. The statue (which is now headless and handless) was flanked by smaller statues representing the Blessed Virgin Mary (of which only the feet and ankles survive) and an unidentified saint (which has been completely removed). The whole structure is currently in a state of bad disrepair. The spring was accessed through a metal gate at the base of the structure. This has filled up with rubble, and no water was present either at the time of the monitoring or in late November 1999.

The well is situated in a triangular area that was at least 0.65m below the surface from which the new development was being built. It is separated from the immediate area by a low metal railing. The perimeter wall behind the well has been decorated with murals and a plaque commemorating the rededication of the site in July 1982.

The trenches were mechanically excavated to a depth of between 0.65m and 0.85m below the existing surface. A similar stratigraphic sequence was recorded over much of the area. The initial 0.3m was composed of loose gravel over a broken tarmacadam surface. The surface sealed a layer of redeposited boulder clay, which consisted here of a sandy clay loam, mid-brown with flecks of brighter yellow/brown. This layer was between 0.35m and 0.5m deep and appeared to be getting thicker towards the south of the site. Undisturbed subsoil was encountered at between 0.75m and 0.85m below the ground surface. It was a yellow, pliable, clayey silt with inclusions of fine sand.

One anomaly noted was a linear feature cutting both the natural and redeposited subsoil, at *c.* 0.42m below the surface, extending from the south-west in a north-easterly direction. This was represented by a fill of organic, black marl containing limestone rubble that had a width of between 2.6m and 2.8m. Hand-excavation of the material at several points along the foundation trenches suggested that it was the base of a flat-bottomed field drain that had been truncated during the redevelopment of the area in the 1970s.

Pre-construction monitoring has not recovered any evidence for significant early activity in the vicinity of St Patrick's Well. Such activity may have been removed with the change in usage of the surrounding area from agricultural to residential since 1948. The truncated linear feature recorded in the vicinity of the well does not appear to be co-linear with field boundaries on early Ordnance Survey maps and was probably a field drain.

*Franc Myles, 9 Ben Edair Road, Stonybatter, Dublin.*

### 245. CONVENT OF THE LITTLE SISTERS OF THE ASSUMPTION, PATRICKSWELL PLACE, FINGLAS
No archaeological significance
99E0345

Monitoring of development works associated with the renovation of the convent of the Little Sisters of the Assumption at Patrickswell Place, Finglas, Dublin 11, was required by Dublin Corporation. The site is within the zone of archaeological potential for Finglas town, SMR 14:66, close to King William's Ramparts, SMR 14:06608, and the site of a medieval episcopal residence established by Archbishop Comyn in 1181. This was succeeded by a large manor or residence recorded as 'Springmount' by the OS map of 1837, the site of which is now occupied by the convent of the Holy Faith Sisters.

Groundworks involved machine-excavation of a foundation trench for a new perimeter wall bounding the western side of the property, as well as excavation immediate to the present convent building. The latter involved the excavation of a lift shaft pit at the northern end of the building, a porch extension on the southern side, and an oratory extension and a new drain on the east side. Excavation in these areas revealed a horizon of made ground overlying geologically deposited strata. The depth of made ground varied slightly but was on average 0.25m.

On the western limit of the property a foundation trench for a wall was opened.

It was 1.1m wide and 1.1m deep and extended for *c.* 75m southwards, from close to the north-western end of the current property up to a wall bounding a modern housing estate. Excavation over the first 70m revealed *c.* 0.33m of topsoil, heavily penetrated by

roots, overlying natural. A post-medieval wall two courses high, constructed of roughly shaped limestone blocks and mortar, was uncovered at the southern end of the trench. Finds associated with the wall were red brick and green and brown glass. Redeposited natural had been thrown on top of the wall. The wall may have been associated with the later 'Springmount' residence, still in existence in the mid-19th century, or may represent an entirely unrelated construction event. The wall was clearly of no archaeological significance, and the development was allowed to proceed.
*Nóra Bermingham for IAC Ltd, 8 Dungar Terrace, Dun Laoghaire, Co. Dublin.*

### 246. PARKWEST, GALLANSTOWN
Early Christian cemetery
O081325
99E0108

During topsoil-stripping before the development of a business park, human remains were revealed on a very low mound towards the north-west of this development in February 1999. A rescue excavation was carried out by Cóilín Ó Drisceoil (Archaeological Consultancy Services), which revealed three east–west-oriented skeletons and disarticulated bone. Two other trenches were opened, and four other individuals were exposed in these. It was thus concluded that the site represented an Early Christian cemetery.

An assessment of the extent of the site was required, and eight trenches were opened encircling the area of the known burials. Six burials were partially exposed but, as agreed with *Dúchas*, were not excavated.

In several trenches a wide, shallow ditch was revealed. Two sections were opened through the ditch in two trenches. It was *c.* 2.5m wide and 0.6m deep as revealed in the trench to the north-west of the first burials found. The other section, opened to the south-east, could not be fully excavated as five burials were revealed that were to remain *in situ*. This feature appears to have been backfilled in antiquity, and subsequently burials were inserted into it, suggesting that the cemetery extended beyond this ditch on the south-eastern side.
*Avril Purcell, Margaret Gowen & Co. Ltd, 2 Killiney View, Albert Road Lower, Glenageary, Co. Dublin.*

### 247. 37 PARK WEST INDUSTRIAL PARK, GALLANSTOWN
Close to cemetery
309640 233060

Monitoring of the excavation of the foundations of an ESB transformer room and site security office was carried out at Site 37, Park West Retail and Industrial Park, Gallanstown, Dublin. Construction work has been ongoing at this site since October 1997, and therefore the site has been very much disturbed. Early in 1999 skeletal remains were excavated by Margaret Gowen & Co. Ltd from the same townland (No. 246 above).

Monitoring revealed that the topsoil in this area had already been stripped down to the natural boulder clay as part of the previous development and a layer of hardcore had been laid over most of the site. The foundation trenches, which were excavated to a depth of *c.* 0.6m, revealed no archaeological deposits or stratigraphy.
*Donald Murphy, Archaeological Consultancy Services Ltd, 15 Trinity Street, Drogheda, Co. Louth.*

### 248. GRACEDIEU
Early Christian cemetery
SMR 7:15, 9–10
31801 25244
99E0217

An assessment and limited archaeological excavation were undertaken at Gracedieu, Co. Dublin, as part of the reinforcement of the Brownsbarn to Ballough Gas Pipeline (formerly known as the Northeastern Pipelines, Phases I and II). The site was first discovered on removal of topsoil during the Phase II pipeline operation in 1988 (Margaret Gowen, *Excavations 1988*, 16–17). The complex is within three fields south of the Ballyboughal Road, *c.* 1.5 miles west of the N1 Swords to Lusk road. During the Phase II pipeline operation an enclosed cemetery comprising 65 poorly preserved individuals, seven of whom were interred in stone-lined and covered graves, was uncovered, as well as enclosure ditches and later medieval settlement and industrial remains. The reinforcement pipeline corridor runs parallel to the existing and archaeologically resolved area of the 1988 NEP II, and it consequently encroached on the constraint area for the site as designated by the SMR.

A geophysical survey was undertaken across the proposed new corridor before the assessment, revealing two enclosures as well as a number of linear and dipolar anomalies that provided targets for the assessment stage investigation.

Ten assessment trenches were opened along the western side of the field over a distance of 175m north–south by 30m east–west. The trenches revealed a number of ditch features including the western circuits of the two enclosure ditches detected through aerial photography and geophysical survey. The south-lying enclosure represents the cemetery enclosure excavated as part of the 1988 NEP II investigation. On the basis of the assessment results it was agreed, in consultation with *Dúchas* The Heritage Service, to clear the topsoil from the proposed corridor at Gracedieu in order fully to address and record the archaeological features that would be affected by the pipe-trench and the drive track.

The proposed line of the pipe-trench was marked out through this area to allow the features crossed to be preserved by total record. East of the proposed pipe-trench an area for the construction drive track was also excavated to assess the impact on archaeological features within this area. The excavation revealed the western ditch circuit of the main, south-lying enclosure, which contained the cemetery remains recorded during NEP II operations in 1988. Here the ditch was found to be V-shaped, at most 4m wide by 2.5m deep. Also uncovered was the ditch of an apparent conjoined D-shaped enclosure, which was known to lie immediately north of the cemetery enclosure through both aerial photography and geophysical survey results. A large north–south-aligned ditch along the western limit of the corridor was found to be largely filled in during the late 17th or early 18th century and appears to represent either the remains of a mill-race or a later boundary feature that may have defined the nunnery precinct during post-medieval times. This feature was directly affected by the line of the pipe-trench and was excavated before construction. Other features of note included at least one multi-directional corn-drying kiln, 4m in diameter, and an ironworking area comprising a spread of waste slag and a pit and post-hole setting surrounding a hearth.

Finds from the excavation were largely 17th-century or later, comprising patterned ceramics and bottles, as well as window glass and copious amounts of butchered animal bone. Several sections of the cemetery enclosure ditch to be affected by the construction were excavated, revealing finds of early medieval date including bone pins and pottery of post-13th-century date. No human remains were recovered from the excavation area.

Agreement with the contractor was reached before the construction of the pipe-trench through Gracedieu to infill and raise the drive track level so as not to affect the enclosure ditches revealed during the assessment. Features such as the corn-drying kilns and the metalworking area were fully recorded before the drive track was constructed, preserving them in situ.

*Malachy Conway for Margaret Gowen & Co. Ltd, 2 Killiney View, Albert Road Lower, Glenageary, Co. Dublin.*

### 249. JAMESTOWN
Pale ditch
32110 22415
**99E0456**

Ten trenches were investigated on the site of the proposed Waste Management Centre in Jamestown townland, Co. Dublin. The work was carried out to resolve some requirements of *Dúchas* before the issuing of an EPA licence for the centre.

Trenches 1–3 investigated sections of substantial field boundaries that run at right angles to the Pale Ditch earthwork on its northern side. Trench 1 revealed a flint thumb scraper in a disturbed context to the west of this field bank. A selection of late medieval and post-medieval potsherds was uncovered within the matrix of the bank material, indicating that the bank is of relatively recent origin. A field drain was observed in Trench 2. No archaeological material was observed in Trench 3.

Trenches 4 and 5 were across existing gaps in the Pale Ditch. These confirmed the survival of the Ditch below the gaps but did not produce objects of archaeological interest. A recent field drain cut into the north fosse in Trench 4.

The remaining Trenches 6–10 were opened c. 7–10m south of the Pale Ditch and ran parallel to it. No archaeological material was observed in these trenches.

*Niall Brady, 2 Vale Terrace, Lower Dargle Road, Bray, Co. Wicklow, for Valerie J. Keeley Ltd.*

### 250. 4–8 BOW BRIDGE, KILMAINHAM
Urban 18th/19th century
31345 23378
**99E0078**

The site is on southern side of the ridge of Kilmainham; the Cammock River flows along its southern boundary. The area is of archaeological interest as it is adjacent to Bow Bridge, which is first recorded in the 12th century. It is known that the flat-topped ridge that overlooks the site from the north was the location of *Cell Maighean*, an important Early Christian monastery. It is thought that Kilmainham was the location of the earliest Viking settlement in Dublin. In the medieval period the Knights Hospitallers had a priory where the 18th-century Royal Hospital still stands. This priory owned a fulling mill on the River Cammock in the 16th century.

This excavation took place in response to a condition in the grant of planning permission for a residential development with basement carpark. The site was formerly occupied by a terrace of 18th-century dwellings with yards extending to the riverbank, which were demolished sometime in the past fifty years. For the past twenty years it has been occupied by a warehouse.

Mechanical excavation of two trenches revealed no archaeological features or remains. Trench 1 ran parallel to the street frontage. A series of basements was uncovered, cut into undisturbed natural. Trench 2 was perpendicular to Trench 1. Here, up to 2.5m of 18th-century fill was found to overlay undisturbed natural and riverine deposits.

*James Eogan, ADS Ltd, Windsor House, 11 Fairview Strand, Dublin 3.*

### 251. 7–11 MOUNT BROWN, KILMAINHAM
Tanning pits
21325 23370
**99E0258**

A series of test-trenches was opened up to the rear of Nos 7–11 Mount Brown, Kilmainham, on 23 June 1999. Three staggered cuttings were dug to the rear of Nos 11 and 10. It was not possible to cut a continuous trench because of water seepage from the Cammock River, situated immediately to the north. The three cuttings were opened to an average depth of 1–2m. The base consisted of yellow daub and loose gravel, consistent with an undisturbed natural ground surface. This was overlain in each trench by a heavy layer of riverine silt averaging 1m deep. The upper layer was consistent with garden soil and debris of 19th- and 20th-century date.

A second series of three staggered cuttings was dug to the rear of No. 8. Cutting A was c. 3m from the end wall of the plot, which abuts the southern edge of the Cammock River. It extended southwards for a distance of 5.8m. A natural daub and gravel horizon was present at a depth of 2.2m. This is overlain by a silt deposit averaging 1.2m thick. A mortared wall, orientated east–west, cuts through the cutting at the north. Its present surface is 1m below ground level, and it extends to a depth of c. 0.8m. A brick-lined sewer extends the entire length of the western section of the cutting. It lies immediately below the concrete ground surface.

During the testing, a series of wooden structures was identified in the rear yard of No. 8 Mount Brown. It appeared to be the remains of two rectangular timber pits or tanks. A clear section of one of the pits was exposed, and part of a second one. Each structure contained a 0.4m-thick deposit of mulch containing wood bark at the base. The structure is made up of vertical square posts with horizontal planking for the sides and base. Some of the base timbers were partly damaged by the digger. The planks and post appear to be of planed timber, and the planks themselves are nailed very tightly and neatly together using what appear to be hand-forged nails of 18th/19th-century type. A sample of wood bark was retrieved from the mulch deposit. It contained an acorn fragment, which suggests that at least some of the bark is oak.

A second 6m-long trench was dug to the rear of No. 8, and a wooden structure was identified close to the surface. It is similar to that previously described and consists of two, possibly three, pits or tanks that extend almost the entire length of the cutting. The walls are made of tightly fitting lengths of planed timber laid horizontally and nailed together using hand-forged nails. They are in turn nailed to upright posts that are square in section. A series of three wooden dividers was present, forming three separate pits or tanks. These were defined by square upright posts of planed timber onto which the horizontal timbers are laid. The central chamber has a tightly fitting planked bottom. It is present at a depth of 1.6m below present ground level. This chamber was filled to a depth of 0.5m with a mulch containing wood bark fragments. The easternmost chamber does not appear to have any bottom, is silt-filled and does not contain a mulch deposit. Its eastern wall face is wooden but has a central gap resembling a sluice-gate of some kind. There appears to be at least one surviving groove to hold a thin sectioned cross timber. The entire wooden structure is cut into the silt layer.

Following the identification of these wooden structures, a full excavation of the rear of No. 8 was undertaken in July 1999. The excavation exposed a two-phase use of the site. The earlier phase consisted of a series of wooden tanning tanks or pits that extended the entire area of the rear yard of No. 8. Two sets of tanks were identified, one larger than the other, separated by a narrow aisle. A number of the wooden tanks extend eastwards into the adjoining property of No. 7 (known as the Band Hall). Narrow gaps in the stonework along the party wall were consistent in size and orientation with the end timbers of the wooden tanks, indicating that the western wall of the Band Hall had been constructed around and over the wooden tanks and had thereby cut through a number of them.

All of these tanks contained an organic mulch deposit. One of the smaller tanks is now part of the National Museum of Ireland's Folklife collection. An examination of this tank revealed that the base timbers were nailed from the base, which indicates that the tanks were not built *in situ*.

The second phase of industrial use on the site consisted of a series of brick tanks. These were built directly on top of the wooden tanks, and in some cases the upper timbers of the wooden tanks were deliberately cut or broken to facilitate the brick tanks. Four of the tanks were connected and were situated at the southern end of the yard. The contents of these tanks indicate that they were used to hold early 20th-century coal and refuse. The primary deposits in each tank, however, consisted of a rope-like fabric that overlay but was partly embedded in the surface of a thick, white deposit of lime. The fabric/rope may have been undergoing some industrial process in these tanks. The presence of lime in the base of the four tanks may be associated with the cleaning of animal hides.

The remaining two were large, single, brick tanks. Both abutted the wall that divided the yard from the Cammock River. One was situated in the north-west corner of the yard. It had an outflow opening with a blocking mechanism at floor level. It also contained a false floor of timber planks. These were the same as the planks used in the wooden tanks and were probably reused here. The base of this tank contained a shallow deposit of light green sludge. The second tank is situated in the north-east corner of the site abutting the river. It was not fully investigated, as part of it appears to extend under the adjoining property of No. 7 Mount Brown. This is significant in terms of establishing a dating sequence because that building, which now houses the Band Hall, was present on an early 19th-century Ordnance Survey map of the area.

This is a tannning yard. Members of the Shannon family were tanners in the Kilmainham area from at least the late 18th century and are listed in various Dublin directories as occupiers of houses in Mount Brown in the early 19th century. Leather-making involves three processes, whereby animal skins are cleaned, tanned and dressed. Tanning is often a highly polluting process that requires a water source, and the Cammock River, immediately to the rear of the yard, is likely to have been the reason for siting the tannery here. There are two ways by which tanning may be effected, using either vegetable tannins or chromium salts. In this case vegetable tanning was used. It involves the soaking of prepared skins in tannic acid. This acid occurs in the bark, wood, fruit and galls of certain trees such as the oak. The function of the tannic acid is essential in the manufacture of leather from hides in that it precipitates gelatine to give an insoluble compound.

The identification of an acorn within the bark fill of the wooden structure in Trench A is consistent with an interpretation that these are soaking pits containing tannic acids in which hides were immersed. The well-preserved condition of the timbers and the position of the structures in the silt layer are also consistent with this view.

The entire area is not yet archaeologically resolved because of access and ownership issues, and it is hoped because of this to return in 2000.
*Erin Gibbons, 45 Daniel Street, Dublin 8, for Arch-Tech Ltd.*

### 252. DEPUTY MASTER'S HOUSE, ROYAL HOSPITAL, KILMAINHAM
Urban
**31327 23384**
**98E0365**

Monitoring took place of the refurbishment and extension of the Deputy Master's House, Royal Hospital, Kilmainham, from August 1998 until February 1999. This house is within the grounds of the present Royal Hospital, erected in the 1680s and built as a hospital and refuge for ex-soldiers. The general area of the present Royal Hospital is reputedly the site of a Knights Hospitallers foundation, granted to the Knights Hospitallers of St John of Jerusalem by Strongbow in 1174. The church of St Maighnenn of Kilmainham, dating from the 7th or 8th century, is also reputed to be close to the present Royal Hospital, and the Kilmainham/Islandbridge area is well known for its Viking burial finds. The present Deputy Master's House was erected in 1763 and replaced an earlier flanker (one of four symmetrical flankers of the main hospital).

Initial test-trenches within the basement of the Deputy Master's House and to the north and east of the present house revealed no archaeological structures. However, the presence of some fragments of late medieval 13th/14th-century tiles from the base of a trench to the immediate east of the house indicated medieval activity in the area. Consequently, full monitoring of all the basement excavations and the extensions and improvements to the north and east were carried out.

Within the basement of the house no trace of any earlier foundations that may have been associated with the earlier flanker built in the 1680s was revealed. The extension to the east of the house, which measured 16m x 8m, was brought down to a depth of 2.5m. There was no evidence for any structures pre-dating the construction of the present house, and this area to the east of the Deputy Master's House appears to have served as a general dump for the kitchen, with various layers of refuse containing a small amount of post-medieval pottery and glass being revealed. There was also considerable evidence for the artificial heightening of this area, with layers of red brick, stone and soil having been brought in to level up what appears to be have been a piece of land that sloped markedly to the east.

Close to the east face of the house the general area had been considerably disturbed by the insertion of later drains. A small box drain was revealed at the northern end of this extension. However, it should be pointed out that a fragment of a line-impressed medieval floor tile was retrieved close to the east face of the house at a depth of 2.5m and close to the location of the medieval tile fragments recovered during the initial trial-trenching.

The area to the immediate north of the house, measuring 12m x 12m, was lowered by 0.5–1m in order to provide a flat surface for landscaping. During the monitoring of the work, several walls, running north–south and east–west, were revealed; all appeared to be contemporary with the present house and seemed to form rooms connected to the basement area. However, a very fine, red brick, arched passageway was revealed in this area. This was 4m long, 2.7m wide and 1.4m high and appeared to back onto some subsurface basement rooms added on to the northern side of the house at a later period. The red brick passage terminated where the southern boundary wall of the sculpture garden is now. It was not possible to investigate this feature fully as it was very unstable and was being backfilled immediately. The roof of the structure had been removed at sometime in the past, and the interior of the passage appeared to be covered with soot.

With the exception of the medieval floor tiles, no evidence was found for any archaeological structures on the site, and no further medieval artefacts or finds were recovered. There was no evidence for the earlier flanker on the site of the current Deputy Master's House, although all traces of this may have been removed with the digging out of the foundations for the present house. The impressed floor tiles suggest a medieval presence in the area, but it was clear that they were not *in situ*. No medieval horizons were found during the monitoring, suggesting that the earlier Knights Hospitallers foundation lies elsewhere on this important site.

*Sylvia Desmond, 25 Rowan Hall, Millbrook Court, Milltown, Dublin 6, for Judith Carroll & Co. Ltd, Pine Forest Art Centre, Pine Forest Road, Glencullen, Co. Dublin, and 13 Anglesea Street, Dublin 2.*

## 253. KILSHANE
Unenclosed cemetery
**31037 24281**
**SMR 14:48**
**99E0220**

An assessment and subsequent monitoring (see No. 161 above) of topsoil removal were undertaken at Kilshane, Co. Dublin, as part of the reinforcement of the Brownsbarn to Ballough Gas Pipeline (formerly known as the Northeastern Pipelines, Phases I and II). The name Kilshane contains the element 'Kil', or *Cill*, signifying a church, while the second element is less certain, but in at least one other instance (in County Limerick) a church site called *Cill Senaig* has been anglicised as Kilshane. That being the case, the County Dublin site may well represent the church of Senach.

The site, first discovered on removal of topsoil during the Phase II pipeline operation in 1988, is in a flat, low-lying area *c.* 0.5 miles to the west of the N2, near St Margaret's. During Phase II pipeline operations an unenclosed cemetery comprising 123 individuals was revealed over a 21m stretch of the pipeline corridor (see report by Margaret Gowen in *Excavations 1988*, 17). Consequent to this discovery, the site was included in the SMR by the National Monuments and Historic Properties Service.

The new reinforcement pipeline corridor runs parallel to the existing and archaeologically resolved area of 1988 and thereby encroached the SMR constraint area for the cemetery site. Geophysical survey of the proposed corridor was undertaken before the assessment.

In summary, the assessment revealed one feature of archaeological potential, and no further features or finds were revealed during subsequent monitoring of topsoil-stripping before pipe-laying.

Magnetic gradiometry and electrical soil-resistivity surveys were undertaken at the site. The former technique indicated strong ferrous (iron) interference within the western area of the survey grid, along with two anomalies representing possible ditch features. One these anomalies is just beyond the disturbance zone caused by the existing gas pipe and is almost certainly ditch F140 revealed in the NEP II 1988 operation. Various clusters of small anomalies were also discerned, along with regular linear-trending anomalies, suggesting changes in the underlying geology. The resistivity survey revealed a number of low-resistance linear trends, which coincide with the magnetic anomalies, indicating possible ditches. However, the majority of the resistivity responses appeared to reflect natural variations in resistance values across the site, especially along the western edge of the survey grid, which would suggest disturbance from the pipe and 1988 construction. The same may also be said of a number of linear trends in the north-eastern corner of the survey grid, which equate with plough action or other modern disturbances.

Four test-trenches were excavated across the proposed 30m wayleave realignment corridor. The trenches were directly east of the area excavated and resolved in 1988. The position of the trenches was largely determined by the anomalous responses from the geophysical survey carried out before the assessment.

Trenches 1 and 2 were conjoined in T-shaped plan, with Trench 1 orientated north-west/south-east and Trench 2 set perpendicular to its centre and extending away in a south-west direction. The position of Trench 1 was determined by the double-ditch-like response from the geophysical survey, which correlates with a ditch excavated at the eastern limit of the 1988 NEP II pipeline corridor and which appeared to mark the eastern boundary of the cemetery. The position of Trench 2 was also determined by geophysical responses, in this case a number of roughly west–east-lying linear anomalies. Trenches 3 and 4 were conjoined in T-shaped plan, as with Trenches 1 and 2, and were positioned south of these. Only a few limited anomalous responses were detected in the southern portion of the survey grid, and the position of Trenches 3 and 4 was largely designed to test a number of these responses as well as to examine areas that failed to give a response.

Trench 1 was positioned 112m from the eastern field boundary and measured 22m by 2m. Removal of topsoil 0.25–0.3m deep revealed two modern drainage features between 0.4 and 0.5m wide and cut directly into subsoil, which in this area was brown, sandy clay containing frequent stones. The eastern half of the test-trench was completely devoid of features and was characterised by grey clay subsoil with less stone than on the western side.

Trench 2, 29m by 2.1m, was conjoined with Trench 1. Several roughly north-west/south-east-aligned features, mostly natural, were revealed on removal of topsoil. Only one item of archaeological significance was revealed, a west–east linear feature, which extended beyond the western limit of the test-trench. The feature, initially defined by several longitudinally set stones, was characterised by a roughly linear spread of dark soil containing charcoal and numerous (apparently heat-shattered) angular stones. The feature, which survived in the trench in a truncated form, was up to 1.9m long by at most 0.75m wide and at its deepest point, the west section, was found to be up to 0.15m deep. A single fragment of iron slag was recovered from the fill of the feature at the western section. The east end of the feature was rounded in plan and delimited by iron staining in the subsoil. It was significantly shallower than the western end and contained a thin lens of grey clay flecked with charcoal, overlying and partially cutting into the brown clay subsoil at this point. The western section of the feature comprised charcoal-flecked, grey clay overlying a deposit of orange, friable ash and a basal deposit of soil charcoal. None of the stones either within or forming the limits of the feature were found to be burnt. It was estimated that the feature could extend, at most, only a further 0.3m beyond the western section face, which was confirmed during later monitoring. In attempting to date this feature, and also taking into account that some possible fragments of bone were associated with the uppermost fill deposit, it would seem that the feature is fairly late, possibly after AD 1700.

The excavation of Trenches 3 and 4 failed to reveal deposits, features or finds of archaeological significance. A simple sequence of topsoil, between 0.25m and 0.3m deep, was found to overlie either yellow/brown clay or grey boulder clay.

No further features were revealed during topsoil removal of the pipeline corridor in late July 1999. The solitary archaeological feature, revealed in Trench 2, appears to be an isolated linear feature, which in the absence of clearly datable finds would appear to be post-17th-century in date.

*Malachy Conway for Margaret Gowen & Co. Ltd, 2 Killiney View, Albert Road Lower, Glenageary, Co. Dublin.*

### 254. KILLEGAR ROAD, KILTIERNAN
No archaeological significance
98E0314

Archaeological testing was carried out in July 1998 in compliance with planning conditions for the proposed development of a house. Several sites with standing remains surround the development area, the closest of which is a megalithic tomb. The assessment was intended to identify subsurface remains associated with these sites.

Any activities associated with known sites had been obliterated by a cultivation system, which has subsequently been levelled by recent ploughing.

*Sarah Cross for Margaret Gowen & Co. Ltd, 2 Killiney View, Albert Road Lower, Glenageary, Co. Dublin.*

**Editor's note:** Though carried out during 1998, the report on this site was received too late for inclusion in the bulletin of that year.

### 255. CASTLEFIELD AVENUE, KNOCKLYON
No archaeological significance
31150 22725
98E0586

Work on the site of a small housing development in Knocklyon was monitored because it adjoined Knocklyon Castle, a late medieval structure restored in the early 19th century and still inhabited. Nothing was found except a layer of recent refuse overlying natural gravel. The area was the site of a hill, apparently that which gave Knocklyon its name, which was levelled in the late 18th or early 19th century to provide gravel for road building. Any earlier remains would have been destroyed at that time.

*Thaddeus C. Breen, 13 Wainsfort Crescent, Dublin 6W.*

### 256. LAMBAY ISLAND
Neolithic axe production with associated activity
O317508
93E0144

This site is an important stone axe production site of Neolithic date with a range of associated features. It is the first axe production site recognised in Ireland or Britain where pecking and hammering rather than flaking were the primary methods of working the rock and where there is evidence of grinding and polishing the axe roughouts at the place of production. The rock quarried on the site is porphyritic andesite (porphyry), which forms the sides of two small valleys. The larger and more easterly valley was the initial focus of excavation. Cuttings 1 and 2 and a series of test-pits (14–21) along the bank of porphyry debitage on the east side of the valley indicate that there was a series of extraction and production episodes. From the results of the 1997–8 seasons (*Excavations 1997*, 57–9; *Excavations 1998*, 62–5) it is clear that quarrying also took place in a smaller valley immediately to the west.

Excavation on the floor of the eastern valley has been centred on a 20m-by-20m area with the purpose of linking the working areas close to the rock face and the features recognised on the valley floor. In the south of this area, excavation in 1999 focused on uncovering more of what had been initially interpreted as a Neolithic occupation surface. In an excavation area of 9m x 6m this context (C904) was revealed as having a considerable surface expression with a very high density of Neolithic finds of a range of materials. It is now clear that this is not an occupation deposit but a deliberately created low monument with a number of distinct zones recognisable on the surface, including zones of beach pebbles, beach gravel and slabs. This monument appears to cover earlier features and to incorporate features that may initially have been discrete. The most notable of the latter are a number of stone settings in a stratigraphic sequence. These resemble somewhat the settings found at passage tomb complexes, and this analogy is strengthened by the character of some of the material in C904. This includes a fragment of an Orkney-type macehead and two jasper pendants. This area has major potential for the understanding of the sequence and duration of activity on the site. It is also of wider significance because of the complexity of the depositional activities.

At the north end of the 20m-by-20m area, excavation of what had been the major focus of work on the valley floor from 1996 onwards was completed (this is the area around Test-Pit 2, Cuttings 5–8, see *Excavations 1996*, 36–7, and references above). In the east of this excavation area the original soil, or palaeosol, is partially preserved, in contrast to the western part of the area, where only truncated Neolithic archaeological features cut into the subsoil survive. On the other hand, the palaeosol was very heavily churned around by rabbit burrow activity, and only the stone fills of features retained any integrity in this area. Excavation of F7 and F11, which before excavation were interpreted as being like F1 (a large, stone-filled pit that had a complex series of structured deposits, a radiocarbon date from charcoal in which indicates a date range of 3965–3383 BC), demonstrated that the 'cairn effect' of these features was created by packing stones and sediment into and over scoops/slots dug into the subsoil. There were deposits of cultural material in both of these features. The stretch of foundation trench immediately to the east and north of F7 could be shown to be stratigraphically earlier than F7.

Quarrying of the porphyritic andesite also took place in the small valley to the west of the larger valley that had been the initial focus of the excavation project. Here, excavation of a transect across the valley (Cutting 11) was completed in 1999. From the excavation, it is clear that quarrying of the porphyry here was concentrated on the lower area of the west-facing outcrop. Here a series of major debitage layers could be recognised, with more localised working indicated by less widespread contexts. On the surface of and in one of the major debitage layers, about midway up the stratigraphic sequence of debitage, were clusters of sherds of Early Neolithic carinated bowl pottery, associated with struck flint.

The fieldwork stage of the excavation will be completed in 2000.
*Gabriel Cooney, Department of Archaeology, University College, Belfield, Dublin 4.*

### 257. SHANGANAGH, LOUGHLINSTOWN (BRAY ROAD)
Geophysical anomalies
O242237
99E0181

Test-trenching was undertaken on the site following a geophysical survey before development. Five anomalies, which possibly represented archaeological features, were highlighted during the geophysical survey. A test-trench was opened in each of the areas of these anomalies. A small spread of charcoal-rich soil was found in one of the trenches; however, a sherd of modern pottery was found *in situ* within this feature.

The site was of no archaeological significance.
*Avril Purcell, Margaret Gowen & Co. Ltd, 2 Killiney View, Albert Road Lower, Glenageary, Co. Dublin.*

### 258. MOUNT ST ANNE'S CONVENT, MILLTOWN
No archaeological significance
SMR 9:28
99E0022

Testing was carried out before the development of a housing scheme. Eight trenches were mechanically opened to natural subsoil with a 0.6m back bucket. Only one feature of possible archaeological interest was recorded (a linear feature that may represent the remains of an earlier field boundary), along with several field drains and a dump of 19th- or early 20th-century rubbish. If there had been medieval occupation in this area, it has been obliterated by the subsequent disturbance of ground levels by later cultivation.

The complex of buildings at the south-eastern corner of the proposed development site, formally the convent of Mount St Anne's, is dominated by Milltown House, which can be dated, from the interior stucco work, to the late 1760s. This structure was built on the site, or in the close vicinity, of

Milltown Castle, which from its description in the mid-17th-century Down Survey would appear to have been a gabled dwelling or possibly a fortified house. Demolition of the buildings to the west and north of the former convent will be monitored in 2000, and further trenching will establish the nature and extent of archaeological strata or structures in this area.

*Franc Myles for Margaret Gowen & Co. Ltd, 2 Killiney View, Albert Road Lower, Glenageary, Co. Dublin.*

### 259. CIANLEA, MOORESTOWN
No archaeological significance
31677 24747
SMR 11:19
99E0536

Testing and subsequent monitoring were carried out at this site. A housing development is being constructed in the vicinity of the building known as Glasmore Abbey. Analysis of aerial photographs revealed a possible enclosure surrounding the building and another circular feature to the south-west. A series of trenches positioned to determine the nature of both of these circular features revealed no evidence to suggest that they were of archaeological importance, rather that the second circular feature was in fact a horse-training ring.

Furthermore, historical evidence suggests that this is not the location of Glasmore Abbey, which, according to the *Martyrology of Oengus*, is situated to the south of Swords. O'Donovan, in the Ordnance Survey Name Books, recorded that the building known as Glasmore Abbey was pointed out to him by a local man.

In the subsequent monitoring programme no material of archaeological significance was identified.

*Rónán Swan, Arch-Tech Ltd, 32 Fitzwilliam Place, Dublin 2.*

### 260. CRUISERATH, MULHUDDART
18th-century house and farmyard
O145339
99E0620

This site at Cruiserath, Mulhuddart, Co. Dublin, was due to be redeveloped for industrial purposes and lay adjacent to an existing, newly developed industrial office park. The site is bounded by Ballycoolin Road to the south, the Goddamendy Industrial Park to the east, agricultural fields to the north and Church Road to the west. An archaeological assessment of the site was requested as a condition of planning permission.

The proposed development was the subject of an environmental impact statement, the cultural heritage research for which included an assessment of the medieval and more recent history of the site. The sources suggested that it had limited archaeological potential. The townland name is derived from the name of its early medieval owners, the Cruise family. Clearly the appendage 'rath' either suggests the pre-existence of a rath within the townland or may refer to a medieval, moated earthwork site. No remains of either type of site can be identified in the cultivated lands of the townland or in the aerial photographs of the site.

The later medieval development of the site was undocumented, but Rocque's map indicated a number of structures/dwellings and an associated garden on the site, which coincided with the position of the access drive to the house from the west. Cruiserath House, as depicted on the 1st edition of the Ordnance Survey, was also undocumented.

The site of Cruiserath House and its adjacent farm buildings saw continuous use, modification and rebuilding from the 19th century. The house appeared to have been demolished in the 1940s or 1950s and replaced with a small, double-fronted house to the south. A very large industrial farmyard was later developed, apparently in the 1970s. The site was evidently cleared of all structures and boundaries, even the recent farm buildings, before the preparation of the environmental impact statement and before the acquisition of the site for development purposes. All that survived were the very extensive concrete yard surface, three large silage pits, the overgrown remains of the tarmac drive to the concrete yard area and the modern house, the foundations of which are easily identified.

The test-trenching was undertaken in two phases during November 1999. Long slit-trenches were opened using a mechanical excavator with a 2m-wide toothless bucket. These were positioned between the remains of the modern house, the supposed site of the earlier house and the modern farmyard. A number of supplementary trenches were later opened in areas where features were revealed.

The test-trenches revealed the very truncated and disturbed remains of a number of masonry and red brick walls and the very well-preserved remains of cobbled surfaces, all of which were found, when superimposed by CAD, to accord remarkably with the layout depicted on the 1st edition of the OS. The remains were too poorly preserved to establish their relative date, and it was not possible, without full excavation, to establish whether any remains of the 18th-century house survived or to what extent it may have been modified. The high level of resolution between the remains record and the OS, however, in spite of the poor preservation of the remains, facilitated the identification of various elements of the house and the early farmyard complex, including the walled garden, kitchen garden and quadrangular farmyard. The structure for the new industrial facility did not impinge on the complex, and to avoid a requirement for full excavation the associated carpark was raised in level in order to preserve the remains *in situ*.

*Margaret Gowen, Margaret Gowen & Co. Ltd, 2 Killiney View, Albert Road Lower, Glenageary, Co. Dublin.*

### 261. RATHFARNHAM GOLF CLUB, NEWTOWN
Burnt mound, burnt spreads
O134255
99E0344

A 20-acre golf-course development on the lower slopes of the Dublin Mountains in Rathfarnham, Co. Dublin, was subject to an archaeological monitoring condition. However, extensive groundworks, involving the stripping of topsoil and excavation into geological strata, had taken place before archaeological attendance. As a result, a damage assessment of the development area was conducted on instruction from *Dúchas*. Following this, all outstanding groundworks were monitored.

Monitoring of soil removal in the north-west corner of the development site revealed a single burnt mound with two smaller spreads of burning that may or may not have been associated with it. Here an existing watercourse was to be altered to form a pond. The watercourse ran east–west across the northern end of the development area to join up with the Owendoher River, bordering the golf-course's eastern edge. It is likely that the watercourse had once been an open stream subsequently altered by agricultural and golf-course activity.

The burnt mound was on a natural knoll just a few metres to the south of the watercourse. The mound was low, had a minimum depth of 0.15m and consisted of burnt stone, charcoal and patches of burnt clay resulting from *in situ* burning. The full extent of the mound was not obtained, as it extended beyond the area excavated for pond construction. Mound material was visible over an area *c.* 15m east–west by 6m north–south. No portable finds were retrieved from the exposed parts of the mound.

Two burnt spreads were identified *c.* 7m to the north-west of the burnt mound, on the northern side of the existing watercourse. Neither had been fully exposed. One was a charcoal spread 1m x 0.8m, and the other was a gritty, grey/blue clay and charcoal spread at least 1.5m x 1m. No artefacts were found in association with these deposits.

During this phase of monitoring, no other features of archaeological significance were uncovered. In several locations over the development area sherds of post-medieval pottery and clay pipe fragments were visible, and a number of field drains and French drains were also identified.

The burnt mound and the two burnt spreads were later fully excavated by Martin Reid. This extension included the monitoring of any additional outstanding groundworks.

*Nóra Bermingham, ADS Ltd, Windsor House, 11 Fairview Strand, Dublin 3.*

## 262. POPPINTREE PARK, POPPINTREE
Site of well
31435 24002
SMR 14:65
99E0469

An assessment was requested before construction of the North Fringe Sewer in north County Dublin. The proposed route of the sewer is through Poppintree Park, close to the site of a historic well marked as Jamestown Well on the 1st edition Ordnance Survey map. The well is not associated with a saint and may be a natural well serving Jamestown House. No visible trace of the well survives on the ground, and it is now built over by tennis courts.

Two test-trenches were opened by mechanical digger along the line of the sewer, both *c.* 14m long.

No archaeological features or deposits were identified in either of the test-trenches. There was no surface evidence of Jamestown Well or other anomalies in the area to the south of the tennis courts.
*Tim Coughlan, Margaret Gowen & Co. Ltd, 2 Killiney View, Albert Road Lower, Glenageary, Co. Dublin.*

## 263. ROBSWALL, PORTMARNOCK
Flint scatter
SMR 26:119
99E0550

Archaeological field-walking and test-pit excavation were carried out at the site of a proposed development north-west of Portmarnock, Co. Dublin, on 27 September 1999. The site is in Robswall townland, *c.* 350m west of the coast road and 160m north of Portmarnock village. The proposed development site is within an area of pasture, with a school immediately adjacent to the south-west. The site is between two recorded archaeological sites: a holy well (SMR 12:38) 350m east of the development and a flint scatter (SMR 12:37) *c.* 140m south-east of the development.

Between 1964 and 1983 a collection of around 2500 prehistoric artefacts was made from this area. It seems likely, however, that this collection contains material from a wider area than it is actually attributed to. In this respect it would include some of the fields on which the proposed development is to be constructed. The quantity of flint recovered from this area led to an excavation of the site in 1983 by David Keeling, 200m north of the proposed development site. A substantial collection of lithic material was recovered from the ploughsoil; however, only scant remains of archaeological features were found cut into subsoil. Two of the features contained charcoal, which gave radiocarbon dates of *c.* 2000 BC. The excavation concluded that intensive ploughing had removed or truncated most of the subsurface archaeological features and in so doing had transferred most of the archaeological material into the ploughsoil. Recent field-walking by Avril Purcell before the development of a site 400m to the north on the coast road recovered a quantity of worked flint (see Appendix No. 1).

The site consists of two fields, of which the western had been ploughed to facilitate field-walking. An initial site inspection on 23 August 1999 recovered several fragments of natural flint, sherds of late 19th-century pottery, red brick fragments and an iron nail. Before this visit a strip *c.* 5m wide, running the entire length of the field, had been stripped of topsoil (maximum depth 0.5m). An access road was being constructed west of the ploughed field, requiring the removal of topsoil and the insertion of a drainage pipe. An inspection of these works revealed a limited depth of topsoil in this area and a thin layer of brown clay overlying rocky outcrops.

Archaeological field-walking and test-pit excavation on 27 September 1999 revealed a flint scatter in the north-west corner of the field, lying largely beyond the area of development. Six 1m$^2$ test-pits were excavated within the ploughed area, their location based on the density and type of lithic material present on the field surface. The material from the test-pits was passed through a sieve to recover lithic and other material. No soils or features of archaeological significance were identified during test-pit excavation. In general the material recovered reflects variations in the natural geology of the area. The test-pit results suggest limited archaeological potential within the proposed development area.

A low-frequency concentration of flint was

noticed within the higher, north-western area of the ploughed field. This area is immediately west of the proposed development. The eastern side of the field had been partially stripped of topsoil that had been banked along the eastern and southern edges of the field. A single end scraper of fairly good quality was recovered from the edge of the remaining section of the ploughed field at a location c. 10m south of the north-lying field boundary. The greatest concentration of flint was found in the north-west area of the ploughed field, corresponding with its highest location. There was a marked fall-off in both the number (frequency) and quality of the flint material to the east, south-east and south of this area. One must conclude that, purely on the basis of the material recovered, there is a low-frequency rate of diagnostic artefact types to that of rubbish and flint spalls, even in the higher, north-west area of the field. The lithic material was evenly distributed throughout the first 0.2m of the topsoil in each of the test-pits, with frequency decreasing with depth. No lithic material nor any indicators of archaeological activity were observed within subsoil at the base of the test-pits. However, this does not preclude the existence of such features, even in truncated form within the field.

*Malachy Conway for Margaret Gowen & Co. Ltd, 2 Killiney View, Albert Road Lower, Glenageary, Co. Dublin.*

### 264. ROBSWALL, PORTMARNOCK
Flint scatter
**32426 24506**
**99E0550 ext.**

Monitoring of topsoil-stripping for this complex of playing pitches was carried out in October–December 1999. This followed an earlier phase of monitoring by Helen Kehoe and field-walking and testing by Malachy Conway (No. 263 above).

Three separate areas/activities were monitored. These included the stripping of topsoil and subsoil for the playing pitches, the excavation of the foundation trenches for the clubhouse building, and an associated service trench.

Within the area stripped for the playing pitches occasional medium-sized and large stones were revealed. Clusters of these were examined to ascertain whether they acted as flint-knapping areas. No indications of such *in situ* activity were revealed. Several pieces of flint were recovered during stripping, although no features that could be associated with this material were observed. A single stone-packed post-hole was revealed toward the centre of the site. Despite cleaning around this, no associated features were found. In the north-east of the site a small hearth was revealed. This appeared to be the result of a single episode of burning.

The excavation of drains for the playing pitches was also monitored. No archaeological finds or features were exposed during their excavation. Excavation of the clubhouse foundations and the associated service trench did not reveal archaeological material.

Some 24 pieces of struck flint were recovered from the area stripped. These appear to have derived from small water-rolled pebbles, collected from the nearby seashore and used for knapping. The collection consists of twelve portions of crudely worked cores and the discarded products of core reduction. Five small flakes were recovered, of which one has slight indications of retouch, although this may equally be damage sustained in the ploughsoil. All of the lithic material found is quite patinated.

*Ian W. Doyle, Margaret Gowen & Co. Ltd, 2 Killiney View, Albert Road Lower, Glenageary, Co. Dublin.*

### 265. ST FRANCIS'S HOSPICE, RAHENY
Site of windmill
**32163 23874**
**SMR 15:85**
**99E0702**

An assessment was carried out at the site of a proposed development at St Francis's Hospice, Raheny, Dublin 5. A planning application was made to Dublin Corporation by St Francis's Hospice to develop lands to the east of the existing hospice building. The site of a possible windmill is recorded in the SMR and in the historical sources, in the vicinity of the proposed development.

The assessment was based on the excavation of five test-trenches opened on 10 December 1999 by mechanical digger. No archaeological deposits were identified.

*Tim Coughlan, Margaret Gowen & Co. Ltd, 2 Killiney View, Albert Road Lower, Glenageary, Co. Dublin.*

### 266. IRISHTOWN ROAD/DERMOT O'HURLEY AVENUE, RINGSEND
Urban
**O183337**
**99E0145**

Five test-trenches were excavated on the site before development. They revealed largely 19th-century material sitting on layers of yellow sand and clay. This material appears to have built up on the site following the growth of this area as a suburb of Dublin during the 19th century.

The site was of no archaeological significance.

*Avril Purcell, Margaret Gowen & Co. Ltd, 2 Killiney View, Albert Road Lower, Glenageary, Co. Dublin.*

### 267. COLDWATER COMMONS, SAGGART
Medieval
**O040258**
**99E0562**

The site is a large expanse of land at the east side of Saggart village. Construction of a golf-course over most of the area is now complete, and the developer intends to construct several areas of golf houses. The site was visited on 8 and 9 September 1999, and test excavation was undertaken from 18 to 20 October 1999, using a mechanical excavator.

Construction of the golf-course was well advanced over most of the site. The site has been landscaped, with hillocks and ponds created, levelled and seeded. All earth-moving that relates to the construction of the golf-course was completed. The area of the development was walked on 9 September 1999, and the edges of drain cuttings, machine tracks and spoilheaps were cursorily examined for indicators of archaeological remains. No features or finds of archaeological interest were noted in the test-trenches. The only finds of interest—medieval pottery and flints—were recovered from the initial field-walking of the site.

Much of the topsoil had been previously removed from the site, particularly in those areas close to Saggart village, where medieval remains would be most expected.

*Claire Walsh, Archaeological Projects Ltd, 25A Eaton Square, Terenure, Dublin 6W.*

### 268. THE OLD BURIAL GROUND, SAGGART
Possible Early Christian
30038 22067
SMR 21:34
99E0229

Test-trenching was undertaken in July on behalf of South Dublin County Council, which intends to extend the existing graveyard to the field to the north-east. The graveyard would appear to incorporate an Early Christian ecclesiastical enclosure within its southern extent.

Two trenches were mechanically opened across the proposed extension. The first was 105m long and extended from the south-eastern corner of the field (adjacent to the early enclosure) to the north-eastern corner. The second trench ran at a right angle to the first and extended for 50m into the north-western corner of the field. They were both opened to double the width of the bucket (i.e. 1.2m).

An examination of the sections did not reveal any evidence for the existence of an outer enclosure associated with the existing site. No bones were recovered from either of the trenches. The evidence from the trenching would therefore indicate that the extent of the Early Christian site is probably within the confines of the enclosure as it exists today and that associated occupation to the north-east of the site (if any such settlement existed) has been obliterated by land improvement.

*Franc Myles for Margaret Gowen & Co. Ltd, 2 Killiney View, Albert Road Lower, Glenageary, Co. Dublin.*

### 269. NEWTOWN LINK ROAD, ST MARGARET'S
Cultivation furrows
O120418
99E0028

A second phase of monitoring of topsoil-stripping was undertaken from 10 to 12 March 1999. The area to be stripped lay outside and to the north of the area that had previously been studied archaeologically for the construction of the new road. The area had to be stripped to allow the laying of a drainage pipe leading from the road north to the stream that flows north-eastwards just east of Connaberry Motte and for the construction of a paddock.

As this area lay outside the study area and was close to Connaberry Motte and Dunsoghly Castle, the topsoil was removed using a toothless grading bucket. A series of cultivation furrows was uncovered. They were aligned roughly north–south and were regularly spaced, 3m apart. They varied from less than 0.1m to 0.55m wide and from 20mm or less to 60mm wide. They were only visible where they cut into subsoil and did not survive in the north-west side of the stripped area, owing to the stony nature of the underlying subsoil there. The furrows were filled with grey, loamy silt, and no finds were retrieved from any of them. However, several sherds of medieval pottery (North Leinster cooking wares and wheel-thrown Dublin wares) were uncovered from the topsoil that overlay them.

The furrows are the remains of ridge-and-furrow cultivation, which is probably of medieval date. The proximity of the site to both the Connaberry Motte and to Dunsoghly Castle means that the cultivation system could have been used by the occupants of either site.

*Claire Walsh, Archaeological Projects Ltd, 25A Eaton Square, Terenure, Dublin 6W.*

### 270. SANDYMOUNT STRAND, SANDYMOUNT
Underwater monitoring
99E0490

Monitoring was carried out of cable-laying for the Esat link along Sandymount Strand in July 1999. The cable was crossing Dublin Bay to Southport in England. The Shipwreck Inventory for County Dublin, held in the office of the Underwater Unit of *Dúchas* The Heritage Service, records a large number of shipwrecks for Dublin Bay including Sandymount Strand.

A large plough systematically cut a furrow and laid the cable along the designated route across the Strand. No archaeology was encountered during the monitoring of the works.

*Connie Kelleher, Underwater Archaeological Unit, Dúchas The Heritage Service, 51 St Stephen's Green, Dublin 2.*

### 271. PHOENIX STREET NORTH/STABLE LANE (PHASE 1), SMITHFIELD
Urban medieval/post-medieval
98E0398

Archaeological excavations were carried out on this site over sixteen weeks ending in March 1999. Audrey Gahan carried out a second phase of excavation at a later stage (see No. 272 below). A series of nine ditches of medieval and post-medieval date, a number of post-medieval drains, medieval and post-medieval pits, and two wells were recorded.

Four areas were excavated in Phase 1: Area 1 (11m x 24m), Area 2 (8m x 8m), Area 3 (8m x 15m) and Area 4 (6m x 11m). A link trench was also excavated between Areas 1 and 3 to ascertain the relationship between the archaeology in them.

*Area 1*
A series of three gullies, one of which is dated to the post-medieval period by the inclusion of red brick in its fills, three possibly medieval ditches and a pit were identified in this area. A considerable depth (up to 1m) of archaeological material, albeit somewhat truncated, survived beneath the 18th-century basements.

It is unclear what purpose the ditches served. They may have been used as part of an overall water management system. It is unlikely that they served as linear pits as the fills were quite consistent in depth and nature throughout their length. The fact that successive ditches survive along similar axes in similar locations may indicate their use as property boundaries. This may be supported by the presence of the post-and-wattle fence, which would have proven too insubstantial to have acted as a revetment but would have been sufficient to demarcate a property line

The finds from this area included shroud pins, coins, a possibly 14th/15th-century silver merchant's signature ring, possible metalworking tools, fabric, leather, metal and leather composite artefacts, chain links, nails, medieval line-impressed tile, pottery, animal bone and slag. This was the only area from which fabric was identified.

*Area 2*
No archaeological features were identified in this area, but distinct post-medieval and medieval contexts were identified. A large quantity of metal artefacts was recovered, a percentage of which would certainly have been lost without the use of a metal-detector on site. However, this method of find retrieval may have biased the archaeological nature in favour of metallic artefacts.

*Area 3*
The archaeology recorded in this area included three brick-lined drains, a well, a gully, a metalled surface, a brick- and stone-lined pit, a series of post- and stake-holes, three north–south-oriented ditches and an east–west-oriented ditch. A number of coins, shroud pins and an amber bead are included in the finds recovered from this area.

The post-medieval drains and well may indicate a level of industrial activity on the site. The nature of this activity is as yet unclear. Historical research will, it is hoped, throw further light on the land use in this area in the post-medieval period.

The sequence of north–south-orientated ditches is interesting in that it displays continuity from the medieval period through to the post-medieval. Their use is unclear, and, like the ditches recorded in Area 1, they may have served as part of an overall water management/land reclamation scheme or as property boundaries.

*Area 4*
The archaeology recorded in this area included an east–west-orientated ditch, two north–south-running linear features and two pits, which yielded probable medieval dates. From the post-medieval period a curvilinear feature, which may have formed part of an enclosing ditch, and a north–south-orientated red brick-lined drain were excavated. As with the rest of the site, no direct evidence for medieval habitation occurred in Area 4. A more definitive explanation for the medieval ditches and linear features than possible water management courses or property boundaries may be uncovered during further excavation

*Finds*
The finds recovered from the excavations include leather, fabric, medieval line-impressed tile, pottery (medieval and post-medieval), shroud pins, coins, a silver seal ring, possible silver ingots, nails, slag, bronze mounts, musket balls, possible strap tags, chapes and blades.

The find retrieval strategy required by the licensing authorities was somewhat unusual in that all possibly medieval deposits were subject to examination with a metal-detector. This method resulted in the recovery of vast quantities of metal but has significant implications for post-excavation analysis and interpretation of the site.
*Una Cosgrave, ADS Ltd, Windsor House, 11 Fairview Strand, Dublin 3.*

### 272. SMITHFIELD
Medieval and post-medieval water management
**1475 1340**
**98E0398 ext.**
During 1999 a second phase of excavation before development was carried out at Smithfield. The archaeology uncovered related to a complex system of water management and drainage within the area, as identified by Una Cosgrave during Phase 1 (*Excavations 1998*, 66). Previous excavations by Alan Hayden at Arran Quay, beside Smithfield, revealed evidence of a wooden quay revetment of late 13th–14th-century date (*Excavations 1990*, 27–8). While no traces of the quay were found during this excavation (it probably extends to the south of this development), the excavated area here is interpreted as deliberate landfill or reclamation behind the quay.

The earliest levels uncovered contained significant amounts of late 13th- and 14th-century pottery, in particular large amounts of roof and floor tile. Overlying these layers were large deposits of redeposited subsoil through which drainage ditches had been cut. The redeposited subsoil layers and the fills of the earliest ditches also contained pottery of late 13th- and 14th-century date. This implies that the deliberate build-up of material and the initial drainage through it occurred during a relatively short space of time. All of these medieval drainage ditches, as well as the later post-medieval examples uncovered, were orientated north–south, draining therefore directly into the River Liffey.

Other features of note uncovered include a medieval ditch that extended across the site in an east–west direction. As it extended parallel to the River Liffey, it probably did not function as a drainage ditch but more likely was a property boundary or division. Also, a large bell-jar-shaped pit of post-medieval date was uncovered partially under the basements of the 18th- and 19th-century buildings that originally stood on the site. Its location suggests that it probably pre-dates the basement construction, and it was dated by its contents to the 17th to early 18th century. Several wells and pits of later post-medieval date were also identified.

Post-excavation work on the material from this site will continue during 2000.
*Audrey Gahan for ADS Ltd, Windsor House, 11 Fairview Strand, Dublin 3.*

### 273. 93–94 MANOR STREET, STONYBATTER
No archaeological significance
**99E0701**
Several test-trenches were opened as part of an assessment of a site on the corner of Stonybatter and Arbour Place, along the western side of one of the main thoroughfares leaving the city from the medieval period onwards. Although the philology of Stonybatter is obscure, there is a possibility that the word has Hiberno-Norse origins. Manor Street, in

turn, is thought to be a reference to the manor of Grangegorman, a little distance to the north-east. At any rate, the site was well developed by the time of John Rocque's survey of 1756, and the possibility remained that archaeological strata were preserved in the substrates.

Four trenches were mechanically excavated across the site where the proposed basement would impinge on substrates. With the exception of one trench in the south-western corner of the site, the insulated foundations of a fish factory had truncated any underlying archaeological strata to natural subsoil. A late 19th-century yard in limestone setts occupied the south-western sector of the site, overlying early 19th-century occupation debris. This activity sealed the subsoil.

Further testing work is to be undertaken in 2000 after the demolition of the existing street-front structures on Stonybatter. The site is to be a mixed residential and commercial development.
*Franc Myles, 9 Ben Edair Road, Stonybatter, Dublin 7.*

### 274. BRIDGE STREET, SWORDS
Quarry site
O179472
99E0320

An initial phase of site assessment works uncovered a stone-cut feature, possibly a ditch associated with the Swords Castle defences. Environmental contamination, in the form of seeping oil and raw sewage, necessitated a site-specific finds-retrieval and section-recording exercise, the results of which proved, beyond reasonable doubt, that the feature is a product of mid-19th-century stone quarrying.
*Eoin Halpin, ADS Ltd, Unit 48, Westlink Enterprise Centre, 30–50 Distillery Street, Belfast BT12 5BJ.*

### 275. WINDMILL LANDS, RIVER WARD, SWORDS
Medieval burials
99E0554

In October 1999 the Underwater Unit of *Dúchas* undertook a rescue excavation following a report from Fingal County Council that a possible human skull was protruding from a riverbank in Swords, Co. Dublin. An intra-riverine inspection verified that the human skull lay within an extensive midden that was exposed for at least 40m along the riverbank. The midden (which consisted mainly of charcoal, shells, animal bone and the human skull) had become exposed during recent flooding of the Ward Valley. Upon removal of the skull, it was apparent that the articulated remains of the skeleton were present within the midden deposit. It was therefore necessary to open a 2m-by-2m cutting to recover the remains of the skeleton. The site is in the flood-plain of the River Ward valley to the south of Swords in the townland of Windmill Lands.

The site produced a number of phases, with the upper levels being quite disturbed and containing a variety of pottery types ranging from transfer print ware and Frechen ware to medieval pottery including Leinster cooking ware and Dublin-type ware. The first undisturbed medieval phase produced both burials and domestic finds. The articulated remains of two individuals were discovered. One of the skeletons was that of a newborn infant, while the other consisted of the upper right long bones and part of the right pelvis of a mature adult. This stratum also produced animal bone remains, metal objects including iron nails, two belt-buckles and two possible socketed arrowheads, and medieval pottery.

The second phase of activity appears to have been associated with some form of nearby settlement as the stratum consisted primarily of the dumping of domestic material. A significant amount of animal bone (cattle, sheep and horse) and medieval pottery including Leinster cooking ware and Dublin-type ware was present. Other finds included mortar and slate, a large quantity of iron nails and an Edward I silver penny. No human remains were recovered from this phase of activity.

The lowest stratum consisted of the midden and the human skull that were originally visible in the riverbank. The midden rested on natural riverine deposits and consisted of large quantities of charcoal, animal bone and shell, including periwinkles, oysters, scallops, mussels and limpets. Excavation of this midden layer revealed three further burials. These individuals had been placed one on top of the other, most likely at the same time. A young female adult was uncovered slightly flexed, with pillow-stones placed around her head. This burial was orientated east–west and was placed more or less on top of an extended older female, whose skull had already been removed from the riverbank. The upper part of the older female had been placed on and had subsequently crushed an infant, who had been the primary interment. The infant remains were orientated in a north-west/south-east direction. The foot bones of another adult were retrieved from the edge of the cutting, and it is likely that the remainder of this skeleton has been long lost to the River Ward. The burials generally tended towards an east–west orientation. However, it is possible that some degree of haste was involved, as it would appear that the bodies were thrown rather than placed with any degree of time and ritual.

The pottery recovered indicates that the site dates to the late 13th and early 14th centuries. This dating is further strengthened by the presence of the Edward I silver penny, which dates to the late 1280s. The dating of the site is not unusual given its location within the medieval borough of Swords. In total, the remains of six skeletons were excavated. Post-excavation work is ongoing.
*Karl Brady and Connie Kelleher, Underwater Archaeological Unit,* Dúchas *The Heritage Service, 51 St Stephen's Green, Dublin 2.*

### 276. KILTALOWN HOUSE, TALLAGHT
Earthwork
98E0118

A survey and small-scale excavation of a tree-lined earthwork at Kiltalown House, Tallaght, were carried out in March 1998. This earthwork was not recorded as an archaeological feature in the Sites and Monuments Record. It was reported to the National Monuments and Historic Properties Service in early 1996 by a local study association, the Heritage Awareness Group. In her response to the Heritage Awareness Group, Geraldine Stout suggested that the earthwork might be identified as part of the Pale boundary earthwork. The aim of the work was to establish the archaeological significance of the earthwork before the proposed widening of the Tallaght–Blessington road, which runs along its southern part.

The earthwork runs for a length of c. 330m and encloses a semi-oval area with a maximum diameter of 160m. Archaeological testing involved the excavation of two trenches. In one cutting, measuring 9.4m north–south by 1.4m, root action had destroyed archaeological levels. The other cutting, measuring 9.2m north–south by 1.7m, was more productive. Positioned alongside the modern roadway in a part of the site threatened by destruction, it embraced the top of the bank and part of the gentle slope of the bank southwards towards the road, as well as the scarp face of the bank on the northern side and the full observed width of the ditch on the north of the bank.

Although the top of the bank had dense roots, on the crest was found a shallow, flat-bottomed gully, 0.8m wide at the top and 0.5m wide at the base. This had been cut directly into the natural soil to an average depth of 0.2m. Thus it appears that the bank was formed not by a mounding-up of material but by the scarping of natural soil to create a ditch to the north. Cut into the base of the gully in the south-east corner of the excavated area was a post-hole measuring c. 0.2m (east–west) by 0.25m at its top. Two stones were positioned on its east and west sides; the former, which was rectangular, had shattered *in situ*, and much of it was removed during excavation. The sides of the post-hole descended nearly vertically to a depth of at least 0.25m; the post-hole had been colonised by roots, and its original depth could not be ascertained. The soil fill of the post-hole was identical to that of the layer immediately above the natural layer in the bank.

The Kiltalown earthwork belongs to the late medieval tradition of protective enclosure that reaches its apogee in the attempted enclosure of the English Pale in 1494–5, and the identification of it as part of the Pale is a reasonable one, but it may equally have enclosed an area of medieval parkland.
*Tadhg O'Keefe, Department of Archaeology, University College, Dublin, for Margaret Gowen & Co. Ltd.*

**Editor's note:** This summary, though of work carried out during 1998, was received too late for inclusion in the bulletin of that year.

### 277. TERENURE COLLEGE, TERENURE
Adjacent to Terenure Castle
31357 22959
SMR 22:95
99E0695

Testing was carried out at Terenure College before the construction of a proposed extension. A single trench was cut along the length of the proposed extension. The stratigraphy revealed reflected the use of this area as a garden, as depicted on the 1st edition Ordnance Survey map. There was no indication of any features or structural remains that could be associated with the castle.
*Rónán Swan, Arch-Tech Ltd, 32 Fitzwilliam Place, Dublin 2.*

### 278. WESTEREAVE
Early Christian cemetery
O313247
SMR 11:84
99E0219

An archaeological assessment and subsequent monitoring (see No. 161 above) of topsoil removal were undertaken at Westereave, Co. Dublin, as part of the reinforcement of the Brownsbarn to Ballough Gas Pipeline (formerly known as the Northeastern Pipelines, Phases I and II). The site is at the top of a long, gentle but prominent, south-east-facing slope to the east of Mount Ambrose House, which rises from the Ward River just north of Skephubble. The site is very close to outcropping shaley slate (which was quarried just to the west of the site). Rocque's map of 1760 shows 'Westrew' as a small settlement at the south-eastern corner of the townland. There is no record of the cemetery, and there are no references to the townland before 1641, so it may have had an earlier name, now lost.

The site was first discovered on removal of topsoil during the Phase II pipeline operation in 1988. Then, a cemetery comprising 52 individuals was revealed over a 27m stretch of the pipeline corridor (see report by Margaret Gowen in *Excavations 1988*, 18). The cemetery consisted of fifteen lintel graves, with the remaining burials interred in simple rock-cut graves. At least two phases of burial were discerned, the earlier phase mainly represented by the lintel graves being enclosed by a penannular gully. Subsequent to this discovery the site was included in the Sites and Monuments Record by the National Monuments and Historic Properties Service.

The new reinforcement pipeline corridor runs parallel to and incorporates part of the existing and archaeologically resolved area of 1988. Geophysical survey of the proposed pipeline corridor was undertaken before an archaeological assessment.

Magnetic gradiometry and electrical soil-resistivity surveys were undertaken at the site before the assessment. Strong ferrous (iron) interference was present within the eastern area of the survey grid, signalling the location of the existing gas pipe. Various isolated, small anomalies were also discerned, along with regular linear-trending anomalies, suggesting changes in the underlying geology. The resistivity survey revealed a number of low-resistance linear trends west of the existing gas pipe, which did not coincide with any magnetic anomalies. These trends indicated possible ditches, which because of their regularity appeared to represent an early modern field division. However, the majority of the resistivity responses appeared to reflect natural variations in resistance values across the site, especially along the eastern edge of the survey grid, which would suggest disturbance from the pipe and 1988 construction.

Three test-trenches were excavated across the proposed 30m wayleave realignment corridor. The trenches were directly west of the area excavated and resolved during the 1988 NEP II pipe-laying operation. The position of the trenches was largely determined by the anomalous responses from the geophysical survey carried out before the assessment. The soil cover was very thin, with the

topsoil lying almost directly over rock over most of the tested areas. No soils, deposits or features of archaeological potential were revealed during assessment.
*Malachy Conway for Margaret Gowen & Co. Ltd, 2 Killiney View, Albert Road Lower, Glenageary, Co. Dublin.*

## FERMANAGH

### 279. MARBLE ARCH RESERVOIR, KILLESHER
Adjacent to souterrain and graveyard
**212163 335087**
Monitoring of topsoil-stripping was conducted on the site of Marble Arch Reservoir, Killesher townland, Co. Fermanagh, on 22 and 23 February 1999. An area measuring 2750m$^2$ was stripped. The northern portion of the site appeared to have been disturbed in the recent past, probably during the construction of the existing reservoir. No archaeological materials were found.
*Cóilín Ó Drisceoil, 6 Riverview, Ardnore, Kilkenny, for Archaeological Consultancy Services Ltd, 15 Trinity Street, Drogheda, Co. Louth.*

### 280. MOLLY MOUNTAIN, MOLLY
Prehistoric
**SMR 259:2**
**H23752801**
The site, which is adjacent to SMR 259:1 (*Excavations 1998*, 72), was on a limestone plateau on the north-western slopes of Molly Mountain, at an altitude of *c*. 180m. The remains of a low circular kerb, 10.75m in diameter, and a cairn were discovered close to two standing stones, 2m and 0.9m high. Structural evidence within the kerb was scant, making classification difficult; however, there was a possible disturbed chamber/passage against the inner south-south-west edge of the kerb. A hut site was found *c*. 10m north-east of the kerb.

Five concentrations of burnt bone fragments were uncovered, with the two main concentrations occurring within the kerb. These were very disturbed and were associated with pot fragments.

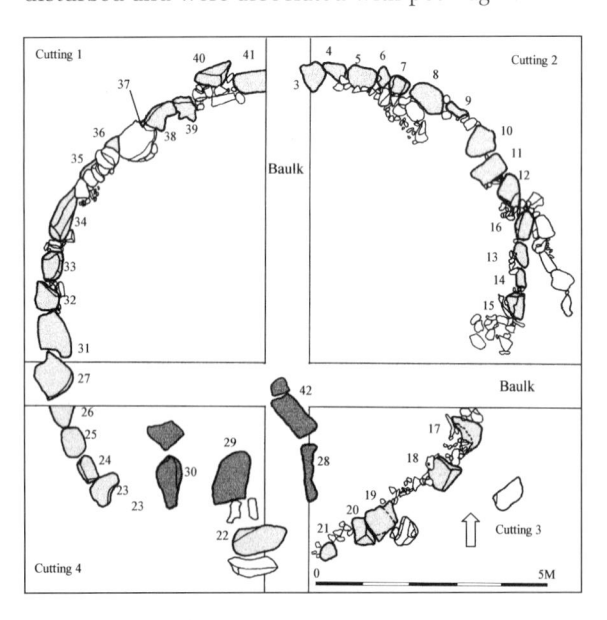

Plan of kerb at Molly Mountain.

Finds from topsoil include a barbed and tanged arrowhead and a hollow scraper.

Post-excavation work is ongoing. Photographs, plans and descriptions of finds and features are available on-line at: http://www.jchanning.com/
*John Channing, 17 Rowan House, Sussex Road, Dublin 4.*

### 281. REYFAD
Post-medieval farm
**H112461**
**SMR 210:72**
The first season of excavation was undertaken during 1998 to establish the nature of an enigmatic earthwork to the east of the Reyfad cup- and ringmarked stones (*Excavations 1998*, 72–3). This work identified a number of structural features, and a cattle astragalus recovered from a layer of heavily compacted clay in the south-west end of Trench 1 was submitted for radiocarbon dating to the Gronigen Laboratory in November 1998. This service was kindly funded by the Environment and Heritage Service of DOE NI and provided a calibrated date range of AD 1683 to 1955. The radiocarbon date and the few artefacts discovered during the first season of excavation suggested a post-medieval date for the monument. However, a combination of map evidence and local oral tradition suggested that there had been no known human occupation here since at least the mid-19th century. Further investigation was therefore required to elucidate the exact date and character of the monument.

In consultation with Brian Williams, Environment and Heritage Service, DOE NI, it was decided that a second, short season of excavation should be initiated and that this work should be directed at those areas of the site that held the greatest potential to address outstanding research questions. To assist this strategy, a programme of intensive geophysical survey was kindly undertaken by Kevin Barton, Shane Rooney and Michael Rogers from the Applied Geophysics Unit, NUI Galway, during May and August 1999. This work involved an EDM topographical survey of the monument and its immediate environs, while ground-probing radar (GPR) and magnetic susceptibility surveys were also undertaken. The topographical and GPR surveys revealed that the raised area in the north-west sector of the monument comprised two platforms. In addition, the magnetic susceptibility survey highlighted a number of large anomalies within the monument and, of greater significance, identified a region of extremely high readings to the immediate west of the earthwork.

The second season of excavation was undertaken on behalf of the Environment and Heritage Service, DOE NI, and the Belcoo and District Historical Society by a volunteer crew during two weeks in August 1999. In light of the results obtained during the programme of geophysical surveying, it was decided that excavation trenches should be opened to investigate two areas. The first trench, Trench 3, comprised a 6m-by-2m opening orientated north-west/south-east to investigate the double platform feature identified during the GPR survey. The second trench, Trench 4, was positioned to the west of the monument and comprised two 2m-by-2m sub-trenches aligned north-east/south-west. This trench was opened to investigate the exceptionally high readings obtained during the magnetic susceptibility survey. A 1m-by-2m section from the south-west end of Trench 1 (investigated during Season 1) was reopened, and an extension of 1m by 2m was added to the north-west. The objective of this exercise was to further elucidate the structure of the possible foundation raft identified in 1998.

The re-examination and extension of Trench 1 confirmed the tentative foundation raft to be a natural feature. Further supporting evidence that a natural crevice occurs in the limestone bedrock along the south-western side of the site had been provided by the GPR survey, and it would appear that this crevice was naturally infilled with limestone boulders and sterile clay. This natural feature formed a firm footing for the clay cap that was placed over it to provide the defining south-west bank of the monument, as revealed during Season 1.

In Trench 3 the upper platform identified during the GPR survey proved to be a natural feature formed by the underlying limestone bedrock. The lower platform would also appear to be a natural feature. However, a concentration of clay and stone found lying over the surface of the lower platform contained a corpus of well-stratified post-medieval artefacts. This layer may represent an attempt to level the ground surface between the upper and lower platforms for agricultural purposes. Alternatively, it may be the remains of a mud wall, originally positioned on the crest of the upper platform, which had collapsed and spilled down over the surface of the lower platform.

Trench 4 was opened to investigate the high anomalies identified in this area of the site during the magnetic susceptibility survey. A level surface of stones was encountered that displayed evidence of having been burnt. This burning may have further enhanced the magnetic susceptibility levels in this area. Beneath this layer of stones was discovered a well-constructed stone-lined drain covered by a roof of large stone slabs. The drain was set in a channel cut into the natural subsoil, and the spoil created during its construction had been thrown downslope to the south-west, where it covered the upper level of the original agricultural land surface. This land surface in turn was set over the natural subsoil. It may be suggested that this was a well-drained haggard for agricultural use.

When taken in conjunction, the geophysical survey, the excavation results, the retrieved material culture and the radiocarbon date all suggest that the site was occupied during the 18th and/or early 19th century and that this was the location of a post-medieval farmstead. The secure stone footings identified during Season 1 in the north-east end of Trench 1 may have been the foundations for a house wall, while the paved area that abuts the stone footings may represent the remains of an inner farmyard. The possibility exists that a further wall of mud and stone crowned the upper platform in the interior of the monument. The stone-lined drain and haggard found to the west of the main site may have been an auxiliary farmyard. The quality of some of the artefacts (including a finely decorated pewter button and a stem from a glass drinking goblet) tend to suggest that the occupants of the settlement were of good standing and that this may have been the home of a strong farmer.

*Colm J. Donnelly and Eileen M. Murphy, School of Archaeology and Palaeoecology, Queen's University, Belfast BT7 1NN.*

## GALWAY

### 282. IVYMOUNT HOUSE, BAUNMORE, ATHENRY
Adjacent to St Bridget's Church
15030 22704
99E0238

The proposed development is *c.* 400m south of the Athenry town wall, close to the 'Spital Gate' entrance. In the front garden of the house to be developed are the remains of St Bridget's Church, which is likely to be medieval in date. The development consisted of the demolition of the porch to the east of the house and the construction of a new extension at this location. In accordance with planning conditions, it was recommended that the excavation of foundation trenches be monitored. No structural remains or features of archaeological significance were evident during monitoring.

*Fiona Rooney, Arch. Consultancy Ltd, Ballydavid South, Athenry, Co. Galway.*

### 283. CHAPEL LANE, ATHENRY
Anglo-Norman town
15022 22770
99E0034

As this development lay in the zone of archaeological potential, pre-development testing in the form of trial-trenches was recommended. The mechanical excavation of six trenches revealed no evidence of features/deposits of archaeological significance. The trenches were excavated to a maximum depth of 1m. In the northern end of the site the stratigraphy consisted of a layer of orange boulder clay, 0.2m deep, overlying a grey, sandy gravel layer. In the southern end the garden soil was found to overlie the grey, sandy gravel layer. The layers present consisted of made-up ground or natural.

*Fiona Rooney, Arch. Consultancy Ltd, Ballydavid South, Athenry, Co. Galway.*

### 284. COURT LANE, ATHENRY
Anglo-Norman town
15022 22771
99E0655

Monitoring of groundworks associated with the installation of new ESB cables along Court Lane, Athenry, Co. Galway, was recommended as this development lay in the zone of archaeological potential and was close to Athenry Castle. Funding for this project was provided by Galway County Council.

A trench was excavated (120m long, 0.5m wide and 0.25–0.45m deep) along an existing stone wall of the park. The stratigraphy revealed little of archaeological significance. The only material of interest was loose stones found in the vicinity of the original town wall. Their presence may indicate disturbance of this feature, but, as the trench excavated was shallow (0.25m), it was not possible

### 285. CROSS STREET, ATHENRY
Anglo-Norman town
15032 22768
99E0070

The proposed development concerned the erection of two stores and the extension to the rear of the present building. The development is within the zone of archaeological potential of Athenry, and therefore pre-development testing was required.

Three trenches were mechanically excavated. The stratigraphy revealed indicated no evidence of features/deposits of archaeological significance. The layers present consisted of a dark brown garden soil overlying the natural.

*Fiona Rooney, Arch. Consultancy Ltd, Ballydavid South, Athenry, Co. Galway.*

### 286. NORTH GATE STREET, ATHENRY
Urban
99E0031

This project involved the demolition of the existing structure and the construction of a new dwelling-house at North Gate Street, Athenry, Co. Galway. As the proposed development was beside St Mary's parish church and within the zone of archaeological potential, the monitoring of foundations was necessary.

The work took place on 23 January 1999. The monitoring revealed no features of archaeological significance. The stratigraphy encountered consisted of 19th/20th-century dump material beneath the concrete surface.

*Martin Fitzpatrick, Arch. Consultancy Ltd, Ballydavid South, Athenry, Co. Galway.*

### 287. CREAGH, BALLINASLOE
Beside 18th-century church and possible medieval parish church
186632 230932
99E0509

The site of the proposed development (four semi-detached houses) is beside an 18th-century church, SMR 88:6. Monitoring of topsoil-stripping was carried out. Stripping of the area of the proposed houses exposed natural boulder clay at a depth of 0.3–0.4m over the entire area. Some modern pottery and glass fragments were recovered, but there were no features of archaeological significance. The development has no impact on archaeological deposits, and no further work is proposed.

*Deirdre Murphy, Archaeological Consultancy Services Ltd, 15 Trinity Street, Drogheda, Co. Louth.*

### 288. PARKMORE, BALLINASLOE
Rath/cashel
18650 23250
SMR 74A:6
99E0265

Monitoring of topsoil-stripping at Ballinasloe, Co. Galway, was carried out in May to June 1999. The proposed development involves the construction of an IDA Business Park and associated services on the Roscommon road in Ballinasloe. The development is close to recorded sites 74A:6 (rath/cashel), 88:8 (church/chapel) and 88:6 (church site).

Monitoring failed to reveal any evidence of archaeological material at the site. However, further work is to be carried out near the ringfort, and it was recommended that this be done under archaeological supervision.

*Donald Murphy, Archaeological Consultancy Services Ltd, 15 Trinity Street, Drogheda, Co. Louth.*

### 289. DUNMORE
Urban medieval
99E0252

A pre-development test excavation was conducted between 23 and 25 June 1999 before the construction of a supermarket and associated facilities. The site was within the zone of medieval archaeology. It lay between an Augustinian abbey and a fording point across the adjacent river. Six 1m-wide test-trenches were dug on the site. These revealed 1–1.5m of landfill, before 1m of river marl was encountered. The base of the trenches consisted of river gravels.

Potential archaeology was encountered on the site's southern aspect. This consisted of a 1.5m-wide east–west-orientated ditch. It lay 9m to the north of the existing structure of the abbey, beneath 0.4m of topsoil. The composition of the ditch's fill showed natural sedimentation above a shallow, charcoal-rich basal layer. No artefacts were recovered. The proximity of the ditch to the abbey would suggest some association between them.

*Niall Gregory, 25 Westpark, Blessington, Co. Wicklow, for Archaeological Consultancy Services Ltd.*

### 290. BARRACK LANE, GALWAY
Urban
1300 2252
98E0021

The full excavation of this site, within and adjacent to the city wall in Galway, which began in January 1998, continued with a further season's work in the summer of 1999. The site contained the remains of a late 16th/early 17th-century house, a 17th-century citadel and an 18th-century military barracks.

The excavation report is ongoing, and it is hoped to include it in the forthcoming *Galway Excavations Project* publication.

*Richard Crumlish, Archaeological Services Unit Ltd, Purcell House, Oranmore, Co. Galway.*

### 291. 33–34 EYRE SQUARE, GALWAY
Urban post-medieval?
12986 22525
99E0119

Two trial-trenches were excavated during pre-development testing at the site of the proposed development. This testing revealed part of an interesting and heretofore unrecorded wall. Although only a short length could be investigated, an examination of its east face has been sufficient to indicate that it may have formed part of the fortifications protecting the east approach to the city. It was not possible to ascertain the width of the wall, and it is difficult to date it. The nature of the wall's construction suggests that it is similar to the late medieval (16th- to 17th-century) walls associated with the walled town defences observed elsewhere.

A narrower wall was exposed for a relatively short distance of 2m, and no indication of its overall height, dimensions or function could be ascertained from the testing. As the development is not intended to impinge on either wall, it was recommended that both walls be covered with approved materials in order to protect them. It was also recommended that any further groundworks at the site be archaeologically monitored.

*Anne Connolly, Archaeological Services Unit Ltd, Purcell House, Oranmore, Co. Galway.*

### 292. THE FAIRGREEN, GALWAY
No archaeological significance
12986 22525
99E0745

Three trial-trenches were excavated to natural by a mechanical digger. Nothing of archaeological significance was discovered.

*Anne Connolly, Archaeological Services Unit Ltd, Purcell House, Oranmore, Co. Galway.*

### 293. CUSTOM HOUSE, FLOOD STREET/COURTHOUSE LANE, GALWAY
Medieval castle, limekiln and building
12986 22525
SMR 94:100
97E0082 ext.

A second season of excavation was undertaken at this site from 8 February to 21 May 1999. The site is c. 10m south-west of the medieval hall that was excavated by this writer in 1997, under the same licence (*Excavations 1997*, 66–9). The excavation took place inside a warehouse complex comprising a large 18th- or early 19th-century warehouse building with a mid-19th-century addition at its north end. Most of the excavation work was concentrated inside the mid-19th-century warehouse building, which is due to be incorporated into the proposed new development at this site. The roof of the warehouse was removed before the commencement of the excavation. The main excavated features comprised portions of a medieval castle, a medieval limekiln and a late medieval building.

*Medieval castle*
The most significant feature of the excavation was a substantial wall (1m high, 1.75m thick) with a pronounced external base batter and traces of internal and external lime rendering. The wall is composed of four courses of large, roughly hewn migmatite and granite boulders (average dimensions 0.45m x 0.3m) and has a clay-bonded core of smaller stones. The excavated portion of this wall extends 6m north-east/south-west, but the wall clearly extends beyond the south-west limit of the excavation. This wall represents part of the south-east wall of a substantial building, possibly the original Anglo-Norman castle at Galway, which is said to have been built c. 1232 and is mentioned in a document recording the death of Walter de Burgho in 1271. The north-east end of the wall was abutted by a buttress (2.2m x 1m) composed of migmatite and granite boulders. A north-east return (1.15m high, 1.25m thick) was encountered, but it was not clearly established whether this represents the original castle wall return. This wall is composed of three courses of unhewn migmatite and granite boulders (average dimensions 0.27m x 0.3m) and rests on two foundation courses of larger boulders that form a rough plinth (average width 0.2m) at the base of the wall. The return is built at an oblique angle to the south-east wall and does not have an external base batter. Furthermore, the internal face of the north-east wall partially abutted that of the south-east wall. It seems likely therefore that the north-east castle wall was substantially rebuilt in the late medieval period.

*Medieval limekiln*
Part of a large bowl-shaped limekiln (diameter 3.5m) was found immediately inside the castle walls. The kiln was internally faced with angular migmatite and granite stones (average dimensions 0.2m x 0.12m), some of which were heat-fractured. A flue opening was found at the south-east, and the stone-lined access to the flue extended across the top of the south-east castle wall. The rebuilt north-east castle wall partially overlay the kiln at north-west. The kiln was excavated to a depth of 1m and was filled with a series of domestic refuse dumps, which contained substantial quantities of animal bone, shells and medieval pottery sherds. Lime deposits were encountered at the limit of excavation.

*Late medieval building*
The north-east castle wall was abutted along its entire excavated length by a late medieval wall (0.75m thick) composed of small, unhewn migmatite, limestone and granite boulders. Excavation indicated that the wall was composed of four courses, and each was separated by a layer of silty clay that yielded sherds of medieval pottery wares. The wall appears to represent the south-west wall of a large building indicated on the 1641 Pictorial Map of Galway. The unusual orientation of the building suggests that it pre-dates the other dwellings indicated on this map. The wall extended 10m from the north limit of the excavation, and a possible return was encountered at its south-east end.

*Medieval stratigraphy and finds*
Late medieval deposits were encountered immediately below the cobbled floor of the mid-19th-century warehouse. These deposits sealed the excavated features and overlay a series of stratified medieval layers that yielded a large quantity of small finds. The finds comprised several hundred sherds of medieval pottery, mainly imported French Saintonge wares, and assorted iron and copper artefacts that have not been identified to date. The pottery is significant as it represents the only substantial assemblage of medieval pottery from early Anglo-Norman Galway. The 13th century is well represented by numerous sherds of polychrome Saintonge wares.

*Post-medieval features*
The existing ground levels inside the large

General view of site at Custom House, Flood Street/Courthouse Lane, from south-east, showing castle walls enclosing medieval kiln.

View of kiln from south-west showing stone-lined flue opening extending across top of south-east castle wall, Custom House, Flood Street/Courthouse Lane.

18th/early 19th-century warehouse building were reduced by *c.* 0.5m in order to facilitate the laying of new concrete floors.

Several post-medieval features including cobbled floors, stone paving and wall footings were encountered during ground reduction in this area. The finds comprised numerous pottery sherds, mainly imported 17th- and early 18th-century English wares, clay pipes and assorted glass fragments (wine bottles etc.) It was also established that late/post-medieval fabric is incorporated in some of the existing warehouse walls and that some of the walls are built directly on late/post-medieval wall footings.
*Dominic Delany, 31 Ashbrook, Oranmore, Co. Galway.*

### 294. FORSTER STREET, GALWAY
Urban
**99E0149**
Pre-development testing was undertaken on the site of a proposed development in Forster Street, Galway City, in March 1999. The site is *c.* 300m outside the medieval walled town. It is currently used as a bus- and carpark.

Four test-trenches were excavated by machine. Three were 25m long, the fourth 14m. All were 2m wide. In Trench 1 underlying the tarmac was a hardcore and rubble fill layer 0.48m thick. A redeposited, natural, stony daub, 0.31m thick, directly underlay this. Underlying the daub was a grey/brown to black garden soil layer, 0.26m thick. This garden soil layer produced some early 20th-century pottery, glass and a 1939 English halfpenny. The natural, grey/light brown, silty daub directly underlay the garden soil.

The stratigraphy within the other trenches was broadly similar to that in Trench 1. No archaeological features or finds were recovered from any of the trenches.
*Gerry Walsh, Rathbawn Road, Castlebar, Co. Mayo.*

### 295. 9 FRANCIS STREET, GALWAY
Urban
**SMR 94:100**
**99E0327**
Pre-development testing was undertaken on the site of a proposed development at No. 9 Francis Street, Galway. The proposed development site is outside the zone of archaeological importance for medieval Galway. This area of Galway, in the vicinity of the Franciscan friary, is depicted as a marshy area on the 1651 Pictorial Map of the city. This was also evident from the trenches dug during the testing. It would appear that this marshy area was reclaimed in post-medieval times, as the sides of the trenches were extremely unstable and were constantly caving in. Because of this subsidence the trenches were *c.* 1.5m wide as opposed to 2m as planned; all were 14m long. Four test-trenches were excavated by machine within the proposed development. They varied from 2m to 3.75m deep.

In Trench 1, underlying the topsoil, 0.8m thick, was a dark brown clay 0.9m thick. This produced some 19th/20th-century pottery. Underlying the dark brown clay was a mid–light brown clay, 0.48m thick. A clay pipe stem, some animal bone and two sherds of 18th/19th-century pottery were recovered from this layer. The natural, white/green daub directly underlay it.

In Trench 2, at the western end, the topsoil, 0.2m thick, directly overlay a brick and mortar layer 0.25m thick. Underlying this was a dark brown clay 0.8m thick, similar to that in Trench 1. A mid–light brown clay, 0.4–0.6m thick, directly underlay the dark brown clay. This clay was similar to that in Trench 1 and directly overlay a natural, grey/white daub. In the eastern half of the trench a mortar and clay layer, 0.83m thick, directly overlay a dark brown clay 1.2m thick, which produced some 18th/19th-century pottery. This overlay a natural, grey/white daub.

In Trench 3, underlying the garden soil, 0.15m thick, was a light brown topsoil with mortar and roots, 0.76m thick. A dark brown clay, 0.7m thick, similar to that in Trench 1, directly underlay the light brown topsoil. Some 19th/20th-century pottery was recovered from this clay. Underlying this was a mid-brown clay, 0.41m thick, which produced some animal bone and some 18th/19th-century pottery. A natural, white daub, 0.17m thick, underlay the mid-brown clay. Underlying the white daub was a natural peat layer 0.38m thick, which in turn overlay a natural, grey daub. The stratigraphy within Trench 4 was similar to that in Trench 3.

No archaeological features or finds were recovered from any of the trenches.

*Gerry Walsh, Rathbawn Road, Castlebar, Co. Mayo.*

## 296. LOUGH ATALIA ROAD/FORSTER STREET, GALWAY

Town (in vicinity of)
12986 22525
SMR 94:100
98E0272 ext.

This site was test excavated in September 1998, and several post-medieval features were identified (*Excavations 1998*, 80–1). The site comprises *c.* 4.5 acres of undeveloped land at the north-east edge of the modern city centre. It consists of three large fields, and an imposing early 20th-century house named 'Ard Patrick' stood on the high ground at the north end of the site. The site forms part of a glacial ridge that originally extended north-east/south-west along the Lough Atalia shoreline but was almost completely removed at north-east as the town expanded eastwards in the 19th and 20th centuries. The site is *c.* 500m east of the medieval walled town of Galway and 350m north-east of Forthill Cemetery, the site of an early 17th-century star-shaped fort. The 1651 Pictorial Map of Galway depicts the site as rough grazing land on the east edge of the medieval town. However, there is a tradition of military encampments along the Lough Atalia shoreline in the 16th and 17th centuries. The high ground bordering Lough Atalia would indeed have been an ideal vantage-point for military encampments, as it overlooked the north-east end of the medieval town and guarded one of its approach routes, now known as Forster Street. The site is also close to the strategically important early 17th-century star-shaped fort. Logan's map of Galway (1818) names the site of the fort 'West Fort Hill' and the area containing the site of the proposed development 'East Fort Hill'. This would seem to confirm the tradition of military activity in this area.

Excavation was undertaken, from 22 February to 2 April 1999, before the proposed hotel development. The excavated features comprised eleven pits, four linear ditches and two stone walls. Six of the pits were securely dated by their pottery finds to the late/post-medieval period. The dating evidence from the remaining five pits was inconclusive, as four of them produced both late/post-medieval and modern finds and one pit failed to produce any datable finds.

Three of the late/post-medieval pits were in a potentially strategic location on high ground on the north-west brow of the ridge. Two were of similar size, shape, profile and composition of fills and are best described as vertically cut, flat-bottomed, subrectangular pits (average dimensions 2.7m x 2.05m, x 0.75m). Excavation did not produce any conclusive evidence to indicate their function, but their strategic location suggests a possible military usage, perhaps as archers' emplacements or observation posts. The third pit was oval (dimensions 4.05m x 1.3m) and contained fills similar to those found in the two subrectangular pits, suggesting that all three are contemporary.

Two irregular pits were also encountered on the north-west brow of the ridge. One was very shallow with a subcircular, round-bottomed depression at the north edge of the base. The pit measured 1.82m by 2.02m and had an average depth of 0.08m, with a maximum depth of 0.28m in the depression. No datable finds were recovered from this feature. The second pit was larger (2.8m x 1.8m) and had an average depth of 0.45m. The sides of the pit were almost vertical, and the base, though slightly uneven, was relatively flat. The fills yielded several sherds of post-medieval pottery wares, and there was a small, central depression at the base of the pit.

Three of the pits on the south-east slope of the ridge were very similar in that they contained very large boulders and a random fill of smaller stones. Two of the pits were similar in size (average dimensions 2.3m x 2m, x 1m), but the third was substantially larger (dimensions 6.2m x 2.2m, x 1m). The dating evidence was inconclusive, but there was a very obvious risk of finds contamination owing to the high degree of voiding that existed between the stones. It is likely that these pits are contemporary post-medieval features, possibly associated with field clearance.

Two large oval/kidney-shaped pits (1: 5.75m x 1.82m, depth 2m; 2: 3.6m x 1.98m, depth 1m) were also excavated on the south-east slope of the ridge. These pits were similar in many respects but contained very different fills. One contained a series of redeposited fills that yielded a substantial quantity of both late/post-medieval and modern pottery sherds. The upper fills of the second pit were modern, but the primary fill securely dates this feature to the late/post-medieval period.

A further large irregular pit (5.58m x 3.74m, depth 0.95m) contained a massive limestone boulder that projected slightly above the top of the pit. This pit appeared to be modern and may have been a garden feature associated with 'Ard Patrick' house.

The excavated linear ditches represent field boundaries, one extending north-east/south-west across the top of the ridge and another running perpendicular to it down the east slope of the ridge. Cartographic evidence suggests that these boundaries were initially established in the post-medieval period and remained in use in modern times. This would appear to be confirmed by the presence of both late/post-medieval and modern finds. A stone wall extending along the south-east edge of the north-east/south-west ditch appears to be an insertion.

*Dominic Delany, 31 Ashbrook, Oranmore, Co. Galway.*

## 297. NATIONAL UNIVERSITY OF IRELAND GALWAY, NEWCASTLE, GALWAY

No archaeological significance
12931 22590
99E0012

Three trial-trenches were mechanically excavated within the site of the proposed development. Nothing of archaeological significance was discovered. Further monitoring was recommended.

*Anne Connolly, Archaeological Services Unit Ltd, Purcell House, Oranmore, Co. Galway.*

### 298. 26 PROSPECT HILL, GALWAY
Town
12986 22525
SMR 94:100
99E0424

Test excavation was undertaken here, before planning, from 11 to 13 August 1999. The site is on a natural elevation on the north-east side of the town. Prospect Hill was originally called *Bóthar Mór*, and the anglicised version of the name (Bohermore) is still applied to the general area. It is clear from the name that this was the principal highway leading to the medieval town. The proposed development site appears to be close to the site of St Brigid's Chapel and the adjoining House of Lepers, both of which are shown and named on the 1651 Pictorial Map of Galway. The House of Lepers was originally founded by Thomas Lynch Fitzstephen in 1543 as a hospital for the poor of the town. It was one of many buildings in the east suburbs that were burned by Hugh O'Donnell in 1596, but it was subsequently rebuilt by Revd Francis Kirwan, who also laid the foundations of St Brigid's Church.

The site (40m north-west/south-east by 30m) was cleared of all upstanding buildings and covered with a layer of gravel chippings in 1998. Testing comprised the mechanical excavation of four trenches. The gravel surface generally overlay a layer 0.25m thick of crushed building rubble and redeposited natural. At the west end of the site this rubble layer directly overlay the natural, light brown, clayey sand, but at the east end a greyish-brown, clayey silt deposit was occasionally encountered. This deposit contained moderate inclusions of animal bone, charcoal flecks, and oyster, mussel and winkle shells. Occasional post-medieval pottery sherds were found in this deposit. It had an average thickness of 0.25m and overlay the natural, light brown, clayey sand.

Several post-medieval features were also encountered. These comprised portions of two oval pits (length *c.* 2m) and three small, round-bottomed pits (1.25–1.75m in diameter). Finds from these features included post-medieval pottery sherds, clay pipe fragments and green glass wine bottle fragments. It was recommended that the site be archaeologically resolved before development.

*Dominic Delany, 31 Ashbrook, Oranmore, Co. Galway.*

### 299. 6–7 QUAY LANE, GALWAY
Town
12986 22525
SMR 94:100
97E0452 ext.

Test excavation was undertaken here, before planning, from 4 to 7 January 1999. The site is at the south end of the medieval town and contains substantial remains of a large late medieval house (11.5m north-east/south-west by 6.6m). The testing formed part of an ongoing archaeological assessment of the site. A detailed survey, comprising the production of scaled elevations of the upstanding late medieval walls, was carried out in May–June 1998, and an impact assessment report was prepared in December 1998.

The upstanding archaeological remains comprise the north-east gable and south-east wall of a late medieval house. The ground floor of the north-east gable is faced with concrete blocks that conceal the site of a large domestic fireplace. The stone surround of the fireplace does not appear to survive, but the large flue opening can be observed behind the concrete walling. The second floor contains a fine late medieval fireplace with a plain flat lintel framed by a simple decorative hood-mould. The fireplace is set in an impressive stepped chimney-stack, which extends the full height of the gable wall. The south-east wall is primarily of late medieval fabric, but sections of the wall have been rebuilt or refaced, and three large windows (now blocked) were inserted at the south end of the wall. The first floor contains a fireplace, similar to the one in the north-east gable but missing its lintelled head. There is a blocked late medieval window embrasure, 1.8m wide, immediately north of the fireplace. The second floor contains the remains of two late medieval windows. The north window is almost complete. It is a mullioned twin-light window with a square head and hood. A single jamb of what was probably a very similar window survives to the south. Other late medieval features include three *in situ* rounded corbels, indicating that each of the three floors was 2.5m high. There is an impressive external chimney stack on the south-east wall. It begins at first-floor level and is supported by three roughly worked corbels (a fourth corbel is missing). The remains of the original string-course can be observed above the late medieval window at the north end of the wall. The fine stone wall façade at Quay Lane is probably of 19th-century construction but contains numerous reused late medieval stones and architectural fragments.

Test excavation comprised the mechanical excavation of three trenches at 6–7 Quay Lane and the manual excavation of two test-pits in the yard at the rear of 8 Quay Lane. Medieval deposits were encountered at an average depth of 0.35m below the old ground levels across the site. They consisted of brown and greyish-brown, silty clays with frequent inclusions of shell (oyster, mussel, limpet and winkle), animal and fish bone, and charcoal flecks. The deposits were not excavated, but trowelling of the upper levels yielded occasional medieval pottery sherds (e.g. Saintonge and Merida wares). The features encountered were part of the rubble foundation of the north-west wall of the late medieval house and a circular, stone-lined well, 0.95m in diameter. The well is faced with roughly hewn limestone boulders and is *c.* 2.5m deep (it was almost completely water-filled when uncovered). Further archaeological work will be required before development at this site.

*Dominic Delany, 31 Ashbrook, Oranmore, Co. Galway.*

### 300. 35 SHOP STREET, GALWAY
Urban
1299 2253
99E0317

The proposed development involved the alteration and extension of the premises to accommodate a retail outlet. The site is within the town wall of medieval Galway and falls within the zone of archaeological potential. Test excavations

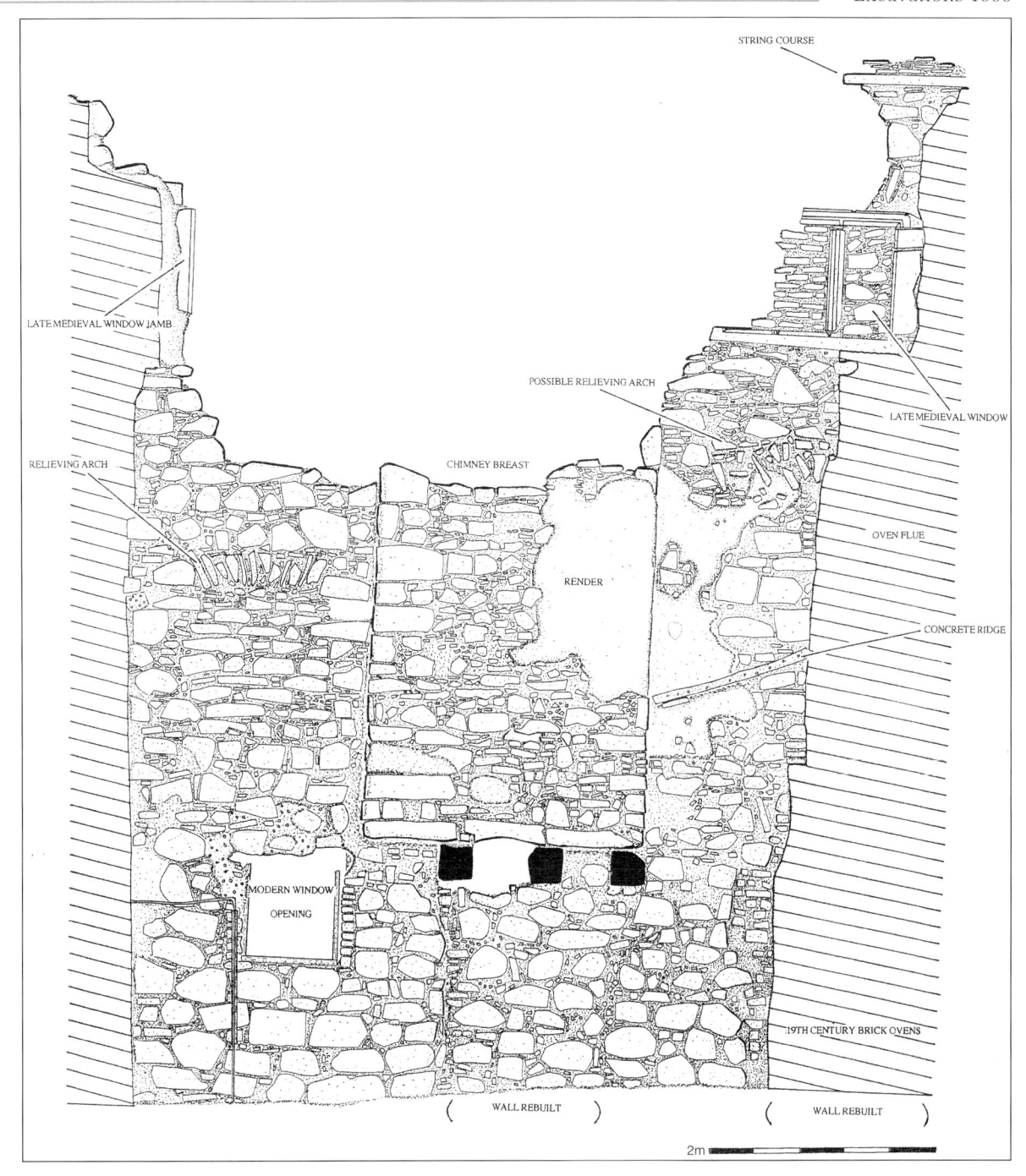

Elevation of outer face of south-east wall of late medieval building at 6–7 Quay Lane, Galway.

undertaken in July involved the excavation of three trenches in the area of the proposed extension.

A black, humic layer was uncovered in all three trenches. This layer contained inclusions of oyster shells and was 0.3m to 1.5m deep overlying the natural, yellow/grey boulder clay.

While no features or artefacts of archaeological significance were uncovered during testing, it was recommended that the boring of the piled foundations be monitored.
*Fiona Rooney, Arch. Consultancy Ltd, Ballydavid South, Athenry, Co. Galway.*

### 301. SPANISH ARCH, GALWAY
Urban
12986 22525
97E0014
A 5m (north-west/south-east) by 3m (north-east/south-west) area was mechanically excavated to a maximum depth of 0.8m below ground level, adjacent to and adjoining the south-west-facing wall at the Spanish Arch. A rubble foundation was revealed, directly underlying the wall. However, no significant dating evidence emerged from material removed under the south-west-facing wall.
*Anne Connolly, Archaeological Services Unit Ltd, Purcell House, Oranmore, Co. Galway.*

### 302. KNOCKROE HILL, GLEENAVEEL
Cairns
99E0629
This project concerned testing on the summit of Knockroe Hill, Abbeyknockmoy, Co. Galway. Recent work erecting telecommunication aerials on the hill resulted in the summit of Knockroe being levelled. The Archaeological Record of County Galway

records the existence of three cairns on the top of this hill; however, only one of these monuments is visible above ground today. The testing was undertaken in an attempt to find the other two monuments. The work was carried out over three weeks from 8 November 1999.

Four trenches were manually excavated revealing no trace of any archaeological monuments or artefacts of archaeological significance. Two cairns, which were recorded some years ago as existing at the summit of the hill, no longer survive. They are likely to have been levelled during work on the summit that resulted in the installation of telecommunication aerials, associated structures and a roadway leading to the hilltop.

*Martin Fitzpatrick, Arch. Consultancy Ltd, Ballydavid South, Athenry, Co. Galway.*

### 303. GEORGE'S STREET, GORT
Urban medieval
14550 20225
99E0274

Test-trenches were excavated to the east of the Cannahowna River to comply with a planning condition. Gort Mart was in the southern section of the development site.

Eight trenches were excavated in the footprint of the foundations of a hotel, houses and a carpark. Trenches 1–4 were excavated in the area of the disused mart. A riverine deposit was recorded overlying the clay subsoil. Trenches 5–8 were excavated in the northern section of the site. This area has been extensively infilled in recent years by the County Council. Ground level has been raised by *c.* 6m in the northern corner of the site.

No archaeological stratigraphy was recorded in any of the trenches, and no artefacts were recovered.
*Jacinta Kiely, Eachtra Archaeological Projects, Clover Hill, Mallow, Co. Cork.*

### 304. BALRICKARD, HEADFORD
Adjacent to castle
1271 2469
SMR 42:21
99E0316

Monitoring of this development was carried out on 17 July 1999, in response to a condition of planning. The development is adjacent to Headford Castle and consisted of the construction of a dwelling-house and associated services at Balrickard, Headford, Co. Galway. The site was less than one-quarter mile south of the village of Headford and was part of the site of an estate house known as Headford Castle, which was owned by the St George family. Lewis's *Topographical dictionary* of 1837 describes the house as 'a handsome modern building, erected on the ruins of the ancient castle'. The grounds are described as an 'extensive demesne'. They consisted of 7495 acres, worth £4460 in 1876. The original castle was built in around 1240–5 by Walter de Ridelsford. The castle was in ruins by 1914. Richard Mansergh-St George was killed by rebels in 1797 (which may indicate that the house dated to the 18th century), while his son, Richard-James Mansergh-St George, was high sheriff of County Galway in 1818. According to a local man, the development site contained the coach-house and stables that were attached to the main house.

The ground disturbance involved the clearing of the proposed location of the dwelling, an area along the road to the north-north-east and a driveway from the road to the north-north-east along the west-north-west site boundary and along the north-north-east side of the dwelling. Only topsoil was removed as the ground was deemed good enough to build on.

The stratigraphy encountered consisted of topsoil, 0.1–0.25m thick, below which was natural subsoil and the foundations of outhouses, associated with the demesne house on the site. The only artefacts recovered during monitoring were red and yellow brick, associated with the foundations of the demesne house.

*Richard Crumlish, Archaeological Services Unit Ltd, Purcell House, Oranmore, Co. Galway.*

### 305. HIGH ISLAND
Early Christian monastery
L501572
SMR 21:26C
95E0124 ext.

In summer 1999 a fifth season of excavation was carried out over nine weeks. Following on from previous years' excavations, a trench 15m east–west x 10m north–south was opened in the area north of the church enclosure wall. This area was chosen for excavation as a small beehive hut, Cell A, within the area is scheduled for reconstruction by *Dúchas* The Heritage Service. Apart from the cell, part of the cashel wall and a previously unknown subrectangular structure were also identified.

Cell A is the earliest of the three structures. A stone-kerbed hearth outside the cell to the south-east appears to be associated with its earliest occupation. Post-dating the construction of the hearth, the cell was surrounded by an annulus that encircled all but its south face, where the entrance was. The annulus was for the most part built of stone, with a good face apparent on its external side. It was relatively well preserved and in places stood almost 0.9m high. No definite dating evidence has been uncovered for this phase of activity; however, the stratigraphic relationship between Cell A and various other structures and features such as the enclosure wall, paved surfaces and the existing church (thought to be 10th-century, based on radiocarbon determination of *in situ* burial) suggests that it is most probably 10th-century or earlier.

Sometime later the monastery seems to have been enclosed by a cashel wall. This was built around the earlier Cell A and effectively incorporated it into its extent.

Post-dating the cashel wall, a subrectangular structure, possibly an enclosure as opposed to a roofed building, was built onto the north side of the wall. Only three walls of this structure were identified. The (east and west) side-walls splayed slightly outwards, yielding internal dimensions of 3.8–4.84m wide east–west. The east wall was 1.9m long, while the west wall was 3.4m long, north–south. No delimiting wall was identified along the south side; however, the cashel wall in this area had been partially robbed out, and it is thought that it may have been deliberately dismantled in this location so as to provide access into the structure.

Excavation inside the subrectangular structure was not completed this year, and its function remains unknown.

As a result of the presence of this new building a passage was cut into the cashel wall on the north-west side; the passage was stepped and paved along its length. Adjacent to the passage the internal face of the cashel wall appeared to have been reinforced with a second face of stone, an apparent attempt to strengthen the wall in this area.

At the end of the previous year's excavation a low wall, standing at most 0.45m high, was exposed on the external side of the north wall of the church enclosure. It was thought at the time that the wall was part of the remains of an earlier enclosure wall. However, excavation in 1999 revealed that the wall, in its excavated form, was of no greater antiquity than the church enclosure wall, and the two walls functioned together by retaining substantial quantities of dumped ash, charcoal, heather and burnt peat, most of which contained food remains. The alignment of the low wall in relation to the church enclosure wall, coupled with its location in this area, nonetheless suggests that its foundations may be of greater antiquity than the overlying courses.

By the mid-12th/early 13th century the monastery was abandoned (dating based upon radiocarbon determination of a burial cut into the church floor), but in the decades, and possibly the centuries, afterwards the site appears to have been frequented possibly by pilgrims or other devotees to the island saints. Traces of transient activity in the form of hearths and small shell middens were uncovered across the excavated area.

Of the small array of finds from the site, the most notable were a number of decorated cross-slabs and two coins. The earliest coin is a debased silver penny thought to have been minted in Norway under King Harold the Hardrada in the mid-11th century, while the later coin is an early 13th-century halfpenny, minted in Dublin under King John (identification, Michael Kenny, NMI).

Conservation and stabilisation work by *Dúchas* was carried out on the west gable of the church and on the south and west walls of the church enclosure. The work is ongoing.

Funding for this excavation was provided by *Dúchas* The Heritage Service.
*Georgina Scally, c/o 81 Upper Leeson Street, Dublin 4.*

### 306. MAINISTIR CHIARÁIN, INIS MÓR
Early Christian/medieval monastery
L810120
96E0081

The fourth season of excavation at Mainistir Chiaráin took place over eleven weeks between late June and mid-September 1999. Two new cuttings were opened this season to provide links between the church construction and Cuttings 1 and 2. Cutting 3 was opened in the baulk between Cuttings 1 and 2, leaving a thin (0.01m) baulk *in situ* to maintain a profile. A 3m-wide extension was also opened to the church in order to provide links between the church construction and the construction level uncovered in Cutting 2 in 1998 (*Excavations 1998*, 84). Cutting 4, measuring *c.* 3m x 3m, was opened between the eastern end of the church and Cutting 2. A 2m-wide baulk was left between Cuttings 3 and 4 to provide support for the church wall.

In Cutting 1 the lower fills of the stone-lined drain exposed in 1998 were excavated. Excavation confirmed that a natural gryke in the limestone was utilised for one side of the east–west section of this L-shaped feature. Large boulders blocked the eastern end of the feature, and limestone slabs lined the sides. To the south several layers of redeposited clay were identified underlying the cobbled surface excavated in 1998, indicating that a clay platform had been constructed here before the cobbled surface was laid. Underlying the clay layers a large, bowl-shaped pit was cut into natural clay. This pit was filled with a charcoal-rich deposit, and the sides were fire-affected. A number of stake-holes were identified surrounding this feature. Samples of charcoal were taken for radiocarbon dating, in addition to large soil samples for flotation. A test-pit excavated around this feature confirmed that the pit was dug into sterile clay.

In Cutting 3 a section of the robbed-out east wall of Building B was identified adjacent to the church. This section consisted of some stone *in situ* as well as a number of socket holes. The east and west cuts of the wall were also identified. In the central area of the cutting a long agricultural furrow provided confirmation of the nature of the disturbance east of Building A. In the southernmost corner of the cutting the line of the south wall of Building B was identified, in addition to a flagstone surface abutting it to the south. This surface provides a link with a similar surface in Cutting 1. A metalled surface was identified extending from the church wall to the south wall of Building B.

The foundation cut for the church was identified underlying the east wall of Building B. This cut was *c.* 1m wide and was filled with a sandy clay with a large amount of rubble. An earlier construction level and foundation trench were found to underlie this secondary cut. This sequence was confirmed in Cutting 4. There were some indications of an earlier construction phase in Cutting 1 in 1998, but because of the wall collapse the cutting had to be backfilled without reaching natural subsoil. Samples of charcoal and mortar were taken for radiocarbon dating from both construction phases.

The large pit identified in the eastern edge of Cutting 2 continued into Cutting 3, and a number of fills were excavated. These consisted primarily of sandy deposits with rubble. The rest of the lime pit identified in the north-west corner of Cutting 2 was also excavated. This small pit was linear rather than circular and was orientated east–west. A small pit filled with a charcoal-rich deposit was identified at the base of the earliest construction surface. Similar charcoal deposits associated with the earlier construction were identified in Cuttings 1 and 4. A third pit was identified in the southern corner of the cutting. This pit underlay the line of the south wall of Building B. It was backfilled with clay.

Cutting 4 provided an opportunity to follow the parallel furrows identified in Cutting 2 in 1998. Excavation adjacent to the church wall confirmed that these were a series of agricultural furrows. An additional furrow, cut at right angles to the three north–south furrows, was also uncovered. The foundation cut for the church wall was also identified. An earlier construction phase, including an earlier cut and deposits of mortar, charcoal and stone, was identified.

This research project is funded by the Heritage Services, Department of Arts, Heritage, Gaeltacht and the Islands, on the recommendation of the National Committee for Archaeology of the Royal Irish Academy, and by the University Research Expeditions Program of the University of California.
*Sinéad Ní Ghabhláin, Research Associate, Cotsen Institute of Archaeology, University of California, Los Angeles, CA 90024, USA.*

### 307. KINALEHIN FRIARY AND ABBEYVILLE
Earthworks
**98E0312**
An open field on the south side of the ruins of the Franciscan monastery of Kinalehin has a complex of earthworks that may represent the cells and cloister of the Carthusian monastery that was founded at this site in the 13th century. A preliminary programme of soil sampling, using a technique devised in the University of Bristol, was carried out in September 1998 in collaboration with Professor Mick Aston and Dr Mark Horton (Bristol). Fist-sized soil samples were taken at 5m intervals and analysed for their heavy-metal content (zinc, cobalt etc.). Concentration of traces of these metals indicated areas of human occupation, and these in turn indicated possible cell sites.
*Tadhg O'Keefe, Department of Archaeology, University College, Belfield, Dublin 4.*

**Editor's note:** This summary, though of work carried out during 1998, was received too late for inclusion in the bulletin of that year.

### 308. KINALEHIN FRIARY AND ABBEYVILLE
Earthworks
**99E0528**
Further investigtions by a joint UCD–University of Bristol team in the field to the south of the ruins of Kinalehin Franciscan friary involved a programme of resistivity survey and the excavation of three trial-trenches. The resistivity survey indicated a possible plan of the Carthusian monastery known to have been founded here in the 13th century. The trenches were laid out to assist in the interpretation of the resistivity survey and to assess the potential of the site for further investigation.

One of the trenches, outside the wall of the Franciscan refectory, contained a fill of stones in a wide ditch, both of indeterminate date. The second trench contained evidence of a robbed wall, and this has provisionally been interpreted as the back wall of the Carthusian monastery. The third trench revealed a deep ditch running at an unusual angle relative to other features on the site, and part of a human bone (probably a femur) was found in its fill. The date of this ditch could not be established.

Resistivity survey and a limited programme of soil sampling for heavy-metal analysis were also carried out at Abbeyville, to the south of the friary ruins but in the same parish. This may be the site of the 'lower house' of the Carthusian monastery—the place where guests and lay brethren stayed. A number of possible house sites are visible as earthworks, and soil analysis confirmed human occupation here.
*Tadhg O'Keefe, Department of Archaeology, University College, Belfield, Dublin 4.*

### 309. ST BRENDAN'S CHURCH, LOUGHREA
Human remains
**99E0491**
Excavations at St Brendan's Church were carried out over three weeks in September 1999. In the town of Loughrea, St Brendan's Church is marked on the third edition of the Ordnance Survey map but not on the first edition. The building, which is currently being converted into the branch library for Galway County Council, is thought to occupy the site of a pre-Reformation church within the walls of Loughrea town. During construction work human bones were uncovered both inside and outside the church building. As a result of these finds and following consultations with *Dúchas* The Heritage Service, it was recommended that all remaining ground disturbance within the church be carried out by a licensed archaeologist.

Five separate areas within the church were excavated during this project. Two of the areas revealed 19th-century cobbled surfaces, but no artefacts of archaeological significance were uncovered in any area. The excavations concentrated in the interior of the building resulted in the recovery of moderate amounts of scattered human remains that had been previously disturbed. While the exact date of the disturbance cannot be defined, it is likely that the construction of the present church building at the beginning of the 19th century resulted in the displacement of buried human remains. While evidence for possible burials pre-dating the church building were uncovered, no features, artefacts or deposits of archaeological significance were encountered to suggest the existence of an earlier church building on the site.

In addition to the excavation work inside the church building, this project involved the cleaning and recording of the section faces of an east–west-running service trench on the north side of the building. Occasional human remains were also recovered from this area. After consultation with the National Museum of Ireland, the human remains recovered from the excavations were delivered to the local minister for reburial.
*Martin Fitzpatrick, Arch. Consultancy Ltd, Ballydavid South, Athenry, Co. Galway.*

### 310. ORANMORE SEWERAGE SCHEME
Various
**98E0375 ext.**
Work on various archaeological sites on the line of the Oranmore Sewerage Scheme continued in 1999. Work carried out here in 1998 was reported in *Excavations 1998*, 84–6. The writer completed several sites started in 1998, and the remaining sites were then excavated or completed by Leo Morahan (see Nos 311–14 below).

*Site XVII, Millplot, mill (site of)*
Work was completed on the site of the millpond and

millpond wall. The millpond wall was shown to have been a stone-faced embankment with man caulking used as a waterproofing layer between the plinth and the lower courses of the wall. Several further pieces of millstones were found in the stone paving that lay on top of the millpond embankment or millpond wall.

Excavation revealed the existence of a rough setting of stones, some further pieces of wattle-like strands and the occasional piece of worked wood. No human bones in addition to the skull found in 1998 (*Excavations 1998*, 85) were discovered. The skull showed several slash marks, and some very sharply incised lines at the back of the skull seem to provide evidence for scalping. The shingled layer contained rounded stones including unworked chert. Several pieces of unworked wood were found. The remainder of the site was resolved.

*Site XXX, Oranmore*
This site, which in 1998 produced a series of pits, several scrapers and debitage of worked flint and chert, as well as fragments of several stone axes and a spindle-whorl, was completed and resolved. Some further pits, prehistoric tools and waste flakes were found.

*Site XXXI, Oranmore*
Work was completed on this site, which had previously produced about half of a Later Mesolithic Bann Flake from a disturbed context. Some chert, much of it unworked, was found. The clearance cairns and embankments proved to be of post-medieval date and produced some late pottery and clay pipe fragments.
*Jim Higgins, 'St Gerard's', 18 College Road, Galway.*

**311. ORANMORE, SITE 28**
Stone-lined features
**99E0120**
During topsoil removal on the Galway–Oranmore sewerage scheme, five stone-lined features were detected. The top of each one was no more than 0.3m beneath the current ground level, and limestone was prevailing. Before excavation, all lay in rocky scrub, and all were close enough to the shores of Oranmore Bay to be affected by very high tides. Four of the features were within 60m of each other at most, with the fifth 400m away to the north.

All features were lined or partly lined by limestone slabs set on edge. All incorporate rock outcrop into some part of their construction. In addition, all their component stones had been heavily burned, while the clay inside these cist-like features, and immediately outside them in many cases, had also been severely baked. Another feature common to all five was part of the internal subdividing line of stones, running parallel to the sides of the 'cists'.

'Cist' no. 1 extended for 7m north–south, measured 2.1 east–west overall and extended to a depth of 0.5m. A foundation trench set in gravel was clearly evident for the north and south side-walls. At its north end the 'cist' opened into an irregular pit full of loose clay, yellow daub and burnt red clay. Finds included one chert scraper from near the upper levels, and some charcoal, shell and baked clay. It appears that the central part of the 'cist' was subjected to the most intense heat.

'Cist' no. 2 was nearly 6m long north-east/south-west by 1.2m wide at most. It had been constructed both against and over some rock outcrop, and the ground it lay on sloped gently to south-west. A small, shallow, stone-lined box *c.* 1m across was built over a sheet of rock against the north-west side of the structure. This 'cist' contained baked clay, charcoal, shell and burnt bone in very small amounts, and these are currently being analysed. The area outside the south-west end contained slight hollows in which some animal bone and teeth were found; these may not be associated with the 'cist'.

'Cist' no. 3 was just 3m to the west of no. 2. Rather poorly preserved, it was aligned north-east/south-west for 4.2m and was 1.4m wide at most. While it contained further charcoal and baked clay, it was shallow, never exceeding 0.28m deep. It was built into rocky, gravelly ground and sloped gently to the south-west. Rock outcrop was most evident at the north-east and south-west ends, beneath some central side-stones.

'Cist' no. 4 was 3m north-west/south-east by 1.5m wide and was the deepest of all at 0.55m. Natural rock formed part of the north-west side and enclosed its south-east side, while it was open to the north-west. While it contained the usual contexts, it also held a large, irregular boulder that had a hole dug for its reception and that had some side-stones of the 'cist' built over it. A number of finds from this included a chert thumbnail scraper, and small amounts of burnt bone and waste flakes.

'Cist' no. 5 ran for 4.35m north-west/south-east and averaged 1.1m wide. This site was furthest from the other four and contained less naturally occurring outcrop. Deposits in its body included baked clay, gravel and lime, while at the north-west end burnt shell, charcoal and further burnt clay were found.

All five 'cists' had parts of their floors formed of a hard, mortar-type substance, also created by the heat. While all five contain some form of internal subdividing line, all of these were set at a slightly higher level to the stones in the sides of the 'cists'. No dates have been returned yet. The intense heat generated here indicates the possibility of crematoria; analysis of the bone may strengthen this.

Whatever the dating of the bones, this area is one that supported intense prehistoric activity, evidenced by a vast array of lithics from around the sites. These included 22 mostly good-quality chert scrapers and three arrowheads of chert. Within 100m of the site, to the south, a polished stone axehead fragment was found in the same landscape.

One unenclosed area of intense burning was found roughly equidistant from four 'cists'. It contained a spread of yellow and red baked clay with one large, heat-stained, irregular stone near the centre. Soil analysis and lithics reports are being prepared, and crude baked clay/pottery from around the site was also sent for analysis.
*Leo Morahan, 110 Cimín Mór, Bearna, Galway.*

**312. ORANMORE, SITE 27**
Bank
**99E0750**
Site 27 was 350m to north of the 'cists'. Part of a bank

that ran west-south-west to a nearby ringbarrow was excavated. Composed of a mixture of brown clay and yellow daub, it contained amounts of waste chert. Traces of an ill-defined fosse 1–1.2m wide and at most 0.3m deep could be made out on either side of the bank. Only 7m length of the bank was excavated.

Within 2m of the bank to south a chert, barbed and tanged arrowhead was found, while from this area two thumbnail scrapers were also found.
*Leo Morahan, 110 Cimín Mór, Bearna, Galway.*

### 313. ORANMORE, SITE 17
Kilns

Two small stone-lined kilns joined by an interconnected flue were dug into the gravel. Both kilns were crude and constructed of drystone, incorporating rock outcrop. They averaged 0.8m to 1.1m across internally. They reached 1.2m deep at most, and the interiors were full up of later rubble. One of the kilns was partly filled with some shell midden material.
*Leo Morahan, 110 Cimín Mór, Bearna, Galway.*

### 314. ORANMORE, SITE 25
No archaeological significance
**99E0751**

A final site at Oranmore was found to consist of a natural, yellow daub material of no archaeological significance.
*Leo Morahan, 110 Cimín Mór, Bearna, Galway.*

### 315. PARKALOUGHAN
No archaeological significance
**14753 21613**
**99E0001**

Pre-development testing was carried out on 13 January 1999 in response to a request for further information on two sites before their development at Parkaloughan, Ardrahan, Co. Galway. The sites were on a low ridge that is orientated roughly east–west, in fair grazing, *c.* 3 miles north-east of Ardrahan village. Lavally Conor Castle (SMR 104:166), a tower-house, was visible a short distance to the north-east, while an enclosure and children's burial-ground (SMR 104:217) lay along the southern boundary of the site to the east.

Six trenches were excavated by machine during the testing, three on each site, to best cover those areas of the proposed development closest to the enclosure and children's burial-ground.

The stratigraphy in all six trenches was the same, topsoil, 0.1–0.4m thick, lying directly above natural boulder clay. No artefacts were recovered during testing, the six test-trenches revealing natural, undisturbed stratigraphy. Nothing of archaeological significance was in evidence.
*Richard Crumlish, Archaeological Services Unit Ltd, Purcell House, Oranmore, Co. Galway.*

### 316. TOWNPARKS (1ST DIVISION), TUAM
Enclosure
**14309 25266**
**SMR 29:170**
**99E0513**

Monitoring of topsoil removal and ground reduction was undertaken before a proposed residential development, from 6 September to 21 October 1999. The site comprises a large green-field area (7.894 hectares), bounded by existing residential developments to the east and south and by agricultural lands to the north and west. The site contains the west half of an enclosure, clearly marked on OS maps but now no longer visible. Testing was undertaken on the east half of the monument by Richard Crumlish in 1995 (*Excavations 1995*, 38, 95E0084).

The monument is at the south-east end of the proposed development site. The recommended margin of 15m to be left undisturbed could not be achieved as the monument is close to the only point of access to the site.

Excavations revealed a uniform stratigraphy across the site. A loose, dark brown, silty clay topsoil, 0.65m thick, overlay a moderately compact, mid-brown, silty sand subsoil. A compacted, cream boulder clay occurred at a depth of 1.15m. Six linear features, representing modern field boundaries and drainage ditches, were encountered during monitoring. No features, deposits or finds of archaeological interest were revealed.
*Dominic Delany, 31 Ashbrook, Oranmore, Co. Galway.*

## KERRY

### 317. ARDFERT COMMUNITY CENTRE, ARDFERT
Adjacent to ecclesiastical site
**78550 12111**
**SMR 20:46**
**97E0302 ext.**

Planning permission was granted for a small extension to the Ardfert Community Centre, which is across the road from the major ecclesiastical site that contains Ardfert Cathedral and two other extant churches. Monitoring of an earlier extension had taken place in 1997 (*Excavations 1997*, 79–80).

The work was carried out on 15 November 1999. Six pits for roof supports were opened. Although all were dug to a depth of *c.* 1m, only one reached boulder clay. No features and only modern finds were noted.
*Isabel Bennett, Glen Fahan, Ventry, Tralee, Co. Kerry.*

### 318. NEW ROAD, BALLYBUNION
Ringfort
**8663 14104**
**SMR 4:32**
**99E0236**

Planning permission to construct a dwelling-house over a partially levelled ringfort at New Road, Ballybunion, Co. Kerry, included archaeological conditions on the development.

A two-week excavation at the site revealed the existence of the ditch, a more recent land drain and cultivation furrows. The site was considered to be a ringfort when surveyed in early 1990, and the results of the archaeological excavation presented no additional information to alter this interpretation. Nothing survived to indicate a bank surrounding the ditch, but it is know that such a structure did exist from the description in the *North Kerry Archaeological Survey* (Toal 1995, 100). The upper stony fills in two of the excavated sections were considered to represent the vestiges of a bank that had been machined into the partially infilled ditch. Further evidence for disturbance to the upper level of the ditch was noted in other sections, where clay pipe stems and modern bottle glass were recovered. All the evidence therefore pointed to considerable disturbance before archaeological excavation.

No intact stratigraphy was encountered, and in many places, particularly within the area of the interior, damage had taken place down to the surface of the boulder clay. Only a small proportion of the interior was exposed, however, and undisturbed archaeological features may survive towards the centre of the enclosure in the adjoining field.

With the exception of a possible hone stone from a disturbed context in the general location of the bank, no firm dating evidence was obtained from the excavation. The presence of burnt animal bones in the base of the ditch is an indicator of human domestic activity, and these could eventually be used to obtain a date for the occupation of the ringfort

*Reference*
Toal, C. 1995 *North Kerry Archaeological Survey.* Dingle.

*Margaret McCarthy, Archaeological Services Unit, University College, Cork.*

### 319. BALLYDWYER WEST
Earthwork
**Q923126**
**99E0131**
Test-trenching took place here before N21 rerouting. One trench was dug by hand into the meandering earthwork, which measured almost 70m in total length. The trench measured 14m by 1m. The strata uncovered in the trench proved to be natural in origin, and therefore the earthwork was deemed not to be of archaeological significance.
*Frank Coyne, Aegis Archaeology, 16 Avondale Court, Corbally, Limerick.*

### 320. BALLYDWYER WEST II
Enclosure
**Q584129**
**99E0132 and exts**
Initially two trenches were excavated by hand here, before the N21 rerouting. They measured 24m in total length and 1m wide and revealed the enclosing element to be composed of clay. The interior of the site, which was entirely filled with peat, sloped dramatically inwards. This suggested that there was an independent water supply in the interior.

It was felt that the site appeared to have similarities to a ritual pond. Therefore a further archaeological dimension had to be considered—that artefact recovery was possible. A further investigation followed as an extension to the licence.

Further trenching was undertaken by hand to assess the depth and nature of the site and to determine conclusively whether it was archaeological in nature. The investigation proved, however, that the site was probably fluvo-glacial in origin and therefore not of archaeological significance.

This licence was also used for the monitoring of the entire N21 rerouting. This included the road itself, *c.* 10km long, and a number of slip roads. Several archaeological features were encountered during the monitoring, all of which were excavated (see Nos 328 and 338 below).
*Frank Coyne, Aegis Archaeology, 16 Avondale Court, Corbally, Limerick.*

### 321. BALLYMACTHOMAS
Enclosure (ringfort)
**8922 11293**
**SMR 29:176**
**99E0262**
The remains of this ringfort lay to the west of the proposed rerouting of the N21. The ringfort had previously been bisected by an older slip road. There was tentative evidence that it may have been bivallate. Thus the line of the rerouted road nearest to the ringfort was tested to ascertain whether the ringfort's enclosing element extended far enough to be affected by the road.

The results of the trenching showed that the enclosing element of the enclosure lay to the west and beyond the line of the road and therefore would not be affected by its construction.
*Frank Coyne, Aegis Archaeology, 16 Avondale Court, Corbally, Limerick.*

### 322. BALLYNABOOLY
Ringfort
**4325 10223**
**SMR 43:218**
**99E0204**
Kerry County Council considered it necessary to carry out road-widening in Ballynabooly townland, near Dingle, in an area considered to be dangerous. The area about which there was most concern was a bend caused by the presence of a univallate ringfort, around which the road skirted. Although no damage to the monument was proposed, it was considered necessary to bring the edge of the road up to the bank of the monument, which necessitated some excavation work in the area of the fosse nearest the road, where a stone wall was to be built. Excavation of this area took place at the end of June 1999.

The area investigated measured 31m by 2.65m. After removal of topsoil by mechanical means, all further work was undertaken by hand, with assistance from staff of the Dingle Depot of the County Council.

Between 0.7m and 1.3m below modern ground level was excavated, and there was much collapse from a break in the bank in this area. Modern artefacts only (including a water pipe at 0.55m below modern ground level) were found. No definite fosse edge was found, although the area excavated may have been too small to encounter it. The only feature noted was a fire-reddened area, up to 0.06m thick, and 0.83m by 0.55m. It seemed to be sitting on the old ground level, but further exploration did not take place owing to the limited brief of the excavation.

The area excavated was trunked with stone, and a stone wall was built upon it, up against the ringfort bank.
*Isabel Bennett, Glen Fahan, Ventry, Tralee, Co. Kerry.*

### 323. BALLYWIHEEN
Burial site
Q352035
SMR 42:94
98E0371

A second season of excavation was undertaken at Ballywiheen from August to September 1999. The monastic site is known locally as *An Raingiléis*, which means 'the site of or ruins of an ancient church'. The site was also used as a *calluragh*, and unbaptised children were buried here within living memory. Archaeological investigation was initially required at Ballywiheen in 1998 following the insertion of a well shaft immediately outside the eastern circuit of the enclosing wall. A number of archaeological deposits and features were uncovered during that season, including a backfilled souterrain and the foundation of a wall (*Excavations 1998*, 89). These were interpreted as being contemporary with the primary use of the monastic enclosure. A later phase of activity was represented by the partial remains of a human burial.

Excavation was necessitated again in 1999 when archaeological monitoring along the line of a pipe-trench extending from the well shaft to the public road led to the discovery of a burial site. The excavation was originally limited to the area of the pipe-trench, but when it became apparent that significant archaeological deposits were present *Dúchas* requested that the full extent of the monument be exposed and excavated. The site is beside the road, *c.* 60m south-east of the monastic enclosure. A modern field boundary bisects the site north–south, and the monument narrowly survived the construction of the road in the early 19th century. The quadrant in the adjacent field lay outside the area of development and was therefore not excavated.

Two phases of activity were discerned. The earlier was represented by a series of pits cut into the natural boulder clay. These varied considerably in size and depth, from over 1m long and 0.65m deep to less than 0.35m in diameter. These smaller pits contained relatively large amounts of charcoal. Bulk soil samples were processed under laboratory conditions for material finds and bones, but, apart from three tiny fragments of calcined bone found in one pit, nothing was recovered. It was not possible to determine whether these bones were human or animal. In the absence of material finds and organic material, the function of the pits remains uncertain. The larger pits may possibly have held crouched inhumations, but no human remains were found to confirm this. The acidic soil conditions prevailing at the site may have resulted in the complete disintegration of the skeletons. Dating of this phase of activity will rely on radiocarbon analysis, and charcoal samples have been submitted to the laboratory in Gronigen.

The second phase of activity saw the insertion of a lintelled grave surrounded by three semicircular stone settings. The inner and outer settings were placed upright in a shallow trench, and the central setting overlay two of the pits associated with the earlier phase of activity. The stone settings were covered by a thin layer of cairn material, which also sealed the earlier pits. The lintelled grave was revealed when the road boundary was removed to create an entranceway into the site. The seven covering slabs survived the construction of the boundary fence and the public road. Excavation revealed a rectangular grave aligned north-west/south-east, carefully constructed of locally derived shale slabs that formed the sides and lintels. There were no flooring or end stones. The grave measured 2.2m by 0.64m and was 0.52m deep. No burial survived, but the acidic soil conditions may have mitigated against organic survival.

Phase 2: stone-lined grave and stone settings at Ballywiheen.

Material finds were scarce but included a hone stone, a spud stone and a loom or net weight. All were recovered from the layer of cairn material. The few artefacts found and the proximity of the burial site to the monastic enclosure point to an early medieval date for the construction of the monument, but the possibility of an earlier origin for the phase of pit digging should not be discounted. Charcoal samples from both phases have been submitted for radiocarbon analysis. The results of the excavation are currently being prepared for publication.
*Margaret McCarthy, Department of Archaeology, University College, Cork.*

Phase 1: pit features at Ballywiheen.

### 324. BRAY HEAD (VALENCIA ISLAND)
Early medieval farm
344736
97E0278 ext.

A third and final season of excavation (see *Excavations 1997*, 81–2, and *Excavations 1998*, 89, for descriptions of the results of previous season's work), funded by *Dúchas*, was undertaken in June and July. Work in 1999 concentrated on the

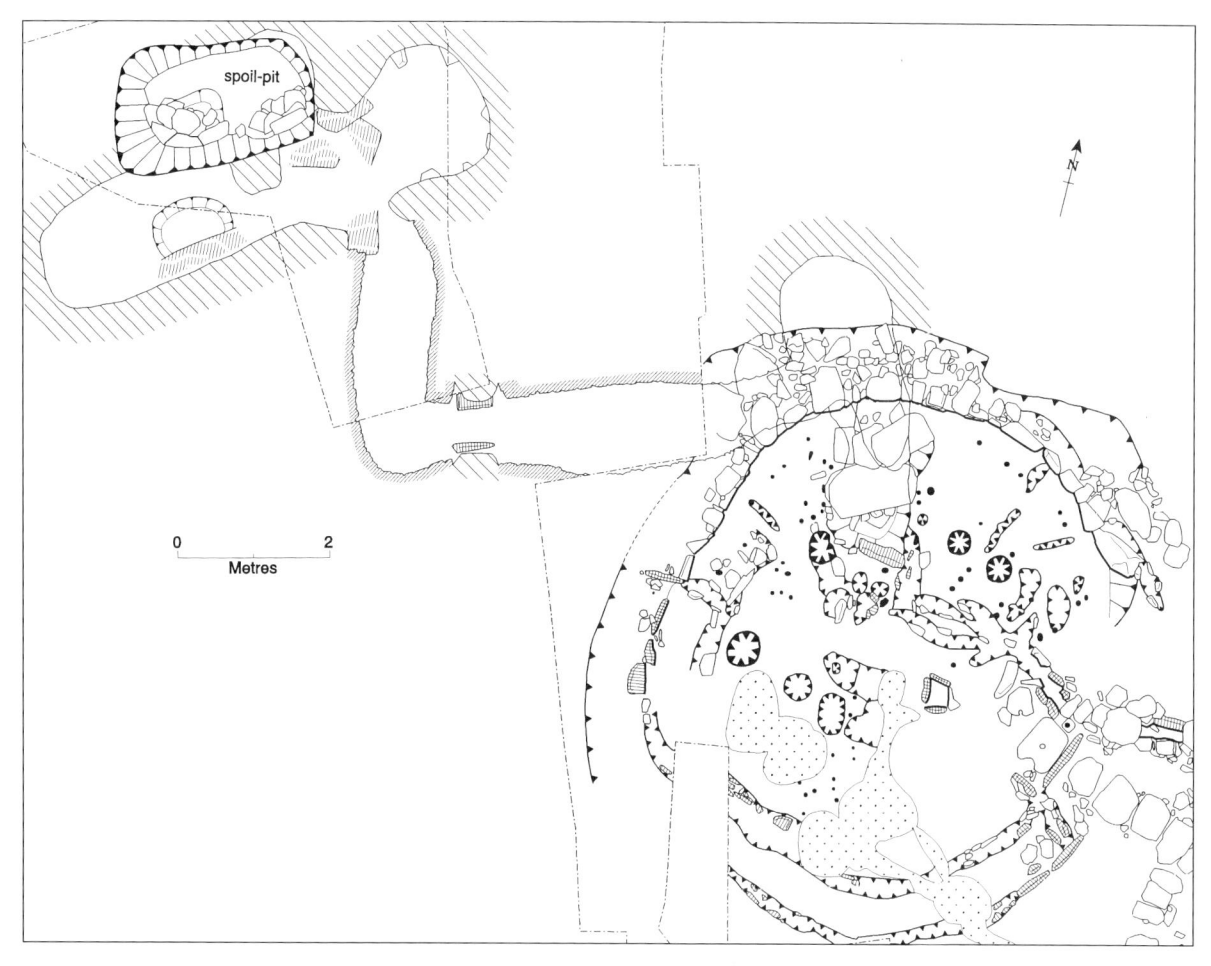

House 4 and souterrain at site at Bray Head.

completion of the excavation of Houses 2, 3 and 6, which were partly excavated in 1998. This work revealed the presence of a further two, very poorly preserved round houses, Nos 10 and 11. Excavation of the souterrain attached to House 4, which was discovered in 1998 but could not be excavated at that time, also took place this season.

The souterrain consisted of a short entrance passage, which turned at right angles into a longer passage. The other end of this passage also turned through a right angle and led to a further passage. This may have been the original end of the souterrain. An air vent opened off the end of this passage. The stone-lined passages were all constructed in individual trenches. There were low creeps between the passages that were constructed by tunnelling through the baulks of subsoil left between the individual trenches. The souterrain appears to have been later expanded. A deep spoil pit was dug, and two narrow tunnels led from its base into a large, earth-cut chamber. The tunnels were blocked with stone when the spoil pit was backfilled. The new chamber was linked to the end of the older souterrain by an earth-cut tunnel.

Parts of the roof of one of the souterrain chambers had collapsed. This and the entrance were covered by reinforced concrete beams and large flat stones after the excavation was completed. The stones were covered in polythene, and then the trenches were backfilled and resodded. This will allow the souterrain to be easily reopened if required.

Other work this year involved excavation of an enclosure, discovered this year, which delimited the northern side of the settlement. The intercutting of the successive levels of houses had suggested that the settlement was enclosed. The corn-drying kiln excavated in 1993 (*Excavations 1993*, 41, 93E0121) lay outside the enclosure. The enclosure consisted of a trench holding upright stones that revetted the downhill side of an earthen bank. It appears to exist only on the northern (uphill) side of the site. A possible entrance was discovered in the north-east side of the enclosure leading to the early medieval routeway known as *Bóthar na Scairte*, which can be traced along the whole length of the island.

In all, an area measuring a maximum of 30m east–west by 28m has been excavated. The remains of eleven houses—six round (one with a souterrain) and five rectangular—delimited on their uphill side by a stone and earthen bank, with a corn-drying kiln lying outside the enclosure, have been revealed and excavated. There may well be further houses immediately west of those excavated, but no funding is available for further work.

*Alan Hayden, Archaeological Projects Ltd, 25A Eaton Square, Terenure, Dublin 6W.*

### 325. BROSNA–KNOCKNAGOSHEL REGIONAL WATER SUPPLY SCHEME
Monitoring
1850 1250
99E0368

Monitoring of the Brosna–Knocknagoshel Regional Water Supply Scheme took place between June and

November 1999. The development encompassed five townlands: Brosna West, Tooreenablauha, Knoppoge, Knockognoe and Knockafreaghaun. No archaeological sites are recorded along the route of the development on the relevant RMP Constraint Maps for County Kerry, Sheets 24 and 32. Contained within Brosna village itself is an ecclesiastical enclosure centred on St Moling's Church and associated holy well. Also within the townland of Brosna West, to the west of the Clydagh River, is a field denoted on the 2nd edition OS map as 'Poulatemple'; this may be of either archaeological or historical importance.

A major focus of the development works is the southern bank of the Clydagh River. The marshy nature of the underlying ground surface is conducive to the location of archaeological sites such as *fulachta fiadh*. During the archaeological impact assessment a potential *fulacht fiadh* was identified 390m north of the proposed Intake Supply Centre. Extensive field-walking by the author could not identify this site, nor were any traces of archaeological stratigraphy noted at this location during the construction works.

The development works relate to the construction of a treatment plant, a reservoir, a pump house and an intake supply centre. The works also involved the construction of 6800m of pipeline and 110 house connections. The larger part of the pipeline followed the course of existing road systems. The trenches had an average width of 1.6m and depth of 1.7m.

Despite the extent and linear arrangement of the development, no subsurface archaeological stratigraphy was identified at any point throughout its course. A single find was retrieved from the bed of the Clydagh River, but this is believed to be a fossil, and a specialist report on it is pending.
*Emer Dennehy, Eachtra Archaeological Projects, 3 Canal Place, Tralee, Co. Kerry.*

### 326. CAHERLEHILLIAN
Early ecclesiastical enclosure
V572835
SMR 70:43
93E0073 ext.

Excavations at Caherlehillian, conducted as part of UCC's programme of training for undergraduate students of archaeology, continued for three weeks during June 1999 (for previous seasons' work, see *Excavations 1998*, 89; *Excavations 1997*, 82; *Excavations 1996*, 47; *Excavations 1995*, 40–1; *Excavations 1994*, 43–4, and *Excavations 1993*, 41–2). Investigations were concentrated in and beneath the *ceallúnach* burial-ground (Area 1), in and around the *leacht*-like structure in the eastern half of the enclosure (Area 8) and in the south-western quadrant of the enclosure (Area 7). Limited investigations were also carried out in Areas 3 and 5.

Further evidence for early medieval activity was uncovered beneath the level of the *ceallúnach* burials in Area 1. A thin lens of soil, which survived in patches, was identified as the early medieval ground surface. A number of adult graves and other features, including a drain and soak-pit, were cut into this layer. One of the graves was lined and covered with slate slabs, and this was stratigraphically earlier than a number of simple dug graves.

In Area 8 a number of *ceallúnach* graves were excavated in the area around the *leacht*-like structure. They were orientated east–west and appear to be post-medieval/early modern in date. One of these graves featured a fragment of a cross-slab reused as a side-stone; on this fragment is carved part of an encircled cross-of-arcs and a stylised peacock.

The two cross-slabs standing adjacent to the *leacht* were excavated, as they were in danger of collapse, and both appear to have been in secondary positions. A large amount of quartz was excavated from the surface of the *leacht*, revealing four slate covering slabs. A cross-inscribed pillar, in two pieces, was identified as one of the two missing corner-posts of the *leacht*-like structure.

In Area 7 the excavation of C8 was completed and the underlying C28 was revealed. This produced a range of finds, including imported pottery (E and B ware), whetstones, spindle-whorls and metal slag. On the removal of C28 a number of post- and stake-holes were revealed.

Excavations will continue in 2000.
*John Sheehan, Department of Archaeology, University College, Cork.*

### 327. CAPPANACUSH EAST
Adjacent to possible standing stone
8335 7020

Monitoring of ground disturbance work for three house sites, a few miles west of Kenmare, was a condition of planning. Work took place between July and September. The site is on the southern slopes of Knockanaskill, between 100m and 150m OD, looking over the estuary of the Kenmare River and across to the Beara Peninsula. It was wet, boggy ground.

Although nothing of archaeological significance was noted in any of the areas monitored (and one site had been cleared without an archaeological presence because of a misunderstanding), a previously unmarked possible standing stone, 0.92m high by 0.6m wide, was noted just 8m to the east of one of the house plots. It was recorded, and the importance of its presence was stressed to the developer.
*Isabel Bennett, Glen Fahan, Ventry, Tralee, Co. Kerry.*

North face of standing stone at Cappanacush East.

### 328. CLOGHERMORE
Ironworking areas
Q905127
99E0130 and exts

Owing to the importance of the limestone reef at

Cloghermore as a probable cave burial site (see No. 329 below), it was proposed to monitor this area before the N21 re-routing, i.e. that part of the road that ran near the outcrop.

An area c. 100m by 40m was stripped by a machine with a flat bucket. Six features of archaeological significance were uncovered. They appeared to be evidence of industrial activity such as iron smelting and were in the form of furnaces and pits. The licence was subsequently extended in order to excavate these features.

All the features were found to be circular in plan and ranged in diameter from 0.55m to 1.45m. Four of the features contained varying amounts of iron slag and charcoal. One pit contained burnt red sandstone and charcoal but no slag. The remaining pit was filled with topsoil and may have been deliberately emptied in antiquity. It is likely that it too was used in some metalworking activity, owing to the evidence of intensive burning in the form of baked boulder clay around the cut. Samples have been taken for scientific analysis and dating purposes.

Further features were uncovered in this vicinity when the monitoring of the main contract commenced. Eleven subcircular features were uncovered that showed similarities to those found previously. They also ranged in diameter from 0.5m to 1.5m. These features were interpreted as bowl furnaces, in varying stages of repair. Some, however, did not show the intense burning of the majority of the features. These may have been forging pits, where the bloom was worked after it was smelted. It is also possible that they were roasting pits, to heat the ore before smelting, which would ensure a more efficient smelt.

*Frank Coyne, Aegis Archaeology, 16 Avondale Court, Corbally, Limerick.*

### 329. CLOGHERMORE CAVE, CLOGHERMORE
Burials in cave
Q906128
99E0431

Following the finding of human bones in 1998, Cloghermore Cave was given National Monument status by *Dúchas*. The minimal rescue excavation was carried out in August 1999, funded by *Dúchas*. The entrance to the cave system is one-third of the way along the length of a large limestone reef that is 180m OD at its highest point and affords expansive views in all directions.

The cave system was surveyed by the Mid-West Caving Club, Limerick, in 1983 and was described as consisting of 375m of fossil passages, which run in a north-west/south-east direction for around half of the length of the system before turning to run in a north–south direction for the remainder (Condell 1985, 52–3).

Entrance to the system was through a narrow cleft on the northern side of the reef. Bones are visible throughout much of the system, but these are mostly animal bone and may have been dragged in by animals or washed into the system from above. However, the two small chambers at the southern end of the system, 'The Two Star Temple' and 'The Graveyard' (Condell 1985, 52–3), contained large quantities of bone.

The route through the system from the existing entrance to the two bone-bearing chambers at the southern end was difficult, and it was clear that this was unlikely to be the route along which the bones placed in these chambers had been carried. It was decided to seek an alternative entrance at the southern end of the system with the help of a radio-location device. This showed that the system terminated inside a D-shaped enclosure, which had been identified in a sloping field on the south side of the reef.

A 1.5m-wide trench was excavated across the enclosing bank at the north-north-east, where the slight depression indicated a possible ditch for a length of 14m. The excavation revealed that the feature consisted of two banks with a rock-cut ditch in between them, while the depression outside the bank was a very shallow, drain-like feature, which can only have been used to divert rainwater flowing down the slope, away from the enclosure.

The radio-location device showed that the system terminated in the middle of the D-shaped enclosure, so a trench measuring 2m x 3m was opened at this point. Three large slabs of limestone were uncovered; two were resting on the flat, while the third was to the western side of the trench and was at an angle, as if it had been disturbed. Voids around the two recumbent slabs clearly showed that they were sealing an entrance of some sort.

Removal of these slabs revealed an almost completely infilled shaft. The shaft was almost D-shaped on the northern side, which was composed of bedrock and some pieces of drystone walling, forming the straight side. The remaining arc of the shaft was composed almost exclusively of drystone walling. It was clear that the walling on the northern side was only necessary to facilitate the placing of the capstones and that the western side had almost completely collapsed into the shaft. However, the walling on the eastern side was intact.

A narrow opening to the cave system below could be seen, but using it would first involve the removal of the collapse and infill from the shaft. Once the shaft had been cleared of soil and stone it could be clearly seen that it allowed entry to the cave system through a narrow opening on its north-north-eastern side.

Apart from the removal of collapse inside the cave entrance, three separate test-pits were dug within the cave system—two in a recess to the east of the entrance, and one in the chamber known as 'The Graveyard'.

An attempt was made to excavate a pit in the chamber known as 'The Two Star Temple'; however, the soil cover here was found to be only 30–40mm deep and rested on a very solid stalagmite floor. The soil from an area measuring 1m$^2$ was removed from the 'Two Star Temple' and sieved. It produced a stone spindle-whorl, an iron arrowhead and some other small iron fragments, as well as small fragments of crushed bone (a result of people walking on the unburnt remains).

The two pits in the recess to the east of the entrance were excavated because of the existence of a thin covering of stalagmite over what appeared to be a substantial area of collapse. It was hoped that this indicated the antiquity of the collapse and that undisturbed archaeological strata were preserved underneath. A few pieces of bone were recovered from the inwashed/collapsed layer in the more westerly of the two pits.

The most productive area of excavation was 'The Graveyard'. The excavation here uncovered large quantities of unburnt bone and two separate stone settings containing substantial amounts of cremated bone and three amber beads. Both settings were capped with flat slabs, while much ash was included with the cremated deposits. However, here too the deposits, though much deeper than in the 'Two Star Temple', rested on a stalagmite floor, which in turn overlay a large amount of collapsed roof stone.

Further investigation of possible deposits beneath this collapse will probably be undertaken next year.
*Michael Connolly, Kerry County Museum, Ashe Memorial Hall, Denny Street, Tralee, Co. Kerry.*

### 330. EMLAGH WEST, DINGLE
Adjacent to ringfort, souterrains etc.
**SMR 53:16**
**99E0495**
Monitoring of all ground preparation work for a proposed guesthouse development took place at this site. Souterrains had recently been discovered nearby (see Michael Connolly in *Excavations 1993*, 43–4, 93E0080), and an ogham stone was also known from the area, as was the site of a ringfort.

Nothing of archaeological significance was noted at the development site.
*Isabel Bennett, Glen Fahan, Ventry, Tralee, Co. Kerry.*

### 331. GORTANEARE
Adjacent to (levelled) rath
**8789 12884**
**SMR 15:57**
**99M0015**
Monitoring of ground disturbance work at this development site (a dwelling-house) took place during March 1999. The development is *c.* 50m north-west of a levelled rath site.

Nothing of archaeological significance was noted at the development site.
*Isabel Bennett, Glen Fahan, Ventry, Tralee, Co. Kerry.*

### 332. LOHER
No archaeological significance
**Q507616**
**SMR 106:7 and 106:16**
**99E0136**
Two engineering test-pits and four associated sub-percolation pits associated with the construction of five houses in the townland of Loher, Waterville, were monitored because of the rich archaeological nature of the entire landscape and the proximity of the proposed development to Kildreenagh ecclesiastical site and Loher stone fort. The site is on the lower western slopes of Farraniaragh Mountain, commanding extensive views of the Loher valley, Ballinskelligs Bay and Skellig Michael.

The exposed material was loose, natural, undisturbed, purple-red sandstone.

No archaeological stratification or artefacts were encountered during this work.
*Laurence Dunne, Eachtra Archaeological Projects, 3 Canal Place, Tralee, Co. Kerry.*

### 333. AGHADOE HEIGHTS HOTEL (PARKAVONEAR TOWNLAND), AGHADOE, KILLARNEY
Adjacent to early ecclesiastical site
**9347 9274**
**SMR 66:16**
Monitoring of ground disturbance aspects of major refurbishment work at the Aghadoe Heights Hotel, Killarney, took place during October–December 1999. The hotel grounds are across the road from the extant remains of a major ecclesiastical site, which is today a graveyard, still in use, with the remains of a 12th-century Romanesque church and a round tower, as well as other features.

It was clear that major landscaping had taken place when the hotel was first built, and the site had been extensively cleared and the gardens laid out. Nothing of archaeological significance was noted during the monitoring.
*Isabel Bennett, Glen Fahan, Ventry, Tralee, Co. Kerry.*

### 334. CARNEGIE LIBRARY, MARKET STREET, KILLORGLIN
Burials
**V776965**
**99E0754**
Human remains were discovered during demolition and construction at the rear of the existing Carnegie Library, Market Street, Killorglin. Consequently, archaeological monitoring was introduced, although only a small zone abutting the rear of the library remained undisturbed. This area measured 18.5m north–south and 6m on average east–west. A truncated burial was discovered. Work was halted, and an emergency excavation licence was applied for. Two severely truncated burials and a quantity of *ex situ* human bone were recovered.

Burial A, the truncated remains of an articulated, *in situ* burial, was discovered extending beneath the south-eastern corner of the Carnegie building. It was therefore necessary to cut a 1.5m-by-1m trench through the concrete floor of the building to enable full recovery of the remains.

This individual had been truncated from the patellae down during recent development work. The left femur and the lower left arm and hand bones were also absent. The skull was lying on the left side, facing north. The individual had been placed extended, with the head at the western end, in a simple dug grave that was orientated east–west. No evidence of a coffin or artefacts survived.

A second *in situ*, articulated but truncated burial, Burial B, was uncovered 1.2m south of Burial A. The right side of the individual had been partially truncated by the southern wall of the library building. The upper torso and skull lay beneath the concrete floor of the building. However, it was deemed structurally unsafe to expose the upper area of this individual by cutting through the floor, as had been possible with Burial A. Therefore, the individual was only partially excavated. Burial B consisted of an extended inhumation aligned west-south-west/east-north-east with the head presumably to the west. The hands had been crossed over the pelvis. This individual had also been placed in a simple dug grave.
*Laurence Dunne, Eachtra Archaeological Projects, 3 Canal Place, Tralee, Co. Kerry.*

### 335. KNOCKANISH WEST
No archaeological significance
Q79361560
SMR 28:83
99E0128

Planning permission to construct a dwelling-house at Knockanish West, The Spa, Tralee, included a condition that pre-development archaeological testing was necessary as the development incorporated a site classified in the RMP as 'unclassified earthwork'. Testing was conducted to determine the nature of a raised area within the site of the development.

A test-trench 13m by 2m was excavated at the southern side of the raised, circular area. A stratum consisting of 70% fractured, coarse limestone pebbles and a stratum containing beach pebbles, fractured limestone, shells and fragments of brick were encountered. This material suggests that spoil from the now-destroyed brick kiln immediately east of the development was dumped in this area. There was no evidence that the raised area was archaeological in nature. No archaeological stratigraphy, features or artefacts were recorded within the area of the test-trench.
*Laurence Dunne, Eachtra Archaeological Projects, 3 Canal Place, Tralee, Co. Kerry.*

### 336. MAGHERABEG
No archaeological significance
99M009

Monitoring of all ground disturbance aspects of a small development at the Sandy Bay Caravan Park, Castlegregory, took place during March. The site is in sand dunes but is c. 450m south-west of the nearest marked archaeological sites, shell middens.

Nothing of archaeological interest was noted during the work.
*Isabel Bennett, Glen Fahan, Ventry, Tralee, Co. Kerry.*

### 337. MAGLASS EAST
Earthwork
Q945120
99E0129

Test-trenching took place here before the N21 re-routing. One trench was excavated by hand across the extent of the earthwork. The purpose of the trench was to ascertain whether the bank was flanked by ditches. No evidence for these was encountered.

A trackway was marked on the 1st edition OS map as traversing the field in question towards Maglass House. This track may have partially used this bank, as it is dry and raised above an otherwise wet and marshy field. It was found not to be of archaeological significance.
*Frank Coyne, Aegis Archaeology, 16 Avondale Court, Corbally, Limerick.*

### 338. ROCKFIELD
Prehistoric burial/ritual
Q931124
99E0323

These features were uncovered during the monitoring of topsoil-stripping in July of the new N21 route between Castleisland and Tralee. Subsequent excavation revealed five subcircular

Cremation pit with elaborate flues at Rockfield, from north.

features, the central one a cremation burial. To the north a stony, amorphous deposit was also excavated. Six metres to the south of the cremation a large cremation pit (1.9m in diameter, 0.4m deep) was exposed. The interior of the pit had been intensely burned, the heat penetrating the boulder clay for up to 0.1m. Two channels, also intensely baked and set in a cruciform arrangement, were cut into the base of the pit. A linear, U-shaped flue extended for 2m beyond the western edge of the pit. Two metres to the south, two truncated post-holes were also excavated.

The baking of the boulder clay in the pit suggests that the heat within it reached high temperatures in order to oxidise it, yet none of the burnt material survived. The cremation, in contrast, showed intensive burning, although the boulder clay beneath it was not burnt. The proximity of the cremation to the pit suggests that the pit may have contained the cremation pyre, the elaborate flues providing the ventilation necessary for high temperatures. Prehistoric dates are anticipated for the features identified.
*Tracy Collins, Aegis Archaeology, 16 Avondale Court, Corbally, Limerick.*

### 339. CASTLEMORRIS, BALLYMULLEN, TRALEE
Adjacent to tower-house
Q846134
SMR 29:163
99E0269

As part of an assessment of the proposed demolition of an existing house and the construction of nine townhouses close to a tower-house at Castlemorris, test excavations were carried out.

Castlemorris tower-house was a Geraldine fortification constructed on the northern bank of the Lee River to protect the southern approach from Gaelic south Kerry and also to protect the first fording point of the Lee from the Tralee Bay approach. The tower-house was constructed in the 15th century by the Morris family. The relict remains of this once-four-floored castle consist of its western, northern and eastern walls only. The ground floor is barrel vaulted, and an intramural stairway is visible in section in the east wall.

Three test-trenches were excavated by hand. Trench 1 measured 5m x 2m; Trench 2 measured 6m x 2m; and Trench 3 measured 4m x 3m. Trenches 1 and 2 were opened along the route of the proposed development foundation areas, and Trench 3 was in the vicinity of the proposed carpark, close to the upstanding remains.

The results in all three trenches were the same. On removal of topsod it was immediately apparent that loose fill had been introduced to raise the ground level in an effort to curb seasonal flooding. The owner confirmed that dredging material from the river had been introduced to level the garden in the 1970s. This fill was on average 0.3m deep. The underlying stratum was black, loose dump material, strewn with bottles, bricks, metal etc. This fill was excavated to an average depth of 1.2m. It appeared to have been introduced to the site in the late 19th or early 20th century. Stratified below this was a layer of grey alluvium clay, no doubt laid down in the course of regular and seasonal flooding from the Lee River.

Excavations did not proceed below this alluvium as the proposed development will have raft foundations, which will not intrude or destroy any subsurface archaeological deposits that may still exist below this level.

Nothing of archaeological significance was found during test excavations to the south of Castlemorris tower-house.

Laurence Dunne, Eachtra Archaeological Projects, 3 Canal Place, Tralee, Co. Kerry.

## 340. BALLYVELLY, TRALEE
Late Neolithic/Early Bronze Age
8220 1460
99E0615

Monitoring of the ground disturbance activities associated with the construction of a new housing development on the outskirts of Tralee town was undertaken in October 1999. During the monitoring six areas of archaeological potential were identified and excavated.

In Area I the trench measured 7m north–south by 5m and was excavated in the rear garden area of House 10. The western limits of the archaeology were heavily truncated by the erection of ESB pylons, and the northern features were truncated through the excavation of the site boundary wall. The excavation highlighted an area of intense activity consisting predominantly of north–south linear arrangements of slot-trenches, posts and stake-holes, with occasional small pits. There is no defined structural pattern, although the large southern slots and posts indicate that it may have been quite substantial. Most of the features excavated produced bone and charcoal, with occasional flint objects and fragments of quernstones also retrieved. The evidence indicates a single-phase structure with limited repairs. Numerous stray finds were retrieved from the surface of the western disturbance by the ESB.

In Area II the trench measured 6m east–west by 4m and was opened along the western boundary of House 10. Because of the location of the trench, a large number of the features could be excavated in section only. The main features were a large pit and a linear furnace. The pit measured c. 3.85m north–south and was 1.1m deep. The fill was quite homogeneous, and the pit was cut to bedrock. A Late Neolithic/Early Bronze Age arrowhead was retrieved from the base of the pit. The pit cuts several east–west slots.

The most visible feature was a linear furnace

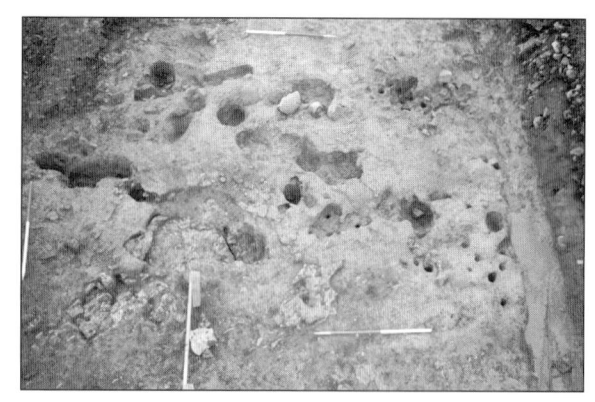

Area I, Ballyvelly, from east.

Area II, Ballyvelly, from south.

heavily truncated by topsoil removal and foundation excavation. However, similar features excavated by Laurence Dunne elsewhere in the same townland (Excavations 1998, 96–7, 98E0240) produced an Iron Age date and appear to have been funerary in function. Several post-holes and stakes surrounded the general area of the furnace, functioning either as spits or as a superstructure.

The Area III trench measured 3m north–south by 3m and was in the western part of House 8. The archaeology in this area consisted solely of a subcircular charcoal-enriched spread delineated by a circular setting of fractured limestone.

The Area IV trench measured 4m north–south by 4m and was in the rear garden area of House 8. The archaeology in this area consisted of two large but shallow stake-holes.

In Area V the trench measured 4m north–south by 4m and was in the rear garden area of House 9. The archaeology in this area consisted of one small, isolated pit, and three large, intercut pits, averaging 1m deep. The fills of the intercut pits were quite homogeneous, although the northern pit produced two distinct deposits of sheep/goat bones.

In Area VI the trench measured 2m north–south by 3m and was in the central part of House 5. A single archaeological feature, a truncated bowl furnace, was excavated in this area.

Emer Dennehy, Eachtra Archaeological Projects, 3 Canal Place, Tralee, Co. Kerry.

## 341. BUNATALLOON, TRALEE
Prehistoric pits
8345 1590
99E0360

Monitoring of all ground disturbance aspects of a

factory site in the Monavalley Industrial Estate, in the northern part of Tralee town, was undertaken to comply with a planning condition. An area of archaeological stratigraphy was noted during topsoil-stripping and was subsequently excavated.

Four pits were excavated. One of the pits, measuring 1.6m north–south by 0.9m and 0.98m deep, was stone-lined on the south-east side. A saddle quern and a rubbing stone had been reused to line the pit. Iron slag was recovered from the upper fill. A second large pit was found 1m to the south-west; it measured 3.1m north–south by 2.7m and 0.8m deep. Two small pits were found to the south and east. They measured 0.8m north–south by 0.76m by 0.2m deep and 0.75m north–south by 0.7m by 0.15m deep.

The material recovered from one of the large pits would suggest that they are prehistoric in date. Post-excavation work is continuing.

*Jacinta Kiely, Eachtra Archaeological Projects, Clover Hill, Mallow, Co. Cork.*

### 342. BUNATALLOON, TRALEE
Prehistoric pit
8356 1600
99E0553

Monitoring of all ground disturbance aspects of a factory site in Monavalley Industrial Estate, in the northern part of Tralee town, was undertaken to comply with a planning condition. An area of archaeological stratigraphy was noted during topsoil-stripping and was subsequently excavated.

A pit, measuring 1.82m north-east/south-west by 0.92m and 0.82m deep, was truncated to the east by a modern drain. The pit contained two fills. The upper fill included 30% of burnt sandstone fragments. The base contained a high percentage of charcoal. Nine stake-holes cut the western end of the base of the pit. They were aligned north-west/south-east. They were on average 0.08m in diameter and 0.13m deep. Two stake-holes cut the eastern end of the base of the pit. They had a similar diameter but were on average 0.4m deep.

Nine stake-holes were clustered to the immediate west of the pit. They were aligned north-west/south-east. It is likely that the stakes to the west and in the western end of the pit functioned as a windbreak, sheltering the pit from the prevailing westerly winds.

*Jacinta Kiely, Eachtra Archaeological Projects, Clover Hill, Mallow, Co. Cork.*

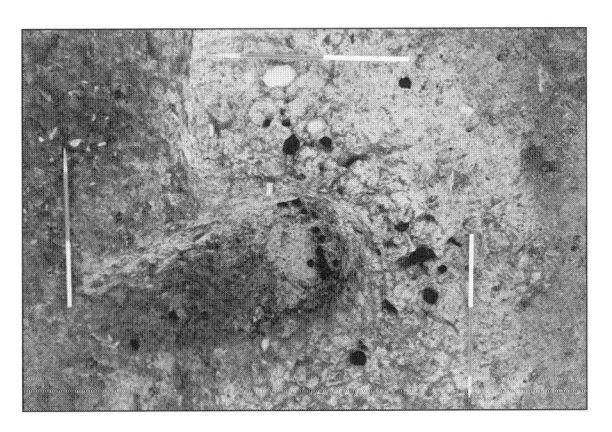

Pit and stake-hole alignment, Bunatalloon, from north.

### 343. CLOON, TRALEE
Test-trenches and monitoring
8400 1373
99E0284

Test-trenching and monitoring of ground disturbance works were undertaken on the northern bank of the River Lee, in Tralee, to comply with a planning condition. The site covers an area of *c.* 18 acres and is bounded by the River Lee to the south and Dan Spring Road to the north. It is south of the zone of archaeological potential for the town.

A possible circular enclosure was identified at the eastern end of the site from an aerial photograph. Two intersecting trenches, 38m by 2m and 45m by 2m, were excavated through the area of the possible enclosure. Modern rubbish overlay the clay subsoil. No archaeological stratigraphy was recorded in the trenches, and no artefacts were recovered. The circular enclosure noted on the aerial photograph is not archaeological in nature. It may have been formed by tethered horses.

Topsoil-stripping in the area of the development site was monitored. The site was then infilled with trunking, and the foundations etc. will be excavated through the trunking. A layer of peat underlay the sod and overlay the clay subsoil. The peat varied in depth from 1m to 3m.

No archaeological stratigraphy was recorded in any of the trenches, and no artefacts were recovered.
*Jacinta Kiely, Eachtra Archaeological Projects, Clover Hill, Mallow, Co. Cork.*

### 344. DROMTHACKER, TRALEE
Adjacent to ringfort
Q154837
97E0022 ext.

Excavations at Dromthacker were undertaken on behalf of the Institute of Technology, Tralee, before the development of a new campus (*Excavations 1997*, 85–6, *Excavations 1998*, 97–8). Part of the planning conditions requires that all ground disturbance be monitored, and as a consequence of this the excavation of ESB trench cables was monitored in August and December 1999. No archaeological feature or find was uncovered during monitoring.
*Rose M. Cleary, Department of Archaeology, University College, Cork.*

### 345. DROMTHACKER, TRALEE
Prehistoric pits
8640 1645
99E0439

Monitoring of all ground disturbance aspects of the entrance and access roads within the area of Kerry Technology Park was undertaken to comply with a planning condition. Four areas of archaeological stratigraphy were noted on the line of the road during topsoil-stripping and were subsequently excavated.

Four pits were excavated on the line of the access road. Pit 1 measured 0.48m north–south by 0.44m and was 0.26m deep. A narrow flue extended from the north-west side and under the baulk. The pit contained cremated bone fragments, which have been identified by Catryn Power as representing the bones of at least one adult individual. The sex could not be determined.

Pit 2 measured 0.6m north–south by 0.4m and was 0.12m deep. Pit 3 measured 0.7m north–south by 0.45m and was 0.3m deep. Pit 4 measured 1.72m north–south by 4.14m and was 0.24m deep. A flue extended from the western side of the pit. It measured 0.35m north–south by 2.2m and was 0.14m deep. Post-excavation work is ongoing.

*Jacinta Kiely, Eachtra Archaeological Projects, Clover Hill, Mallow, Co. Cork.*

### 346. KILLEEN, TRALEE
Adjacent to 17th-century house
**8485 1600**
**99E0335**

Monitoring of ground disturbance aspects of the first phase of a housing development in the townland of Killeen, to the north of Tralee town, was undertaken to comply with a planning condition. The development site consists of disused parkland. To the immediate south of the area are the relict remains of a 17th-century estate house, built by a Cromwellian named Bateman.

All ground disturbance associated with the excavation of Access Roads B and D and House Sites 46–74 was monitored. An area of cobbling, 5.3m north–south by 3.4m, was recorded 3.3m north-east of the entrance. A sherd of blackware was associated with the cobbles. A flint scraper was recovered from the topsoil.

Two test-trenches, measuring 18m and 14.5m, were excavated on the line of the boundary wall that will separate the modern housing estate from the remains of the 17th-century house. The topsoil overlay a yellow/brown, silty clay in both. No archaeological stratigraphy was recorded in the trenches.

*Jacinta Kiely, Eachtra Archaeological Projects, Clover Hill, Mallow, Co. Cork.*

### 347. KNOCKNACUIG, TRALEE
Monitoring
**8220 1470**
**99E0608**

Monitoring of all ground disturbance aspects of the first phase of a housing development in the townland of Knocknacuig, to the west of Tralee town, was undertaken to comply with a planning condition. The site is to the east of Lohercannan hillfort, SMR 29:112, and to the north of an enclosure, SMR 29:117. Ground disturbance aspects were monitored in the area of Courtyard A, House Sites 1–14, and Courtyard B, House Sites 1–14.

A flint scraper was recovered from the topsoil. Four areas of stratigraphy were investigated. They were geological in nature. There are a number of limestone sinkholes in the area of the site.

*Jacinta Kiely, Eachtra Archaeological Projects, Clover Hill, Mallow, Co. Cork.*

### 348. MARKET PLACE, TRALEE
Urban
**Q83551456**
**SMR 29:119**
**99E0179**

Monitoring of ground disturbance works associated with the demolition of an existing building and the construction of a shop and store was conducted at the southern side of the present-day Market Street, Tralee. The development is within the area of archaeological potential for the medieval town of Tralee. The market was moved to this location in the 1840s, where it remained until recent years.

Upon the discovery during monitoring of a cobbled surface and what appeared to be the truncated remains of the bowl and flue of a furnace, an excavation licence was applied for.

A 3.5m area around the furnace was cleaned. This revealed that the flue ran under the site boundary. Both the furnace and the flue exiting from it were severely truncated, and the fill averaged just 0.02m deep. The fills produced no material that could indicate the function and/or date of the furnace. Some fragmentary pieces of charcoal were discovered at the base but were insufficient to obtain a $^{14}C$ date. A large, heat-altered limestone on the southern edge of the furnace may have functioned as a standing platform.

Although the lack of finds or datable material makes dating the furnace difficult, the depth at which it was found and its location within the remains of a burgess plot would seem to indicate that the structure is related to medieval activity in Tralee.

*Laurence Dunne, Eachtra Archaeological Projects, 3 Canal Place, Tralee, Co. Kerry.*

### 349. MONAVALLEY, TRALEE
In vicinity of prehistoric burial activity
**Q842157**
**98E0127 ext.**

Most of this housing development had been monitored in 1998 (*Excavations 1998*, 98). However, the licence was reactivated in 1999 for the remaining portion of the site to be stripped and the development to be completed.

During the original monitoring, several circular pits that had been severely truncated had been discovered in the western quadrant of the site. These had been excavated, and five were found to contain minute flecks of burnt bone. Unfortunately, these remains were too small to be positively identified as human or animal. A small amount of charcoal was also recovered but was not from a secure context and so proved unsuitable for dating purposes.

During the second phase of the monitoring, nothing of further archaeological significance was encountered.

*Frank Coyne, Aegis Archaeology, 16 Avondale Court, Corbally, Limerick.*

### 350. CLOCH AN OIGHAIR, (CARRIGEENDANIEL TOWNLAND), MOUNTHAWK, TRALEE
No archaeological significance
**8231 1156**
**97E0456 ext.**

In July 1999 a further extension to this housing development was commenced. Monitoring, mainly of access roads and of a sewerage pipe trench, took place. Nothing of archaeological interest was found, and the topsoil was cleared to boulder clay or bedrock, to an average depth of 0.5m below modern ground level.

*Isabel Bennett, Glen Fahan, Ventry, Tralee, Co. Kerry.*

# KILDARE

### 351. ATHY (CO. KILDARE)–STRADBALLY (CO. LAOIS)–PORTLAOISE (CO. LAOIS) GAS PIPELINE
Monitoring
99E0384

Monitoring was carried out during the excavation of the pipeline trenches required by An Bord Gáis for the Athy–Stradbally–Portlaoise Feeder Main on the L109 (between Athy and Stradbally) and the T16 (between Stradbally and Portlaoise). The trenches for the feeder main were opened along the public roadway and the road verge from the northern perimeter of Athy, through Stradbally and terminating on the eastern side of Portlaoise—a total length of *c.* 27km. No archaeological features or artefacts came to light during mechanical excavation of the pipeline trench. A number of subsidiary gas-pipe trenches in certain streets in Athy town were also monitored; no material of archaeological interest was noted.

*Breandán Ó Ríordáin, Burgage More, Blessington, Co. Wicklow, for Valerie J. Keeley Ltd.*

### 352. CONVENT LANE, ATHY
Urban
S689944
99E0596

Archaeological monitoring for the excavation of foundations for a new building at Convent Lane, Athy, was undertaken on 29 October 1999. The site measures *c.* 250m$^2$, set well back from the frontage of Duke Street. The projected line of the medieval town wall, as depicted by Bradley *et al.*, extends a short distance to the south of the property being developed. The exact line of the town wall is, however, unknown.

The sides of the existing structure were widened, while the line of the existing gable ends was to be retained. The foundation trenches were 1.1m wide and 0.4–0.5m deep. The material removed consisted of tarmac and hardcore, red brick rubble and cement, and topsoil with bottles, crocks etc. No deposits were present that pre-dated the 20th century.

*Claire Walsh, Archaeological Projects Ltd, 25A Eaton Square, Terenure, Dublin 6W.*

### 353. GARTER LANE, ATHY
Urban medieval
268171 193945
99E0221

Trial-trenching was undertaken at the site of a proposed apartment development at Garter Lane, Athy, on 1 May 1999. The work was undertaken in compliance with recommendations issued by *Dúchas* in relation to a pre-planning enquiry regarding the development. The site is on the eastern bank of the River Barrow and immediately to the north of White Castle.

Six trial-trenches were excavated by machine in order to determine the nature and extent of any subsurface archaeological features, deposits or finds that may have existed within the boundaries of the proposed development area.

No structural features or finds of archaeological interest were uncovered. However, a black, silty layer was revealed in all the trial-trenches. Subsequent borehole investigations indicated that this layer was at least 0.6–1m thick. The highest level on the surface of this layer was 53.1m OD.

It is suggested that the silty layer is the remnants of both the Barrow riverbed and the bed of the former mill-race that existed in this area in antiquity. Furthermore, the uppermost layer represents a fill material, introduced into the area in the mid-19th century when the area was reclaimed.

*Martin E. Byrne, 31 Millford, Athgarvan, Co. Kildare.*

### 354. BALLITORE
Medieval settlement
99E0202

Three phases of investigation were carried out along the route of the Moone–Timolin–Ballitore Hill N9 Realignment Scheme. Initially test-trenching at four potential sites (Sites 25, 36, 37 and 45) took place. (The numbering system used for the sites followed that used in the report: *Archaeological assessment N9 Realignment Moone–Timolin–Ballitore Hill, Co. Kildare*, by Dr Niall Brady of Valerie J. Keeley Ltd, February 1999.) Test-trenching at Sites 25, 36 and 37 took place between 13 May 1999 and 11 June 1999 and produced no finds or features of archaeological significance.

Testing at Site 45 took place between 14 and 30 May 1999. Nine hand-dug trenches were excavated within the area of the road-take. Trenches 1, 2 and 9 produced significant amounts of medieval pottery and the possible remains of medieval structures. It was clear that further excavation would be required to resolve the nature and extent of the features exposed.

The second phase involved excavation of Site 45. Trenches 1, 2 and 9 were extended and excavated over eight weeks between 30 June and 25 August 1999. The sod and topsoil were removed by machine under archaeological supervision. Further medieval finds and features were uncovered during this phase. However, despite the extended cuttings, the archaeology was not fully resolved.

The final phase involved topsoil-stripping of Site 45. It was recommended that large-scale sod and topsoil-stripping of the two fields within the area of the road-take be undertaken to ascertain the nature and full extent of the site. This was carried out using two machines, under archaeological supervision, before the construction phase of the road began. A full team was employed to excavate features that were exposed. This phase commenced on 26 October 1999 and was completed on 21 January 2000.

Site 45 lay in the townland of Ballitore at Chainage 144. It was defined as a circular earthen enclosure, lying on the western edge of the land-take of the proposed route. It was identified during field inspection and consisted of a raised central area with a further embankment to the south. It had an overall diameter of *c.* 41m. Three later field boundaries now trisect the site. A low-lying, boggy marsh area lies to the far south of the area, while the site itself has a prominent hilltop setting.

Remains of a significant medieval settlement were uncovered. The main feature identified was a large enclosing ditch, sweeping around the side of the hill/embankment. It began as three separate ditches, which ran for *c.* 25m, before all three joined to form one ditch. This was traced for a further 45m, giving an overall length of 70m. It varied from 3m to

4m wide and was c. 1m deep. Large amounts of animal bone and medieval pottery were recovered from the fill.

A series of ploughmarks and minor ditches was found outside this enclosing ditch, probably representing associated agriculture and drainage features. They extended up to, but not beyond, the ditch, suggesting that they respected the line of the already-existing ditch. These too contained finds of medieval pottery.

Within the area enclosed by the ditch were further small gullies and ditches, as well as the remains of two possible house structures. These structures consisted of the remains of foundation trenches with large packing stones. However, these were badly disturbed and difficult to trace, probably as a result of later ploughing activity. They were c. 12m long by 4.5m wide. Again, large amounts of medieval pottery were associated with these structures. These consisted mainly of Leinster cooking ware and local green-glazed wares, although some English and French wares were identified amongst the sherds.

*Hilary Opie, 103 Cherrywood Drive, Clondalkin, Dublin 22.*

### 355. PLUNKETT ROAD, BALLYMORE EUSTACE
No archaeological significance
N934082
99E0533

Test excavation of the site of a new dwelling was undertaken on 2 October 1999. Three trenches were opened by mechanical excavator, using a toothless bucket. No traces of medieval cultivation furrows survived here; however, the profile of potato ridges was apparent. Straight-sided ridges, which were up to c. 0.45m wide and varied from 0.3m to 0.6m deep, extended into the subsoil. In confirmation of their late date, glazed pottery dating from the 18th century onwards was recovered from the lowest levels of the cultivation soil in the trenches. Several small, abraded sherds of glazed medieval pottery were also recovered from the topsoil.

No features of archaeological interest were present.

*Claire Walsh, Archaeological Projects Ltd, 25A Eaton Square, Terenure, Dublin 6W.*

### 356. PLUNKETT ROAD, BALLYMORE EUSTACE
Medieval borough
293931 209822
99E0586

An archaeological evaluation was undertaken at a proposed development site at Plunkett Road, Ballymore Eustace, Co. Kildare, on 20 October 1999. The work was carried out in compliance with a condition included in the grant of planning in relation to the construction of a bungalow on the site.

Four trenches were excavated by machine. The site is to the east-south-east of the medieval borough of Ballymore and within the designated zone of archaeological potential. However, no features, deposits, structures or finds of archaeological interest were uncovered.

It is presumed, based on the results of the testing, that levels within the area of the site were reduced in the 19th century before the site was levelled with a shale gravel. This process resulted in topsoil being removed and may have also led to some disturbance to the natural, sandy subsoil. Given the location of the site, it was expected that, at a minimum, sherds of medieval pottery would have been uncovered. However, it is probable that any such material was removed from the site during groundworks associated with the construction of a previous dwelling.

*Martin E. Byrne, 31 Millford, Athgarvan, Co. Kildare.*

### 357. NORTH CROSS, ST JOHN'S, BALLYMORE EUSTACE
High cross
N933099
99E0143

Peter Harbison noted in his study of *The high crosses of Ireland*, published in 1992, that the north cross in St John's Church of Ireland churchyard at Ballymore Eustace was leaning at a 'perilous angle'. In 1998 a site inspection gave rise to fears that the situation was deteriorating, and a decision was made to take down the cross and rectify the problem.

The large granite cross, 3.5m high, was set in a granite base that was almost completely buried in the ground. The cross was removed from the base by the National Monuments staff of *Dúchas* The Heritage Service, and the main reasons for the 'perilous' angle of the cross shaft were immediately evident. An examination of the mortice showed that the shaft was sitting in the base without any mortar, and there was a gap of c. 20mm on three sides between shaft and mortice. The cross shaft had no tenon and sat loosely in the mortice to a depth of c. 0.3m. The mortice was over double that depth but bellied inwards at c. 0.3–0.35m below the upper surface, resulting in a narrowing of the mortice, which did not permit the shaft to be seated securely in position. The gap between the shaft and the mortice had allowed an old iron key, probably for the church door, to slip down into the bottom of the mortice, which was filled up with soil, dead leaves and water.

A small excavation took place around the base to facilitate its removal and to prepare the area for the re-erection of the cross. The base consists of a large granite boulder that had been worked to create a stepped pyramidal shape on its upper surface. It is crudely cut, and the steps are of uneven height. The lower part of the stone is unworked, and the eastern side is steeply concave. The base was sitting on the undisturbed natural esker and was propped on the east by a number of stones overlain in places by mortar.

Excavation was confined to the area immediately around the base so that no stratified burials would be disturbed, although a number of cuts for burials were recorded. The lack of significant stratigraphy or any great depth of burial would suggest that this area of the graveyard has not been extensively used. The finding of two sherds of medieval pottery, slag, a bronze binding strip and a small quantity of animal bone would seem to indicate some medieval occupation activity in the area before its use as a burial-ground.

*Heather A. King, National Monuments and Historic Properties Service, Dúchas The Heritage Service, 6 Upper Ely Place, Dublin 2.*

### 358. BALLYSAXHILLS
Area of burning
2815 1908
99E0704

Monitoring of soil-stripping was carried out at the proposed quarry site at Ballysaxhills, Kilcullen, Co. Kildare, on 1 December 1999 on behalf of Kilsaran Concrete Ltd in order to comply with the planning permission granted by An Bord Pleanála.

The soil-stripping had been preceded by an extensive programme of geophysical testing and archaeological test-trenching, carried out on this portion of the site in 1995 by Margaret Gowen, the results of which were reported to the National Monuments and Historic Properties Service (August 1995 and 4 December 1995, *Excavations 1995*, 43–4, 95E0256).

The depth of soil in the area monitored varied from 0.25m on the upper portion of the site to the east, to a maximum depth of over 0.4m towards the west. The deposits consisted mainly of a light brown topsoil overlying natural gravel, with occasional pockets of boulder clay extending to a depth of over 0.45m. These deposits were consistent over the total area of soil-stripping, and, apart from the partly backfilled test-trenches from the earlier testing programme, no anomalies were noted.

A small area of burning was noted overlying the natural deposits at a point just north of the most southerly extent of the soil-stripping. In depth the burning varied from 10mm to 15mm, but no reddening of the underlying deposits was noted. The burning consisted of a spread of charcoal, with some small fragments, consistent with the clearance by burning of light vegetation.

No other features were noted, nor were any deposits or material of archaeological significance revealed.

*Daniel Leo Swan, Arch-Tech Ltd, 32 Fitzwilliam Place, Dublin 2.*

### 359. BALLYVASS
*Fulacht fiadh*
99E0453

Excavation of a *fulacht fiadh* site took place before Bord Gáis pipeline development. The site encompassed an area of 55m$^2$ of undeveloped land. The site was revealed during archaeological monitoring as a spread of burnt stone and charcoal-rich soil. Excavation revealed three shallow pits and two complete troughs. The pits consisted of a primary ash layer fill, followed by charcoal-rich soil mixed with burnt stone. Both fills were found to extend beyond the edges of the pits. The *fulacht fiadh* site extended southwards beyond the area of excavation, where the northern portion of two further pits were excavated. They had the same fill as the other pits. However, the base of one of them contained two flint scrapers.

One of the troughs consisted of a steep-sided oval hollowing of the natural subsoil. Its fill was similar to that of the pits. The other trough was circular. While it had the same fill as the other trough and pits, it also had a cladding of redeposited natural subsoil. Removal of this revealed that the subsoil that was dug into to create the trough was of a sandy and therefore porous composition. The cladding would have served to retain water in the trough.

*Niall Gregory, 25 Westpark, Blessington, Co. Wicklow, for Margaret Gowen & Co. Ltd.*

### 360. BISHOPSLANE, SITE 4
No archaeological significance
SMR 29:11
97E0370

Between 16 and 22 February 1999 archaeological monitoring was carried out at Site 4, Bishopslane, Ballymore Eustace, Co. Kildare. The proposed development involved the construction of a single-storey dwelling in the northern end of the site, set back roughly 18m from the road.

The proposed development lay within the zone of archaeological potential as outlined by the Urban Archaeological Survey. Archaeological monitoring of topsoil-stripping and the excavation of all foundation trenches were requested by *Dúchas* as a condition to any planning permission granted.

Recent archaeological fieldwork at Bishopslane, Sites 1–6, by Alan Hayden (*Excavations 1997*, 90, 97E0370 and 97E0425), revealed the remains of possible medieval structures in the north and south of the site, with medieval agricultural furrows occurring between them. These results would appear to indicate that this area is within the boundaries of the medieval settlement of Ballymore Eustace.

Along the northern foundation trench of the proposed development two substantial cut features, C17 and C29, were identified. Both these features cut the natural geology and were filled with redeposited natural and mixed clays containing 19th–20th-century china.

It seems probable that C17 and C29 were parts of the same feature and represented the sides of a natural hollow measuring roughly 10m east–west x 6m, which had been subsequently backfilled. This suggests that the north-east corner of the site had been levelled off within the last 100–200 years.

Based on the results of the archaeological monitoring, it can be stated there were no significant archaeological features or deposits within the land-take of the proposed development.

*Rob Lynch, IAC Ltd, 8 Dungar Terrace, Dun Laoghaire, Co. Dublin.*

### 361. BROADLEAS COMMONS
Environs of stone circle
292790 207417
99E0140

A watching brief was undertaken on 27 March 1999 at a single dwelling-house development, at Broadleas Commons, Ballymore Eustace, Co. Kildare. The work was undertaken in compliance with a condition included in the grant of planning in respect of the development.

The development site is to the east and in the immediate environs of a stone circle (SMR 29:23) known as 'The Piper's Stones'. The monument consists of 28 stones, all of which lie on their long axes. The diameter of the site is *c.* 30m, and it is postulated that it may have been formed by up to 49 stones. All but three of the surviving stones are of granite, and there is a slight platform within the ring.

All levels' reduction, including those required for service trenches, house, driveway, soak holes,

septic tank and percolation areas, were monitored. No structures, deposits or finds of archaeological interest were uncovered during the work.
*Martin E. Byrne, 31 Millford, Athgarvan, Co. Kildare.*

### 362. BROWNSTOWN/CARNALWAY
No archaeological significance
**N857112**
**99E0416**

Monitoring of soil-stripping took place at this site before gravel extraction. The site is in the townlands of Brownstown and Carnalway, near Kilcullen, Co. Kildare. The area is gently undulating, generally sloping from north to south, and mostly low-lying (from $c.$ 140m to $c.$ 120m OD). The site was under open pasture at the commencement of soil-stripping.

The site was stripped using a mechanical excavator fitted with a 2.5m-wide toothless bucket, working tracks of $c.$ 13m wide (the reach of the digger arm). Four features were identified. In addition, a small flint scraper was found lying on the surface of the redeposited topsoil bund, but it was not possible to determine from which part of the site it had been taken.

Feature 1 was an irregularly shaped area of dense, charcoal-rich soil measuring $c.$ $6m^2$. No finds were recovered from this feature, and no other features were noted during the soil-stripping in its vicinity. The shape and content of this feature suggest that it was an *in situ* burnt-out tree root.

Feature 2 was an area of staining containing animal bones and burnt material. It is in the southern half of the field and was first noted as a distinct spread of darker soil. It is slightly curved, $c.$ 6m long and 0.4m wide in the middle, widening to $c.$ 1m at the northern end and $c.$ 1.5m at its southern end. The northern portion of the feature is subcircular; the southern portion is irregularly oval. The visible surface of the feature consists of a dark grey/brown, friable silt, with a small clay content and possibly a small ash component. It contains very little charcoal. There are small, irregularly shaped concentrations of animal bones at both the northern and southern portions, and on the eastern side of the southern end is a thin band of heat-reddened soil at the boundary of the feature.

To the north of Feature 2 is a further area of darkened soil, consisting of a linear feature 2.5m wide by at least 15m long, running north-east to south-west (Feature 2.1). It ends sharply at its south-west end but may continue for a further 30–40m to the north-east. It has the appearance of a remnant field boundary. Feature 2 was covered in plastic, and it and Feature 2.1 were fenced off for further examination.

Feature 3 was a small, subcircular concentration of charcoal, $c.$ 0.2m in diameter, surrounded by a broader area of brown to yellow sand with charcoal flecks. The spread of charcoal-flecked sand fades out less than 1m from the centre of the feature. The concentrated area of charcoal ran to a depth of only $c.$ 40mm, with a vague zone of darker brown, charcoal-flecked sand underlying it. The feature contained no other material or finds.

Feature 4 was a similar discrete concentration of charcoal $c.$ 20m to the south-east of Feature 2. It is subcircular and $c.$ 0.2m in diameter, with a spread of charcoal flecks thinning out away from the centre. Because of its proximity to Feature 2, and the fact that it is in an area of the development that will not be further disturbed in the short term, this feature was covered in plastic and marked out for further examination.
*Finola O'Carroll, Cultural Resource Development Services Ltd, Campus Innovation Centre, Roebuck, University College, Belfield, Dublin 4.*

### 363. CHURCH ROAD, CELBRIDGE
No archaeological significance
**29736 23308**
**SMR 11:01 201**
**99E0256**

Testing was carried out before the extension of an existing 19th-century two-storey cottage, the foundations of which were expected to be dug to a depth of 0.8m. The site is within the Celbridge zone of archaeological potential and is relatively close to the Early Christian foundation of St Mochua, the enclosure of which is less than 100m to the west. While the modern Ordnance Survey maps suggest that the site is just to the east of the enclosure (as evidenced in the pronounced curve on Church Road), the 1939 edition suggests an outer enclosure to the south-east of the church, now built upon. A projection of this line to the north would bisect the proposed development.

Two trenches were opened by hand along the extent of the new walls. Both trenches encountered bedrock that dipped from between 0.25m and 0.68m below the surface, which was sealed by 19th-century deposits.
*Franc Myles, 9 Ben Edair Road, Stonybatter, Dublin 7.*

### 364. 17 AND 18 MAIN STREET, CELBRIDGE
Urban
**9605 3302**
**99E0557**

Archaeological monitoring took place here over several weeks in December 1999. While foundations that related to the two 18th-century houses that had been demolished were revealed, nothing of any archaeological interest was recovered. A considerable amount of the site, which fronted onto Main Street, Celbridge, and backed onto the River Liffey, was very disturbed, owing to the erection of outhouses and a garage on the site in modern times.
*Sylvia Desmond, 25 Rowan Hall, Millbrook Court, Milltown, Dublin 6, for Judith Carroll & Co. Ltd, Pine Forest Art Centre, Pine Forest Road, Glencullen, Co. Dublin.*

### 365. CHURCHTOWN SOUTH
Deserted settlement site
**264469 195052**
**SMR 34:6**
**99E0192**

Test-trenching was carried out at a proposed development site in Churchtown South, Athy, on 20 May 1999. An assessment had already been carried out in response to a request for further information from the planning authority, and that report recommended that testing be conducted as a condition of planning. The proposed development is within an SMR site listed as KD34:6 and is defined as a possible deserted settlement. It is depicted on the 2nd edition Ordnance Survey map as a linear ridge but does not appear on the 1839 edition of this map.

Four test-trenches were inserted in the areas of greatest impact from the development. Stratigraphy was similar throughout most of the site, with topsoil occurring to a depth of 0.15–0.2m and lying directly upon a light brown subsoil that continued to the maximum depth to which the test-trenches were excavated. Occasionally pockets of red clay were found within this subsoil, but these were interpreted as being of natural origin. The southern end of Test-trench 1 showed a variation in this stratigraphy, with the red clay subsoil becoming more prevalent. The areas of red clay in Test-trench 1 also showed signs of modern disturbance, particularly in the form of deeply buried layers of red brick. According to local memory, the area was the site of a brickworks in earlier times, but the precise location of the factory is not known. This fact would certainly account for the occurrence of deposits of red brick and may also explain the concentration of red clay toward the southern end of the site, as the occurrence of this clay may have been the determining factor in the choice of location for the brickworks.

No features or artefacts of archaeological interest were identified, and it is possible that many of the surface irregularities in the field were caused by disturbance resulting from the former existence of a brick factory in the general area.

*Clare Mullins, 31 Millford, Athgarvan, Co. Kildare.*

### 366. ABBEYLANDS, CLANE
Vicinity of Franciscan friary
287857 227464
99E0386

The site is in the townland of Abbeylands, to the immediate south-east of the modern village of Clane. Within the property is an almost square graveyard within which are the partial extant remains of Clane Abbey, a Franciscan friary established *c.* 1258. It is likely that the friary was founded by Gerald Fitz-Maurice (Fitzgerald, Lord of Offaly) and, according to Gwynn and Hadcock (1970, 245), 'he is said to have been buried in the Friary in 1287'. In 1345 a general chapter, held at the friary, made important decisions about Irish custodies. In 1433 an indulgence was granted as the establishment was in need of repair. However, following the Dissolution of the Monasteries, portions of the friary—including the church chancel and part of the dormitory—were destroyed by order of Lord Leonard Grey, late king's deputy, for the purpose of repairing the king's castle at Maynooth. Fragments of the nave, chancel and south aisle still survive, as does a mutilated effigy said to be of Gerald Fitz-Maurice. In addition, aerial photographs of Clane show a linear cropmark running south from the south-west corner of the graveyard. This has been interpreted as a possible roadway.

An assessment of the site by the writer suggested that as much of the site as possible should be subjected to geophysical surveying in order that further areas of archaeological interest could be identified. The results of such a survey could be used to determine what areas should be subjected to archaeological testing by hand- and machine-excavation.

The geophysical investigations were undertaken by GeoArc Ltd from 21 to 24 June. A total of 35 20m-by-20m grids were surveyed by means of magnetic gradiometry. An area measuring 40m x 40m, to the north of the existing graveyard, was also subjected to investigation by means of resistivity survey. This particular area was chosen as it had been identified as the most likely location of the remaining friary buildings, given the typical layout of such establishments. The results of the magnetic gradiometry survey indicated the existence of a number of linear and circular anomalies, of unknown origin, as well as a number of additional anomalies that may have been produced by previous burning. The resistivity results displayed a number of rectangular and subrectangular positive anomalies, which were interpreted as being produced by the masonry foundations of several buildings, most likely associated with the friary.

The results from the surveys were used to determine the locations of test-trenches in order to investigate the various detected anomalies. The areas that could not be subjected to such survey methods were likewise investigated by means of trial-trenches. Such testing was undertaken from 22 to 28 July, with additional testing carried out on 11 August. Furthermore, monitoring of pipe-trench excavations along the northern boundary of the site, associated with the servicing of an adjacent development, was undertaken in November 1999

The results of the testing programme confirmed the presence and extent of the subsurface wall features to the north of the existing graveyard and indicate that these appear to be linked with the extant features of the friary. In addition, a number of burials were revealed to the north, west and south of the existing graveyard boundary walls. Furthermore, additional walls were revealed to the south and south-west of the graveyard. A gravel surface was also uncovered to the south-west of the graveyard, which may be the remains of the road feature identified in aerial photographs. A number of areas of burning were also uncovered, the locations of which were broadly similar to those detected by the magnetic gradiometer investigations. One unusual feature was a stone-built tunnel with an arched roof, running south-west from the south-eastern corner of the graveyard. This feature had been truncated by a modern sewerage pipe. While the structural nature of the feature is not representative of classic souterrain construction methods, this possible interpretation cannot, as yet, be ruled out.

A number of artefacts were recovered during testing, including sherds of medieval pottery, fragments of roof tiles and fragments of decorated floor tiles, all of which are probably related to the friary.

*Reference*
Gwynn, A. and Hadcock, R.N. 1970 *Medieval religious houses: Ireland.* Dublin.

*Martin E. Byrne, 31 Millford, Athgarvan, Co. Kildare.*

### 367. JONES'S PUB, MAIN STREET, CLANE
No archaeological significance
**N876276**
**98E0510 ext.**
The site of the development at Jones's Pub, Main Street, Clane, is within the zone of archaeological potential highlighted in the recent Medieval Urban Survey. The village is also the location of the monastery of Clane, or *Cloenath*, founded by St Ailbe at *Cluain-damh* on the River Liffey. It appears in the early historical records in 549 and 782, and in 1162 Gelasius, archbishop of Armagh, held a synod at the monastery.

Three test-trenches were machine-excavated in October 1999. The first was opened along the approximate centre line of the long axis of the second phase of development, to the south of the first (*Excavations* 1998, 102). The second and third were placed in the footprint of a proposed carpark development to the west of the main construction area. Nothing of archaeological significance was noted.
*Eoin Halpin, ADS Ltd, Unit 48, Westlink Enterprise Centre, 30–50 Distillery Street, Belfast BT12 5BJ.*

### 368. MOAT COMMONS, CLANE
Vicinity of motte
**N879271**
**98E0185**
A condition of the planning permission required a site assessment before development.

The site was tested in two stages. The first stage (May 1998) tested the area closest to the field containing the motte and the northern portion of the site. The remaining trenches were excavated in September 1999.

The site fell into three sections. Trenches 1–4 were in the field closest to the public road. They showed evidence for deposition of material, presumably in an attempt to raise the original ground level, as the surface of the field appeared to have been very wet and may have been prone to flooding by the stream that runs between the field and the public road. The redeposited material was modern. In Trench 2 there was also evidence for the insertion of modern drainage pipes. These trenches were separated from the rest of the site by a public road.

Trenches 5–9 were placed in the field closest to the motte, which showed least sign of previous disturbance. The alignment of the field fence between the motte and the development site hinted at the earlier presence of an enclosing feature associated with the motte. However, the test-trenches did not show any evidence for such a feature. It is possible that the excavation of the modern field drain obliterated the remains of this feature, if such had survived. The fill of the drain was a brown clay that was consistent throughout its depth. Trenches 8 and 9, which were excavated further out in the field, produced no archaeological material.

Trenches 10–11 tested the location of the previous dwelling-house and its outhouses. In this area there was evidence for introduction of material and for excavation of pipes for drainage purposes. There was also evidence for contamination by diesel oil and for removal of the original ground surface during the demolition of the dwelling-house. Archaeological material was not exposed in those areas where it was anticipated that it may have survived, i.e. the area closest to the motte. Archaeological strata were not exposed elsewhere in the test-trenches.
*Rosanne Meenan, Roestown, Drumree, Co. Meath.*

### 369. CORBALLY
Proximity to Neolithic settlement
**N8513**
**98E0094**
Limited topsoil-stripping was undertaken to the north-west of where substantial Neolithic deposits were previously revealed, including the remains of three Neolithic houses (*Excavations 1998*, 103–4). No features or finds of archaeological significance were revealed during this phase of topsoil-stripping.
*Avril Purcell, Margaret Gowen & Co. Ltd, 2 Killiney View, Albert Road Lower, Glenageary, Co. Dublin.*

### 370. CORBALLY
Proximity to Neolithic settlement
**N852125**
**99E0486**
Topsoil-stripping was undertaken on a small area several hundred metres east of where substantial Neolithic deposits were revealed in 1998 (*Excavations 1998*, 103–4, 98E0094). No features or finds of archaeological significance were revealed.
*Avril Purcell, Margaret Gowen & Co. Ltd, 2 Killiney View, Albert Road Lower, Glenageary, Co. Dublin.*

### 371. CURRAGH
No archaeological significance
**27765 21145**
**SMR 23:76**
**99E0739**
The Curragh was a focus of activity associated with the disposal of the dead during prehistory. Some of this activity involved the construction of burial mounds; a considerable number of these sites are known to have existed on the summit of the ridge that is now largely occupied by the Curragh Camp.

This work was commissioned by the Department of Defence in order to address the archaeological implications of the proposed expansion of the Defence Forces Training Centre, which includes the construction of a new swimming pool. This development will take place on a site within an archaeological complex, KE23:76; the site is currently occupied by a carpark and basketball court. It lies at the foot of the ridge on its southern side.

The assessment was carried out on the basis of documentary research and the excavation of four test-trenches on the site of the proposed swimming pool. Nothing of archaeological significance was noted. The foundations of a running track, which formerly occupied the site, were uncovered.
*James Eogan, ADS Ltd, Windsor House, 11 Fairview Strand, Dublin 3.*

### 372. CURRAGH CAMP, CURRAGH
Environs of archaeological complex
**276483 218333**
**97E0388 ext.**
Monitoring of groundworks associated with the

upgrading of services—Ammunition Depot, Curragh Camp—was undertaken in compliance with recommendations from *Dúchas* The Heritage Service. The work was carried out at various dates from April to September 1999. The development area is in the environs of a number of archaeological sites and was tested in 1997 (*Excavations 1997*, 92–3).

No features, deposits or structures of archaeological or historical interest were uncovered during the work. The only find of significance was a length of chain-link (copper alloy), which may be part of a ceremonial lanyard or horse decoration of 19th/early 20th-century date.
*Martin E. Byrne, 31 Millford, Athgarvan, Co. Kildare.*

### 373. 'THE RACE OF THE BLACK PIG', THE CURRAGH
Earthwork
98E0059

Ordnance Survey 6-inch maps of the Curragh record as pathways or access ways two linear features that are marked as 'Site of Ancient Road (called the Race of the Black Pig)'. In February 1998, before the laying of gas pipelines, three cuttings were made along the line of this putative monument. No evidence of a pre-modern earthwork was found.
*Tadhg O'Keefe, Department of Archaeology, University College, Belfield, Dublin 4, for Valerie Keeley Ltd.*

**Editor's note:** This summary, though of work carried out during 1998, was received too late for inclusion in the bulletin of that year.

### 374. CURRAGH/POLLARDSTOWN
Black Pig's Race
27551 21431
99E0645

Before cable-laying through the Curragh for Telecom Éireann, a small investigation trench extended across the alignment of the Black Pig's Dyke in a location that had been recently landscaped. The trench was *c.* 13m long, 0.6m wide and 1m deep. No archaeological features or artefacts were observed.
*Niall Brady, 2 Vale Terrace, Lower Dargle Road, Bray, Co. Wicklow, for Valerie J. Keeley Ltd.*

### 375. CURRYHILLS I
Fire-pit
283778 227782
99E0569

Topsoil-stripping associated with the Prosperous Sewerage Scheme, which had commenced before the preparation of the associated archaeological assessment report, revealed a distinct area of burning.

Clearance of the basal remains of topsoil cover across the site indicated that the site consisted of a localised area of burning. The feature was irregular in plan, with rounded corners, and measured up to 1.74m x 1.14m, with the long axis orientated north-west/south-east. There was evidence of scorched/burnt soil along portions of the edges of the feature.

Removal of the charred material, which consisted of ash and charred/burnt wood fragments, revealed a depression in the subsoil. The extent of the depression coincided with the extent of the charred material. The depression was cut into the sloping subsoil, and the cut was very obvious on the south-east and north-east edges of the feature. These edges generally had a sharp break in slope with the base, while the break in slope along the remaining edges was not perceptible. The base itself was relatively flat, although it sloped from north-west to south-east. The feature had a maximum recorded depth of 0.13m.

A number of areas of scorched/burnt soil, orange/red, were revealed along portions of the edges and base of the feature.

The nature of the depression, with its rounded corners and the fact that it was cut into the sloping subsoil, indicates that the feature is not natural and is likely to be the basal remains of a pit. The fill indicated that it was used for burning. Furthermore, patches of scorched soil indicate that the heat intensity was irregular, hotter in some areas than others. Given the nature of the feature, it is probable that it is the truncated remains of a fire-pit.

A sample of the fill has been sent for wood analysis, after which it will be submitted for $^{14}$C dating. Furthermore, it is proposed to submit another sample of the fill for environmental analysis. It is hoped that the wood and environmental studies, coupled with the $^{14}$C dating, will determine the nature and function of the feature and help in establishing a context for the site in terms of the archaeology of the region as a whole.
*Martin E. Byrne, 31 Millford, Athgarvan, Co. Kildare.*

### 376. CURRYHILLS II
No archaeological significance
283678 227536
99E0570

The site was first noted as an area of burning during field-walking associated with the preparation of an archaeological assessment report in relation to the Prosperous Sewerage Scheme. The area to be disturbed by the scheme had been stripped of topsoil before the commencement of the report. However, the extent of the site was not readily identifiable when first discovered, and no attempt was made to determine this until the appropriate licence was issued by *Dúchas* The Heritage Service.

Clearance of loose topsoil cover, the result of previous topsoil-stripping, across the site indicated that the site consisted of a localised area of burning. The feature was irregular in plan (dog-legged) and measured up to 1.28m x 1.16m, with the long axis orientated north-east/south-west. There was evidence of scorched/burnt soil along portions of the south-west edge of the feature.

A trench measuring 1.1m x 0.4m was excavated through the burnt material. This revealed that the burnt material was 20–30mm thick and was made up of ash and lengths of cereal stubble. Most of the stubble was charred, but some unburnt and partially burnt stubble was in evidence. Furthermore, some fragments of burnt paper were also recovered. There was no evidence that the material occupied a depression or pit.

The nature of the evidence indicated that the feature was relatively modern, probably associated with cereal crop production, and no further archaeological investigation was undertaken.
*Martin E. Byrne, 31 Millford, Athgarvan, Co. Kildare.*

### 377. DONAGHMORE
No archaeological significance
29638 23711
SMR 6:5
99E0675

The development, a temporary storage facility, was c. 170m west of ecclesiastical remains (SMR 6:5) and a rectangular enclosure site (SMR 6:12). The soil-stripping consisted of the removal of topsoil varying from 0.25m to 0.6m deep, over an area measuring c. 130m x 75m. No features, remains or deposits of archaeological significance were encountered.
*Christine Baker, Arch-Tech Ltd, 32 Fitzwilliam Place, Dublin 2.*

### 378. EASTON
No archaeological significance
29840 23600
99E0733

An irregularity in a field boundary adjoining a curve in a road on the line of the proposed Celbridge Interchange was investigated in case it represented traces of a destroyed earthwork. Three cuttings were excavated, two on the edge and one in what would have been the interior. No traces of any archaeological remains were found.
*Thaddeus C. Breen, 13 Wainsfort Crescent, Dublin 6W, for Valerie J. Keeley.*

### 379. KILRATHMURRAY, ENFIELD
No archaeological significance
2654 2406
99E0230

The site, where soil-stripping before quarrying was taking place, was in an area of hilly pasture comprising a gravel ridge running north-east/south-west. A feature was revealed and subsequently excavated (see No. 380 below). The soil-stripping revealed a consistent stratigraphy with variations in depth (0.3–2.3m) reflecting the undulating topography. Several areas of burning were uncovered but were not considered of archaeological significance.
*Christine Baker, Arch-Tech Ltd, 32 Fitzwilliam Place, Dublin 2.*

### 380. KILRATHMURRAY, ENFIELD
Non-antiquity—animal pen?
2654 2406
99E0286

The feature identified during a programme of monitoring (see No. 379 above) was at the base of the slope of a gravel ridge and was open to the south only. It appeared as a reverse L-shape, measuring 6.6m north–south by 4.8m. It ranged in width from 0.7m to 1.5m. Set into a matrix of grey sand, the feature comprised three trenches with fills of sandy clay varying from orange to brown and with an average depth of 0.25m. Finds were limited to a sherd of brownware and a piece of clay pipe stem. Given its location, the nature of associated finds and the subsequent agricultural usage of the land, the feature is best defined as an open animal pen or shelter and assigned to the early/mid-19th century.
*Christine Baker and Rónán Swan, Arch-Tech Ltd, 32 Fitzwilliam Place, Dublin 2.*

### 381. GLEBE SOUTH (A)
Environs of medieval borough
282752 206678
SMR 28:49
99E5041

An archaeological evaluation was undertaken at a proposed development site at Glebe South, Old Kilcullen, Kilcullen, Co. Kildare, on 25 September 1999. The site is to the south-south-west of the Old Kilcullen ecclesiastical remains and adjacent to the postulated location of a gate associated with the medieval borough.

Five trenches were excavated by machine. Two distinct layers were uncovered. Layer 1, 0.24–0.32m thick, was interpreted as a topsoil layer. The sterile and undisturbed nature of Layer 2 indicated that it represented the 'natural' subsoil horizon.

No features, structures or finds of archaeological interest were uncovered during the evaluation, and it was recommended that no further archaeological involvement was required at the site.
*Martin E. Byrne, 31 Millford, Athgarvan, Co. Kildare.*

### 382. GLEBE SOUTH (B)
Environs of medieval borough
282699 206677
SMR 28:49
99E0729

An archaeological evaluation was undertaken at a proposed development site at Glebe South, Old Kilcullen, Kilcullen, Co. Kildare, on 18 December 1999. The site is to the south-south-west of the Old Kilcullen ecclesiastical remains and adjacent to the postulated location of a gate associated with the medieval borough.

Five trenches were excavated by machine. Two distinct layers were uncovered. Layer 1, 0.28–0.33m thick, was topsoil. The sterile and undisturbed nature of Layer 2 indicated that it represented the natural subsoil horizon.

No features, structures or finds of archaeological interest were uncovered during the evaluation, and it was suggested that no further archaeological involvement was required at the site.
*Martin E. Byrne, 31 Millford, Athgarvan, Co. Kildare.*

### 383. GRANEY EAST
Adjacent to nunnery
281742 183906
99E0052

Monitoring was undertaken at a quarry site at Graney East, Castledermot, Co. Kildare, in February and July 1999. The site is c. 3.7km to the south-west of Castledermot. The immediate area surrounding the development is rich in archaeological sites, with a 17th-century house (SMR 40:13) to the north-west, a cross site (SMR 40:44) to the immediate north and a holy well site (SMR 40:14) immediately to the west. In the western third of the field in which the proposed quarry lies is the site of a nunnery (SMR 40:15) that was founded c. 1200 for nuns of the order of Arrouaise and was recognised as an abbey by 1476. The abbey was suppressed in 1539. The area is densely covered with low earthworks and fragments of walls. It is possible to distinguish a driveway and small fields to the east of the driveway, as illustrated on the 1st edition OS 6-inch map. Most of the earthworks are concentrated to the west of this driveway. The graveyard is not recognisable, and a small quarry had been excavated, at some unknown time in the past, near the western boundary. To the east of the earthworks is a long, linear earthwork-like feature. It is possible that this feature represents the remains of the eastern boundary of a garden depicted on the 1837 map. However, without excavation it is difficult to determine the relationship between this feature and the nunnery.

In addition, a mill-race, serving a mill in Graney West td, is illustrated on the 1837 map. A section of this mill-race runs through part of the field in which the development lies and, though now dry, is relatively intact. The remains of a sluice were found at the junction formed by the river and mill-race. The mill-race was constructed and lined with stones and ran from its junction with the Graney River in a general north-westerly direction towards a mill in Graney West td. The present ruins (SMR 40:43) include a date stone of 1799, but the main standing building, which is partly demolished, includes the lower ten or so courses of a previous structure from which, projecting from the north side, the foundation courses of an even earlier building are visible. The existence of such an earlier mill is mentioned in the Civil Survey of 1654–6.

An assessment of the project, prepared by the writer, suggested the inclusion of appropriate buffers along the line of the mill-race, as well as between the nunnery and the edge of the development area. These buffer areas were subsequently agreed with both the NMHPS and Kildare County Council and were conditions of the grant of planning.

Monitoring of soil-stripping in an area of c. 2 acres undertaken in February 1999 revealed no features or deposits of archaeological interest; a total of ten sherds of medieval/post-medieval pottery were recovered.

Additional topsoil-stripping was undertaken in another c. 2-acre area of the site in July 1999, during which a single skeleton was uncovered. Following discussions with both the NMHPS and the NMI, it was decided initially to undertake testing in the general area surrounding the skeleton in order to determine whether it was part of a graveyard. The results of this were negative, and it was agreed that the skeleton should be excavated and removed.

The skeleton was orientated east–west, with the skull to the west. It lay in an extended position with the legs flexed. The skull was damaged, and it was not possible to ascertain how it lay. The right arm was extended, and the left arm was positioned across the ribcage. The legs were flexed towards the south, and the right leg lay over the left. An examination of the skeleton (Clare Mullins, pers. comm.) indicated that it was a female, aged late 20s/early 30s.

The skeleton lay in and on a sandy gravel material, and it was not possible to determine a grave-cut. The skeleton lay 834mm (101.418m OD) below the present ground surface.

Five additional sherds of medieval/post-medieval pottery were recovered during this phase of monitoring, four from the topsoil and one from the material surrounding the skeleton.

Additional monitoring will be undertaken during 2000.
*Martin E. Byrne, 31 Millford, Athgarvan, Co. Kildare.*

### 384. GRANGEROSNOLVAN
Burnt spread
**99E0473**
Topsoil-stripping during monitoring of a Bord Gáis pipeline initially revealed a burnt spread at the junction of the topsoil and the natural subsoil. However, surface clearance of it showed indistinct patches of burnt soil over an area of 2m$^2$ that were up to 10mm deep. There was no distinct cut or deposition. Nothing of an artefactual nature was recovered.
*Niall Gregory, 25 Westpark, Blessington, Co. Wicklow, for Margaret Gowen & Co. Ltd.*

### 385. GREAT CONNEL
In vicinity of standing stone
**SMR 23:15**
**99M0034**
Monitoring was undertaken at this site, as a private residence is being constructed within 50m of the standing stone. During the digging of the foundation trench for the southern wall of the internal courtyard, 2m from the western end of the wall, bone was recovered from the digger bucket. This bone was highly fragmented, but the skull was almost complete; the bone fragments were very crumbly and brittle.

The bones were recovered from within a clay matrix—fine, mid- to light brown with few stones (those present <50mm in diameter), flecks of charcoal and also two fragments of snail shell.

There was no sign of a cut or an obvious differentiation in the fill within which these bones were recovered.

The cutting of the foundation trenches for the western wing of the house did not reveal any cuts, indication of cuts, artefacts or other human remains, or evidence of further burial. Therefore these bones seem to be a discrete burial. Given the absence of a differentiated fill and the fact that these bones were recovered from the digger bucket, it is not possible to determine whether they were originally buried in this location or were reburied at a subsequent date.

Examination and analysis of these skeletal remains have now been completed by L. Buckley. The skeleton has been identified as belonging to a female aged around 25 years. The pattern of decay is consistent with that of an individual dating from the medieval or Early Christian period. A post-medieval date is possible, but a 20th-century date has been ruled out.

This programme of monitoring recovered a possible Early Christian skeleton and a fragment of rotary quern, which may also date to the Early Christian period. This may suggest that the site itself was an Early Christian one and therefore may support the contention that the standing stone is in fact a cross shaft.
*Daniel Leo Swan, Arch-Tech Ltd, 32 Fitzwilliam Place, Dublin 2.*

### 386. KILCULLEN
Monitoring
**98E0418**
The upgrading of the Kilcullen Sewerage Scheme involved the excavation of trenches varying from over 3m to 1m deep, on the route extending northwards on rising ground from Kilcullen town to

the suburbs and estates on the road leading to Naas.

This particular area was characterised by the presence of a considerable stratum of sandy soil and gravel immediately below the tarmac and road metalling. This feature had resulted from the fact that the original humus and topsoil had been removed in earlier times during construction of the main thoroughfare that was the first turnpike road in this region. It was noteworthy that the original boulder clay overlying the sand and gravel deposits had not been removed from the more level ground leading southwards from Kilcullen town centre towards the Athy road.

Whilst a number of relatively modern concentrations of domestic spoil and bric-à-brac were encountered during trenching in areas adjoining the River Liffey close to the town bridge, no material of archaeological interest was recovered during the monitoring carried out between January and mid-June 1999.

*Breandán Ó Ríordáin, Burgage More, Blessington, Co. Wicklow, for Valerie J. Keeley Ltd.*

### 387. KILDARE
Urban medieval
98E0574

Approximately 2900m of gas pipeline was laid within Kildare town over fourteen weeks between 30 November 1998 and 19 March 1999. Most of this was within the zone of archaeological potential, although several short stretches of pipeline just outside the zone were also monitored.

Evidence of medieval activity was found at two locations, though on a limited scale. Both of these were in the Market Square area. The trench running from the junction of Bride Street northwards towards the Cathedral contained seven sherds of medieval pottery, along with a cut antler, an iron nail, red brick, several pieces of cremated bone, and unburnt animal bone and teeth. The trench running from the junction of Station Road to Dublin Street contained four sherds of medieval pottery, all from the extreme north-west end of the trench.

The remains of several stone-built culverts and walls were also uncovered along the route. These all appeared to be 19th- and 20th-century in date on the evidence of their construction and the finds found in association with them.

In general the trenches contained modern gravel infill, representing road foundation material, and were regularly cut by modern service pipes and cables. This, and the shallow nature of the trenches (less than 1m deep), meant that the likelihood of hitting archaeological deposits was limited. As a result, no evidence of the medieval town walls, the gatehouses or the earlier monastic enclosures was uncovered.

*Hilary Opie, 103 Cherrywood Drive, Clondalkin, Dublin 22.*

### 388. BOTHAIRÍN NA gCORP, KILDARE
No archaeological significance
99E0183

An archaeological evaluation was undertaken at a proposed development site at *Bothairín na gCorp*, Kildare, on 17 April 1999. The work was carried out in compliance with a request from *Dúchas* as a portion of the site is within the designated zone of archaeological potential associated with Kildare town, being in the north-western quadrant of the town.

The mechanical excavation of eleven trenches took place. The trenches were set out in a gridded fashion. No features or deposits of archaeological interest were uncovered, and two shreds of medieval pottery were recovered from the topsoil horizon.

*Martin E. Byrne, 31 Millford, Athgarvan, Co. Kildare.*

### 389. BRIDE STREET (REAR OF), KILDARE
Urban medieval
271774 211919
99E0187

An archaeological evaluation was carried out at a proposed development site at Bride Street, Kildare, on 24 April 1999. The work was undertaken in compliance with a request from the NMHPS, *Dúchas*, as the site is within the designated zone of archaeological potential associated with Kildare town.

Five trenches were mechanically excavated within the confines of the site. The results indicated that the entire site had previously been disturbed. There is a probability that the levels across the site had been reduced sometime in the past and that the area had been subsequently filled. The relatively flat surface of the site in comparison with the existing slope on Bride Street, the difference in levels between the surface of the site and the area to the immediate north, and the 'modern' nature of the fill material (Layer 1) would all appear to testify to this conclusion. It is possible that the levels were originally reduced in order to provide soil to level up the school site to the immediate north.

Two sherds of probable medieval pottery were recovered from a disturbed context.

*Martin E. Byrne, 31 Millford, Athgarvan, Co. Kildare.*

### 390. BRIDE STREET, KILDARE
Urban medieval
99E0099

An archaeological excavation was conducted on the site of the proposed development of the new Kildare Credit Union at the junction of Bride Street and Bangup Lane. The excavation was carried out over eight weeks between 6 April and 26 May 1999. It involved general ground reduction to a depth suitable for construction throughout the south-western part of the site. Further test areas were excavated to the east and north-east.

Excavations revealed the presence of a large, north–south-aligned ditch feature in the western part of the site. The ditch showed up as a dark, organic clay upper fill against an olive-yellow subsoil. No trace of a bank survived at the surface. A roughly square, possibly defensive, stone-built structure was later constructed at the southern limit of the site, the origin and date of which are difficult to determine. It was separated from the later medieval activity by a build-up of redeposited, natural, yellow, compact, sandy clays. The structure comprises four roughly hewn, random-coursed limestone walls, the parallel, east–west-aligned walls abutting a larger, north–south-aligned wall. The larger wall appears to be the earliest.

The subsequent activity on the site consisted of a series of medieval cobbled surfaces, related pits and other features. Later, in more recent times, a series of large linear cuts and pits indicates extensive excavations relating to a nearby butcher's yard.

After consultation with *Dúchas* The Heritage Service, it was recommended that the structure be left *in situ* and that alternative designs for the proposed building be prepared. A conservation project with regard to the structure is ongoing at the time of writing.

*Declan Moore, 8 Yewland Green, Renmore, Galway, for Mary Henry & Associates, Clonmel, Co. Tipperary.*

### 391. MEDICAL CENTRE (REAR OF), BRIDE STREET, KILDARE
Urban medieval
271858 211920
99E0556

An archaeological evaluation was undertaken at a proposed development site to the rear of the Kildare Medical Centre, Bride Street, Kildare, on 9 October 1999. The site is within the designated zone of archaeological potential associated with Kildare town.

Two trenches were mechanically excavated within the confines of the site. Nothing of archaeological interest was uncovered. Accordingly, it was recommended that no further archaeological involvement was required at the site.

*Martin E. Byrne, 31 Millford, Athgarvan, Co. Kildare.*

### 392. BRIDE STREET/BANGUP LANE, KILDARE
Urban medieval
272580 212273
SMR 22:29
99E0099

An archaeological evaluation was carried out at a site at Bride Street/Bangup Lane, Kildare, on 4 and 5 March 1999. Testing was carried out in response to a condition of planning.

Three test-trenches were inserted, positioned to best represent the stratigraphy of the overall site. Excavations were commenced using a toothless bucket. However, this soon had to be abandoned in favour of a normal, toothed foundation bucket as the high density of stone within the general fills tended to counteract any positive effects of the ditching bucket.

The results of the test-trenches indicate the survival, to a depth of *c.* 0.7m, of what seemed to be medieval deposits towards the rear (south-west) of the site. These deposits consisted of layered arrangements of redeposited natural and silty clay mixed with stone and fragmentary slate. They produced oyster shell, animal bone and several sherds of medieval pottery. It was clear that these deposits extended for some distance northwards, but they seemed to be at least partially disturbed towards the extreme northern end of the site. The archaeological deposits were covered by up to 1m of stony rubble. These deposits were largely denuded towards the front (east) of the site, where the rubble generally came directly down upon the natural, but here some deposits, which seemed to occupy a cut into the natural, survived around the central area.

A number of wall foundations associated with the recently demolished structure were uncovered. Other wall foundations discovered were more difficult to explain. However, the general impression from the stratigraphy was that all walls, with the exception of the possible wall aligned east–west in the northern part of the site, post-dated the layer of rubble and therefore probably belong to the 18th or 19th centuries.

The absence of modern debris over the site was noteworthy, while there was also a scarcity of identifiably post-medieval finds. This is unusual on an urban site and clearly suggests an absence of modern disturbance. This absence of modern material also served to more firmly contextualise the medieval sherds as deriving from an *in situ* location within the stratigraphy.

Full archaeological excavation was recommended in mitigation of the archaeological potential of the site.

*Clare Mullins, 31 Millford, Athgarvan, Co. Kildare.*

### 393. KILDARE CREDIT UNION, BRIDE STREET, KILDARE
Urban
99E0099 ext.

During archaeological excavation of the site by Declan Moore (No. 390 above) a large linear ditch of possible Early Christian date and the base of an Anglo-Norman tower were recorded in the south-west corner.

An extension to the licence was granted to monitor construction foundation work for the building and to ensure that existing archaeological features remained intact.

A culvert comprising a cover of limestone slabs and a slate base was exposed for 9m of its length at

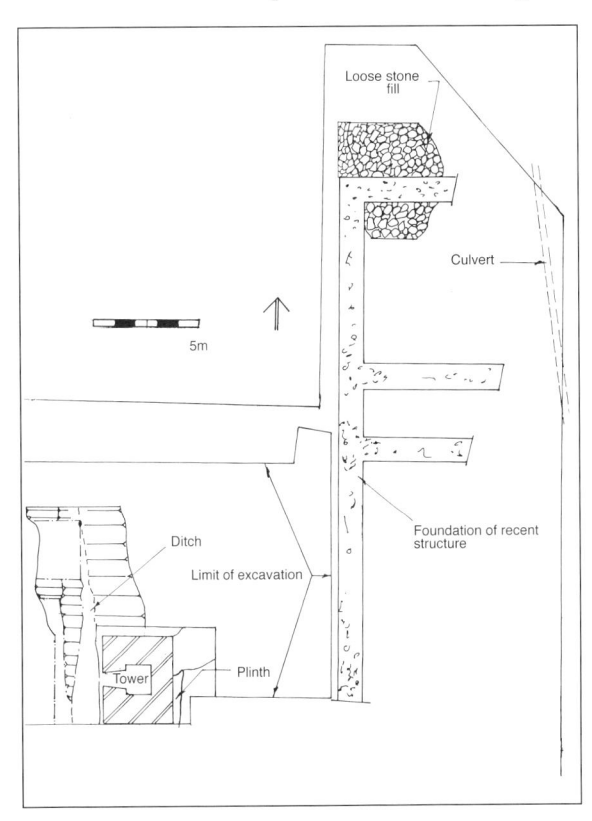

Plan of existing features at Kildare Credit Union, Bride Street.

the north-east of the site. It was 0.65m high and 0.4m wide. The side-walls were constructed of mortared cut limestone, and the culvert was surrounded by a loose stone fill.

The reinforced concrete foundation of a recent building was uncovered on the east half of the site. It overlay a large loose stone area of fill at its extreme north end and extended to the south boundary.

No further archaeological features were recorded.
*Frank Ryan, 28 Cabinteely Way, Dublin 18.*

### 394. ROUND TOWER HOUSE (REAR OF), DUBLIN STREET, KILDARE
Urban medieval
272726 212179
99E0121

An archaeological evaluation was undertaken at a proposed development site at the rear of Round Tower House, Dublin Street, Kildare, on 8 May 1999. The site is within the designated zone of archaeological potential associated with Kildare town.

The mechanical excavation of two trenches took place within the confines of the proposed apartment complex, carpark and associated access road, all of which will be constructed during Phase 1 of the development.

The results of the trenching indicated that the site had been levelled up sometime in the past, probably during the late 19th/early 20th century. The fill used in this procedure appears to have been dumped directly upon the original topsoil, which, in turn, lay directly upon the natural sterile subsoil. No features, deposits or finds of archaeological interest were uncovered during the work.

Further investigations will be undertaken in 2000 following the demolition of buildings fronting onto Dublin Street.
*Martin E. Byrne, 31 Millford, Athgarvan, Co. Kildare.*

### 395. MAIN STREET, KILL
Environs of medieval church
293774 223909
99E0396

An archaeological evaluation was undertaken at a proposed development site at Main Street, Kill, Co. Kildare, on 31 July 1999. The site is within the boundaries of the urban area of archaeological potential for Kill and to the immediate east of the site of the medieval parish church.

Six trenches were mechanically excavated within the confines of the site. No features or structures of archaeological interest were uncovered.

Two sherds of probable medieval pottery were recovered from the disturbed topsoil, and it was recommended that no further archaeological involvement at the site was required.
*Martin E. Byrne, 31 Millford, Athgarvan, Co. Kildare.*

### 396. KILLHILL
Enclosure
305752 223793
SMR 20:1
99E0243

Monitoring of topsoil-stripping associated with the construction of a dwelling was undertaken on 12 June 1999. The work was carried out in compliance with a condition included in the grant of planning. The site is within the boundaries of a large enclosure (KD20:1) that encompasses the base of Killhill. Also on Killhill is a smaller enclosure site (KD20:2).

Monitoring involved the supervision of the topsoil-stripping/levels' reduction associated with the house and associated yard, driveway, septic tank and percolation area.

No features or finds of archaeological interest were uncovered during the work.
*Clare Mullins, 31 Millford, Athgarvan, Co. Kildare.*

### 397. RIVER GREESE, KILKEA LOWER AND GRANGEROSNOLVAN UPPER
No archaeological significance
27550 18730
99D012, 99R030 (diver survey and detection device licences)

An underwater inspection and licensed metal-detector survey of the River Greese was carried out on 24 August, on behalf of Margaret Gowen & Co. Ltd, at the location where Bord Gáis Éireann's Ballyvass to Athy Pipeline will cross the river in Kilkea Lower, Co. Kildare. This did not reveal any objects or features of archaeological interest. The survey area extended from *c.* 15m upstream of the proposed crossing-point to a point *c.* 40m downstream of that point.
*Niall Brady, 2 Vale Terrace, Lower Dargle Road, Bray, Co. Wicklow, for Valerie J. Keeley Ltd.*

### 398. KILMEAGE
Vicinity of church
N775231
99E0625

The development site is to the north-west of the Church of Ireland church in Kilmeage village. The site slopes steeply upwards, eastwards from the Kilmeage–Allenwood road, and is bounded on the north-west side by the Kilmeage–Robertstown road and on the south-east side by a large sand and gravel quarry. There are good views westwards to the Hill of Allen and southwards towards the Wicklow Mountains. The major portion of the site at the back of the existing bungalow is currently under grass. The portion of the site fronting the Allenwood road is overgrown with vegetation and may have been quarried out in the past, as suggested by a steep scarp downwards from the boundary fence of the existing bungalow.

The church is reputed to have been built on the site of an earlier church, although the site is not marked on the Sites and Monuments Record for County Kildare.

The village of Kilmeage was laid out in the 1830s. There is a tradition that a large quantity of human bone was found when the houses south-west of the church and across the road were being built, suggesting that a graveyard originally surrounded the church. There is also a tradition that the northern and western limits of the original graveyard extended further outwards than today's boundary.

Ten trenches tested this development site. Four of them were in the vicinity of the graveyard, to establish the presence/absence of burials and/or an early enclosing feature around the church. Such remains were not found. The scarcity of human bone was noteworthy, as disturbed human bone is generally found in the vicinity of graveyards. Very few fragments were found in these trenches.

The other trenches tested the wider development area. Two pit-like features were exposed. It was suggested that one of them (in Trench 5) may have been a hand-dug test-pit for quarrying purposes. The function and date of the other, in Trench 10, were not clear. Ash had been thrown into it, and it may have had some kind of domestic function.

No human burials were exposed. There was no evidence for the remains of an enclosing ditch associated with an earlier church on the site.
*Rosanne Meenan, Roestown, Drumree, Co. Meath.*

### 399. KNOCKSHOUGH GLEBE
Monitoring
**2723503 212000**
**98E0288 ext.**

Monitoring was carried out during the topsoil-stripping for a trial cutting on the proposed Kildare Bypass. The trial cutting measured 30m x 30m and lay in Knockshough Glebe townland. The work was carried out on 20 October 1999.

The site selected was an area of relatively flat grassland. The mechanically excavated trial cutting was opened to a depth of over 7.5m, in connection with ongoing water-table studies. The soil profile consisted of 0.4–0.6m of grass-covered topsoil overlying silty marl and, at lower levels, gravel, stones and sand. No artefacts or structures of archaeological interest came to light during this work.
*Breandán Ó Ríordáin, Burgage More, Blessington, Co. Wicklow, for Valerie J. Keeley Ltd.*

### 400. LEINSTER LODGE
Hearth
**99E0474**

Topsoil-stripping during monitoring of a Bord Gáis pipeline revealed a burnt spread at the junction of the topsoil and natural subsoil. The spread covered an area of 1.5m² that lay within a shallow, subrectangular pit. The fill consisted of charcoal-rich soil over a burnt soil base. No artefacts were recovered from the site that could have indicated its age.
*Niall Gregory, 25 Westpark, Blessington, Co. Wicklow, for Margaret Gowen & Co. Ltd, 2 Killiney View, Albert Road Lower, Glenageary, Co. Dublin.*

### 401. BARN HALL, LEIXLIP
In proximity to a bridge site
**29922 23417**
**SMR 11:11**

Monitoring was carried out on 21 October 1999 on the site of a proposed extension to the existing club house at Barn Hall. The site is immediately to the north-west of a bridge built in 1308 by John le Decer, mayor of Dublin.

On removal of the concrete, a 0.1m layer of rubble sat directly on the natural, yellow/brown boulder clay. Examination of the site indicated that this area had previously been cut into the natural bank along the river's edge, thus destroying any stratigraphy that may have existed here.
*Donald Murphy, Archaeological Consultancy Services Ltd, 15 Trinity Street, Drogheda, Co. Louth.*

### 402. MAINHAM
No archaeological significance
**28684 23019**
**99E0133**

Twelve trenches were mechanically excavated to natural, undisturbed levels during pre-development testing. No conclusive *in situ* archaeological remains were revealed.

As a result of the proximity of the proposed development to extant archaeological sites, it was recommended that all ground disturbance at the site be monitored by an archaeologist during the construction phase.
*Anne Connolly, Archaeological Services Unit Ltd, Purcell House, Oranmore, Co. Galway, for Valerie J. Keeley Ltd.*

### 403. MAYNOOTH
Urban
**N938377**
**97E0353**

Cable-laying on behalf of Esat Telecom extended east–west along a route from within the University's gate lodge, alongside the castle's gatehouse, and on up the north side of Main Street to its junction with Stratton Road, at which point the route headed south. An extension also ran south along the west side of Leinster Street from the Leinster Mills, crossing Main Street to terminate at its junction with Leinster Street.

One sherd of local ware was recovered from the trench close to the junction of Main Street and Fagan's Lane. Two small fragments of stone window mouldings and a substantial window mullion were recovered beneath the castle façade, from which they clearly fell at some point in the past.
*Niall Brady, 2 Vale Terrace, Lower Dargle Road, Bray, Co. Wicklow, for Valerie J. Keeley Ltd.*

### 404. THE ROOST BAR, LEINSTER STREET, MAYNOOTH
Urban
**99E0188**

Archaeological testing was carried out at the Roost Bar, Leinster Street, Maynooth, from 26 April to 3 May 1999 to supply additional information about the nature of any archaeology present on the site in accordance with recommendations from the County Council. Two test-trenches, one with lateral extensions, were excavated at the site.

Test-trench 1 was positioned in the western area of the site of proposed development and was c. 11.8m long on an east–west axis x 1.4m (maximum) wide. Beneath modern rubble and concrete was a layer of bitumen that had burning on its uppermost surface. There were also the remains of black pitch and redeposited, red, natural clay. The remains of a pit, filled with iron objects such as horseshoes, door hinges, nails and bolts, were uncovered at the centre of the test-trench. The bottom of the test-trench was composed of natural deposits of red clay. Beneath this lay a natural deposit of grey clay.

The remains of a stone wall were uncovered in the middle of Test-trench 1. It ran along a north-west/south-east axis and was uncovered immediately beneath the concrete and rubble. Only the northern-facing surface was exposed. The wall was constructed on a stone foundation and was a maximum of 4.8m long (including the projection of the wall in that area of the site where it had been destroyed by the erection of a modern concrete pillar), 0.4m thick and 0.4m deep. Because of the presence of a substantial amount of mortar on its exposed surface, it was not possible to determine how many courses it contained.

The northern extension of Test-trench 1 was c. 3m long x 0.75m (maximum) wide. The extension was only partially excavated, and only the modern concrete and its associated rubble were uncovered. No archaeological features were revealed.

The southern extension of Test-trench 1 was c. 4m long x 0.8m (maximum) wide. It was only partially excavated and was made up of modern concrete with associated rubble and concrete foundation. A layer of bitumen lay directly beneath the concrete foundation.

The only archaeological feature uncovered in this area was the remains of a wood-lined stone trough/drain. This feature on its northern side consisted of one stone lying on its side. This stone was c. 0.3m deep and 0.1m thick. The southern side of the trough/drain was partially destroyed, but one stone, c. 0.1m deep, was still preserved. The remains of an internal lining of wood were uncovered. The base of the stone trough/drain was made up of hard bitumen. A large quantity of rusted iron objects was uncovered during the excavation of the fill of the trough/drain. According to local information, there had been a blacksmith's forge next door to the site until quite recently. It would seem highly likely that the iron objects uncovered in the fill of the trough/drain are the waste materials from this metalworking process.

Test-trench 2 was positioned in the eastern area of the site of proposed development and was c. 9.6m long on an east–west axis x 0.65m. Test-trench 2 was also made up of a layer of modern concrete that lay immediately above a layer of rubble stone and concrete pieces. At the western extremity the test-trench was composed of four layers of soil of varying colours, which sealed the remains of a wall. This was uncovered immediately beneath the modern concrete at the extreme northern end of the trench and was only excavated to 0.4m deep, the depth of a cobble surface/floor. Three courses of the wall were exposed. The cobble surface/floor was uncovered throughout the entire length of the trench. The cobblestones were on average less than 0.1m long, and it is clear that they were laid down in a deliberate manner.

One large sherd of early modern pottery was uncovered in Test-trench 2, in a disturbed context. In addition, a large range of modern pottery, glass, red brick fragments, bottles and pieces of mortar and an assortment of metal objects were uncovered in this trench.

*Eoghan Moore for Arch-Tech, 32 Fitzwilliam Place, Dublin 2.*

## 405. MAYNOOTH CASTLE, MAYNOOTH
Prehistoric and early medieval settlement and Anglo-Norman castle
**N934375**
**96E0391 ext.**

Excavation of the whole of the interior of the late 12th-century keep was undertaken for *Dúchas* The Heritage Service, from October to December, before the development of the ground floor as an exhibition space. Archaeological assessment of the site had been undertaken in 1996 (*Excavations 1996*, 52). Post-excavation work is ongoing at the time of writing, and the results of carbon dating of the earliest phases of activity uncovered are awaited. Seven main phases of occupation of the site were evidenced.

Part of a rectangular prehistoric building was the stratigraphically earliest structure uncovered. No finds were associated with it; however, a stone axehead and unfinished macehead, as well as a number of waste flakes of flint, were uncovered in early medieval contexts and may derive from the structure.

At least two small post-and-wattle round houses, each c. 5m in diameter, were constructed over the prehistoric remains and are probably of early medieval date. No datable finds were recovered from them, but excellent carbon samples were retrieved from their hearths and post-holes. The latest of the round houses appears to have had a curving wooden stockade added to one side of it. The house would appear to be contemporary with the beginning of the cultivation of the site, which was evidenced by regularly spaced shallow furrows. The cultivation later overwhelmed the house and continued until the arrival of the Anglo-Normans.

The site appears to have fallen into Norman hands in around 1175. The remains of a mound of sod c. 1m high were uncovered dating to the beginning of the Anglo-Norman occupation. The remains of a rectangular post-and-wattle building survived on top of the mound, which was delimited by a stout wooden fence with an entrance in its east side. An arrowhead, an iron spur and a scabbard chape were amongst the finds from this level. Pottery consisted of Ham Green ware. It is not clear into what category of site the settlement fits.

The initial construction of the stone keep, probably in the late 1180s, was evidenced by thick mortar slicks. The original keep was divided into two rooms by three piers that supported the first floor.

The ground floor of the castle was radically altered, most likely in the early 15th century. The ground floor was roofed with two wicker-centred barrel vaults, which were supported on a new spine wall that linked the older internal piers. A second mortar slick and the sockets of timber supports for the arch centring marked this activity. A well was found in the west half of the keep. It was infilled, possibly when the ground floor was altered, and another was opened in the western half of the keep. The keep continued to be occupied until the 16th century, when it fell in the Silken Thomas Rebellion and was badly damaged.

Slight evidence of the reoccupation of the castle in the 17th century was uncovered.

In the 18th and 19th centuries the keep was again reused, but this time one half of the ground floor was used to store coal. The eastern doorway was blocked up (the outside of the keep being used as a handball alley), and a new doorway was opened in its western wall. A stone staircase was built and led, via a breach in the vaulting, up to the first floor.

A good assemblage of medieval pottery (including several largely complete jugs) and wooden objects (the latter from the well) were uncovered. The animal, bird and fish bone assemblages would appear to be of interest as they include fallow deer from the deer park as well as immature seal bones and other oddities.

*Alan Hayden, Archaeological Projects Ltd, 25A Eaton Square, Terenure, Dublin 6W.*

### 406. MOONE
No archaeological significance
27937 19224
99E0691

An assessment excavation before road development established that a circular cropmark was a glacially derived natural feature. No further investigations were required at this site before road construction.

*Christine Tarbett-Buckley, c/o Valerie J. Keeley Ltd, 29–30 Duke Street, Athy, Co. Kildare.*

### 407. MOONE ABBEY, MOONE
Early Christian monastery
27895 19267
98E0276

Excavations, before conservation and funded by *Dúchas* The Heritage Service, were completed in 1999 with a second season of ten weeks' duration. Two areas were investigated—the eastern end of the church (21.5m x 7.1m) and outside the south wall (19m x 2m).

Further exploration was carried out this season on the small 10th- to 11th-century stone church, associated with the Columban monastery. The foundations supporting the west wall and southwest anta were laid down on an apparently undisturbed stratum. They were built of local slate, with traces of mortar bonding evident in the upper courses. Most of the north-west anta foundation had been removed in the early 17th century.

The random-coursed masonry in the walls of the church had distinctive Early Christian punch dressing in vertical and diagonal strokes on several of the blocks. In addition to the sharpening marks (noted in *Excavations 1998*, 108–9), examples of incised designs were present on the original walling. An interesting circular geometric pattern was laid out with a compass.

A rectangular foundation or plinth (2.4m long, 1.7m wide, 1m deep), built on undisturbed soils, was discovered 10m west of the Early Christian church, underneath the 13th-century nave wall. The masonry consisted of uncoursed mortared slate, forming an offset beneath a single random course. Its function has not been determined, but it would appear to date to the occupation of the Columban monastery.

The construction of the nave and the conversion of the earlier church into the chancel most likely date to the 13th century, when it became the manorial church serving the Anglo-Norman borough at Moone. Loose, moulded stones belonging to this building phase were discovered in the excavations. Two deep exploratory cuttings were investigated on the line of the north nave wall. No evidence was found for either the foundation or the wall, all traces having been removed in the 19th century. In the south-eastern corner of the nave a 13th- to 14th-century deposit of silt mixed with sand produced pottery, a fragment from an iron vessel and a quern.

Moone Church continued in use for worship after the Reformation, but this had ceased by the early 17th century, when a masonry crypt was built by the Archbold family beneath the north-west of the chancel. The crypt was recorded in order to evaluate both the structural features and the deposits within. The rectangular interior (2.8m x 2m) was roofed with a tunnel vault. A ledge and holes incorporated into the side-walls indicated that a wooden shelf to support coffins had spanned the width of the crypt. Disarticulated human skeletal remains and coffin fragments were lying scattered on the floor. Investigations within the eastern entrance revealed evidence for four stone steps descending to the original crypt. The inscribed limestone plinth, belonging to a memorial monument associated with the crypt, was fully uncovered in the corner of the chancel. Other carved and inscribed fragments from this monument were reassembled for conservation.

Following the building of the crypt, the church interior was used for interment, and the latest small finds from the burial soil were of 18th-century date. The chancel was standing at this time, but the collapse of the north chancel wall in the early 19th century resulted in damage to the entrance and roof of the Archbold crypt. In a second construction phase the entrance was lengthened and the eastern end of the roof was repaired with granite lintels covered with reused masonry. Two lead coffins, deposited in the mid-19th century, were lying on the surface within the crypt. The doorway was subsequently sealed with masonry blocking.

*Miriam Clyne, Templemartin, Craughwell, Co. Galway.*

### 408. RIVERS BOTHOGE AND GREESE, MOONE/TIMOLIN/CROOKSTOWN UPPER
Timber feature
27935 19284, 27550 18730, 27950 19353, 28005 19533, 28013 19710

Before Kildare County Council's realignment of the N9 between Moone, Ballitore and Crookstown, an underwater inspection and licensed metal-detector survey of the Greese and Bothoge rivers took place at five locations between 12 and 16 April, where works will impinge on the riverbanks.

A timber feature was observed protruding into the riverbed upstream and away from one work site in Timolin townland. No further items of archaeological interest were observed.

*Niall Brady, 2 Vale Terrace, Lower Dargle Road, Bray, Co. Wicklow, for Valerie J. Keeley Ltd.*

### 409. MOAT CLUB, ABBEY STREET, NAAS
Adjacent to motte
289139 219409
99E0391

An archaeological evaluation was undertaken at a proposed development site to the rear of The Moat Club, Abbey Street, Naas. The work was carried out in compliance with a request from the National Monuments and Historic Properties Service and Naas Urban District Council, following a pre-planning enquiry. The site is within the boundaries of the urban area of archaeological potential for Naas and in the immediate environs of the motte.

Two trenches were mechanically excavated. No finds of archaeological interest were recovered during the testing. However, two walls were revealed. One was relatively modern, being of shuttered concrete construction, and it appeared to have formed part of a building block associated with former school buildings on the site. The other wall appears to be of 19th-century date and is illustrated in a plan of the site dating to 1872.

The natural subsoil was found to slope down to the east and south, reflective of the existing topography of the area as a whole.

No features, structures or artefacts of historical or archaeological interest were recovered during the work, and therefore it was recommended that no further archaeological involvement was required at the site.
*Clare Mullins, 31 Millford, Athgarvan, Co. Kildare.*

### 410. DUBLIN ROAD, NAAS
Town wall
289616 219578
99E0111

Testing was undertaken at the site of a proposed rear extension to a premises on Dublin Road, Naas, on 13 and 14 March 1999. The work was carried out in compliance with a condition attached to the grant of planning in relation to the proposed development. Two trial-trenches and one trial-pit were excavated within the boundaries of the rear yard.

Four distinct layers were uncovered, all but one (Layer d) of which appeared to be post-medieval or modern in origin. Layer d produced a number of sherds of late medieval pottery, and the nature of the deposit indicated that it was late medieval in origin. A wall was uncovered in Trench 2. It was truncated both by the foundation trench of the existing cottage and a service pipe-trench. The wall was up to 1.5m long and at least 1.1m wide, although its exact width could not be measured as it appeared to continue into the adjacent property. Two rough courses of stone were revealed, standing to a maximum height of 0.43m. Given the apparent width of the wall, coupled with the fact that it appears to be associated only with Layer d, it is interpreted that the feature is the basal remains of the town wall defences.

Some fragmented disarticulated human bones were recovered both from Layer d and from the foundation trench of the existing cottage. Investigations by Clare Mullins (*Excavations 1995*, 47, 95E0279) revealed the presence of a cemetery *c.* 10m north-east of this site. It is speculated that this cemetery is associated with the Augustinian priory, situated, by tradition, outside the town defences. Given that the town defences may be later than the priory, it is probable that the disarticulated human bone comes from the cemetery site and that some of the skeletons were disturbed when the town wall was constructed, with some of the loose bone being deposited on the town side of the wall only to be disturbed once more when the present cottage was constructed.

Monitoring of groundworks associated with the development was undertaken on 3 May. No additional features were uncovered during this work, although additional human bone fragments were recovered, again from the backfill of the foundation trench associated with the existing cottage.

Arrangements were put in place to ensure the continued *in situ* preservation of the wall feature.
*Martin E. Byrne, 31 Millford, Athgarvan, Co. Kildare.*

### 411. FRIARY ROAD, NAAS
Urban medieval
64798 12182
SMR 19:30
98E0468 ext.

Excavations for the foundations of a building in the south-west corner of a development site on Friary Road, Naas, proceeded in early 1999. Testing and an earlier phase of monitoring had been carried out the previous year (*Excavations 1998*, 110).

Two features were noted during monitoring in this area. Feature A was originally revealed during test-trenching as a rectangular deposit of layers of red and yellow ash mixed with burnt clay, measuring 1.5m north–south by 0.5m deep. The excavation of the foundation trench revealed a maximum east–west dimension for this feature of 1.3m.

Feature B extended for a distance of 3.2m along the southern foundation trench in this area. It consisted of a layer of burnt red/orange clay 0.05–0.14m thick, over a layer of black, charred material 0.1–0.23m thick. This lay directly upon the natural gravels. The natural did not show any indication of burning. The entire feature was covered by 0.7m of gravel fill containing inclusions of red brick. Both features are probably associated with early modern domestic structures that stood on the site.
*Clare Mullins, 31 Millford, Athgarvan, Co. Kildare.*

### 412. MAULDINS, NAAS
Unknown
N919212
99E0468

The development site is *c.* 1.7km north-east of the centre of Naas, on the main Dublin road. Maudlins House is a large, two-storey house with an extension at the back and a verandah on the north side. It is listed in the County Kildare Development Plan. It would appear to be 18th/19th-century in date; a cursory examination of the exterior did not reveal features that would suggest an earlier date.

The development site, 3.15 acres, comprises the dwelling-house, with sheds on the other site of the driveway from the house and gardens surrounding the house on all other sides. There is a tennis court in the garden. There has been some landscaping in the garden, with terracing stretching northwards from the house. The site is surrounded by industrial estates on all sides.

The development comprised renovation and extensions to Maudlins House, along with the construction of office buildings and warehouses. An underground carpark is also planned. The sheds will be demolished. There will be access from the adjoining industrial estates.

The developer was required by the planning authority to carry out archaeological testing on the development site. The nearest recorded monument is SMR 19:21, which is listed as a 'graveyard site' and marked as a 'cemetery' on the OS 6-inch map. This lies c. 650m south-west of the development site, on the road into Naas. While there are no other known monuments marked for the townland, the townland name 'Maudlings' indicates that there may have been activity in the medieval period

Ten trenches tested the site. Glacial deposits ranging from pure gravel to pure sand were exposed. In the vicinity of the house was evidence for introduction and dumping of material associated with landscape terracing. Further away from the house the glacial deposits were overlain by topsoils and garden soils. Archaeological deposits were not observed.

*Rosanne Meenan, Roestown, Drumree, Co. Meath, for ADS Ltd.*

### 413. NEWBRIDGE ROAD, NAAS
Possible medieval
99E0259

Two trenches were opened north–south and east–west, by mechanical excavator, to assess the site for potential archaeological features before construction of a small development measuring 20m by 11m.

No evidence of an archaeological nature was revealed during the site assessment. Trench fill consisted of rubble infill with modern inclusions.

*Helen Kehoe, c/o Margaret Gowen & Co. Ltd, 2 Killiney View, Albert Road Lower, Glenageary, Co. Dublin.*

### 414. NEW ROW (REAR OF)/SOUTH MAIN STREET, NAAS
Urban medieval
288569 218970
99E0333

An archaeological evaluation was carried out at a proposed development site to the rear of New Row/South Main Street, Naas, on 17 July 1999. The work was undertaken in compliance with a request from the NMHPS, *Dúchas* The Heritage Service, following a pre-planning enquiry. The site is within the boundaries of the urban area of archaeological potential for Naas and is in the general environs of the presumed line of the town wall.

Ten trial-trenches were mechanically excavated within the confines of the development site. No features or structures of archaeological interest were uncovered during the testing.

*Martin E. Byrne, 31 Millford, Athgarvan, Co. Kildare.*

### 415. TONE'S PUBLIC HOUSE, 1 NORTH MAIN STREET, NAAS
Urban
99E0027

Testing was carried out at Tone's Public House, 1 Main Street, Naas, on 11 January 1999. One test-trench was mechanically excavated. It measured c. 2.8m x 0.65m on a north–south axis and was excavated to the depth of the upper surface of a natural shale deposit. No archaeological features were uncovered.

*Eoghan Moore for Arch-Tech, 32 Fitzwilliam Place, Dublin 2.*

### 416. 19 NORTH MAIN STREET, NAAS
Urban medieval
289161 219554
SMR 19:30
99E0055

An archaeological evaluation of a site at 19 North Main Street, Naas, was carried out on 13 March 1999 in response to a condition of planning. Planning permission had been granted for the demolition of the existing three-storey building and the construction of a three-storey over basement building. Testing was carried out following the demolition of the previously existing structures.

The property boundaries in the area appear to preserve the medieval burgage plot pattern. The site consists of a rectangular street-frontage property measuring c. 6m along the street front by 12m from front to rear. Testing was limited to the rear half of the site, as a basement already existed towards the street front.

Four small test-trenches were excavated along two proposed trench lines. The total area opened during testing was somewhat restricted because of the unstable nature of the gable walls of the adjoining buildings. In the main, the remaining soil profile within the test-trenches was undisturbed natural. However, what was interpreted as a layer of archaeological material was identified on the south-western side of the site at a distance of c. 4m from the rear site boundary and 1.2m from the side boundary on the south-west. This layer was a brown/black, silty clay with stone, containing inclusions of animal bone and shell. It occurred at a depth of 1m beneath the existing ground surface, which corresponded with the floor level of the recent building. It was a minimum of 0.3m deep, and it appeared that the layer was bottoming out at this level. The layer appeared to be localised within the site. A similar but less well-defined layer was found in another test-trench c. 2m to the north-east, but it could not be determined conclusively whether this represented an archaeological layer as there had been some disturbance in this area.

Construction of the proposed building and associated basement was to involve the reduction of levels on the site. Accordingly, excavation of the archaeological layer identified in Test-trench 4 was recommended, as well as archaeological monitoring of all ground reduction. Because of the apparent localised nature of the archaeological layer that was identified, and also because of the unstable state of the gable walls of the properties adjoining the site, it was recommended that excavation of this archaeological layer be carried out in conjunction with the general reduction of levels on the site.

*Clare Mullins, 31 Millford, Athgarvan, Co. Kildare.*

### 417. 19 NORTH MAIN STREET, NAAS
Urban medieval
289161 219554
SMR 19:30
99E0055 ext.

Following testing at Naas Credit Union, where an isolated pocket of archaeological layers was identified (see No. 416 above), excavation commenced in April 1999. Because of the isolated and apparently nebulous nature of the archaeological layers, and also because of the unstable nature of the gable walls of the surrounding buildings, excavation was carried out in conjunction with monitoring of ground-level reduction of the surrounding area.

The archaeological layer identified during testing proved to represent the upper layer of a pit that extended to a depth of 1.4m. The top of this pit was at a depth of 0.6m beneath the present ground surface and, while the edges of the pit were difficult to define, it was irregularly square with dimensions of c. 1.4–1.6m each way. The pit had been truncated on the north and east sides, and there was a tendency to over-cut the remaining edges, but the southern side of the pit showed an almost sheer-vertical drop.

Three distinct layers could be discerned within the fill. The uppermost was a sandy, stony clay with occasional charcoal flecks. The central and most distinctive layer followed the contours of the cut; it consisted of a dark brown, silty clay mixed with natural and contained inclusions of frequent charcoal flecks, frequent animal bone and some oyster shell; this layer produced several sherds of medieval pottery, all found close to each other. The lower layer was almost indistinguishable from the natural, being composed of a sandy gravel, and would have been dismissed as natural were it not for the occurrence of a conspicuous lens of mortar running almost horizontally through it close to the base. Another lens of mortar occurred as an interface between the central and basal layers of the pit. The pit lay beneath 0.5m of disturbed soil, which formed the floor level of the pre-existing building.

Monitoring of general ground-level reduction and the excavation of two column bases within the boundary of the property to the south were also undertaken. The results of monitoring did not reveal further archaeological material.

*Clare Mullins, 31 Millford, Athgarvan, Co. Kildare.*

### 418. ST MARY'S COLLEGE, NAAS
Urban medieval
**289090 219493**
**99E0689**

An archaeological evaluation was carried out at a proposed development site at St Mary's College, Naas, Co. Kildare, on 27 November 1999. The work was undertaken in compliance with a request from the NMHPS, *Dúchas* The Heritage Service. The development, which consists of a two-storey extension to existing school buildings, is in the immediate environs of the town defences and Dominican friary and to the immediate north-west of a motte.

Three trenches were excavated by machine. The development is on the edge of existing basketball courts, the groundworks of which reduced the area by up to c. 1m below the original ground surface.

No features, structures or deposits of archaeological interest were uncovered during the evaluation, although a base sherd of medieval/post-medieval date was recovered.

*Martin E. Byrne, 31 Millford, Athgarvan, Co. Kildare.*

### 419. PROSPEROUS–ROBERTSTOWN WATER IMPROVEMENT SCHEME
Within zones of archaeological potential
**SMR 13:7–10, 13:13, 13:14, 13:16, 13:17**
**99E0085**

An archaeological assessment was conducted in March 1999 on a section of the Prosperous to Robertstown Water Improvement Scheme, which bisected Mulhall's Fort (SMR 13:17) along an existing road. The southern half of the fort and a segment of the northern portion remained extant, while the road and two houses and gardens had greatly disturbed its interior. The assessment was conducted before further disturbance, as it was anticipated that deeper archaeological strata may survive below the road. The fort itself measures 80m in maximum diameter.

Two trenches were excavated along the proposed pipeline and road verge to a depth of 1.4m. Two body sherds of 19th-century ceramic were recovered from one trench amongst disturbed boulder clay. The second trench crossed the western extent of the fort. No features or artefacts associated with the fort were uncovered. That the ditch was not exposed would suggest that the area had been greatly disturbed by the road construction. Consequently, it was recommended that archaeological monitoring of the route would be sufficient to identify any further features of archaeological significance along the proposed route.

A single trench, 1m wide, was excavated by machine along the route of the pipeline to accommodate a single water main and four telecom ducts within the road and verge to an average depth of 1.4m.

A 2km stretch of the scheme, between Prosperous and Blackwood crossroads, was monitored between 8 November 1999 and 30 January 2000. The natural glacial sand and gravel were exposed directly below the tarmac and hardcore layer of the roadway at an average depth of 0.3m. No archaeological features or deposits were uncovered.

The remainder of the scheme was monitored from 8 January to 15 March 2000 from Blackwood crossroads to Mulhall's Fort. A single trench 1m wide and up to 1.5m deep was excavated along the road and the road margin. The tarmac and hardcore extended to a depth of 0.3m and overlay the natural glacial sand, gravel and boulder clay. The final stretch of the pipeline between Mulhall's Fort and Robertstown was completed on 15 March 2000. Monitoring of this stretch revealed that the tarmac and hardcore deposits of the bog road extended to a depth of 0.25m and overlay an extensive layer of natural, black peat. This extended to an average depth of 1.4m and overlay the natural, grey, marly clay. No archaeological features were exposed, and no finds were recovered.

The excavation of the trench close to the various recorded sites along the route and through Mulhall's Fort did not reveal any archaeological stratigraphy. Similarly, the excavation of the pipe-trench across the dry canal bed did not reveal any features, deposits or finds.

*Ian Russell and Donald Murphy, Archaeological Consultancy Services Ltd, 15 Trinity Street, Drogheda, Co. Louth.*

### 420. MULLATINE, RATHANGAN
Adjacent to urban medieval area
**266956 219069**
**99E0728**

Monitoring was undertaken at a residential development site at Mullatine, Rathangan, Co.

Kildare, from 3 to 12 November 1999. The site is immediately to the south of the zone of archaeological potential of Rathangan (SMR 17–11), a town with early medieval origins and subsequent Anglo-Norman activity.

The monitoring of ground reductions associated with the development indicated that the topsoil was 0.25–0.4m deep. In addition, the undisturbed subsoils were reduced by up to 0.1m.

No features, structures or deposits of archaeological interest or potential were uncovered during the monitoring. However, a total of 56 sherds of pottery were recovered. It is probable that such pottery was introduced to the site from the nearby village. Analysis of the pottery sherds, undertaken by Clare McCutcheon, indicated that 25 were medieval (Leinster cooking ware and locally(?) made glazed and unglazed wares) and one was a 17th-century sherd from North Devon, with the remainder dating to the 18th/19th centuries.

*Martin E. Byrne, 31 Millford, Athgarvan, Co. Kildare.*

## 421. TIMOLIN, SITE 10
No archaeological significance
28035 19625
99E0203

This was one of a series of archaeological investigations carried out on the proposed route of the N9 Realignment at Moone–Timolin–Ballitore Hill. An irregularity in a field boundary, partly enclosing a circular area, was noted in the initial paper survey. It was not on the line of the proposed road, but a series of ten cuttings, measuring 10m by 1.8m, was mechanically excavated along the line of the road. Nothing of archaeological significance was found in any of the cuttings, and the field boundary proved to be a hedge enclosing a disused sandpit.

*Thaddeus C. Breen, 13 Wainsfort Crescent, Dublin 6W, for Valerie J. Keeley.*

## 422. TIMOLIN, SITE 38
Scatter of medieval pottery
27980 19340
99E0203

This was one of a series of archaeological investigations carried out on the proposed route of the N9 Realignment at Moone–Timolin–Ballitore Hill. A series of low earthen banks or mounds was noted in the initial paper survey. Four cuttings were excavated, investigating different parts of the feature. No structural remains were found: the 'banks' and 'mounds' were irregularities left by gravel-digging. Some scattered medieval pottery was found in the topsoil, along with a few metal objects of unknown date.

*Thaddeus C. Breen, 13 Wainsfort Crescent, Dublin 6W, for Valerie J. Keeley.*

## 423. TIMOLIN, SITE 42
Earthwork
27955 19355
99E0203

This was one of a series of archaeological investigations carried out in connection with the N9 Realignment at Moone–Timolin–Ballitore Hill. Ancillary drainage works will pass between the stream known as Bothoge and a raised, D-shaped or circular area that appears to be an artificial earthwork. Seven cuttings, measuring 10m by 1.8m, were mechanically excavated along the area to be affected. The field is marshy, and the cuttings uncovered successive layers of gravel and peat.

One of the cuttings extended into the edge of the D-shaped feature, although the latter seemed rather irregular at this point. It consisted of gravel, which appeared to be undisturbed, with stones within it following a natural bedding as though laid down under water. The only find from this site was an iron horseshoe of uncertain date.

*Thaddeus C. Breen, 13 Wainsfort Crescent, Dublin 6W, for Valerie J. Keeley.*

## 424. TIMOLIN, SITE 43
Bronze Age cemetery and medieval pottery scatter
27980 19385
99E0203

This was one of a series of archaeological investigations carried out on the proposed route of the N9 Realignment at Moone–Timolin–Ballitore Hill. Site 43 proper was a low mound, half of which was on the line of the road, but, as cist burials had previously been found on either side of the line of the road, it was decided to investigate the entire area. The site of a slip road adjoining the present road was also investigated because a further cist grave was said to have been found at the foot of a standing stone near the present road.

A geophysical survey of the relevant areas pinpointed a number of potential features, and eight cuttings, 2m x 2m, were dug by hand on the sites indicated. Only one of these showed any structural remains, and that appeared to be a recent feature, near the present road. However, a large amount of medieval pottery was found here in the topsoil. It may be significant that the Fair Green is recorded as having been near here.

After the eight cuttings had been excavated, the relevant parts of the route were completely stripped by machine. Two small burnt spreads were found, as well as traces of drains and lazy-beds that had been shown in the geophysical survey. Further medieval pottery was found scattered around the field, presumably spread by ploughing.

When Site 43 proper, a low circular mound, was being stripped, a pit burial was exposed, and the remainder of the half of the mound to be affected by the road was excavated by hand. A further pit and two cists were found.

The first pit, Feature 6, was subrectangular, 1.3m x 0.9m, and 0.2m deep. It contained the remains of a child, five to seven years old. The bones were not burnt but were broken and disarticulated. This appeared to be the result of later disturbance, as some of the bones were found between three overlapping flat stones that had collapsed into the pit.

The second pit, Feature 8, was also subrectangular, 1.9m x 1.1m, but the lower part was smaller and almost triangular. The overall depth was 0.43m. Some flat slabs of stone were found near the top. This pit had certainly been disturbed, as only two fragments of cremated bone were found in it, along with part of a clay pipe stem.

One cist, Feature 7, comprised four stone slabs forming the walls (1.2m x 0.8m) and a capstone that was somewhat bigger than the cist proper. There was no floor stone. It contained a crouched inhumation, with no grave-goods. The skeleton lay on its right, facing west, with the head at the southern end. It was identified as the remains of a woman aged 25–35.

The second cist, Feature 9, was polygonal, with a stone base. No capstone was present, but there was an outer wall of slabs sloping inwards at an angle of about 30°. The cist was shallow, only 0.2–0.23m deep, and was filled with a mixture of soil and cremated bone. Cremated bone was also found beneath the floor stone and between the inner and outer walls. The cremation represented the remains of two adults and one child. They were accompanied by two pots: an upright vase and an undecorated vessel, inverted. The cist proper measured 1.4m x 0.86m; the overall dimensions including the outer walls were 1.6m x 1.4m.

*Thaddeus C. Breen, 13 Wainsfort Crescent, Dublin 6W, for Valerie J. Keeley.*

### 425. TIMOLIN
Possible castle site
280015 193289
SMR 36:026
99E0558

An archaeological evaluation was carried out at a proposed development site at Timolin, Co. Kildare, on 7 October 1999. The work was undertaken in compliance with a request for additional information in respect of a planning application to construct six houses on the site.

Six trenches were excavated by machine at the site, which is within the confines of a castle site. No features, deposits or structures, either associated with or independent of the castle, were uncovered. However, a total of eighteen sherds of pottery, all of which appear to be of medieval date, were recovered during the evaluation. Consequently, it was recommended that monitoring of groundworks should be undertaken if planning permission was granted.

*Martin E. Byrne, 31 Millford, Athgarvan, Co. Kildare.*

## KILKENNY

### 426. BAUNLUSK–BALLYCONRA GAS PIPELINE
Monitoring
2434 1720–2486 1495
99E0388

Archaeological monitoring of a Bord Gáis Éireann gas pipeline from Baunlusk to Ballyconra townlands, Co. Kilkenny, was carried out between July and September 1999. The development connects the Glanbia Factory at Ballyconra, near Ballyragget, with an interconnector at Baunlusk, on the main Dublin to Cork gas main, 5km south-west of Kilkenny City. Construction involved the excavation of a 22.5km-long and 20m-wide corridor.

The pipeline covered a total of 26 townlands and 9 parishes in the baronies of Crannagh, Fassidinan, Galmoy and Shillelogher, within the ancient kingdom of Ossory. As a result of the initial environmental impact statement and subsequent archaeological monitoring of this development, thirteen (possibly fourteen) previously unrecorded archaeological monuments were discovered, consisting of *fulachta fiadh,* possible ring-barrows, a flat cremation and an ironworking site.

Monitoring of construction produced eight previously unknown archaeological sites. Seven of these were excavated under separate licences and are detailed in separate reports below (see Nos 427, 430, 431, 433, 437, 459 and 460). The remaining site, Parkmore 1, was backfilled, fenced off and avoided by development. This site was a possible *fulacht fiadh* (NGR 248062 151684, 77.41m OD) consisting of a burnt mound over 12m long and 6m wide, possibly orientated east–west, running into the south and west bulks. The site is in the northern corner of the field. Five individual, isolated pit or post-hole features were also revealed, which represent either outlying features of further archaeological sites or isolated activity.

*Paul Stevens for Margaret Gowen & Co. Ltd, 2 Killiney View, Albert Road Lower, Glenageary, Co. Dublin.*

### 427. BONNETSTOWN
*Fulacht fiadh*
245686 158793
99E0601

This site was revealed during archaeological monitoring of a Bord Gáis Éireann gas pipeline development (see No. 426 above). The site was 5km north-west of Kilkenny City, at an elevation of 148m OD, the highest on the pipeline. Bonnetstown townland is on an eastern ridge of the Slieve Ardagh foothills, overlooking Kilkenny City and the Nore valley. Excavation was carried out in August 1999 before development.

This site extended east and west beyond the area of excavation and consisted of a heavily denuded *fulacht fiadh* with a thin spread of ash and burnt mound material and a small oblong trough or pit, bisected by a modern field boundary. The underlying natural was limestone bedrock and glacial, orange/brown boulder clay, with steeply undulating peaty soils and rough pastureland.

A small pit feature (possibly representing a trough), towards the west of the site, was oblong in plan with a concave profile. It was orientated north-east/south-west, was 1.5m long, 0.75m wide and 0.2m deep, and contained a backfill of burnt mound material of fire-cracked sandstone (50%, 0.06–0.15m in individual diameter) and silty clay (50%). A stake-hole was found 0.37m to the south-east of this pit and was circular in plan with a U-shaped profile.

The denuded burnt mound was irregular and patchy, with areas of dark grey ash and charcoal, fire-cracked sandstone (0.15–0.06m in individual diameters), gravel and dark brown silt. The mound, which was not visible before excavation, covered an area of 9m+ east–west (continuing under the west baulk), 11m north–south and 0.1m in truncated depth.

The insertion of a bank and ditch field boundary, post-dating the 1839–40 1st edition OS map, both bisected and levelled this site. A scattered layer of mound material, builders' rubble and gravel represented the construction phase of the field boundary.

*Paul Stevens for Margaret Gowen & Co. Ltd, 2 Killiney View, Albert Road Lower, Glenageary, Co. Dublin.*

### 428. TINNANAMOONA, CHAPEL LANE, CALLAN
Urban medieval and post-medieval
24149 14325
99E0232

An archaeological assessment was requested to provide additional information ahead of granting planning permission for a proposed housing development at Tinnanamoona, on the edge of Callan. The site was a field between the line of the inner town wall and the line of an outer defence (on a map of 1681).

Four trenches were opened, and two boundary walls (on the lines of the town walls) were recorded. There were no visible remains of the medieval town walls (or fosses) around any side of the site.

The excavation of test-trenches against the east and south boundary walls and in the footprint of the proposed houses suggests that the field was never occupied by town suburbs. The outer defence on the 1681 map would have enclosed green fields.

An infilled ditch c. 2m wide was uncovered close to (and below) the south boundary, on the line of the outer defence, but with no sign of an upcast bank in the field. The ditch may have been a defensive trench with a bank upcast on the outside but is more likely to have been an open field drain or a roadside drain. The town defence may be completely obscured by the present road.

The trench against the east boundary wall, on the line of the inner defence, uncovered a ditch close to the wall. An upcast bank may be under and beyond the wall. The ditch was exposed but not excavated, and no finds were recovered.

A large hollow intercepted in the south-east corner of the site with a burnt clay edge, infilled with recent material, is likely to be associated with quarrying and industrial activity. Further excavation ahead of the development and monitoring of groundworks was recommended by Dúchas.
*Jo Moran, ArchaeoGrafix, Church Lane, Stradbally, Co. Waterford.*

### 429. MILL STREET, CALLAN
Urban medieval
99E0053

Test-trenching was carried out on the site of Callan Credit Union, on the northern side of Mill Street, in compliance with a condition of planning. The site was within the zone of archaeological potential for Callan town. The medieval street-plan of Callan is cross-linear, and Mill Street forms the western route.

A trench, 5m north–south by 5m and 1m wide, was opened on the footprint of the foundations of the proposed extension. A mixed layer of rubble had accumulated on a horizon of brown and yellow clays. No archaeological stratigraphy was recorded in the trench.
*Jacinta Kiely, Eachtra Archaeological Projects, Clover Hill, Mallow, Co. Cork.*

### 430. CASTLEBLUNDEN
Flat cremation pit
247265 154044
99E0756

This site was revealed in Castleblunden townland, 4km south-west of Kilkenny City, during archaeological monitoring of a Bord Gáis Éireann gas pipeline development (see No. 426 above). Excavation was carried out in August 1999 before development. Castleblunden townland is part of St Patrick's parish and takes its name from the Cromwellian Overington Blunded, who was granted the lands in 1653.

A single cremation pit was found 38m south of the source of the Stony Stream. The underlying yellow, glacial boulder clay was cut by the small, partially truncated, circular pit, which had a concave profile and measured 0.5m in diameter and 0.1m in depth. The pit contained a uniform charcoal-rich fill with occasional pebbles and small stones, with 40% of the deposit composed of crushed cremated human bone, measuring 5–20mm in diameter, distributed throughout the fill but with concentrations to the middle and sides.
*Paul Stevens for Margaret Gowen & Co. Ltd, 2 Killiney View, Albert Road Lower, Glenageary, Co. Dublin.*

### 431. CASTLEINCH: 1
*Fulacht fiadh*
247534 153117
99E0603

This site is in the townland of Castleinch, or Inchyolaghan, in the parish of Castleinch, 4km south-west of Kilkenny City. The area is a flat plain stretching east of the Slieve Ardagh Hills to Kilkenny City and the Nore valley, and the site is 60m south of the Breagagh River. The site was partially exposed during archaeological monitoring of a Bord Gáis Éireann gas pipeline development (see No. 426 above). Excavation was carried out in August and September 1999 before development.

The site was a partially truncated *fulacht fiadh* with stratified burnt mound continuing east of the area of excavation. The site contained two troughs, a possible working surface, a mound of unused boiling stones, a buried sod and a smaller boiling pit. The underlying limestone bedrock was covered by yellow/brown boulder clay, with areas of iron-panning.

Trough A was to the north-west of the site and was an irregular ovoid or pear-shaped pit with vertical north and east sides, a straight, steep southern side and a flat base. It was 1.1m long, 0.75m wide and 0.5m deep, orientated north-east/south-west, but was possibly recut and may have originally been circular or square. It contained a primary silting of fine, grey sand with charcoal, sealed by large, sub-rounded stones (sandstone cobbles: 20% fire-cracked) and fragmented cattle bone in grey/black, silty sand, possibly representing the last firing of this trough. This in turn was sealed by an upper backfill of burnt mound material.

Trough B was 3m south-east of, and post-dated, Trough A. It was a shallow, subrectangular pit with square profile and flat base, measuring 1.8m+ in excavated length, 1.5m in width and 0.25m in depth. Four post-holes and two stake-holes were cut into the base of this trough around the western edge in an irregular pattern, and two were cut across the centre, possibly representing the staves or sails of a decayed or removed wooden lining. Each post-hole was filled by a grey/black, silty clay with fire-cracked stone and charcoal. All these cuts had tapering profiles, suggesting that the uprights they contained were sharpened. The trough was filled by a single, uniform backfill of burnt mound material, the basal part of which was substantially wetter than the upper part, suggesting that the trough successfully cut below the water-table.

An oval pit with concave profile was found north of Trough B, within the area of the burnt mound. It was over 0.6m long, 0.5m wide and 0.2m deep, orientated east–west. It contained a dark grey/brown, sandy silt clay with occasional fire-cracked stone, charcoal and gravel and produced a possible bronze swan-necked pin.

A scattered area of similar-sized, partially heat-affected sandstone (with very occasional limestone measuring less than 0.2m) represented a collection of unused boiling stones (C18). The stone, selected for geology and size, was heated but not cracked through contact with cold water and therefore either not used in the boiling process or used only once in the latter stages of the simmering process and not reused.

An intermittent layer of mid-brown, silty clay (C19) lay north-east of the stone scatter and represented a soil dump, possibly associated with a residual buried sod, measuring 2m in exposed length, 1.5m in width and 0.1m in depth.

A possible platform or working surface was found to the east of Trough B, covering C18 and C19. The surface consisted of a compacted area of redeposited, natural boulder clay with occasional charcoal flecks, measuring 4m in exposed length, 3m in exposed width and 0.2m in depth.

The partly truncated oblong and concave mound sealed these features and continued under the baulk to the west. The mound (which was not visible before excavation) covered an area of over 10m north–south, 7m+ east–west, with a truncated depth of 0.45m, and was made up of fire-cracked sandstone (0.1–0.25m in individual diameter), charcoal and silt. Within the top of the mound were isolated lenses of dark grey clay, 0.1m thick. These and the mound were sealed by a layer of compacted, grey/brown, friable, silty sand with charcoal, gravel and fire-cracked stone, 3m in diameter, 0.1m deep, possibly representing a buried sod line or soil dump.

Modern activity on this site was evidenced by two pipe-trenches cutting across the northern and western portion of the site.

Paul Stevens for Margaret Gowen & Co. Ltd, 2 Killiney View, Albert Road Lower, Glenageary, Co. Dublin.

### 432. ARCON MINE (GALMOY), CASTLETOWN
Proximity to *fulachta fiadh* and medieval castle
**226930 172790**
**99E0753**
Monitoring of topsoil-stripping and associated plant excavations was carried out at the Arcon Mines, Galmoy, Co. Kilkenny. The topsoil-stripping formed part of the works associated with the construction of a new tailings pond at the mine. During the construction of the first tailings pond in 1996, a number of *fulachta fiadh*/burnt mounds were recorded, as well as a corn-drying kiln with associated industrial activity.

No archaeological features were identified during the monitoring in 1999, but three possible *fulachta fiadh* sites were identified in January 2000, which will require excavation.

Tim Coughlan, Margaret Gowen & Co. Ltd, 2 Killiney View, Albert Road Lower, Glenageary, Co. Dublin.

### 433. CLONMANTAGH CASTLE, CLONMANTAGH LOWER
Settlement
**23484 16388**
**SMR 13:2**
**98E0597 ext.**
Monitoring of excavations for services and drainage was undertaken at Clonmantagh Castle from 12 to 26 January 1999. The proposed development comprised the refurbishment of a 19th-century farmhouse and part refurbishment of the adjoining late medieval tower-house. The refurbishment programme was undertaken by the Irish Landmark Trust.

No archaeological deposits were encountered during monitoring, but this is hardly surprising given the extensive ground disturbances associated with the construction of the farmhouse and subsequent farmyard developments. However, the excavations did provide the opportunity to observe the foundations of the west and south walls of the tower-house. The foundations are composed of two to four courses of unhewn limestone boulders. They are 0.75m high and rest on the light brown, natural, sandy clay and gravel. The top of the foundation forms a plinth, 0.2m wide, at the base of the tower. It was also established that the modern concrete-framed window at the east end of the south wall of the tower occupies the site of an earlier door, which was probably inserted when the adjoining farmhouse was built. The threshold of the 19th-century doorway survives. A ditch feature, 3.8m wide and *c.* 1.5m deep, possibly representing an infilled moat, was observed in the trench section immediately outside the east wall of the bawn. Unfortunately the narrowness of the trench and unstable ground conditions prevented detailed examination of this feature.

A number of interesting observations were made during the refurbishment project. It is clear that there was originally a large rectangular building, a hall or soft house, attached to the east side of the tower. The roof-line of the west gable of the 'hall' is visible on the east wall of the tower, and the north wall of the 'hall' is incorporated into the 19th-century farmhouse (this is evident from the thickness and pronounced batter of this wall). Examination of the north-east and south-east angles of the tower indicates that the 'hall' was bonded to the tower immediately above the top of the base batter. This is particularly evident at the north-east, where some of the tie-stones project from the angle of the tower. The angle immediately above the batter at the south-east is rebuilt with roughly hewn blocks. It seems likely that the original tie-stones were deliberately removed and the angle rebuilt to preserve the uniform appearance of the angle of the tower. The fact that the 'hall' was bonded to the tower suggests that the buildings are contemporary. Excavations on the site of the south wall of the 'hall' revealed only slight traces of its foundation, suggesting that it was removed when the farmhouse was built.

A dendrochronological report on oak wood samples from the castle suggests that the tower-house was built *c.* 1525 (David Brown, The Queen's

Roof line of hall on east wall of tower at Clonmantagh Castle.

University of Belfast, February 1999). This date supports Carrigan's (1905) assertion that the castle belonged to Piers Butler, earl of Ormond (d. 1539). It is interesting to note that the closest parallel for the tower and hall structure at Clonmantagh is found in the 15th-century enclosure castle at Granny, Co. Kilkenny, which was also built by the Butler family.

*Reference*
Carrigan, W.C.C. 1905 *The history and antiquities of the Diocese of Ossory.*

*Dominic Delany, 31 Ashbrook, Oranmore, Co. Galway.*

### 434. CASTLETOWN, GALMOY
17th-century earthen fortification
226966 172747
99E0205

A possible Cromwellian or Jacobean earthwork fort was discovered during an envrionmental impact study for the Arcon Lead–Zinc Mine at Galmoy. The fort was archaeologically tested but revealed no evidence of date (Gowen 1990). Subsequent monitoring of construction (Pollock 1996) revealed ten *fulachta fiadh*, as well as late medieval/early post-medieval activity south-west of the fort. Archaeological excavation of this site took place in May and June 1999, to facilitate the proposed expansion of the existing tailings pond facility.

Excavation confirmed the site to be an earthen outwork fortification or 'redoubt', probably 17th-century in date, with a pentagonal plan, two demi-bastions on one side and a hornwork protecting the entranceway.

Two opposing quadrants of the site (Areas 1 and 2) were initially stripped of topsoil. Excavation of Area 1 had concluded when all work was halted in favour of preservation, and the site was fenced off from any development. Three phases of this site were identified.

Phase 1 represented the pre-construction levels of the site. Natural was a fine, grey, glacial sand overlain by yellow/orange, sandy boulder clay and cut by several isolated features that pre-dated the fortification. These included several furrows, a buried sod line and two undated post-holes.

Phase 2 represented the construction and use of the earthwork. The interior was lowered by deliberate removal of the old sod and subsoil. There was no evidence of structures or occupation layers within the interior, and the limited artefactual evidence suggested that the site was not in use for a prolonged period. The main defensive bank partially survived as an intermittent concave mound, 0.6m in maximum height. The bank was made of successive deposits of cobbles, gravel and redeposited, natural sand. These were piled up against a supporting palisade fence, evidenced by a number of post-holes and stake-holes including the main corner posts, braces and supports for a retaining timber palisade across the inner ditch face.

The enclosing ditch turned through 60° to give a diamond-shaped/pentagonal plan. Two salient-angled demi-bastions were noted at the north and west corners of the circuit. Five deep trenches were excavated through this V-shaped ditch. Each demi-bastion face was 7.5m long and protruded into the ditch. The base of the recess between the demi-bastions was flat, with a low bank within the base of the ditch, continuing the line of the ditch. The outer face of the north-west ditch was steep, 5m wide and 2m deep, and contained two basal fills of orange, sandy clay silt and stony, silty clay with bone. The north-eastern ditch was parallel-sided and V-shaped in profile and was 5.5m wide and 2.6m deep. Here, it cut a buried sod line and was itself truncated by modern activity. The basal fills for this portion of the ditch were iron-panned, stony, coarse sand with large cobbles.

A metalled surface extended through a break in the ditch, which was protected by a small, east–west, linear gully, 15m long, 1.3m wide and 0.6m deep, terminating at a large post-hole. This represented one side of an outer defensive hornwork and gatepost.

Evidence of a low, truncated outer 'counterscarp' bank survived along the north-west face of the fort, made up of various dumps of earth and possibly revetted with stone. It was 2.6m wide and 0.3m deep. Behind the counterscarp bank was evidence for an outer palisade constructed to form a 'covered way'. Elsewhere evidence was truncated by modern disturbance.

Phase 3 represented the destruction of the site. The fort was burned and partially levelled by pushing the inner and outer banks into the partially silted-up ditch, probably a deliberate act by the builders. It is also possible that the fort was destroyed in battle; however, no cannon or musket balls were found in this excavation.

The quality of the bastions and the crude hornwork both suggest that the site was hastily thrown up and not meant to be permanent. A larger bastioned fortification at Longford Pass, Co. Tipperary, is 13.5km south of the site and was built before 1654. This is referred to as 'Fort Ireton', after Henry Ireton, who was involved in Cromwell's campaign of 1650 and 1651 (Kerrigan 1995, 133).

Castletown townland and Coady's Castle (SMR 3:4/1–5) were reportedly forfeited by E. Shee under Cromwell (Carrigan 1905, 281). Local legend tells of a grant by Cromwell to Pierce MacOdo (Coady) of all the land he could see (including Castletown) (Dowling 1978, 24). The earthwork therefore probably formed part of the refortification of Coady's Castle after 1655, which included the addition of a spear-shaped defensive bastion.

Excavation produced a small assemblage of animal bone and some military and domestic artefacts, tentatively dated to the 17th or 18th centuries. In addition, a number of sherds of prehistoric coarseware and a possible rubbing stone for a saddle quern were also recovered from the upper ditch fills, suggesting prehistoric occupation close by.

*References*
Carrigan, W.C.C. 1905 *The history and antiquities of the Diocese of Ossory.*
Dowling, A. 1978 *An outline of Galmoy (Gabbal Maoth) Parish situated in the Kingdom of Ossory.*
Gowen, M. 1990 Trial investigation of a possible archaeological site at the Galmoy Prospect, Co. Kilkenny. Unpublished report.
Kerrigan, P.M. 1995 *Castles and fortifications in Ireland 1485–1945.*
Pollock, D. 1996 Archaeological monitoring of topsoil removal at Galmoy, Co. Kilkenny. Unpublished report.

*Paul Stevens for Margaret Gowen & Co. Ltd, 2 Killiney View, Albert Road Lower, Glenageary, Co. Dublin.*

### 435. ST MARY'S CHURCH, GOWRAN
Medieval church
26325 15345
98E0112

Holes were cut in the floor of the roofed chancel at St Mary's Church, Gowran, to take underfloor heating and foundations for relocated tombs. The roofs of two burial vaults (early 19th century) were exposed on the north side; elsewhere excavations to c. 0.4m did not reach the base of demolition material associated with rebuilding the chancel in the early 19th century.

*Dave Pollock, ArchaeoGrafix, Church Lane, Stradbally, Co. Waterford.*

### 436. GRAIGUENAMANAGH
Urban medieval
99E0033

Two test-trenches were opened in January 1999. Following the removal of topsoil to a depth of 0.15m, subsoil was reached. Nothing of an archaeological nature was noted.

*Sheila Lane, 1 Charlemont Heights, Coach Hill, Rochestown, Cork.*

### 437. GRANGE
*Fulacht fiadh*
243472 169597
99E0600

This site is 1.5km south-west of Ballyragget and was revealed during archaeological monitoring of a Bord Gáis Éireann gas pipeline development (see No. 426 above). Excavation was carried out in August 1999 before development. The site lay within a significant cluster of archaeological sites, all within 1km of the site: two or three other possible *fulachta fiadh*, two possible ring-barrows, a ring-ditch complex and five enclosure sites.

This site extended beyond the area of excavation and consisted of a heavily denuded *fulacht fiadh*, with patches of burnt mound spread, a large and a small truncated circular trough and a small pit feature, all partially truncated by modern and post-medieval drainage activity. Natural subsoil on the site was orange/brown boulder clay. The underlying topography was undulating land along the western flood-plain of the River Nore. The site was also 75m south of a small stream.

Trough A was a heavily truncated subcircular trough, situated to the west, with a concave profile and a flat, regular base. It measured 2.5–3.6m in diameter and 0.75m in depth and contained a deliberate backfill of burnt mound material, which decommissioned the trough.

Trough B was a small pit-trough, within the centre of the site, partly truncated by a pipe-trench. It was oval with concave sides and a flat base. It measured 1.5m north–south by 1.3m by 0.3m deep and was also deliberately backfilled by burnt mound material, with a high charcoal content.

A third feature was a small, circular pit stratigraphically sealed by the burnt mound, 0.6m south of Trough A. It had a concave profile and measured 1m in diameter and 0.3m in depth, filled by a dark grey, silty clay with burnt mound material inclusions.

The truncated and heavily ploughed-out roughly circular mound was made up of fire-cracked sandstone measuring between 0.2m and 0.15m in individual diameters, with charcoal lumps and dark brown, silty clay. The mound, which was not visible before excavation, covered an area of over 12.5m east–west (continuing under both baulks), 12m north–south and 0.1m in truncated depth.

Following the decommissioning of the site (by pushing the mound into the troughs), the resulting hollow silted up with a dark grey, silty peat post-dating the burnt mound. Modern and possibly earlier, post-medieval drainage activity on this site was evidenced by a number of pipe-trenches and drainage ditches criss-crossing the site.

*Paul Stevens for Margaret Gowen & Co. Ltd, 2 Killiney View, Albert Road Lower, Glenageary, Co. Dublin.*

### 438. GRANNY AND AGLISH NORTH
Burnt spread
99E0466

Monitoring of topsoil-stripping was carried out as part of the Kilmacow Quarry Development and pursuant to planning permission. The monitoring commenced in late August 1999 and continued very occasionally throughout autumn 1999. Works ceased in winter 1999 and will resume in spring 2000.

Two areas that required monitoring measured 140m by 50m and 350m by 220m. Between 15% and 20% was monitored during 1999, with the remainder to be monitored in 2000. The nearest point in the larger area is 8m from the outer edges of the constraint area for an archaeological site (SMR 43:02301 and 43:02302—two *fulachta fiadh*).

A total of 0.6m of topsoil and the upper level of subsoil were removed. Other than the occasional stray finds, modern pottery (chinaware, porcelain and kitchen delph), modern glass and broken clay pipes, nothing of archaeological significance was found in the smaller of the two areas looked at. However, in the second, larger area, nearest the archaeological site, a spread of charcoal was found beneath the topsoil. It measured 0.6m by 0.4m and was 0.15m thick and 0.15m below ground level. It had no clear or defined shape. A small number of burnt stones were in the midst of the charcoal. The burning appeared to occur *in situ*. It was not possible to determine whether it could be associated with the *fulacht fiadh*, *c.* 200m away.

Work will resume in spring 2000.

*Mary Henry, 24 Queen Street, Clonmel, Co. Tipperary.*

### 439. EVAN'S HOME, BARRACK LANE, KILKENNY
Urban medieval
25080 15610
SMR 19:26:68
99E0662

Archaeological assessment was carried out in December 1999 to the rear of Evan's Home, immediately north-west of St John's Priory. The site is on the eastern bank of the River Nore at the northern corner of the medieval suburb of St John's. The remains of the Blessed Lady Chapel of the priory (*c.* 1290) were incorporated into the present Church of Ireland St John's Church in 1817. Evan's Home is a fine, large, two-storey building built *c.* 1750 as the Infantry Barracks and converted to Evan's Asylum in 1818.

Three test-trenches were opened across the site; Trench 1 extended parallel to Evan's Home, 1.3m from the boundary wall with St John's Priory. It revealed stratified medieval layers, which contained a number of medieval floor tiles, pottery and bone. These were cut by a limestone wall, 1m thick and rendered front and rear, containing a protruding, chamfered sandstone door-jamb. The wall had a packing fill of alternating mortar and silt with a large quantity of medieval pottery, iron and animal bone. This wall was almost certainly part of the medieval priory chapel. It was sealed by a universal layer of mortar, rich in post-medieval brick and pottery, representing the building level of Evan's Home.

Trenches 2 and 3 were perpendicular to Trench 1 and close to the north and east wings of Evan's Home. Both trenches revealed limestone-mortared walls associated with the barracks building and representing a rear wall between the two rear wings and an internal basement wall. One isolated deposit in Trench 2 produced a single sherd of late 16th- or 17th-century German stoneware, suggesting some truncated activity after the initial medieval phase.

*Paul Stevens for Margaret Gowen & Co. Ltd, 2 Killiney View, Albert Road Lower, Glenageary, Co. Dublin.*

### 440. 1 GREENHILL, KILKENNY
Urban medieval/post-medieval
SMR 19–26
99E0522

The site is just to the east of the River Nore and north of Irishtown in the city of Kilkenny.

Testing was carried out before the construction of two semi-detached houses and associated site works. Four test-trenches were opened manually on the imprint of the proposed development. The only archaeological remains uncovered dated to the early modern period, i.e. post-1700.

The upper level of the site was dominated by a thin cover of poor-quality topsoil. It appeared to have been imported to the site. A cobbled surface was uncovered towards the rear of the site. The surface occurred below the topsoil at a depth of 0.27m and abutted a poorly built wall. The cobbled surface and wall may have been part of the remains of an outdoor yard and retaining wall. Where the cobbled surface did not occur, there was a deposit of very compact, hardcore-like material beneath the topsoil. In one location the hardcore sealed a pocket of tarmacadam. Elsewhere the hardcore overlay a deposit of ash with inclusions of smashed bottle glass. The ash was dumped over a new layer of cobbled surface. This cobbled surface was 0.6m below ground level, and the cobbles were set into a mixture of mortar, ash and a dark yellowish/brown, silty clay. This deposit was 0.9m thick and overlay naturally deposited subsoils. A wall belonging to the building that previously stood on the site dominated the trench opened along the front and through the centre of the development.

*Mary Henry, 24 Queen Street, Clonmel, Co. Tipperary.*

### 441. NEW ROAD, GREENSBRIDGE, KILKENNY
Urban
25050 15603
99E0618

Archaeological assessment of an extension to the Nore Bar public house included the excavation of two test-trenches in the area of the development. No archaeological materials were found.

*Cóilín Ó Drisceoil, 6 Riverview, Ardnore, Kilkenny.*

### 442. GREEN STREET, KILKENNY
Urban medieval
25040 15616
SMR 19:26
99E0042

The proposed development site comprises a mill on Green Street with some associated buildings and a large garden to the rear. It is proposed to refurbish the mill and an associated house and to build apartments in the garden to the rear. According to the Urban Archaeological Survey for Kilkenny, the line of the city wall ran through the site under the rear wall of the mill. The garden area lies outside the city wall.

Thirteen test-trenches were opened in February 1999. One trench was opened on the line of the city wall to a depth of 1.4m, and no evidence for the wall was found. The other trenches were opened in the garden area on the footprint of the proposed building. Garden soil was removed to a depth 1.5m, and below this was natural, light brown clay.

Nothing of an archaeological nature was noted.
*Sheila Lane, 1 Charlemont Heights, Coach Hill, Rochestown, Cork.*

### 443. GREEN STREET, KILKENNY
Urban medieval
**SMR 19:26**
**99E0713**

The site is on Green Street, Kilkenny, just to the north of the city centre in the area known as Irishtown, only 45m from the River Nore.

Pre-construction testing was carried out before the construction of three dwelling-houses and associated site works. Five test-trenches were opened on the site, on the imprint of the proposed development.

Archaeological deposits were uncovered 1m below ground level, occurring at levels of between 44.2m and 44.5m OD. The upper deposits were of post-medieval date. The deposits at the lower levels may have been of medieval date. They occurred at levels of between 43.3m and 43.5m OD. They consisted of dark, organic-rich material and appeared to be built-up dumped deposits. The inclusions in the dark, heavy and organic-smelling deposits included charcoal, small pieces of wood, decayed vegetable matter, animal bedding and waste, and the occasional fragmented animal bone. No datable finds were recovered to conclusively date the lower deposits. However, they were sealed by deposits of post-medieval date.

The archaeological deposits were left *in situ*, and it was recommended that a raft foundation be used to preserve the deposits below the 1m level.
*Mary Henry, 24 Queen Street, Clonmel, Co. Tipperary.*

### 444. JAMES'S STREET, KILKENNY
Urban medieval
**98E0427 ext.**

Limited excavation was carried out at a site fronting on to James's Street, Kilkenny, between 12 and 15 January 1999. An archaeological assessment carried out in 1998 by Paul Stevens (*Excavations 1998*, 116, 98E0427) had identified a number of potential medieval features. As the foundations of the proposed development would be interfering with the known level of archaeology, only the extreme northern portion of the site, a small area measuring 16m east–west by 2m, was excavated. Because the foundation for the proposed building would be very shallow, a number of identified archaeological features were left *in situ* as they were situated well below the required 0.4m buffer zone. The remains of a limestone and red brick wall in the western half of the cutting were left *in situ*, as it extended north under the footpath.

The earliest phase of activity on the site comprised two large pits cutting the natural subsoil. The westernmost pit, sealed under a thick layer of redeposited natural, was filled with sub-spherical cobbles and yielded a single sherd of Saintonge pottery. Most of this pit and the redeposited natural were left *in situ*. The other pit, found roughly in the centre of the area excavated and extending north under the road, was filled with a dark, silty clay, animal bone and Anglo-Norman pottery.

In the eastern portion of the cutting a series of features indicating likely structural activity was identified and excavated. A linear wall trench orientated east–west measured 7.7m by 0.4–0.6m. It varied between 0.2m and 0.25m deep and was filled with a loose mix of heavy clay and medium-sized to large cut stone and cobbles. It yielded animal bone, charcoal and a few sherds of Anglo-Norman pottery. A number of deposits, consisting of intervening layers of clay and thin spreads of charcoal, were confined to the area north of the wall trench and extended north beyond the limit of excavation. These layers yielded no finds but contained small quantities of animal bone and oyster shell. It is likely that these deposits were contemporary with the wall trench and indicate the remains of flooring and/or occupational debris. Another wall trench, parallel and likely contemporary to that already described, was identified in the north-facing section but was not excavated.

A large pit in the western end of the site, cutting the redeposited natural, was filled with a loose deposit of small stones and organic material, which yielded some animal bone, charcoal and oyster shell, in addition to a few sherds of Anglo-Norman pottery and a single piece of worked bone. This pit and the structural features identified to the east were sealed by thick layers of medieval and then post-medieval garden soil.
*Christopher Read, Northwest Archaeological Services, Cloonfad Cottage, Leitrim Village, Co. Roscommon, for Margaret Gowen & Co. Ltd.*

### 445. TYNAN'S BRIDGE HOUSE, JOHN'S BRIDGE, KILKENNY
No archaeological significance
**S507559**
**99E0025**

An assessment took place in January 1999 for a proposed development in the south-eastern sector of the medieval city, on the west bank of the River Nore. The development involves a rear extension on the site of the present garden. The assessment, which consisted of three parallel, linear test-trenches opened by hand, revealed no archaeological deposits or soils.
*Paul Stevens for Margaret Gowen & Co. Ltd, 2 Killiney View, Albert Road Lower, Glenageary, Co. Dublin.*

### 446. BRIDGE HOUSE, 87–89 JOHN STREET LOWER, KILKENNY
Urban medieval
**25080 15570**
**SMR 19:26–17/67**
**95E0053 ext.**

Archaeological monitoring was carried out, in April 1999, of service trenches for a petrol sump, water and gas main and several retaining-wall trenches during construction of the Kilkenny River Court Hotel. The hotel is behind Bridge House (*Urban Archaeological Survey*, Map 4c, 67), overlooking the River Nore. The site was subject to previous survey and archaeological testing (by M. Gowen, *Excavations 1995*, 49, and E. O'Donovan, *Excavations 1998*, 116–17), and development was subsequently relocated away from the identified area of archaeological potential.

Most of the features noted during monitoring related to early modern stable buildings and a cobbled yard (recorded before development). However, a number of archaeological features were revealed, which were recorded and preserved *in situ*.

Bridge House is likely to have been built by the Ormond Butlers, as Charles Butler, earl of Arran and brother of the second duke of Ormond, was in possession of the building in 1704. It was almost certainly the Butlers who rebuilt the house at the end of the 18th century, when the bow and new John Street façade were added and it became the Dower House of the Ormond family. It was extensively refurbished at this stage, with the insertion of a fine stucco plasterwork ceiling.

The site is on the eastern bank of the River Nore, adjacent to St John's Bridge and within the medieval suburb of St John's, which grew up around St John's Priory, thought to have been under the Bridge House site (Finn and Murphy 1962, 35). William Marshall founded the priory in 1211 for the Cannons Regular of St Augustine (also called the Brethren of the Hospital of St John). The monks' first foundation, near John's Bridge, continued in use until 1325, when it moved to its present location at the eastern end of the suburb.

The earliest records of defensive walling around the suburb occur in the early 16th century, when there are references to a stone and lime wall, and a turret in 1570 (Thomas 1992). The medieval suburb of St John's is mentioned in Cromwell's account of the Siege of Kilkenny in 1650. The town wall was evidently in existence from at least the mid-16th century and continued in use through to the end of the 17th century. The line of the suburb town wall and ditch was found in testing to the rear of No. 86 (by E. O'Donovan, *Excavations 1998*, 116–17), and elsewhere the ditch was revealed by the writer, partly running under Maudlin Street to the small mural tower on that street (*Excavations 1998*, 117–18). The eastern suburb wall survives along part of the rear property plots of John Street and was found at the rear of Nos 68 and 69 John Street by E. O'Donovan (*Excavations 1996*, 68–9, 96E0131).

A large, truncated ditch feature was partially revealed in the north-west corner of a petrol-sump tank trench. The partly exposed ditch was parallel to John Street Lower, 11m to the rear of Bridge House, and had a steeply sloping concave profile. It measured 3m in exposed width and 3m in depth and contained a very dark blue, organic fill with wood fragments. Though wider, this ditch appeared to be the continuation of the medieval suburb defensive ditch noted in Trench D, to the rear of No. 85 John Street (see O'Donovan). The ditch was removed within the trench by the remains of a 19th-century outbuilding, constructed on a substantial deposit of brick rubble shored up by a contemporary retaining wall, parallel to the River Nore. The ditch was preserved only under an area of modern cobbling and garden soils.

A possible medieval wall was revealed under John Street, orientated north-east/south-west, aligned with the earlier line of the street leading to an earlier bridge south of the present John's Bridge (shown on J. Rocque's 1758 Map of Kilkenny). This lime-mortared limestone rubble, 0.9m thick and 0.5m+ in exposed depth, was abutted to the south by a deposit of gravel and cobbles, possibly representing an original road surface or foundation. It was also abutted to the north by a very large, concrete water tank, which removed all trace of any associated features or deposits.

The wall was revealed in a gas and foul-water mains trench that extended across John Street through the archway between Nos 87 and 88 and terminated in the hotel carpark area. The trench, 1m wide and 0.5–0.75m deep, contained a number of other features including a stone-lined drain of uncertain date, walls of the 18th/19th-century stables and associated cobbled surfaces. Excavation of this trench also revealed several architectural fragments including a Tudor window lintel and Tudor door-jamb, both originating from Bridge House. A dressed sandstone fragment of possible medieval date was also revealed and may provide evidence of an earlier medieval structure.

Demolition of a brick partition wall and removal of the plaster from the rear of No. 88 John's Street revealed two Tudor window-jambs reused within the fabric of the wall.

*References*
Finn, J. and Murphy, J.W. 1962 John Street—north and south sides. *Old Kilkenny Review* **14**, 25–39.
Thomas, A. 1992 *The walled towns of Ireland* (2 vols). Dublin.

*Paul Stevens for Margaret Gowen & Co. Ltd, 2 Killiney View, Albert Road Lower, Glenageary, Co. Dublin.*

### 447. 24 JOHN STREET UPPER, KILKENNY
Urban post-medieval
**SMR 19:26**
**99E0564**

The site is in the centre of Kilkenny and to the north-east of the River Nore. It is just 20m to the east of the St John's Abbey, an Augustinian priory.

Existing buildings were demolished on the site, and testing was undertaken before construction of a large, two-storey licensed premises. Four test-trenches were opened. The first was along the proposed new gable wall, at the nearest point to the nearby Augustinian priory. Its upper levels were dominated by a mixture of loose rubble fill and hardcore. At a depth of *c.* 0.25–0.3m below ground level (45.96m OD) a drystone wall was uncovered in the northern half of the trench. Abutting one side of the wall and near its base was a cobbled surface. The wall appeared to be a garden or boundary wall, with the cobbled yard running up to its side. The remainder of the trench was dominated by post-medieval deposits. The deposits were mixed and contained fragmented red brick, oyster shell, animal bone and one rimsherd of post-medieval date. A thin band of redeposited boulder clay separated the post-medieval deposits from a series of riverine sand and gravel deposits with a high content of water-rolled pebbles and small stones. The riverine deposits occurred at a level of 45.1m OD and extended to the base of the trench.

The second test-trench was along the east gable of the proposed building. Underlying a deposit of dark brown fill were riverine deposits. The riverine deposits occurred at high levels along the east part of the site, 46.98m OD.

It was noted from the opening of the third trench, in the middle of the site, that the riverine deposits rose quite noticeably in a west–east direction, from 45.1m OD along the west to 45.64m OD in the middle and 46.98m OD in the east part of the site. In this trench a large pit truncated the riverine sand and gravel deposits at 0.6m below ground level. The upper fill in the cut was very mixed, with inclusions of wood, mortar and rubble, garden soil, red brick and small stones. The underlying fill was redeposited, yellowish-brown, coarse sand. It overlay a dark, greyish-brown, silty sand. It contained frequent amounts of small stones, extensive charcoal, occasional fragmented red brick and oyster shell, crushed mortar and a small quantity of animal bone. One sherd of slipware was recovered from the fill. The primary fill was very dark, greyish-brown sand and silt. It contained charcoal and mortar.

The final trench was to the back of the development site. A soak pit dominated one half of the trench. The soak pit truncated a deep, post-medieval deposit. This deposit was quite homogeneous and extended to the riverine deposits, 44.65m OD. The riverine deposits were at much lower levels at the rear of the site than those along the east, middle or western sides. It was possible that the level of the riverine deposits had been reduced here and infilled with the post-medieval deposits, the later soak pit reflecting the post-medieval activity on the site.

No medieval deposits, features or structures were found on the site, nor was anything found that could be associated with the nearby Augustinian priory. The closeness of riverine deposits to ground level was the most noticeable feature.

*Mary Henry, 24 Queen Street, Clonmel, Co. Tipperary.*

### 448. 1 THE PARADE, KILKENNY
Urban
**SMR 19:26**
**99E0584**

Two test-trenches were opened here in October 1999. Nothing of an archaeological nature was noted.
*Sheila Lane, 1 Charlemont Heights, Coach Hill, Rochestown, Cork.*

### 449. KILKENNY CASTLE, THE PARADE, KILKENNY
12th–19th-century castle
**2508 1557**
**SMR 19:26**
**E000627 and 99E0481**

From 1991 to 1993, a series of excavations was conducted by the writer in order to facilitate the restoration of the central wing of the castle, which is a historic property in state care (*Excavations 1991*, 29–30; *Excavations 1992*, 39–40; see also *Old Kilkenny Review* (1993), 1101–17). From February 1995 to February 1998 a second series of excavations was conducted in and around the south tower to facilitate the restoration of the parade wing (*Excavations 1997*, 102–4). From October 1998 to November 1999 a third phase of excavations was conducted. This concentrated on two areas of the castle.

*Area A: the south-west half of the castle yard*
Here an extensive series of cuttings was excavated for the laying of services. Some of these extended beyond the castle yard. Although the eight cuttings involved were dug at different times over the space of one year, each adjoined at least one other. This helped to provide a broader picture of stratigraphy below ground.

Cutting 17 was a long, linear trench that was excavated from the south-west side of the castle yard, in a south-west direction, through the passageway of the gateway in the parade wing and out into the middle of the parade in front of the castle. The north-east half of the cutting revealed a great deal of modern disturbance, particularly from pipes etc. running beneath the passage of the gateway.

Nevertheless, the findings from this cutting confirmed some of those revealed in cuttings from the earlier programmes of excavation in the vicinity. For example, it showed that the façade of the present gateway, which dates from *c.* 1700, was inserted through the curtain wall of the 13th-century stone castle. Furthermore, it confirmed that this façade is built on the top of the base batter of the demolished section of the curtain wall.

The cutting also confirmed that the 13th-century base batter truncates the rampart of the earlier earthwork castle of *c.* 1170. On the outside of the present gateway the base batter descends into the moat. Previous excavations have shown that the latter was filled in during renovations carried out in the second half of the 17th century and sealed with a metalled surface when the present parade was laid out in front of the castle. The ground level was subsequently raised, with the laying of a series of metalled surfaces. These were encountered during the excavation of Cutting 17.

At the south-west end of the cutting the excavation was deepened to 3.65m, beneath the present road surface, to reveal a large, stone-built culvert. This runs in a south-east/north-west direction along the middle of the parade and appears to date to the 18th century. It was set into a deep trench, which was dug from the level of one of the later metalled surfaces.

Cutting 18 was in a corridor in the parade wing, to south-east of Cutting 17, at the north-west of the south tower. The excavation was required for the laying of underfloor services. At the south-west end, where the 13th-century curtain wall and adjoining south tower had been truncated, the top of the underlying base batter was exposed. Throughout the rest of the cutting, the remains of the rampart of the 12th-century earthwork castle were exposed. The latter had been truncated by the foundations of the parade wing, which was constructed in the 1860s.

Cuttings 19, 25, 26 and 27 were a series of adjoining cuttings, in the castle yard, which extended south-east from the north-east end of Cutting 17 on the inside of the gateway, to the line of the missing south-east curtain wall of the 13th-century castle, at the north-east of the south tower. They were delineated on the north-east side by Cutting 25, a shallow, linear trench, which was excavated to 0.75m deep. The other cuttings varied between 0.3m and 1.6m deep.

At the south-east end, Cuttings 25 and 27 were on either side of Cutting 14, which was excavated in 1995. These exposed the remains of the base batter of the missing south-east curtain wall. The outer face had been destroyed by the construction of a parallel underground passageway, which was built in 1862.

Running parallel to the inside of the destroyed curtain wall, all three cuttings revealed the remains of the foundation of a destroyed 17th-century building that formerly ran along the south-east side of the castle yard. Along with the curtain wall, it was demolished during the second half of the 18th century.

Both the above foundation and the 13th-century base batter truncated the rampart of the 12th-century earthwork castle. To date, the three programmes of excavation have revealed that the 13th-century curtain wall was built along the outside of the ridge of the earlier earthen rampart. The latter was constructed of redeposited glacial material excavated from the fosse surrounding the 12th-century fortress. This appears to have been a ringwork, built by Earl Strongbow and burnt down in 1173 (see *OKR* 1993, 1108–11).

The excavations to date have shown that the ground level in the interior of the earthwork fortress was raised by redeposited glacial material, thus burying the old ground surface. This may have been carried out during the building of the stone castle, when the outside of the rampart and the underlying inner slope of the fosse were truncated by the construction of the towers and the base batter of the curtain wall. On the inside of the demolished south-east curtain wall, the original ground level is *c.* 1.3m beneath the present castle yard.

Approximately 15m to the north-west of the south-east curtain wall and *c.* 9m from the north-west one, in Cuttings 19 and 26, beneath the redeposited layers of glacial material, two layers of silty clay and organic material were encountered, totalling 0.33m thick. They contained flecks of charcoal, charred wood fragments and chippings. This horizon overlay a metalled surface, which was 1.6m beneath the present castle yard. No datable artefacts were recovered from these lower levels, which were only briefly investigated before being backfilled to facilitate the laying of services, but they would appear to date from the time of the earthwork castle.

Cutting 23 was a continuation of service trench/Cutting 25, extending south-east from the outside of the demolished south-east curtain wall of the 13th-century castle, for a distance of 43.3m, across the park to an oil house. It was 0.75m wide and contained a 0.6m-thick layer of building waste and redeposited clay. Beneath this, towards the south-east end, a metalled surface was encountered, which was covered by the above layer in the later 18th century. The excavation of the trench stopped at this level.

Cutting 24 was a wide trench, the north-east side of which was a continuation of Cutting 25 to the south-east. It extended north-west from the north-east end of Cutting 17 to the north-west corner of the castle yard. This area had been partially excavated (Cutting 9) in 1992. A great deal of disturbance was encountered owing to the laying of earlier services. The undisturbed stratigraphy consisted mainly of layers of redeposited glacial material. Beneath this the pre-1170 sod was revealed.

At the north-west end of the cutting the remains of a medieval stone passageway were encountered. Previous excavations (Cutting 3) carried out in 1992 showed that this feature ran in a north-west direction, beneath the present central wing of the castle towards a 13th-century sallyport, which was excavated during 1991 and 1992 (Cuttings 5 and 7). It truncated the redeposited glacial layers and overlay an earlier passageway that appears to have had a timber revetment on either side.

*Area B: the north-west side of the castle*
These cuttings were a continuation of excavations that were carried out during 1991 and 1992.

Cutting 5A was an extension of Cutting 5, which was excavated beneath a 19th-century cellar, to the north-east of the west tower. Here the lower 12th-century rampart layers and the underlying original ground level were found.

Cuttings 7 and 8 were excavated in 1991–2 and were extended during 1999. They were beneath the floor of a 19th-century, semi-underground passageway that runs north-east from the west tower. The excavations here exposed the base batter of the 13th-century curtain wall and a contemporary sallyport. The work during 1999 exposed the remains of a post-medieval terrace that was built on the base batter and was demolished when the moat was being filled in during the renovations of the second half of the 17th century.

The extension of Cutting 7 from the south-west side of the sallyport, as far as the west tower, revealed a stairway that gave access to an outward projection from the above terrace.

Cuttings 10A, 20 and 21 were in the rose garden to the north-west of the castle. Here a deep cutting (10) had been excavated in 1992 (*OKR* 1993, fig. 3), which exposed the bottom of the 13th-century base batter down in the moat. The work in 1999 involved the excavation of deep service trenches extending from Cutting 10. In these the stratigraphy removed came from the upper build-up of ground over the moat, which dated to around 1700.

Cutting 22 was in the ground chamber of the west tower. It was a shallow trench, which exposed a horizon of redeposited ash and occupation material that produced finds dating to the later 17th century. A similar horizon was encountered in the excavation of the interior of the south tower (Cutting 15), where it was used as a bedding for the laying of a cobbled floor. Accordingly, it is likely that the present 19th-century flagged floor replaced a cobbled one.

*Ben Murtagh, Primrose Hill, Threecastles, Co. Kilkenny.*

## 450. STATHAM'S GARAGE, PATRICK STREET, KILKENNY
Urban medieval
**SMR 19:26**
**99E0757**
Three test-trenches were excavated in the site of

Statham's Garage in Patrick Street, Kilkenny, to comply with a request from Kilkenny Corporation before a grant of planning. The proposed development site is on the eastern side of Patrick Street within the zone of archaeological potential for Kilkenny City. The site is vacant at present. The 18th-century cartographers John Rocque and Samuel Byron illustrate a large building fronting onto Patrick Street on this site.

The trenches were opened on the footprint of the foundations of the proposed development. Trench 1 was T-shaped in plan and measured 7m north–south by 6m. Eight pits were recorded cutting the subsoil. Trench 2 measured 7m east–west by 2m. A ditch aligned east–west was recorded cutting the subsoil. Trench 3 measured 6m east–west by 2m. Two possible pits were recorded cutting the subsoil. The stratigraphy in the trenches was planned and recorded. No archaeological excavation took place.

*Jacinta Kiely, Eachtra Archaeological Projects, Clover Hill, Mallow, Co. Cork.*

### 451. 26 PATRICK STREET, KILKENNY
Urban medieval
SMR 19:26
99E0165

Excavation was undertaken before the construction of an extension to the rear of 26 Patrick Street, Kilkenny. The site is within the area of the medieval walled city.

The excavation uncovered the foundations of a post-medieval building and a number of medieval features to the west of its foundations. A trench, 20m by 13m, was excavated. Five medieval pits, which varied in size, were excavated in the western section of the site. The average pit measured 1.2m north–south by 1.85m by 0.4m deep and contained one or two fills. The most substantial pit measured 1.8m north–south by 3.5m by 1m deep and contained twelve fills. The fills included the bones of sheep, cattle and pig, medieval pottery sherds and oyster shells. Two pin fragments were also recovered. The pits most likely served as refuse pits, and the faunal remains recovered from them would support this. They occur in the area of the medieval burgage plots.

A linear feature, possibly a ditch, measuring 4.6m north–south by 0.9m by 0.7m deep, was found to the west of the wall foundations. It contained the bones of cattle, sheep, pig and horse and sherds of pottery.

Excavation at 26 Patrick Street, Kilkenny, from south-west.

The basal layers of a number of post-medieval red brick and limestone walls were recorded in the eastern section of the trench. There were a number of pits associated with the walls.

*Jacinta Kiely, Eachtra Archaeological Projects, Clover Hill, Mallow, Co. Cork.*

### 452. BURGERMAC, 20 ROSE INN STREET, KILKENNY
Urban
99M0027

Monitoring was carried out here between 11 February and 1 March 1999 and involved a total of seven days on site.

A building survey was carried out by Declan Murtagh on 20 June 1998 to assess the historic fabric of the upstanding remains, which consisted of a terraced, three-bay, three-storey house with a steep pitched roof, constructed *c.* 1800.

The modern Rose Inn Street was an important axis in the medieval city of Kilkenny. The curve of the street from St John's Bridge towards High Street may delimit the original outer defences of the castle. Situated to the south of the early 13th-century St Mary's Church, the site of No. 20 Rose Inn Street, and the adjoining plots, represents a break in the continuity of medieval burgage plot alignment that ran perpendicular to High Street (Bradley 1990, 69). Later historical sources document the presence of properties fronting onto Rose Inn Street. A composite map derived from the major cartographic sources for the city shows the site of the late medieval tavern The Sheaf Inn in the vicinity of the site under investigation (Hogan 1860–1, 350). The Urban Archaeological Survey notes that Bishop Rothe's College, in existence between 1642 and 1650, was in the vicinity of Nos 20–21 Rose Inn Street (1993, 82). However, the exact location of these buildings has yet to be identified.

It was recommended that all below-ground site works be subject to an archaeological monitoring condition. Monitoring involved general ground reduction to a depth of *c.* 0.6m at the western end of the building and the excavation of foundation trenches to an approximate depth of 0.6m in the eastern end of the building.

Ground reduction at the rear (western end) of the site revealed the presence of six negative features cut into natural subsoil. Development did not have any adverse physical impact on the below-ground archaeological resource, as the negative features were all revealed *c.* 50mm below the level of mechanical excavation. The six features were revealed through limited hand-excavation undertaken across the entire site, after mechanical excavation had stopped. Hand-excavation involved only removal of loose material accumulated over the archaeological features as a result of the mechanical excavation and did not involve any excavation of the *in situ* negative features.

Discussion with the Excavation Licences Section of *Dúchas* The Heritage Service regarding the preferred management strategy for the archaeological resource was undertaken at the time of fieldwork. This resulted in all of the recorded archaeological features being preserved *in situ* as the development failed to have an adverse impact on these archaeological remains.

No archaeological features or portable finds were recorded from the eastern part of the site. The natural subsoil was sealed by a mixture of brown/grey, gravelly clay and modern rubble with occasional charcoal flecking and fragments of oyster shell. These are interpreted as representing redeposited archaeological layers, thus extending the image of meaningful archaeological deposits previously surviving across the full extent of the site.

The recording of potentially redeposited archaeological deposits along with six negative features testifies to the presence of meaningful cultural remains from within the general development area. As a number of these cuts extend beyond the development site in both a northerly and a southerly direction, it is recommended that any future developments in the area be undertaken in conjunction with a detailed archaeological management plan.

*References*
Bradley, J. 1990 Medieval Kilkenny City. In W. Nolan and K. Whelan (eds), *Kilkenny: history and society*.
Hogan, J. 1860–1 Map of the city of Kilkenny. *Journal of the Royal Society of Antiquaries of Ireland*, 350–4.

*Dermot Nelis, IAC Ltd, 8 Dungar Terrace, Dun Laoghaire, Co. Dublin, for ADS Ltd.*

### 453. ST CANICE'S PLACE/VICAR STREET, KILKENNY
No archaeological significance
**S504653**
**99E0057**

An assessment took place in February 1999 for a proposed development in the north-eastern sector of the medieval city, on the west bank of the River Nore and south-east of St Canice's Cathedral. The development involves the construction of a petrol service station and shop on the site of an existing petrol station, demolished before this assessment.

Three linear test-trenches were opened across the site. These revealed no archaeological deposits or soils. The site appeared to have been substantially truncated during construction of the existing structure sometime in the last 20–30 years.

*Paul Stevens for Margaret Gowen & Co. Ltd, 2 Killiney View, Albert Road Lower, Glenageary, Co. Dublin.*

### 454. ST FRANCIS'S ABBEY BREWERY, KILKENNY
Urban medieval
**S565505**
**99E0148**

Monitoring and test excavation were carried out on the Smithwicks Brewery Fermentor Block Expansion Stage VIII. The test excavation was within the precincts of St Francis's Abbey and adjacent to the military barracks established at the site at the beginning of the 18th century.

The test excavation revealed a deposit model that mirrored earlier phases of work by the writer (*Excavations 1997*, 105, 97E0099) and by Margaret Gowen (*Excavations 1996*, 58, 95E0242, and *Excavations 1998*, 123, 98E0069). A thin layer of gravel was identified over boulder clay. This was overlain by a layer of soft, silty, organic material that has consistently produced occasional post-medieval finds, such as red brick and pottery. The layer appears to have accumulated naturally from the early post-medieval period. It directly underlies a mortar layer representing barracks activity. The monitoring confirmed the archaeological profile established during the test excavation.

*Edmond O'Donovan, Margaret Gowen & Co. Ltd, 2 Killiney View, Albert Road Lower, Glenageary, Co. Dublin.*

### 455. RIVER BREAGAGH AT ST FRANCIS'S ABBEY BREWERY, KILKENNY
Urban
**S570510**
**99E0385**

Archaeological survey and the inspection of engineering test-pits were undertaken along the Breagagh riverbed where it crosses through St Francis's Abbey Brewery, Kilkenny, in order to establish a baseline against which the impact of proposed excavation works on the riverbed could be measured for archaeological and conservation purposes.

The riverbed level is to be reduced by bulk excavation to remove residual PCB contamination before the commencement of work on the Office of Public Works River Nore Flood Alleviation Scheme, which will also involve works in the River Breagagh. The PCB contamination was substantially cleaned up at the time of a spillage from a refrigerated unit over twenty years ago and has remained stable ever since, but removal of any surviving contaminated material is now required to prevent its movement and spread, through scouring action, after the reduction in level of the Nore as part of the flood-relief scheme.

The river and the masonry wall along its southern side formed the boundary of the medieval friary precinct, which, like other ecclesiastical establishments, was located at the limits of the town. The precinct of St Francis's Abbey occupied the north-eastern sector of the medieval Hightown, bounded by the Breagagh River on the north and the Nore on the east. Originally known as the North Quarter, it was owned by the bishops and only ceded to the Marshalls in 1207 (Thomas 1992, 131–2). Because of its function within the medieval town, and as part of the friary boundary, the river is a significant archaeological feature, and its deposits have significant archaeological potential.

The masonry wall on the southern side of the river was probably first built in the 14th century. It has been altered and repaired in antiquity, especially during the 17th century, and more recently and substantially as part of the development of the modern brewery facility. The masonry wall extended from, and formed part of, the circuit of medieval town wall in this location. A small defensive tower, Evan's Tower, stands at the confluence of the Breagagh with the Nore, and the wall does not appear (from present inspection) to extend along the bank of the Nore. There are no records apart from Rocque's map to suggest that the Nore river frontage ever possessed a wall.

In all, six test-pits were opened, primarily to assess the depth of the medieval wall foundations but also to establish the nature and content of the deposits on the riverbed. These were excavated in pumped, sand-bagged locations roughly 1–1.5m², which remained dry in the relatively shallow water flow of the river. Of these, four were opened along the medieval wall and two were opened on the opposite side adjacent to the modern concrete wall. The first attempted pit was abandoned because of an inability to control the water flow (all pumped water had to be tanked for disposal offsite). The exposed riverbed was composed of gravel and small washed stones with occasional larger blocks. On either side, banks of gravel and sands have accumulated in three locations. These had significant reed growth on them at the time of survey, and their vegetation-covered surfaces had a high silt content.

Excavation on the southern side, against the medieval wall, revealed that the gravel extended down for at least 0.8–1m and that it possessed modern debris to that depth. No medieval material was noted in any of the material excavated along this side, although large quantities of modern bottles, some delph, plastics and some metal objects were removed for identification. This material, along the medieval wall, appears to be quite modern, and the gravel and sands have been significantly and dynamically reworked.

On the opposite, northern, side the profile differed. In both pits a thin spread of gravel overlay a virtually stone-free, organic-rich silt (exposed to the limit of excavation), which yielded two fragments of medieval ceramics. This was interpreted as the primary riverbank, wh ich has seen very limited erosion or reworking in the area investigated.

A second phase of investigation involved the examination of trial borings. These were monitored by Paul Stevens (see No. 456 below).

*Reference*
Thomas, A. 1992 *The walled towns of Ireland* (2 vols). Dublin.

*Margaret Gowen, Margaret Gowen & Co. Ltd, 2 Killiney View, Albert Road Lower, Glenageary, Co. Dublin.*

### 456. RIVER BREAGAGH AT ST FRANCIS'S ABBEY BREWERY, KILKENNY
Urban medieval/riverbed
25050 15640
SMR 19:26
99E0385 ext.

Monitoring of geotechnical trial boreholes within the River Breagagh took place in September 1999. The trial bores were in the Smithwicks Brewery complex, from the junction of the River Nore, along the length of the town wall and Evan's Turret, up to the site of Cotteral's Bridge.

No archaeological deposits or artefacts were noted within the core samples analysed. However, analysis of the relative depth of each borehole sample showed anomalies in the data, possibly caused by obstructions of large boulders, probably fallen from the town wall or the Horse Barracks buildings adjacent to the river. Finds from this site consisted mostly of modern or early modern pottery, glass and metal, with undated brick, mortar and animal bone from a large mammal (probably relating to activity associated with the 19th-century Horse Barracks).

*Paul Stevens for Margaret Gowen & Co. Ltd, 2 Killiney View, Albert Road Lower, Glenageary, Co. Dublin.*

### 457. MOONHALL
Adjacent to archaeological complex
25940 15681
SMR 20:22
99E0703

Archaeological assessment of a residential development within an archaeological complex at Moonhall, Clifden, Co. Kilkenny, included the excavation of four test-trenches in the area of the development. A deserted medieval village, enclosures associated with the village, a ringfort, a castle and a well form the archaeological complex.

No archaeological materials were found in the test-trenches.

*Cóilín Ó Drisceoil, 6 Riverview, Ardnore, Kilkenny.*

### 458. PARKSGROVE: 1
Burnt mound and ironworking site
243523 170491
99E0597

This site was revealed during archaeological monitoring of a Bord Gáis Éireann gas pipeline development (No. 426 above). The site is in Parksgrove townland, 1.5km south-west of Ballyragget, within the western flood-plain of the River Nore. Excavation of the site within the wayleave corridor was carried out between July and August 1999 before development.

*Ironworking site*
The site centred on a small, circular pit, cutting natural boulder clay subsoil and possibly used as a furnace bowl for ironworking. It was 1.2m in diameter and 0.3m deep and was filled with a stony clay containing iron slag and charcoal. Associated with but post-dating this was a large, thin, circular spread of hard, mixed, orange, coarse sand and clay, with some fire-cracked limestone, also containing a number of iron nail fragments. The spread measured 15m north–south by 9m+, was 0.18m deep and continued west of the excavation area.

Within the site, and cutting the ironworking pit and spread, was a large linear gully, orientated south-west/north-east (continuing to the west), which turned east and terminated with a V-shaped profile and rounded terminus. The ditch was otherwise concave in profile, 1.6m wide and 0.45m deep, and contained a clay fill and burnt mound material. This was sealed by a subcircular spread of burnt mound material also extending under the west baulk, measuring 10m north–south by 8m+ and 0.3m deep. The spread was heavily truncated by later ploughing and may have been deliberately pushed into the ditch.

A number of fragments of iron objects, slag and charcoal suggested use of the site for ironworking. However, stray finds from the site, including a fragment of clay pipe, modern porcelain and a modern padlock, suggest substantial modern intrusion.

*Burnt mound*
Eight metres to the north of the ironworking site was a small spread of charcoal-rich soil, fire-cracked stone (90% sandstone/10% limestone) and silt, possibly representing a separate burnt mound or the continuation of the above feature. This mound measured 2m east–west by 4m and 0.15m deep and continued to the west of the excavation. It cannot be ruled out that this is a separate burnt mound or Bronze Age *fulacht fiadh* site.
Paul Stevens for Margaret Gowen & Co. Ltd, 2 Killiney View, Albert Road Lower, Glenageary, Co. Dublin.

## 459. PARKSGROVE: 2
*Fulacht fiadh*
243545 170304
99E0598
This site was revealed during archaeological monitoring of a Bord Gáis Éireann gas pipeline development (see No. 426 above). The site is in Parksgrove townland, 1.5km south-west of Ballyragget, within the western flood-plain of the River Nore. Excavation of the site within the wayleave corridor was carried out in August 1999 before development.

Natural, orange boulder clay was cut by three separate troughs, which clustered in the centre of this site. Trough A was a subcircular pit with a concave profile, 2.2m in diameter and 0.8m deep, containing a truncated lining of light grey putty clay, 0.8m thick, at the very base of the trough. The pit was deliberately backfilled with redeposited, sandy, natural clay and burnt mound material, and a single post-hole was found immediately south of the trough.

Trough B, 1m west of Trough A, was a subcircular pit with U-shaped profile, 1.7m in diameter and 0.9m deep. Four stake-holes were cut around the base of the trough, possibly representing the sails of a wicker lining. This trough was also deliberately backfilled by a single, uniform layer of burnt mound material and also had an associated post-hole immediately east of it.

Trough C, immediately north of Trough B, was a rectangular pit with square profile and rounded edges, measuring 2.8m by 1.6m by 0.5m deep. It contained a truncated lining of bright grey putty clay, 0.3m thick, in turn sealed by a deliberate backfill of burnt mound material. A small, tight cluster of shallow stake-holes and a further isolated stake-hole were found at the eastern edge of this trough. A small whetstone was retrieved from its lower backfill.

The troughs were sealed by a burnt mound, which was circular in plan with a concave profile. The mound consisted of fire-cracked stone (sandstone 95%/limestone 5%), charcoal lumps and black silt and covered an area of 21m north–south by over 11m, continuing to the west, and 0.25m in maximum truncated depth. An informal hearth area, south of the trough complex, was sealed within the burnt mound. Later ploughing of the site and modern drainage activity reduced the level of the top of the mound.
Paul Stevens for Margaret Gowen & Co. Ltd, 2 Killiney View, Albert Road Lower, Glenageary, Co. Dublin.

## 460. PARKSGROVE: 3
*Fulacht fiadh*
243523 170044
99E0599
The site was revealed during archaeological monitoring of a Bord Gáis Éireann pipeline development from Ballyconra to Baunlusk, Co. Kilkenny (see No. 426 above). Parksgrove townland is situated along the western flood-plain of the River Nore, with undulating farmland and patches of reclaimed boggy ground. Excavation of this site took place in August 1999. The underlying natural was glacial boulder clay.

The site consisted of a partially exposed spread of fire-cracked sandstone and charcoal-rich, silty sand, continuing west of the edge of excavation, representing part of a denuded *fulacht fiadh*. The exposed semicircular deposit measured 8.5m by 6m and 0.2m in maximum depth and was heavily truncated by later ploughing. Two large areas of burnt soil lay to the east of the mound and were interpreted as an informal hearth and a second hearth and platform area, for heating stones to use in the *fulacht fiadh*. The hearth was circular with tiny fragments of manganese oxide and occasional small stones and gravel, 3.5m by 3m and 0.1m deep. The platform and hearth contained several dump deposits of pink ash, white ash and an irregular, disturbed limestone and sandstone spread, measuring 12m by 6m and 0.22m deep.
Paul Stevens for Margaret Gowen & Co. Ltd, 2 Killiney View, Albert Road Lower, Glenageary, Co. Dublin.

## 461. KILMURRY CASTLE, SLEIVERUE
Late and post-medieval
2633 1140
SMR 43:037002
99E0210
The site is at the south end of the county, just 2km to the north-east of Ferrybank, in Waterford City, and almost the same distance to the north of the River Suir. It consists of a small late medieval tower-house, with an adjoining two-storey dwelling-house, surrounded by farm buildings. Further to an application to Kilkenny County Council to renovate the dwelling-house, the owner engaged the writer to conduct an assessment of the building. This was carried out during 1988.

The assessment revealed that the dwelling-house incorporated a later medieval church or chapel that was attached to, and built at the same time as, the tower-house. An original doorway at ground level gives access between the two buildings. In parts of late medieval Leinster, tower-houses were built at the west end of some churches, as a residence for clergymen. Kilmurry Castle is such an example. Documentary evidence suggests that it may have been built in the 1430s.

During the 16th century and first half of the 17th century the site was the property of the Fitzgerald O'Dee family of nearby Gurteens Castle. The church was a chapel of ease. Internally it measures 9.15m x 4.62m. Inside and to the east of the south doorway is a stoup. In the south-east corner is a piscina. The east window is a large single-light with an ogee head.

Subsequent to the Cromwellian Settlement the chapel was renovated with the use of clay-bonded masonry. It was turned into a dwelling, adjoining the tower-house (Phase 2). In effect the two buildings functioned as a single house. In the later 18th or early 19th century they underwent a programme of renovations (Phase 3), and again about a century later (Phase 4). Further work (Phase 5) was carried out before the 'Castle' was abandoned in 1955.

On foot of the building's assessment, planning permission was granted to proceed with the proposed renovations with conditions, one being that the late medieval chapel would be preserved within the fabric of the dwelling-house. A limited archaeological excavation was also required for the laying of a new floor within the building and for the laying of services outside. This work was carried out during 1999. Before its commencement it was not known whether a disused graveyard existed within and around the old chapel. The excavation was conducted in three areas.

Area A involved the excavation of a linear trench running from the south-east corner of the old chapel, across the yard to the south, for a distance of 17.8m, to the south boundary wall. It was dug to a depth of 1.2m and was c. 0.9m wide. Beneath a layer of topsoil a cobbled surface was encountered, which dated to the Phase 3 renovations. This in turn overlay a layer of topsoil, in which some late 18th- or early 19th-century artefacts were found. Underlying this was a thin layer of subsoil, which in turn overlay very hard glacial clay. No evidence of a graveyard was found.

At the north end of the trench it was found that the south-east corner of the old chapel rested directly upon the natural clay, while in the southern half a wide and shallow cut was encountered, which was a late feature.

Area B was within the interior of the old chapel. During the later renovations this area had been subdivided into two rooms. The floor of the eastern room (kitchen) was 0.15m lower than that of the western one. It was proposed to replace these with one level floor.

The concrete floor of the kitchen was removed to reveal a cobbled surface underneath. The excavation found that beneath the western flagged floor was a thick layer of loose material, consisting mainly of ash and other material from fire hearths. This layer ran east beneath the cobbled floor of the kitchen and was a bedding for cobbles. This shows that the Phase 4 flagged floor of the western room replaced a cobbled one. Artefacts recovered from the bedding layer included many wine bottle fragments of post-1750 date.

The work also showed that the bedding layer overlay the natural glacial clay, indicating that the original (Phase 1) floor of the chapel, as well as the Phase 2 floor, had been destroyed during the Phase 3 renovations (later 18th/early 19th century). At the west end it was found that the offset footing of the tower-house was built into a foundation trench, which was dug into the glacial clay. The natural ground slopes away to a stream to the east of the present dwelling-house. The foundation of the chapel slopes with this gradient. It was also found that the east wall was built directly on the natural clay. As was the case in Area A outside, no human burials were encountered within the chapel.

Area C was in the modern extension to the east of the old chapel. On the ground floor this consists of a single room. Here it was found that the Phase 3 extension overlies the remains of a Phase 2 lean-to shed, constructed with clay-bonded masonry. Within the room the excavation found that the natural clay had been dug into for the laying of the same bedding layer that was found within the chapel (Area B), for the setting of Phase 3 cobbles. The latter had been removed by the laying of later floors. Again, as in areas A and B, no human burials were encountered in Area C.
*Ben Murtagh, Primrose Hill, Three Castles, Co. Kilkenny.*

### 462. MILL STREET, THOMASTOWN
Urban medieval/post-medieval
**SMR 28:40**
**98E0176**
Testing was undertaken before the construction of a residential dwelling at Mill Street, Thomastown, Co. Kilkenny. The site of the development is immediately to the south-east of the centre of Thomastown, fronting the National Primary Route linking Waterford to Dublin and on the east bank of the River Nore. It is to the south-east of the walled town and to the periphery of the zone of archaeological potential as defined by the Urban Archaeological Survey.

Four test-trenches were opened on the site. Two were opened in 1998 (*Excavations 1998*, 124), and two in 1999. The trenches were opened with great difficulty, as much of the site had been infilled with building debris and rubble and it is on the east bank of the river, which flows c. 8m beneath.

The building debris extended to a depth of 3m in the trenches opened. It was not possible to excavate beneath the 3m level in the two trenches opened in 1998. The two trenches opened in 1999 extended to depths of between 3.5m and 4m. However, no archaeological remains were uncovered between the 3m level, the base of the infilled rubble material, and the limit of the excavation in both trenches.
*Mary Henry, 24 Queen Street, Clonmel, Co. Tipperary.*

### 463. THE QUAY, THOMASTOWN
No archaeological significance
**SMR 28:40**
**99E0068**
The site for proposed development is within the zone of archaeological importance established for Thomastown; consequently, monitoring of all construction work was requested as a planning condition. Proposed works consisted of the erection of a roofed area to an existing yard. Nine foundation pits were dug at the periphery of the site. There was no indication of archaeologically significant material.
*Cathy Sheehan, Hillview, Aglish, Carrigeen, Kilkenny.*

## LAOIS

### 464. AGHABOE ABBEY, AGHABOE
Archaeological complex
23314 18574
**SMR 22:19**
**99E0592**
Monitoring of excavations was undertaken before a

proposed development at Aghaboe Abbey, from 13 to 15 October 1999. The development comprised the provision of toilet facilities in the existing carpark and the installation of a floodlighting system in the grounds of the Dominican friary. The carpark site was tested by the writer in 1994 (*Excavations 1994*, 141), and part of the Dominican friary was excavated by Anthony Candon before a conservation project in 1986 (*Excavations 1986*, 22).

Excavations in the carpark related to the site of the proposed toilets, septic tank, percolation area and part of the ESB cable trench, which will extend from the toilet building to the church grounds. This area was stripped of topsoil and gravelled when the carpark was developed in 1994. The gravel generally overlay a yellowish-brown, clayey sand subsoil, 0.1m thick, and this overlay a natural, light brown, clayey sand. Some fragments of human bone were found in the disturbed subsoil close to the carpark entrance. The cable trench, 0.2m wide and 0.2m deep, inside the church grounds, was manually excavated. The first section extended along the base of the enclosing boundary wall, and the topsoil consisted of a dark greyish-brown, sandy clay with moderate inclusions of stone, mortar, modern pottery sherds and glass fragments. Occasional fragments of animal and human bone were also found. The most notable find from the topsoil was a late medieval chamfered limestone jamb (0.4m x 0.17m x 0.14m). A disturbed, yellowish-brown, clayey sand subsoil was occasionally encountered at a depth of 0.25m.

The trench at the base of the boundary wall terminated at a point directly opposite the southwest corner of the church. From here the trench was taken across the gravelled area outside the west gable of the church, through the west doorway and, finally, across the gravelled interior of the church. All of this area had been archaeologically excavated and backfilled during the 1984–6 conservation project. A fragment of a rebated limestone jamb (0.23m x 0.21m x 0.1m) represented the only find of archaeological interest from the rubble fill.

*Dominic Delany, 31 Ashbrook, Oranmore, Co. Galway.*

### 465. KILMINCHY
Possible site of castle
**SMR 13:88**
**99E0390**

Pre-development test-trenching was undertaken at Kilminchy, near Portlaoise, where an area of 150 acres of farmland is being developed. The land is gently undulating, and the soils are generally light and sandy. Some features had been noted in the extant farm buildings that suggested the possibility that they incorporated earlier structures (Sweetman *et al.* 1995). The work was undertaken at the request of the managing director, Mr Colman Buckley, who had noted an arc of a stone wall now incorporated into a modern hayshed, which may be part of Kilminchy Castle, location now unknown, or of the Mail Coach Stables that subsequently existed on the site.

Five trenches were excavated at different locations on the site by mechanical digger using a ditching bucket. No material of medieval date was uncovered. The arc of a wall was not of medieval construction but was the inner face of a three-sided bay with projecting buttresses. This was constructed of roughly coursed random rubble, and the buttresses were both built of squared, dressed blocks. The wall survived to a depth below present ground level of 2.25m and was clearly a foundation level. This appeared from the map evidence to be the central bay of a building that also had projecting bays at either end. The wall had been broken through by the insertion of a slurry tank on the east side and was not followed on the west side.

A survey of the cartographic evidence for the area showed that, while a possible tower-house was indicated on the Down Survey map of the area, drawn *c.* 1650, the symbol for a 'gentleman's residence' was used on Taylor and Skinner's map of 1778 (Taylor and Skinner 1783), with the note 'FitzGerald Esq.'. Based on parallels with other such features, for example at Anneville, Co. Westmeath (Craig 1976, 103–4), a building date in the mid-18th century is likely.

An ongoing programme of field-walking as the fields are ploughed is being carried out as part of the archaeological investigations of the site as a whole.

*References*
Craig, M. 1976 *Classic Irish houses of the middle size*. London.
Sweetman, P.D., Alcock, O. and Moran, B. 1995 *Archaeological inventory of County Laois*. Dublin.
Taylor, G. and Skinner, A. 1783 *Maps of the roads of Ireland*.

*Finola O'Carroll, Cultural Resource Development Services Ltd, Campus Innovation Centre, Roebuck, University College, Belfield, Dublin 4.*

### 466. JESSOP STREET/COOTE STREET, PORTLAOISE
Town
**24713 19848**
**SMR 13:41**
**99E0392**

Test excavation was undertaken here before planning, from 16 to 20 July 1999. The site is north-west of the remains of the 16th-century fort and church of Maryborough (now Portlaoise). Much of the site was formerly occupied by a large, early 20th-century ironworks known as 'Kelly's Foundry'. The foundry buildings were cleared in the early 1990s. The site was covered with hardcore fills, crushed rubble and concrete slabs at the time of testing.

Testing comprised the mechanical excavation of ten test-trenches. The hardcore, crushed rubble and concrete slab surfaces occasionally overlay modern deposits but more frequently overlay the light yellowish-brown, clayey sand subsoil, which was encountered at an average depth of 0.4m. The subsoil yielded occasional modern and post-medieval pottery sherds. It had an average thickness of 0.3m and overlay the orange or reddish-brown, natural, clayey sand.

Two post-medieval linear features were encountered. A linear feature at least 22.5m long, in Trench 2, probably represents a post-medieval field or property boundary, but the origin of a short

(5.65m) linear feature in Trench 9 could not be established. Both features were relatively shallow and sterile and would appear to be of limited archaeological interest. A series of walls (2m high, 0.4m wide) and a stone-lined drain were encountered in Trench 6. The walls represent a subsurface structure, but their origin could not be established. They are very distinctive in that they are almost entirely faced with rounded cobblestones, an unlikely building material. However, this is not unusual for Portlaoise, as many of the surviving 19th-century sheds and outbuildings in the town are similarly constructed.

*Dominic Delany, 31 Ashbrook, Oranmore, Co. Galway.*

## LEITRIM

### 467. AGHAVAS
Medieval lacustrine habitation site
21884 30086
99E0555

Following the report of a previously unknown site discovered during afforestation, an emergency inspection of the site recorded an unfinished quern (*Archaeology Ireland* No. 49, 17) and medieval crannog ware. A more detailed survey before reconstitution of the site showed it to be several small mounds of ash and charcoal, roughly oval, 17m north-east/south-west by 11m and 0.5m deep. The site had been found at the margins of a former lake, and, although construction appears unclear, it seems that roundwood timbers were placed directly onto peat and the mound was consolidated by vertical timbers at the edge. Some slabs possibly showed evidence for paving. Animal bones, in association with the other artefacts, suggest a late medieval lakeside settlement.

*Victor Buckley and Aidan O'Sullivan, c/o Dúchas The Heritage Service, 6 Ely Place Upper, Dublin 2.*

### 468. GARADICE HOUSE, BALLINAMORE
17th-century house
21790 31199
SMR 25:51
99E0332

Testing before an extension to an existing building at Garadice House, Ballinamore, Co. Leitrim, was carried out in July 1999. It is proposed to change the use of this 17th-century house from a dwelling to a hotel, through renovation and the construction of an extension.

Two trenches were excavated to determine the location and extent of the former west wing, which was demolished early in the 20th century. The testing confirmed the extent of the west wing and indicated that it had a basement similar to that under the main block. Demolition material was used to raise ground level on the west side of the house, which is at least 1m above surrounding ground level. A culvert was exposed extending in a north–south direction outside the west wall of the west wing and had a pitched roof of stone lintels. It was 0.3m wide and 0.3m deep and was similar to 17th-century examples found in Portumna Castle, Co. Galway. The proposed extension will not have a significant impact on the

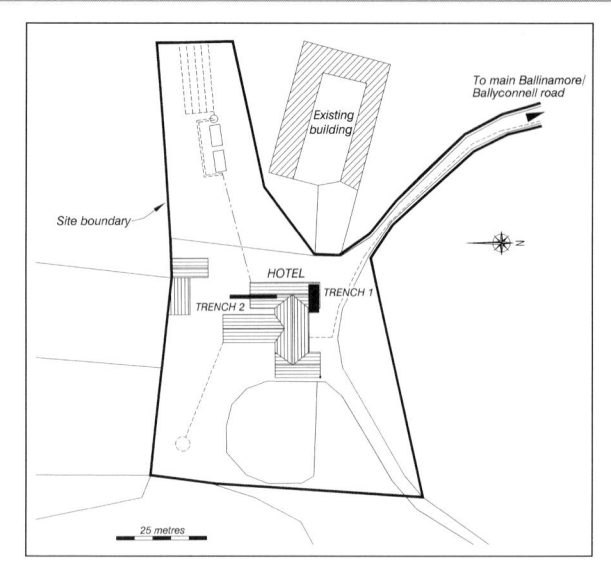

Detail of site showing location of trenches at Garadice House, Ballinamore.

intact basement of the former west wing.

*Donald Murphy, Archaeological Consultancy Services Ltd, 15 Trinity Street, Drogheda, Co. Louth.*

### 469. BRIDGE STREET, CARRICK-ON-SHANNON
Urban
SMR 31:5
99E0257

Pre-development testing was undertaken on the site of a proposed development off Bridge Street, Carrick-on-Shannon, Co. Leitrim. The site is within the zone of archaeological importance for Carrick-on-Shannon. Six test-trenches were excavated by machine within the proposed development. All were 12m long and 2m wide, except Trench 6, which was 5m long.

The stratigraphy within Trench 1 consisted of a sod/topsoil layer 0.48m thick, which directly overlay a black, peaty layer 0.32m thick. Underlying the black peaty layer was a light brown peat 0.15m thick. A sherd of modern glazed pottery was recovered from this layer. It directly overlay the natural, grey, stony daub.

At the northern end of Trench 2 the sod/topsoil, 0.35m thick, directly overlay a light brown clay, 0.13m thick, which produced some red brick. The light brown clay directly overlay the natural, orange, stony boulder clay. In the southern half of the trench the sod/topsoil layer, 0.32m thick, overlay a mortar and clay layer 0.27m thick. Underlying the mortar and clay layer was a black, peaty layer 0.5m thick, which produced some red brick. The black, peaty layer directly overlay the natural, orange boulder clay.

At the northern end of Trench 3 the sod/topsoil, 0.3m thick, directly overlay the natural, orange, stony boulder clay. In the southern half of the trench the sod/topsoil, 0.32m thick, directly overlay a mortar and clay layer 0.64m thick. Underlying the mortar and clay layer was a black, peaty layer 0.15m thick, which produced some modern white-glazed pottery. The black, peaty layer directly overlay a natural, grey daub 0.25m thick, which in turn directly overlay a natural, orange, stony boulder clay.

At the northern end of Trench 4 the sod/topsoil, 0.3m thick, directly overlay the natural, orange, stony boulder clay. In the southern half of the trench the sod/topsoil layer, 0.1m thick, directly overlay a mortar and clay layer 0.49m thick. Underlying this was a dark brown, peaty clay layer, 0.27m thick, which directly overlay the natural, orange, stony boulder clay.

In Trench 5 the sod/topsoil layer, 0.4m thick, directly overlay a natural, orange stony, boulder clay.

In Trench 6 the sod/topsoil layer, 0.19m thick, directly overlay a stone flag floor 0.08m thick. Underlying the stone flag floor was a loose clay and stone layer 0.43m thick. A layer of redeposited, natural, orange daub, 0.21m thick, directly underlay the loose clay and stones. A grey, sticky daub, 0.2m thick, directly underlay the redeposited, natural, orange daub. Underlying the grey, sticky daub was a brown, peaty clay, 0.22m thick, which produced two clay pipe stems, some animal bone and two sherds of 18th–19th-century pottery. The brown, peaty clay directly overlay a natural, sandy gravel.

No archaeological features or finds were recovered from any of the trenches.
*Gerry Walsh, Rathbawn Road, Castlebar, Co. Mayo.*

### 470. MAIN STREET, CARRICK-ON-SHANNON
Urban medieval/post-medieval
**SMR 31:5**
**99E0521**
The site is at the east end of the Main Street in Carrick-on-Shannon. Before construction works for a two-storey building it was necessary, in accordance with planning permission, to undertake testing of the site.

Three test-trenches were opened. One had to be abandoned following the exposure of an unmarked, high-voltage, live ESB cable at 0.3m below ground level. The other two trenches were opened to natural deposit levels, which occurred between 0.7m and 0.8m below ground level.

Little was revealed of archaeological significance. In one of the trenches the natural soil consisted of peat, 0.75m below ground level. This was not surprising as much of Carrick-on-Shannon and its environs is dominated by peat. The strata in the two trenches consisted of disturbed topsoil between the tarmacadam surface and associated build-up and the subsoils. It consisted of disturbed and loose garden soil with inclusions of red brick, flecks of charcoal, mortar and frequent stones.

There were no traces of any archaeological remains that could be associated with the 17th-century Plantation town.
*Mary Henry, 24 Queen Street, Clonmel, Co. Tipperary.*

### 471. PRIEST'S LANE, CARRICK-ON-SHANNON
Urban
**SMR 31:5**
**99E0223**
Pre-development testing was undertaken on the site of a proposed development off Priest's Lane, Carrick-on-Shannon, Co. Leitrim. The site is within the zone of archaeological importance for Carrick-on-Shannon.

Four test-trenches were excavated by machine within the proposed development. Two were 5m long, two were 13m long, and all were 2m wide. No archaeological features or finds were recovered from any of the trenches.
*Gerry Walsh, Rathbawn Road, Castlebar, Co. Mayo.*

### 472. FAIR GREEN, MANORHAMILTON
Adjacent to Manorhamilton Castle
**18841 33979**
**99E0571**
The Fair Green is to the west of Manorhamilton Castle, which dates to the 17th century. The local community proposes to develop the Fair Green into an amenity area. It was recommended by the National Monuments and Historic Properties Section, *Dúchas* The Heritage Service, that pre-development testing be carried out.

Four trenches were mechanically excavated in the area of the proposed development. Two of the trenches were opened at right angles to the castle wall in order to ascertain whether a ditch survived. No evidence of a ditch was revealed during the trial-trenching.

Excavations in the trench along the southern perimeter of the Fair Green revealed the remains of a sunken well. Only the east side of the well was exposed, and no further work was carried out at this stage.
*Fiona Rooney, Arch. Consultancy Ltd, Ballydavid South, Athenry, Co. Galway.*

## LIMERICK

### 473. N20/N21 ROAD IMPROVEMENT SCHEME, ADARE/ANNACOTTY CONTRACT 2
Monitoring
**98E0506 ext.**
This is a summary of the licensed monitoring attendance during the construction phase of Contract 2 of the Adare to Annacotty Road Improvement Scheme, from September 1998 to November 1999.

The dual carriageway extended for 14km from the townland of Kilgobbin in the south-west of the county (on the northern edge of the town of Adare) to the townland of Rathbane South, to the south-east of Limerick City. The road improvement scheme required the construction of twelve bridges and a number of ancillary roads. The clearance work consisted of the removal of 276,431m$^3$ of topsoil. The townlands of Ashfort, Attyflin, Ballybronoge South, Ballycummin, Ballygeale, Barnakyle, Cloghacloka, Derrybeg, Derryknockane, Fortetna, Gorteen, Kilgobbin, Monearla, Rathbane South/North, Rineroe and Rossbrien were all subject to monitoring attendance during the construction phase of Contract 2.

A variety of sites were discovered during the monitoring of the topsoil clearance, ranging from prehistoric settlement and burial sites up to 19th-century rural and industrial sites. Of the 24 archaeological sites discovered during topsoil clearance for the road scheme, excavation was carried out on 21. Sites at Fortetna townland and at Rathbane South townland did not require archaeological excavation, but they were recorded. It was decided, following consultation with *Dúchas*, that a *fulacht fiadh* discovered at Rossbrien townland could be covered in a geotextile material, sand and earth, as it lay in an area outside the main construction works and so would not be affected by the development.

The following is a list of sites that were

discovered and investigated during the construction phase of the road scheme, all in County Limerick:

*Fulacht fiadh* and Beehive well, Barnakyle, excavated by Ciara MacManus, see No 490 below;

*Fulacht fiadh*, Attyflin, excavated by Ciara MacManus, see No. 479 below;

*Fulacht fiadh* remains, Derryknockane, excavated by Ciara MacManus and Damian Finn, see No. 500 below;

*Fulacht fiadh* remains, Cloghacloka, excavated by Mary Deevy, see No. 496 below;

Corn-drying kiln, Gorteen, excavated by Ciara MacManus, see No. 504 below;

Two *fulachta fiadh*, Rossbrien, excavated by Mary Deevy, see No. 533 below;

Two *fulachta fiadh* and a stone-lined well, Gorteen, excavated by Mary Deevy, see No. 505 below;

Ring-ditch, Ballybronoge South, excavated by James Eogan and Damian Finn, see No. 481 below;

*Fulacht fiadh*, Attyflin, excavated by Mary Deevy, see No. 478 below;

Tree-circle at Fortetna, National Grid coordinates 15262 14919, recorded by Damian Finn;

*Fulacht fiadh* at Rossbrien, National Grid coordinates 15777 15334; following consultation with *Dúchas*, it was agreed that geotextile material, sand and stone would be sufficient protection for the site, as road construction will not be affecting the site completely;

Spread of archaeological material, Ballybronoge South, excavated by James Eogan and John (Sinclair) Turrell, see No. 481 below;

Undated field boundary and pits, Ballygeale, excavated by James Eogan and John (Sinclair) Turrell, see No. 486 below;

Possible prehistoric settlement, Ballygeale, excavated by James Eogan and John (Sinclair) Turrell, see No. 485 below;

Pits and post-holes at Kilgobbin, excavated by Ciara MacManus, see No. 508 below;

Subcircular pit, Kilgobbin, excavated by Ciara MacManus, see No. 508 below;

*Fulacht fiadh* remains, Rineroe, excavated by Mary Deevy, see No. 532 below;

*Fulacht fiadh*, Rossbrien, excavated by Catherine McLoughlin, see No. 534 below;

Artificial platform and possible *fulacht fiadh*, Rathbane South, excavated by Catherine McLoughlin, see No. 529 below;

Bridge footings at Rathbane South, National Grid co-ordinates 15860 15410, recorded by Damian Finn;

*Fulacht fiadh*, Rathbane South, excavated by Catherine McLoughlin, see No. 531 below;

*Fulacht fiadh*, Rathbane South, excavated by Catherine McLoughlin, see No. 530 below.

*Damian Finn, Ballycurreen, Glounthaune, Co. Cork, for ADS Ltd.*

### 474. BLACK ABBEY, ADARE
Medieval monastery
**R468465**
**99E0500**

The digging of a foul-water main connected to a temporary classroom at St Nicholas's school in the grounds of the former Augustinian friary, or Black Abbey, of Adare was monitored in October 1999. The groundwork associated with this development was extremely limited and superficial, and nothing of archaeological interest was uncovered.

*Kenneth Wiggins, 17 Vartry Close, Raheen, Co. Limerick.*

### 475. MAIN STREET, ADARE
Urban medieval
**14692 14638**
**SMR 21:32**
**99E0084**

The Adare Main Street Improvements Scheme was processed under Part X of the Local Government (Planning and Development) Regulations, 1994. The work entailed pipe-laying and upgrading the road surface over a length of 480m from the Dunraven Arms Hotel carpark at the eastern end of the village to just beyond the junction for the Askeaton road at the western end of the village. On foot of an archaeological assessment, licensed monitoring, which consisted of a trench through the length of the village, was in place for the first phase of the work (March–May 1999). Archaeological deposits and cut features were recorded in the section of the trench for 260m from the eastern end of the village. When the work recommenced in September 1999, to dig out for the foundation of an improved road surface, archaeological excavation proceeded before the construction. The excavation was carried out in two sections: the northern carriageway (8 weeks, October–December 1999) and the southern carriageway (8 weeks, January–February 2000).

Archaeological deposits survived from the eastern end of the village to a point east of the stream that crosses the Main Street near the centre of the village. The insertion of a stone bridge/culvert in the 19th century had removed all older deposits in this area. West of the stream post-medieval/modern material was recorded between the existing road foundation and the underlying boulder clay or bedrock.

Over the eastern half of the excavation, archaeological layers had been scarped and only isolated pit cuts survived. Towards the centre of the village, deposits up to 0.2–0.3m survived. The earliest feature excavated was a large, stone-lined culvert that traversed the road. The capstone was between 0.86m and 1m below existing ground level. The culvert measured 0.6m x 0.5m internally and was built in a large trench. It was covered by redeposited boulder clay that had been cut by medieval pits. The culvert may have served to direct a water source to the Trinitarian abbey (13th-century foundation).

On the northern side of the main street a variety of materials comprised a road surface that extended for 116m. This was made up of levelled-out bedrock, metalling, rough cobbling and a more formal stone surface. The rough cobbling occurred particularly over the fills of pits that lay beneath the road. The formal stone surface was excavated in the centre of the village and extended for 18m. The stones were set in a clay bedding. An earlier, similar stone surface was recorded beneath, but this was protected and remains undisturbed.

*Sarah McCutcheon, Limerick County Council, PO Box 53, County Buildings, 79–84 O'Connell Street, Limerick.*

### 476. ARDANREAGH
Adjacent to possible rectangular enclosure
16314 13879
SMR 32:190
99E0268

Testing was carried out on 8 June 1999 following a request by *Dúchas* to the applicant, as the development site was within SMR 32:190, an enclosure or subrectangular platform, defined on the east, north and west sides by a ditch and on the south side by the field boundary. It may be a medieval moated site. The development, to the west of the R512 on flat grazing land, consisted of a dwelling-house, garage, septic tank, percolation area, entrance and boundary wall, which were east of the enclosure, the boundary being only 2m from the outer edge of the ditch at the south-western corner. The site measured 61m from the centre road line by 30.5m north–south.

Within the development site the only feature noted was an earthfast boulder close to the northern fence. A second, similar boulder was found north of the site, close to the road bank. Eight 1m-wide cuttings were made to coincide with the various elements of the proposed development.

No features, deposits or finds that could be identified as archaeological were noted in any of the cuttings. There did not, therefore, appear to be any archaeological reason why the development should not proceed.

*Celie O Rahilly, Limerick Corporation, City Hall, Limerick.*

### 477. ATTYFLIN, SITE AR7
Medieval settlement
15110 14778
SMR 21:25
96E0380 ext.

A complex of earthworks on the summit of a low hill (37m OD) was identified in the environmental impact statement for the proposed N20/N21 Road Improvement Scheme in Attyflin townland.

The earthworks are very low; the main feature is a subrectangular enclosure defined by a low, rounded bank *c.* 80m long (north–south) and 48m wide; there is an entrance in the south-east corner. The north-west quarter of the enclosure is occupied by a slightly raised, level, rectangular platform, *c.* 23.5m north–south by 19.5m. The remains of a field system, including a possible trackway, have been identified east of the enclosure. There is a *cillín* with associated field system on the other side of the present Patrickswell–Croom road (N21).

The realignment of the N21 necessitated the excavation of the western part of the enclosure before construction of the road. In addition, topsoil was stripped by mechanical excavator under archaeological supervision from areas extending 100m south of the site and 50m north of the site. Seven test-trenches were previously excavated in March 1997 by the writer and in December 1997 by Paul Logue (*Excavations 1997*, 111–12, 97E0477).

The enclosure was found to be a two-phase construction. The Phase 1 enclosure was 85m long. It was surrounded by a ditch that varied from 1.5m to 3m wide and averaged 0.6m deep. This ditch was cut through the underlying limestone bedrock in places. The Phase 2 enclosure involved the filling of the northern enclosure ditch and the digging of a ditch parallel to it 15m to the north, thereby extending the enclosed area from *c.* 2400m$^2$ to *c.* 3200m$^2$. The entrance was midway along the western side of the Phase 1 enclosure; it consisted of a 2m-wide causeway. Two pairs of substantial post-holes defined an entrance 1.5m wide internally. A line of smaller post-holes extended across the enclosure from the northern side of this entrance. This suggests that the enclosure was internally subdivided by a wooden fence

Within the enclosure there was a clear difference in the intensity of ancient activity. Relatively few features were found in the southern part, while in the northern half a series of large pits was uncovered. Four were quarry pits that were broader than they were deep and were filled with stones. It is thought that originally these pits were dug to extract clay for building purposes, the stony fill resulting from the sorting on site of the material dug out of the pit. Three rubbish pits were found. They are deeper than they are broad and contained organic-rich fills. Two of these pits cut one of the quarry pits. No clear evidence for structures was found within the enclosure, nor were any hearths uncovered, although a considerable amount of ash had been dumped into the northern ditch of the Phase 1 enclosure.

About 40m north of the main enclosure a series of ditches was uncovered during topsoil-stripping. These represent at least two phases of enclosure of which there was no surface trace. The Phase 1 enclosure was 35m long (north–south) and had a 2m-wide entrance gap midway along its western side, which was flanked by a pair of post-holes. The Phase II enclosure was roughly the same size as the earlier one, although the ditch that defined it was less substantial. Within these enclosures a series of pits was found. Two of them were quarry pits, and there was one substantial rubbish pit; however, there was also a series of less substantial pits, one of which contained more than 100 oyster shells.

Most of the features uncovered contained sherds of glazed medieval pottery. The vast majority of the pottery assemblage is locally made Adare ware; imported ceramics are solely represented by Saintonge green-glazed ware (C. Sandes, pers. comm.). A number of iron knives, one of which retained part of its wooden handle, were found. There are examples of both whittle tang and plate tang among the assemblage. A small iron slash hook was found. A decorated copper-alloy stick-pin and a simple copper-alloy ring brooch were found in one of the rubbish disposal pits. A single-edged composite bone comb was found in the backfill of the Phase 1 enclosure ditch. These finds all suggest a date in the 13th–14th century for the occupation on this site.

*James Eogan, ADS Ltd, Windsor House, 11 Fairview Strand, Dublin 3.*

### 478. ATTYFLIN
Isolated trough
1517 1488
99E0459

The site is in Attyflin townland, *c.* 9km south-west of Limerick City, east of the N20. The site was

Pit/trough(?), Attyflin (No. 478), half-sectioned from south.

uncovered during archaeological monitoring of topsoil-stripping before road construction on the N20/N21 Adare to Annacotty road scheme. A rescue excavation was carried out over three-and-a-half weeks in August–September 1999. The site was close to marshy ground within which a *fulacht fiadh* (see No. 479 below) was excavated.

Two phases of activity were identified. The earliest phase consisted of a subsoil-cut subcircular pit that may have been a trough. This pit measured 1.8m in maximum diameter and 0.3m in maximum depth. There was evidence for a wooden structure in the form of stake-holes in its base and surrounding its upper edges. It was filled with black, charcoal-rich soil with frequent fragments of degraded sandstone. There was also a series of shallow, irregular-shaped, subsoil-cut pits and depressions, all with an upper fill of black, charcoal-rich soil with frequent fragments of degraded sandstone. It is unclear, however, whether any of these were hearths, owing to the lack of evidence for *in situ* burning. No artefacts or animal bone were recovered from any of these features.

The second phase of activity consisted of ploughmarks running in three directions, east–west, north–south and north-west/south-east.
*Mary Deevy, ADS Ltd, Windsor House, 11 Fairview Strand, Fairview, Dublin 3.*

### 479. ATTYFLIN
*Fulacht fiadh*
**99E0171**
Monitoring of topsoil-stripping along the proposed route of the N20/N21 Limerick bypass resulted in the discovery of a *fulacht fiadh* within the townland of Attyflin, Co. Limerick. The site was c. 500m east of the N21 road, within the vicinity of a number of known areas of archaeological activity, including New Site B (c. 500m to the east), AR7 (No. 477 above, c. 2km to the south-west) and AR6 (c. 3km to the south-west).

The site survived as an elongated mound 17m long x 9m wide x 0.35m high. Excavation of the mound revealed it to be an accumulation of dump material, consisting of a mix of heat-shattered limestone stones and charcoal-rich soil, characteristic of this type of site.

A small trough was uncovered under the south-west quadrant of the mound. The trough was rectangular (2.1m long, 1m wide, 0.28m deep) and orientated north-west/south-east, with steep sides and a flat base.

Another, more substantial subsoil-cut feature was found 1.3m to the north of the trough. Excavation of this feature revealed the existence of a large, oval pit, 0.14m x 2m x 1.2m deep. The pit was orientated north-east/south-west, with the southern half appearing to have a stepped side, while the northern sides were more vertical. It had been filled by a number of deposits of burnt and shattered limestone rocks, along with a number of silt deposits. A few small fragments of animal bone were recovered from these fills, along with two fragments of wood, neither of which had been visibly worked.

Around the east edge of the pit, where the break of slope for the pit cut was gentlest, twelve stake-holes were uncovered and excavated. There was very little pattern to the stake-holes in plan, except for one possible line of double post-holes running north–south along the edge of the pit. Disturbance on the opposite side of the pit in the form of later drains meant that it was not possible to tell whether there was a corresponding set of post-holes on the west edge. However, it is suggested that these stake-holes represented the remains of either a windbreak or a structure spanning the width of the pit.
*Ciara MacManus, c/o ADS Ltd, Windsor House, 11 Fairview Strand, Dublin 3.*

### 480. BALLINACURRA (HART)/BALLINACURRA (WESTON)/ROSSBRIEN SOUTH/RATHBANE/BANEMORE
Monitoring
**1600 1543–1555 1555**
**99E0643**
Monitoring of topsoil-stripping for the Limerick Main Drainage Southern Interceptor pipeline wayleave commenced in October 1999 and is scheduled to continue for 12–18 months. Small sections of the pipeline corridor are opened consecutively, and these are archaeologically monitored as they become available. The pipeline crosses several townlands on the southern outskirts of Limerick City, runs close to two known monuments (SMR 13:15 and 13:20) and will tunnel under the site of Ballinacurra Bridge (SMR 13:12). The pipeline runs for 5.26km from the proposed Pumping Station at Corcanree, opposite the Dock Road by Roche's, to the Bawnmore estate in Banemore Townland.

To date, topsoil-stripping has been carried out over 1.46km, with a wayleave width of 16m, from the Dock Road through the racecourse to Ballinacurra Bridge. No archaeological soils or features were encountered, and monitoring is ongoing.
*Paul Stevens for Margaret Gowen & Co. Ltd, 2 Killiney View, Albert Road Lower, Glenageary, Co. Dublin.*

### 481. BALLYBRONOGE SOUTH
Ring-ditch
**15110 14840**
**99E0324**
This site was discovered during the monitoring of topsoil clearance before construction of the Adare to Annacotty N20/N21 Road Improvement Scheme in July 1999.

Excavation revealed a penannular ring-ditch with a U-shaped profile. The ring-ditch had a maximum external diameter of 7m and a maximum depth of 0.5m. The pattern of silting in the ditch suggests that there may have been an external bank. The main fill of the ditch was a charcoal-rich silt in which fourteen token deposits of cremated human bone were found. One of the deposits contained part of a decorated bone artefact that is similar stylistically to a gaming-piece found in a cremation under a barrow at Cush, Co. Limerick. A copper-alloy spiral ring was also found in this fill.

These artefacts suggest a date in the Iron Age for the filling of the ditch and the deposition of the cremations.

The site had been partially destroyed by a machine-excavated engineering test-pit before archaeological investigation.

*James Eogan and Damian Finn, ADS Ltd, Windsor House, 11 Fairview Strand, Dublin 3.*

### 482. BALLYCLOGH
Linear earthwork
R642566
99E0040

Test-trenching took place here before construction of the Southern Ring Road. The area investigated was a linear earthwork running in a north–south direction through poor-quality grassland. The first edition OS map records it as a roadway, but it is not marked on the second edition.

One trench was opened by hand, measuring 10m by 1m, across the earthwork, to ascertain the nature of the feature and to find out whether it was flanked by ditches.

The trenching proved that this earthwork was the original roadway of the first edition OS map. The finds, which included pottery sherds and a glass fragment, showed the feature to have a late 18th–early 19th century date, and it is therefore not archaeological in nature.

*Frank Coyne, Aegis Archaeology, 16 Avondale Court, Corbally, Limerick.*

### 483. BALLYCUMMIN
*Fulachta fiadh* and 19th-century trackway
15530 15230
SMR 13:151
98E0433

Various stages of archaeological investigation were undertaken at Ballycummin between September 1998 and May 1999 in association with the construction of a new computer factory by Dell Products (Europe) B.V. and in compliance with a condition of planning permission issued by Limerick County Council. The investigations also covered the installation of a dual carriageway connecting the factory with the new Loughmore link road and associated storm and foul drains by Shannon Free Airport Development Company Ltd.

Phase 1 involved the pre-development testing of seven potential archaeological sites noted in the environmental impact statement and on aerial photography of the factory site. A single trench was mechanically excavated at each site, six of which were 15m long, with the remaining trench 10m long. No archaeological evidence was noted during this work.

The factory construction site is on the demesne of Roche Castle—an early 19th-century house. Most of the features encountered in the monitoring of groundworks (Phase 2) relate to farming activity associated with the house. However, to the south-west of the site a *fulacht fiadh* was uncovered in the digging of a trench for a temporary telecom supply to the contractor's compound. The ploughed-out burnt spread lies immediately under the sod and is 15–19m long and 0.1–0.55m thick. The feature is outside the area of development, and the trench was backfilled following examination and recording.

Phase 3, construction of the dual carriageway to the factory and an ancillary road, necessitated the removal of portions of a trackway, SMR 13:151. A metal-detector survey was undertaken over the stretches of trackway to be removed, which totalled 120m in length. Of 570 readings recorded, 565 were ferrous. Three trenches, each measuring 10m x 1m, were excavated by hand across the feature. These revealed a stone construction, with an elaborate French drain underneath in one of the cuttings. The artefacts recovered include delftware, stoneware sherds, clay pipes, red brick, mortar pieces, glass and iron objects. The trackway is 19th-century in date and may have been used to ferry stone from a nearby quarry to Roche Castle.

Four *fulachta fiadh* were uncovered during monitoring of the construction of the dual carriageway, ancillary road and associated storm and foul drains (Phase 4). All the sites were subsequently excavated by hand, as two were within the area of road construction while the other two lay close to inserted drains that would affect the hydrology of those sites. All of the *fulachta fiadh* were evident as ploughed-out spreads and were further interfered with by 19th-century tillage furrows and French drains.

*Fulacht fiadh* 1 was a rectangular trough measuring 2.6m x 1.65m and 0.35m deep dug into the subsoil. The burnt spread, with an overall diameter of 8.5m, though close by, was completely separate from the trough.

*Fulacht fiadh* 2 was close to No. 1. The burnt spread measured 9.5m x 7.5m and covered eleven hollows of varying shapes and sizes. Some of these are likely to have been natural depressions; some may have been modified; and others are likely to have been entirely man-made.

*Fulacht fiadh* 3 consisted of three separate burnt spreads measuring 11m x 4.5m, 10m x 3m and 5.5m x 4m. Two large pits were connected with one of the spreads, one of which is likely to be modern.

*Fulacht fiadh* 4 was a rectangular trough measuring 2.4m x 1.4m and 0.35–0.4m deep dug into the subsoil. The presence of stake-holes indicated that it was originally timber-lined. The trough was surrounded by a burnt spread measuring 12m x 8.5m.

*Noel Dunne, Newtown, Rathangan, Co. Kildare.*

### 484. HOWMEDICA LINK ROAD, BALLYCUMMIN
Monitoring
15510 15220; 15550 1526 (between these points)
99E0376

The Howmedica link road is 500m east of the N20

road and 250m south of the Raheen Industrial Estate. It was constructed as part of the infrastructure for the new Dell Computers European Manufacturing Facility (EMF 3). The road corridor is 30m wide and covers a distance of c. 550m.

The area is one of high archaeological potential. Four *fulachta fiadh* and a 19th-century trackway have been excavated by Noel Dunne in the surrounding area (see No. 483 above).

The only archaeological feature uncovered in the monitoring of the topsoil clearance was a 48m-long section of the trackway (SMR 13:151).
*Damian Finn, Ballycurreen, Glounthaune, Co. Cork, for ADS Ltd.*

### 485. BALLYGEALE, SITE 1
Settlement activity of unknown date
15127 14760
99E0341

This site was c. 2km from Patrickswell, on the east side of the existing road to Croom (N20). It lies in a poorly drained area at the foot of a ridge on the top of which (in Attyflin townland) were a field system and habitation site dating to the medieval period. It is c. 200m north of Ballygeale 2 (No. 486 below), which was excavated concurrently. The site was discovered in June 1999 during monitoring of topsoil-stripping on the N20/N21 Road Improvement Scheme.

After removal of a thin layer of topsoil, a number of features were exposed, including part of a penannular ditch, post-holes, several burnt areas and a linear ditch. Most of them were filled with a very dark soil that contained a considerable amount of burnt stone and charcoal. Most of the features were very shallow, with the notable exception of a large pit (3.35m x 3.5m) to the east of the penannular ditch, which proved to be a stone-lined well.

The ditch varied from 0.5m to 0.9m wide and most likely represents the wall trench of a circular structure c. 10m in diameter with an entrance to the south. There may have been a ring of posts around the outside of the ditch, supporting the walls, and an inner ring of posts, supporting the roof. There was a central hearth, while the presence of a number of stake-holes suggests other internal features. The very shallow stratigraphy made it difficult to assess the relationships between features and the phases of activity; the site was limited to the east and west by modern disturbance. A series of post-holes north of the well and some hearths may be from an earlier phase than the structure, which is probably contemporary with the well and the majority of the hearths and pits. Another set of hearths and pits, together with a linear ditch, seems to be a later feature.

The well was excavated to a depth of 2.4m, a limit set by time and safety considerations. The shaft was 0.6m in diameter and was lined with large, undressed stones set in clay. Some flat stones were placed around the mouth of the well to provide access. There was a considerable amount of burnt stone in the fill and in the clay lining of the well. Some animal bone and wood were found in the lower fill of this feature.

No pottery or artefacts were found that would give an indication of date, although it is anticipated that wood, bone and charcoal samples will provide enough material for radiocarbon dates.
*James Eogan and Sinclair Turrell, ADS Ltd, Windsor House, 11 Fairview Strand, Dublin 3.*

### 486. BALLYGEALE, SITE 2
Undated field boundary and pits
15127 14745
99E0342

This site was c. 2km from Patrickswell, on the east side of the existing road to Croom (N20). It lies just below the crest of a low, flat-topped, north-facing ridge, 200m south of Ballygeale 1 (No. 485 above), which was excavated concurrently. The site was discovered in June 1999 during monitoring of topsoil-stripping on the N20/N21 Road Improvement Scheme.

The surface of the site was cleaned to reveal a number of features appearing as largely brownish-orange fills against a mixed, natural subsoil consisting of loose gravel and brownish-grey, sandy silt clay.

Excavation revealed a shallow, c. 1m-wide ditch running across the site for 21m in a south-west/north-east orientation, merging with a shallow pit at the eastern limit of the site. Immediately north-west of this pit was a shallower, slightly wider ditch at right angles to the first, which was traced for 5.5m. These ditches seem to form the corner of a rectangular enclosure. With the exception of two isolated features, all the activity on the site was concentrated within the angle formed by these ditches.

The first ditch was cut by an irregular, shallow pit, midway along its length. There was a line of four small post-holes in the bottom of this pit and a further two in its south-west corner. North-west of this was a shallow depression that had post-holes along its north-eastern edge. These, together with several adjacent post-holes (some of which contained packing stones), form a roughly subrectangular pattern (c. 2m x 4m) and may define a small, rectangular structure.

Some 3m south-west of the longer ditch was a shallow, squarish (1.2m x 1.1m) feature that was lined with stones; this may have been a hearth. Finally, a single pit was identified c. 15m south of the other features. This pit was circular in plan (1.6m diameter) and had steeply sloping sides and a regular, slightly dished base. The basal fill was composed of many successive layers of coloured ash. There was a small post-hole on the north edge of the pit and a somewhat larger one dug into its base. The pit may have had another function before being used to dump ash in.

The ditches can be interpreted as field boundaries, while the other features may indicate that there was some small-scale domestic or industrial activity in the corner of a field, as suggested by the charcoal-rich pit and hearth. The finds from the excavation consisted solely of some small scraps of animal bone. It is hoped that these, together with charcoal and ash samples, will provide enough material for radiocarbon dates.
*James Eogan and Sinclair Turrell, ADS Ltd, Windsor House, 11 Fairview Strand, Dublin 3.*

### 487. BALLYSIMON II
Watermill
16149 15543
SMR 5:41
98E0607

This site is in the path of the Limerick Southern Ring Road, and before its demolition it was proposed architecturally to survey the extant structure. Ballysimon Mill first appeared on the 17th-century Down Survey Map. From the survey it was found that no original 17th-century features remained. In fact the entire structure appeared to have been rebuilt over the years. A large farmhouse of Georgian style in the vicinity of the mill was also due for demolition. Aegis recommended that this too should be photographically surveyed, and this was subsequently carried out.

It was then agreed that the extant mill structure should be test-trenched to see whether it was built on the earlier foundations of the 17th-century mill. The only free space in which to trench by hand was in the interior of the extant mill, because of the surrounding concrete yard. The unstable nature of the building meant that only one test-trench could be dug.

The mill building was two-storeyed and rectangular, measuring 4m east–west by 5.5m. The trench measured 1.4m by 3.5m. The west end of the trench abutted a portion of ashlar masonry, which was interpreted as an early part of the building. Overburden in the form of modern debris and building rubble was encountered, beneath which was the original cobbled stone floor, containing one large limestone flag that appeared to have been a reused step. This overlay the red boulder clay, interpreted as the natural parent material of the site. No artefacts of archaeological significance were recovered. The test-trenching concluded that the extant structure did not stand on an earlier site.

*Tracy Collins, Aegis Archaeology, 16 Avondale Court, Corbally, Limerick.*

### 488. BALLYSIMON IV
No archaeological significance
R618552
99E0005

This site was identified by Celie O Rahilly (Senior Archaeologist, Limerick Corporation) during field-walking, as part of an environmental impact statement on the proposed Limerick Southern Ring Road from Adare to Annacotty. The site consisted of two conjoined circular depressions in the townland of Ballysimon, 4km south-east of Limerick City.

The first depression measured 18m x 18m, and the second measured 15m x 15m. Two test-trenches were excavated by hand. Test-trench 1 measured 1m by 7m and ran in a north–south direction, from the outer area of the more northerly depression, down towards its centre. Test-trench 2 measured 1m by 4m and ran in a north–south direction, across the outer area of the more southerly depression. The test-trenches failed to reveal any deposits, features or finds of archaeological interest. The depressions may have been the result of localised quarrying in the 18th or 19th century.

*Ken Hanley, 44 Eaton Heights, Cobh, Co. Cork, for Aegis Archaeology Ltd.*

### 489. BALLYSIMON
Medieval enclosure (adjacent to church site)
16231 15764
SMR 13:26
99E0422

The site is *c.* 1 mile south of Limerick on the north side of the main Limerick–Tipperary road and is on the west edge of a terrace overlooking a bend in the River Groody. A subcircular enclosure was uncovered at this location during test-trenching by Fiona Rooney (*Excavations 1998*, 130, 98E0487) before the construction of the Southern Ring Road. This initial investigation revealed an enclosure ditch, which produced a single sherd of medieval pottery. A second trench in the interior of the enclosure demonstrated that it had been disturbed by cultivation activity.

A full excavation of this enclosure was carried out from September to December 1999 by the writer. It was also agreed with the client that two 50m-long strips of the road-take would be mechanically stripped to natural on either side of the enclosure in order to investigate the possibility that associated archaeological features existed outside the confines of the enclosure.

*The enclosure*

The subcircular enclosure was delimited by a ditch, averaging 4m wide and 1.5m deep, which was absent on the west side, where the enclosure was delimited by the riverside edge of the terrace. The internal area of the enclosure measured *c.* 35m in diameter, and an entrance causeway was found in the north side of the ditch. There were no extant remains of an enclosing bank, which appeared to have been backfilled into the ditch, and based on the ditch dimensions the bank may have originally been very substantial. Apart from a moderate amount of unhewn limestone boulders recovered from the southern extent of the ditch, there was no evidence to suggest that the bank had been revetted.

The ditch contained evidence for two phases of activity. The initial ditch cut (Phase 1) was flat-bottomed apart from a basal gully in the north-east corner. This ditch became infilled with collapsed bank material and backfilled dump material, including animal bones and charcoal-rich deposits.

These fills were then cut by a shallower and narrower ditch (Phase 2) that followed the line of the earlier ditch and disturbed the original entrance causeway. After the Phase 2 ditch had been almost completely infilled it was sealed by a redeposited layer of natural subsoil, perhaps originating from remaining bank material that was pulled over the ditch by later cultivation activity.

There was no evidence to indicate that the interior of the enclosure had been raised by material upcast from the ditch, as it was lower than the surrounding area, and all of the internal structural features were cut into the natural boulder clay horizon.

The foundation slot-trenches of two circular timber huts were uncovered near the centre of the enclosure. These were sealed by the ploughsoil layer, and both huts were disturbed by later cultivation activity. The central structure (Hut A) measured 7.8m in diameter, with a cobbled entrance surface uncovered on the north side of the hut. An earlier hut structure (Hut B), 6.8m in diameter, was uncovered to the north of Hut A. No finds were recovered from Hut B, but it was found to have been disturbed by the construction of Hut A.

A large number of post- and stake-holes were uncovered in the area between Hut B and the causewayed entrance, suggesting the presence of another structure in the north end of the site. Also, three small ironworking pits and one cooking pit were uncovered in the interior of the enclosure.

*Monitoring of soil-stripping to the west and east of the enclosure*
Two 50m-long strips of land on either side of the enclosure were mechanically stripped to the natural boulder clay. No archaeological features were uncovered to the west of the enclosure, within the river flood-plain below the terrace. A hut structure (Hut C) and small kiln were uncovered to the east of the enclosure, and both of these were excavated.

The circular hut was *c.* 10m to the east of the enclosure. It measured 7.7m in diameter and was of a similar construction to the huts within the enclosure. There was a break in the east side of the delimiting slot-trench, indicating the presence an entrance in this area.

A keyhole-shaped corn-drying kiln was uncovered *c.* 5m to the east of the hut entrance. This was a shallow, stone-lined feature 4.7m long and 2.1m wide. It was orientated north–south, with the bowl at the north end of the kiln and the fire-spot at the south end of the flue. There was no evidence of baffle stones or lintel stones in the flue. A shallow pit, with a charcoal-rich fill, lay 0.7m to the south of the kiln.

*Artefacts*
The ditch fills contained occasional finds such as animal bone, medieval pottery and iron nails. Finds from the interior of the site included medieval pottery sherds (both local and imported), dating to AD 1250–1350, a quernstone fragment and a stone mortar. Saintonge pottery sherds were uncovered in the fill of the Phase 2 ditch and in Hut A, the latest structure in the enclosure. The quernstone and stone mortar were both recovered from the make-up material of the cobbled entrance to this hut. The shallow pit to the south of the corn-drying kiln produced a sherd of locally produced medieval ware of a similar type to the sherds recovered from within the enclosure. No finds were recovered from the Phase 1 ditch fills or from Hut B, although it is intended to submit charcoal from both features for dating.

*Preliminary conclusions*
This enclosure has been interpreted, on the basis of its finds, morphology and siting, as a medieval ringwork. Later cultivation activity has transformed the morphology of the site, but it was clearly a subcircular enclosure delimited by a substantial ditch crossed by a causewayed entrance on the north side. The ditch was absent in the west side, where the enclosure was delimited by the edge of the terrace. The soil profile in the ditch was also disturbed, but the presence of redeposited natural subsoil towards the base and top of this feature indicated that the enclosure was once delimited by a bank that has since become levelled.

The artefactual evidence recovered from the enclosure shows that it was occupied in the late 13th/early 14th centuries. The enclosure is to the north of the site of a 14th-century church, currently in use as a graveyard, and the two sites may have been contemporary. This position of the enclosure, on the edge of a river terrace and close to the site of a medieval church, is indicative of a medieval ringwork. The artefactual assemblage supports such an interpretation.

The artefacts and features uncovered at Ballysimon suggest that this was a settlement site, with the occupants living in circular timber huts and carrying out their own ironworking and grain processing in what appears to have been a defended farmstead. The absence of the bank means that it is difficult to assess the precise defensive nature of the site. The evidence from the ditch and interior of the enclosure indicates that the occupation of the site continued into the 14th century, when it appears to have been abandoned. No artefacts were recovered from the Phase 1 basal ditch fills or the earliest interior structure (Hut B), and therefore the dating of the establishment of the site awaits the dating of charcoal and animal bone samples recovered from these features.

Tony Cummins, Aegis Archaeology, 16 Avondale Court, Corbally, Limerick.

## 490. BARNAKYLE
*Fulacht fiadh*
99E0067

The excavation of a *fulacht fiadh* within the townland of Barnakyle, Co. Limerick, was carried out over seven weeks from 10 February 1999. The site was discovered during monitoring of topsoil-stripping and drainage installation along the proposed route of the N20/N21 Limerick bypass and lay *c.* 5 miles to the south of Limerick City and *c.* 500m to the west of the N20 main road.

The *fulacht fiadh* survived as a mound of burnt stones and charcoal-rich soil, 18.94m long, 14m wide and 0.5m at its highest, under which a number of subsoil-cut features survived. Excavation and removal of the mound revealed three phases of activity on the site.

The first phase was the initial use of the site as a cooking area, with the construction of at least one trough, and associated build-up of mound material. The trough was elongated, 2.12m long, 1.48m wide and 0.43m deep, and was filled with a charcoal-rich, peaty deposit. Another possible trough lay to the north-east of the first one. Again, it was elongated (1.8m x 0.86m x 0.45m deep) and filled with a charcoal-rich material and numerous burnt stones. The resultant mound material then covered these earlier features.

The second phase of activity included the building of a substantial stone hearth structure over part of the earlier trough and the excavation of a secondary trough. The stone hearth was 2.6m long and 1.86m wide and consisted of two large stones, slabs of limestone, bounded by a ring of upright limestone blocks and divided in the middle by elongated slabs of limestone set on their sides. The two main slabs of stone were burnt and heat-shattered, along with many of the other stones that made up the hearth. The secondary trough was uncovered along the west edge of the mound and survived as a large, elongated pit (4.85m long, 3.18m wide and 0.99m deep) with a north-west/south-east orientation. The trough was filled by a number of deposits, ranging from soft, peaty layers to soft clays, and appeared to be lined by a layer of small stones set into the edge. During this phase, the build-up of the rest of the mound material occurred. At this stage it was possible to identify an area within the mound where the rake material from the hearth had been dumped to the north-east of the hearth.

The last phase of activity on the site resulted in the construction of a beehive-shaped well, which was sunk into the north-east end of the mound. The well was of drystone construction, comprising roughly hewn blocks of limestone.
*Ciara MacManus, c/o ADS Ltd, Windsor House, 11 Fairview Strand, Dublin 3.*

### 491. BAURNALICKA
No archaeological significance
SMR 21:73
99E0331

Test-trenching on the site of a proposed extension to a private house, in the vicinity of an enclosure, revealed no features or deposits of archaeological significance.
*Brian Hodkinson, Annaholty, Birdhill, Co. Tipperary.*

### 492. BOHERGEELA
No archaeological significance
R575388
SMR 31:62

The development is within the RMP site number LK031—062-01/04. The archaeological remains are to the north of the present development. Trial-trenching did not uncover any archaeological remains or finds.
*Rose M. Cleary, Department of Archaeology, University College, Cork.*

### 493. CAHIRGUILLAMORE, BRUFF
No archaeological significance
99E0298

Test-trenching was carried out before a private (residential) development. Nothing of archaeological significance was identified. Monitoring had been recommended because of the proximity of a number of known archaeological sites of varying dates. No further action was taken.
*Una Cosgrave, ADS Ltd, Windsor House, 11 Fairview Strand, Dublin 3.*

### 494. CASTLEMUNGRET
Adjacent to monuments
15341 15408
99E0306

It is proposed to develop the site at Castlemungret as a County Council graveyard. An assessment was carried out because of its proximity to a variety of SMR sites. Dúchas had recommended that all topsoil-stripping be monitored as the site was large. To facilitate early availability for burial, the first area in which interments are to take place was extensively tested instead. Five trenches were opened using a mechanical excavator with a toothless bucket. These were 2m wide by over 30m long. The ground was reduced to boulder clay. No archaeological remains were uncovered in the test excavations.
*Sarah McCutcheon, Limerick County Council, PO Box 53, County Buildings, 79–84 O'Connell Street, Limerick.*

### 495. CASTLEROBERTS
Vicinity of enclosure
R490448
SMR 21:58
99E0638

A test excavation was carried out in November 1999 before the construction of a dwelling-house in a field adjacent to the surviving north-western quadrant of an enclosure. The cuttings revealed natural, grey sediment and limestone boulders beneath the topsoil. There was no indication in the cuttings of any material of archaeological origin.
*Kenneth Wiggins, 77 Vartry Close, Raheen, Co. Limerick.*

### 496. CLOGHACLOKA
Trough and adjacent pits
1540 1507
99E0364

The site was c. 8km south-west of Limerick City and 1km to the south of the N20. It was uncovered during archaeological monitoring of topsoil-stripping before road construction on the N20/N21 Adare to Annacotty road scheme. A rescue excavation was carried out over four weeks in July, during which four phases of activity were identified.

The earliest phase consisted of one large and two shallow pits, all filled with charcoal-rich soil and fragmented sandstone. The three pits were probably all troughs. Associated with the troughs were a number of very shallow pits or depressions filled with the same burnt material, some of which may have been hearths. Evidence for wooden structures was recovered in the form of stake-holes in the corners of the two shallow troughs and a short row of stake-holes nearby, which may have been a windbreak. No artefacts or animal bone were recovered from any of these features.

The second and third phases of activity were represented by three straight, linear ditches, which were relatively modern field drains. The fill of part

Troughs at Cloghacloka, half-sectioned.

of one of these ditches was composed of displaced burnt material, indicating that the earlier, Phase 1, features had been disturbed at some stage by land development. It may be that a shallow mound or spread of burnt material was originally present and that Phase 1 represents the basal remains of a badly truncated *fulacht fiadh*. Another phase of activity was represented by a series of furrows. These were later than Phase 1, but it was not possible to identify their chronological relationship with Phases 2 and 3.
*Mary Deevy, ADS Ltd, Windsor House, 11 Fairview Strand, Fairview, Dublin 3.*

### 497. CLOGHAST
Monitoring
172555 125193
99E0295

Planning permission was granted by An Bord Pleanála for the construction of a telecommunications mast, associated buildings and an access road. The development site is on the south-eastern slopes of a peak known as 'The Pinnacle' and was covered with thin mountain peat. The development site is in the vicinity of a stone circle (SMR 49:95). Planning conditions imposed on the development required the presence of an archaeologist to monitor all excavation works.

No archaeological material was encountered during monitoring.
*Meriel McClatchie, Archaeological Services Unit, Department of Archaeology, University College, Cork.*

### 498. CROOM
Ring-ditch
15134 14006
SMR 31:135
97E0399 ext.

This project involved the full excavation of a ring-ditch in the townland of Croom, *c.* 0.5 miles south of the town of Croom, Co. Limerick. It was associated with the Croom Bypass and was funded by Limerick County Council and the National Roads Authority. The site, first identified during fieldwork, was a circular platform of raised ground 24m in diameter.

Archaeological investigations of the monument were first carried out by Thaddeus Breen in 1997 (*Excavations 1997*, 113). The investigations concluded that the site represented a circular, ditched enclosure with possibly associated features outside the ditch.

The original licence was extended to allow full manual excavation of the monument and the monitoring of topsoil-stripping to its north and south.

Removal of the sod and topsoil revealed the upper fills of a ditch and drain feature and an area of archaeological activity in the central raised area. During excavations it was found that the ditch had been greatly disturbed by a series of drains that followed the line of the ring-ditch. Here the stratigraphy consisted of a layer of orange/grey, silty clay overlying the stone drains. The original cut of the ditch had been altered by this disturbance. The basal fill of the ditch survived below the drains and contained inclusions of animal bone. In the east of the site (along the road boundary) an area 20m long had not been disturbed by land reclamation, and here the ditch and entranceway survived. The original ditch cut was 2.8m wide and *c.* 1m in maximum depth. Removal of the orange/grey, silty clay layer revealed the basal layer of the ditch and a deposit of stones in the north and south terminals. The deposit of stones contained inclusions of animal bone, charcoal flecks and a fragment of a lignite bracelet. The ditch was U-shaped in section.

In the eastern half of the central raised area the remains of a possible structure were revealed. It was defined by two linear slot-trenches, both of which ran in an east–west direction. The fill of the trenches was a stony, grey/brown, silty clay with coarse components of animal bone and animal teeth. Within the area defined by the slot-trenches a number of shallow pits and post-holes were revealed. A scatter of cremated bone was also revealed below the topsoil within the dark, blackish-brown, silty clay deposit.

The excavations revealed the remains of a ring-ditch consisting of a subcircular central area measuring 33.3m north–south by 31.4m, raised *c.* 0.4m above the surrounding ground. This was enclosed by a ditch that had been reused in more recent times for land reclamation purposes.

Finds from the site included modern pottery, glass and clay pipe fragments, which came from the ditch, the drains and the topsoil. Coarse components from the structure consisted primarily of animal bone, some cremated bone and the occasional fragment of slag. A small pin was found in the disturbed area of the ditch, and a fragment of a lignite bracelet was discovered in the undisturbed context in the south terminal.

Monitoring of the mechanical excavation of the topsoil revealed a number of drains, some of which were the same as those found during the manual excavation of the ring-ditch. Some of the drains appeared to run below the level of the road, therefore pre-dating its construction. Altogether, eleven drains were revealed: five ran in a north–south direction and were machine cut, two ran in an east–west direction, and the others ran along the line of the ring-ditch; all were manually cut. Modern glazed pottery fragments were the only coarse components revealed during the excavation of the drains.
*Fiona Rooney, Arch. Consultancy Ltd, Ballydavid South, Athenry, Co. Galway.*

### 499. CROOM
Enclosure
15128 14024
SMR 30:134
97E0400 ext.

This project concerned the excavation of a site along the route of the Croom Bypass, Co. Limerick. Funding for the project was provided by Limerick County Council and the National Roads Authority. In the townland of Croom, this site was first identified by Celie O Rahilly during fieldwork. It is a subcircular area measuring 27.4m north–south by 25m, which is raised *c.* 0.5m above the surrounding ground. A low scarp defined the site in the north and south, while traces of a second, similar site were visible to the immediate north-west. Investigation of the monument in 1997 by Thaddeus Breen found that it represented a circular, ditched enclosure, possibly a bivallate ringfort, with a second ringfort adjoining it (*Excavations 1997*, 113). These monuments had been levelled in the 19th century.

The line of the road-take impinged only on the area to the east of the site and included a possible ditch and external bank feature to the north-east. Stripping of topsoil from the remainder of the field was monitored.

The removal of topsoil in the area of the monument exposed a low bank feature that had been apparent in the survey of the monument. Lying to the north-east of the site, it was 6.5m long, 4.2m wide and 0.48m high. A drainage channel ran north–south through the bank, while a further drain bisected the bank in the south. The bank is made up of a compact, brown, natural subsoil. The survey conducted before excavations shows that this bank feature, while appearing to run from the second enclosure, follows the line of the larger enclosure and may represent a terminal feature associated with the monument.

Immediately south of the bank, excavation revealed a possible ditch that was disturbed by numerous features. The ditch was cut into the grey, natural layer and was filled with an orange/brown, clayey silt. Finds from the fill included numerous fragments of modern glass and animal bone, as well as modern iron fragments. The ditch cut was most definite at the north edge and west face, where it was steep-sided and had a round bottom. A drain feature ran along the east side of the ditch, while further disturbance was evidenced by two drains that ran east–west through the ditch and into the monument. At the south end the ditch feature was further disturbed by a large, stone-filled soak pit. While the ditch feature in the north end appears to be original, the continuation of this ditch through to the south is not definite as it has been substantially disturbed. It may be that the original ditch feature ran for the length of the adjoining bank but was later extended to aid the significant drainage operation that saw the insertion of stone-filled drains throughout the field.

The monitoring of topsoil-stripping revealed numerous drains that acted as drainage channels laid down in the not-too-distant past.
*Martin Fitzpatrick, Arch. Consultancy Ltd, Ballydavid South, Athenry, Co. Galway.*

### 500. DERRYKNOCKANE
*Fulacht fiadh*
**99E0093**

The partial remains of a *fulacht fiadh* were discovered in the townland of Derryknockane, Co. Limerick, in February 1999, 5km south-west of Limerick City and *c.* 1.5km south-east of the existing N20 road. The site was uncovered during monitoring of topsoil-stripping for the proposed N20/N21 Limerick Bypass and survived as a spread of charcoal-rich soil and burnt stones.

Excavation of this spread revealed the existence of a large, subrectangular trough pit, 2m long, 1.2m wide and 0.4m deep, with an east–west orientation. A smaller, linear pit (1.6m x 0.65m) lay to the east of the trough, and a large, subcircular pit (1.2m diameter) lay 1.6m to the south-east of the trough.

The trough had been filled by various deposits, which included a sealing layer of redeposited subsoil, over which lay the main fill of charcoal-rich, blackened material containing a large number of burnt stones.

The trough had been positioned upon a small ridge surrounded by marshy land, which sloped off to the west. Much of the dump material from the use of the trough appeared to have accumulated down, and to the base of, this slope, evidenced by a 0.13m-thick spread of mound material in this area.

Only the partial remains of a *fulacht fiadh* were uncovered during these excavations; the rest of the site was presumably destroyed by agricultural activity in the past. The remains of a linear plough furrow to the east of the trough and those of a large French drain to the west of the trough confirm this destruction.
*Ciara MacManus, c/o ADS Ltd, Windsor House, 11 Fairview Strand, Dublin 3.*

### 501. FANNINGSTOWN
Enclosure (ringfort)
**15056 144620**
**SMR 21:62**
**97E0408 ext.**

This site, a mound 22m in diameter with no enclosing element extant, was first test-trenched by Colin Gracie before construction of the Croom Bypass. Its archaeological merit was proved by the identification of a ditch associated with it and by a medieval stick-pin recovered from one of the trenches (*Excavations 1997*, 114).

It was suggested by the client, the Roads Design Office of Limerick County Council, that the only intrusive works at the site would be the digging of two parallel toe drains, 180m and 120m long and 1.5m wide. The proposed location of the drains was dug by hand, and any archaeological material was recorded and removed.

The longer of the drain trenches ran adjacent to the enclosure, but no archaeological features were encountered. Two artefacts of interest were recovered from the topsoil in the trench: an iron Jew's Harp and a fragment of medieval local ware.

The second trench cut the eastern edge of the enclosure for a length of 30m. The remainder of the trench yielded only modern features and finds. It was found that the enclosure was encircled by a ditch, which appeared on the north and south side of a platform interpreted as the interior of the ringfort. Approximately 10m south of the enclosure ditch a second ditch was discovered, but, owing to the narrowness of the trench, its relationship with the enclosure was unclear. The northern ditch cut was 0.9m deep, 3.8m wide and U-shaped in profile, with five distinctive fills. The ditch on the south side was much larger and appeared to have been recut twice. Its first phase had a U-shaped cut and three fills. The second phase also had a U-shaped cut and three fills. The first phase was 1.8m deep and 9.9m wide, a very large ditch by ringfort standards. The recut of the ditch was 0.8m deep and 2.9m wide. It appears that this recut could have functioned as a field boundary ditch rather than being related to the enclosure.

Despite the narrowness of the trench, it may be suggested that there were two phases of activity in the interior of the enclosure. Phase 1 dug into the layers of a natural mound and was represented by two probable curving slot-trenches and a house floor.

These features seemed to have been deliberately covered by a layer of clay into which the second phase of activity was cut. This phase was also represented by two U-shaped trenches, tentatively interpreted as house slots. In turn these features were sealed by a layer that marked the abandonment of the site as a place of habitation.

Unfortunately, no diagnostic artefacts were recovered from the excavation and none were found in sealed features. Also, the nature of the trenches dug provided a narrow view of the archaeology, which made interpretation difficult. It was impossible to say whether the slot-trenches represented circular or rectangular structures.

*Tracy Collins, Aegis Archaeology, 16 Avondale Court, Corbally, Limerick.*

### 502. FANNINGSTOWN
Possible enclosure
**115056 14443**
**SMR 21:160**
**99E0213**

This potential site was first identified in 1995. It appeared on the ground as two linear, low banks and possible associated shallow ditches, which were tentatively identified as a possible enclosure.

Two trenches were dug by hand before construction of the Croom Bypass. Trench A measured 10m by 1m and ran east–west across the parallel ditch features. Trench B measured 8m by 1m and ran north–south across the features. Excavation revealed that the features were composed of topsoil and mixed boulder clay with lenses of grey marl. At the base of the shallow ditches small stones were found, and so the features were interpreted as drains. Finds were scarce and all modern. No features of an archaeological nature were discovered.

*Tracy Collins, Aegis Archaeology, 16 Avondale Court, Corbally, Limerick.*

### 503. FANNINGSTOWN
Possible enclosure
**15054 14408**
**SMR 21:161**
**99E0263**

This potential archaeological site was first identified in 1995 before construction of the Croom Bypass. Subsequently, the client commissioned a topographical survey of the potential site, and the southernmost portion was archaeologically investigated by Colin D. Gracie, but it proved to be negative (*Excavations 1997*, 114, 97E0410).

Aegis was contracted to investigate the northern part of the site. Two trenches were dug by hand to investigate an area of high ground, in order to establish its archaeological merit. Neither of the trenches produced anything of archaeological significance, and the site was proven to be natural.

*Michael Connolly, Aegis Archaeology, 16 Avondale Court, Corbally, Limerick.*

### 504. GORTEEN
Possible corn-drying kiln
**SMR 21:17 (adjacent to)**
**97E0230 ext.**

Further archaeological investigations were undertaken around the area of monument AR2, a moated site (SMR 21:17) in Gorteen townland, Co. Limerick, during May 1999. This work was carried out during construction of the N20/N21 Road Improvement Scheme, in addition to the work carried out on the monument from November 1998 to January 1999 (*Excavations 1998*, 132–3). This further monitoring of topsoil-stripping revealed the existence of what may be a corn-drying kiln, *c.* 20m to the north of the moated site.

The site first appeared as two large spreads of black, charcoal-rich material. Excavation of these spreads revealed that those within the northern portion of the site overlay the remains of the kiln, which had survived only to ground level. The cut of the kiln was orientated west–east, was 3.5m long and varied from 1.28m to 1.9m wide. The western half of the cut was more bulbous than the eastern, which was elongated, giving it an hourglass shape. The base of the pit was somewhat undulating, although within the more circular, eastern end the base was more bowl-shaped.

Roughly hewn blocks of limestone lined the sides of the kiln, forming the foundations for the main structure. The stones survived as two courses along the eastern half of the pit sides, as well as along the southern edge of the pit. The bulbous, eastern end of the pit and the more elongated, western end of the pit were divided in section by a column of loosely stacked stones. The fill of the pit contained charcoal-rich deposits and stone rubble collapsed from the upper half of the structure.

Approximately 2.3m south of the kiln another large spread of material was uncovered. This spread was roughly 4.5m long and 2.5m wide and consisted of charcoal-rich material. Investigation of the spread suggested that this was the remains of dump material from the kiln.

Although no recognisable grain was recovered from the deposits, the kiln was probably used for drying corn, as it is similar in shape and construction to those previously excavated. Although no dating material was recovered from the site, the kiln's proximity to the moated site and its similarity to other kilns of medieval date give it some link to the enclosure.

*Ciara MacManus, c/o ADS Ltd, Windsor House, 11 Fairview Strand, Dublin 3.*

### 505. GORTEEN
*Fulachta fiadh* and stone-lined well
**1496 1478**
**99E0307**

The site is in Gorteen townland, *c.* 10km south-west of Limerick City, near Adare, to the south of the present N21. The site was uncovered during archaeological monitoring of topsoil-stripping before road construction on the N20/N21 Adare to Annacotty road scheme. A rescue excavation was carried out over twelve weeks between July and September. Excavation revealed two *fulachta fiadh* on either side of a dried-up river channel, possibly a tributary of the River Maigue.

A stone well had been cut through the larger *fulacht fiadh*, Site B, which was on a natural spring. The well was subrectangular and measured 1.8m by 1.2m. It was of drystone construction, composed of large, rectangular blocks of limestone. This stone structure was surrounded on all sides by rounded cobblestones, which filled the cut excavated through the *fulacht fiadh* mound for the well. The spring flowed very strongly, filling the well and flowing out of a specially constructed stone drain towards the low ground between the two *fulachta fiadh*.

The smaller site, Site A, had a very shallow spread of burnt material (rather than a mound) that measured 7.5m in diameter and 0.15m in maximum depth. One cut feature uncovered beneath the spread may originally have been a trough; however, this was impossible to determine as it was badly truncated on its northern side. This side of the burnt spread had also been disturbed and displaced, probably by water action during the rising and falling of the adjacent river.

Site B was a much larger site with a mound measuring *c.* 12m in maximum diameter and 0.73m in maximum depth. It had also been very disturbed by water action on its southern and south-western side, again the side exposed to the fluctuating river levels. A number of distinct phases of activity were identified on this site. The earliest were a number of subsoil-cut features, some of which may have been natural, while others were stake-holes in a linear arrangement aligned east–west at the northern end of the site. These features were separated from the *fulacht fiadh* activity by a layer of peat and in some places by a layer of finely crushed shells. A second phase of activity is represented by a deep, rectangular pit (2.7m x 0.8m and at least 1m deep) dug through the peat and the underlying subsoil. The fill of this pit was a mixture of redeposited subsoil and peat, indicating that it had probably been backfilled shortly after it had been dug, during which time a small, polished stone axehead was deliberately placed in the fill.

No other artefacts or animal bone were recovered from either of these *fulachta fiadh*. No additional pits, which could have served as troughs, survived. It is possible that the trough had occupied the position of the natural spring and was destroyed during the insertion of the stone well, for which a large cut was excavated through the mound.
Mary Deevy, ADS Ltd, Windsor House, 11 Fairview Strand, Fairview, Dublin 3.

### 506. BARRYSFARM, HOSPITAL
Holy well(?)
R706362
SMR 32:147
99E0182

Testing was carried out on the site of a proposed new GAA clubhouse, at St John's Park, Barrysfarm, in the medieval village of Hospital, Co. Limerick. The development is near St John's Well (site of), to the west of the main village road, *c.* 42m north of St John's Church (in ruins) and east of the existing Sports Ground. Six test-trenches were inserted, four (A–D) along the foundation lines of the proposed clubhouse building and two (E and F) along proposed service lines to the north and south. Testing was carried out from 1 to 3 May 1999.

Trench A revealed two cut features of unknown age; however, these were found below the level of proposed disturbance. Trench B revealed a field drain, which continued north through Trenches C and E. Trench C exposed three post-medieval/modern pits and a deep furrow cut. Trench D produced no features except for a small, localised cluster of weathered stone. Trench E revealed the continuation of the sub-linear field drain from Trench B.

Most of the southern end of Trench F contained recent disturbance; however, a limestone wall was identified towards its northern end. The wall was quite substantial, and no associated finds were recovered. It could not be determined whether this undated feature formed part of St John's Well, the site of which is believed to have been in this general vicinity. However, according to local opinion, the well is believed to have been under the existing carpark, some distance to the east of Trench F. Realignment of a proposed drainage pipeline was recommended to avoid the structure in Trench F.
Ken Hanley, 44 Eaton Heights, Cobh, Co. Cork.

### 507. INCHMORE
No archaeological significance
R606544
99E0006

This site was identified by Aegis Archaeology staff during fieldwork for an archaeological reconnoitre report, which detailed the rewalking of the route of the proposed Limerick Southern Ring Road from Adare to Annacotty. The site was a circular mound, measuring 45m in diameter, rising to a maximum height of 2m, in the townland of Inchmore, 4km south-east of Limerick City. No enclosing element, such as a bank or ditch, was identified. The site was not marked on the 1st edition OS map.

A single hand-dug test-trench, 1m by 16m, was inserted in a north–south direction, from the outer area of the mound towards its centre. No deposits, features or finds of archaeological interest were identified, suggesting that the mound was an entirely natural feature. Several finds of early modern/modern date were retrieved from the topsoil.
Ken Hanley 44 Eaton Heights, Cobh, Co. Cork, for Aegis Archaeology Ltd.

### 508. KILGOBBIN
Pits
99E0423

Excavation of an area of potential archaeological interest in Kilgobbin townland, Co. Limerick, took place over two weeks in July. The area lay along the line of the proposed N20/N21 road realignment and had been discovered during topsoil-stripping monitoring. The site survived as a roughly circular ring of black, charcoal-rich soil, *c.* 5m in diameter, with a small, circular pit to the south of this. Approximately 50m to the east of the site another large circular pit was found and excavated.

Excavation of the spread revealed the existence of three very badly truncated pits, set out in a triangle, all filled by a charcoal-rich, silty clay, and a number of small random post-holes. As the pits were so badly truncated, it proved difficult to determine their extent and even more so their function. The presence of the small post-holes on site suggests that this may be the remains of a structure, where perhaps the spreads represent the remains of slots as opposed to pits.

As no immediately datable material was recovered from the site, it is not possible at present to tell what period this activity is from.
*Ciara MacManus, c/o ADS Ltd, Windsor House, 11 Fairview Strand, Dublin 3.*

### 509. ABBEY FARM, KILMALLOCK
Historic town
R601282
99E0105

Monitoring took place at Coláiste Iosaef at the northern end of Kilmallock in March and April 1999, following the demolition of the old eastern wing of the building and during the construction of a new extension. A convent was built on the site in 1933, and it is *c.* 40m north-east of the line of the north-eastern corner of the town wall and *c.* 215m north-west of the well-preserved ruins of the Dominican abbey.

No evidence of archaeological habitation or activity was revealed during groundwork on the site, with the exception of two small pits of unknown date uncovered in one of the foundation trenches.
*Kenneth Wiggins, 17 Vartry Close, Raheen, Co. Limerick.*

### 510. SHEARS STREET, KILMALLOCK
Urban medieval
99E0056

Testing was carried out before a private housing development to the south of Shears Street, Kilmallock, Co. Limerick. The site, which measured 67–110m long x 27–48m wide, lay inside the town wall. A proposed estate road would link onto Sarsfield Street, *c.* 12.5m to the south of King's Castle.

Ten test-trenches were inserted, Trenches 1–8 in the main field site and Trenches 9 and 10 along the proposed estate road. The work was carried out on 30–1 January 1999 and 6–7 February 1999.

Overall, the ten test-trenches revealed a substantial amount of archaeological activity. There were clear stratigraphic similarities between all of the trenches. In general, sod and topsoil cover thickened from east to west across the site. Below this was a widespread, mid-grey/brown, silty clay, which appeared to form a stratified 'garden soil' horizon. This occurred at various depths, ranging from 86.17m OD (Trench 2) to 87.88m OD (Trench 7). Finds from this layer suggest a medieval origin, with some modern (probably agricultural) disturbances. This general layer sealed a substantial quantity of cut features, consisting mostly of pits and plough furrows. Pottery retrieved from some of these features pointed to a medieval date.

Field ditches were also identified running through Trenches 2–5 and 9. These lined up with existing property divisions leading from the main street and would appear to have represented medieval property or garden allotments. Several furrow cuts and pits pre-dated the field ditches, suggesting a medieval subdivision of earlier holdings.

There was no evidence of any substantial structural activity, apart from an occasional stake- or post-hole and a crude wall in Trench 3. A solitary foundation wall was uncovered in Trench 10. Trench 1 produced tentative evidence to suggest that a large quantity of clay was introduced to raise the ground level inside the town wall.

Based on these findings, further archaeological monitoring and excavation were recommended before the development.
*Ken Hanley, 44 Eaton Heights, Cobh, Co. Cork.*

### 511. KILMALLOCK
Urban medieval/post-medieval
99E0363

A small-scale excavation was carried out on subsoil-cut features discovered during the monitoring of topsoil-stripping of a carpark area during the ongoing drainage scheme at Kilmallock, Co. Limerick. The site lies just beyond King John's Castle and is enclosed by the town wall. The excavation was carried out in tandem with the drainage scheme, monitored by J. O'Connor.

As the area was to be used as a carpark, it was agreed with the relevant authorities in *Dúchas* that the exposed features would be recorded in plan and a small sample investigated; the remaining features were sealed with terram and gravel. Investigations suggested that these features dated to the 13th/14th centuries and had subsequently been cut through by post-medieval cultivation furrows.

A large, post-medieval ditch was excavated running north–south through the middle of the site. Excavations showed that this ditch had followed the line of an earlier ditch, which, though narrower, was much deeper than the post-medieval one. The earlier ditch was filled with a noxious-smelling, black/grey clay and has been dated by the associated finds to the early medieval period. It is likely, given the location and dimensions of this ditch, that it was part of the original town defences.
*Cia McConway, ADS Ltd, Unit 48, Westlink Enterprise Centre, 30–50 Distillery Street, Belfast BT12 5BJ.*

### 512. KILRODANE
No archaeological significance
SMR 28:131
99E0124

Six test-trenches were excavated on the footprint of a single dwelling-house and at associated percolation areas to the immediate south-east of the site of Kilrodane church and graveyard. No extant remains of the church or graveyard are visible. Ballyfraley stream separates the site of the church from the house site. No archaeological stratigraphy was recorded in any of the trenches, and no artefacts were recovered.
*Jacinta Kiely, Eachtra Archaeological Projects, Clover Hill, Mallow, Co. Cork.*

### 513. KILSHANE
Adjacent to friary
14183 13646
SMR 29:112
99E0573

The proposed private house development is adjacent to Kilshane Friary. Trial-trenching of the footprint of the house and two trenches across the line of the proposed driveway revealed no features or deposits of archaeological interest.
*Brian Hodkinson, Annaholty, Birdhill, Co. Tipperary.*

### 514. ATHLUNKARD STREET/ISLAND ROAD (SITE K.I.33), LIMERICK
Part of historic town
15803 15765
SMR 5:17 (part of)
99E0135

The site was at the eastern end of the block defined by the Northern Relief Road/Island Road to the east, Athlunkard Street (formed in 1824) to the south, Athlunkard Villas (at the southern end of Bishop's Street) to the west and St Ann's Court to the north. Apart from three houses fronting west onto Athlunkard Villas, the properties faced south onto Athlunkard Street, with their backyards opening onto St Ann's Court.

The site was just outside the town wall to the east of the Englishtown. The wall extended south from the Island Gate, parallel to the Island Road. Thirty metres to the north of the site, two stretches of standing remains of the wall survive at St Peter's Cell, with another, defaced, 9m stretch extending east–west along the southern side of St Ann's Court. During pipe-trenching in 1996 the line of this wall was followed eastwards for 20m (*Excavations 1996*, 70, 96E0134). It then turned northwards on the alignment of the standing remains of the town wall at St Peter's Cell. There is cartographic evidence for a gate, Little Island Gate, at the eastern end of St Ann's Court. No trace of this was noted during the trenching, but this may have been due to the limited size of the cut. It is possible that the remains, which may consist of a simple arched ope, survive at a deeper level.

The site consisted of three properties, Nos 9B, 10 and 11 (now open space), on Athlunkard Street. The northern end of the westernmost of these, No. 9B, abutted the town wall, just south of where this gate was positioned. This property was 6m wide.

Extending eastwards on the same line as the town wall was a previously unknown wall, identified below the Island Road (*Excavations 1996*, 70). This was aligned exactly with the east–west portion of town wall on St Ann's Court. It was battered on its northern face, and there were medieval deposits associated with it.

With regard to the standing remains on the site itself, the cartographic evidence would suggest that the buildings fronting Athlunkard Street are 19th-century, while those to the rear are post-1760s.

Five cuts were opened across the site on 19 March 1999. Cut 1 was not fully excavated as its purpose was to find the wall. Once this was identified, no further digging occurred. No other structural remains were noted in any of the trenches. Cut 3 was the only one where a possible natural level was reached, at a depth of 2.7m. This consisted of a grey, silty clay, with decayed vegetation and loose gravel—all of which could constitute an old foreshore level. Common to Cuts 2–5 was a light brown, compacted, turfy, organic layer, which in Cut 5 had medieval pottery sherds. This occurred at a depth of 2m in Cut 3, 2.8m in Cut 2, and 3m in Cuts 4 and 5. Overlying this layer were silt in Cut 4 and sand in Cut 5. No finds were recovered from these, and they may represent a flood level. An ash deposit occurred in Cut 2 at a depth of 2.6m.

Post-medieval deposits occurred in Cuts 2–5. The material was very similar to that noted in the pipe-trenching during the pre-construction of the Northern Relief Road, both on the Island Road (Phase 1) and south of Athlunkard Street (Phase 2). Given the thickness of these deposits, they do not appear to have been formed by occupation but rather by the material being dumped, which would be in keeping with their location outside the town wall. Between 0.7m and 1.2m of early modern rubble/debris was recorded.

*Celie O Rahilly, Limerick Corporation, City Hall, Limerick.*

### 515. BROAD STREET/GEORGE'S QUAY/ABBEY RIVER, LIMERICK
Urban medieval
15806 15735
SMR 5:17
98E0581

Three cuttings were excavated on George's Quay and one at Broad Street before construction activity associated with the Limerick Main Drainage Scheme. In addition, a programme of excavation (50 trenches) was initiated in the Abbey River before the first phase of pipe-laying in the riverbed. Phase II of the construction work will see river gravels being investigated for archaeological structures and artefacts at the mouth of the Abbey River at its confluence with the River Shannon and another short programme of land-based excavation in the Potato Market.

*George's Quay*
A small excavation, Cutting 1, was carried out on George's Quay in front of Barrington's Hospital. The cutting measured 4m east–west by 3.5m and was excavated to a depth of 2.5m below ground level. The trench revealed a sequence of 18th-century reclamation that is likely to be associated with the construction of the existing quay, built in 1760. The current quay was built parallel to, and outside of, the town wall.

The excavation uncovered twelve distinct layers of deposition/reclamation above an 18th-century culvert contemporary with George's Quay and a later stone culvert cut through it. The town wall was not encountered in this cutting. The excavation was not carried to the base of archaeological deposits because of the limited impact of development in this location.

Cutting 2 was at the junction of George's Quay and Mary's Street. The cutting measured 6m east–west by 8.5m and was excavated to a depth of 5m below the existing quay. The excavation was at the junction of the medieval bridge, the town wall and a defensive tower defending the northern end of the bridge on the town wall. The stretch of town wall was 6.8m long and 2.45m wide and stood to a height of 4.45m. The springing arch of the medieval bridge was identified at the easternmost external end of the town wall. A walkway or sconce was identified, behind and inside the town wall. This led to an arched entrance into the tower. No surface trace of the structures was visible above ground level before the excavations.

The historical sources suggest that the medieval defences survived up to 1760, when the present quay was constructed; the bridge was replaced in 1830. No medieval archaeological layers were recorded adjacent to the walls. The layers that abutted the structures were 18th- and 19th-century in date and were deposited as a result of reclamation and quay construction.

A small excavation, Cutting 4, was carried out on George's Quay at the bottom of Creagh Lane. The cutting measured 9m east–west by between 3.5m and 4.5m and was excavated to a depth of 2.25m below ground level. The trench revealed a similar sequence of 18th-century reclamation to that seen in Cuttings 1 and 2 associated with the construction of the existing quay built in 1760. However, a corner section of mural tower on the town wall was identified along the length of the cutting. The section of town wall was identified 1.3m below the street. The masonry structure was 1.05m wide and extended a further 0.95m beneath the existing road level. Full excavation was not carried out to the base of archaeological deposits as a result of an alteration to the design to the proposed development in response to the archaeological discovery.

*Broad Street*
Excavations at Broad Street (Cutting 3) uncovered two medieval bridge piers under the junction of Broad Street and Charlotte Quay. These structures formed part of the medieval bridge (on the site of Baal's Bridge) that formed the vital link between the Irishtown and the Englishtown on King's Island. When the Anglo-Normans launched their assault on Limerick in 1175 there was no bridge in the location later occupied by Baal's Bridge. Giraldus Cambrensis records that the attackers found a ford across the Abbey River and he 'hurled himself headlong into the swiftly flowing river…' and managed to cross to the opposite bank. It would appear that the bridge linking King's Island to the mainland to the south, on the site of what is now called Baal's Bridge, was non-existent when the Anglo-Normans arrived in Limerick in 1175.

The excavations at Broad Street indicated a long archaeological sequence commencing in the mid-13th century up to the present day. The cutting measured 6.35m east–west by between 5m and 8.25m and was excavated to a depth of 4.5m below the street level. Three samples from oak timbers that revetted one of the bridge piers were submitted for dendrochronological dating (David Brown, The Queen's University of Belfast). The results suggested that the bridge piers were constructed in the early 13th century.

Organic deposits were identified abutting the bridge piers. Environmental analysis of macrofossil plant and insect remains (by Eileen Reilly and Penny Johnston of Margaret Gowen & Co.) has demonstrated that the deposits around the bridge piers accumulated slowly as a result of the dumping of organic refuse and the accumulation of river silts. The organic deposits originated from natural silting and contemporary settlement in the medieval city during the 13th and 14th centuries. The excavation revealed evidence for the growth and development of Broad Street, with evidence of house floors dating from the 14th/early 15th century built on top of ground reclaimed from the riverbed. This expansion of the Irishtown towards the Abbey River is likely to have been associated with renewed town wall building extending into the Abbey River. The uppermost archaeological deposits in the cutting consisted of post-medieval cobbling, drains and culverts. The medieval bridge was demolished in 1830 before the construction of the current Baal's Bridge.

*Baal's Bridge*
Extensive excavations of the riverbed from Matthew Bridge to Baal's Bridge have been completed. These involved opening a large cutting under Baal's Bridge and fifty smaller trenches upstream and downstream of the ford on which the bridge is sited. The river gravels (c. 1m deep) in these locations are rich in archaeological artefacts. While no *in situ* structures have been uncovered, a large, important and eclectic collection of archaeological objects was found. The trenches were excavated *in situ* in the riverbed, and the artefacts were recovered layer by layer.

A preliminary summary of the artefacts found includes objects dating from the prehistoric period (worked flint) to the post-medieval period. To date, no Bronze Age objects have been recovered. Several pre-Viking Age artefacts have been recovered, including a possible Iron Age horse bit, an Early Christian bronze zoomorphic object and a spiral-headed pin. A number of Viking Age stick-pins and a coin (c. 1035), minted in London for King Cnut, were also found. Medieval and post-medieval artefacts include beads, coins, horse equipment, pins, brooches, tools and weapons. A small assemblage of locally manufactured and imported medieval pottery has been recovered from the riverbed. Fifty medieval coins dating from 1200 to 1540 have been recovered; they are largely Irish, although Scottish, French and English coins are also included. An early post-medieval (c. 1600) seal bearing the 'Lymerick Port' coat of arms was also recovered from the riverbed. Objects dating from the Williamite siege of the city, including iron and stone cannon, musket balls of various sizes, gun flints, spurs, fragments of iron mortar bombs, grenades,

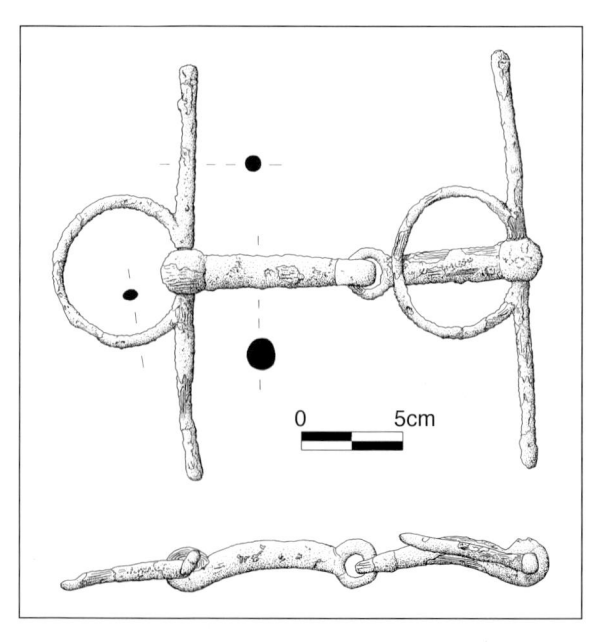

Medieval horse bit from the Abbey River, Limerick.

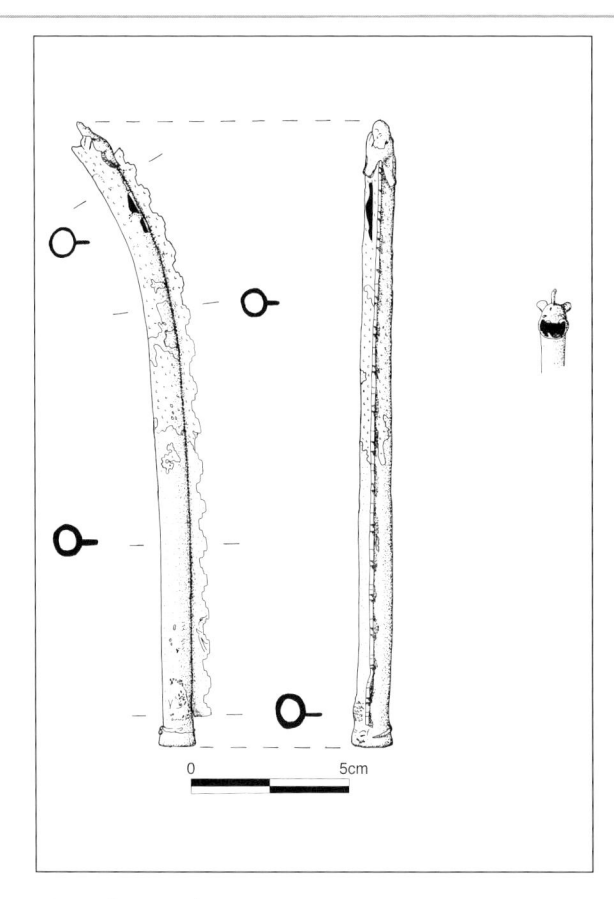

Early Christian/Viking Age zoomorphic bronze artefact from the Abbey River, Limerick.

iron bayonets and coins (Jacobite gun money), have been retrieved.

*Edmond O'Donovan, Margaret Gowen & Co. Ltd, 2 Killiney View, Albert Road Lower, Glenageary, Co. Dublin.*

### 516. CHARLOTTE'S QUAY, LIMERICK
Urban medieval
R580573
99E0094

Monitoring and excavation work were carried out before construction of a multi-storey carpark and ancillary works at the rear of Charlotte's Quay, Limerick. The site is between St Michael's graveyard and an extant portion of the medieval town wall. Some previous archaeological investigation in this area revealed large-scale post-medieval disturbance, with limited pockets of archaeological activity (Lynch 1984).

Monitoring and testing in February 1999 identified only two areas of archaeological activity. Area A was outside the south-eastern end of the existing graveyard boundary wall, within an area of substantial post-medieval disturbance. Skeletal remains were identified (at *c.* 5.45m OD and 5.8m OD), within pockets of an undisturbed clay horizon. Area B was a small area in the extreme north-eastern corner of the site. This consisted of an extremely thin band of charcoal-flecked, grey clay overlying natural boulder clay. No datable finds were recovered; however, the deposit appeared to be a residual, undisturbed archaeological layer.

The monitoring and testing suggested that *c.* 95% of the site had been disturbed by post-medieval activity, caused principally by 19th-century gasworks. The only archaeology of any substance was in a small area at the south-west corner of the site. Several design changes were made to the proposed development, in consultation with the NMHPS, the NMI and the developer, which minimised the impact on the areas of known archaeology.

In March 1999 a limited archaeological excavation was carried out at the extreme south-western corner of the site (Area A). This revealed that St Michael's graveyard continued well beyond the south-eastern limit of the existing boundary wall. *In situ* burial remains were identified in shallow, earth-cut graves. A maximum of eight individuals were identified, both articulated and disarticulated (specialist report by Clare Mullins). Pottery associations suggested a 13th/14th-century date.

*Reference*
Lynch, A. 1984 *PRIA* **84**C, 281–331.

*Ken Hanley, 44 Eaton Heights, Cobh, Co. Cork.*

### 517. CLANCY'S STRAND, LIMERICK
Environs of medieval mill
15763 15761
**SMR 5:19**
**98E0578**

Test excavation was carried out near the site of a medieval/post-medieval mill. The site is indicated on the 1st edition Ordnance Survey map but is not marked on the 2nd and 3rd editions. The mill is illustrated at the western edge of Curragour Falls on Phillips's map of 1685.

A single test-trench was opened at the manhole shaft on Clancy's Strand. It was 10m long and revealed a 19th-century soil profile over natural. The deposits were interpreted as ground reclamation for the construction of the road adjacent to the River Shannon. No walls or other archaeological indicators suggesting the presence of a structure were found during the assessment. Archaeological monitoring is to be carried out during the construction phase of the project.

*Edmond O'Donovan, Margaret Gowen & Co. Ltd, 2 Killiney View, Albert Road Lower, Glenageary, Co. Dublin.*

### 518. 5–7 JOHN'S GATE, LIMERICK
Part of historic town
**SMR 5:17 (part of)**
15822 15698
**99E0362**

This site was at the eastern end of the south side of St John's Square, abutting the last house. It was within the town wall, to the west of the site of John's Gate. It was to have been tested with two cuttings.

However, on arrival at the site following the demolition on 5 August 1999, it was found that a machine cutting had already been opened without archaeological supervision. The trench was approximately central to the site. The western section was cleaned off and drawn at 1:10. A panel along the base of the section was also cleaned. In this, one sherd of local medieval pottery was found at the southern end. Tight against the base of the section was a small cavity through stones. This was not opened. A post-hole was 0.18m from the baulk, and there was a pit that was partially excavated. Three bands of layers were identified in the section. The upper one was post-medieval, and the next, identified by the pottery, was of medieval date. There were no finds from the lowest one.

Given the presence of such archaeological material, the decision was taken to omit the proposed cellar from the new development.

*Celie O Rahilly, Limerick Corporation, City Hall, Limerick.*

### 519. KILRUSH CHURCH, LIMERICK
Environs of Early Christian church
SMR 5:9
15571 15681
98E0579

Test excavation was carried out before the construction of the Northern Lower Interceptor Sewer pipeline at Kilrush Church. The church site is in Derravoher townland off the North Circular Road within Limerick's Municipal Boundary and dates from the Early Christian period. It consists of a fine, pre-Romanesque (9th- to early 12th-century) stone church, at the centre of modern housing estate. The church is likely to have been enclosed within a defensive ditch and would have been associated with a cemetery and other monastic or secular buildings. No trace of any other associated monuments survives in the vicinity of the church.

A single test-trench was opened c. 40m from the church on the North Circular Road in an attempt to find and evaluate any outlying archaeological features. No archaeological deposits or indicators were found in the test-trench, where a natural, sterile soil profile was identified immediately under the existing road surface. Archaeological monitoring is to be carried out during the construction phase of the development.

*Edmond O'Donovan, Margaret Gowen & Co. Ltd, 2 Killiney View, Albert Road Lower, Glenageary, Co. Dublin.*

### 520. 36–39 NICHOLAS STREET/1–3 PETER STREET (SITE K.I.24), LIMERICK
Part of historic town
15790 15762
SMR 5:17 (part of)
94E0071 ext.

The site was within the Englishtown, on the east side of Nicholas Street and north of Peter Street. The latter, positioned opposite the northern end of St Mary's Cathedral, was formed between 1840 and 1870 and presumably was so named as it led to Peter's Cell, off Bishop's Street to the east. Nicholas Street was the main street and has its origins in the medieval town.

There were four properties in the site, Nos 36–39 (consisting of two buildings, each subdivided into two units), facing onto Nicholas Street, and a range of three cottages extending down the northern side of Peter Street.

Building 1 (Nos 36 and 37), to the north, was a three-storey, two-bay building, 9.5m deep by 6m wide. The front wall, on Nicholas Street, was a mixture of brick- and blockwork. The rear wall was mass concrete. These units were inserted between the standing remains of two stone side-walls of a late medieval house, the southern one containing, at first-floor level, the sides and part of the lintel of a late medieval fireplace. The sides were finely carved limestone, with the eastern side intact but the western side damaged. It was obvious from the vertical building breaks in the two side-walls that the walls of the medieval house did not originally extend as far as the present street line but c. 4m short of it. Between the two side-walls, towards the rear of the property, were the remains of a vaulted undercroft (*Excavations 1994*, 58–9; *Excavations 1995*, 56). The Urban Archaeology Survey also mentions 'a round headed doorway with chamfered limestone jambs in the north wall between Nos. 35/36' (Bradley et al. c. 1989–90, 263, House B). At the rear of the property was another building, of which only the northern gable and eastern side-wall survive.

Building 2 (Nos 38 and 39), to the south, was a two-storey, two-bay building at the corner of Nicholas Street and Peter Street. The original building was 8.5m wide and 6.5m deep. At the rear the northern unit had a lean-to (total depth 3.5m and 1.5m wide) against the party wall with a tiny open space beyond it. The remainder of the area was covered with an extension, measuring 7m north–south by 3.75m, accessed from Peter Street.

The Peter Street range consisted of three single-storey houses (artisan dwelling type), each with a central door and one window on either side. All opes were defined with brick arches set in stone walls. The total length was 21.5m, and they were 5m wide. At the rear, between the house walls and the party wall to the north, were sheds/outhouses. The three houses were at the same floor level, which was at street level at the west end of the street, but, given the drop in the latter, there was a flight of five steps to the footpath at the eastern end of the third house. Both the Peter Street cottages and the building on the corner were built between 1840 and 1870, but Nos 36 and 37 dated to the 1930s.

The recent work on this site, in April 1999, following the demolition of Nos 36 and 37, consisted of a cutting, Cut 9, and limited access to the undercroft. A report was prepared incorporating an account of all the archaeologically supervised work done, together with historical and cartographic research, 18th-century descriptions and a brief inventory of comparative structures in Limerick. The standing remains of the medieval walls were recorded photogrammetrically, and structural analysis by an architectural historian is pending.

Cut 9 was 2.3m east of the front wall, parallel to the dividing wall of Nos 36 and 37, and extended eastwards as far as the mass concrete back wall. There was a possible cross-wall 5m from the front of the property. It was very poorly built, with a layer of soft, cement-like substance with underlying brick, and its total width was 1m. Given its instability, it appears unlikely to have been load-bearing. West of this wall the cut was 2.7m long and 1.4m wide. There was 2m of rubble overlying soft, brown, silty fill with a high bone content. This may be of archaeological significance, although no finds were recovered that could be used to date it. Given the unstable nature of the rubble fill, no further digging was done. To the east of the cross-wall the cut was 1.6m wide and 2.7m long, and the fill consisted of a high amount of large stones, slabs and brick. The base of the back wall was 1.3m below the floor level and was set on a stone plinth from the base of which a cut and carved stone was recovered, identical to one *in situ* in the mantelpiece.

The dividing wall of Nos 36 and 37 defined the southern side of the cut. To the west of the cross-wall it was of a very poor quality, mainly brick, which curved vertically, possibly because it was vaulted (?cellar). It was 1.6m high. East of the cross-wall it was built with 0.25m of concrete overlying courses of brick. The total exposed height was 0.45m.

Given the instability of the dividing wall, it is unlikely that the 1930s buildings had separate cellars. It is possible, however, that there was a single cellar for the building they replaced, with an arched longitudinal dividing wall. The underlying fill was very loose, which would suggest that the preceding building was demolished into an existing cavity. Apart from the dividing wall with possible vaulting, no other cellar walls were identified, and it was not possible for reasons of safety to make a cutting close to the side-walls. Given that the two side-walls relate to the original late medieval house, if there was a cellar belonging to the 18th/19th-century building it is likely that it was a conversion of the existing undercroft, with an extension westwards, as it would have been structurally very difficult to have inserted a cellar at a later stage.

The vaulted undercroft was initially identified towards the rear of the property, where its eastern end wall was found. This consisted of a blocked arch, with the blocking done in two parts, northern and southern. The wall itself may be original, but this was not confirmed. At the western end the vault, or at least the central part of it, was partly destroyed by the levelling of the area immediately east of the mass concrete wall of the 1930s building, in order to accommodate the concrete floor of their backyards. It was clear from the accumulation of debris here and on both sides of the eastern end wall that it was backfilled with household-type rubbish that, judging by the pottery, was dumped in the 18th and 19th centuries.

*The undercroft*
It had been intended to record the undercroft. To do this it was necessary to reduce the ground level east of the end wall. The access ramp, first made in 1995, extended from the south, through the existing gap in the property wall at the rear of the last house on Peter Street. It then curved westwards down the centre of the plot to meet the arch just north of its centre point, cutting a thick deposit of sand. The front wall of the building at the rear of the property (on the 1840 and 1870 OS plans) was identified during the removal of this fill. Its base was cut into the upper layers of the sand, at a depth of 0.5m, implying that, once the end wall of the undercroft was blocked, the area was infilled with sand before the construction of the house. This building used the end of the northern late medieval wall as its northern gable.

Visible in the northern section of the ramp was 0.35m of overburden over 0.5m of sand. Nearer the arch, however, was 0.9m of dump material under the sand. This material consisted of brick, mortar etc., with 18th/19th-century pottery, over 0.55m of brown sand with bits of slate and some stones. This fill pattern was also identified when the blocking wall was exposed in 1997. Below this and at the level of the base of the blocking wall (into the undercroft), was 0.3m of debris, including bricks and mortar overlying a layer of cobbles. An area of these measuring 0.9m east–west by 0.65m was exposed in the gap created by the removal of the northern part of the blocking wall. The vertical divide between this and the southern one was central, i.e. under the keystone. The northern side was built with tightly packed stones with some brick and some larger stones. It was topped with three larger stones, and the space between them and the base of the arch was partly filled with bricks and stones wedged in to support the actual arch. It had an internal batter and measured 0.4m wide at the top and 0.5m wide at the base.

To the south the blocking wall was composed of small, loosely packed, unbonded rubble stones. The upper 0.6m was particularly loose; below this the wall was more solid. The total height was 1.9m. Fill obscured the inside face, so it was not possible to determine whether it was battered. Externally abutting the arch, 0.2m south of the keystone, was another wall extending east–west. The top of this was 0.3m above the underside of the arch. It was a maximum of 0.4m high and 0.85m thick and underlay 0.5–1m of overburden. Just east of the arch the underside of this wall had collapsed. There were three to four courses of masonry, but only one survived *in situ*. Behind this wall was a stony clay, and below it was 1.2m of 18th/19th-century debris, with no trace of any sand. Given its poor quality, it was unlikely to have been load-bearing, and it probably represents the garden wall for the northern property as depicted on the 1:1000 OS plan.

The arch keystone was a piece of red (?)sandstone. The maximum height from the cobbles to the keystone was 1.85m. To the south a single voussoir was visible; the rest was obscured by the garden wall etc. The northern side of the arch consisted of around thirteen to fourteen narrow limestone voussoirs, almost rectangular. Immediately inside the arch, on the northern side, was 0.85m of debris, made up of 0.5m of cindery, black fill containing much 19th-century pottery over 0.35m of building debris, brick, stones, mortar etc. This overlay a brown, organic silt at the level of the cobbles.

The rest of the area was packed with 2.2m high of dumped material, which, judging by its shape, was poured in from an opening in the roof just behind the keystone, where the roof had collapsed. This material extended west for 2.4m and was spread over half the width of the undercroft (2.5m). This volume of the material would have to be removed before the original floor level (the layer of cobbles?) could be exposed. Given the unstable nature of the southern side of the vault, with the hole behind the keystone and another hole further west, it was decided that the undercroft should remain as it is until a proper resolution of the whole site was carried out.

*Late medieval house remains*
The two side-walls of the late medieval house, i.e. the north wall of No. 36 (31m long) and the south wall of No. 37 (25m long), survived. The walls were 0.8m and 1m thick respectively, and this facilitated any repairs or refacing. The vertical building breaks on both walls at all three levels are evidence for the lengthening of the houses by *c.* 4m at the Nicholas Street end. At ground level the additional length was built with stone, and the portion facing the street was finished with square-cut ashlars. There was a recess at each level in both houses, also part of the addition. This extension westwards must have been in place by 1840, which suggests that the house was 'converted', in the late 17th or 18th century, perhaps in the Dutch style (Barry 1894).

At the ground level east of the recesses, on both walls, were panels of reasonably good stonework. On the north wall was a very well-defined vertical break, the east side of which corresponded with the base of the straight 'arch' in the original wall. On the south wall the corresponding stonework has either been covered with or replaced by a small fireplace surrounded with mass concrete. The two upper storeys had similar fireplaces. There has also been a considerable amount of repair work, in stone, brick and mass concrete, to the original walls, particularly around these late fireplaces. Where such work was done in stone, it is difficult to determine with accuracy what was original and what has been repaired. Both walls were plastered within the two latest buildings. Where this render was applied to the stone or brick, it came away relatively easily, but not where it was applied to concrete.

The northern face of the southern wall appears to have undergone more intensive restructuring, with large areas of infilled brickwork but only one area of concrete. The late medieval fireplace, probably 17th-century, was found at first-floor level in the southern wall, 11m from Nicholas Street. At the eastern end, at the same level, was a blocked, rectangular through-ope, which is stone on the southern side but brick on the northern. Given the extensive brick repairs along this wall, it would appear that at some point between 1654 and 1840 a large house occupied the corner site.

On the northern wall the straight 'arch', 5m long, started at the first-storey floor level, rising to a height of 2m above it. It terminated at another vertical break corresponding with the rear (east) wall of No. 36, where there was a curved recess. The remainder of the wall to the east was sloped from a height of 8m to 2.9m over a distance of 5m. It continued at approximately the latter height eastward for the length of the plot. There were two blocked opes: one possibly a large window at the floor level of the top storey, just east of the rear, mass concrete wall; and a smaller one further east, at what would have been the top of the ground-floor level. It is uncertain whether these were through-opes or just recesses, but the ope in the northern face of No. 35, mentioned above, may coincide. At the eastern end the face of the wall protruded. This was the northern gable of the house at the rear.

The Civil Survey (Simington 1938) plot information was revised for this part. Reference no. 160 applies to Nos 36 and 37 Nicholas Street, with Dr Dominick Fitz-David Whyte listed as the proprietor. He was mayor in 1629 and 1643 (Lenihan 1866, 153). Reference no. 159, Nos 38 and 39, is described as a waste plot. This description does not necessarily mean that there was not some kind of structure here in the late medieval period. Street frontage was usually always occupied. The length of the properties from the town wall to the Nicholas Street frontage was calculated and found to fall 15–25ft short of the present Nicholas Street line. On the 1870 OS plan Peter Street extended from Nicholas Street eastwards across what would have been plot ref. no. 158, the stone and cagework house. East of the last house on Peter Street it curved northwards to link up with Peter's Cell. This situation lasted until the early 20th century, when it is shown as straight (1938 revision). Given that the dimensions of Nos 38 and 39 Nicholas Street, with their outhouses at the rear, are identical on all plans from 1870, it is probable that they were the same buildings as those demolished in 1995.

*References*
Barry, J.G. 1894 Report from the Hon. Local Secretary for Limerick. Galwey's Castle/Ireton's House. *JRSAI* **24**, 386–9.
Bradley, J. *et al.* *c.* 1989–90 Urban Archaeology Survey. Part XVII (iii). Limerick City. Unpublished, OPW.
Lenihan, M. 1866 *Limerick: its history and antiquities, ecclesiastical civil and military.* Dublin.
Simington, R.C. 1938 *Civil Survey 1654–56, County of Limerick.* Dublin.

*Celie O Rahilly, Limerick Corporation, City Hall, Limerick.*

### 521. SIR HARRY'S MALL, LIMERICK
Urban medieval
15763 15761
SMR 5:19
98E0577

The Franciscan abbey in Limerick is in the south-eastern corner of King's Island, immediately outside the town wall. The De Burgo family founded the abbey in 1267. At the Dissolution of the Monasteries (*c.* 1540) the abbey is recorded as consisting of a church, dormitory, cloister, hall, kitchen, three chambers and a garden of one acre. A substantial building is indicated on Phillips's map of 1685 on the site of the abbey, along with an illustration of what may be the precinct walls enclosing the land of the friars. The Englishtown wall wraps around the south-western edge of the abbey, suggesting that this portion of the town wall was constructed respecting the extent of the property after it was founded in 1267. In addition, the map illustrates a boundary wall/ditch south of, and parallel to, the present alignment of Meat Market Lane and River Lane. This would appear to be the northern boundary that survived up to the end of the 17th century. The Abbey River acted as the northern boundary of the site.

Four test-trenches were excavated to the east of the site along the Abbey River on Sir Harry's Mall. The trenches were aligned on proposed manholes.

The test excavation uncovered a uniform deposit profile indicating that the Mall was constructed on land reclaimed from the river. The test excavation did not reveal any evidence for the precinct wall of the abbey, which is likely to be further west, under the existing houses fronting onto Sir Harry's Mall.
*Edmond O'Donovan, Margaret Gowen & Co. Ltd, 2 Killiney View, Albert Road Lower, Glenageary, Co. Dublin.*

### 522. SIR HARRY'S MALL/LONG LANE/FISH LANE (SITE K.I.16), LIMERICK
Part of historic town
15812 15749
SMR 5:17 (part of)
99E0433

This site was at the south-eastern end of the area known as the King's Island/Englishtown, within the zone of archaeological potential for Limerick City as defined on both the Recorded Monuments Map and the Urban Archaeology Survey. It was defined to the north by Long Lane, to the east by Sir Harry's Mall/Abbey River, to the south by Fish Lane and to the west by the new Northern Relief Road. Both Long Lane and Fish Lane were of medieval origin.

This work was carried out in December 1999 before proposed construction, in order to identify the archaeological implications of the site, which, for development purposes, includes the area south of Fish Lane (partially excavated previously by Kenneth Hanley, see *Excavations 1997*, 118–20, 96E0334). As yet, there has been no planning application/permission. Any proposed development will impinge on known structural archaeological remains and is also likely to affect deposits. The identification of these would allow the implementation of a proper mitigation strategy at the design stage. It should be noted that this work involved the clearance of 1–1.5m of late fill, which was sufficient to expose the features described below.

The 1840 OS plan shows that a small part of this site, east of Sheep Street and north of Fish Lane, was partly within the walled area of the medieval town. The area between the town wall and Long Lane was possibly part of St Francis's Friary. The area east of the wall was likely to have been the bank of the Abbey River, and it was not until it was reclaimed, in around the 1770s, that it was developed. Number 16 Sir Harry's Mall is possibly the only original structure from this time that survived to the recent past.

The town wall, encountered during monitoring for the Northern Relief Road (*Excavations 1996*, 70–1, 96E0213), was exposed heading eastwards (Wall A) and then southwards to Fish Lane (Wall B). Also exposed, abutting the outside face of the town wall, were two walls, C and D, and an associated area of cobbling, E. Possibly associated with these walls was a portion of a wall, F, found directly on Wall A. Six shallow cuttings were made, owing to the flooding.

Work commenced to the west of the site, where Wall A was exposed just below the existing surface. It extended west–east for 25.5m, parallel to but south of Long Lane (4.75–3.96m OD). This wall was a continuation of the 2m-wide wall identified further west, below the Northern Relief Road, where the external face was exposed to a height of 2.5m. It extended south-east from the Gaol Lane/Long Lane intersection. Its internal face was found flush with the northern edge of Sheep Street. Wall A maintained its width of 2m as far as the eastern end, where it terminated with a very well-defined projection, battered on the northern and eastern sides, which represented the remains of the base of a corner tower (4.43–3.4m OD). The presence of a corner tower in this location is confirmed by the representations on the various early maps of Limerick.

At the western end the upper courses of the external face of Wall A had been removed by the insertion of a later wall. Judging from the cartographic evidence, this insert can be dated to the early 19th century. There was also evidence to suggest that, further east, there was some rebuilding of the upper courses, but the internal face would appear to be original. Under the Northern Relief Road the exposed external face rested on a plinth found 2.7m below the exposed top. On the internal face, however, the plinth occurred at 0.6m below the top, at 4.697m OD. There was a distinct difference between above and below the plinth: above consisted of close-fitting, evenly faced, well-cut blocks; below was formed with roughly faced, randomly coursed, ill-fitting stones. Towards the eastern end, Wall A was 1.55m of similarly faced wall above the footing (or plinth?). This occurred at *c.* 2.41m OD. It would appear, therefore, that the town wall followed a downslope from west to east, as presumably the plinth or footing would have occurred below the ground level as it existed at the time of its construction. There is no evidence, so far, for a precise construction date for the town wall in this part of the Englishtown. There were grants of land 'within/below' and 'without' the walls of Limerick in 1198 (Lenihan 1866, 48), and in 1237 'a toll was granted for the purpose of enclosing the city with a wall' (Lenihan 1866, 53).

Extending southwards for 15.7m from Wall A's internal face (just west of the remains of the corner tower) a second wall, Wall B, aligned north–south, was exposed (3.92–3.66m OD). At the northern edge of Fish Lane it terminated with a finished end, which may represent the side of a simple arched gate, on the lane. Though narrower and of a different build, it appeared to be bonded to the masonry of the internal face of Wall A. This difference may be the result of either the town wall having been built in stages or Wall B being a precinct wall for the Priory of the *Fratres Cruciferi*, or Crutched Friars. The exact foundation date for this is not known, but it was mentioned in the Pipe Rolls for 1211–12 (Hodkinson 1990, 41) and is listed in Gwynn and Hadcock (1988, 210) as founded before 1216. This wall aligned with a small section of wall exposed at a low level on the site south of Fish Lane (*Excavations 1997*, 118–20, 96E334, Cutting 2A, Phase 1). Here, also, the southern limit of the walled town was identified by another wall, at a higher level, running east–west parallel to, but just south of, Little Fish Lane.

The external face of Wall B was, judging from its masonry, of a single build. However, it had its own

Plan of walls and cuts at Sir Harry's Mall/Long Lane/Fish Lane, Limerick.

separate internal face, B1, positioned approximately central to the core. This face extended from Fish Lane north to where the north wall of No. 16 Sir Harry's Mall crossed Wall B. North of this point the internal face appeared to be of a different build, bearing a closer resemblance to the lower internal face, B2. There was what appeared to be a secondary spread of unfaced masonry at the northern end. This obscured the upper internal face, but its line can be seen to continue behind it.

If, as suggested above, the ground level at the time of the construction of the town wall dropped, the original external facing of Wall B1 may not have been exposed by the present work. Alternatively, it is possible that the two parts of the wall, B1 and B2, are the result of later modification, possibly relating to the presence, in the angle of the town wall, of the two houses described in the Civil Survey of 1654. These could have been built after the Dissolution (1537) and the laicisation of the priory.

Externally abutting Wall A, two apparently contemporary parallel walls, C and D, were exposed heading northwards (4.23–3.9m OD) for c. 4.8m but were not fully cleared of the overburden of late fill. They were similar in construction and dimensions. Abutting the west face of Wall C was a second wall, C1, of a later build. As the location of C and D did not correspond with any walls or lanes on the OS maps, they may be earlier; it is possible that they are the side-walls of a building depicted on the 1590 map in this location. This was apparently associated with St Francis's Friary. Their association, if any, with Wall F, on top of (and overhanging) Wall A, needs to be clarified. This may be the southern gable of this structure.

An area of cobbling, E (c. 3.65m OD), was exposed west of Wall D, just below the level of its plinth. This had an east–west line defined by larger, rectangular cobbles. As there was no cartographic evidence for a lane in this location, it would appear to be reasonable to identify it as a floor, but this can only be confirmed by excavation. The southern end of the cobbled surface was disturbed by a trench, noted in the section of Cut 3, extending east–west, parallel to the town wall. Again, only by excavation will it be possible to determine the relationship of this trench with Wall A and the cobbles, but it may be related to the rebuilding of the external face.

No structural remains were identified internal to the town wall, and the only area where the fill was reduced to a possible medieval horizon (2.02m OD) was along the internal face of Wall A, where it had been defaced.

There was a complex of connecting walls north of Fish Lane, some or all of which are likely to be related to the house fronting the Mall, No. 16. Three of these, G, H and I, formed a cellar; two more, J and K, defined the northern edge of the lane; and the third, L, was a three-sided structure abutting Wall B1 externally (3.83–3.25m OD). The cellar's western wall, G, had an impressive external batter and extended northward beyond the northern wall of the cellar, H. Similarly battered walls, dating to the 18th century, were identified by K. Hanley (pers. comm.)

on the site to the south. Also possibly associated with this building was the three-sided structure, L. Judging by its poor construction, this was not a substantial structure and may have been either a latrine or some kind of garden feature. The northern boundary wall of No. 16, removed during the clearance, crossed Wall B. As noted above, there appeared to be a change in the internal facing of Wall B1 north of the crossing-point. At its western end this boundary wall angled northwards, and then turned west on Wall A. The section of *in situ* Wall F here was left in order to clarify its relationship with Walls C and D, the two parallel walls mentioned above. At its eastern end, Wall D aligned exactly with the return aligned north–south. At the western end Wall C was aligned with the vertical line of blockwork, with every second stone recessed as if there had been a return northwards. Beyond this line the remainder of Wall F was definitely later.

Two walls, J and K, appear to have been inserted to define the northern side of Fish Lane or may be the foundations for buildings or property boundaries part-fronting the lane. Their exact date of construction is uncertain; they were definitely in place in the early 19th century but may be earlier. Also exposed on both sides of the town wall were other foundations identified on the 19th-century OS plans.

Cut 1 was at right angles to the external face of Wall A, near the Northern Relief Road. It was 4m long, 1.5m wide and 0.8m deep (the level of the blue-grey clay), at which point flooding occurred, 1.85m from the top of the town wall. The exposed height of Wall A was 1m of faced stones, with 0.9m of defaced wall core. The fills visible in the western section were all semi-modern; the pottery recovered was 18th/19th-century brownware and glazed red earthenware.

Cut 2 was dug parallel to the western side of Wall C1, abutting the external face of Wall A, 2.2m from it, in order to determine the depth of foundations of Wall C1. Only the western face of this wall was exposed, as its eastern face was built against the western side of Wall C, the possible Friary-related structure. This cut was 2.5m long and 1.75m wide. The base of Wall C rested on late fills.

Cut 3 was opened between Walls C and D, the two parallel walls abutting the external face of Wall A, 2.15m east of Wall C and 1.8m west of Wall D. It was 2.1m long, 1.2m wide and 0.9m deep. A possible trench, cut parallel to Wall A, was identified. In the eastern section this was against the face of Wall A, but in the western section the cut was further north. The fills varied in both but, judging by the amount of brick etc., still appeared to be late.

Cut 4 was parallel to the eastern end of the corner tower of Wall A. It measured 2.7m north–south by 0.9m by a maximum depth of 0.35m. The fill consisted of a mixed debris with sand and brick and may have been a form of reclamation fill.

Cut 5 was dug at right angles to Wall B1, 1.25m south of the tower. It was opened in order to determine the depth of the face of the wall, but flooding occurred almost immediately. It measured 2.1m east–west by 1.1m. The fill was identical to that in Cut 4.

Cut 6 was dug in Fish Lane, parallel to the walls defining its edge, Walls I, J and K. At the west end, below tarmac and hardcore, a double layer of cobbles was visible in the northern section only. Below this was late demolition rubble, not the original lane stratigraphy. At the eastern end mixed debris overlay a thick layer of pure, grey/brown clay.

The presence of the layer of dense, pure clay may explain the lack of original stratigraphy in Fish Lane; this was the same thick, dense clay layer identified on both the adjacent sites that appears to have been deposited as an impermeable layer to lessen the effects of the tidal flooding before the development of this area in the 18th century. South of Fish Lane it pre-dated the houses constructed by Sir Harry Hartstonge, *c.* 1777. Presumably the ground level in this area was reduced, the town wall destroyed and clay put in place. 'Sir Harry Hartstonge...made an embankment at Sluice Island, at a great outlay of money, and built a mall, and several fine houses, which, being without the walls, were free at the time from Corporate claims, or other city taxes...[c]alled sir Harry's Mall—now gone to complete ruin—the site of its fine houses utterly neglected' (Lenihan 1866, 368–9). It is now known that the houses on Sir Harry's Mall were built not 'outside the town wall' but partly over it (*Excavations 1997*, 118–20, 96E0334).

The cartographic evidence shows the gradual expansion, after the mid-18th century, of the town beyond the limits of the town wall. Before this, while there is evidence for dwellings external to the wall, the wall itself remained functional and its line was respected. After this it can be seen that the areas external to the wall, to the south and east of the site, were being reclaimed and built on. By about 1786 even the wall seems to have been omitted south of Fish Lane and along the southern side of the site, and it was also cut through by the lane leading north to the County Court House and Hospital located on the site of the friary.

By the 19th century there was extensive development along the southern side of Long Lane, but the area in the angle, internal to the town wall, remained open until the late 19th century. By this stage the Georgian houses (built in 1777) were gone. The early 20th century saw the maximum development of the site, which situation has remained until recently.

*References*
Gwynn, A. and Hadcock, R.N. 1988 *Medieval religious houses: Ireland*. Dublin.
Hodkinson, B.J. 1990 The priory of the Hospital of Sts Mary and Edward, King and Martyr, known as Holy Cross, OSA, near the Bridge of Limerick. *NMAJ* **32**.
Lenihan, M. 1866 *Limerick: its history and antiquities, ecclesiastical civil and military*. Dublin.

*Celie O Rahilly, Limerick Corporation, City Hall, Limerick.*

### 523. THOMOND GATE, LIMERICK
Urban post-medieval
15806 15735
SMR 5:17
99E0407
The medieval defences of the city included an

extramural gate at the western end of Thomond Bridge, hence the etymology of the placename 'Thomond Gate'. The gate was on the bridge and has been illustrated on early maps of the town, including Hardiman's map, dated 1590. Speed's map, dated 1610, illustrates a star-shaped fort outside Thomond Gate. These post-medieval earthen fortifications are further illustrated on Greenville's map, c. 1640, and are likely to have been developed and altered to withstand the various 17th-century sieges of the city. The modern streetscape (Mass Lane, Castleview Avenue and Halloran's Lane) around Thomond Gate may reflect the line of elements of these earthworks. However, little consistency exists in the cartographic sources on the layout and exact location of the earthen defences around the Thomond Gate area.

Test excavation was carried out at Thomond Gate. Five test-trenches, 4–6m long, were excavated on the location of manhole shafts within the zone of archaeological potential at the western end of Thomond Bridge. River gravels or natural boulder clay was encountered in all of the trenches; no archaeological indicators were found above these deposits.

The assessment was limited to the construction corridor of the Main Drainage Scheme and as a result could not shed any further light on the nature of the post-medieval earthwork defences in the Thomond Gate area. It is proposed to monitor all construction work in the zone of archaeological potential.
*Edmond O'Donovan, Margaret Gowen & Co. Ltd, 2 Killiney View, Albert Road Lower, Glenageary, Co. Dublin.*

### 524. CASHEL'S LANE, THOMONDGATE, LIMERICK
Part of historic town
15749 15785
SMR 5:017 (part of)
99E0008

This work was carried out on 16 February 1999 before construction of a local authority housing development. The site was on the west side of the Shannon River, fronting the northern side of the old road, Thomondgate, leading to Thomond Bridge. It was not included in the zone of archaeological potential as defined by the Urban Archaeological Survey. It was, however, included within the area defined on the Recorded Monuments Map. The area measured 7.5m north–south by 22m. The site sloped down from west–east.

Three cuttings were made. No archaeological features, deposits or finds were identified in any of them. It seemed that the previous buildings, constructed in the 19th century, were put directly on the natural gravel, which occurred at 0.5–0.7m below the present ground level. The looseness of this natural deposit implied that it was never subject to any significant load-bearing pressure or interference.
*Celie O Rahilly, Limerick Corporation, City Hall, Limerick.*

### 525. CASTLE DEMESNE, NEWCASTLE WEST
Historic town
12796 13374
SMR 36:67
99E0222

The proposed development was at the Ballygowan water plant, Newcastle West, Co. Limerick, which is within the zone of archaeological potential for Newcastle West as identified in the Urban Archaeological Survey of County Limerick. Excavations on site were monitored on 19 May 1999.

The proposed development involved the relocation to another part of the site of a water and $CO_2$ tank, the excavation of a plinth to support a new water tank and the excavation of a services trench.

Before arrival on site, much of the development area had been excavated to the level of the natural geology as part of an earlier development.

The results of the monitoring indicated that the area had been extensively landscaped at some point in the past and that any additional excavation associated with the development would impinge only on previously disturbed ground. Based on these results, it was decided that further ground disturbance associated with the development would not require archaeological monitoring.
*Rob Lynch, IAC Ltd, 8 Dungar Terrace, Dun Laoghaire, Co. Dublin.*

### 526. OLD ABBEY
Adjacent to church and graveyard
SMR 19:100
99E0667

Test excavations took place before the grant of outline planning permission for the construction of two dwelling-houses. The proposed development in the townland of Old Abbey is immediately adjacent to Kilmoylan Church and graveyard. The proposed development site is on the summit of a low hill commanding extensive views of the surrounding undulating pastureland, with Foynes town and Aughinish Island clearly visible to the north.

Three test-trenches were excavated; two on the footprint of the proposed house foundations and one in the vicinity of the percolation areas. Trench 1 was at the north-east corner of House 1. It was L-shaped in plan and measured 5m north-east/south-west by 10m, with an average width of 1.5m. Trench 2 was at the south-west corner of House 2. It was L-shaped in plan and measured 5m north-east/south-west by 10m north-west/south-east, with an average width of 1.5m. Trench 3 was linear in plan and incorporated the two percolation areas to the east of Houses 1 and 2. It measured 30m north–south and had an average width of 1m.

In all trenches topsoil was removed to an average depth of 0.25m, exposing a light yellow/brown, compact clay subsoil. No stratigraphy or artefacts of an archaeological nature were identified while monitoring the ground disturbance activities.
*Emer Dennehy, Eachtra Archaeological Projects, 3 Canal Place, Tralee, Co. Kerry.*

### 527. BALLYCUMMIN, RAHEEN
Vicinity of enclosure
R559524
SMR 15:59
99E0116

A test excavation was carried out before a large-scale office development in the Raheen Industrial Estate, adjacent to a large enclosure. An aerial photograph indicated the presence of a potential site to the north of the enclosure, directly below the site of the proposed office block. The test excavation was carried out in March 1999, and each of the cuttings revealed naturally occurring sand and stone directly below the topsoil. No archaeological features or habitation layers were revealed.

Archaeological monitoring of the groundwork associated with the development was conducted in August 1999. Despite the great extent of the area disturbed and its proximity to the enclosure, no archaeological features or deposits were found to exist.

*Kenneth Wiggins, 17 Vartry Close, Raheen, Co. Limerick.*

## 528. RAHEEN
No archaeological significance
**R633391**
**99E0398**
The development is adjacent to the Lough Gur area. Trial-trenching did not uncover any archaeological remains or finds.

*Rose M. Cleary, Department of Archaeology, University College, Cork.*

## 529. RATHBANE SOUTH
Artificial platform and possible *fulacht fiadh*
**15843 15452**
**99E0525**
Monitoring of topsoil-stripping along the line of the N20/N21 Limerick Bypass uncovered a spread of burnt stone within a charcoal-rich matrix in an area of extremely wet ground. Further investigation and excavation of the area began on 30 September 1999 and ended on 15 October 1999.

The site was an artificial platform of brushwood, peat and clay. The brushwood base was horizontally laid, with no evidence for vertical pegs to hold the larger timbers in place. The timbers were very poorly preserved and showed no signs of toolmarks. They were laid on top of an apparently natural peat layer and were concentrated underneath a peaty redeposit in an area measuring *c.* 8.5m east–west by 3.5m.

Above the layers of timber and peat a thin deposit of tacky, grey clay formed an artificial ground surface above the natural water level. This clay layer was cut in the north-western quadrant of the platform by a shallow, subcircular pit that had a maximum depth of 0.4m and a mean diameter of 1.24m. The pit was filled by two peaty deposits but yielded no artefacts.

The pit, its fills and the grey clay surface were sealed beneath a charcoal-rich layer of heat-shattered sandstone, with a maximum depth of 0.3m. Although this layer conforms to the classic definition of *fulacht fiadh* material, no further evidence, such as a definite trough feature or traces of on-site burning, indicate the use of the site as a cooking area. The presence of an extensive *fulacht fiadh c.* 100m to the east (see No. 530 below) suggests that the stony, charcoal-rich layer may have been transported to the site to refurbish the artificial platform following the abandonment of the pit.

No datable artefacts were recovered from the site.

*Catherine McLoughlin and Emmet Stafford, ADS Ltd, Windsor House, 11 Fairview Strand, Dublin 3.*

## 530. RATHBANE SOUTH
*Fulacht fiadh*
**15858 15442**
**99E0633**
Archaeological monitoring of topsoil-stripping along the line of the N20/N21 Limerick Bypass uncovered a spread of burnt stone within a charcoal-rich matrix. This lay *c.* 70m south of 99E0634, another *fulacht fiadh* (see No. 531 below) The site was a roughly circular spread of black soil and heat-shattered stone that measured 7.5m east–west by 8.5m and was *c.* 0.2m deep. Several pits were found beneath the burnt spread, as well as a trough and fire-pit.

The trough was an oval cut into the subsoil and measured 2.6m north–south by 1.9m. The depth of the cut varied but at its maximum was 0.4m, and it was filled by burnt mound debris. The fire-pit was 0.5m to the east of the trough. It measured 1.7m east–west by 1.2m and had a maximum depth of 0.35m. The base of the cut was filled by an extremely charcoal-rich layer with some burnt stone. Twelve stake-holes ran between the trough and the fire-pit, which would have acted as a windbreak. Several other pits were found in the vicinity of the trough and fire-pit, none of which produced any artefacts. All these features were sealed beneath the burnt spread, which was cut by a later gully and several lazy-beds. The gully was linear and orientated east–west. No artefacts were recovered from the fill to suggest a date for its use.

*Catherine McLoughlin, ADS Ltd, Windsor House, 11 Fairview Strand, Fairview, Dublin 3.*

## 531. RATHBANE SOUTH
*Fulacht fiadh*
**15857 15448**
**99E0634**
Monitoring of topsoil-stripping along the N20/N21 Limerick Bypass uncovered a spread of burnt stone within a charcoal-rich ploughsoil. The spread measured 14m north–south by 28m. Further archaeological investigation and excavation began on 18 October 1999 and concluded on 5 November 1999.

The site consisted of several layers of soil, all of which had been disturbed by ploughing. These contexts, which contained varying levels of burnt stone and charcoal, overlay a series of subsoil-cut features. Unfortunately, the relationship between some of these features had been obscured by pre-construction engineering test-pits.

The main phase of activity on the site was represented by a rectangular pit that held evidence of *in situ* burning. This pit, which had straight sides and a flat base, had a mean depth of 0.5m, measured 2.75m by 1.8m and was immediately identified as the trough or central feature of the site.

A large circular pit with a maximum depth of 1.35m and an average diameter of 3.9m was immediately to the west of the trough. This feature was lined with a layer of clay, indicating that it had a water-holding function. The pit may have been used as a cistern to store the water necessary for the cooking process in the adjacent trough. This possibility is supported by the absence of naturally rising or running water in the immediate vicinity of the site, which was within an area of dry, natural gravels.

Another feature, which ran diagonally across the site along a south-east/north-west direction, was also identified as having a water-management function. This gully, which fell steadily toward the north-west, had steep sides and a gently rounded bottom. It had an average width and depth of 1.1m and 0.48m respectively and ran for a recorded length of 15m. In common with the large pit, which was a minimum distance of 2m to the west, this gully had an applied clay lining. Unfortunately, the relationship between the two features was obscured by a pre-construction test-pit.

Several smaller features (pits and stake-holes) were identified and excavated below the level of the burnt material; no archaeological features were identified beyond the spread of burnt stone. Although the various fills of the large pit mentioned above contained bones from both wild and domestic animals, no artefacts datable without scientific analysis were recovered from the site. A second, smaller *fulacht fiadh* c. 70m to the south (see No. 530 above) was excavated in tandem with this excavation.
*Catherine McLoughlin and Emmet Stafford, ADS Ltd, Windsor House, 11 Fairview Strand, Dublin 3.*

### 532. RINEROE
Modern field drains
1488 1476
99E0451

The site is in Rineroe townland, c. 12km south-west of Limerick City, near Adare, to the north of the present N20. The site was uncovered during archaeological monitoring of topsoil-stripping before road construction on the N20 Adare to Annacotty road scheme. A rescue excavation carried out over one week in August revealed three straight, narrow, parallel ditches, two of which were stone-filled. These were all interpreted as field drains, which were likely to be relatively modern in date.
*Mary Deevy, ADS Ltd, Windsor House, 11 Fairview Strand, Fairview, Dublin 3.*

### 533. ROSSBRIEN
*Fulachta fiadh*
1574 1534
99E0235

The site is in Rossbrien townland, c. 2km south of the centre of Limerick City. It was uncovered during monitoring of topsoil-stripping before road construction on the N20/N21 Adare to Annacotty road scheme. A rescue excavation was carried out over six-and-a-half weeks between May and July. Excavation revealed two *fulachta fiadh*, c. 15m from each other, alongside the Ballynaclough River.

Both sites had very shallow 'mounds' consisting of circular spreads of charcoal-rich soil with heat-shattered limestone and sandstone. In Site A the burnt spread measured c. 10m in diameter and 0.1m in depth. A large, subrectangular trough was found beneath the spread on the western side of the site. The trough measured 2.5m by 1.9m and 0.55m in maximum depth. It was filled with burnt mound material. Evidence for a wooden structure in the

Site B, Rossbrien, trough from south-west.

trough was recovered in the form of three small stake-holes in the base of the trough. The western side of the site was badly disturbed by water action from the flooding river and by tree root action.

In Site B the charcoal spread was much smaller, 5.5m in maximum diameter and 0.1m deep. A subrectangular trough was found immediately adjacent to the spread, again on its western, i.e. river, side. The trough measured 2.2m by 2.1m and 0.5m in maximum depth. It was mainly filled with burnt mound material. Inside the trough at its eastern end a rectangular slab of limestone stood upright on the base of the trough, while there was a row of stake-holes along the southern side and in a cluster beside the slab on the northern side of the trough. The natural subsoil on which these sites were found was very stony. However, it was clear that the large amount of natural stones had been augmented and consolidated on the western side of Site B to form a fairly flat stone surface between it and the river. Site B was truncated by two linear ditches running perpendicular to each other, which were probably field drains. No artefacts were recovered from either site.
*Mary Deevy, ADS Ltd, Windsor House, 11 Fairview Strand, Fairview, Dublin 3.*

### 534. ROSSBRIEN
Possible *fulacht fiadh*
15788 15436
99E0524

Monitoring of topsoil-stripping along the line of the N20/N21 Limerick Bypass uncovered a spread of burnt stone within a charcoal-rich soil, in low-lying, boggy ground. Burnt stone was mixed through the topsoil, which contained numerous finds of modern pottery, glass, metal objects, animal bone and shell. Three stone beads were also recovered from the topsoil. The excavated material was a series of deposits primarily made up of burnt stone and charcoal-rich soil, measuring 30m north–south by 17m, with a depth of no more than 0.3m. One subsoil-cut feature lay to the south-west of the main spread of material, but as this was sealed under a thin layer of peat it was not related to the burnt spread. The burnt spread itself lay on top of this thin layer of peat. Limestone bedrock protruded through the whole area, and no other features were present.
*Catherine McLoughlin, ADS Ltd, Windsor House, 11 Fairview Strand, Fairview, Dublin 3.*

### 535. SHANID LOWER
Adjacent to raised rath
**SMR 19:76**
**99E0590**
Test-trenching was carried out at this proposed development site, which is *c.* 35m from a probable raised rath. Two trenches were opened, to test the proposed house location. Nothing of archaeological significance was noted at the site.
*Isabel Bennett, Glen Fahan, Ventry, Tralee, Co. Kerry.*

### 536. TOWLERTON
Circular mound
**R609559**
**98E0608**
This site, at Towlerton, Kilmurry, was identified during a rewalking of the route for the Limerick Southern Ring Road. It was viewed as a circular mound 8m in diameter and 0.4m high. A trench measuring 5m by 1m was dug by hand in order to test the top of the mound and to see whether there was any enclosing element. It became clear that the site was of natural origin. Nothing of archaeological interest was found.
*Tracy Collins, Aegis Archaeology, 16 Avondale Court, Corbally, Limerick.*

### 537. WOODSTOWN III
Circular depression
**R648568**
**99E0038**
This site was identified as a circular depression with a low, interior mound during field-walking by Aegis along the route of the Limerick Southern Ring Road. Three trenches were dug by hand to ascertain whether the site was of archaeological significance. Trenches A and B measured 8m by 1m, while Trench C was 2m by 1m. The trenching proved that that site was not of archaeological significance.
*Frank Coyne, Aegis Archaeology, 16 Avondale Court, Corbally, Limerick.*

### 538. WOODSTOWN IV
Circular mound
**R650572**
**99E0039**
One trench measuring 8m by 1m was opened at this site before construction of the Southern Ring Road. It proved that the site was not of archaeological significance.
*Frank Coyne, Aegis Archaeology, 16 Avondale Court, Corbally, Limerick.*

## LONGFORD

### 539. MAIN STREET, BALLYMAHON
Adjacent to church and graveyard
**215729 256612**
**99E0441**
Testing was undertaken at a proposed development site on 7 August 1999. The site is adjacent to a church and graveyard (SMR 27:3) and on the northern bank of the River Inny. There were two mill buildings on the site, consisting of an extant cornmill and associated kiln/store. These buildings were the subject of an industrial archaeological/architectural survey undertaken by Colin Rynne.

Three trenches were mechanically excavated within the confines of the development site. No features, structures or finds of archaeological interest were uncovered, although the backfilled remains of a mill-race, associated with the extant mill, were uncovered.

It was recommended that no further archaeological involvement was required at the site.
*Martin E. Byrne, 31 Millford, Athgarvan, Co. Kildare.*

### 540. RATHCRONAN, GRANARD
Town
**23327 28097**
**SMR 10:55**
**99E0566**
Test excavation was undertaken here before planning, on 16 November 1999. The site is at the south edge of the town and close to a motte and bailey, SMR 10:08001, an enclosure, SMR 10:08002, and a church and possible graveyard, SMR 10:05501. Most of the proposed development site is also within the urban zone of archaeological potential for Granard. The site comprises *c.* 14 acres of undulating pastureland, and it was not feasible to test the entire area before development. Following consultation with *Dúchas*, it was agreed that testing would be limited to the area of the proposed development that is closest to the recorded monuments and that monitoring of topsoil removal would be undertaken at construction phase.

The motte and bailey are strategically sited on the hilltop immediately north-west of the proposed development site. This is the castle built by Richard de Tuit in 1199, and it is also likely that this was the inauguration site of the chiefs of Anghaile, mentioned in 1475. Aerial photographs suggest that the motte and bailey occupy part of a much larger enclosure, perhaps a hillfort or monastic boundary.

Testing comprised the mechanical excavation of two 55m-long trenches, at locations corresponding to the north-west limits of the proposed development. A moderately compact, mid-brown, silty sand topsoil, 0.55m thick, overlay the subsoil, which varied from a light grey, clayey sand to an orange, clayey silt. No features, finds or deposits of archaeological interest were encountered.
*Dominic Delany, 31 Ashbrook, Oranmore, Co. Galway.*

## LOUTH

### 541. ARDEE LINK ROAD
Monitoring
**99E0200**
A considerable number of sites were identified during monitoring of the Ardee link road, which covers a distance of 7km from Ardee town through the Dee valley to the M1 motorway under construction at Charleville. The work was carried out for Louth County Council. The site names (Richardstown 1 etc.) listed below correspond to numbers given to all sites investigated under monitoring licence 99E0200. Some were excavated under that licence, while the larger sites were excavated under separate licences. Excavations

under licences 99E0200, 99E0465 and 99E0458 were carried out by Matthew Seaver. Further excavation was undertaken in Broadlough and Richardstown townlands by Carmel Duffy (see No. 547 below).
*Matthew Seaver for Valerie J. Keeley Ltd, 29–30 Duke Street, Athy, Co. Kildare.*

### 542. 16–18 CASTLE STREET, ARDEE
No archaeological significance
**N96199080**
**99E0304**

Monitoring of ground reduction works within gardens to the rear of 16–18 Castle Street, Ardee, Co. Louth, was undertaken before the construction of a carpark. The site is to the north-east of the urban tower-house known as the Courthouse, SMR 17:7.

Monitoring was undertaken between 22 October and 2 November 1999. An irregular-shaped area, comprising two former gardens to the rear of the properties, was mechanically cleared of topsoil and reduced to the top of the clay subsoil, which lay on average 0.5m below present ground level. The northern garden area was retained behind a limestone wall, north of which at a reduced level lay an access roadway to commercial premises. A sparse hedge and fence line forming the south boundary at the western side of the proposed development were removed under supervision to allow the construction of a concrete block wall, the foundation depth of which was 0.8m.

Topsoil was dark brown loam overlying yellow boulder clay with a sandy texture, containing numerous limestone boulders of irregular and water-rolled form. Fragments of slate, red brick and modern patterned ceramics were found within the topsoil removed from the western portion of the development. Remains of a former garden partition wall were uncovered extending through the western portion of the proposed development and as far as the cross-over point between the east and west portions of the proposed carpark area. The wall, 0.5m wide and constructed of mortared limestone, was set into the clay subsoil.

The eastern portion of the development had been used as a small apple orchard, and a modern shed foundation with associated drain was revealed directly on removal of the sod at an angled point along the north perimeter wall of the garden. Removal of rich, black topsoil, containing only a few fragments of butchered animal bone, to an average depth of 0.55m revealed the yellow boulder clay. The excavation of a sump measuring 2m by 2m and 1.5m deep immediately east of the area stripped for the carpark revealed fairly homogeneous, yellow clay with inclusions of very large, undressed boulders.

The development did not reveal any deposits, features or finds of archaeological significance. The enclosing walls along the north and east perimeters of the site were retained, the only alteration to site boundaries being the replacement of a sparse hedge with a block wall along the south side of the western area of the development site. The pronounced and elevated level of these former gardens, by c. 2m above the surrounding ground level, appears to be linked with possible redeposition of the clay subsoil. A stage of deliberate dumping of clay, possibly in the late 19th or early 20th century during construction of dwellings fronting Castle Street and/or in the surrounding area, appears to be likely. If the clay subsoil on the site is redeposited, there is a possibility that deposits, features or finds of archaeological potential survive below a level of 1.5m from the existing garden level (102.9m OD).
*Malachy Conway, Archaeological Consultancy Services Ltd, 15 Trinity Street, Drogheda, Co. Louth.*

### 543. O'CARROLL STREET/BLACK RIDGE/OLD CHAPEL LANE, ARDEE
Urban medieval
**N2964729081**
**SMR 17:217**
**99E0642**

A pre-development assessment was undertaken before a planning submission at a 6-acre green-field site bounded by O'Carroll Street/Black Ridge and Old Chapel Lane, Ardee, Co. Louth, on 12 November 1999. The proposed development site is at the north-east corner of the town, within the area of archaeological potential as outlined in the Urban Archaeological Survey of Ardee. The site lies directly along the supposed line of the medieval town wall and is adjacent to the site of Cappocks Gate at its south-east corner.

Topographically, the field is split-level, higher on the western side than the east, and this is most apparent across the centre of the proposed development site, where a subtle bank and ditch feature crosses the field south-east to north-west, representing a former land division. Excavation of five test-trenches was undertaken with the aid of a tracked mechanical excavator with a 2m-wide ditching bucket.

Trench 1 was positioned north-west/south-east along the western side of the proposed development site and measured 134m by 2.2m. A simple stratigraphic profile was revealed comprising dark brown topsoil on average 0.3m deep, overlying a dark brown clay/loam between 0.1m and 0.2m deep, in turn overlying a mottled, orange/brown, stony clay subsoil. A number of west–east-aligned field drains were revealed, cut into clay subsoil, and a naturally formed area of very stony subsoil comprising numerous boulders was found between 50m and 70m from the south end of the trench. The latter feature corresponds with a noticeable natural rise in the field surface in this area. No features, deposits or soils of archaeological potential were revealed. A number of brownware sherds were recovered from the deposits over the clay subsoil.

Trench 2 was positioned north-west/south-east along the south-eastern corner of the proposed development site and measured 66m by 2.2m. Dark brown topsoil, on average 0.3m deep, overlay dark brown clay loam between 0.1m and 0.2m deep, which lay in turn over mottled, orange/brown, stony clay subsoil. A number of features of archaeological potential were revealed towards the southern end of the trench, cut into clay subsoil.

F1 comprised a rectangular pit, 0.9m by 0.65m, 0.8m from the south end of the trench. The feature was cut directly into the clay subsoil and was filled with a homogeneous, dark brown loam with no obvious inclusions of archaeological significance.

The eastern edge of a second cut feature, F2, with similar fill to that in F1, was revealed extending into and beyond the western edge of the trench.

F3 consists of a west–east linear spread of dark brown loam between 8m and 9.9m from the southern end of the trench. This deposit contains fragments of animal bone and sherds of post-medieval or early modern pottery. The deposit, up to 0.2m deep, lies 0.5m below existing ground level and at its northern end overlies a limestone wall foundation, F4, consisting of an interrupted setting of flat limestone slabs and stones. F4 extends 1.44m into the trench from the western section, and, although it apparently ends at this point, a stone in the eastern section at a depth of 0.55m suggests that the feature may continue east. The wall foundation was found to be only one stone deep and would appear to be no more than 0.3m in surviving depth. The southern edge of F3 is characterised by F5, a linear spread of fine mortar 0.65m wide, extending through the trench. This deposit is up to 0.2m deep and runs parallel to the remains of the limestone wall 1.1m to the north.

Remains of a possible stone-filled field drain, F6, were found 1.5m north of and parallel to F3, consisting of a narrow, linear setting of water-worn stones.

At a location between 46m and 50m from the southern end of the trench lies F6, a roughly east–west linear deposit of dark brown soil with numerous stones. This represents the remains of a former field boundary extending west.

Finds from this trench were largely derived from F3 and comprised a small quantity of butchered animal bone and several sherds of post-medieval or early modern character.

Trench 3 was positioned approximately south-west/north-east along the south-east edge of the proposed development site, measuring 88m by 2.2m. Dark brown topsoil, on average 0.3m deep, overlay dark brown clay loam between 0.2m and 0.3m deep. Mottled, orange/brown, stony clay subsoil lay below this level (0.6–0.7m+). The remains of a former, north–south-aligned field boundary were revealed c. 50m from the eastern end of the trench, coinciding with a marked linear surface feature defining a split level between the higher, western and lower, eastern sides of the field. The surface expression of this feature was a subtle, south-east/north-west-running bank, comprising two parallel ridges with the intervening area sunken and with a shallow ditch to the east. The subsurface remains, F7, consisted of a deposit of very stony subsoil, 5m wide, composed of numerous boulders and stones. A shallow ditch up to 4m wide lay immediately east of this feature. No features, deposits or soils of archaeological potential were revealed.

Trench 4 was orientated approximately south-west/north-east and measured 100m by 2.2m. Dark brown topsoil, on average 0.35m deep, overlay dark brown clay loam up to 0.55m deep. Grey, gravelly clay subsoil lay below this level east and west of the former land division (0.9–1.1m+), interrupted on the west by an outcrop of light orange/brown, sandy loam, 5m wide and 4m from the former field division. Remains of this former north–south field boundary (see Trench 3 above) lay c. 52m from the eastern end of the trench and also coincided with the linear surface feature mentioned above. The subsurface remains, F8, consisted of a deposit of very stony subsoil 5m wide comprising numerous boulders the same as F7. A shallow ditch up to 4m wide lay immediately east of this feature. No features, deposits or soils of archaeological potential were revealed.

Trench 5 was positioned south-west/north-east along the northern edge of the proposed development, roughly parallel to the line of O'Carroll Street/Black Ridge. The trench measured 50m by 2.2m. Dark brown topsoil on average 0.4m deep overlay a dark brown clay loam 0.1m deep. Mottled, grey/brown, stony clay subsoil lay below this level (0.5m+). No features, deposits or soils of archaeological potential were revealed.

Several features of archaeological potential were revealed towards the southern end of Trench 2 including an apparent wall foundation (F4). Although the material overlying this feature (F3) appears to be post-17th-century in date, the proximity of features F1 to F5 to the site of Cappocks Gate suggests that they may be related. The width of F4 alone would not be consistent with that of a medieval fortification wall or a gatehouse; however, it may represent an ancillary building of contemporary date, with the deposition of post-medieval material possibly representing the period of its demolition.

The most obvious topographic expression on the field surface is the line of a former field boundary in Trenches 3 and 4, through F8 and F9. The eastern margin of the site is characterised by a linear strip of land on average 8m wide, which lies immediately beyond the area of proposed development, extending from O'Carroll Street/Black Ridge to a series of gardens at the south-east corner of the site. The margin has been reduced in level, and much waste and domestic debris has accumulated along its length. Although it appears to have been set aside for horticultural purposes, its width and linear appearance suggest that it may represent an older landscape feature, possibly a trace line of the former town wall or a feature parallel to it.

The assessment results recommended further archaeological investigation in the south-east area of the site, before groundworks, as a condition of full planning permission.

*Malachy Conway, Archaeological Consultancy Services Ltd, 15 Trinity Street, Drogheda, Co. Louth.*

### 544. HAGGARDSTOWN, BLACKROCK
Various
J678236
SMR 12:9, 27
99E0683

Planning permission for a housing development was granted subject to licensed monitoring of soil-stripping. The site consisted of two fields, the long axis of which is north–south. This is a low-lying area, mostly below 15m OD. The ground was highest in the north-west, and there is an area of waterlogged ground along its eastern boundary. A possible souterrain is listed on the site of the development. Jordan (1934) made reference to the removal of stones from an underground passage. Previous testing by Kieran Campbell (*Excavations 1994*, 64–5,

94E0197; and Campbell 1995) concentrated on the north-west corner and revealed the presence of a roughly circular, ditched enclosure, most likely a ringfort, of *c.* 40m in outer diameter. No evidence of a souterrain was uncovered at this time. This area, with an additional buffer zone of 15m radius, was excluded from the development.

Monitoring of the soil-stripping of this *c.* 16-hectare site revealed a number of features of note.

Feature 1 was a substantial shell midden, spoon-shaped in cross-section and irregular, elongated oval in plan, covering a horizontal area of at least 4m east–west by *c.* 1.5m north–south and with a maximum depth of 0.2m. There was no burnt material associated with the shells, and underlying the shell-rich lens was a thin layer of fine, water-rolled gravel, suggesting that this feature was a natural marine deposit.

Features 2 and 3 were in the southern part of the site. They were noted first as a spread of burnt soil, with a second, distinct spread 8m to the east of the first. Initial cleaning of the two spreads showed that the burnt soil was contained within two apparently discrete features cut into subsoil. Feature 2, on the west side, was contained in a roughly circular pit *c.* 2.5m in diameter and 0.6m deep, and Feature 3 was narrower and shallower, *c.* 1.4m wide, 4.5m long and 0.4m deep. Feature 2 was the ash-pit for a corn-drying kiln that lay immediately to the west of it and ran on the same east–west axis as Features 2 and 3. This was mostly covered by a layer of mid-brown,

Feature 2, Haggardstown, Blackrock, from west.

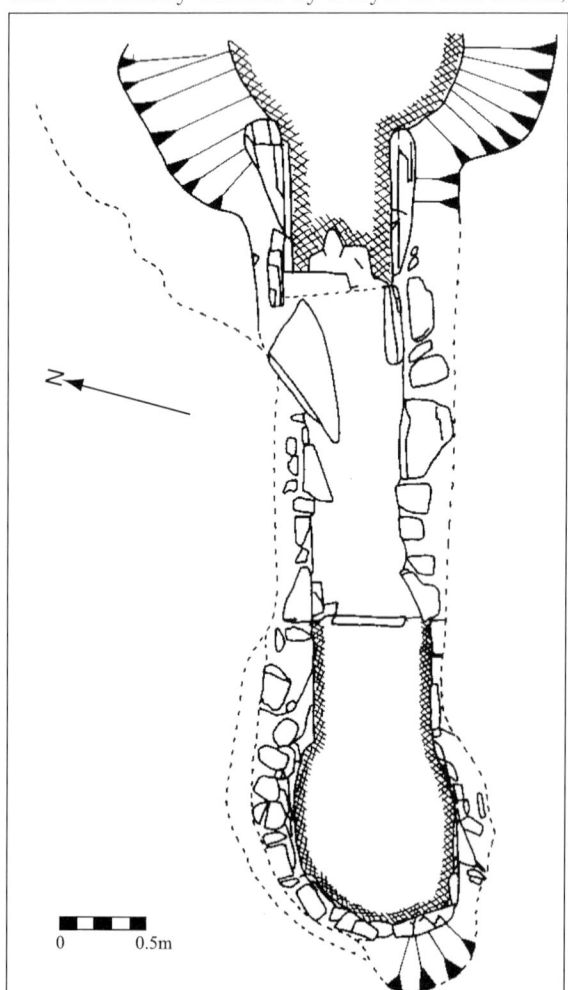

gravelly clay, which resembled natural boulder clay but was redeposited.

The kiln was of the keyhole type, built of drystone walling, consisting in the main of local sandstone and limestone, with the occasional use of flat slabs of local sandstone as vertical walls and also as lintels, although only two collapsed examples of the latter were present. Its overall length was 4.6m: the circular bowl was 1.1m x 1m and the flue was 3.5m by 0.6m. It survived to a maximum height of 0.65m, with up to seven drystone courses surviving in the bowl. The flue consisted of courses of drystone walling at the western end; at the eastern end the initial 1.45m was occupied by vertical stone slabs resembling small orthostats. These were between 0.5m and 0.58m high. The entire floor of the flue was paved with similar, thin stone slabs. In the eastern end of the flue the floor and wall slabs were heavily fire-damaged, scorched to a dull red colour and shattered through intense heat. The ash-pit lay immediately to the east.

The bowl was floored with marl that was probably derived from the marshy ground to the east. This floor was compacted, was laid directly on the natural gravels and was a maximum of 60mm thick. A similar layer of marl, which also contained stones, overlay it; this appeared to represent collapsed roofing material. There were no deposits of charcoal or charred grain on the floor, and, although some inclusions occurred within the floor material, these are probably not derived from the use of the kiln.

No associated paving was noted such as has occurred in other similar kilns (see Hurley 1997, 22–4; Hurley and Scully 1997, 276–7). This absence

Plan of Feature 2 at Haggardstown, Blackrock.

of paving may have been due in part to the intensity of the agricultural activities in the area.

The ash-pit immediately to the east of the kiln contained layers of ash and charcoal, although again no deposits of grain were noted. It survived to a maximum diameter of 2.65m on the north–south axis and was 0.56m at its deepest. It included fragments of shells and an upper layer, thickest in the centre, consisting of a mixture of clay with marl in it, beige but with ash and charcoal inclusions.

Feature 3 had the appearance of a shallower and narrower version of the ash-pit with a similar fill. It was 8m to the east of Feature 2 and was noted as a spread of burnt earth 4.5m east–west by 1.3m. It too contained a layer of heavily charcoal-flecked soil, and lenses of orange (burnt) soil containing a high percentage of ash. The lenses containing shells were thicker, and the quantity of shells, principally limpets, was greater in this area. The upper layer in both Features 2 and 3 was a mixture of clay with marl in it, beige but with ash and charcoal inclusions, and this also extended over the corn-drying kiln. This was found to extend to the east and west of these features and had the appearance of a field boundary or drain. To the east it merged into the sandy subsoil, although it was visible in it.

It appears most likely that the kiln and associated pit were inserted into an existing feature, possibly a field boundary, and that debris from the kiln was spread into the ditch. After the kiln ceased to be used, the ditch may have continued in use and then either silted up or was filled in.

The finds recovered came from the upper levels of the features and were possibly associated with the field boundary. A fragment of a post-medieval skillet handle, one rimsherd and one body sherd of post-medieval date, one fragment of Staffordshire slipware and one (broken) rimsherd of earthenware crock with a dull red glaze were recovered. One flint core was also recovered from the ploughsoil overlying the feature. Two unrecognisable iron pieces were noted but not retained.

Feature 7 survived as a lens of charcoal-stained soil up to 50mm thick but on average 20mm thick, overlying the gravel and clay subsoil. It had an irregular shape and was 0.79m in maximum length and 0.52m in maximum width. A number of flint pieces, including a scraper, were recovered from the charcoal-stained soil, as well as a tiny fragment of heavily abraded pottery. In cleaning the adjacent area, a thin skin of unburnt soil overlying gravel, a further three pieces of struck flint were recovered. Again, one of these, a small side scraper, was worked. Unfortunately, no other features survived in the vicinity of Feature 7. Although it was directly overlying subsoil, and the topsoil in the immediate area was a minimum of 0.5m thick and a possible maximum of 1m thick, it is impossible to say whether it was the base of a cut feature. Alternatively, it may indicate human activity in the area before the development of the considerable depth of topsoil. The field had been extensively and deeply ploughed, and the subsequent activity involving heavy machinery had entirely obliterated any other detail.

Feature 8 comprises a number of features identified over an area of c. 50m north–south by 30m east–west, on the east-facing slope of the slight hill immediately below the ringfort investigated by Campbell. Approximately 0.5m of topsoil was removed.

The area was assessed by systematically walking through it both north–south and east–west. Thirteen individual features were identified, and many incidences of bone, shells, charcoal and other material were recorded. Planning permission has not been obtained for building within this area, so the features were not disturbed.

The soil in this area is varied but in general is dark brown, water-saturated and dense; it is visibly distinct from the soil in the remainder of the development, which is lighter in colour and less water-saturated. The area has been truncated to the east and north by the construction of the roads for the development. Soil has been removed from the northern end and added to the east in the construction of these roads. There has been extensive ploughing in the area, the most recent phase relating to potato crops, and the furrows ran approximately north–south.

There is a central zone that is in line with the possible entrance to the ringfort as described by Campbell (1995). The concentration of archaeological material within it is significantly denser than that in the remainder of the area. This is c. 30m wide (north–south) and runs down the slope of the hill to the east for c. 30m.

Soil-stripping in the area to the south-east of the ringfort and immediately south of Feature 8 uncovered a zone of soil (Feature 9) that in general is dark brown and visibly distinct from the soil in the remainder of the development. The brown soil was charcoal-flecked and had a high clay content, containing grit and some gravel, and it proved to be confined to a band running east–west down the slope, roughly 18m long and 2.5m wide, though irregular in shape. Four sherds of post-medieval pottery were recovered from this feature, as well as one piece of slag.

The feature appears to have been an early field boundary, consisting of a bank containing stones or a stone facing, and possibly an associated shallow ditch. The latter feature, represented by a shallow scoop into the natural, may simply have been the surviving portion of the area dug out to create the bank, which may then have been capped with stones. The intermittent nature of the stones, and the occasionally inverted soil profile where the brown, charcoal-flecked soil was covered by redeposited natural, appears to have been caused by deep ploughing.

On the western end of the field boundary a narrow gully running roughly north–south was noted. This was 1.75m long, between 0.15m and 0.2m wide and 50mm deep. It was filled with a brown, wet, sterile soil, which did not contain any charcoal. No finds were recovered from it. It had the appearance of a possible furrow that may have related to the field boundary described above.

Feature 10, in the north-west area of the northern field, was a spread of burnt soil contained in a pit 1.3m long, running roughly east–west, and 1m in maximum width. The pit was 0.2m deep and was filled with a dark, loamy soil containing burnt stones. There was an extension to the west end of the pit that was 0.4m wide and 0.8m long. The sides of the cut for this feature were steeper than for the pit, and the western end was very straight. It had a layer, 50mm thick, of the dark, loamy soil overlying a fill 0.12m deep of burnt soil that was reddish-brown. It had the general appearance of a flue. No finds were recovered from this feature, and no other features were noted during the soil-stripping in its vicinity. However, the topsoil in this area was *c.* 0.2m deep, and again plough damage may have removed any associated features not cut into subsoil.

Feature 11 was also a pit cut into subsoil containing burnt stones in a matrix of reddish, burnt soil. The pit was 1.1m east–west by 0.64m. It had a maximum depth of 0.24m. The sides were quite steep, although it was quite irregular in shape. No finds were recovered, and there was no layer of dark soil as occurred in Feature 10. No other features were noted in its vicinity.

In summary, monitoring resulted in the identification of eight archaeological features or spreads of features. Seven of these were in areas directly affected by the proposed development, and these were examined and recorded. Feature 8, a complex of features to the east of the ringfort, was in an area omitted from the developer's planning permission.

Apart from Features 2 and 3 (the corn-drying kiln) and Features 8 and 9 (the complexes of features to the east of the ringfort), the remaining features are quite enigmatic. The time span over which there was human activity on the site is possibly of the order of 4500 years, or longer.

*References*
Campbell, K. 1995 *Archaeological report on site investigations at Haggardstown, Dundalk, Co. Louth.*
Hurley, M.F. 1997 *Excavations at the North Gate, Cork, 1994.* Cork
Hurley, M.F. and Scully, O.M.B. 1997 *Late Viking Age and medieval Waterford: Excavations 1986–92.* Waterford.
Jordan, J. 1934 Townland of Haggardstown. *County Louth Archaeological Journal* **8**, 210–14.

*Finola O'Carroll, Cultural Resource Development Services Ltd, Campus Innovation Centre, Roebuck, University College, Belfield, Dublin 4.*

### 545. BRAGANSTOWN
*Fulacht fiadh*
303421 294468
97E0475 ext.

A burnt spread was discovered during monitoring of topsoil-stripping associated with the construction of the Dunleer–Dundalk Motorway. Excavation took place from 26 April to 17 May 1999.

An area 10m x 10m was identified for excavation. The burnt spread was a hard, black, sandy silt with frequent angular, disaggregated stones, ash and charcoal. Initial examination of the stone suggests that red sandstone formed the bulk of the deposit. Ploughing and machine disturbance had severely levelled the deposit to a subrectangular shape and a depth of 0.2m. It measured 8.4m x 4.56m. When the burnt spread was removed, a hearth, a trough and two pits were revealed beside an area of rough paving.

The hearth was subcircular, 0.11m deep x 0.92m x 0.78m, and filled with charcoal and burnt stone. It lay 1.45m to the north of the trough. This was trapezoidal in plan, 0.45m deep x 3.5m x 0.8m. The base of the trough was lined with a tangentially split oak plank (wood identification by Ellen O'Carroll), some of which had decayed. A slight protruding 'lip' on the top of the west side of the trough suggests that the sides may also have been wood-lined. The trough was filled with soft, black, clayey silt with frequent disaggregated stone, ash and charcoal.

Two pits were also investigated, one to the south and the other on the east side of the trough. The latter was oval in plan and 'stepped' in section. It was 0.43m deep and 1.51m x 0.97m. The pit was filled with friable, light grey, sandy silt, charcoal, ash and burnt stones. The former pit was oval, 0.3m deep and 0.41m x 0.38m. Again, this was filled with ash and burnt stone. The trough and pits all truncated a compact, light grey/brown, sandy silt. Disturbance of the burnt spread above had compressed a large quantity of burnt stone into this deposit.

Thirty-three flint artefacts were recovered from this deposit, including a leaf-shaped arrowhead, a barbed and tanged arrowhead, three round scrapers and two cores. The remaining flints consisted of primary flakes and debitage. The artefactual evidence suggests that this was the 'occupation' surface, the colour and composition of which may have been changed over time by leachate from the burnt mound above.

A large quantity of unburnt stones was deposited along the west side of the burnt spread. Some of these were placed on top of the surface and may be interpreted as an area of rough paving. Some 60% of the flint artefacts recovered were found close to this paving, suggesting that this was a knapping area. The site produced no other artefacts.

Because the plank recovered from the base of the trough was tangentially split, it was not possible to submit it for dendrochronological analysis. It is hoped, however, that radiocarbon dates will be obtained from charcoal samples recovered.

*Cóilín Ó Drisceoil, 6 Riverview, Ardnore, Kilkenny, for Valerie J. Keeley Ltd.*

### 546. BROADLOUGH 2
Trough
297333 290953
99E0200

This site was *c.* 10m east of the east bank of the River Dee. This area was being excavated for piling, which would be used to support a new river-crossing. The material above the site was a silty, orange/brown clay that contained frequent manganese and iron staining and occasional decayed stones. This would suggest that the deposits were formed by riverine deposition.

The site was a burnt spread 1.5m east–west by 1.3m. It comprised a spread of charcoal-rich clay with frequent heat-cracked stone. A wooden stake, 0.1m by 0.8m, penetrated the centre of the spread. This was surrounded by a cut 0.32m by 0.35m. The stake was relatively recent in date. The burnt deposit was 0.28m deep. It overlay a subrectangular trough that had sloping sides.

The trough was 2.12m north–south by 1.5m. It had a maximum depth of 0.18m. It was truncated by four large post-holes. In the north-east corner a

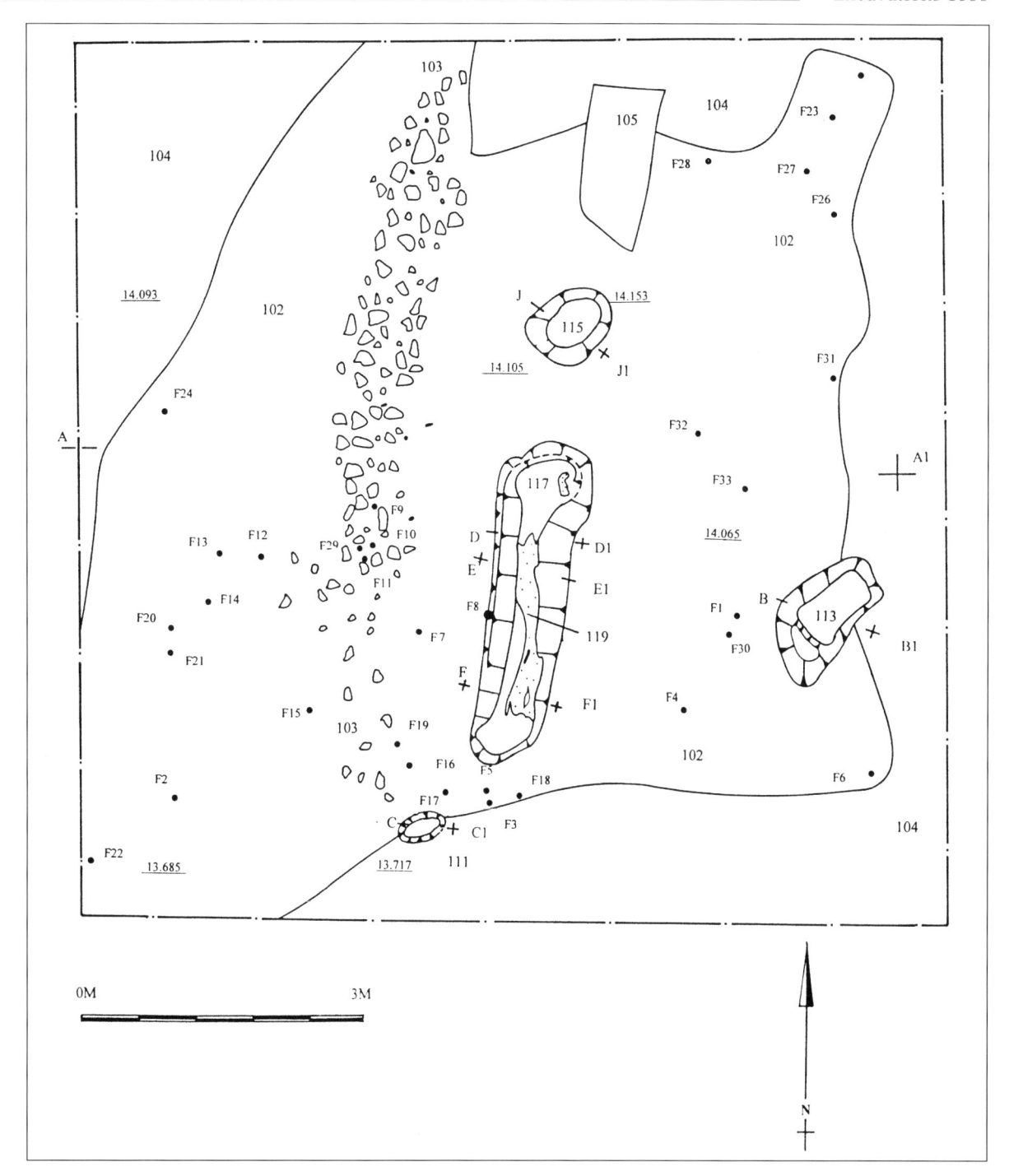

Post-excavation plan of site at Braganstown.

circular post-hole, 0.18m by 0.19m, was uncovered. This was up to 0.17m deep. It was flush with the corner of the trough. In the south-east corner a subcircular post-hole, 0.22m by 0.18m, was excavated. It was c. 0.14m deep. Both of these post-holes were filled with the burnt material.

In the south-west of the site a subcircular post-hole, 0.2m by 0.22m, was 0.16m deep. In the north-west an irregular-shaped post-hole, 0.4m by 0.3m, was found. This comprised a subcircular post-hole measuring 0.3m by 0.26m with a 'lip' facing east. It was up to 0.22m deep. Both of these post-holes were filled with blue-grey, silty marl with frequent charcoal flecks. The extreme west of the trough did not have a definite edge and dropped away into a linear gully. These features were sealed under the blue/grey marl, which contained occasional heat-shattered stones. A single, small, rounded stone was found within this gully.

The gully was flat-bottomed with gently sloping sides. It was up to 1.2m wide at the top and 0.22m deep. It ran north–south and seemed to curve to respect the trough. It was traced for a length of 15m. It had a shallow terminal at its southern end, while the northern stretch continued beyond the area of excavation. It appeared to be heading in the direction of the river. The blue/grey marl was much purer to the south and contained no burnt stone. The trough, gully and post-holes were all cut into a compact, light yellow/brown, stony, sterile clay. A sample is currently being processed for radiocarbon dating.

*Matthew Seaver for Valerie J. Keeley Ltd, 29–30 Duke Street, Athy, Co. Kildare.*

### 547. BROADLOUGH
Pit, possibly part of *fulacht fiadh*
**99E0460**

The pit came to attention during monitoring of machine clearance for the construction of the Ardee link road. Two flints were recovered at the base of the topsoil.

The pit was subrectangular, 1.75m x 1.4m and 0.2m deep. The fill was burnt stones, many of sandstone, *c.* 0.15m across, angular and most often fairly flat, comprising 80% of the material. In the interstices was black clay and some charcoal, which was sampled.

Examination of the surrounding area revealed no further archaeological evidence. Numerous *fulacht fiadh*-type sites, large and small, were identified during monitoring of the Ardee link road and have been excavated; the full conclusions are not yet clear.
*Carmel Duffy, The Mill Road, Umberstown Great, Summerhill, Co. Meath, for Valerie J. Keeley Ltd.*

### 548. CAPPOCKSGREEN
Burnt spread
**99E0458**

Excavation took place from 20 August to 1 September 1999 on a possible *fulacht fiadh* exposed during topsoil-stripping for the Ardee link road.

The site is on a broad bend of the River Dee, 140m from the present course of the river at the western margin of the original flood-plain. A spread of heat-fractured stones in a charcoal-rich soil lay in an apparent arc, 6.6m long by *c.* 2.3m wide, around a further concentration of burnt stones in a subrectangular pattern, 1.15m by 0.75m. The archaeological deposits were sealed by ploughsoil and lay on the surface of, and sloped into, a light brown, sandy clay that formed a 0.5m-thick deposit over the underlying natural subsoil of sand and gravel. The sandy clay is probably the result of inundations from the river.

Excavation revealed that the burnt stone deposits were no more than 0.08m thick. The subrectangular concentration of stones was removed onto a smooth surface of charcoal with some ash, possibly a hearth. A second, similar setting of burnt and unburnt stones overlying a charcoal-stained surface, 0.67m by 0.55m, was found 2m to the south-east of the main burnt spread. However, no evidence was found for a trough at the site, which was eventually expanded to an area 18m by 13m.

A waste flint flake from the arc of burnt stone was the only artefact recovered.
*Matthew Seaver for Valerie J. Keeley Ltd, 29–30 Duke Street, Athy, Co. Kildare.*

### 549. CARLINGFORD TOWN AND ENVIRONS
Urban
**98E0161**

Rescue excavation and archaeological monitoring continued in Carlingford, Co. Louth. This involved the completion of the excavation at Castle Hill adjacent to King John's Castle (see *Excavations 1998*, 139–40) and the monitoring of sewer, water main, Telecom and ESB services at Newry Street, Castle Hill, Market Street, Shore Road and Old Quay Lane.
*Dermot G. Moore, ADS Ltd, Windsor House, 11 Fairview Strand, Fairview, Dublin 3.*

### 550. CASTLE HILL, CARLINGFORD
Urban medieval
**31885 31198**
**99E0234**

An assessment of a proposed development involving the construction of a mews house and a terraced house was carried out at Castle Hill, Carlingford, Co. Louth. The site is to the west of Newry Street, inside the line of the town wall.

Two trenches were excavated. The first, at the north end of the site, consisted of topsoil above natural gravel, which was exposed at a depth of 0.15m below the surface. The second was excavated at the south end of the site in an area where the ground has been made up and is 1.5m above road level. Two walls of relatively recent date (18th–20th century) were exposed in the trench and were cut into a post-medieval deposit. This layer extended to a depth of 2.2m and overlay the natural gravel. To the north of these walls a brown, loamy soil containing stones and shell was evident at a depth of 1.5m. This deposit almost certainly represented a former garden soil, but no finds were present that could help to date it. Natural gravel was exposed at a depth of 2m in this area.

As the proposed mews house was not to impinge on the garden soil, no further work was necessary.
*Donald Murphy, Archaeological Consultancy Services Ltd, 15 Trinity Street, Drogheda, Co. Louth.*

### 551. CASTLE HILL, CARLINGFORD
Urban medieval
**O186121**
**99E0299**

The site was tested before submission of the planning application so that the results could accompany the application for the construction of a dwelling-house. It is just inside the area of archaeological potential in Carlingford as defined by the Urban Survey for County Louth. The line of the town wall is thought to have extended east–west along the northern boundary of the proposed development site, and a mural tower was immediately east of this site

Three trenches tested this small site for evidence for the town wall. No such evidence was found. The stratigraphy comprised modern fill and building rubbish possibly deriving from demolition of a structure(s) on the site. The present boundary wall at the back of the site was built on top of layers of 19th-century fill. The fill layers extended southwards into the site, and no archaeological material was observed.
*Rosanne Meenan, Roestown, Drumree, Co. Meath.*

### 552. CASTLE HILL, CARLINGFORD
Urban medieval
**31869 31196**
**99E0421**

An archaeological assessment of a proposed residential development was carried out at Castle Hill, Carlingford, Co. Louth, on 4 August 1999. The site is within the medieval town of Carlingford, close to King John's Castle and the line of the town wall.

Three test-trenches were excavated on the site using a mechanigal digger with a 3ft bucket. The trenches excavated revealed only modern garden soil

covering the natural subsoil. No archaeological features were revealed in any of the trenches, and no finds of archaeological interest were recovered. No further archaeological excavation is therefore necessary at the site.
*Deirdre Murphy, Archaeological Consultancy Services Ltd, 15 Trinity Street, Drogheda, Co. Louth.*

### 553. CHURCH LANE, CARLINGFORD
Medieval(?) burials
J18991141
98E0161

During monitoring of the ongoing Main Drainage Scheme in Carlingford, human skeletal remains were discovered in Church Lane, outside the eastern gate of the Holy Trinity Church. Work on the drainage scheme was halted to facilitate the excavation of the remains.

Four human skeletons were discovered lying just outside the modern walls of the graveyard. All four lay within the natural beach gravel; there was no evidence of coffins. It was determined that the skeletons were at least several hundred years old, but in the absence of associated datable artefacts a more accurate age cannot be estimated at this time.

The lower legs of all four skeletons had already been removed with the construction of a cobbled surface—presumably a path/roadway. Three of the skeletons lay within a single grave-cut, and there was evidence to suggest that the first burial had been pushed or moved slightly to allow for the second, which in turn partially underlay the third. The fourth burial lay to the south of these and within a much shallower grave-cut.

Pathology analysis was carried out on site by L. Buckley, who has determined that all four were young adult males and all bore sword cuts on their skulls. One individual had a healed head wound in addition to the fresh sword mark. Given this evidence, it is likely that these four individuals were infantry men, struck down from horseback in a late medieval/early post-medieval skirmish.
*Cia McConway, ADS Ltd, Unit 48, Westlink Enterprise Centre, 30–50 Distillery Street, Belfast BT12 5BJ.*

### 554. HOLY TRINITY HERITAGE CENTRE, CARLINGFORD
Post-medieval
J18861172
99E0686

The planned addition of a kitchen extension to the Church of the Holy Trinity, Carlingford, now the Holy Trinity Heritage Centre, was subject to an archaeological monitoring condition.

The Heritage Centre is in the south-east corner of the town and stands on the top of a hill, surrounded by a graveyard and enclosed by a stone-built wall. The church is believed to be within the confines of the medieval town of Carlingford, and the site may have been that of the parish church first referred to in documents dating from the early 13th century. At the eastern end of the church stands a tower that may have been built in the late 16th or early 17th century. The church itself may have been added later in the 17th century and underwent extensive refurbishment at the start of the 19th century.

The required groundworks covered an area *c.* 4m by 4m. Building construction necessitated the ground to be reduced by 0.3m in the area of the new floor and up to 0.8m along the line of the building's foundation trenches. Ground reduction was carried out using a mechanical excavator fitted with a toothless bucket.

Two burials and two drains were uncovered. On instruction from *Dúchas*, these features were excavated and the burials were removed. The burials were extended inhumations, oriented east–west, and had been placed into shallow graves, which, at the time of excavation, were unmarked. The presence of nails indicates that these skeletons were originally contained in coffins. The western end of one of the burials truncated the eastern end of the second. This earlier burial was only excavated from below the knee, as the rest of the burial extended outside the development area. Apart from coffin nails, there were no grave-goods found in association with these burials, although a bone pin/handle was found in the machined-off topsoil within a metre of the later of the two burials.

Drains had truncated each burial; several bones were missing from the upper skeleton, and the skull had been crushed. At least one of the drains dated from the 19th century and was more than likely constructed as part of the 19th-century programme of renovation. The second drain was either late 19th- or early 20th-century in date.

Excavations undertaken within the church by Dermot Moore and Carol Gleeson in 1992 (*Excavations 1992*, 44–5) uncovered burials yielding radiocarbon dates of AD 1442–1650 and AD 1517–1666. Twenty burials were excavated, all of which were unmarked within shallow graves. The absence of coffin nails or any trace of wood suggests that the burials were simple inhumations in which coffins were not used. These burials had been disturbed by 19th-century renovation works.

It is possible that the two burials most recently investigated are contemporaneous with the burials excavated by Moore and Gleeson, as they share a number of similarities. The use of coffins, however, in the burials external to the church may indicate a slightly later date.

No medieval archaeological structural evidence or burials were revealed. If evidence for the earlier church survives, it remains to be found.
*Nóra Bermingham, ADS Ltd, Windsor House, 11 Fairview Strand, Dublin 3.*

### 555. CHARLEVILLE
Pit
303118 291097
97E0475 ext.

A pit was discovered during monitoring of topsoil-stripping along the route of the Ardee link road. Excavation took place from 2 to 4 November 1999.

The pit was subrectangular and measured 2.7m x 0.85m x 0.5m diameter. Much of the sides and base was scorched red. The pit was filled with two distinct deposits. The earlier was a dark brown, silty clay with frequent charcoal and burnt clay inclusions; the later was a mid-brown, sandy clay with frequent large stones. No finds were recovered.
*Cóilín Ó Drisceoil, 6 Riverview, Ardnore, Kilkenny, for Valerie J. Keeley Ltd.*

### 556. NUNS WALK, COLLON
Medieval borough
299850 282181
99E0018

An assessment of a proposed residential development at Nuns Walk, Collon, Co. Louth, was carried out in January 1999. The proposed development involves the construction of 21 houses, and four trenches were excavated in the area of the development. No archaeological deposits or features were found, and it is likely that the medieval borough of Collon was not in this area. It was probably situated south-west of the site, near the remains of a medieval church. The proposed development will not have any archaeological impact.

*Donald Murphy, Archaeological Consultancy Services Ltd, 15 Trinity Street, Drogheda, Co. Louth.*

### 557. SCHOOL LANE, COLLON
Medieval borough
29996 28169
SMR 20:23
99E0397

An assessment of a proposed residential development site was carried out on 17 August 1999 at School Lane, Collon, Co. Louth. The site is at the south end of the present-day village of Collon and lies partially within the zone of archaeological potential, which represents a medieval borough/town. The site comprises a large area measuring 225m east–west by 200m and lies to the rear of properties fronting onto Drogheda Street. The site consists for the most part of an open grass field that slopes from the north end towards the Mattock River, which runs east–west c. 25m from the southern boundary of the site. There is a prominent knoll at the eastern edge of the site, close to the school. A modern barn and the ruins of a 19th-century farmyard occupy the north-central area of the site. The barn stands on the site of a large house that was formerly the Church of Ireland rectory and to which the yard was attached. An enclosed area immediately in front of the rectory consisted of a walled garden and orchard.

Six test-trenches with an overall length of 349m were excavated using a tracked excavator fitted with a 1.5m-wide bucket. The trenches were concentrated in the northern half of the site, within the area due to be disturbed by the proposed development. No significant deposits of archaeological interest were uncovered. Five sherds of medieval pottery were recovered but were found in association with post-medieval sherds. All features recorded were found to be of relatively recent date. The stone walls in Test-trench 3 could be identified as belonging to the 19th-century ruins still standing on the site.

Testing was restricted by the presence of buildings in the north-west area of the site, but it is likely that the construction of the farmyard has already reduced the ground surface below natural. Natural boulder clay was exposed at depths of between 0.3m and 0.55m below rubble and a brown loam. No further archaeological investigation is considered necessary.

*Donald Murphy, Archaeological Consultancy Services Ltd, 15 Trinity Street, Drogheda, Co. Louth.*

### 558. DAWSONS DEMESNE
Medieval settlement/possible site of friary
N965907
SMR 17:101.20
99E0061

A private house was to be built close to the banks of the Dee River, on the east side of Ardee. This area is believed to be a possible location of the Carmelite friary, founded in 1302. Fourteen test-trenches were excavated by mechanical digger in the footprint of the proposed house.

The trenches demonstrated that river silts were present along a line parallel to the present line of the river but 10m to the north of the existing bank at a depth of between 0.45m and 0.55m below the modern surface. There were no indications of any structures in this area, and the only objects found, fragments of roof-tile, may have been incorporated into the soil from further to the south-west, possibly at the initial stages of the remodelling of the riverbank.

*Finola O'Carroll, Cultural Resource Development Services Ltd, Campus Innovation Centre, Roebuck, University College, Belfield, Dublin 4.*

### 559. DAWSONS DEMESNE
Irregular pit
297227 290712
99E0200

A small site was discovered close to the motte at Dawsons Demesne and was excavated on 24 June 1999. It was patch of dark brown/black, silty clay, which contained frequent small lumps and flecks of charcoal and fragments of shattered stone (up to 30% of its content), measuring 0.5m north–south by 0.8m. The deposit contained a single sherd of poorly fired coarse pottery with a dark core and a light orange/brown exterior fabric. The deposit was found to fill an irregular-shaped shallow pit with gently sloping sides up to 0.08m deep. This cut a reddish-brown, sandy clay that contained frequent shattered and decayed stones such as mudstone and sandstone.

The deposit was natural in origin and probably derived from glacial processes. The sherd and a charcoal sample are currently being processed.

*Matthew Seaver for Valerie J. Keeley Ltd, 29–30 Duke Street, Athy, Co. Kildare.*

### 560. CARRICK ROAD, DONAGHMORE
Possible site of graveyard/church
J237654
SMR 7:60
99E0063

The site was on the shoulder of a hill with views to the east and south and more restricted views to the west. The ground sloped upwards to the north. Pre-development testing was undertaken at the site using a ditching bucket, with two trenches excavated along the main axes of the proposed house. Monitoring of the subsequent soil-stripping of the site was also undertaken. Nothing of archaeological interest was uncovered, either in the test-trenches or during soil-stripping.

The site owner stated that a souterrain had been uncovered during the building of the existing house in the 1970s and that this had been recorded and filmed by staff from the Office of Public Works.

Unfortunately, no record of this souterrain under this townland name could be found in *Dúchas*, and no evidence of its existence was recorded during testing or monitoring. The site is adjacent to an area believed, according to local tradition, to have been a graveyard, although there is no surface evidence to support this.

*Finola O'Carroll, Cultural Resource Development Services Ltd, Campus Innovation Centre, Roebuck, University College, Belfield, Dublin 4.*

### 561. 20 BOLTON SQUARE, DROGHEDA
Urban medieval
30873 27544
99E0369

An assessment of a proposed commercial development was carried out at Bolton Square, Drogheda, Co. Louth. The site is just inside the northern town wall boundary on the north side of Bolton Square. This area of the town was probably not extensively settled during medieval times and was most likely reserved for industrial purposes.

The assessment involved the excavation of two trenches. They did not reveal any evidence of archaeological stratigraphy. Upon the removal of a concrete yard, boulder clay was exposed all over the site.

*Deirdre Murphy, Archaeological Consultancy Services Ltd, 15 Trinity Street, Drogheda, Co. Louth.*

### 562. BOLTON STREET, DROGHEDA
Urban medieval
30863 27536
99E0250

An assessment of a proposed commercial development involving the demolition of an existing shop unit and the construction of a new one was carried out at Bolton Street, Drogheda, Co. Louth. The site is on the west side of Bolton Street, inside the medieval town of Drogheda, close to the western line of the town wall. This area was probably not extensively settled during the medieval period.

Two trenches were excavated following the removal of a concrete floor. A thick layer of garden soil was evident in the trenches and directly overlay the subsoil, which was exposed at an average depth of 1m. There was no evidence of archaeological stratigraphy in the excavated trenches, and it was clear that this site was the back garden of a house fronting onto Bolton Street.

*Deirdre Murphy, Archaeological Consultancy Services Ltd, 15 Trinity Street, Drogheda, Co. Louth.*

### 563. 1 BOLTON STREET/SQUARE, DROGHEDA
Urban medieval
30868 27546
SMR 24:41
99E0742

An assessment was carried out on a proposed two-storey extension at 1 Bolton Street/Square, Drogheda. The site is just inside the north-west angle of the medieval town wall. One trench was excavated by machine along the western wall of the proposed development. A dark brown layer containing stone was exposed below the topsoil at an average depth of 0.45m. This layer contained a number of 19th-century pottery sherds and clay pipe fragments and probably represents a layer of demolition material that was spread over the site to raise the ground level. This in turn overlay the natural, orange boulder clay at an average depth of 0.95m. No archaeological features or deposits were uncovered.

*Ian Russell, Archaeological Consultancy Services Ltd, 15 Trinity Street, Drogheda, Co. Louth.*

### 564. THE GATE LODGE, SIENNA CONVENT, CHORD ROAD, DROGHEDA
Medieval suburbs
310263 275918
97E0149

The site of this proposed residential development lies to the east and outside the medieval town wall of Drogheda and consists of the gate lodge of the nearby Sienna Convent, an imposing, three-storey over basement, yellow brick building from 1792, built in the style of a large country house.

Two trenches were excavated along the east and west sides of the lodge, close to the foundations of the proposed new two-storey dwelling. Trench 1, excavated on the west side of the lodge, measured 7m by 1.2m and was 1.5m deep; it revealed a mix of stony gravel, sandstone, tarmacadam and red brick fragments that probably constitutes the foundations of the convent driveway; no features or finds were uncovered in this trench.

Trench 2, excavated on the east side of the lodge, measured 8m by 1.2m and was 1.6m deep, revealing sod and topsoil to a depth of 0.4m overlaying a layer of mortar to a depth of 0.5m. Under this lay a black clay loam to a depth of 1.4m containing fragments of red brick glass and two pieces of delft plate. Below this layer the natural gravel was exposed. No features were evident, and the finds recovered were of post-medieval date.

No evidence for archaeological stratigraphy was revealed in either trench, and therefore no further archaeological work is proposed.

*Deirdre Murphy, Archaeological Consultancy Services Ltd, 15 Trinity Street, Drogheda, Co. Louth.*

### 565. 103/104 DULEEK STREET, DROGHEDA
Adjacent to town wall
O091747
SMR 24:41
99E0399

Pre-development testing was carried out on a proposed development site at 103/104 Duleek Street, Drogheda, Co. Louth. The site is opposite Millmount motte and is in the angle of Duleek Street and Mount St Oliver. The ground slopes downwards to the street at the base of the motte. The line of the town wall is known to run beneath the rear boundary wall of both properties, which were immediately inside the wall. The rear gardens of Nos 103/104 Duleek Street would be affected by the proposed development.

Three test-trenches were dug using both a ditching bucket and a clawed bucket in the garden of No. 103 Duleek Street, and the line of the town wall at the rear boundary of this and the adjacent property was examined.

Test-trench 1 was dug to a depth of 1.5m. Beneath the humus was over 1.5m of redeposited material that included modern china, bottles, iron and a sheet of galvanised iron. Lenses of clay were visible, and there was also a lot of clinker and some clay pipes. Medieval pottery was noted from close to the surface, but at 1.5m the soil was more uniform, a dark grey/brown, silty, friable soil similar to garden soil. Here the finds consisted predominantly of some fragments of early (12th–13th-century) medieval pottery, although one fragment of brown-glazed ware was recovered at this level.

Test-trench 2 ran for 25m east–west from the rear of the garden. Yellow boulder clay was uncovered immediately under the sod at the fence, and the humus and topsoil thickened to a depth of 0.4m at the eastern end of the trench. There were few finds, mostly modern glass or china.

Test-trench 3 was placed crossing the west end of Test-trench 1 and ran north–south for a distance of 6m. This was dug to ascertain the natural slope of the subsoil. A distance of 4m separated Test-trenches 1 and 2, and subsoil was not found in Test-trench 1, although it was over 1.5m deep, but occurred at 0.4m in Test-trench 2. The subsoil profile recorded in Test-trench 3 showed that it dropped a total of 1.4m over a distance of 4m and was a maximum of 2.2m below the sod line. The finds recovered were similar to those from Test-trench 1, although they were fewer. Immediately above the line of the subsoil no pottery was recovered but some animal bone (cattle) was noted. There was no evidence for an undisturbed medieval horizon, as the finds continued to be mixed, until the point where they ceased to occur and only bone was present.

Clearance of the overburden of vegetation along the boundary fence to the rear of 103 Duleek Street revealed a number of stones of irregular shape. None was fixed in position, and all were sitting directly on subsoil. At most they could be taken to represent the remnant of the rubble core of a wall, as nothing that could be considered to be facing was discerned. A cut into the subsoil was observed to the west of the line of the stones. This was not investigated as it lay outside the properties being developed. It may be some form of ditch, as it did not appear to be natural. Further to the north, where the ground begins to fall away steeply, clearance along the boundary where the ground level inside the garden remained high showed the same kinds of stones, also sitting directly on the subsoil, but again no trace of a clear line or of facing-stones was found. There is a block wall to the rear of No. 104 Duleek Street, and the town wall is believed to run beneath or beside it. Without removing the wall, which may not be necessary to the development, no further investigations could be made.

Test-trenches 1 and 3 produced material indicating that the ground level in this property was considerably raised by the introduction of soil and other fill. There is no definite indication of when such filling commenced, although it clearly continued until relatively recently.

The town wall is completely reduced to the rear of No. 103 and most likely also to the rear of No. 104, although this could only be confirmed by demolishing the existing boundary wall. Local information suggested that there had been cottages running along Mount St Oliver and therefore in the garden of No. 104 Duleek Street. This has not been confirmed by any map or photographic evidence, although small structures are shown on the west side of the town wall at this point on the map of 1861.

Undisturbed *in situ* archaeology was not uncovered in any of the trenches opened. The original slope of the hill was altered by bringing in fill, but there was no evidence that any stepping of the original surface occurred. This fill contained both medieval and post-medieval material, but nothing of earlier date was noted. However, animal bone did occur at subsoil level.

The map evidence clearly indicates that the street now known as Mount St Oliver is a relatively recent creation, possibly related to the remodelling of Mill Mount during the Napoleonic 'threat'. Thus, during the medieval period the gardens to the rear of Nos 103 and 104 Duleek Street were more than likely also gardens or common ground. In the 1835 manuscript map of Drogheda the town wall is indicated by a heavy line. It is shown as a long, straight line to the rear of Duleek Street, but it is not shown on this map as carrying across the last plot, equivalent to the garden of No. 104, presumably having been demolished when the new street was made.

*Finola O'Carroll, Cultural Resource Development Services Ltd, Campus Innovation Centre, Roebuck, University College, Belfield, Dublin 4.*

**566. DYER STREET, DROGHEDA**
Urban medieval
30896 27502
99E0242

An assessment of a proposed commercial development at Dyer Street, Drogheda, was carried out in September 1999. The development involves the construction of a basement carpark and an overhead commercial premises. The site is on the north bank of the River Boyne, along the south side of Dyer Street in the centre of the medieval town, in an area of high archaeological potential.

The site was cleared of existing buildings, and a concrete yard and 19th–20th-century topsoil were removed under archaeological supervision. Following the removal of this debris, features became evident on the surface almost immediately. In the south-east corner of the site a series of timber tanning boxes was exposed at a depth of 1m, and north of these a stone wall extending in an east–west direction was evident. In the southern half of the site a substantial stone and brick building of post-medieval date was noted, and a possible brick kiln survived inside the structure. To the west of the building was a post-medieval stone culvert.

Twelve trenches were excavated. They revealed the presence of medieval stratigraphy over most of the site. To the north, deposits were exposed that consisted of medieval floors and surfaces. In this area stratigraphy survived to a depth of 1m below present ground level but was not undisturbed and was cut by later features such as walls, culverts and basements. To the east of the site two east–west walls of possible medieval date may form part of a single structure, and north of this feature a substantial stone wall of late medieval date was encountered. An upright timber post of medieval date in the same area may form part of a revetment along an earlier riverbank. This feature also divides the site

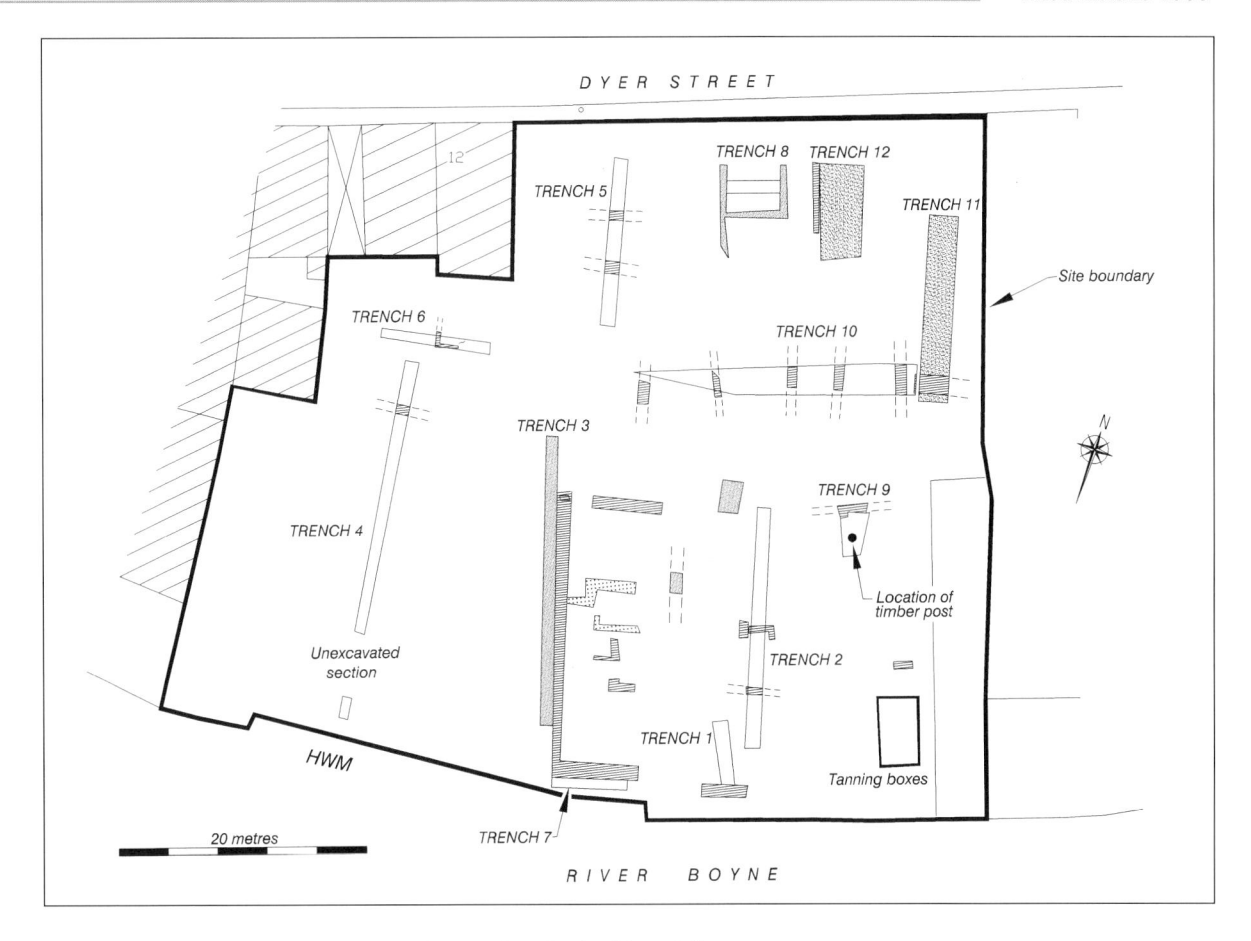

Location of trenches on site at Dyer Street, Drogheda (No. 566).

north–south, and the southern half contains a black, organic layer over 1m thick, below stratified deposits. This layer contained timber, leather and sherds of medieval pottery. The scale of the proposed development has not yet been finalised, and it was recommended that the site be excavated before any development.
*Donald Murphy, Archaeological Consultancy Services Ltd, 15 Trinity Street, Drogheda, Co. Louth.*

### 567. TOWN CENTRE, DYER STREET, DROGHEDA
Urban medieval/post-medieval
30886 27507
SMR 24:41
99E0248

An excavation was conducted during six weeks from 2 September to 15 October 1999 to the rear of Farney Villa and Distillery House, Dyer Street, Drogheda. An area measuring 25m east–west by 35m was excavated to a depth of 0.5m before construction of a proposed carpark and extension to the existing Drogheda Town Centre.

The site was covered in a brown, post-medieval layer that lay directly below the concrete and hardcore to the rear of Farney Villa. Within this layer a number of post-medieval bonded stone walls were exposed to the north and east of the site. These represented the foundation walls for 19th-century storerooms that were originally part of the whiskey distillery of Preston Bros and are clearly marked on the 1870 OS map of Drogheda. One of these storerooms was constructed above two post-medieval well shafts. These had been deliberately covered with large slate slabs and sealed beneath the brick and mortar floor of the storeroom. An extensive brick drain network was also exposed within this layer, which radiated throughout the site and was also 19th-century in date.

A second post-medieval brown loam was exposed below this layer and was also spread throughout the site. Two slate-roofed culverts were exposed within this layer running north–south; these were also post-medieval in date. Four additional areas measuring c. 7m by 5m were excavated to a depth of 1.4m in the areas to be disturbed by the insertion of ground-beams. A dauby clay of medieval date was exposed in three of these trenches at an average depth of 1.4m, below the post-medieval brown loam. A possible medieval culvert and clay-bonded wall were exposed in the north-east corner of the site, in association with a medieval, brown, gravelly clay that may represent a floor. A small test-hole measuring 0.5m by 0.5m was excavated to a depth of c. 0.7m in this area, to determine the depth of natural deposits. A dark grey, organic layer was exposed below the gravelly clay, which in turn lay above a medieval, organic, peaty layer.

The excavation revealed that extensive post-medieval deposits and walls survive at an average depth of 0.5m over much of the site and are clearly associated with the whiskey distillery that stood here. In addition, significant medieval deposits survive at an average depth of 1.5m. The proposed foundation layout has been revised in order that the archaeological material not be affected.
*Donald Murphy, Archaeological Consultancy Services Ltd, 15 Trinity Street, Drogheda, Co. Louth.*

### 568. STAR AND CRESCENT CENTRE, FAIRGREEN, DROGHEDA
Urban
309327 275944
SMR 24:41
99E0475

Monitoring of the construction of a small extension and new entranceway at the Star and Crescent Centre, Fairgreen, Drogheda, was conducted in August 1999 to fulfil a requirement of the planning permission. Six narrow trenches were excavated by machine along the lines of the proposed foundations to an average depth of 1.4m. In all of the trenches the natural sand was exposed at an average depth of 0.8m below a spread of modern, brown clay. A number of stone and brick walls uncovered to the south-west of the site were also post-medieval in date.

It was clear that no archaeological stratigraphy existed on the site and that the brown clay exposed consisted of a modern, redeposited clay above the natural sand. The variety of finds from the site, ranging in date from the late medieval to the late 20th century, confirm that the area was heavily disturbed in the recent past, possibly during the construction of the current Star and Crescent Centre.

*Donald Murphy, Archaeological Consultancy Services Ltd, 15 Trinity Street, Drogheda, Co. Louth.*

### 569. GREEN LANES, DROGHEDA
No archaeological significance
30884 27543
99E0654

The proposed development site is on the north side of Green Lanes, towards its eastern end, in the parish of St Peter's in Moneymore townland. The street, which runs from Bolton Street (west) to Magdalene Street (east), was previously known as Irish Street and consisted of two alleys or rows of weavers' houses, demolished by the local corporation in 1970. The rows, said to have been erected by Alderman Chester in around 1774, were known as Chester's Buildings and consisted of a series of white-washed houses, each with an extra room to accommodate a loom and with thick walls to withstand the vibration when it was in operation. During the earlier 17th century the Dominican friary and St Peter's Church, both of which figure on Newcomen's map of 1657, had dominated this part of the town.

The site, formerly a gas shop and storage area, is 200m north-west of a recent archaeological assessment at 41 Magdalene Street (see No. 577 below). The site of a possible pottery kiln was uncovered through the recent discovery of vast quantities of 13th-century pottery from a site towards the western end of Green Lanes by Donald Murphy.

Assessment across the area of proposed development was carried out on 27 October 1999. Three trenches were excavated using a mini-digger with a 2ft bucket.

Trench 1 was along the northern end of the site, measuring 4m by 0.8m (west–east) and excavated to a maximum depth of 0.9m. Removal of rubble overburden mixed with brown soil to an average depth of 0.4m revealed a fairly mixed deposit comprising patches of orange clay, black humic soil (containing fragments of shell), broken stone and red brick, between 0.4m and 0.5m deep. Orange clay subsoil containing numerous angular and rounded stones lay at a depth of 0.8m below present ground level. The remains of a low north–south-aligned rubble foundation wall, containing red brick fragments, were revealed lying above the clay subsoil 2.2m into the site from the eastern perimeter wall. The wall survived to 0.8m wide and no more than 0.35m high, lying 0.4m below ground level, and was overlain by rubble overburden. It would appear to represent the remains of a partition wall.

Trench 2 was c. 5m south of Trench 1 towards the northern end of the site, measuring 4m by 0.8m (west–east) and excavated to a maximum depth of 0.8m. Removal of rubble overburden mixed with brown soil to an average depth of 0.55m revealed a fairly mixed deposit of redeposited orange subsoil, black humic soil (containing shell fragments), broken stone and brick, at most 0.3m deep. Orange clay subsoil containing numerous angular and rounded stones lay at a depth of between 0.7m and 0.8m below present ground level. Remains of a low, north–south-aligned deposit of stone rubble, mainly comprising large, rounded limestone boulders, was revealed lying above the clay subsoil at a location 2.5m into the site from the eastern perimeter wall. This comprised a rough structure, 1m wide and up to 0.4m high, which lay 0.17m below present ground level and was overlain by rubble. The structure appears to be a continuation of the rubble partition wall foundation uncovered in Trench 1.

Trench 3 was towards the southern end of the site, measuring 3.5m by 0.8m (west–east) and excavated to a maximum depth of 0.9m. Removal of a thin rubble overburden mixed with brown soil to an average depth of 0.25m revealed a fairly homogeneous deposit of light brown clay loam containing occasional fragments of red brick and broken stone, up to 0.6m deep. Orange clay subsoil containing numerous angular and rounded stones lay at the base of the trench, 0.85m below present ground level.

No archaeological features or finds were uncovered during the assessment.

*Malachy Conway, Archaeological Consultancy Services Ltd, 15 Trinity Street, Drogheda, Co. Louth.*

### 570. HORSE LANE, DROGHEDA
Just outside medieval town
30832 27535
99M0097

Monitoring of the digging of foundations for a house and garage was conducted on this site, which is outside the medieval walls of Drogheda to the south side of Trinity Street. Excavation of the trenches revealed a mix of garden soil and modern fill. Foundations did not exceed 0.6m deep, and the only finds recovered were 18th/20th-century pottery together with some sherds of brown-glazed earthenware and some animal bone. No archaeological stratigraphy was uncovered during the excavation of the foundations.

*Deirdre Murphy, Archaeological Consultancy Services Ltd, 15 Trinity Street, Drogheda, Co. Louth.*

### 571. JOHN STREET, DROGHEDA
Urban post-medieval tannery
**98E0250 ext.**

This report describes the results of a fourth phase of test excavation at the proposed development site on John Street that is part of the Drogheda Town Centre Bridge Development. The site is adjacent to the McDonalds restaurant on the southern side of the River Boyne. This phase of excavation was carried out between 6 and 9 September 1999 under an extension to an existing licence issued to Edmond O'Donovan for assessment at the site (*Excavations 1998*, 143). The purpose of the additional test excavation was to find the position and, in particular, the level of the old town wall and its external ditch. It also sought, without damaging them, well-preserved masonry elements of the 19th-century tannery on the site, to more fully address the context and date of other possible masonry features uncovered in earlier assessments (O'Donovan, Phases I–III).

Previous attempts to test the site were significantly hampered by the amount of rubble on site, and without open-area ground reduction an interpretation of possible features was not feasible in slit-trenches. An extremely cautious approach to the presentation of level information was taken as a result, and some levels quoted for possible features in Phases I, II and III had actually been taken from heavy, bonded rubble in the test-trenches.

The Phase IV assessment was designed to record in as comprehensive a manner as possible the archaeological potential of the site, focusing on the level to which structures survived in order to finalise the structural engineering design and impact assessment.

The assessment required the ground reduction of an area measuring *c.* 400m$^2$ to the base of a rubble infill across the site. The large site possesses the substantial subsurface remains of the old tannery. Before assessment, the site had a slightly raised surface that has been grassed over. A deep deposit of rubble fill derived from the demolition and clearance of the tannery buildings and dumping connected with the John Street Road Improvement Scheme and the main drainage schemes covered the entire site.

During Phase I testing, masonry walls were revealed in two of the trenches (11 and 12). The wall from Trench 11, at the north-east corner of the site, was 4m long and 1.5m wide and was found at 4m OD. In Trench 12 the top of a 1.12m-wide wall was found 1.27m below ground level (3.25m OD). This wall comprised limestone bonded with mortar and was found along the line of the town wall. The Phase II archaeological assessment saw further trenches excavated across the site (Trenches 15–17). Masonry walls were revealed in two of the trenches (16 and 17), along with the remains of a possible stone platform (Trench 15). The wall from Trench 16 lay at 2.1m below ground level; however, it was not possible to determine its orientation or indeed its full dimensions. In Trench 17 the uppermost deposit was clay loosely mixed with red brick and large, angular limestone blocks, 1.4m deep, which overlay a masonry structure (likely to be a wall). This wall appeared to be 1.2m wide and was oriented roughly north–south. It was built from large limestone blocks and was bonded with a sandy, crumbly mortar; red brick was present, bonded onto the upper surface of the structure. Trench 15, at the north-east corner of the site, 8.2m long and 2.4m wide, revealed what was initially thought to be a substantial curved masonry wall and surviving element of a medieval mural tower. The feature comprised a substantial, level, 8.2m-wide masonry platform lying at between 3.53m and 3.73m OD. The platform had a rough masonry surface built from tightly packed angular limestone blocks and was covered by deposits of loose, modern demolition rubble and dump made up of clay loosely mixed with limestone blocks. These deposits were between 0.9m and 0.7m deep.

The projected line of the town wall and ditch bisects the proposed development site. The town wall remained intact up to 1837, shortly after which a large tannery was developed on the site; however, the line of the wall remains evident within the tannery and can be identified on the 1862 OS map. The tannery and any remaining upstanding fragments of the town wall were demolished with the construction of the new Drogheda inner-relief dual carriageway along John Street.

The substantial wall uncovered in Trench 12 and the masonry identified in Trench 11 were interpreted as possible constituents of a circular feature and therefore as possible elements of the medieval defences of the town. Clays and pits thought to be of medieval date were also identified at the eastern end of Trench 12. No clear sign of a ditch or moat was revealed to the west of the projected line of the town wall, a portion of which was uncovered during the excavations carried out before work on the Drogheda Main Drainage Scheme by ACS Ltd. Phases I–III testing was unsuccessful in establishing whether the structures exposed belonged to the tannery or were earlier in date.

*Phase IV*

An area measuring a maximum of 102m (west–east) by 38m was reduced in level. The supervised mechanical removal of the site's rubble overburden revealed the base level of disturbance, invariably exposing the truncated and foundation remains of the 19th-century tannery. The assessment was directed not to disturb the intact remains of the tannery, and no masonry structures were to be dismantled.

The site was covered by heavy, compacted rubble, representing the collapsed remains of the old tannery, accompanied by dumps of rubble derived from demolition that occurred as part of the John Street Road Improvement Scheme. This overburden varied from 1.5m to 2.4m deep, with a notable concentration of large masonry debris through the central portion of the test area, corresponding with the possible stone platform revealed in Phase II, Trench 15. As a result, no remains of a mural tower were found, and on removal of the rubble, which most certainly had been interpreted as the possible remains of a tower base, the truncated remains of the tannery were found.

Two buildings belonging to the old tannery (Structures 1 and 2) were revealed west and east of the projected line of the town wall. A wall (Structure 4) was found running along the projected line of the town wall, flanked on the west by a covered stone drain (Structure 3) and to the east by a masonry structure (Structure 2) from the tannery. At the north end of this combined structure, extending into the northern section on the western side, lay a series of limestone steps (Structure 5). Lying immediately west of the covered drain, Structure 5 appears to correspond to a section of masonry revealed in Phase II, Trench 17.

*Structure 1*
A series of conjoined and interrupted walls of a two-roomed tannery structure was revealed along the northern part of the site, west of the projected line of the town wall. The structure was oriented west-south-west/east-north-east and was 32m long (west–east) and 10m wide, with 0.5–0.9m-thick walls, the top of which lay between 2.23m and 2.29m OD. The remains of a path consisting of flat slabs were found adjacent to the western gable end. There was at least one doorway in the north wall. The walls were constructed of rough limestone blocks in double-wall form with a limited rubble core, bonded with a gritty lime mortar and occasionally augmented or repaired with red brick. The interior of the structure was characterised by a 'floor' or spread of tannery waste, including cinder, charcoal and slag, as well as crushed stone and brick, not over 0.1m thick. The internal floor levels were recorded at 2.09m OD on the west, rising to 2.51m and 2.2m OD on the east. This building is immediately west of Structures 5 and 4, flanked by a stone-/brick-lined drain (Structure 3) that lies directly along the projected line of the town wall. The lack of correspondence to any of the structures depicted on the 1862 25-inch OS map confirms that the building represents a later tannery construction.

*Structure 2*
A series of three conjoined walls with a further interrupted stretch represents a building 14m long by 9m wide. Its alignment, similarity of construction to Structure 1 and associated context define this building as part of the tannery, even though, as with Structure 1, it does not correspond to any of the structures depicted on the 1862 25-inch OS map. Clearly the mapped layout of the tannery changed or, more accurately, was developed over time. The walls of Structure 2 were between 0.5m and 0.9m wide and at least 1.1m high (top between 2.46m and 2.05m OD; base exposed at 1.78m OD). They were constructed of rough limestone blocks in double-wall form with a limited rubble core, bonded with a gritty lime mortar occasionally augmented or repaired with red brick. The interior faces of the conjoined walls were lime-washed, with the 'plaster' surviving up to a thickness of 0.05m. Partial removal of the 'fill' of the structure revealed limestone and brick rubble on the western side and large, compacted, water-rolled stones and boulders on the east. The interior of the structure was quickly inundated with water from the River Boyne during excavation.

*Structure 3*
Structure 3 comprised the remains of a stone- and brick-lined drain running parallel to a wall (Structure 4) and overlying Structure 5. The drain, which lay directly along the projected line of the town wall, was exposed for a length of 30m, extending beyond the excavated area to the north and south. It was 0.5m wide and up to 0.18m deep. It was built of irregularly shaped limestone and half-bat red brick, portions of which were mortared, and it had a possible cobbled floor. The top of the drain lay at 2.66m OD at highest and 2.29m OD at lowest. The drain lintels were a mixture of flat limestone slabs, slate and large iron plates and bars. The interior of the drain was partially filled with rubble and tannery waste, including fragments of glass, leather, wood and patterned ceramics.

*Structure 4*
Structure 4 was a limestone masonry wall lying directly along the projected line of the old town wall, flanked on the west by a covered stone-lined drain and by the western corner and wall of the tannery building. In stratigraphic terms Structure 4 pre-dates both adjoining structures, although the dimensions, build and form of the wall strongly suggest that while it lies along the projected line of the town wall it is not a medieval wall. It is nevertheless quite reasonable to assume that both Structures 3 and 4 may encapsulate part of the foundation of the original town wall or, at the very least, were built on its foundation. That the town wall was demolished before the construction of the tannery is not in question; what is questionable is the degree of removal of this structure before the construction of the tannery. The 1862 OS map of the site clearly shows a major north–south wall running through the tannery along the line of the old town wall. A 0.9–2m-wide section of the wall was exposed for a distance of 36m (north–south). The top of the wall was higher to the south, 2.68m OD, and lower to the north, 2.52m OD. Four modern steel uprights, equidistantly spaced at 3.07m, were found driven into the wall. These fixtures are of the type used in modern steel railings and would suggest that, at a late stage in the use of the tannery, the wall, which likely functioned as a boundary, was partially demolished and replaced with metal fencing.

*Structure 5*
Structure 5 is at the northern end of the excavated area, over the projected line of the old town wall. The constituent masonry remains, though partially disturbed, comprise a series of steps at the southern end. They lie below the drain identified as Structure 3, but their relationship with the adjoining wall, Structure 4, was not fully established, as this would have required the partial dismantling of Structures 3 and 5. On plan, however, it would appear that the drain forms the top step of Structure 5, and, while there are no corresponding steps to traverse the adjoining wall (Structure 4), it would appear that Structure 5 extends beyond the section to the river wall, linked with the drain (Structure 3). In the Phase II assessment, Trench 17, the excavator revealed the remains of a wall up to 1.2m wide, oriented roughly north–south and built of mortared limestone blocks augmented with red brick at a depth of 1.4m below ground level (3.9m OD). Phase IV assessment has now established that this feature

represents the continuation of combined Structures 3–5, and possibly Structure 1. The top of Structure 5 corresponds with the top of the drain, being 2.33m OD at highest and 2.29m OD at lowest, and would appear to lead to a series of quayside steps depicted on the 1862 OS map.

*Tannery pits*
On clearance of the rubble overburden from the site, spreads or deposits of cinder, charcoal and slag measuring on average 10m by 6m were revealed. The deposit varied between 0.05m and 0.12m thick and was also found as floor material within Structure 1. It was found mainly in regular, rectangular spreads to the south of Structure 1, between 2.33m and 2.21m OD, and also to the east of Structures 2, 3 and 4. In the latter area, in particular, regular spreads of this waste material between 2.35m and 2.31m OD suggested the surviving remains of tanning pits/areas, the former containment of which was either by wooden frame, as found in the north-east corner of the excavated area, or stone wall. The position of these tannery pits corresponds with those depicted on the 1862 OS map. Once found, excavation below these structures was avoided, except at one location, where a test-pit was excavated to establish whether the town ditch lay parallel to the projected line of the wall.

*Revetment*
A test-trench *c.* 9m by 9m was excavated through the level of the tannery pits/waste spreads to establish whether the town ditch survived in this area. The ditch was not found. However, below an orange clay layer 0.8m deep (essentially the foundation for the tanning pits) lay remains of a wooden, east–west-aligned revetment. The exposed remains comprised a large upright wooden post 0.7m in diameter (1.63m OD) with an upright split wooden plank held or braced by a narrow wooden post set at 45 degrees to the plank. At the western side of the test-trench a split wooden plank, lying horizontally, was found at 1.7m OD. To the north of the line of the revetment was a deposit of grey/blue, compact, estuarine clay, and to the south of the revetment lay wetter, blue clay, also estuary-derived. Nineteenth-century pottery was found within the estuarine clay immediately north of the revetment.

*Deposit stratigraphy*
In general, immediately below the thin layer of sod that covered the site lay a mixed, rubble-filled deposit comprising loose, brown clay and sand with copious amounts of brick, stone and concrete rubble, as well as quite a number of very large limestone boulders. In most cases the rubble deposit overlay the demolished remains of structures or the truncated remains of tannery pits. Therefore the top of these structures invariably reflects the basal level of the rubble horizon across the site. It should be pointed out that several of the possible structures identified within the test-trench programmes of Phases I–III were misinterpreted as structural remains, owing to the size of the trenches opened, when in fact they represented collapsed and dumped sections of brick or limestone walling. The invariably restrictive nature of the process of narrow test-trenching can, for this site at least, be shown to be insufficient in determining the nature, context, relationship and even the verification of structures.

*Summary*
No medieval masonry structures were revealed within the excavation area. Of the five building structures recorded, two were tannery buildings, one was a covered drain with associated 'walkway and steps', and one was a north–south wall that, though on the projected line of the old town wall, was in fact an internal division wall within the tannery complex. It seems likely, given the location of Structures 2 and 4, that some remnants of the town wall survived on the site before the construction of the tannery. If this were the case, it is possible that the medieval town wall was used to provide a foundation for later tannery walls.

At the same level as the tannery walls and pits, lay regular spreads of cinder mixed with charcoal, slag and crushed brick (between 2m and 2.35m OD). In the north-east corner of the excavation area, in particular, these spreads, which were largely of cinder, were contained within wood-lined tanning pits. Elsewhere this material, occasionally augmented with fine sand or yellow clay, could be clearly seen cutting into a layer of orange clay. This was most notable to the west of Structures 3 and 4, where the orange clay, up to 0.8m thick in places, was also cut by the foundation of Structure 1. Occasional spreads of light brown/orange, mottled clay were found at the interface between the tannery horizon and the underlying clay 'cap' (2.23m OD). Finds from this particular deposit contained mainly post-18th-century debris; however, a least two sherds of medieval character were recovered. It is possible that this material was redeposited and therefore contaminated with later material; it remains unclear from where it derives. Below the orange clay, on the western side of the excavation, lay several deposits of estuarine clays or silts (2.42m OD) further characterised by the discovery of part of a timber revetment. Material recovered from beneath the orange clay, within the estuarine silt, was post-18th-century in date.

The excavation strategy required that the levels below the rubble be left intact, so, apart from the single test-pit on the western side of the excavation, no further intrusive work was carried out. Medieval deposits, possibly reclamation material, certainly survive at a lower level but will not be affected owing to the proposed construction rafting over the surviving tannery remains.

*Malachy Conway for Margaret Gowen & Co. Ltd, 2 Killiney View, Albert Road Lower, Glenageary, Co. Dublin.*

### 572. 40 JOHN STREET, DROGHEDA
Urban medieval
**99E0019**

Two stages of archaeological assessment were undertaken at 40 John Street, Drogheda, Co. Louth. In Lagavooreen parish on the north side of John Street, the site was formerly a workshop and garage. The street is first described in 1230 as the 'Royal Way', becoming 'St John's Street' by 1317. The first reference to properties along the street is made in

1363, and by 1574 the first depictions of buildings, including warehouses along John Street quayside, is made by Goche. Archaeological deposits have been recorded from along the street from 1976, including sections of the town wall. Fourteenth-century material was recovered at a depth of 1.8–2.3m below the present street level by Georgina Scally at 48 John Street (*Excavations 1996*, 76, 96E0339), and successive investigations at a site adjacent to the McDonalds restaurant revealed archaeological remains at 3.25m OD (E. O'Donovan in *Excavations 1998*, 143, 98E0250, and No. 571 above)

Five trenches were excavated, three in Stage I and two in Stage II after on-site structures had been cleared. Trench 1 was excavated through an overgrown yard in the south-west corner of the site, and Trenches 2 and 3 were excavated within the standing garage building along the north side of the site.

Trench 1, aligned north–south, revealed rubble overburden, including red brick and roof slate, to a depth of 1m lying over compact, buff clay containing red brick and cinder fragments and a sherd of brownware pottery (late 18th century), 0.2m deep. Earlier stratified deposits were light brown clay 0.1m deep, black clay containing fragments of slate, bone and shell 0.2m deep, brown clay containing oyster shells and cinder 0.2m deep, over a buff, waterlogged clay and gravel mix containing fragments of shell at a maximum depth of 1.7m. Two red brick walls (F1–F2) and a modern drain were revealed in the upper horizon. A single sherd of glazed medieval pottery was recovered from the light brown clay deposit (depth 1.15m).

Trench 2 (west–east) was excavated within the north-west area of the garage building. Here, below a floor of reinforced concrete and hardcore fill, 0.4m deep, lay gravelly, brown clay mixed with large and small, angular and water-worn stones, containing fragments of red brick, modern pottery and butchered animal bone up to 0.55m deep. Gravelly clay soil similar to the overlying deposit but with less of a rubble component extended a further 0.85m deep, overlying sterile, gravelly clay.

Trench 3 (west–east) was positioned 6.5m east of Trench 2 and 3.6m south of the northern perimeter of the site. Removal of a double concrete floor interspaced with hardcore and rubble 0.4m deep revealed a deposit of red brick rubble 0.22m deep. Underlying deposits were gravelly, brown clay mixed with large and small, angular and water-worn stones, containing red brick fragments 0.7m deep. The basal level reached was gravelly clay containing occasional fragments of shell at a depth of 1.30m to 1.65m+.

Trench 4 (12m north–south by 1.3m) was excavated from the south perimeter of the site to the quay wall. The trench was excavated to the base of the rubble overburden Deposit 1. Two test-pits were excavated below the rubble backfill, providing stratigraphic profiles. The findings in Pit 1 were: Deposit 1, consisting of a rubble backfill including red brick and slate 1.8m deep (top 3.29m OD), overlying Deposit 2, a black, organic layer containing fragments of red brick and patterned ceramics (19th/20th century) 0.3m deep. Below this was Deposit 3, yellow clay containing numerous small stones 0.4m deep, overlying Deposit 4, a black, organic layer containing oyster shell, wood fragments, occasional fragments of butchered animal bone and small stones 0.4m deep (top 2.04m OD). Basal Deposit 5, grey marl, was encountered at a depth of 2.8–3.3m+ below surface (extends below 0.52m OD). A red brick foundation wall F4 was found 6m from the southern end of the test-trench. Though badly preserved and crumbling, it survived to 0.4m high and 0.9m wide; it was aligned west–east 1m below surface level, cut into the top of Deposit 2.

In Pit 2 were: Deposit 1, rubble backfill 0.9m deep (top at 2.83m OD) over Deposit 3, yellow clay containing numerous small stones 0.3m deep. Deposit 4, a black, organic layer containing oyster shell, wood fragments and occasional fragments of butchered animal bone 2m deep, overlay Deposit 5, grey marl clay at a depth of 3.2m below ground level. A limestone rubble wall F5 was found between 9.65m and 10m from the southern end of the trench. The wall, aligned west–east, survived to 0.3m high and 0.35m wide, constructed of roughly cut and irregular-shaped limestone blocks bonded with a lime-based mortar. The wall lay below Deposit 1 at 1.93m OD, cut directly into Deposit 4 (top at 1.71m OD to the north of F5).

Trench 5 (7.5m west–east by 0.8m) was excavated 2.7m east of Trench 4 along the projected line of F5. The north-facing line of F5 was traced extending west below rubble Deposit 1, was at 2.35m OD and was exposed for a distance of 4.3m, at which point the wall returns north (top at 1.96m OD) towards the quay wall. The wall was 0.4m high and 0.7m wide. Two test-pits (3 and 4) were excavated through the black, organic Deposit 4, one on each side of the northern return of the wall, to establish the depth of the deposit and to confirm a date. Within Test-pit 3, Deposit 4 was found to extend from a depth of 1m to a maximum depth of 3.1m, where grey, gravelly clay was encountered. The deposit contained oyster shell, wood, leather and bone fragments including a plain bone stick-pin. Two medieval glazed sherds of Saintonge ware were also recovered. In Test-pit 4 the black, organic Deposit 4 was found to lie between 1.5m and 2.9m below ground level. Oyster shell, wood (including a bucket or tub stave) and butchered bone fragments were recovered, along with a glazed strap handle from a medieval jug, possibly of 14th- or 15th-century date. Significantly, a large worked timber was also found within this deposit (top at 1.01m OD). This object was found set almost vertically within Deposit 4. The timber is 1.66m long, roughly squared in section, *c.* 0.2m x 0.16m, tapering to a rounded but pointed end with a crescent-shaped mortice hole 0.1m wide by 0.09m deep, which is cut into the side of the timber close to the pointed end.

A significant deposit of archaeological potential, Deposit 4, containing material of 13th-, 14th- and possibly 15th-century date was revealed. Deposit 2, of a similar type to Deposit 4 but contaminated with debris of late 19th- or early 20th-century date, probably represents redeposition of Deposit 4 material during construction of red brick walls that were revealed in Trenches 1 and 4. The rubble limestone foundation walls (F5–F7) post-date

Deposit 4 (14th/15th-century date), and on the basis of construction and type of mortar used, it is suggested that these walls are most likely 16th- or early 17th-century in date. A late 16th-century depiction of the town by Goche (1574) clearly shows stone-built houses or warehouses along the north side of John Street.

The organic Deposit 4, containing material of 13th/15th-century date, appears to represent a reclamation deposit, necessitated by periodic rises in the Boyne river level and paralleled at other sites along the north and south bank of the river, where reclamation deposits have been shown to reflect episodes of dumping or ground-heightening dating from the 13th through to the 17th century. The discovery of a large vertical-set wooden post may represent part of a former revetment at the site.

The top of the reclamation deposit (4) was found to lie at 2.04m OD towards the street frontage, rising to 3.76m OD towards the back (north end) of the site, while to the east the deposit lay between 1.29m and 1.01m OD. The base of the deposit lay at around 0.52m OD. This suggests that the deposit is deepest along the western half of the site and that it has been partially truncated by the 19th/20th-century developments along the southern side of the site at the street frontage.

*Malachy Conway for Margaret Gowen & Co. Ltd, 2 Killiney View, Albert Road Lower, Glenageary, Co. Dublin.*

### 573. JOHN'S BRIDGE, JOHN'S STREET, DROGHEDA
Medieval town wall and 19th-century tannery
O009075
99E0744

An extensive archaeological assessment had already being conducted on the site to determine the level at which structural remains survived (see No. 571 above). Thus, all structural remains were preserved *in situ*.

Ground reduction was taken to a level at which the top of some of the surviving tannery walls were flush with the reduced ground level. None of the walls was exposed, and no archaeological finds were revealed.

*Avril Purcell, Margaret Gowen & Co. Ltd, 2 Killiney View, Albert Road Lower, Glenageary, Co. Dublin.*

### 574. FORMER DROGHEDA GRAMMAR SCHOOL, LAURENCE'S STREET, DROGHEDA
Urban medieval
309065 275294
98E0544

An excavation took place at the site of the former Drogheda Grammar Gchool, (St) Laurence's Street, Drogheda, before the construction of a retail and commercial development. The site of the proposed development fronts onto William Street to the north and (St) Laurence's Street to the south, both of which are medieval in date, and it incorporates part of Freeschool Lane, also a medieval street. Buildings dating from the 18th–20th centuries have destroyed archaeological deposits in various parts of the site. The southern boundary of the site is dominated by two Georgian buildings, Dr Clarke's Freeschool and Singleton House, both constructed between the 1730s and 1740s. As both buildings have basements, they have obliterated archaeological deposits in the southern part of the site. In the late 19th century an extension to the east of Singleton House, to accommodate a dining hall for the former Drogheda Grammar School, also involved an element of destruction to archaeological deposits. However, as this building did not have a basement, some archaeological deposits survived.

The middle section of the site directly north of these buildings, where the former gardens of Drogheda Grammar School and Singleton House were laid out, had remained undisturbed, and in this area of the site deposits ranging in date from the 13th to the 20th century were evident. In the northern third of the site, along the east of Freeschool Lane, foundations of an 18th-century building formerly known as the Balfour Hall were evident. Directly north of this area and bordering Freeschool Lane and William Street a series of stone buildings and basements dating to the late 18th and early 19th century have, for the most part, destroyed archaeological deposits in this part of the site. The north-eastern corner of the site had been greatly disturbed by the construction of a swimming pool during the 1940s.

The excavation was divided into four separate areas, three of which were excavated in sequence, and the fourth area, which borders Palace Street to the east, remains to be excavated. Area 1 comprised the main part of the site east of Freeschool Lane and included the former Grammar School buildings. Following site clearance to the north of Singleton House, the remains of three terraced buildings were evident. These buildings most likely represent the backs of houses that fronted Laurence's Street and may be those represented on a drawing of the town of 1718 by the artist Van der Hagen. Of these buildings, only one had a basement, and finds recovered from the floors of these structures would suggest that they were 17th-century in date. They were subsequently destroyed by the construction of Singleton House. To the east of these houses and Singleton House the external western wall of the archbishop's palace was exposed. This residence was built by Primate Christopher Hampton in 1613, and part of the bricked floor of this building survived in the south-eastern corner of the site. However, most of this structure was destroyed by the construction of the dining hall extension in the late 19th century. The floor of the 17th-century palace sealed medieval surfaces of 13th- and 14th-century date, which were probably floors of earlier houses along Laurence's Street. The western wall of the palace also reused an earlier medieval wall as its foundation. A post-pit, rubbish pits and a hearth were also exposed in this area of the site.

Extensive layers of garden soil dating from the 13th to the 18th century were exposed north of the buildings. These layers, which collectively measured over 1.3m, contained large amounts of animal bone and numerous sherds of pottery. The uppermost layer, which is probably of early 18th-century date, contained large amounts of dumped material and may relate to the Grammar School phase of this site. Along the eastern side of Freeschool Lane and set in this garden soil, a series of flower-bed features was evident. These were laid out in a 'Celtic cross' pattern and were bordered by leg bones of sheep placed upright in the ground. They are partially covered by a mortar layer that may have formed part of a pathway. The garden soil also sealed a series of exceptionally large rubbish pits, which contained a large quantity of Staffordshire and Sgraffito slipware and black-glazed earthenware pottery (almost 2000 sherds). Garden soils of late 14th-century date sealed earlier features on this site: medieval cellars, two medieval houses, a limekiln, two medieval corn-drying kilns, a series of medieval rubbish pits and an early cobbled pathway.

The two houses were revealed at the western area of the site, close to Freeschool Lane. The first fronted onto Freeschool Lane, and the east wall of the laneway was constructed above its western foundation. This building was 15.7m long and 4.6m wide. The east and west walls were present, but the north wall was partially destroyed by the construction of the Balfour Hall, and the south wall was destroyed by the construction of a post-medieval limekiln. The eastern wall was 15.7m long and 0.8m wide, and the western wall was 16.8m long and 0.8m wide. Both walls were clay-bonded, and a doorway was evident in the western wall. Successive phases of cobbled and mortar floors were evident inside the house. A rusty iron key was recovered from the western wall, near the area of the doorway.

To the south-east of this a second house was exposed, 8.4m long and 6.8m wide. It had a mortar floor, and a hearth was evident in the north-eastern corner of the room. The northern section of this house was destroyed by a large medieval pit. The house was positioned along the western side of a north–south cobbled pathway that directly overlay the natural boulder clay. This pathway was exposed at a depth of 16.419m OD and was 18m long (north–south) and 1.9m wide. A cellar revealed along Freeschool Lane and constructed of substantial stone walls with a battering at the base may be associated with the famed Frumbole's Inn. It was 4.2m long (east–west), 2.5m wide and 2.9m deep (12.764m OD). Putlog holes were evident in the south face of the northern wall, where a probable stairwell or wooden floor existed.

A second cellar or basement was evident in the north-eastern corner of the Balfour Hall. This structure was medieval in date, measuring 4.2m by 2.5m, and was backfilled before the construction of the Balfour Hall. A corn-drying kiln was exposed in the western part of the site, and a more substantial one was evident in the eastern part. The former measured 3.9m by 2.2m, and the latter measured 3.4m by 1.6m. Burnt animal bone and teeth were recovered from the interior of the structure, which was stone-lined at its eastern end.

North of this kiln a cruciform drystone limekiln of probable 14th-century date was exposed. This structure was quite substantial and consisted of a large circular bowl area with a diameter of 3.4m and four stone-lined flues at the north, south, east and west.

The area to the west of Freeschool Lane was almost devoid of archaeological stratigraphy. A post-medieval cobbled surface measuring 3.1m by 3.5m, together with a stone drain and associated stone well with a diameter of 1m, was exposed over post-medieval garden soil. This layer extended over the

Medieval cellar to the east of Freeschool Lane, Drogheda (Frumbole's Inn).

Four-flued late medieval limekiln, Laurence's Street, Drogheda, after excavation.

largest part of the site and was cut by the foundations of a 19th-century building. The layers sealed a series of late medieval rubbish pits that was excavated into the natural boulder clay. Freeschool Lane, which was 3.4m wide, was destroyed by the construction of an 18th-century culvert that extended in a north–south direction down the centre of the medieval laneway. Further excavation is required in the eastern part of the site in the area that fronts onto Palace Street.

*Deirdre Murphy, Archaeological Consultancy Services Ltd, 15 Trinity Street, Drogheda, Co. Louth.*

### 575. 23/24 LAURENCE STREET, DROGHEDA
Urban medieval
309145 275272
**99E0173**

An assessment of a proposed commercial development at Laurence Street, Drogheda, was carried out in April 1999. The site is at the east end of Laurence Street, just inside the medieval town wall, close to the barbican of St Laurence's Gate.

Four trenches were excavated by hand inside the existing basements of two buildings. A single layer of medieval garden soil was exposed at a depth of 0.2m below the surface in the easternmost basement. As the proposed development involved only the replacement of basement floors, it was established that there would not be any impact on the archaeology.

To the east of the basement of No. 24 Laurence Street and directly below the present-day Palace Street a stone undercroft or cellar with a very shallow, barrel-vaulted roof was discovered. The walls were constructed of stone averaging 0.3m in size and were bonded with mortar that had a very high gravel content. The cellar had maximum dimensions of 4m east–west by 2.96m and an internal height of 2.7m. A window or ope was evident in the west and south walls of the structure and was most likely medieval in date. As the cellar underlies a public street and is outside the area of the development, it will not be interfered with in any way.

*Donald Murphy, Archaeological Consultancy Services Ltd, 15 Trinity Street, Drogheda, Co. Louth.*

### 576. LOUGHBOY, DROGHEDA
Medieval monastic
**98E0285**

Testing was carried out in June 1998 to determine the extent of a previously identified early medieval monastic site. Earlier investigations had recorded burials and souterrains associated with an enclosure close to a holy well associated with St Buite. The extent of the archaeological complex was unclear because there was a possibility of an outer enclosure and because there may have been activity outside of the enclosed area.

The site is on a slope running down to the River Boyne. The steep gradient had two effects on the site. Firstly, there may have been deliberate levelling of the site associated with its primary use. Secondly, the steep slope has caused soil creep, which may have damaged archaeological deposits.

Archaeological features relating to at least two phases of human activity were recorded in two test-trenches on either side of a zone protecting the archaeological complex. Substantial ditches interpreted as an outer enclosure were recorded in both trenches. The eastern trench had a small number of shallow features, which have been disturbed by soil creep. The western trench had a broader range of features, including possible structural remains and a substantial pit beyond the limit of the outer enclosure.

The archaeological deposits recorded in the assessment were not particularly rich, and there were no significant finds. They have, however, broadened the understanding of the history of the site. It is now clear that there was an outer enclosure at the site. It is also clear that a wide range of activities took place here in at least two phases. The draw of the river and the holy well was strong enough for people to overcome the obstacles of building on a steep slope.

A number of questions cannot be answered by the archaeological work carried out to date. The most important of these relates to the integrity of the complex. Although the date of the previously recorded souterrains and burials is not in question, there are at least two phases of activity represented in the material recorded in this assessment. The relationship between the initial features, the enclosure and the other, more ephemeral features cannot be determined at this point.

*Sarah Cross for Margaret Gowen & Co. Ltd, 2 Killiney View, Albert Road Lower, Glenageary, Co. Dublin.*

**Editor's note:** Though carried out during 1998, the report on this site was received too late for inclusion in the bulletin of that year.

### 577. 41 MAGDALENE STREET LOWER, DROGHEDA
No archaeological significance
**30890 27636**
**SMR 24:41**
**99E0543**

An assessment of a proposed residential development at 41 Magdalene Street, Drogheda, Co. Louth, was undertaken on 27 October 1999. The site is on the east side of Magdalene Street, which dates from around 1250, was the main road to the North Gate and features on most of the early maps of the town. The site, which formerly contained garages and part of a dwelling that were demolished before the assessment, is within the line of the town walls of Drogheda, within the zone of archaeological potential. It lies *c.* 40m west of St Peter's Church of Ireland church, which dates from 1748, and is on the site of St Peter's Collegiate Church (SMR 24:16), originally founded before 1186.

The three west–east-orientated test-trenches were excavated across the areas of proposed dwelling construction using a mini-digger.

Trench 1 was at the northern end of the site, measuring 4m by 0.8m and excavated to a maximum depth of 0.9m. Rubble overburden mixed with brown soil was found to an average depth of 0.4m over a mixed deposit comprising patches of orange clay, black humic soil (containing fragments of shell), broken stone and red brick between 0.4 and 0.5m deep. Orange clay subsoil containing numerous angular and rounded stones lay 0.8m below present ground level. The remains of a low, north–south-aligned rubble foundation wall containing red brick fragments were revealed lying above the clay subsoil 2.2m from the eastern perimeter wall. The wall, 0.8m wide and no more than 0.35m high, lay 0.4m below ground level and would appear to represent the remains of a partition wall associated with the previous property on the site. A further stretch of this rubble wall was also found in Trench 2.

Trench 2, measuring 4m by 0.8m, was *c.* 5m south of Trench 1, towards the northern end of the site, and was excavated to a maximum depth of 0.8m. Rubble overburden mixed with brown soil on average 0.55m deep overlay a fairly mixed deposit of redeposited orange subsoil, black humic soil (containing shell fragments), broken stone and brick at most 0.3 deep. Orange clay subsoil containing numerous angular and rounded stones lay at a depth of 0.7–0.8m below present ground level. Remains of a low, north–south-aligned deposit of stone rubble, mainly comprising large, rounded limestone boulders, were revealed lying above the clay subsoil 2.5m into the site from the eastern perimeter wall. This comprised a rough structure, 1m wide and up to 0.4m high, which lay 0.17m below present ground level and is a continuation of the partition wall foundation uncovered in Trench 1.

Trench 3, measuring 3.5m by 0.8m, was close to the southern end of the site and was excavated to a maximum depth of 0.9m. Rubble overburden mixed with brown soil on average 0.25m deep overlay a fairly homogeneous deposit of light brown clay loam containing occasional fragments of red brick and broken stone up to 0.6m deep. Orange clay subsoil containing numerous angular and rounded stones lay at the base of the trench, 0.85m below present ground level.

In summary, no archaeological features or deposits were revealed in any of the trenches, and no finds were recovered
*Malachy Conway, Archaeological Consultancy Services Ltd, 15 Trinity Street, Drogheda, Co. Louth.*

### 578. 49 MARY STREET, DROGHEDA
Urban medieval
30922 27487
99E0658

An assessment of a proposed residential development at 49 Mary Street, Drogheda, was carried out in November 1999. The site is on the west side of the street, just outside the line of the medieval town wall. Mary Street was constructed *c.* 1810, at which time the town wall was demolished and the new road was excavated into the side of the hill.

The site was cleared of houses, and immediately the boulder clay was visible over most of the site. A trench 30m long and 2m wide was excavated north–south along the centre of the proposed development site. It failed to reveal any evidence of archaeological stratigraphy, and, as boulder clay was visible elsewhere on the site, it was clear that the proposed development would not have any archaeological impact.
*Donald Murphy, Archaeological Consultancy Services Ltd, 15 Trinity Street, Drogheda, Co. Louth.*

### 579. MILLMOUNT, DROGHEDA
Motte and 19th-century Martello tower
309007 274782
SMR 24:25
98E0194

A second phase of work was undertaken at Millmount, Drogheda, during the restoration and refurbishment of the Martello tower (see *Excavations 1998*, 144, for first season's report). Monitoring was conducted in August of the mechanical removal of 0.6m of earth from the top of the mound. A dark brown, rubbly loam containing early 20th-century finds was exposed directly below the sod and is clearly associated with the destruction of the Martello tower during the Civil War. Five substantial, bonded stone walls, *c.* 0.6m wide, were exposed below this layer radiating outwards from the base of the tower and were found in association with a number of beam-slots along the lower footing of the tower. These were clearly the supporting walls for a suspended wooden floor or decking that surrounded the tower. The remains of a small square structure were exposed to the south-west of the tower, which may be the remains of a sighting/viewing platform that was used for artillery ranging. No archaeological stratigraphy or deposits were revealed that pre-dated the construction of the Martello tower.
*Donald Murphy, Archaeological Consultancy Services Ltd, 15 Trinity Street, Drogheda, Co. Louth.*

### 580. 2–3 OULSTER LANE, DROGHEDA
Medieval town suburbs
30939 27544
99E0185

An assessment of a proposed residential dwelling was carried out at 2–3 Oulster Lane, Drogheda. The site is to the east of and outside the medieval town, possibly within the suspected eastern suburbs and west of the medieval church of St Laurence The Martyr.

Two trenches were excavated but did not reveal any evidence of archaeological stratigraphy. The subsoil is very close to the surface along the western section of the site, and it would appear that ground level was made up at the eastern end through the introduction of *c.* 1m of topsoil. There will be no archaeological impact at this site.
*Donald Murphy, Archaeological Consultancy Services Ltd, 15 Trinity Street, Drogheda, Co. Louth.*

### 581. 10 PALACE STREET/FRANCIS STREET, DROGHEDA
Urban medieval/post-medieval
30917 27533
SMR 24:41
99E0637

An assessment was carried out to the rear of 10 Palace Street, Drogheda, on 10 November 1999 to fulfil a condition of the planning permission for the erection of a new townhouse on the site. The site is within the area of archaeological potential of Drogheda, *c.* 50m north of St Laurence's Gate, but outside the medieval walls of the town.

Two trenches were excavated by machine within the area of the proposed development. Trench 1 was excavated east–west, was 5.5m long and 1.4m wide and contained a number of post-medieval layers. A large, post-medieval wall, 0.95m thick, was uncovered below a variety of post-medieval garden soils. An internal cobbled surface was revealed at the east end of the trench, overlying a series of post-medieval hardcore deposits.

Trench 2 was excavated perpendicular to Trench

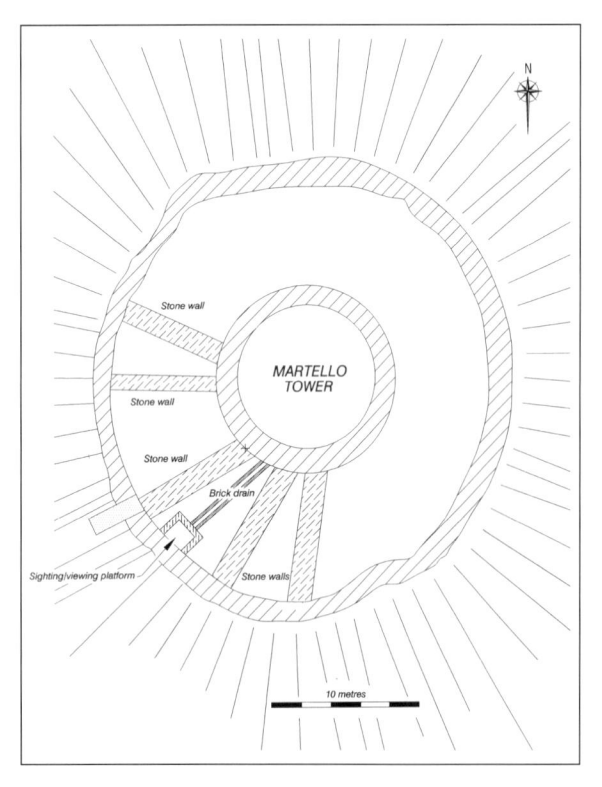

Detail of stone walls and brick drain at Millmount, Drogheda.

1, north–south, and was 3m long and 1.3m wide. A possible medieval wall and hard cobbled surface were exposed at a depth of 1.4m, below a number of later, 19th-century demolition material deposits.

A number of post-medieval finds, along with three sherds of medieval ware, were recovered from the base of Trench 2. No other significant archaeological features or deposits were found, and the development will not have any archaeological impact.

*Ian Russell, Archaeological Consultancy Services Ltd, 15 Trinity Street, Drogheda, Co. Louth.*

### 582. 11 PALACE STREET, DROGHEDA
No archaeological significance
309180 275328
99E0088

Testing was carried out at 11 Palace Street, Drogheda, before a proposed residential development. This small site, 6.5m east–west by 6.1m, is just outside the line of the medieval town wall. Three trenches were dug in the site. A concrete floor was removed in all trenches.

In Trench 1 this overlay cobbles that in turn overlay several layers of building debris up to 1.5m thick, containing red brick fragments and 17th–18th-century pottery. These overlay a hard mortar floor.

Trench 2 was in the west of the building. The concrete overlay a dark brown loam containing mortar flecks that was up to 0.2m deep. Below this was red brick rubble in brown, sticky clay up to 0.46m deep. It overlay a hard mortar floor.

The third trench was in the south of the building. The concrete floor overlay sandy clay containing red brick fragments, mortar and uncut limestone up to 0.06m thick. Below this was thick mortar and red brick up to 0.1m thick. It overlay dark brown loam containing mortar flecks up to 0.14m thick. These overlay a layer of light brown sand and gravel containing mortar flecks and roughly cut limestone up to 0.21m thick. Nineteenth-century pottery was found in this layer. This sat on the hard mortar floor.

*Matthew Seaver for Archaeological Consultancy Services Ltd, 15 Trinity Street, Drogheda, Co. Louth.*

### 583. SCARLET STREET, DROGHEDA
Urban medieval
309200 275650
98E0527 ext.

An assessment of a proposed retail development was carried out in April 1999. The site is to the north of the medieval town on the site of an old gaol that dates to 1818.

Four trenches were excavated and revealed that the site consisted of made-up ground above boulder clay. There was no archaeological stratigraphy present, and the proposed development will not have an archaeological impact.

*Donald Murphy, Archaeological Consultancy Services Ltd, 15 Trinity Street, Drogheda, Co. Louth.*

### 584. SHOP STREET/DYER STREET, DROGHEDA
Urban
308990 275080
99E0249

The site, which lay within the medieval town of Drogheda, extended from Shop Street on the east along the north street frontage of Dyer Street. The excavation was carried out to fulfil the requirements of *Dúchas* The Heritage Service before redevelopment of the site as commercial and residential units.

Pre-development testing of the site by Donald Murphy in 1996 indicated the presence of *in situ* archaeological deposits (*Excavations 1996*, 78, 96E0115). Walls of probable medieval date were identified, along with cobbled and red brick surfaces of post-medieval date. The current excavation sought to record the location and nature of all the *in situ* walls. Once the walls were exposed the pile layout was amended to ensure that they were avoided when construction recommenced. All of the archaeological remains lay beneath the proposed ground-beam level, and therefore it was only the piles that would affect the archaeology.

Excavations at Dyer Street in 1996 by Donald Murphy, during the Drogheda Main Drainage and Waste Disposal Scheme, revealed the remains of several medieval houses on the north side of the street (*Excavations 1996*, 76–7, 96E0160). One of these was very substantial and lay at the east end of the street, close to the Shop Street junction. The walls of this building stood 0.9m high, were 1.35m wide and were dated to the mid-1200s. The current excavation at Dyer Street was immediately to the north of the site of this substantial house.

The excavation revealed the remains of a substantial east–west-orientated wall that extended along the south side of the site. At its west end this wall turned south, forming a corner. The wall was on average 1.3m wide and survived to a maximum height of 1.2m. A narrow plinth was evident on both sides of the wall. The wall probably represents the back wall of the medieval house that was excavated in 1996. An internal garderobe chute was found 5.6m from the west end of the wall. The remains consisted of a vertical opening in the core of the wall (0.4m by 0.44m), which was linked to an ope in the southern face of the wall (0.34m by 0.4m) by a diagonal chute. It is likely that the chute fed one of the drains that were found inside the house during the 1996 excavation to the south. An external garderobe chute was evident on the north side of the wall 1.3m from its west end. The remains of the chute measured 0.44m by 0.2m by 0.44m deep. It is not clear whether this feature was original to the construction of the wall, as it fed into a walled, post-medieval refuse pit.

The remains of two other medieval walls were evident to the north of the house. These had been subject to modern disturbance, and their exact function and relationships are unclear, but they may have been boundary walls.

The majority of the excavated deposits were outside—to the north of—the medieval house, with most of the surviving internal deposits being outside the limit of the excavation. The deposits to the south of the wall consisted largely of redeposited boulder clays interspersed with thin bands of organic material. A number of pits were identified. Some of these were used as general refuse/cesspits, and the function of others remains unclear.

*Tim Coughlan, Margaret Gowen & Co. Ltd, 2 Killiney View, Albert Road Lower, Glenageary, Co. Dublin.*

### 585. 2–3 MILL ROW, TRINITY STREET, DROGHEDA
Urban medieval
308405 275320
99E0017

An assessment of a proposed extension to a commercial premises at 2–3 Mill Row, Trinity Street, Drogheda, was carried out in January 1999. The proposed development site is outside the West Gate of the medieval town on the south side of Trinity Street. The street consists of a group of purpose-built mill cottages associated with the nearby flax mill, which was later converted to a boot factory.

One trench measuring 7m by 1.2m was excavated. This revealed that the existing building was constructed above a layer of red brick rubble and a layer of cobbles of 18th–19th-century date. There was no evidence of archaeological stratigraphy, and hence the proposed extension would not have any archaeological impact.

*Donald Murphy, Archaeological Consultancy Services Ltd, 15 Trinity Street, Drogheda, Co. Louth.*

### 586. 9 WEST STREET, DROGHEDA
Medieval town
30890 27513
99E0515

The site of the development is at the corner of West Street and Meatmarket Lane within the medieval town of Drogheda. The development includes a two-storey extension to the rear of an existing pharmacy on West Street. Two trenches were dug: one was excavated externally by machine to the rear of the new extension; and one was hand-dug internally, in the floor area of the new extension.

Trench 1 measured 6.1m by 2m and was 1.05m deep. It was excavated 0.6m from the southern wall of the new extension. A layer of concrete extended to a depth of 0.4m, below which a black, sandy clay with rubble and red brick fragments extended to a depth of 0.6m, sealing a 0.1m-thick layer of mortar. Below the mortar a layer of dark brown, loamy garden soil flecked with red brick, charcoal and mortar was visible to a depth of 0.95m. Below this a layer of light brown to green garden soil with shell and charcoal was exposed. A single sherd of green-glazed Saintonge pottery was recovered from this layer. No other finds or features were encountered in this trench.

Trench 2 was excavated in the floor of the new extension and was 1.1m long, 1.3m wide and 1.7m deep. A concrete floor, block wall and foundation associated with the present extension extended to a depth of 1.18m, below which rubble fill extended to 1.42m. Below this a compacted layer of rubble composed of red brick and stone extended to a depth of 1.72m. No features or finds were evident in this trench.

In conclusion, medieval garden soil was revealed at a depth of 1m to the south of the extension, although the extension itself has been built on a previously disturbed area.

*Deirdre Murphy, Archaeological Consultancy Services Ltd, 15 Trinity Street, Drogheda, Co. Louth.*

### 587. 26 WEST STREET, DROGHEDA
Urban medieval
308782 275155
SMR 24:41
99E0476

Monitoring was to be carried out during the excavation of a number of strip foundation trenches for a proposed extension to the rear of 26 West Street, Drogheda. However, it was decided by the architects to construct a raised raft foundation instead. Consequently, no archaeological work was required on this site.

*Donald Murphy, Archaeological Consultancy Services Ltd, 15 Trinity Street, Drogheda, Co. Louth.*

### 588. DROMIN
Adjacent to church/graveyard
O03038944
SMR 18:14
99E0508

The site is adjacent to a church and graveyard on a small rise. Pre-development test-trenching was undertaken for a proposed house, 17m to the east of the church and graveyard site.

Five trenches were excavated by mechanical digger. Initially, trenches were excavated along the foundation plan of the house, but on the discovery of archaeological deposits on the west side of the site, testing was extended a further 8.5m to the east.

Trenching demonstrated the existence of intact features of probable medieval date. These were a hearth that was partly exposed by the trench and, in a second cutting, a layer of grey, silty loam containing animal bone and some medieval pottery overlying a stony surface that overlay subsoil. These features, and a possible cut for a ditch that abutted them and had a separate stony fill, extended into a third cutting. They occurred over an area *c.* 10m x 6m and coincided with the level ground that was also the highest part of the field. Accordingly, the location of the house was moved an additional 10m to the east of its original position.

There were no intact features on the east side of the site, and the decreasing depth of topsoil in that direction indicates that recent ploughing, which had left visible ploughmarks in the subsoil, would have severely impinged on surviving features.

*Finola O'Carroll, Cultural Resource Development Services Ltd, Campus Innovation Centre, Roebuck, University College, Belfield, Dublin 4.*

### 589. DROMISKIN
No archaeological significance
99E0076 and ext.

In connection with building work two areas were monitored; these were at either end of an existing dwelling-house and were close to SMR 12:47.

To the north side of the house an area 8m by 26m was opened. This was flat ground that had been kept as a lawn adjacent to a house. The work, which was carried out by mechanical means, initially involved the stripping of the humus over the entire area. This proved to be 0.2m in average depth. It was homogeneous humus devoid of any features. Immediately beneath were glacial gravels. No evidence for any features or finds came to light. In order to test the material further, four pits, *c.* 2m x 5m, were dug at different points to a depth of 0.6m. These confirmed that this material was natural.

To the south side of the house an area, a lawn with shrubs, was prepared for a carpark extension. This was somewhat trapezoidal in shape and measured 36m by 9–13m. The work was carried out

by mechanical means. After stripping the sod, it was clear that the area had been interfered with at the time that the house was constructed, around 1974. On top of the original surface a build-up, consisting largely of building debris, took place. This fill averaged 0.3–0.4m deep at the western end but increased to c. 0.6m over the northern portion. Trenches for sewerage and electricity were also dug across the site. The modern fill was removed to the natural surface. This was scraped, but no archaeological features or finds came to light.
*George Eogan, Knowth Project, University College, Earlsfort Terrace, Dublin 2.*

## 590. DROMISKIN
Cemetery and possible trackways
30542 29812
SMR 12:47
99E0330

The site is on the south side of the road leading eastwards from Dromiskin village, lying south of the former ecclesiastical enclosure (SMR 12:46). The curving line of the roadway probably represents the trace of an inner enclosure around the early monastic site. There is a substantial amount of marshland along and to the south of the proposed development area, which probably formed a natural boundary for the monastic site to the north. The proposed development incorporates the site of cist burials discovered in 1862 in the west corner of a field to the south-east of the monastic graveyard.

Two stages of assessment were carried out. Stage I was undertaken by Donald Murphy between 20 and 22 July 1999, consisting of thirteen test-trenches, of which four revealed archaeological potential. The grave-cuts of at least six west–east-aligned burials were revealed in Trench 3, a possible wooden trackway in Trench 4, and a wooden platform or trackway in Trench 5. Artefacts recovered included a sherd of local medieval ware from the top of a possible pit in Trench 6. The Stage II assessment was undertaken to verify the nature, context and extent of the trackway and platform features revealed in Trenches 4 and 5 respectively. This work was carried out by Malachy Conway under an extension to the licence, between 29 October and 4 November 1999.

Trench 3 was excavated to a depth of 0.3m, revealing natural, grey silt (OD 8.34m) into which had been cut at least six west–east-aligned graves. The burials appeared to have been cut into a sandy, brown loam 0.5–0.1m thick, which overlay the natural, grey, silty sand. All six grave-cuts were fairly regularly spaced, c. 1.5–1.8m apart, and were 1m wide. The presence of stones along the edges of three grave-cuts, at the northern end of the trench, indicates possible long cists. The graves are all concentrated in the area of a slight hillock in this corner of the site, and it is likely that the cemetery originally extended further west below the adjoining houses and perhaps north under the road towards the cemetery itself. The burials did not continue further to the south into the wetter, marshy ground. At the south end of the trench a very shallow ditch was exposed, which may have been the original extent of the cemetery. The only find recovered from the trench was a small body sherd of Beauvais, which came from the topsoil above the graves. The ditch at the south end of the trench was extremely shallow, just 0.15m deep, and it is possible that it represents a later plough furrow rather than an enclosing feature around the burials.

Trench 4, measuring 12.5m by 2m, was excavated north–south along the modern field boundary. The trench was excavated to a depth of 1m (OD 7.1m), at which point a series of timbers was exposed along the eastern side of the trench, lying in a north–south direction. These appeared to consist of some irregular planks up to 0.43m wide apparently laid on irregularly placed branches that sat on a peaty soil. Re-excavation in Stage II extended the trench a further 16.5m south to examine deposits and stratigraphy in this area. Measuring 29m north–south by 1.7m, Trench 4 was excavated to a depth of between 1m (7.1m OD) and 1.25m. Fragments of butchered animal bone were recovered from the interface of the brown loam that overlay the peat deposit. At this level a roughly north–south-running field ditch (0.7m wide and 0.6m deep), parallel to the existing hedge line, ran for a distance of 9m from the north end of the trench.

The possible wooden trackway feature uncovered in Stage I was found to consist of branches and wood fragments apparently dumped or washed into the upper fill of the hedge-line ditch. A series of roundwood branches (birch and possibly alder) and fragments of tree roots was found irregularly set into the water-saturated peat fill of the ditch, flanked along its western margin by a mixed deposit of grey, gravelly clay, compacted peat and limestone. No ancient dressed timbers or planks were uncovered. Fragments of butchered animal bone and a sherd of early modern pottery were recovered from the upper fill of the ditch, which also contained small twigs, leaves and possibly reeds or rushes to a depth of 0.6m. The south end of the ditch terminated at an area or deposit of waterlogged peat, and it is possible that the ditch operated as a water channel or drain into a naturally wet and marshy area along the eastern side of the field. The material is clearly naturally accumulated debris and waste within a boundary ditch. A fallen tree stump, possibly of oak and associated with several fragments of animal bone, was found across the line of the trench, 23.5m from the northern end.

Stage I, Trench 5, measuring 64m by 2m, was excavated west–east. Natural, grey, silty sand was exposed at the west end of the trench at a depth of 0.65m (OD 7.47m). The top 0.2m of the trench consisted of sod and topsoil over a brown loam with small stones, 0.25m deep. A rimsherd of medieval local ware was recovered from this loam, which possibly represents medieval/post-medieval ploughsoil over this part of the site. This brown loam sat directly on a loose, brown, peaty clay 0.2m deep, which in turn overlay natural, grey, sandy silt. A fragment of a medieval tile with green/brown glaze was recovered from this layer.

At a distance of 15m from the west end of Trench 5 a layer of grey, stony, sterile clay was exposed, sitting directly on the peaty layer and below the ploughsoil. This layer was c. 0.2m deep towards the middle of the trench. The natural, grey, sandy silt was exposed at a much deeper level over the eastern end of the trench, and the brown, peaty layer became far more extensive. It is possible that the grey, stony

Location of burials and possible platform area, Dromiskin (No. 590).

layer was purposely deposited above the peat on what was formerly wet ground, to consolidate the ground for use. There is a substantial drop in ground level to the south of Trench 5, where the ground is extremely wet. At a distance of 30.5m from the west end of the trench, a series of timbers and branches was exposed sitting on the peat at a depth of 1.1m (OD 6.4m) and was found to extend eastwards for 10m.

Stage II excavation over the area of this possible trackway or platform, to a maximum depth of 1.3m, revealed a sequence of topsoil 0.2m deep over brown loam, with small stones towards the base of the deposit, 0.25–0.35m deep. The upper level of the peat deposit (6.7m OD) was characterised by irregularly arranged branches and root fragments, mainly of birch, as well as possible reeds or rushes. Much of this material was both fragmented and compacted, and it was sampled for analysis. This deposit of 'debris' overlay a more waterlogged peat horizon within which were set a number of longitudinal and transverse timbers, as well as more irregularly arranged roots and branches. The extent of this deposit, at least 11m west–east by 12m, was established along the northern and western edges of the assessment area, where the peat ran onto the natural clay marl, and to the east of the trench, where the peat deepened and was substantially water-saturated and where the wood remains appeared to end.

In general the arrangement of this material does not correspond with any type of trackway. The western side of the deposit was characterised by at least one large, straight, longitudinal (north–south) oak timber (possible remains of sapwood) with remains of its root ball at its northern end and a curious, A-frame-type arrangement of two further possible oak timbers at its southern end. At least one further possible oak timber lay in transverse fashion, roughly perpendicular to the longitudinal one, and extended as far as the edge of the clay marl c. 1.2m west, while roundwood branches, possibly alder, were similarly arranged towards its northern end. The eastern side of the deposit is also characterised by a straight, roughly north–south, longitudinal oak; however, several further possible oaks of narrow width lie roughly parallel along its west side. A number of tree stumps (alder) survive, standing in the peat within the area defined by the longitudinal oaks, and that on the east side had surviving and extensive roots extending from the stump. The remainder of the material contained within the area comprised numerous branches (alder and birch) and occasional tree trunks (alder and possibly oak). No dressed timbers or tooling marks could be found on any of the exposed timbers. The oaks, straight and without branches or knots on the trunks, would appear to be derived from a managed woodland. Such managed oak woodland was common from the early historic period, and, as oak provided the main source of building material for construction, it was a valuable and managed commodity. Such a maintained woodland would have been enclosed by other tree species, namely birch and alder. The site was visited by archaeologists from the Irish Archaeological Wetland Unit (UCD), who confirmed the timber species and that none of the timbers bore any toolmarks.

Trench 6 contained a pit cut into the natural, grey, sandy silt at a depth of 0.4m from ground level and 2m from the west end of the trench. The pit measured 1m in diameter and was filled with ploughsoil and stones. A single sherd of medieval local ware was recovered from the top of the unexcavated fill.
*Donald Murphy and Malachy Conway, Archaeological Consultancy Services Ltd, 15 Trinity Street, Drogheda, Co. Louth.*

### 591. DROMISKIN
*Fulachta fiadh*
30518 29815
99E0549

The site is in Dromiskin village, to the west of the former ecclesiastical enclosure that is an Early Christian monastic site containing the remains of a round tower and high cross. Nearby are six possible souterrains and an earthwork, SMR 12:43. The monastery was founded by St Patrick in around 433, with numerous abbots recorded from the 8th/10th centuries before it was abandoned in around 1065.

The proposed development is for ten houses with associated services, and the site is to the north of the road leading from Dromiskin to the nearby coast. A *fulacht fiadh* was found in 1996 in marshland to the south of the site, and two cist burials were discovered nearby in 1862. Four trenches were excavated in the area to be disturbed by the development.

Trench 1 was excavated in an east–west direction in the northern section of the site. It measured 37.5m by 1m and was 0.9m deep. Sod and topsoil extended to a depth of 0.2m, below which a black clay extended to a depth of 0.7m, at which point the natural, grey boulder clay was exposed. The middle layer contained a single sherd of blue and white patterned, tin-glazed earthenware. At 7m from the western end of the trench an old field drain extending north–south was exposed at a depth of 0.3m, 0.6m wide and 0.3m high. The field drain contained fragments of red brick and water-rolled stones.

Trench 2, in the western section of the site, extended north–south, measured 32m by 1m and was excavated to a depth of 1.3m. The sod and topsoil extended to a depth of 0.15–0.2m. Below this a yellow, sandy clay extended to a depth of 0.4m, and this rested on a layer of stony, grey, rich ploughsoil that extended to a depth of 1.1m. The natural horizon was a grey/white, dauby boulder clay that lay at a depth of 1–1.1m. No features were evident in this trench, and no finds were recovered.

Trench 3, in the eastern section of the site, extended north–south, measured 45m by 1m and was excavated to a depth of 0.9m. The sod and topsoil extended to a depth of 0.2m and overlay the ploughsoil, which was similar to that encountered in Trenches 1 and 2. At the northern end of the trench natural boulder clay lay at a depth of 0.85m, but 5m from the northern end of the trench boulder clay rose to 0.3m below the surface. At 12.5m from the southern end of the trench an area of black, burnt soil was visible in both trench baulks at a depth of 0.7m and was 3.5m long. A small amount was hand-excavated, revealing large amounts of burnt stone that may represent the remains of a ploughed-out *fulacht fiadh*. No finds were recovered from this trench.

Trench 4, in the southern section of the site, extended in an east–west direction, measured 21m by 1m and was excavated to a depth of 1.5m. The sod and topsoil extended to a depth of 0.2m, below which the boulder clay was exposed. At 1.5m from the east end of the trench, sod and topsoil extended to a depth of 0.4m and overlay a sandy ploughsoil extending to a depth of 0.78m. Below this lay a layer of black, burnt clay with tiny fragments of orange, fire-cracked sandstone. This burnt layer measured 3.5m east–west and was visible in the north and south sections of the trench. Hand-excavation revealed that this layer extended to a depth of 0.78–1.05m, at which point the boulder clay was exposed. This feature was identified as the remains of a ploughed-out *fulacht fiadh*. A single piece of animal bone was recovered from the burnt layer.

In conclusion, the presence of the remains of two *fulachta fiadh* that would be truncated by proposed foundations requires a recommendation for excavation of these features before development.
*Donald Murphy, Archaeological Consultancy Services Ltd, 15 Trinity Street, Drogheda, Co. Louth.*

### 592. DRUMLECK
Pit
303981 296262
97E0475 ext.

A pit discovered during monitoring of topsoil-stripping along the route of the Dunleer–Dundalk Bypass Motorway was excavated on 25 May 1999. It was an isolated circular pit, 1.5m in diameter, filled with charcoal and burnt stone. No finds were recovered.
*Cóilín Ó Drisceoil, 6 Riverview, Ardnore, Kilkenny, for Valerie J. Keeley Ltd.*

### 593. DUNDALK
No archaeological significance
99E0225

Testing was carried out in connection with the Dundalk Sewerage Scheme upgrading project. The testing took place along Lines 7 and 9, east and west of the Dublin road in the suburbs to the southern side of the town. An assessment carried out in November 1997 by Valerie J. Keeley Ltd identified this area as archaeologically sensitive, as the sewerage pipeline runs through an area where flint scatters and what may be a Late Neolithic/Early Bronze Age settlement site were found.

Eight trenches were dug, each 10m x 2m, up to a maximum depth of 1.9m. Trenches A1–3 lay in an old Iarnrod Éireann yard and had evidence of railway activities in them. A2 contained an old storm-water pipe. A3 contained part of a wall, 1m high, 16.5m long and 0.5m thick. The wall was earthbound on the southern side and was probably part of a construction associated with the railway. A4 and A7 contained peat growth. A5–7 all had a similar soil profile: modern stone infill; black silt with stones; brown clay with small, angular stones; red boulder clay; brown clay with modern artefacts—pottery, glass and bone; boulder clay and grey-green sand to the bottom.

This generalised profile seems to characterise how the railway embankment was constructed, and a similar pattern was observed during monitoring of the laying of the sewerage pipe further along the embankment.

None of the eight investigation trenches contained anything of archaeological significance.

*Carmel Duffy, The Mill Road, Umberstown Great, Summerhill, Co. Meath, for Valerie J. Keeley Ltd.*

### 594. 35 ANNE STREET, DUNDALK
No archaeological significance
304431 306850
99E0104

Monitoring took place of an extension to a residence at 35 Anne Street, Dundalk. The site was within the medieval area of the town identified in the Urban Archaeological Survey. The current buildings on site date from the mid-19th century. The existing building was demolished. The foundation trenches were up to 0.58m deep. No archaeological material was encountered.

*Matthew Seaver for Archaeological Consultancy Services Ltd, 15 Trinity Street, Drogheda, Co. Louth.*

### 595. CASTLEBLANEY ROAD, DUNDALK
Medieval borough
302835 308620
99E0216

An assessment of a proposed residential dwelling at Castleblaney Road, Dundalk, Co. Louth, was carried out in May 1999. The site lies to the north side of the Castleblaney Road in the area of the Anglo-Norman settlement at Castletown.

Two trenches were excavated but did not reveal any archaeological deposits. The gravelly subsoil was exposed at an average depth of 0.4–0.5m below present ground level, and no finds or features were recovered.

*Donald Murphy, Archaeological Consultancy Services Ltd, 15 Trinity Street, Drogheda, Co. Louth.*

### 596. CASTLETOWN ROAD, DUNDALK
Medieval cobbled road
30308 30857
SMR 7:118
99E0454

On 4 August 1999 the remains of a well-constructed cobbled road were exposed during the excavation of Line 1 of the Dundalk Sewerage Scheme, Contract No. 3. It was found *c.* 10m east of the entrance to Castle Park Estate, Castletown Road, Dundalk. The site was within the zone of archaeological potential for Castletown as outlined in the Urban Archaeological Survey for Dundalk. The archaeological remains of the area span from the Bronze Age to the later medieval period, and this was the location of the first Anglo-Norman settlement in the environs of Dundalk.

The pipeline trench was orientated east–west along the line of the Castletown Road before it turned sharply to the south at the entrance to Castle Park. The trench was 1.2m wide and up to 2.5m deep.

The excavation ran from 10 August to 1 September 1999. It uncovered the remains of a substantial, east–west-orientated, 12th–13th-century cobbled road with two phases of construction. This was sealed by 1–1.1m of ploughsoil and modern road construction. The cobbling was exposed along its length (east–west) for 10m and across its width for 7m. The cobbles appeared to turn off the line of the pipeline trench to the east, and they extend beyond the limit of excavation to the north and west. To the south the road was delimited by a drystone-built drain.

The road, as would be expected in a non-habitation context, yielded very few finds. Artefacts recovered included several horseshoes, two sherds of pottery and what appears to be a highly corroded iron stick-pin.

The cobbling and drain overlay the northern edge of a large, 12th-century ditch/pit and a possible flattened bank. This cut feature was 2.7m wide and 1.8m deep and had an east–west orientation. The possible bank was represented by several layers of clay sloping from south to north with a maximum depth of 0.26m.

*Rob Lynch, IAC Ltd, 8 Dungar Terrace, Dun Laoghaire, Co. Dublin.*

### 597. 17/19 CHAPEL STREET, DUNDALK
Close proximity to medieval friary
J05090749
99E0514

Testing of a proposed residential development was carried out. The site is within the zone of archaeological potential and is close to the medieval friary of St Leonard's, SMR 7:53B. During construction work in 1911, burials were found near this location, presumably from a cemetery belonging to the friary.

Two trenches were excavated by machine in the area to be disturbed. Both revealed hardcore extending to depths of 0.18–0.3m, below which a brown/black garden soil extended to a depth of 0.5m and contained fragments of red brick and stone. This overlay a stony, grey, sandy soil that probably represented natural subsoil. The garden soil in Trench 1 contained some animal bone, possibly horse bone, and two sherds of black-glazed earthenware. No other finds or features were uncovered.

There was no evidence for human burial in either trench, and it is probable that St Leonard's cemetery was further east of this site.

*Deirdre Murphy, Archaeological Consultancy Services Ltd, 15 Trinity Street, Drogheda, Co. Louth.*

### 598. AIB BANK, 96 CLANBRASSIL STREET, DUNDALK
Post-medieval features
3047 3075
98E0456 ext.

Excavation was undertaken at this site on behalf of Allied Irish Bank Plc. AIB is undertaking significant renovations to the existing bank on Clanbrassil Street. During the initial programme of testing (*Excavations 1998*, 148), a cobbled layer was identified. The objectives of the current programme were to attempt to elucidate the nature and date of that cobbled layer and to determine the nature of the deposit into which the cobbles were set.

Owing to safety considerations, it was not possible to excavate the entire area of the proposed extension; instead, it was decided to excavate a central area, 4m wide and 8m long, and to monitor any subsequent soil removal.

The stratigraphy revealed was consistent with that seen in the previous testing programme, i.e. rubble and backfill overburden, overlying a black layer, overlying a dump of stones, which in turn overlay a cobbled layer.

The stratigraphy demonstrates that the site has been extensively disturbed by recent activity, namely drainage and cellarage. This disturbance is further evidenced by the manner in which both medieval and post-medieval sherds of pottery were recovered from similar contexts (Sandes, unpublished). Environmental analysis of the deposits through which these drains were cut suggests that this was a garden belonging to the building fronting onto Clanbrassil Street (Plunkett, unpublished). The drains were cut through the cobbled layer (C4); nonetheless, this cobbling survived intact over much of the site.

The results of the environmental analysis indicate that the natural deposits were exposed for a period of time during the 17th century, which allowed for the deposition of the *pinus* pollen. The historical record for this particular area of Dundalk shows that it was subject to an intensive attack on at least one occasion during the 17th century. It is possible that, in the aftermath of these disturbances, this area were cleared and attempts were made to consolidate the area between Clanbrassil Street and the surrounding town ditch. This is supported from the archaeological record by the presence of pit features that may be interpreted as having a drainage function. The layer of cobbling was a subsequent effort at reconsolidation.

This programme of excavation has shown that the features identified in the initial testing programme may be dated to the latter part of the 17th century.
*Rónán Swan, Arch-Tech Ltd, 32 Fitzwilliam Place, Dublin 2.*

### 599. DEMESNE/TOWNPARKS, DUNDALK
Urban medieval
30435 30742 (centred on)
SMR 7:105 (vicinity of)
99E0311

All ground disturbance works associated with the Dundalk Sewerage Scheme, Contract No. 3, were to be monitored. The scheme is a local authority development to be undertaken by Dundalk Urban District Council and includes the construction of foul sewers and surface-water pipelines and required upgrading of the existing sewerage system. The total length of pipeline to be constructed is c. 19,125m, with roughly 230 manholes. Pipe sizes vary from 150mm to 1700mm in diameter. Trenches on average will be up to 2m wide with depths varying from 2m to 6m. The approximate time limit for completion of the scheme is sixty weeks.

To date, the monitoring of pipeline excavations has revealed significant archaeological material, resulting in several programmes of archaeological fieldwork. These are: 99E0312, test-trenching in various locations in Dundalk town centre before pipeline excavations (No. 600 below); 99E0454, excavation of a medieval cobbled road at the western end of the Castletown Road (No. 596 above); 99E0516, test-trenching following the discovery of a cobbled road of unknown date on the Dublin road (No. 601 below); 99E0627, excavation of a cobbled road of unknown date on the Dublin road (No. 602 below); 99E0737, test-trenching in various locations in Dundalk town centre before pipeline excavations—licence suspended until February 2000.

Monitoring of pipeline excavations is ongoing.
*Rob Lynch, IAC Ltd, 8 Dungar Terrace, Dun Laoghaire, Co. Dublin.*

### 600. DEMESNE/TOWNPARKS, DUNDALK
Urban post-medieval
30435 30742 (centred on)
SMR 7:105 (vicinity of)
99E0312

Between 19 and 29 July 1999 and September and October 1999 a total of 21 test-trenches were excavated along pipeline routes 3, 4, 5, and 8 of the proposed Dundalk Sewerage Scheme, Contract No. 3. These trenches formed part of an archaeological assessment that incorporated both desk-based research and an extensive programme of test-trenching to identify the archaeological constraints of the pipeline routes. The assessment was undertaken on behalf of Dundalk Urban District Council

A desk-based assessment of the scheme by Valerie J. Keely & Co. Ltd had identified a number of pipeline routes running through several archaeologically sensitive areas. Lines 3 and 5 cross the projected line of the town defences, and Line 4 runs outside but parallel to the town wall. The northern end of Line 8 runs through an area known to contain Bronze Age flint scatters.

The test-trenching revealed no significant archaeological features or deposits. There was no evidence of the town defences in the areas tested along Lines 3 and 5. The only archaeological material of note discovered were the remains of one or more 18th–19th-century metalworking areas along Patrick Street.

Line 3 runs north–south along St Nicholas Avenue and crosses the projected line of the medieval town defences. Six trenches were excavated. Nothing of archaeological significance was discovered. To the south the stratigraphy consisted of c. 0.4m of 19th-century clays deposited over natural geology. To the north of the street, which is adjacent to the Castletown River, up to 2m of dumped 19th-century clays was recorded. These had been deposited during land reclamation.

Line 4 runs north–south along Philip Street. It runs outside but parallel to the medieval town defences and through the former Lord Rodin's demesne. Five trenches were excavated. Nothing of archaeological significance was discovered.

Line 5 runs east–west along Patrick Street. It crosses the projected line of the medieval town defences at the junction of Patrick Street and Laurels Road and proceeds into the medieval town along the eastern half of Patrick Street. Five trenches were excavated in this area.

The current line of Patrick Street also has its origins in the 20th century; constructed as part of the Dundalk Housing Scheme during the 1920s, it is first seen in the 1940 edition of the OS map of Dundalk. It was preceded by Shiel's Court, a small cul-de-sac of structures orientated east–west and between the rear of the buildings fronting onto Bridge Street to the east and Lord Rodin's estate to the west. Shiel's Court had its origins in the 18th century and is visible on Taylor and Skinner's 1777 map of Dundalk. The southern side of Shiel's Court continued to develop in a linear fashion through the 19th century until it met the boundary wall of Rodin's estate. Shiel's Court was preceded by burgage plots associated with the buildings fronting onto Church Street, which are visible on 16th- and 17th-century maps of Dundalk. It is likely that these burgage plots respected earlier property boundaries dating to the medieval period.

Two distinct phases of activity were identified within the test-trenches excavated on Patrick Street.

Phase 1 was present in Trenches 9 and 20. It consisted of the accumulation of 0.6–1.3m of 17th–18th-century garden soils associated with the burgage plots mentioned above.

Phase 2 was recorded in Trenches 8, 9, and 20. It represented the 18th- and 19th-century development of what was then known as Shiel's Court. Trench 8 measured 2.6m (north–south) x 1.2m and contained evidence of the remains of an 19th-century metalworking area, in the form of limestone-built walls, a flagged floor and a deep deposit of cinders and corroded metal. Trench 9 measured 5m (east–west) x 1.2m and contained an east–west-orientated limestone wall in its north-facing section. This wall was constructed over the 17th-century garden soils and was probably the remains of an 18th–19th-century structure that fronted onto Shiel's Court. Trench 20 measured 5m (east–west) x 1.2m and contained evidence of two phases of 19th-century industrial activity in the form of cobbled floors, internal red brick walls and several deep deposits of cinders and ash. Both these phases were constructed over 17th-century garden soils.

Line 8 was orientated north–south and ran along a footpath on the south side of Long Avenue, parallel to a culvert containing the Ramparts River. A number of Late Neolithic/Early Bronze Age flints have been recovered from this area in the past. Four trenches were excavated, and nothing of archaeological significance was discovered. In general, stratigraphy consisted of modern dumped clays overlying several deposits of alluvial clay.

Rob Lynch, IAC Ltd, 8 Dungar Terrace, Dun Laoghaire, Co. Dublin.

### 601. DUBLIN ROAD (PRIORLAND/MARSHES LOWER), DUNDALK
Cobbled road
30483 30608 (vicinity of)
SMR 7:114 (vicinity of)
99E0516

Test-trenching on Line 8 of the proposed Dundalk Sewerage Scheme, Contract No. 3, was requested by Dundalk Urban District Council following the discovery of the remains of a substantial cobbled surface during the monitoring of pipe-laying (see No. 599 above). Three trenches were excavated between 21 and 23 September 1999.

Line 8 is a 450mm-diameter foul sewer that runs along the route of the Dublin road for 300m before turning south-west along Priorland Road. The pipeline trench will be c. 1.2m wide and up to 4m deep. The site was outside Crossan's garage on the Dublin road, to the south of the town centre.

Trench 1 was 21m south-west of the area of cobbling exposed during monitoring. A continuation of the cobbled surface was recorded at 1.1m from present ground level. Trenches 2 and 3 contained no evidence of cobbling.

The results of the test-trenching, coupled with the evidence provided by the monitoring, indicates the presence of a roughly constructed cobbled surface stretching for between 35m and 45m south-east from the manhole MH 110. It could also be seen to extend beyond MH 110 to the north-east, where MH 110 will link with an extension of Line 8 that follows the line of the culvert containing the Ramparts River on the east side of Hill Street. The cobbled surface would seem to be present only in the low-lying and waterlogged area at the north-western end of Line 8, around Crossan's garage. The cobbles would appear to give way to the more stable and dry boulder clay that lay upslope, to the south-east.

Rob Lynch, IAC Ltd, 8 Dungar Terrace, Dun Laoghaire, Co. Dublin.

### 602. DUBLIN ROAD, (PRIORLAND/MARSHES LOWER), DUNDALK
Cobbled road
30483 30608 (vicinity of)
SMR 7:114 (vicinity of)
99E0627

An excavation was carried out along Line 8 of the proposed Dundalk Sewerage Scheme, Contract No. 3, between 8 November and 15 December 1999. This followed the discovery of the remains of a substantial cobbled surface during the monitoring of pipe-laying (99E0311) and a later programme of test-trenching (99E0516), see Nos 599 and 601 above.

Line 8 is a 450mm-diameter foul sewer orientated roughly north–south along the route of the Dublin road. The pipeline trench will be c. 1.2m wide and up to 4m deep. The site itself was outside Crossan's garage on the Dublin road, to the south of the town centre. The Dublin road at this point bisects an area known locally as Balmers Bog and referred to on early maps as The Great Bogg. The ground is relatively low-lying and rises gradually to the north.

The excavation area measured 53m x 1.2m and revealed the remains of a rough stone surface with two phases of construction in places, stretching northward for 49m from the southernmost point of the cutting. The surface was very uneven and loose in places, in particular to the north of the site, where cobbles gave way to a thin layer of stony clay that has been interpreted as a metalled surface. The southernmost 10m of the surface overlay a sub-base of rounded cobbles 0.12m deep. This area of the site was low-lying and constantly under water, which may suggest the need for a sub-base. Further south, in a dryland environment, the surface directly overlay the natural geology. Excavation of the stone surface yielded no datable artefacts, but it is hoped that a quantity of animal bone sealed by it may provide a *terminus ante quem* for the feature.

The surface was sealed by 0.3m of silt that had been deposited in several episodes, the lowest levels of which contained several sherds of 18th-century

pottery. This material was further sealed by 0.6m of relatively modern, dumped clays, which had presumably been deposited in an effort to stabilise the surrounding ground before the construction of the modern road.
*Rob Lynch, IAC Ltd, 8 Dungar Terrace, Dun Laoghaire, Co. Dublin.*

### 603. DUBLIN STREET, DUNDALK
Urban medieval
30456 30686
99E0189

An assessment of a proposed commercial development at Dublin Street, Dundalk, was carried out in April 1999. The site is to the south of the medieval town, in an area of archaeological potential. The proposed development involved the demolition of a workshop and the reconstruction of an open shed with ancillary services.

Three trenches were excavated on the site. Trench 1 revealed the presence of garden soil in the south-east area, which contained brick, stone and animal bone. It extended to a depth of 1.1m, below which a sterile, grey clay was evident that may be of natural origin. The excavation of Trench 2 revealed disturbed soil containing concrete, brick and stone above a sterile, sandy gravel at 0.6m. Trench 3 revealed a sandy rubble layer containing brick, stone, mortar and fragments of earthenware pipes, overlying a layer of shale and stone at a depth of 1.35m. The natural horizon was not exposed. The garden soil exposed in Trench 1 probably represents the gardens of houses that stood in the area until the 20th century. The foundations for the proposed building will be excavated to a depth of 0.9m and therefore would not have an archaeological impact.
*Deirdre Murphy, Archaeological Consultancy Services Ltd, 15 Trinity Street, Drogheda, Co. Louth.*

### 604. 3 DUBLIN STREET, DUNDALK
Urban post-medieval
J460694
99E0567

Monitoring was carried out during the excavation of foundation trenches for a store at the rear of 3 Dublin Street, Dundalk. The site is in the angle formed by Dublin Street and Anne Street, close to the junction of these streets with Park Street, and is within the area of the late medieval suburb of Upper End. The store had maximum dimensions of 5.5m x 5.5m.

Foundation trenches, 0.55m wide, were excavated to a depth of 0.45m through an existing concrete surface and underlying rubble fill. A deposit of dark grey silt with brick fragments and shells was encountered at a depth of 0.3m. A sherd of black-glazed earthenware from this deposit was datable to the 18th or 19th century.
*Finola O'Carroll, Cultural Resource Development Services Ltd, Campus Innovation Centre, Roebuck, University College, Belfield, Dublin 4.*

### 605. 59 DUBLIN STREET, DUNDALK
Urban post-medieval
J460676
99E0661

Monitoring took place during the excavation of foundation trenches for an 8m-by-5m extension to the rear of a *c.* 1930s red brick terraced house. The site is outside the late medieval suburb of Upper End, *c.* 30m south of the site of the Dublin Gate as determined by Gosling (1995).

Trenches, 0.9m wide and 0.6m deep, were excavated for the north, east and south walls of the extension, through black garden soil that produced pottery of 20th-century date at all levels. Stone paving slabs, uncovered at a depth of 0.44m in the northern trench and left *in situ*, probably relate to the previous house on the site. Natural subsoil, a greenish-grey clay, was exposed at a depth of 0.55m in the southern trench.

*Reference*
Gosling, P. 1995 *From Dún Delca to Dundalk.* Monaghan.

*Finola O'Carroll, Cultural Resource Development Services Ltd, Campus Innovation Centre, Roebuck, University College, Belfield, Dublin 4.*

### 606. 80 DUBLIN STREET, DUNDALK
Urban
304431 306850
99E0160

An assessment was carried out at 80 Dublin Street, Dundalk, before a proposed commercial development. The site is within the area of archaeological importance defined by the Urban Archaeological Survey, and archaeological investigation was required as a condition of planning permission. The site was a narrow plot, only 4m wide.

After demolition of the existing 19th-century building two test-trenches were opened on the proposed north and south foundation walls in March 1999. Both were 15m long and 1m wide. A layer of modern demolition waste up to 0.18m thick was removed from Trench 1 and overlay a layer of light brown clay up to 0.29m deep, which contained 18th-century pottery. This overlay a sterile, grey gravel and sand. In the centre of the trench a modern ceramic sewer pipe had heavily disturbed these deposits. Trench 2 revealed the same stratigraphical sequence. No deposits of archaeological significance were encountered, and it appeared that post-medieval activity had removed any traces of medieval activity.
*Matthew Seaver for Archaeological Consultancy Services, 15 Trinity Street, Drogheda, Co. Louth.*

### 607. FARRANDREG, DUNDALK
Souterrain
30343 30784
SMR 7:34
99E0624

In October 1999 a programme of test-trenching was undertaken to define, as far as was reasonably possible, potential adverse affects on the archaeological resource resulting from the proposed extension of the Farrandreg Drainage System, which is part of the Dundalk Sewerage Scheme. Five test-trenches were excavated across the site on behalf of Dundalk Urban District Council.

The route of the proposed pipeline is within an area of archaeological potential and runs within *c.*

10m of a known souterrain. The monument is orientated north–south and runs parallel to the proposed pipeline route. However, an aerial photograph taken in 1979 indicated the existence of a possible cropmark adjacent to the souterrain.

The test-trenches revealed the substantial remains of a multi-chambered souterrain extending across the full width of the proposed development and for an undefined distance along its length.

Trench 1 measured 5m x 3m. The western end contained a substantial north–south-orientated cut. This cut the natural clays, was 1.8m wide and extended beyond the northern and southern limits of the trench. It narrowed to 0.9m wide to the north of the trench, which may represent either the terminus of the feature or simply a narrowing of the passage. It was interpreted as representing the foundation trench of a souterrain chamber.

Trench 2 was 6m south of Trench 1 and measured 5m x 3m. It contained the intact remains of a substantial souterrain at 0.4m below present ground level. It consisted of two visible passages, one orientated east-south-east/west-north-west, and the other a north–south passage perpendicular to the first.

The east-south-east/west-north-west passage was visible above ground for 2.2m, at which point it ran beneath the level of the excavation. Its line was marked by an east–west-orientated cut that extended beyond the southern and eastern limits of the trench.

A dislodged capstone allowed for a visual inspection, which revealed that the souterrain was drystone-built and had a corbelled roof. The western end of the passage was blocked by rubble. It was not possible to measure the eastern end of the passage; however, its length was estimated as roughly 20m. The eastern end was met by a further north–south-orientated passage running perpendicular to it.

Trench 3 was 1m to the south-east of Trench 2 and measured 3m x 2m. A cut feature extended across the width of Trench 3 and continued beyond the eastern limit of excavation. The northern edge only of the cut was recorded, as its southern edge lay beyond the southern limit of the trench. It cut the natural clay and clearly represented an eastern continuation of the souterrain foundation cut recorded in Trench 2.

Trenches 4 and 5 contained no archaeological features or deposits.

It is highly likely that the monument described above forms part of the souterrain recorded by Paul Gosling in the early 1980s. If this is the case it would indicate that the monument, as currently understood, consists of at least one east–west passage running downslope to the east for a distance of *c.* 30m, with a further three, north–south-orientated passages of uncertain length running perpendicular to it.

It must also be concluded that it is unlikely that such a monument occurred in isolation. Therefore it is probable that it forms part of a wider habitation area, which was most likely represented by the presence of a ringfort. Despite the fact that the site has been ploughed extensively in the recent past, it is likely that the truncated remains of such a habitation site survive below the ploughing horizon; this is borne out by the possible cropmark identified in the aerial photograph in 1979.

*Rob Lynch, IAC Ltd, 8 Dungar Terrace, Dun Laoghaire, Co. Dublin.*

### 608. LINENHALL STREET, DUNDALK
No archaeological significance
30486 30798
99E0657

An assessment was carried out at a site in the north-west quadrant of a block defined by Linenhall Street (west), Fairgreen Row (north) and Wolfe Tone Terrace (south) in the north-east corner of the town, within the area of archaeological potential as outlined in the Urban Archaeological Survey of Dundalk. The north perimeter of the site is defined by a series of terraced houses and one large, detached property. The western line is defined by a terrace that includes a former public house. Access to the site is from Linenhall Street through a narrow, arched laneway, which gives access to the rear of the properties fronting Linenhall Street and Fairgreen Row. A north–south property division with the gardens/yards of terraces lying immediately east of the site delineates the eastern perimeter of the site. The southern perimeter of the proposed development site is characterised by a substantial stone wall extending from the rear of the south-lying property as far as the eastern perimeter. Excavation of four test-trenches was undertaken using a mini-digger on 2 December 1999.

Trench 1, positioned north–south along the western side of the eastern proposed apartment block, measured 10m by 1m. A concrete slab 0.2m thick and a thin hardcore fill up to 0.1m deep overlay natural, yellow, sandy clay, found to be over 0.7m deep.

Trench 2, positioned west–east along the northern side of the eastern proposed apartment block, perpendicular to the end of Trench 1, measured 8m by 1m. A rubble and hardcore surface 0.2m thick overlay dark brown garden soil up to 0.4m deep. Natural, yellow, sandy clay lay below this level, with a depth of over 0.5m.

Trench 3, positioned north-west/south-east along the line of the drainage/services from the proposed apartment block, measured 4m by 1m. A hardcore and gravel surface 0.5m thick overlay dark brown, sandy soil containing red brick rubble and a disused drain up to 0.3m deep. The rubble deposit lay on a deposit of wet, dark brown, gravelly clay, 0.4m deep, below which lay a deposit of sandy clay at a depth of 1.2m+.

Trench 4, positioned west–east along the line of the foundation of the western proposed apartment block, measured 4m by 1m. A hardcore and gravel surface 0.5m thick overlay dark brown, sandy soil containing red brick rubble and sewer pipe up to 0.3m deep.

No features, deposits or soils of archaeological potential were revealed in any of the trenches.
*Malachy Conway, Archaeological Consultancy Services Ltd, 15 Trinity Street, Drogheda, Co. Louth.*

### 609. XEROX/ESB ELECTRICITY SUBSTATION, MULLAGHARLIN, DUNDALK
No archaeological significance

Owing to the construction of an Electricity Substation for Xerox Limited by Uniform Construction Limited, a large area, comprising *c.* 32,000m$^2$, was to be topsoil-stripped before any building work began on the site. As the site is within an area of high archaeological potential—a number of souterrains have been noted in the surrounding area—it was suggested that monitoring of the topsoil-stripping be undertaken to find and define archaeological activity, if any, on the site.

The topsoil was stripped by a large-tracked machine (Hymac) and by bulldozer. It was then banked up in large spoilheaps that would eventually be used to create large, landscaped berms around the proposed building. Investigation of the topsoil, which had a variable depth of 0.2–0.3m, and the exposed orange, slaty, gravelly subsoil, yielded no subsoil-cut archaeological features.

Nothing of archaeological significance was uncovered during the topsoil-stripping, and development was able to proceed.
Dermot G. Moore, ADS Ltd, Windsor House, 11 Fairview Strand, Fairview, Dublin 3.

**610. MULLAGHARLIN/HAGGARDSTOWN, DUNDALK**
Various
30543 30420
98E0440 ext.
Pre-development testing was carried out in October 1998, by Dermot Moore and then Audrey Gahan, of c. 100 acres on the site of the proposed Xerox Technology Park, just south of Dundalk. A total of 28 trenches were examined, two of which yielded archaeology in the form of spreads of *fulacht fiadh* material (*Excavations 1998*, 152).

In January 1999 full-scale topsoil-stripping commenced, monitored by a team of archaeologists. In addition to the areas of archaeology found previously, eight other areas were found and completely excavated, under the previous licence.

*Area 1: truncated fulacht fiadh*
This area was found in the October 1998 testing of the site and consisted of two spreads of *fulacht fiadh* material that were extensively ploughed out. The larger of the two spreads measured 4.25m north–south by 2.5m. It survived to a maximum depth of 0.4m and was made up of a deposit of friable, silty, charcoal-rich soil with frequent inclusions of burnt stone. The second spread measured 2m by 1.25m and was made up of the same deposit as the larger spread. Four subsoil-cut pits were found close to the *fulacht fiadh* spreads. The largest of these was probably cut as a trough. It measured 3m by 1.35m and was a maximum of 0.4m deep. It was filled initially by *fulacht fiadh* debris and then by silt. The other pits were not suitably diagnostic to suggest a function.

*Area 2: pit*
This area was found in the October 1998 testing of the site and consisted of an oval, subsoil-cut pit measuring 1.4m by 0.9m and 0.16m deep. It was filled with a black, charcoal-rich, friable, silty clay. The feature was revealed in a waterlogged hollow, with no other traces of archaeology surviving in the immediate vicinity.

*Area 3: Bronze Age hearth*
This area was discovered in January 1999 and comprised a hearth and stake-hole complex with associated pits. All the features underlay topsoil and cut the subsoil. The hearth measured 1m north–south by 0.7m and had a maximum depth of 0.19m. The basal fills contained burnt material that was overlain by a layer of flat stones; this in turn was overlain by an extremely charcoal-rich layer. The hearth was surrounded on all sides by nineteen stake-holes. A sizeable pit had been cut to the west of the hearth. This measured 1.04m east–west by 1.36m and had a maximum depth of 0.15m. This truncated feature contained several sherds of Bronze Age pottery.

To the north of the hearth several more features survived. Two of these were pits, one of which also contained Bronze Age pottery, and the third was a linear gully that was traced for a length of 20m north–south. This gully measured c. 0.4m east–west, was 0.5m deep and cut one of the above pits.

*Area 4: fulacht fiadh*
This area was found in January 1999 and comprised several spreads of *fulacht fiadh* material and associated pits. The pits appeared to have been cut in a random fashion around a natural hollow that was fed by a spring. There were thirteen subsoil-cut pits, most of which were quite substantial. One of these conformed to classic trough morphology; it was subrectangular, measuring 2.37m north-west/south-east by 1.2m and 0.35m deep. A stake-hole had been cut into each of the corners. There were no finds from these features.

All the features cut the subsoil, and the majority were overlain by black, clayey silt that contained frequent inclusions of burnt stone and charcoal. This had a maximum depth of 0.2m. Three of the pits had also been cut by a linear gully that was traced for c. 20m and was orientated in a north-west/south-east direction. It was 0.8–1m wide and 0.3m deep. No artefacts were retrieved to suggest a date for its use.

Several of the other pits had also been cut by post-medieval field drains that criss-crossed the whole area, including the vicinity of Area 3 above.

*Area 5: corn-drying kiln*
This area was discovered in January 1999. It was a corn-drying kiln that had been abandoned in antiquity, with a substantial amount of debris accumulated within it. The kiln had been cut into a north-facing slope and was orientated north-north-west/south-south-east. It was subrectangular and 4m long. At its widest it was 1.6m, and at its deepest 0.5m. The cut had three distinct parts. At the northerly end was a narrow, sloping cut that probably acted as a flue. This gave way to a fire-pit in the centre. The kiln was completed by a flat-bottomed chamber at the southern end, and the structure consisted of drystone walling on all sides. It did not survive above ground level. Several stake- and post-holes were found to the north-west of the flue. The kiln had been cut through a small, backfilled ditch that was 1.1m wide and was traced for a length of 8.5m. It was orientated north-west/south-east.

A subrectangular cut measuring 8m north-north-west by 1.1m south-south-east and 0.25m deep was found 2.5m to the south of the kiln structure. The function of this feature was not immediately obvious, but it may have been a cut for a kiln that had been abandoned. At its southern end this feature cut a previous ditch that had much the same dimensions as the ditch upslope, except that it was badly truncated. No finds were recovered from any of the features.

*Area 6: ditch*
Area 6, discovered in January 1999, was 25m to the south-east of Area 5. It contained a ditch that measured 12m and was orientated north-north-west/south-south-east. The northern end terminated in natural bedrock, and the southern extent was unknown owing to severe truncation. The maximum width of the ditch was 2.3m, and it was 0.4m deep. The base of the ditch had been cut towards the southern end by a pit. This measured 1.65m north–south by 1.35m and was 0.3m deep. The pit was filled by copious quantities of slag. A hearth was found 2.5m south-west of the northern terminus of the ditch and was made up of a layer of flat stones with charcoal-rich soil.

*Area 7: ditch and fulacht fiadh spread*
Area 7, found in January 1999, was a linear ditch measuring 24m as found. It was severely truncated and, as it survived, was 2.5m wide and 0.5m deep. It was orientated north-east/south-west. Several spreads of charcoal-rich, silty clay with burnt stone, typical of *fulacht fiadh* debris, were found to the north-east of the ditch. These spreads were no more than 0.2m deep. No artefacts were recovered.

*Area 8: Bronze Age structure*
Area 8, discovered in January 1999, measured *c.* 38m north–south by 35m. It contained the remains of one, or possibly two, Bronze Age structures. Structure 1 was a circular feature measuring *c.* 8m north–south by 9m. It was made up of two rings of post-holes, many of which were stone-packed. There may have been an entrance at the north-east, as evidenced by a large gap in the inner ring of post-holes. However, the structure had been truncated on its northern side, so it is difficult to say for certain whether an entrance existed here. Inside the area enclosed by the post-holes several non-structural pits existed.

Structure 2 was to the south-west of Structure 1. The area enclosed by this ring of post-holes measured 7m east–west by 6m. Whilst outer structural post-holes could be discerned, the interpretation of this area is more problematic than that of Structure 1, as the area also contained a dense concentration of pits and stake-holes that, in the absence of stratigraphy, makes interpretation difficult.

A small, linear ditch lay immediately to the west of Structure 2. This was traced for a length of 10m running north–south and was on average 1m wide and 0.5m deep. This ditch was not found anywhere else around the area, so is probably not related; rather, its similarity to the other small ditches found over the whole development may place it within an as yet undated field system. No artefacts were recovered from the fill.

The two structures appear not to have been enclosed, although several other scatters of post-holes were in evidence within the excavated areas. One of these created an arc and was made up of five deep post-holes. Other pit and post-hole scatters the function of which is unclear lay apparently randomly throughout the area. Several post-holes, both within the structures and outside them, contained large sherds of coarse Bronze Age pottery (exact type as yet unidentified). Other finds included small pieces of quartz and lumps of granite.

*Area 9: ditch*
This area was found in January 1999 and contained the remains of an extremely truncated ditch. This was linear, orientated north-east/south-west, and was traced for a length of 20m. Its maximum surviving depth was 0.2m, and it was on average 1m wide. Several pits were found along the line of this ditch, one cut it and two were cut by it. No artefacts were recovered.

*Area 10: souterrain, associated features and ditch*
Area 10 was discovered in January 1999. Excavation began in April 1999 after negotiations with *Dúchas*. The souterrain lay *c.* 40m south of a horseshoe-shaped enclosure noted in the SMR (7.95). The souterrain was damaged by machine action. It was constructed of roughly coursed drystone walling. As it survived it consisted of an entrance passage that ran east–west for 3m and contained a slot with two post-holes, probably to hold a door; several other post-holes were excavated at the point where the entrance passage turned north–south. It continued in this direction for 7m and was 1m wide until near the terminus, where it widened slightly into an end chamber. The roof survived here and showed the passage to have been *c.* 1m high. Another passage was offset from the first at right angles 5m along the east wall of the north–south passage. This passage was raised from the level of the north–south passage by 0.3m. It initially ran east–west but curved gently toward the north. It was *c.* 5m long and ended in an intact chamber that had finely corbelled upper coursing and roof and measured 2.5m north–south by 1.5m east–west at its widest. At its greatest height it measured 1.5m. The roofing along the rest of the souterrain was a mixture of lintels and corbelling. Finds included an amber bead, a probable loom weight, half a lignite(?) bracelet and a quantity of animal bone. Several metal objects were also recovered, one with traces of enamel.

The north–south passage had been cut through the base of an earlier linear ditch. This ditch ran in a north-north-west/south-south-east direction toward the horseshoe-shaped enclosure and measured 47m as found. A test-trench was opened within the protected area of the monument and showed that the ditch continued toward the terminal of enclosure. It did not run beyond the enclosure. The ditch had an upper width of *c.* 3m; on the west it was steep-sided. On the east a small cut through subsoil (*c.* 0.2m) led to a shelf *c.* 1m wide. This then dropped sharply, and the base of the ditch measured 0.4–0.6m. The ditch showed very little evidence of silting and instead was mostly backfilled by brown, silty clay that probably came from a bank, although no archaeological evidence of this survived. No artefacts were recovered from the fill.

Approximately 3m north of the souterrain a large, irregular-shaped feature, consisting of a central linear section with two crescent-shaped arcs projecting at either end, had been cut into the subsoil. The north-eastern arc measured c. 8m and was fairly shallow (c. 0.1–0.2m). On average it was 1m wide. At the southern terminal a shallow grave contained the partial remains of an articulated skeleton. This arc turned west and ran as the central linear section for c. 18m. The width of the feature here varied a great deal (0.75–3.5m), and the depth was c. 0.5m. The second arc turned south and ran for a length of 7m. The fill was dark brown/black, charcoal-rich, silty clay, which contained several sherds of souterrain ware. The linear band of the feature was revetted on its southern side by a line of rough boulders. This was to keep out the upcast formed by the digging of the cut, which had been placed immediately to the south of the feature. Several pits of indeterminate nature were cut through the upcast. From the line of the revetment a large pocket of seeds was recovered. This irregular feature also cut the backfilled ditch.

*Catherine McLoughlin, ADS Ltd, Windsor House, 11 Fairview Strand, Fairview, Dublin 3.*

### 611. 10 NEW STREET, DUNDALK
Urban
J05090601
99E0251

Assessment of an extension to a house in New Street, Dundalk, included the excavation of two test-trenches in the area of the development. No archaeological materials were found.

*Cóilín Ó Drisceoil, 6 Riverview, Ardnore, Kilkenny.*

### 612. 87–88 PARK STREET (TOWNPARKS), DUNDALK
No archaeological significance
304662 306916

Monitoring was conducted before a proposed commercial extension at Rogers Garage, 87–88 Park Street, Dundalk, Co. Louth, in March 1999, within an area of archaeological potential as identified by the Urban Archaeological Survey. The existing buildings on the site were demolished, and their shallow foundations were removed by machine. These overlay a mid-brown loam, which contained red brick and mortar fragments. A total of 0.3m of this material was removed to provide an adequate level for construction. No archaeological features or deposits were exposed, and no finds were recovered. The development had no archaeological implications.

*Donald Murphy, Archaeological Consultancy Services Ltd, 15 Trinity Street, Drogheda, Co. Louth.*

### 613. RODEN PLACE, DUNDALK
Urban medieval
30497 30736
99E0186

Testing of a proposed commercial development on the north side of Roden Place was carried out in April 1999. The site is in an area of archaeological potential as identified in the Urban Archaeology Survey of County Louth.

Following the demolition of existing buildings on the site, two trenches were excavated before development. These revealed the presence of a substantial layer of garden soil over the northern two-thirds of the site, behind existing buildings fronting onto Roden Place. An intensive examination of the deposit produced a single sherd of 13th-century local ware, and there was a complete absence of bone. The natural, grey marl was exposed at depths ranging from 1.1m to 1.3m. From an examination of the plans it was concluded that the proposed development would not impinge to any significant degree on the garden soil.

*Donald Murphy, Archaeological Consultancy Services Ltd, 15 Trinity Street, Drogheda, Co. Louth.*

### 614. 5 SEATOWN, DUNDALK
Medieval cemetery
J051075
91E0008 ext.

Assessment and excavations in 1991 revealed the presence of skeletal remains believed to be associated with the nearby priory and hospital of St Leonard (*Excavations 1991*, 33–4). Additional developments on the site were assessed in January 1999. Further disarticulated skeletal remains were uncovered; however, modifications to the foundation scheme and alterations to the service lines meant that significant disturbance to the archaeological remains was avoided.

*Eoin Halpin, ADS Ltd, Unit 48, Westlink Enterprise Centre, 30–50 Distillery Street, Belfast BT12 5BJ.*

### 615. TANKARDSROCK, DUNDALK
Archaeological landscape
30165 30750
SMR 7:30–2
99E0616

An assessment was carried out on the site of a proposed dwelling-house and associated groundworks at Tankardsrock, Dundalk, Co. Louth, between 26 and 29 November 1999 to fulfil a condition of the planning permission. The site is within a prehistoric landscape as defined by a number of recorded monuments (a ringfort, SMR 7:30, and two recorded standing stones, SMR 7:31 and 7:32) and is clearly within an area of archaeological potential.

Twelve trenches were excavated in the areas of proposed ground disturbance, to an average depth of 0.7m. In all of the trenches the natural boulder clay was exposed at a consistent depth of 0.25m below the sod and topsoil. A number of 19th–20th-century finds were recovered from the topsoil and from the ploughsoil in Trenches 9 and 11. The site would appear to be devoid of archaeological stratigraphy, as no archaeological features or deposits were evident and no other finds were recovered.

*Ian Russell, Archaeological Consultancy Services Ltd, 15 Trinity Street, Drogheda, Co. Louth.*

### 616. 16 WYNNE'S TERRACE, DUNDALK
Urban medieval
304520 306795
99E0293

An assessment of a proposed extension to an existing dwelling was carried out at 16 Wynne's Terrace, Dundalk. The site is on the east side of Wynne's Terrace, within the possible suburbs of the medieval town.

A single trench was excavated following the removal of a concrete yard. The ground was

disturbed and consisted of demolition debris above a sterile, sandy soil. There was no evidence of archaeological features or artefacts at this site.
*Donald Murphy, Archaeological Consultancy Services Ltd, 15 Trinity Street, Drogheda, Co. Louth.*

### 617. DUNLEER
Urban
30580 28799
98E0348

Testing was carried out in Main Street, Dunleer, in July 1998 before commencement of the Dunleer Sewerage Improvement Scheme (*Excavations 1998*, 150) to establish the presence of an enclosing feature around the Early Christian monastic site or any other early settlement features. No such features were exposed in three test-trenches.

The Underwater Archaeological Unit carried out an underwater survey of the banks of the White River.

Following a recommendation by *Dúchas* The Heritage Service, monitoring was carried out by the writer for two months at the beginning of 1999. The monitoring was then taken over by Cara Murray for IAC Ltd, who completed the project for Louth County Council (see No. 618 below).

The construction work monitored by the writer involved the excavation of: an access road along or close to the west bank of the river; a large area close to the existing sewage plant on the west bank of the river for a new treatment plant; a pipeline down to the river west of the railway station to the site of Syphon Chamber 1; Pumphouse 1 and associated piping down to the bank of the river; pipelines along the Dundalk and Barn roads and a pipeline within the green-field area north-west of the treatment plant site; and a small test-trench beside the graveyard before constuction of a manhole there.

All the numbers in the text and in the headings for each section refer to manhole numbers used as reference points.

*Access road (202–43)*
This road, allowing access from Main Street into the treatment plant site, was excavated along the west side of the river. This comprised soil-stripping to a depth of 0.3–0.5m. The topsoil was a grey/brown clay. Subsoil was generally a yellow/brown boulder clay containing shattered limestone stones. Remains of an east–west stone wall were exposed in the vicinity of 203. This was the foundation of an unmortared rubble wall, 0.5m wide at the lowest course. This wall was probably the remains of a farm outhouse. Nothing of archaeological significance was found here

*Treatment plant*
An area 80m x 60m was excavated to a depth of 6m to accommodate the construction of the treatment plant. A feature, A, filled with chunks of sandstone, was exposed underlying the topsoil. This feature comprised an extent of black soil filled with red sandstone, measuring 1.5m (north–south) by a maximum of 1.3m. Along the southern and western sides the cut was 0.3m deep, but on the other sides the edges were much less clear-cut. The feature bottomed onto the underlying natural, grey, coarse sand/fine gravel.

After further cleaning, the feature became more complex. A shallow trench could be seen running westwards from Feature A. This was filled with loose, grey clay, 0.15m deep and 0.8m wide, with a more defined edge on the north side. Occasional small pieces of sandstone were contained within the grey clay. There were no artefacts within the fill. Feature A was cut into the trench.

A similar pit, B, was exposed to the north of A. This was filled with the same loose, black soil and sandstone. When excavated out, it was found to have a flat bottom and was 0.24m deep. This feature was not associated with the shallow trench.

The function of these shallow pits and the trench was not clear. Although the soil was loose and black, there did not seem to be a high charcoal content; in A there were roots in the loose, black clay. Red sandstone was found in an engineer's test-pit dug on the Ardee Road to the west, explaining the occurrence of red sandstone in a general limestone area. There did not appear to have been concentrated burning here. The trench was shallow, and there was no organic content at the base; there were no finds in the fill.

The site of the treatment plant was excavated to a depth of 6m before steel and concrete foundations were put in place.

*Syphon Chamber 1 and associated pipe-laying (62–66 and down to riverbank)*
An east–west embankment was built here when the railway was laid in the 19th century, giving access from Main Street to the railway station. Soil-stripping was carried out parallel to the embankment and at its base. A trench, 0.5m deep, was excavated through fill and also through natural, the fill representing slippage from the embankment. The trench was then backfilled with hardcore in order to provide a stable base for the pipes. Archaeological material was not exposed here.

At the top of the slope (65) the pipeline turned southwards, still cutting though higher and higher ground. At this point the trench was dug only to a depth of 0.2m through a deposit of yellow clay that lay at the bottom of the slope here. Turning eastwards again, a series of larger, deeper holes (63, 64) was excavated for manholes. The excavation for 63 was 3–4m deep. A pre-existing sewage pipe was already in place there, making the ground very unstable. The pipeline was brought out to the Barn Road, cutting through ground that had already been disturbed by excavation for the earlier sewage pipe and by excavation for the front garden of the private dwelling-house here.

*Pumphouse 1 and associated piping down to the bank of the river (107–115)*
The corridor for the pipe from the location of Pumphouse 1 (on the Dundalk road) down to the riverbank (115) was stripped, and the trench for the pipe was excavated.

The channel of the river had altered over the years, and there was evidence for riverine deposits comprising pure sands and gravels. One such layer, of grey sand, contained charcoal flecks. The layer was 9m wide along the length of the trench and

0.4–0.5m deep. It ran eastwards from 114 and underlay the brown ploughsoil. There were no defining limits to the layer; no features were observed in it, and no finds were recovered from it. Its function was not clear.

*Excavation of pipelines along the Dundalk (202–102) and Barn (60–62) roads*
This commenced at Pumphouse 1 and ran northwards. The trench was excavated through hardcore overlying a layer of gravel in a light brown clay matrix; this stratigraphy remained fairly consistent along the length of the trench. The trench varied in depth from 1.5m to 4m depending on the design of the pipe-work. Three drainage features were the only features observed along this length. All were continuations of drains running westwards under the road, from the east side of the road, and were modern in date. All three drains were between 104 and 103. No archaeological features or layers were observed along this stretch of pipeline.

Excavation of the pipeline took place along the Barn road (60–62), rising up with the natural slope here. Brown boulder clay lay under the road surface to a depth of 2.5m. However, moving eastwards rock was exposed closer and closer to the surface until eventually it was exposed immediately under the road surface and progress became very slow. No archaeological features or layers were observed along this stretch of pipeline.

*Excavation of pipeline (35–41) westwards to the Ardee road and from 41 northwards to the treatment plant area (41–43)*
Sod clearance and topsoil-stripping generally down to depths of 0.5–0.7m were carried out along this line. A succession of grey, coarse and fine sand and gravel layers was exposed.

In the area of 39 was a widespread deposit of organic material at the uppermost levels. This had been caused by the dumping of slurry and farmyard waste from the adjoining cowsheds. Moving westwards past 36 towards 35, the natural underlying material was more clayey in nature, brown and containing large stones. It was dug to a depth of 1m.

A spur from 38 to 47 was excavated through natural sands and gravels to a depth of 1.5m.

The mixed, grey and brown gravel layers were also present in the 41–43 length.

*Test-trench beside the graveyard*
A small test-trench was excavated beside the wall of the present graveyard, as a manhole was proposed for this location. The trench measured 2m (east–west) x 3m and was 1.4m deep. The stratigraphy was as follows: hardcore, overlying rubbish mixed with loose, brown clay, overlying dark brown garden clay. These combined layers were 0.9m deep. They overlay natural layers of grey, stony gravel overlying light brown, sandy clay.

Sherds of modern pottery were found in the three uppermost layers, but there were no finds in the lower levels. No fragments of human bone were found here.

No features or burials associated with the Early Christian monastic site were exposed here.
*Rosanne Meenan, Roestown, Drumree, Co. Meath.*

### 618. DUNLEER
Vicinity of ecclesiastical enclosure
**98E348 ext.**
Monitoring was carried out as part of the Dunleer Sewerage Scheme. Little of archaeological significance was uncovered. No indication of the enclosure, which is solely retained in the street pattern, was evident in monitoring. A small portion of pipe-trench within the enclosure indicated 18th-century garden soil deposits in the outer area of the enclosure and an undated clay floor in the inner ward. Post-medieval metalled and cobbled surfaces and drains, associated with the railway and the Black Mill (AD 1845), were recorded.
*Cara Murray, IAC Ltd, 8 Dungar Terrace, Dun Laoghaire, Co. Dublin.*

### 619. ATHCLARE CASTLE, DUNLEER
Tower-house
**30556 28625**
**SMR 18:40**
**99E0337**
The site of Athclare Castle is south of the town of Dunleer. The castle itself is built of coursed limestone and greywacke rubble with limestone quoins. It has a batter and is three storeys high over a north–south barrel vault. The proposed development is an extension to the west side of the castle on the site of a previously demolished building.

Test-trenching was carried out on the site. Trench 1 was excavated parallel to the existing building in a north to south direction and was 8m long, 1.1m wide and 0.55m deep. Modern driveway gravel extended to a depth of 0.1m, below which a layer of red brick and stone rubble extended to 0.35m, where yellow boulder clay was exposed. No features or finds were evident.

Trench 2 was excavated parallel to Trench 1 in the area of the proposed development and was 10m long, 1.1m wide and 0.6m deep. Gravel extended to 0.1m, with brick, stone, sand and rubble extending to 0.25m. Directly below this lay natural, yellow boulder clay. No features or finds were evident.

Trench 3 was excavated in the area of the proposed septic tank and was 3.2m long, 1.4m wide and 2.1m deep. The sod extended to a depth of 0.1m and overlay a stony topsoil that extended to 0.35m and rested directly on natural, yellow boulder clay. A field drain was uncovered at a depth of 0.35m, composed of loose stones (0.05–0.1m) running north-east to south-west. The boulder clay extended to a depth of 1.1m, at which point rock was evident. Apart from the drain, no other features were evident, and no finds were recovered.

Trench 4 was excavated north-west of Trench 3 and was 1m long, 1m wide and 0.8m deep. The sod extended to a depth of 0.12m, below which a stony layer extended to 0.3m and rested directly on boulder clay. No finds or features were evident.

Trench 5 was excavated on the proposed percolation area and was 1m long, 1m wide and 0.8m deep. The sod extended to a depth of 0.12m, below which a stony, brown layer of clay extended to a depth of 0.3m, where the boulder clay was exposed. No features or finds were evident.

In conclusion, it would appear that the earlier

dwelling and its foundation were destroyed in their entirety. Owing to the absence of archaeological deposits in the area, no further work is required.
*Deirdre Murphy, Archaeological Consultancy Services Ltd, 15 Trinity Street, Drogheda, Co. Louth.*

### 620. DROMIN JUNCTION, DUNLEER
Near possible earthwork
30377 29040
SMR 18:58
99E0418

Monitoring took place of two proposed dwellings at Dromin Junction, Dunleer, Co. Louth. The site is to the south of a possible earthwork. The area of the proposed houses and septic tanks was stripped by mechanical excavator. The natural, yellow/brown shale boulder clay was revealed at an average depth of 0.2–0.4m below sod and topsoil. No features of archaeological significance were exposed in the area stripped, and no finds were recovered with the exception of a single sherd of modern ceramic. No further archaeological work was required.
*Donald Murphy, Archaeological Consultancy Services Ltd, 15 Trinity Street, Drogheda, Co. Louth.*

### 621. MAIN STREET, DUNLEER
Proximity of Early Christian monastic site
30581 28800
SMR 18:64
99E0443

The site of the proposed development, an extension to the front of an existing retail unit together with a first-floor apartment overhead, is on Main Street, Dunleer, inside the town. It is close to an Early Christian monastic site, a motte and a possible souterrain.

Monitoring of the excavation of foundation trenches revealed a layer of made-up sand and gravel extending to a depth of 1.4m. Excavation ceased at this point, as the foundation trenches were deep enough. No archaeological stratigraphy or finds were encountered. Further archaeological work is not required for this proposed development.
*Donald Murphy, Archaeological Consultancy Services Ltd, 15 Trinity Street, Drogheda, Co. Louth.*

### 622. MAIN STREET UPPER, DUNLEER
Possible early ecclesiastical/medieval
3057 2879
99E0696

Testing was carried out at Upper Main Street, Dunleer, from 6 to 9 December 1999 on the site of a proposed commercial and residential development.

The site is a short distance south-west of the parish church with its surrounding churchyard, which has been identified as the probable location of an early medieval ecclesiastical site. This identification is strengthened by the occurrence here of a number of Early Christian cross-inscribed slabs. The nearby motte and the 14th/15th-century church tower confirm the continuance of the site through the later medieval period into recent and modern times.

Nine cuttings were opened, eight in the main area of the site and the ninth extending the length of the access road. Of particular concern was the possibility of any surviving medieval structures or features associated with the street frontage.

A consistent stratigraphy was revealed across the entire site, with topsoil overlying a ploughsoil that in turn came down onto natural deposits. This reflects the almost exclusive use of the site for tillage and cultivation. In the south-eastern corner of the site, immediately adjacent to an existing house, was evidence of concrete slabs that are probably the remains of animal sheds. There was no evidence of any previous structures associated with the street frontage.

As no archaeological features, deposits or artefacts were recovered from the trenches excavated, this site can be considered as having been archaeologically resolved.
*Daniel Leo Swan, Arch-Tech Ltd, 32 Fitzwilliam Place, Dublin 2.*

### 623. DUNLEER–DUNDALK MOTORWAY
*Fulachta fiadh*, pits, souterrain and rath
97E0485 ext.

Monitoring of topsoil-stripping and drainage works associated with the Dunleer–Dundalk Motorway continued. Seven previously unrecorded archaeological sites were found and excavated. They are described under their townland headings: Braganstown (No. 545 above), Charleville (No. 555 above), Drumleck (No. 592 above), Newrath (Nos 629 and 630 below) and Whiterath (No. 642 below).
*Cóilín Ó Drisceoil, 6 Riverview, Ardnore, Kilkenny, for Valerie J. Keeley Ltd.*

### 624. FAUGHART UPPER
Earthwork site (possible)
230619 231272
SMR 4:38
98E0541

Monitoring of topsoil-stripping for a proposed residential development was conducted on this site, which is at the bottom of the east slope of Faughart Hill, on which stands the significant Early Christian monastic foundation of St Brigid. It is close to two ringforts.

Stripping by mechanical excavation revealed sod and topsoil coming down directly onto shelly boulder clay at average depths of 0.15–0.3m. No archaeological features were exposed, and no finds were made.
*Donald Murphy, Archaeological Consultancy Services Ltd, 15 Trinity Street, Drogheda, Co. Louth.*

### 625. HARRISTOWN
*Fulacht fiadh*
300019 290971
99E0498

Monitoring on the Ardee Link Road led to discovery of the site. It was excavated over twelve weeks from September to November 1999. The site was fully excavated within the take of the road, but part of the archaeological deposit ran off the road.

The burnt stone deposit was up to 25m long, 10m wide and 1.5m deep. A trough and hearth were excavated on the highest part of the site, close to the north edge of the road-take. A charcoal sample recovered from the hearth has been sent for dating.

Two curvilinear ditches were cut into the burnt stone mound on the southern edge of the site, and some stretches cut into the underlying subsoil. These features contained substantial quantities of metal slag, which were also present in the main part of the burnt mound.

Numerous flints, several sherds of Bronze Age pottery and a part-polished stone macehead were recovered from the *fulacht fiadh* material.

Interpretation is incomplete pending expert reports, carbon dating and placing the site in a broader context with the numerous other sites discovered during construction of the Ardee Link Road.

*Carmel Duffy, The Mill Road, Umberstown Great, Summerhill, Co. Meath, for Valerie J. Keeley Ltd.*

### 626. MARSHES UPPER
Adjacent to archaeological complex
J06380455
SMR 7:120–7:127
99E0112

Monitoring of groundworks associated with a science service centre adjacent to an archaeological complex was undertaken. Five souterrains and two enclosure ditches, which were excavated by M. Gowen in 1982 (*PRIA* 92C (3), 55–121), form the archaeological complex. No archaeological materials were found.

*Cóilín Ó Drisceoil, 6 Riverview, Ardnore, Kilkenny, for Archaeological Consultancy Services Ltd.*

### 627. MONASCREEBE
Ringfort
30460 31312
SMR 4:20
99E0417

Monitoring of a proposed residential dwelling was carried out at Monascreebe, Dundalk, Co. Louth. The development site incorporates a ringfort that exists at the southern end of the field.

A buffer area of 20m was created around the monument, and the northern area of the site was stripped of topsoil. Monitoring of the stripping revealed the presence of subsoil at a depth of 0.3m below the surface. No archaeological features were encountered in the proposed development area, and no further work was required.

*Donald Murphy, Archaeological Consultancy Services Ltd, 15 Trinity Street, Drogheda, Co. Louth.*

### 628. RIVER BOYNE, MORNINGTON
Boat of unknown date
313012.14 275613.46
99E0064

An underwater investigation was carried out at two locations on the River Boyne, Cos Meath and Louth, on behalf of Drogheda Port Authority. A swim search was conducted at the site of a geophysical anomaly close to the Maiden Tower at the above coordinates. An underwater video system and lighting were used to watch the activities of divers. A series of arcs ranging from 3m to 20m was walked around a shot line, which was placed on the location of the anomaly by a global positioning system. Nothing was found that would explain the anomaly.

Archaeological trial-trenching was undertaken north of Mornington village in the river channel. The excavated material was brought to the surface through a dredge and was deposited in a sieve that was monitored by the archaeologist. Four trenches were excavated. Trenches 1–3 were excavated to between 0.5m and 0.75m deep and consisted of sand with frequent water-worn stones overlying pure estuarine sand. Trench 4 was excavated 3m below the surface, and timbers were noted protruding from the estuarine sand. Visibility was poor; however, thirteen ribs measuring 0.12m by 0.12m were noted up to 0.1m above the riverbed. They contained circular dowel-holes. The distance across the vessel from rib to rib was 2.5m. The site lay in the current shipping lane and was marked with underwater buoys. The date of the vessel is currently unknown.

*Matthew Seaver for Archaeological Consultancy Services Ltd, 15 Trinity Street, Drogheda, Co. Louth, and Management, for Archaeology Underwater, Tullamore, Co. Offaly.*

### 629. NEWRATH
*Fulacht fiadh*
303982 296472
97E0475 ext.

A burnt spread was discovered during monitoring of topsoil-stripping associated with construction of the Dunleer–Dundalk Motorway. Excavation took place from 17 to 31 May 1999.

An area 11m x 8m was identified for excavation. The east and west limits were bounded by a drainage ditch and a field boundary ditch respectively. The burnt spread was a soft, black/grey, clayey silt with frequent angular, disaggregated stones, ash and charcoal. Initial examination of the stone suggests that red sandstone formed the bulk of the deposit. One large flint flake was recovered. Ploughing and machine disturbance had severely truncated and levelled most of the deposit into four shallow, isolated spreads.

When the burnt spread was removed a trough, two hearths and two pits were revealed cut into the subsoil. The trough was subcircular, 2.5m x 1.95m x 0.75m deep, and was interpreted as such based on its size. It was filled with redeposited subsoil, ash, charcoal and burnt stone.

Two hearths were revealed near the trough. One of these was subcircular, 1.89m x 1.13m x 0.3m deep. The base of the cut was scorched orange, and it was filled with dark brown, clayey silt with frequent charcoal, ash and burnt stone inclusions. The second hearth was of irregular shape, 1.37m x 0.75m x 0.2m deep. The cut was filled with ash and charcoal.

Two small pits were found 3.9m away from the trough and hearths. The larger of these was truncated by the modern field ditch and measured 0.84m x 0.51m x 0.22m deep. The second pit was oval and measured 0.52m x 0.42m x 0.26m deep. Both pits were filled with light grey, sandy silt containing burnt stone, ash and charcoal.

An unidentified coin and white chinaware were found in the fill of the field boundary ditch, and three flint flakes were found in the topsoil. It is hoped to obtain radiocarbon dates from charcoal samples recovered.

*Cóilín Ó Drisceoil, 6 Riverview, Ardnore, Kilkenny, for Valerie J. Keeley Ltd.*

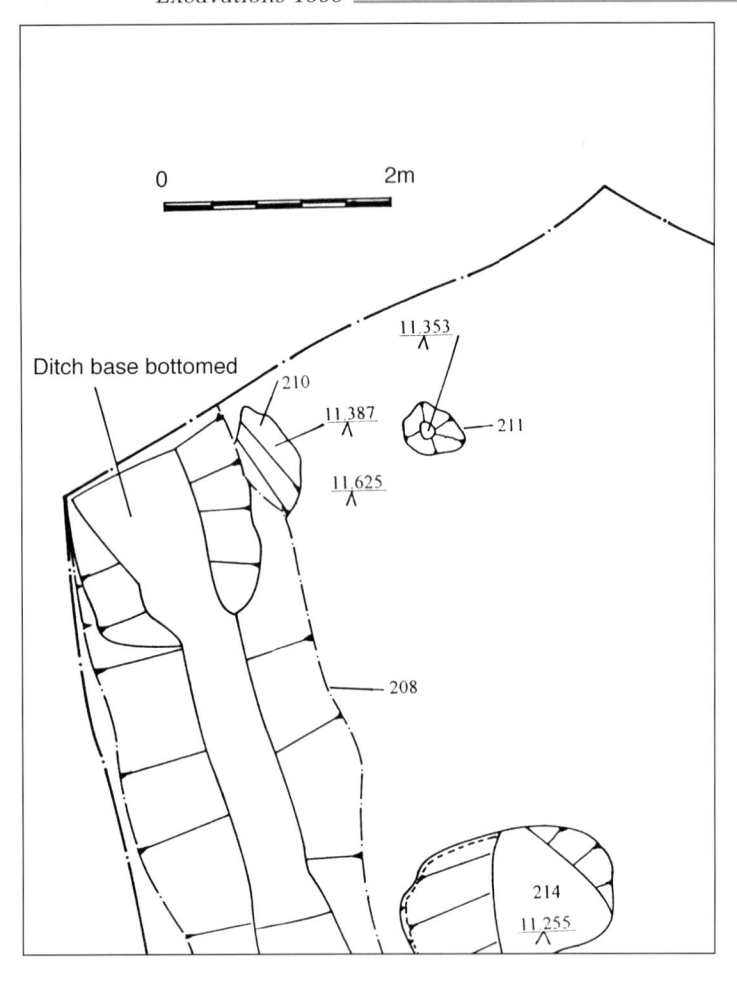

Post-excavation plan of site at Newrath (No. 629).

**630. NEWRATH**
Pit
304003 296511
97E0475 ext.

A circular pit was discovered during monitoring of topsoil-stripping along the route of the Dunleer–Dundalk Bypass Motorway. Excavation took place on 13 and 25 May 1999 and uncovered an isolated circular pit, 1.25m in diameter x 0.1m, filled with charcoal and burnt stone. No finds were recovered.

*Cóilín Ó Drisceoil, 6 Riverview, Ardnore, Kilkenny, for Valerie J. Keeley Ltd.*

**631. PHILLIPSTOWN**
Vicinity of holy well
O010683
99E0280

There is a record of a holy well in the townland of Phillipstown (Mosstown parish), Dunleer, Co. Louth, with the tradition that it was 'by the roadside to N. of R.C. church' (notes from SMR files for SMR 17:64), but its precise location was not noted.

The development in question comprises a dwelling-house with associated services. The house is one of a set of three that are to be placed along the side of the road here. This is the westernmost of the three sites, and the developer was requested by *Dúchas* to carry out a site assessment.

The site is on the top of a ridge that slopes down to the north and to the west. There is marshy ground outside the site, to its north.

In December 1998 the site of the first house (easternmost of the three) to be built here was tested (*Excavations 1998*, 152, 98E0584). Nothing of archaeological significance was exposed.

Two trenches tested the areas of the back and front of the house. A third trench tested the location of the septic tank, and a series of small pits tested the percolation area.

The same stratigraphy was exposed in all of the test-trenches and test-pits. It comprised grey topsoil 0.3–0.4m deep underlying the sod. This came down onto very sticky boulder clay, mottled grey and light brown and containing many stones. The trenches were dug to a depth of 0.8–1m, and the stratigraphy did not change through depth.

Archaeological material was not observed in any of the trenches.

*Rosanne Meenan, Roestown, Drumree, Co. Meath.*

**632. RICHARDSTOWN 1**
Isolated pit
301578 290922
99E0200

A burnt spread was discovered under topsoil and was excavated on 7 July 1999. It consisted of a spread of mid-brown, silty clay measuring 1.05m north–south by 1.25m, with frequent flecks and sparse small lumps of charcoal. On excavation a shallow, irregular-shaped pit up to 0.08m deep was uncovered. It cut through natural till. No artefacts were recovered, and a sample is currently being processed for radiocarbon dating.

*Matthew Seaver for Valerie J. Keeley Ltd, 29–30 Duke Street, Athy, Co. Kildare.*

**633. RICHARDSTOWN 3**
Isolated pit
302735 291068
99E0200

A burnt spread of dark brown, charcoal-stained, silty clay was revealed under topsoil and was excavated on 20 July 1999. It measured 0.2m north–south by 0.2m and contained frequent lumps of charcoal and fragments of burnt stone. It filled a roughly circular pit with gently sloping sides that was up to 0.1m deep and had been cut through the light brown, sandy, natural clay. No artefacts were recovered, and a sample is currently being processed for radiocarbon dating.

*Matthew Seaver for Valerie J. Keeley Ltd, 29–30 Duke Street, Athy, Co. Kildare.*

**634. RICHARDSTOWN 4**
Subrectangular pit
302214 290894
99E0200

This site was found during stripping in the east of Richardstown townland. It was a dark brown/black spread of charcoal-stained clay, 2.02m east–west by 1.9m. The deposit was up to 0.2m deep and filled a subrectangular trough cut through orange/brown, sandy, natural clay.

To the north of this a soft, orange, silty clay was revealed. A test-trench dug into this clay revealed a narrow channel filled with grey, charcoal-flecked marl at 24.768m OD. The two features did not appear to be contemporary. No further features were uncovered in this area.

No artefacts were recovered, and a sample is currently being processed for radiocarbon dating.
*Matthew Seaver for Valerie J. Keeley Ltd, 29–30 Duke Street, Athy, Co. Kildare.*

### 635. RICHARDSTOWN 6
Circular pit
300197 290954
99E0200

This site was at the western boundary of the townland, a short distance west of a large burnt mound at Richardstown. It was in an area of low-lying ground and consisted of a subcircular spread of charcoal-stained clay containing occasional heat-cracked stones. This measured 0.62m east–west by 0.42m.

Excavation revealed a subcircular pit 0.1m deep at 20.465m OD. The northern side of the pit had straight edges, while the southern side sloped gradually. The pit was cut through a thin layer of brown, peaty soil that contained frequent wood fragments c. 0.02m thick. It also cut the underlying light yellow/brown, compact, sandy clay.

To the south-west of the pit was a fan-shaped cut filled with silty, brown clay with no inclusions. This opening connected to the pit and bottomed at 20.537m OD. No artefacts were recovered, and a sample is currently being processed for radiocarbon dating.
*Matthew Seaver for Valerie J. Keeley Ltd, 29–30 Duke Street, Athy, Co. Kildare.*

### 636. RICHARDSTOWN
Burnt mound
301352 291028
99E0465

This site was uncovered during monitoring of a drainage pipe close to the River Dee. It consisted of a substantial portion of a burnt mound of fire-cracked stone and charcoal-stained clay measuring 9.8m east–west by 11.5m. This underlay up to 0.6m of ploughsoils and silts that had probably resulted from flooding. The mound was up to 0.38m thick and had probably been considerably higher in the past but had been lowered through agricultural activity. The mound was cut to the south by a substantial east–west ditch that pre-dated the 19th century.

The burnt mound overlay a layer of grey marl that was cut by a subrectangular trough 2.4m long and 1.4m wide. It was lined with a charcoal layer that probably represented a burnt wooden lining. The base of the trough was cut by fourteen post-holes 0.08–0.1m wide and 0.1–0.19m deep. The post-holes mirrored each other on either side of the trough. The burnt stone overlay a thin layer of peat that contained some bone and charcoal. This in turn overlay natural gravels. No hearth was found during the excavations. Part of the mound remained unexcavated as it lay outside the land-take.

A range of samples was taken, including geological, wood and charcoal samples for species identification and radiocarbon dating. It is also hoped to calculate a minimum number of uses for the mound from the remains.
*Matthew Seaver for Valerie J. Keeley Ltd, 29–30 Duke Street, Athy, Co. Kildare.*

### 637. RICHARDSTOWN
Archaeological complex
291050 299894
99E0526

In September 1999 archaeologists monitoring the line of the new Ardee to Dunleer road reported the discovery of an area of intense prehistoric activity on a low gravel ridge, overlooking the River Dee (*An Níth*). The site was first identified as a series of cut and burned features exposed during small-scale quarrying on the top of the ridge. A rescue excavation was undertaken on behalf of *Dúchas* The Heritage Service.

An area measuring 15m x 30m was excavated. Although the features on the site were severely truncated by ploughing, three distinct phases of activity were identifiable. Although definitive $^{14}$C dates have yet to be obtained, the phases have been putatively dated to the Neolithic and Bronze Age periods on the basis of the material assemblage found in the features.

The partially burnt remains of a subrectangular plank-built structure, probably a house, represented the earliest phase of activity on the site. The house was defined on three sides by a foundation or bedding trench. The northern side of the house was markedly curved. Its long axis was orientated north-north-west/south-south-east, and it measured 11.4m

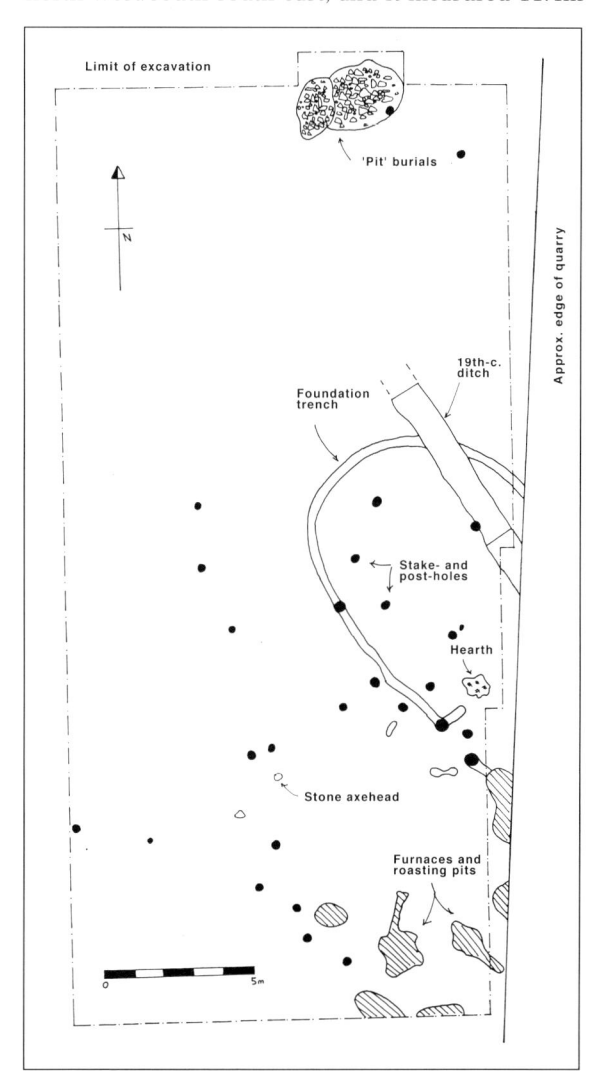

Preliminary sketch plan of site at Richardstown (No. 637).

x 7.54m. It had an internal arrangement of at least six large post-holes and had at least two, if not three, external post-holes. There were also three large post-holes along the line of the foundation trench. The full extent of the structure was not recovered, however, owing mostly to the damage caused by the quarrying, as well as to interference from the Later Bronze Age pits. The surviving portions of the house indicate that it consisted of at least one large room, and probably two, with a short internal division extending at a right angle from the foundation trench near its south-western end. The entrance or doorway appears to have been at the same point, as indicated by a gap in the trench and two large, flanking post-holes. A small hearth was found just inside the doorway. Neolithic artefacts recovered from these features and associated pits include retouched flint blades and a polished sandstone axehead.

Bronzeworking was the second phase of activity on the site. The features uncovered, some of which cut across the house, include what appears to be a quatrefoil-shaped furnace with four flues and a vent, an irregular, bowl-shaped furnace, two large roasting pits and three pits filled with ash and charcoal-rich soil. Bronze slag and a number of sherds of coarseware pottery were found in the fill of the furnace.

The third phase of activity on the site may also date to the Bronze Age. It consisted of two large pit burials, one clearly post-dating the other, at the highest point of the ridge to the north of both the house and bronzeworking area. A token deposit of cremated bone was recovered from the base of the second, later pit, but there were no surviving human remains in the first. A number of flint flakes were found in the stone- and clay-filled upper fill of both pits. A stake-hole on the southern edge of the earlier pit suggests that the burials were also marked in some way above ground.

The line of a 19th-century field drain that ran across the area of the house was also uncovered and partly excavated.

After the excavation was completed, the site was returned to the landowner, who, it is understood, intended to continue quarrying.
*Emmet Byrnes for* Dúchas *The Heritage Service, 6 Ely Place Upper, Dublin 2.*

## 638. SHEETLAND ROAD, TERMONFECKIN
Anglo-Norman palace
**313823 280282**
**99E0077**

An assessment of a proposed residential development at Sheetland Road, Termonfeckin, was carried out in February 1999. The site is to the west of the bawn of the medieval Archbishop's Palace on the north side of Sheetland Road. The proposed development involves the construction of 36 houses, and thirteen trenches were excavated across the site.

No archaeological features or objects were recovered in any of the trenches, and it would appear that this area was outside the medieval settlement. It was concluded that the proposed development would not have any archaeological impact.
*Donald Murphy, Archaeological Consultancy Services Ltd, 15 Trinity Street, Drogheda, Co. Louth.*

## 639. STRAND ROAD, TERMONFECKIN
Early Christian monastery
**O14148044**
**98E0406 ext.**

An assessment carried out at Strand Road, Termonfeckin, in December 1998 revealed the presence of archaeological deposits and features on the site of a proposed residential dwelling (*Excavations 1998*, 153–4). Further work was carried out in March 1999 under an extension to the existing licence. The site is within the suggested outer enclosure of the Early Christian monastery of St Feichin, to the south of the site of the high cross and to the north of a holy well. The site has been under cultivation since the 1840s and probably before.

Twelve trenches were excavated in the area of the proposed development. These indicated the presence of deposits over much of the site. A medieval ploughsoil horizon was evident over much of the middle part of the site, and it was clear that several features cut into the boulder clay occurred below this level. Two pits in Trenches 4 and 8 appeared to represent medieval activity, while linear cuts in Trench 4 indicate the presence of plough furrows also of possible medieval date. Redeposited boulder clay and stone settings evident in Trench 6 were undated but probably form part of structural remains such as those of a house. A deposit of charcoal and oxidised clay was evident below a loam layer containing shell and animal bone in Trench 7. Linear cuts in Trenches 11 and 12 are probably medieval or earlier in date.

Further archaeological excavation and monitoring were recommended for specific areas of the site before further development.
*Donald Murphy, Archaeological Consultancy Services Ltd, 15 Trinity Street, Drogheda, Co. Louth.*

## 640. KNOCKABBEY, THOMASTOWN
Tower-house
**N929988**
**SMR 11:80**
**99E0260**

Monitoring was carried out at Knockabbey, Thomastown, Co. Louth, in July and August 1999. Knockabbey is the former residence of the Bellews, the Tennisons and the O'Reillys, and the estate house is made up of five phases of building and alteration, dating from the 15th to the 20th century.

Phase I, medieval, *c.* 15th/16th century, is the construction of the tower-house. Phase II, post-medieval, around the mid-17th century, is the construction of a T-shaped building to the west of the tower-house and the subsequent enlargement of the fenestration (Phase IIa, *c.* 1700). Phase III, around the mid-18th century, is the renovation of the T-shaped building. Phase IV, around the mid-19th century, is the construction of new wings to the south and east of the tower-house; and Phase V, *c.* 1925, is the rebuilding of the southern range and the interior of the tower-house after an extensive fire.

This monitoring relates to the Phase I building, which was subject to renovation work between July and August 1999. The focus of the monitoring was on the removal of the flagged floor at ground-floor level in the tower-house, to prevent rising damp. The flagged floor was relaid *in situ* after the insertion of a new damp-proof course.

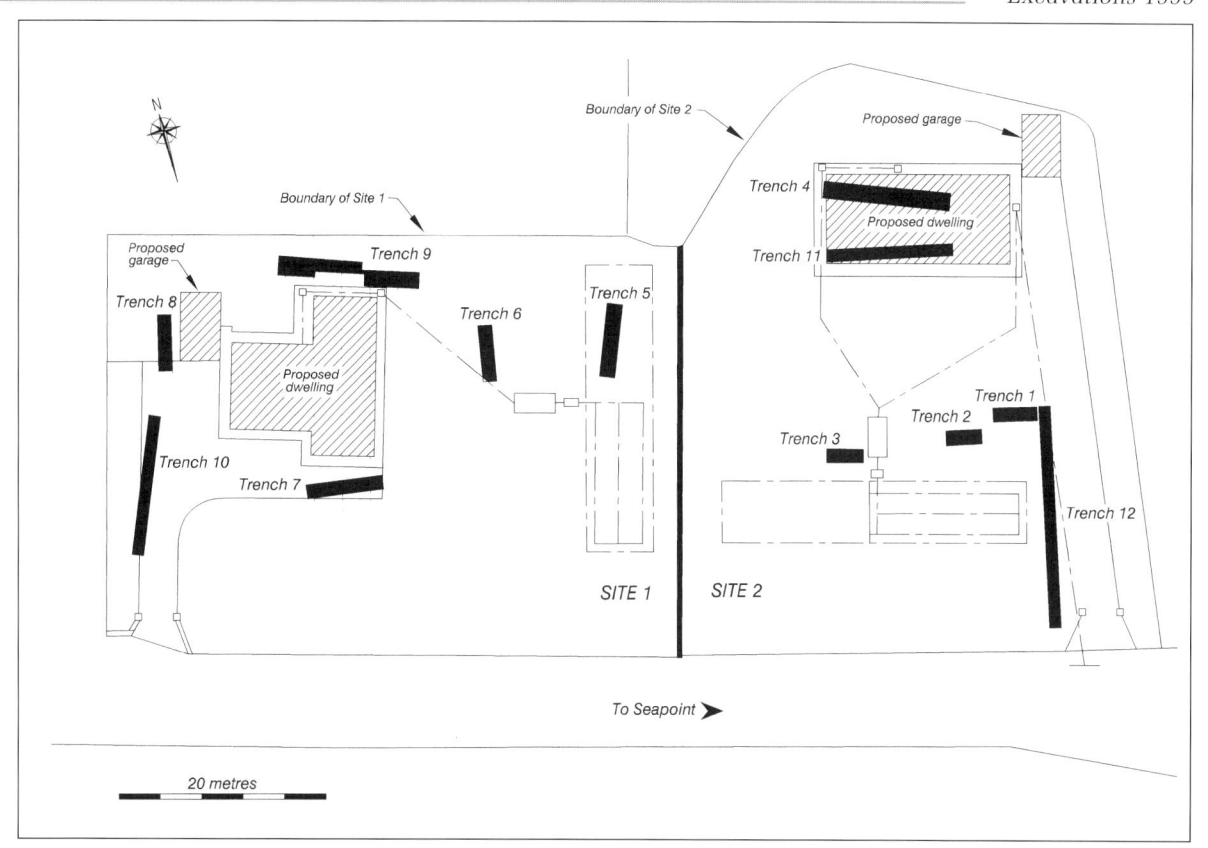

Detail of site at Strand Road, Termonfeckin, showing location of trenches.

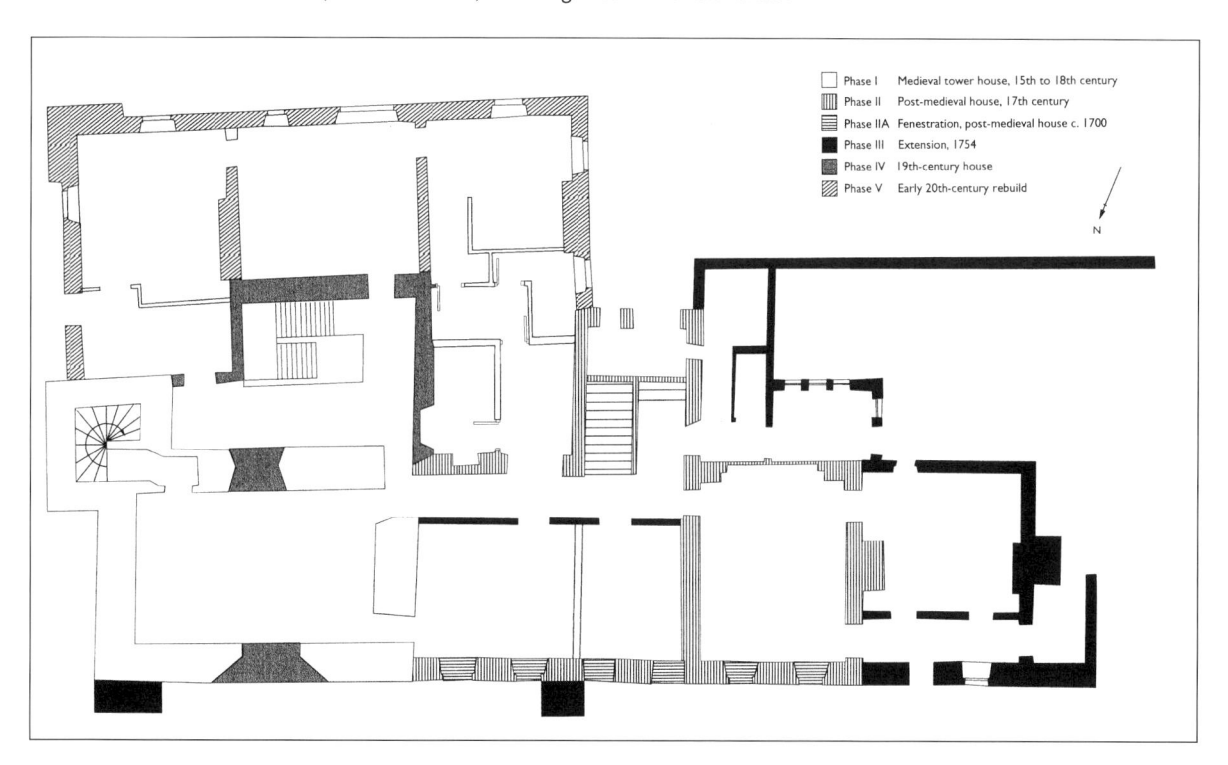

Plan of Knockabbey, Thomastown.

Plasterwork was removed from the internal walls in the upper floors of the tower-house, and portions of the external, rendered, six-bay façade of the 17th-century T-shaped building fell away to reveal evidence of the early fenestration of the building. It is suggested that, stylistically, the fenestration is Queen Anne in date (*c.* 1700).

The monitoring at ground-floor level in the tower-house revealed that natural boulder clay formed the foundation for the tower-house. A relatively uniform layer of clay that may have formed an earlier floor surface pre-dating the flagstones overlay the natural clay; however, no datable finds were identified. The surface of the possible clay floor was altered and overlain by sand and mortar layers that formed the bed for the stone-flagged floor. These deposits included red brick and stone that indicated a *terminus post quem* for the floor in the post-medieval period. The surface below the sand and mortar layers was rough, and no evidence for occupation (charcoal flecking etc.) was revealed during the monitoring.

*Edmond O'Donovan, Margaret Gowen & Co. Ltd, 2 Killiney View, Albert Road Lower, Glenageary, Co. Dublin.*

### 641. CHAPEL LANE, TULLYALLEN
Vicinity of church
N969518
99E0329

A condition of planning permission required a site assessment before development. The development site was *c.* 80m east of the site of a late medieval church (SMR 24:1) surrounded by a graveyard, which may be built on the site of an earlier church. There are four holy water stoups in the graveyard (SMR 24:2:4), which may also be late medieval.

Two trenches tested the locations of the front and back walls of the proposed bungalow. In both trenches black garden soil overlay a grey/brown, silty material that produced fragments of brick and a sherd of black-glazed pottery, thereby suggesting an earliest date of the late 18th century. Natural was an orange/brown, stony boulder clay, and no archaeological features or artefacts were observed.

The grey/brown, silty material may have been laid down to provide a level surface in this location—the laneway to the west slopes down from north to south, while the development site is flat, suggesting that the site had been levelled artificially. This proposition is further strengthened by the fact that the grey/brown, silty material was deeper in Trench 1, at the south of the site. The previous landowner informed the writer that similar levelling had been carried out when an orchard was cleared about 25 years ago.

The spoil from the trenches was examined, but no material from any period earlier than the late 18th/19th century was observed.

*Rosanne Meenan, Roestown, Drumree, Co. Meath.*

### 642. WHITERATH
Rath and souterrain
298525 304195
99E0485

A rath and souterrain were uncovered during monitoring of topsoil-stripping associated with the construction of the Dunleer–Dundalk Bypass Motorway, along the route of a realignment of the County Road 185. Excavations are continuing at the time of writing, and a full report will be included in *Excavations 2000*.

*Cóilín Ó Drisceoil, 6 Riverview, Ardnore, Kilkenny, for Valerie J. Keeley Ltd.*

## MAYO

### 643. ASKILLAUN
No archaeological significance
SMR 85:28
99E0415

Pre-development testing was undertaken on the site of a proposed development in Askillaun, Louisburgh, Co. Mayo. The site is within the archaeological constraint of ecclesiastical remains. Five test-trenches were excavated by machine within the proposed development site. They varied between 8m and 20m long and were 1.5m wide. In all, the topsoil overlay a natural, sandy gravel. No archaeological features or finds were recovered from any of the trenches.

*Gerry Walsh, Rathbawn Road, Castlebar, Co. Mayo.*

### 644. BALLINA WASTEWATER TREATMENT PLANT, BELLEEK, BALLINA
No archaeological significance
SMR 30:53
99E0117

Mayo County Council proposes to extend and refurbish the existing wastewater treatment plant in Belleek, Ballina, Co. Mayo. The proposed development is within the archaeological constraint of SMR 30:54, a cairn. No remains of this cairn are evident above present ground level in the area marked on the constraint map. A small cairn of stones *c.* 10m in diameter lies on top of the earthwork (SMR 30:53) immediately to the north of 30:54. It may be the case that the area circled for 30:54 is the same as that for 30:53, i.e. a cairn on top of an earthwork. SMR 30:53 is over 100m from the northern edge of the proposed development.

Before testing, a subcontractor commenced work and stripped some topsoil from the proposed location of one of the trenches. The subcontractor also stripped some topsoil and commenced the digging of foundations for a sludge dewatering building outside the southern boundary of the existing treatment plant. The area stripped measures 60m x 30m and includes the compound for the temporary site offices. The partially in-place foundations of the sludge dewatering building measure *c.* 30m x 20m. The sod/topsoil layer in this area was on average 0.64m thick and lay directly above a natural, orange boulder clay. No archaeological features or finds were observed in this area.

Three test-trenches were excavated by machine, between 24m and 30m long and 2m wide. Trench 1 was inside the northern end of the existing treatment plant. It was clear from the excavation that the ground here had been disturbed and landscaped, presumably when the plant was built in 1984. No archaeological features or finds were recovered from it or any of the other trenches.

*Gerry Walsh, Rathbawn Road, Castlebar, Co. Mayo.*

### 645. ABBEY STREET, BALLINROBE
No archaeological significance
1193 2645
SMR 118:22
99E0240

Pre-development testing was carried out on 27 May 1999 in response to conditions of planning for a development consisting of the construction of two townhouses, one apartment and three garages at Abbey Street, in the northern outskirts of Ballinrobe town, Co. Mayo. These conditions were included as Ballinrobe town is a recorded monument and the site is adjacent to a 13th-century Augustinian abbey. The Augustinian abbey and its graveyard were across the road to the north-north-west, 20m from the development site. A dwelling and outhouse of modern date had recently been demolished on the site.

Two trial-trenches were excavated by machine. They were orientated north-west/south-east and were 21.2–22m long, 0.9–1.3m wide and 0.25–1.8m deep. The stratigraphy uncovered was similar in both trenches, consisting of rubble above concrete, cobblestones, wall foundations, a manhole, a soakage pit, topsoil and natural subsoil.

The rubble represented the foundation and fabric of the dwelling and outhouse recently demolished. The cobbles represented the original floor of the outhouse that stood at the north-west end of the site. The topsoil was a part of the garden between the dwelling and outhouse. The three wall foundations were associated with the building just demolished, as were the manhole and the soakage pit.

All the evidence from the testing was of modern occupation and activity at the site. Modern artefacts only were recovered.

*Richard Crumlish, Archaeological Services Unit Ltd, Purcell House, Oranmore, Co. Galway.*

### 646. ABBEY STREET, BALLINROBE
No archaeological significance
**SMR 118:22**
**99E0400**
Pre-development testing was undertaken on the site of a proposed development off Abbey Street, Ballinrobe, Co. Mayo. The site is within the zone of archaeological importance for the medieval town of Ballinrobe. Four test-trenches were excavated by machine within the proposed development site.

Trench 1 measured 35m x 1.5m. The stratigraphy consisted of a sod/garden topsoil layer 0.27m thick directly overlying a natural, silty gravel.

Trench 2 measured 35m x 1.5m. At the western end of the trench a garden topsoil 0.3m thick directly overlay a stony topsoil 0.45m thick, which produced some modern glass and white-glazed pottery. The stony topsoil directly overlay a natural, orange boulder clay. Midway along the trench the garden topsoil 0.84m thick directly overlay a natural, orange boulder clay. At the eastern end of the trench the sod and stony topsoil 0.3m thick directly overlay a natural, orange boulder clay.

Trench 3 measured 10m x 1.5m. Approximately 0.1m depth of garden topsoil had been stripped from this area and replaced by a layer of stone (0.15m thick) by the developer. At the northern end of the trench the natural bedrock directly underlay this stone layer. In the remainder of the trench underlying the builder's stone layer was a layer of large boulders and stone fill up to 1.3m thick. This is of relatively recent origin and may have come from the dredging of the adjacent River Robe. Directly underlying the boulder layer was the natural limestone bedrock and in places a natural, orange boulder clay.

Trench 4 measured 30m x 1.5m. At the western end of the trench the garden topsoil 0.2m thick directly overlay a sheet of natural limestone bedrock Midway along the trench a redeposited natural boulder clay 0.15m thick directly underlay the garden topsoil. An old sod layer 0.21m thick, which produced some tin and plastic, directly underlay the redeposited boulder clay. Underlying the old sod layer was a light brown clay 0.55m thick, which produced some modern glass. The light brown clay directly overlay a natural, orange boulder clay. At the eastern end of the trench a light brown, sticky clay 0.8m thick directly underlay the garden topsoil. This sticky clay, which directly overlay the natural limestone bedrock and in places a white, silty gravel, produced some modern white-glazed and Willow Pattern pottery.

No archaeological features or finds were recovered from any of the trenches.

An examination of all the other areas on the site where construction work had taken place produced no evidence of any archaeological features or finds.
*Gerry Walsh, Rathbawn Road, Castlebar, Co. Mayo.*

### 647. BALLINSMAULA
*Fulachta fiadh*
**99E0106**
Two *fulachta fiadh* and two burnt spreads were excavated under this licence, which was initially issued for testing a possible *fulacht fiadh* identified by Gerry Walsh in the environmental impact statement for the Ballinsmaula/Knock/Claremorris Bypass. Hand-testing confirmed the suspected site as a *fulacht fiadh,* and the licence was extended to cover full excavation of this site and three other burnt spreads revealed by topsoil removal in the immediate vicinity of the first site. Excavation was carried out between the beginning of March and the end of August 1999.

Site I was found during topsoil removal and consisted of a thin layer of fire-shattered stones. It was a flat deposit with no suggestion of a mound structure, varied from 0.28m to 0.2m deep and measured 8m east–west by 4.8m. Although this was a deposit of burnt stone, there was very little trace of the usual sooty/charcoal matrix normally associated with such deposits. The site was crossed by drains, some of which seemed to be part of a large herringbone system draining the fields around the site. Redeposited boulder clay was noted on the north-west end of site. The site, including redeposited boulder clay, was resting in a wide hollow in the natural; it appears that all this material was dumped here to level off the field.

No archaeological features were found. Struck chert pieces including some scrapers were recovered, but none were in direct association with the burnt stone deposit.

Site II was found during topsoil removal and occupied an area measuring 26m north–south x 15m. It consisted of three discrete pockets of burnt stone revealed at the south, west and north ends of the site; the intervening area between these pockets was filled with featureless peat. Four pits were found dug into the boulder clay, three were adjacent to/under the north pocket of burnt stone, and one was adjacent to the west pocket. The site was crossed by two drains that were part of the large herringbone system crossing these fields; a third, older drain crossed the site on the west side. One of the pits, at the north end, had been slightly cut by digger toothmarks, and the west pit was truncated by the third drain. None of this disturbance was obvious before excavation, suggesting that it all occurred before road excavation. This, and the patchy nature of the burnt stone here, was probably caused by drainage and land-levelling in the area.

Site III was noted at environmental impact statement stage by Gerry Walsh and identified as a possible *fulacht fiadh*; test excavation was recommended. It was the classic kidney-shaped mound running north–south with a depression on its west edge indicating a possible trough. A test-trench cut from north to south across the mound revealed burnt stone, and the licence was extended to cover full excavation. A large mound of burnt stone was revealed, measuring 29.55m north–south by 18.7m with a maximum height of 0.68m. A large, nearly perfectly circular boiling pit was found on the west edge of site, with maximum dimensions of 1.5m north–south by 1.53m and 0.24m deep. Two wooden stakes were found driven into the boulder clay on the south-east and north-east edges of this pit; the cutmarks that sharpened these stakes were obvious, and they both retained bark. A smaller pit was also found; it was no more than 1m in diameter and was revealed on the south-east edge of the site. Underlying the burnt stone, more or less at the centre of the mound, were two layers of burnt timbers.

Finds from the site were pieces of struck chert and flint including some scrapers.

Site IV was discovered during topsoil removal; it was on the edge of the road-take, on a shoulder of peat left by road excavation. It was an extremely disturbed spread of burnt stone running alongside a field boundary; its maximum dimensions were 7m north–south by 4m and it rested on peat that rose to a height of 1.5m above natural. The deposit was varied, only patches of charcoal/sooty clay matrix were apparent, and most of the burnt stone was resting in peat. This and the position of the deposit on top of such a depth of peat suggested that the spread of burnt stones had been redeposited here, possibly when the farmer's drain abutting the site to south was being constructed.

Running out north from under this burnt material and visible in the section of the road excavation was a linear arrangement of timbers. These were set at a depth of 0.77m below sod level and ran northwards for a distance of 15.6m. In section the timbers suggested the presence of a bog trackway, but excavation revealed that this was not the case and that they were probably deposited by river action. No archaeological features or artefacts were found.
*Joanna Nolan, c/o Bypass site office, 'Thornhill', Ballyhaunis Road, Claremorris, Co. Mayo.*

### 648. BALLINSMAULA
Enclosure
13595 27708
SMR 101:27
99E0176

This site is designated as an enclosure on the 1st edition 6-inch OS map. It is marked as a quarry on the 2nd edition OS map and in the Sites and Monuments Record. The 1984 GSI aerial photograph shows the area as a large quarry. When the site was initially inspected in 1994 the area of the site and a large part of the surrounding ground were an open quarry. Since then, the whole area was backfilled, levelled and reseeded; no surface traces of quarrying or of the archaeological site survived.

Testing was carried out on behalf of Mayo County Council within the area where the enclosure once stood, before the construction of Phase 1 of the Knock–Claremorris Bypass. Three test-trenches were mechanically excavated. The deposits revealed in all three trenches suggested several episodes of quarrying, backfilling and finally levelling.

Topsoil-stripping of the area was monitored during road construction. No archaeological finds or features were revealed on the site.
*Angela Wallace, Margaret Gowen & Co. Ltd, 2 Killiney View, Albert Road Lower, Glenageary, Co. Dublin.*

### 649. BALLYGLASS
No archaeological significance
G094379
99E0496

A one-day pre-development test excavation was undertaken at this site, which was not recorded as a monument but is 100m to the west of the smaller court tomb in Ballyglass excavated by Seán Ó Nualláin in 1968 and 1972. The site appeared as an irregular-shaped earthen mound with maximum dimensions of 14m by 19m and up to 1m high.

Two trenches revealed the mound to be redeposited gravel material with no clear structure or stratigraphy and no features such as a bank or surrounding ditch, and it was of no archaeological significance.
*Gretta Byrne, Céide Fields Visitor Centre, Ballycastle, Co. Mayo.*

### 650. BARRACK STREET, BALLYHAUNIS
Monitoring
99E0551

Monitoring of pipe-laying in Barrack Street, Ballyhaunis, was undertaken over two weeks in September–October 1999. This street was added to the Ballyhaunis Sewerage Scheme, where Martin Byrne was previously licensed (*Excavations 1998*, 154–5, 98E0032). A 200m stretch of pipe-laying in the street was monitored. The pipe-trench was *c.* 1.5m wide.

No archaeological features or small finds were recovered from the pipe-laying.
*Gerry Walsh, Mayo County Council, Castlebar, Co. Mayo.*

### 651. CAHERDUFF
No archaeological significance
SMR 121:38
99E0591

This development site was close to a cashel. Three trial-trenches were dug before house construction, but nothing of an archaeological nature was encountered. All trenches were extremely shallow, as the limestone rock outcrop is high in the ground here.
*Leo Morahan, 110 Cimín Mór, Bearna, Galway.*

### 652. CARROWNLOUGH
No archaeological significance
14021 26859
99E0389

Two trenches were mechanically excavated down to natural subsoil at Carrownlough, Irishtown, Co.

Mayo. Both were archaeologically sterile. Further monitoring was recommended.
*Anne Connolly, Archaeological Services Unit Ltd, Purcell House, Oranmore, Co. Galway.*

### 653. CASTLEGAR
Ringfort
**SMR 101:26**
**99E0037**

A rescue excavation was carried out at Castlegar, Claremorris, on behalf of Mayo County Council before road construction for the Knock–Claremorris Bypass. The excavation site, a recorded monument, is classified as an enclosure. Before excavation an inner bank and outer ditch were seen to delimit the site. The ditch was shallow, and the bank had been reduced to a scarp except for a short distance at the south-west.

Quarrying had removed sections of the enclosing bank, and a relatively large area of quarrying had occurred at the north and the south. The enclosing element had been reused, since the 1848 OS 6-inch edition, as a field boundary. A magnetic gradiometry survey also revealed the remains of ridge and furrow cultivation overlying the entire site.

The chamber of a souterrain, built of drystone walling, is in the south-west quadrant of the interior.

The enclosure encompasses the apex of a small hillock, and in order to facilitate the road-cut a section through the western edge of the hillock was to be removed. A rectangular area 60m x 30m corresponding to the outer limits of the site was excavated before its removal by the road development. This corresponded to the outer edge of the enclosure on the western side and a small section of the interior.

The excavation revealed a widely splayed V-shaped fosse, cut into the gravel hillock, defining the outer edge of the enclosure. The fosse averaged 1.8m wide at the upper levels, tapering to 0.3m at the base. It reached a maximum depth of 2m. The ditch was backfilled in three stages. The upper fill appeared to be modern, while the layers below appeared to have been a deliberate backfill, perhaps in antiquity. Sandy clay at the base of the ditch indicated that it had been open for some time before the primary ditch fill.

There was no evidence found during the excavation for an internal bank. Along the northern edge of the site the bank had been removed by quarrying. Elsewhere in the excavation the bank is likely to have been levelled during the construction of tillage ridges that were seen to cover the excavation area once the sod had been removed.

A subcircular pit averaging 1.3m in diameter and 1.2m deep was revealed 15m west of the enclosing ditch, on the outer edge of the excavation area. There were no finds within the pit fill to indicate a probable date or function, and it may have been an extraction pit. There were no other features outside the line of the ditch, and natural gravel was reached quickly in this area once the topsoil had been removed.

Limited excavation of the interior revealed the remains of a creep and a second souterrain chamber extending at a lower level in a north-east direction. A narrow cobbled pathway was also uncovered leading towards the creep. The souterrain chamber and the area around it were backfilled, and the features within the interior were not fully resolved.

The finds were blue glass beads, a fragment of a decorated glass bracelet, whet stones and a bone knife handle. The broken base of a rotary quern and a holed stone, which may be a loom weight, were also uncovered. Animal bone was found within sealed contexts of the ditch fill. Worked chert was found in the topsoil, and clay pipe stems and modern pottery were found in association with the disturbed areas of quarrying.
*Suzanne Zajac, 1, Chapel Lane, Killala, Co. Mayo.*

### 654. CASTLEGAR
Heat-fractured stone deposits
**99E0051**

Testing for archaeological remains was undertaken at this location on the Knock–Claremorris Bypass, Co. Mayo, as the route of the proposed road passed close to earthworks of possible archaeological significance. An area of 125m by 46m was stripped to undisturbed subsoil. Surface finds retrieved from the area before testing were a fragment of a decorated rotary quern and a fragment of roughly hewn sandstone masonry.

Testing showed that the area had been substantially quarried out and then filled over in the recent past. No features or deposits associated with the possible earthworks were present. A deposit of peat, the only *in situ* natural layer apart from the subsoil to survive within the test area, was identified at the edge of the quarry. Removal of the peat revealed two disturbed deposits of heat-fractured sandstone. These were fully excavated by hand under an extension to the licence.

The largest deposit of heat-fractured stone reached a maximum length of 7.5m and was 0.1–0.2m thick. Recent machine-dug pits cut both of the deposits. Most of the burnt material was affected by modern disturbance. The excavation did not identify any other features, finds or deposits.
*Paula King, Westport Road, Castlebar, Co. Mayo.*

### 655. CASTLEGAR
Mound
**99E0072**

This site was identified by Gerry Walsh during the assessment of the route of the Knock–Claremorris Bypass as being of possible archaeological significance. It consists of a mound that measures 17.75m north–south by 14.35m. It reaches a height of 0.73m above the surrounding ground surface.

The route of the proposed road encroached on the eastern edge of the mound. Testing, followed by excavation, incorporated an area of 17m east–west by 12.5m at the eastern side of the site. The remaining part of the mound was not investigated. All testing and excavation were carried out by hand. The investigation identified but did not remove features of possible archaeological significance, as they were not affected by the development.

The excavation revealed modern features and ones of possible archaeological significance. The modern features were a series of furrows and a later stone feature, possibly a robbed-out wall. Part of a kerb-like curved line of large stones at the base of the mound at the western edge of the excavation area is of possible archaeological significance. Seven large stones ranging in size from 0.3m by 0.3m to 0.5m by 0.8m were exposed and recorded. The remains indicated that the stones continued outside the excavation area. It was not possible to arrive at a definitive interpretation of the feature. Artefacts retrieved by the excavation included several pieces of worked chert and chert debitage from disturbed contexts.

The investigation indicated that the mound is a site of probable archaeological significance.
*Paula King, Westport Road, Castlebar, Co. Mayo.*

### 656. CLARE
*Fulachta fiadh*
**M355756**
**98E0551**

Three adjacent sites of burnt stone deposits were excavated under this licence; all were found during monitoring of topsoil removal on the route of the first phase of the Knock–Claremorris Bypass.

Site I was revealed as a low mound of fire-cracked stones resting in a sooty, charcoal-stained clay matrix; its initial flattish appearance suggested disturbance, and local information confirmed that land improvement works had occurred here in the 1960s. It is on the edge of deep bog and survived as a thin (maximum depth of burnt stone: 0.35m) deposit resting partly on boulder clay and partly on peat. It was excavated between the end of October and 4 December 1998. The *in situ* portion of the site still resting on boulder clay was a shallow spread of burnt stone measuring 5.76m north-west/south-east by 4.54m. Excavation showed that the rest of the site was disturbed; apparently it was levelled and partially pushed towards the south and south-west; disturbed patches of burnt stone mixed through the adjacent peat were encountered on this side of the site. A roughly circular boiling pit cut into the boulder clay was found on the north-east edge of the site, outside the limit of the surviving burnt stone. Finds from the site were several pieces of struck chert, including scrapers, and a polished stone axe.

Site II was a flat, fairly shallow spread of heat-fractured stone lightly mixed with charcoal-stained peat/clay. It was subrectangular with its long axis running roughly north–south. The spread measured 9m north–south by 7.8m and had a maximum depth of 0.3m. It was resting on peat that road excavation revealed reached a maximum depth of 2.8m. This, and a pocket of redeposited boulder clay abutting and partly overlying the burnt stone on the north-east, showed that this was only a redeposited spread, probably deriving from nearby drainage works that were in place before road excavation commenced. No finds were recovered.

Site III was a small, roughly circular, low mound of burnt stone revealed by topsoil removal. It lay directly on a sloping shelf of boulder clay at the edge of deep bog where the peat reached a depth of *c.* 3m. This site was excavated in January 1999.

The mound measured 4.35m north–south by 5.1m. It was a very shallow deposit ranging from 0.17m to 0.22m deep. The charcoal content in the burnt stone deposit varied; there was very little charcoal in the upper levels of the site, especially towards the centre of the mound, whereas the basal layer of the burnt stone was resting in charcoal-rich, sooty clay. This suggested that the site had suffered exposure and leaching of its uppermost layers. A roughly circular pit was found on the west edge of the site, just clear of the burnt stone deposit; it was cut into the boulder clay and had filled up with peat. No finds were recovered.
*Joanna Nolan, c/o Bypass site office, 'Thornhill', Ballyhaunis Road, Claremorris, Co. Mayo.*

**Editor's note**: Although this site was excavated during 1998, the report was not received in time for inclusion in the bulletin of that year.

### 657. LEEDAUN, CLAREMORRIS
Adjacent to Bronze Age settlement site and levelled *fulacht fiadh*
**99E0035**

This excavation was carried out before pipe-laying on the Claremorris Sewerage scheme. The site had been discovered and excavated by Gerry Walsh during a previous scheme in 1995 (Appendix 2). The wayleave for the sewerage scheme was kept as far west as the level of the land would allow, to minimise the impact on the archaeological area.

The area immediately adjacent to the previous excavation was excavated by hand. Four 5m-by-12m trenches were excavated to natural subsoil or rock. The area was disturbed by modern furrows. No definite features of archaeological interest were uncovered. A number of pieces of worked chert and flint were recovered from the topsoil, and some prehistoric pottery was recovered from the surface of the subsoil.

In addition to this excavation, twenty trial-trenches measuring 3m x 12m were opened across the wayleave at 10m intervals to the north and south of the hand-excavated area. Subsequently, the areas between the trial-trenches were stripped of topsoil. The whole area was stripped to natural subsoil or rock except for three areas that merited further investigation by hand.

These were two areas with evidence of burning. The larger measured 3.5m by 1.3m by 0.12m thick. The third was a curved cut in the subsoil with associated deposits of iron slag.
*Richard Gillespie, Westport Road, Castlebar, Co. Mayo.*

### 658. DOWAGH WEST
No archaeological significance
**11874 25558**
**SMR 121:92**
**99E0699**

Pre-development testing was carried out on 8 December 1999 in response to conditions of planning imposed on the proposed development at Dowagh West, Cross, Co. Mayo, as the proposed development is within the recorded constraint of an enclosure. The development consisted of the construction of a dwelling-house, septic tank and garage. The site was on a ridge that runs in an east–west direction across a field of good grazing land along the main Cross–Ballinrobe road (R334).

Four trenches, 10.3–22.7m long, 1–1.2m wide and 0.4–1.4m deep, were excavated by machine

The stratigraphy in three of the trenches was natural and undisturbed. The stratigraphy in the fourth consisted of topsoil, below which was natural subsoil and a thin layer of stones along a 5m section at the south-west end of the trench. Below the natural were grey boulder clay and bedrock. This layer of stone was probably the remains of a field clearance cairn that was itself cleared at a later date.

Two modern pottery sherds were recovered during the testing, which revealed no archaeological evidence. The enclosure marked in the RMP was not visible; the hachure on the OS 6-inch sheet represented a bank that was barely perceptible, if at all.

*Richard Crumlish, Archaeological Services Unit Ltd, Purcell House, Oranmore, Co. Galway.*

### 659. KILCASHEL FORT, KILCASHEL
Stone fort
**99E0531**

This stone fort in the townland of Kilcashel is marked on the first and subsequent editions of the Ordnance Survey maps. The excavations were carried out in conjunction with a programme of consolidation work on the cashel walls and in the interior of the monument undertaken by *Dúchas*. The excavations, which were concentrated on the entrance to the fort, were carried out in September–October 1999.

A trench 5.4m long and 1.25–1.3m wide was excavated through the entranceway. The removal of sod and topsoil revealed a loose layer of stones (C4) that formed the surface of the entrance passage. A spud stone at the east end was associated with this surface and indicates that a gateway or doorway spanned the entranceway. At the west end of the entranceway two post-holes suggest the presence of a doorway/gateway at this side also. Removal of C4 exposed a well-defined paving layer that extended for the length of the passage. This layer was made up of large, flat stones in the centre with smaller, rounder stones at either side. Below the paving layer, excavation revealed the original earthen surface layer of the entrance passage. Two post-holes in this layer indicate a possible door/gate feature in the east, while further activity in the west was suggested by the presence of two large pit features.

*Martin Fitzpatrick, Arch. Consultancy Ltd, Ballydavid South, Athenry, Co. Galway.*

### 660. KILTULLAGH HILL, KILTULLAGH
See No. 769 below, under County Roscommon.

### 661. KNOCK NORTH
Adjacent to souterrain
**SMR 121:42**
**99E0440**

Testing was before road realignment on the Garracloon road was carried out by Mayo County Council. An area of 70m x 8–10m was tested. The area was excavated with a mechanical digger to undisturbed subsoil or rock, which was at a maximum depth of 1m. Nothing of archaeological interest was uncovered.

*Richard Gillespie, Westport Road, Castlebar, Co. Mayo.*

### 662. LISCROMWELL
No archaeological significance
**SMR 79:1**
**99E0387**

Pre-development testing was undertaken on the site of a proposed development in Liscromwell, Castlebar, Co. Mayo. An enclosure is in the field of the proposed development, around which a buffer zone of *c.* 15m will be fenced off and left undeveloped.

Five test-trenches were excavated by machine outside the buffer zone. Each was 20m long by 1.5m. No archaeological features or finds were recovered from any of the trenches.

*Gerry Walsh, Rathbawn Road, Castlebar, Co. Mayo.*

### 663. LISDUFF/CLARE/CASTLEGAR/ BALLINASMAULA/BARNEYCARROLL/ BALLYNABREHON SOUTH
Monitoring
**98E0304**

Monitoring of topsoil removal took place on the route of Phase I of the Knock–Claremorris Bypass. This portion of the bypass was a 6km-long corridor running east of the town of Claremorris, Co. Mayo. It ranged from 40m to 60m wide, and the terrain varied from topsoil averaging 0.3–0.6m deep to bog reaching maximum depths of 4m.

The route crossed what had previously been agricultural land, and all topsoil removal was monitored. Monitoring was carried out between 30 November 1998 and 30 April 1999. Although most of the route was well away from built-up areas, a good deal of disturbance was evident. Land improvement and drainage activities had been carried out in many locations along the route, and some of the bog had been used in the past as an unmanaged dump, therefore much of the material recovered had been subject to significant disturbance before being revealed by road excavations.

Several previously unknown sites were uncovered and dealt with under separate licences. These were 98E0412, a partially destroyed *fulacht fiadh* at Clare td (excavated by Suzanne Zajac, *Excavations 1998*, 155–6); 98E0551, two partially destroyed *fulachta fiadh* and a disturbed spread of burnt stones at Clare td (see No. 656 above); and 99E0106, two *fulachta fiadh* and two disturbed burnt spreads at Ballinsmaula td (see No. 647 above). Known and suspected sites previously identified by the environmental impact statement were dealt with under separate licences (99E0037, Castlegar, see No. 653 above; 99E0051, Castlegar, see No. 654 above; 99E0072, Castlegar, see No. 655 above; 99E0106, Ballinasmaula, see No. 647 above; and 99E0176, Ballinasmaula, see No. 648 above).

*Joanna Nolan, c/o Bypass site office, 'Thornhill', Ballyhaunis Road, Claremorris, Co. Mayo.*

### 664. MAYO PARKS, MAYO ABBEY
No archaeological significance
**SMR 90:100**
**99E0049**

Pre-development testing was undertaken on the site of a proposed development in Mayo Parks townland, Mayo Abbey, Co. Mayo, in February 1999. The proposed development site is within the archaeological constraints for SMR 90:100, ecclesiastical remains.

Three test-trenches, between 20m and 28m long and 2m wide, were excavated by machine on the site of the proposed development. No archaeological features or finds were recovered from any of the trenches.

*Gerry Walsh, Rathbawn Road, Castlebar, Co. Mayo.*

### 665. MOYHASTIN
No archaeological significance
**SMR 88:50**
**99E0700**

The four foundation trenches for this house were monitored, and all contained rich topsoil overlying yellow daub or gravel. Topsoil contained some recent animal bones, various modern pottery sherds and fragments of tile. Nothing of an archaeological nature was detected.

*Leo Morahan, 110 Cimín Mór, Bearna, Galway.*

### 666. MUCKLAGH
Ringfort
**9578 28683**
**SMR 76:26**
**99E0254**

Testing was undertaken before the construction of two semi-detached holiday cottages at Mucklagh, Westport, Co. Mayo. The remains of part of an overgrown ringfort occur in the same field as the proposed development.

Four test-trenches were opened on the imprint of the two cottages. One was sited at the entrance to the development, and another was sited along the proposed avenue to the houses.

No archaeological remains, associated with the nearby ringfort or not, were uncovered during testing.

*Mary Henry, 24 Queen Street, Clonmel, Co. Tipperary.*

### 667. RAUSAKEERA NORTH
No archaeological significance
**SMR 118:144**
**99E0731**

Pre-development testing was undertaken on the site of a proposed development of three houses in Rausakeera North, Kilmaine, Co. Mayo. Part of the proposed development site is inside the zone of archaeological importance for a souterrain. Nine test-trenches were excavated by machine within the site. They varied between 10m and 20m long, and all were 2m wide. In all, the sod/topsoil overlay natural gravel or boulder clay. No archaeological features or finds were recovered from any of the trenches.

*Gerry Walsh, Rathbawn Road, Castlebar, Co. Mayo.*

### 668. ROBEEN GRAVEYARD, ROBEEN
No archaeological significance
**SMR 110:48**
**99E0278**

Pre-development testing was undertaken on the site of a proposed extension to Robeen graveyard, Robeen, Co. Mayo. The proposed extension is within the area of SMR 110:48, ecclesiastical remains. Four test-trenches were excavated by machine on the site of the proposed extension.

All trenches measured 54m x 1.5m. The stratigraphy within Trenches 1–3 consisted of a sod/topsoil layer 0.34m thick, which directly overlay a natural, light brown/white, silty gravel and in some places a natural, orange boulder clay.

At the southern end of Trench 4 the sod/topsoil, 0.4m thick, directly overlay a natural, orange boulder clay. Four metres north of the southern end of the trench the natural, light brown/white, silty gravel replaced the natural, orange boulder clay. In the northern half of the trench the sod/topsoil 0.35m thick directly overlay a natural, orange boulder clay.

No archaeological features or finds were recovered from any of the trenches.

*Gerry Walsh, Rathbawn Road, Castlebar, Co. Mayo.*

### 669. SHRULE
No archaeological significance
**SMR 122a:4 and 122a:16**
**99E0735**

Pre-development testing was undertaken on the site of a proposed development in Shrule, Co. Mayo. The development is inside the zone of archaeological importance for a church (SMR 122a:4) and an earthwork (SMR122a:16). Eleven test-trenches were excavated by machine within the proposed development.

The trenches varied in length from 11m to 20m, and all were 2m wide. In general, the stratigraphy consisted of topsoil overlying natural gravels or boulder clay. No archaeological features or small finds were recovered from any of the trenches.

*Gerry Walsh, Rathbawn Road, Castlebar, Co. Mayo.*

### 670. THE DESERTED VILLAGE, SLIEVEMORE (ACHILL ISLAND)
Multi-phase landscape
**5918 30770**
**SMR 41:00802; 42:10914**
**91E0047**

The tenth season of survey and excavation at the Deserted Village in Slievemore took place over eight weeks from 26 June to 18 August 1999. The 1999 season continued the excavation in Cuttings A, B and C in the vicinity of House #36 and at the Monk's Garden in the village of Tuar. The instrument survey continued in Tuar Riabhach and in the neighbouring village of Faiche.

*Cutting A*
Excavation continued in Trench F18 outside the north gable of House #36. Previously, a French drain had been noted here, suggesting pre-planning before the construction of this house (*c.* 1800).

Further excavation revealed an abundance of finds, all of late 19th-century date and probably belonging to the 'booley' phase of occupation, *c.* 1860–1940.

*Cutting B*
The deposits in this area have been interpreted as lazy-beds that on stratigraphical evidence seem to pre-date the construction of House #36. Underneath a mixed organic deposit were two long, rectangular deposits of a rich, orange ash that extended north–south across the cutting. This deposit appears

Cutting B, Slievemore, at the end of the 1999 season.

to have been laid down before the setting of the lazy-beds, for the purpose of 'flattening' this area for reasons unknown at present. The lazy-beds are of a fairly substantial nature but were deliberately shortened as they approached the western end of Cutting B and seem to be related to the presence of the French drain referred to above.

Excavations in F13 of Cutting B produced two tiny beads, one white and the other pale blue, parts of two shoes with metal heels and leather soles, a burnt fragment of a clay pipe stem, pieces of slag, glass, pottery and metal, and fragments of wood and charcoal. A portion of red brick had a small area of glaze on one surface.

*Cutting C*
Excavations in Cutting C revealed a series of small pits that were successively dug and refilled at different rates and at different times. It is even possible that that some were dug into previously refilled pits, such is the complex nature of the stratigraphy in this area. The function of these pits is unknown as, apart from one fragment of hematite, no diagnostic artefacts have been found. Two of the pits were covered with very similar large boulders, and there was evidence of slag adhering to the rims of two of the pits.

*Monk's Garden excavation*
Excavation this year was concentrated inside the souterrain and in the area immediately outside the entrance. The fill inside the souterrain was removed to reveal two side-walls made up of large orthostats, while the roof consisted of three large lintels that descended in height towards the rear. Underneath the innermost lintel is a 'wall' of compact clay, and below this are two upright stones set into the fill on either side of the passage. The passage curves to the east, and it is possible that it descends into a 'drop-hole' creep.

The excavation will continue in 2000.
*Theresa McDonald, St O'Hara's Hill, Tullamore, Co. Offaly.*

### 671. STREAMSTOWN
No archaeological significance
**99E0003**
Mayo County Council wishes to widen the road at a dangerous bend in Streamstown, Westport, Co. Mayo. A strip of land 4m wide is to be acquired for the scheme. The writer had noted a possible archaeological mound adjacent to the area to be acquired. This mound is not a recorded monument.

Pre-development testing of the area to be acquired was undertaken March 1999. Four test-trenches were excavated by hand. Each measured 4m by 2m. No archaeological features or finds were recovered from any of the trenches.
*Gerry Walsh, Rathbawn Road, Castlebar, Co. Mayo.*

### 672. TURIN
Tower-house
**1275 2574**
**SMR 122:01702**
**99E0719**
Pre-development testing was carried out on 14 and 15 December 1999 in response to recommendations made by *Dúchas* The Heritage Service following receipt of an impact assessment report on a proposed development at Turin townland, Kilmaine, Co. Mayo. The proposed development consisted of the restoration of Turin Castle, its conversion to a residence, including associated services, and the reduction in level of a raised area in the immediate vicinity of the tower-house. The castle stands on undulating, good-quality grassland, 2.5km south-east of Kilmaine village.

Seven trial-trenches were excavated by machine during the testing. They were 10–25.4m long, 1.1–2m wide and 0.4–1.1m deep.

The stratigraphy in the three trenches farthest from the tower-house was natural and undisturbed. The stratigraphy in the remaining four test-trenches, adjacent to three sides of the monument, consisted of topsoil above a rubble deposit 0.2–0.9m thick, above grey boulder clay and bedrock.

The artefacts recovered from the rubble deposit were red brick fragments, mortar, cut and dressed limestone blocks, several animal bone fragments, occasional oyster shells, one modern glass fragment, one modern base sherd and one clay pipe bowl fragment.

The rubble deposit was part of a raised area in the immediate vicinity of the tower-house and consisted primarily of stone, with a small amount of mortar. It would appear to be fabric from the tower-house, attested by the cut and dressed blocks recovered. The upper sections of the walls of the tower-house, which are missing, must have collapsed or been tossed onto the ground below. The modern artefacts recovered from the rubble would suggest that the collapse/demolition occurred in the last 200 years.
*Richard Crumlish, Archaeological Services Unit Ltd, Purcell House, Oranmore, Co. Galway.*

## MEATH

### 673. BALLINAVALLEY
Vicinity of archaeological complex
**N583787**
**99E0328**
The site is in the townland of Ballinvalley, which is south of the two Carnbane hills on which the Lough Crew passage tomb cemetery lies. Ballinvalley townland and Drumsawry townland to its west contain a large number of recorded monuments of all

periods. The development site is close to a dense cluster of monuments to its north-west, west and south-west. These were a cairn, cists within a barrow, and a cist (SMR 9:55) that contained vase food vessel burials, the capstone of which was decorated—this last site is the closest recorded monument to the development site. There are also standing stones and an enclosure. Three ringforts are recorded to the east of the site.

The planning permission granted by Meath County Council for a bungalow with associated septic tank, garage and driveway required pre-development testing and an archaeological impact statement to be submitted to *Dúchas* before site preparation work.

Five trenches tested the major components of this proposed development. The trenches were placed as close as possible to the foundation trenches of the house, septic tank, garage and driveway.

Trenches 1 and 3–5 did not reveal archaeological material.

A charcoal-filled feature was exposed in Trench 2, which tested the back wall of the house. Its maximum dimensions were 0.8m x 0.65m x 0.15m deep. It was found at the bottom of the ploughsoil but overlying the gravelly subsoil. Its sides were gently sloped and uneven and did not appear to have been deliberately cut. The fill was a charcoal-enriched soil with some loose stones. There were no finds. The purpose of the feature was unclear, and there were no means whereby it could be dated. No associated features were exposed in the rest of the trench.

Following the exposure of the charcoal-filled feature, monitoring was carried out during ground reduction and foundation trenching. No further features associated with the charcoal (or elsewhere on the site) were exposed.
*Rosanne Meenan, Roestown, Drumree, Co. Meath, for ADS Ltd.*

### 674. BECTIVE, SITE S
No archaeological significance
**99E0698**

The site had been selected for investigation during an earlier assessment, by Valerie J. Keeley, of the proposed realignment and widening of the R161 Trim–Navan road by Meath County Council from Bective to Balreask, carried out during February 1999. It appeared as a small basin, 50m east–west by 40m, with a number of low, curved bank features.

Five trenches, 10m x 2m, were opened by machine. The general soil profile was sod and topsoil, red/brown clay and grey gravel.

None of the trenches contained any archaeological material.
*Carmel Duffy, The Mill Road, Umberstown Great, Summerhill, Co. Meath, for Valerie J. Keeley Ltd.*

### 675. BECTIVE, AREA 1
No archaeological significance
**99E0722**

The site was selected as a potentially sensitive area during an archaeological assessment carried out by Valerie J. Keeley (1999) for the proposed realignment and widening by Meath County Council of the R161 Trim–Navan road from Bective to Balreask.

The County Council proposes to widen the existing bridge over the River Clady, and after consultation with *Dúchas* it was agreed to dig two investigation trenches, one on either side of the river.

The trenches were 10m x 2m. The northern one was 1.4m deep and contained up to 0.6m of modern rubbish building up the riverbank, underlain by red/brown clay 0.1m deep, grey silt 0.2m deep, and grey gravel in the floor of the trench, which was at the water-table. The grey silt was most likely the former flood-plain of the river. The southern trench was 1.05m deep and contained sod and topsoil, underlain by grey/brown clay up to 0.45m deep, beneath which was red/brown peat 0.4m deep, underlain by grey/green gravel, again at the water-table.

Neither trench contained any archaeological evidence, finds or structures.
*Carmel Duffy, The Mill Road, Umberstown Great, Summerhill, Co. Meath, for Valerie J. Keeley Ltd.*

### 676. BECTIVE ABBEY
No archaeological significance
**28594 25996**
**99E0095**

Before proposed road-widening and the installation of a carpark at Bective Abbey, Co. Meath, four areas were investigated in the field to the south-west of the abbey, close to the road. Four trenches, 10m x 3m, had their sod and overburden removed, but no archaeological deposits nor any material that would indicate human activity here were recovered.
*P. David Sweetman, Dúchas The Heritage Service, 6 Ely Place Upper, Dublin 2.*

### 677. BELLEWSTOWN
Mound, possible ring-ditch or barrow
**N75485475**
**SMR 36:34**
**99E0520**

Owing to quarrying by the owner of this site, a rescue excavation was carried out. The site was initially inspected by Michael Moore of *Dúchas* on 4 August 1999, who noted two ditch-like features in the southern face of the area that had been quarried. By the time the licence was issued those features had been destroyed. The site, a recorded monument, is classified as a mound 6.5m in diameter and 1.1m high surmounting a hillock of sand *c.* 8m high.

Three trenches were hand-excavated in the remaining section of the mound in the south-west quadrant of the hillock. Trench 1 was 24m long, 1.1m wide and 4.8m deep. A 0.1m layer of sod and topsoil overlay an orange/grey, sandy ploughsoil varying from 0.2m to 0.3m thick. The mound material, an orange, sandy clay, was exposed at a depth of 0.6m and extended to a depth of 0.8m. Apart from a cluster of large stones, this trench contained no features or finds.

In Trench 2, topsoil had been stripped right up to the eastern edge of the mound, exposing a ditch feature cut into the sand. The trench was excavated westwards through the mound and was 1.5m long, 1m wide and 1m deep. The ditch was 1.75m wide with an average fill depth of 0.3m, consisting of brown clay loam with a few small stones. No finds were recovered from this trench.

Trench 3 was 2.1m long, 2.1m wide and 0.8m

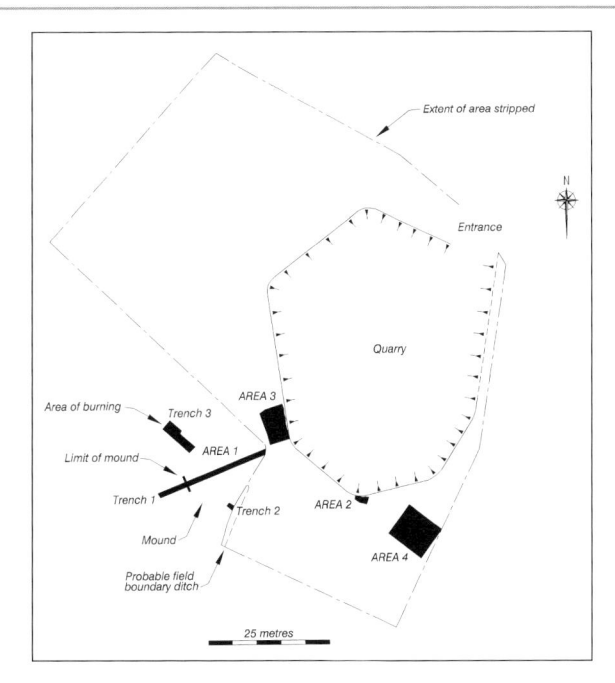

Excavated areas at site at Bellewstown.

deep. It was opened along the western part of the mound. Sod and topsoil extended to a depth of 0.45m and overlay a uniform layer of brown, dauby soil (0.42m thick) that contained a stone feature running east–west, 2m long and 0.5m wide, tapering to 0.2m at its west end. A hearth and several pits were exposed. The hearth measured 1.3m by 1.1m and contained fragments of bone and a probable tooth. A charcoal sample was taken for radiocarbon dating.

In Area 1 the remains of a stone structure of probable late medieval origin were exposed by topsoil-stripping east of the mound in the south face of the quarry. It was 1.7m long by 0.6m wide, constructed of limestone rubble and bonded with mortar. A layer of debris was visible on the floor of the quarry, probably representing the demolished wall. A bone and a 17th-century button were recovered from this debris. No further finds or features were recovered in this area.

Area 3 was a ditch and pit to the north-east of the mound, visible in the south-west face of the quarry. The features were cleaned back, revealing a semicircular pit with a stony, yellow/grey sand and a 0.05m-wide ditch of c. 0.3m depth. Both features were destroyed before proper excavation could take place.

Area 4 was some distance east of the mound in an area that had been topsoil-stripped. It measured 8m north–south by 6m and consisted of a possible timber structure with evidence of burning and numerous post-holes. A layer of yellow, fine, compacted sand was exposed, which contained frequent inclusions of charcoal and evidence of burning in places. Three burnt timber planks were removed and sent for radiocarbon dating. Near the centre a circular hearth was visible with a small cluster of stones on top. Fourteen post-holes with diameters of less than 0.2m were found in the northern section of this area, varying up to 0.5m deep. A trench pit, 2.1m by 0.16m, was also visible. All these features were obvious as brown, sandy clay staining the grey sand.

In conclusion, it is clear that both the mound and the sandy hillock are archaeologically sensitive. Indeed the areas to the east and west of the site are likely to contain other deposits. The results of this partial excavation suggest that this monument is in fact a burial mound. However, the site is under a direct threat from quarrying. It was therefore recommended that no further work be permitted on the hillock or in the immediate area.

*Deirdre Murphy, Archaeological Consultancy Services Ltd, 15 Trinity Street, Drogheda, Co. Louth.*

### 678. CABRAGH
No archaeological significance
99E0175

Archaeological monitoring was required for excavations of a private house development. The site lies c. 600m from the known monuments on Tara Hill.

The topsoil was stripped off 25m² where the house was to be built, to a depth of 0.35–0.45m, and off a 4m-wide driveway to a depth of 0.7m. It was a dark brown, sandy silt with less than 20% stones up to 0.1m across and contained nothing of archaeological significance. The foundation trench, 1m wide and up to 0.7m deep, was excavated into the subsoil. The subsoil was red/brown boulder clay and was archaeologically sterile

*Carmel Duffy, The Mill Road, Umberstown Great, Summerhill, Co. Meath.*

### 679. COLP WEST
Unknown
31179 27415
99E0472

An assessment of two possible archaeological features identified in an earlier environmental impact statement took place. The proposed development entails the construction of a new residential neighbourhood on a 130-acre site. Colp is first referred to in the Lives of St Patrick as 'Colpdai'. It contains a large number of registered monuments, including a cemetery, an enclosure, a *fulacht fiadh* and a probable medieval borough. Colp townland is within an area of archaeological potential identified in the Urban Archaeological Survey as an Anglo-Norman settlement. References are made in the Llanthony Cartularies (records of a religious foundation established in Colp in the 13th century) to a considerable number of houses, ditched field systems, roads, a millstream, a church cemetery and a causeway. Several known sites exist within the core area, including a church and enclosure, a mound, a grange and a castle.

Two features were tested: three low-visibility linear depressions 1m wide running north–south (Trenches 1–4) and a low, arcing bank up to 0.8m high (Trench 5).

Trench 1 was excavated east–west across the linear depression and measured 10m by 1m and 1m deep. Sod and topsoil extended to a depth of 0.2m and overlay the natural boulder clay. No features or finds were exposed.

Trench 2 was excavated south-west to north-east across the linear feature, measured 4m by 1m and was excavated to a depth of 0.7m. Sod and topsoil extended to 0.2m, below which orange boulder clay was exposed. No features or finds were exposed.

Trench 3 was excavated east–west across a

second linear feature, measured 4m by 1m and was excavated to a depth of 1m. Sod and peaty topsoil extended to a depth of 0.3m and directly overlay the natural boulder clay. No features or finds were recovered.

Trench 4 was excavated north of Trench 3 across a linear feature in a marshy area bounded by an east–west, waterlogged ditch. It measured 5m by 1m and was excavated to a depth of 1.3m. The sod and topsoil directly overlay orange boulder clay. No features or finds were recovered.

Trench 5, 16m long, was excavated through the 0.8m-high arced bank to a depth of 1.3m. The northerly section of the trench revealed topsoil to a depth of 0.3m above boulder clay. Within the arced bank itself the topsoil extended to a depth of 0.55m and overlay boulder clay. No features or finds were recovered.

Neither feature proved to be significant. The linear features were possibly shallow field drains or ditches, whereas the arced bank probably represents a mound of dumped material created during ploughing. As the development is very extensive and as most of sites in Colp townland have no surface trace, monitoring of all topsoil-stripping has been recommended.
*Donald Murphy, Archaeological Consultancy Services Ltd, 15 Trinity Street, Drogheda, Co. Louth.*

### 680. CORMEEN
Proximity to fort
N73688969
99E0477

The site of the proposed development is in Cormeen, *c.* 2 miles from Moynalty, close to SMR 5:60, a ringfort known locally as 'Fools Fort', measuring 39m north–south by 37m.

The proposed development consists of a bungalow, garage, septic tank and associated services. A monitoring condition was imposed by Meath County Council. Area 1, consisting of the proposed dwelling, garage and services, was stripped to a depth of 0.5m. Topsoil extended to a depth of 0.34m, below which orange boulder clay was exposed. No features or finds were evident. Area 2 was a long, narrow stretch along the south-west corner of the site in the area of the proposed driveway. Directly inside the existing gate along the west section of the site were the remains of an old shed and yard, below which a layer of manure was visible to a depth of 0.5m, below which the orange boulder clay was exposed. Further east the topsoil extended to a depth of 0.2m and directly overlay orange boulder clay.

Monitoring failed to reveal any archaeological stratigraphy. There is no visual or archaeological impact on the monument, and therefore no further archaeological work is required.
*Deirdre Murphy, Archaeological Consultancy Services Ltd, 15 Trinity Street, Drogheda, Co. Louth.*

### 681. LARRIX STREET, DULEEK
Early Christian monastic site
30452 26859
SMR 27:15
99E0464

An assessment was carried out on the site of eight proposed dwelling-houses, associated services and an access road. The site is on the south side of Larrix Street, Duleek, Co. Meath, within an area of archaeological potential as identified in the Urban Archaeological Survey of County Meath, and is a recorded monument. An Early Christian monastic site and enclosure are evident in the present street pattern around Duleek.

Four test-trenches were excavated by machine. Trenches 1–3 were excavated within the area of the proposed houses, and Trench 4 was excavated parallel to Larrix Street, crossing the line of the earlier ditch.

Trench 1 was excavated north–south to the west of the site and measured 19m by 0.7m. The sod and topsoil extended to a depth of 0.2m and lay above a post-medieval, light brown, dauby clay, which in turn lay above the natural boulder clay at a depth of 0.36m. At the south end of the trench a section of ditch was exposed extending in a south-west to north-east direction; it was at least 3m wide but extended southwards beyond the trench. The ditch was 1m deep and was visible at a depth of 0.3m below the surface. A small dump of loose stone was exposed at the north side of the ditch, which may have formed part of a collapsed drystone wall. Two sherds of 19th–20th-century pottery were recovered from the sticky, brown clay fill.

Trench 2 was excavated in the south-west corner of the site, measured 20m by 0.7m and was excavated to a maximum depth of 1.2m. A layer of light brown, sticky, moist clay was exposed at a depth of 0.3m below the sod and topsoil. This contained a single clay pipe stem, extended to a depth of 0.4m at the east end of the trench and 0.9m at the west end and lay directly above the natural boulder clay. No features were evident, and no other finds were recovered.

Trench 3 was excavated to the south of the site, measured 34m by 0.7m and was excavated to an average depth of 0.65m, with one section excavated to a depth of 2.2m. The sod extended to a depth of 0.14m and overlay a layer of fine, brown, sandy clay that contained three fragments of post-medieval pottery and a single rimsherd of unglazed medieval ware. This layer extended to the top of the natural boulder clay at a depth of 0.4m. A section of ditch

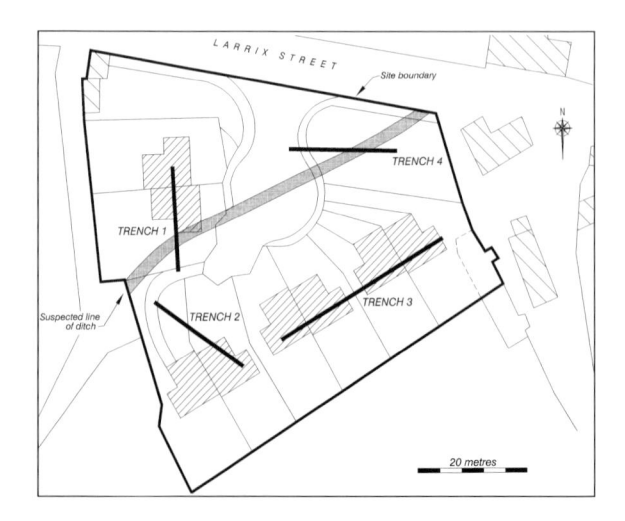

Detail of site at Larrix Street, Duleek, showing location of trenches and suspected line of ditch.

was exposed *c.* 6m from the east end of the trench, extending in a north-west/south-east direction. It was visible below the fine, brown, sandy clay and had been cut into the natural boulder clay. It was 1.8m deep, 2.7m wide at the top and 1m at the base. The fill was a grey, boulder-clay-like, wet clay, and no finds were recovered.

Trench 4 was excavated in a roughly east–west direction close to the existing entrance to the site, measured 20m by 0.7m and was excavated to a depth of 0.6m except where the ditch crossed the trench, where it was excavated to a depth of 1.6m. The sod extended to a depth of 0.2m and overlay a layer of fine, light brown clay. This in turn overlay the natural boulder clay at a depth of 0.3m. A section of ditch was exposed *c.* 5m from the east end of the trench. This appeared to extend in a south-west/north-east direction and was presumably part of the ditch that was uncovered in Trench 1. The ditch was cut into the natural boulder clay and was exposed directly below the light brown clay. It was 1.3m deep and 5m wide. All the finds recovered from the dark grey, heavy clay fill were modern in date.

Trenches 2 and 3 failed to reveal any archaeological stratigraphy, and the natural boulder clay was exposed at an average depth of 0.4m. The ground above appears to have been heavily ploughed, thereby obliterating any features that may have existed. All the finds recovered were relatively modern in date, with the exception of a single sherd of medieval ware. However, this came from a disturbed context. The ditch exposed at the end of Trench 3 may relate to the Early Christian enclosure but in all likelihood is not an enclosing ditch but an old field drain.

The ditch exposed in Trenches 1 and 4 would appear to follow the line of the Early Christian enclosure. However, this ditch appears to have been interfered with in the north-east corner of the site towards Larrix Street. Human memory records the presence of a drain in this area of the site, and the ditch was probably backfilled early in the early 20th century, as indicated by the relatively modern finds that were recovered. It is clear, therefore, that, while the ditch follows the line of the Early Christian enclosure, it has been altered in the north-east corner, where it was probably used as a drain.

The proposed development will impinge slightly on the enclosing ditch, and it was recommended that the sections of the ditches that will be disturbed by the proposed house foundations be excavated and that all ground disturbance works associated with the development be monitored.
*Deirdre Murphy, Archaeological Consultancy Services Ltd, 15 Trinity Street, Drogheda, Co. Louth.*

## 682. DUNMOE, N51 ROAD REALIGNMENT
Close to monastic complex and earthworks
**8848 6977**
**SMR 25:15**
**99E0480**

An assessment was carried out from 23 to 25 August 1999 on four sites identified in the environmental impact statement along the proposed realignment of the N51 road at Dunmoe, Co. Meath. The first of these sites was within the road-take adjacent to the Donaghmore monastic complex (Site A) but within the townland of Blackcastle Demesne. Site B was also within the townland of Blackcastle Demesne and was identified during a field inspection. It was an oval mound defined by a U-shaped ditch. A third site (Site C), also within Blackcastle Demesne, was identified during a field inspection and was an earthen-banked, linear feature 0.3–0.4m high, running north-east to south-west for *c.* 20m; this appeared to be a road or pathway. Site D was identified during a field inspection in the townland of Dunmoe and was visible as a circular spread of nettles with a diameter of 9m.

Sites A and D were tested by machine to determine whether archaeological deposits were present. Sites B and C were clearly man-made features and were tested by hand-excavation.

### Site A, Blackcastle Demesne
A trench 100m long by 1m was excavated parallel to and to the south of the existing roadway, within the road-take of the proposed road realignment adjacent to the Donaghmore monastic complex. The trench was excavated to a depth of 0.5–0.6m, to the top of natural boulder clay. Approximately 0.5m from the northern end of the trench a shallow ditch that had been cut into the natural boulder clay was exposed, running towards the road, and represented a relatively modern field boundary. This was indicated on the various Ordnance Survey maps and is not linked with the monastic site. The ditch was *c.* 2m wide and 0.5–0.6m deep. The trench consisted entirely of ploughsoil right down onto the natural boulder clay, indicating that this field had been extensively ploughed in the recent past. No archaeological material was exposed, and no finds were recovered. The proposed road realignment will therefore not affect any archaeological deposits in the area.

### Site B, Blackcastle Demesne
This site was identified during field inspection as an oval mound surrounded by a ditch on all sides with the exception of the side next to the roadway. Following the clearing of the vegetation from the site, it became apparent that this feature was a quarry that had been excavated into the side of the hill. Other, similar disused quarries occur in the immediate area, some of which are indicated on the Ordnance Survey map. A trench was excavated to the natural boulder clay through the feature and through the ditch along the south-western side. This confirmed the feature to be a quarry, partially backfilled with material dumped there in the last ten to twenty years. Finds recovered from the mound included mineral cans, whiskey and gin bottles, and fragments of tarmacadam. This feature is therefore not of archaeological significance and appears to be of recent date.

### Site C, Blackcastle Demesne
Site C was visible on the ground heading south-eastwards from the present roadway for a distance of 30m before returning southwards towards the River Boyne. A trench was excavated across this feature north-east to south-west within and parallel to the land-take of the proposed roadway. The sod and

topsoil came down directly onto the natural boulder clay at an average depth of 0.2–0.25m. No archaeological features or material were exposed. This feature is clearly marked as an old field boundary on the Ordnance Survey map. It is of no archaeological significance, and no further archaeological work was deemed necessary.

*Site D, Dunmoe*
A trench was excavated through a spread of nettles that had been identified as a possible archaeological feature within the land-take of the proposed road. This trench was excavated north-east to south-west and exposed the natural boulder clay at an average depth of 0.15–0.2m below a layer of sod. A small dump of manure immediately on top of the sod probably accounts for the growth of the nettles. The site is of no archaeological significance, and no further work was recommended.

The excavation of trenches within the four sites revealed that there are no known features of archaeological significance along the proposed route of the new road. All four sites proved to be archaeologically sterile, and no further archaeological work is required. Monitoring of the entire road realignment has been requested by *Dúchas*.
*Donald Murphy, Archaeological Consultancy Services Ltd, 15 Trinity Street, Drogheda, Co. Louth.*

### 683. DUNSHAUGHLIN
Vicinity of monastic enclosure
N970527
99E0114

A condition of the planning permission required a site assessment before development.

The development site is on the north side of Dunshaughlin village, *c.* 100m to the north-east of the church of St Secundinius. According to tradition, the church was founded in the mid-5th century, and there are references to it in sources in the 9th century and later.

Four two-storey dwellings are planned for the site, which is at present under grass. Six trenches tested the area of the proposed development, five of which were perpendicular to the boundary wall on the west side. They were positioned to coincide with the walls of the proposed houses.

Evidence for a ditch was exposed in Trenches 2, 4 and 6, and possibly Trench 3. Its upper layers were characterised by a loose, black or dark grey clay that was distinct from the underlying gritty boulder clay. It appeared to be *c.* 4m wide. It was at least 1.7m deep, probably deeper, and there were indications in Trench 2 that the lower levels were waterlogged, as evidenced by the survival of a timber plank. At the level where excavation ceased in Trench 2 the ditch appeared to be *c.* 2m wide at its lower levels.

The ditch in Trench 6 did not appear to lie in the same arc as formed by the ditch in Trenches 2 and 4. This hinted at the possibility of the survival of two ditches, although if that had been the case the two would have been very close to each other. In this case the ditch exposed in Trenches 2 and 4 would be an inner ditch and that exposed in Trench 6 an outer ditch.

It is also possible that the ditch was not originally excavated as a regular circle.

There was no obvious evidence for a bank on the inner side of the edge of the ditch.
*Rosanne Meenan, Roestown, Drumree, Co. Meath.*

### 684. MAIN STREET, DUNSHAUGHLIN
No archaeological significance
N969518
99E0283

Monitoring was a condition of planning permission. The development site is at the south end of Main Street, Dunshaughlin, within the area of archaeological potential as defined by the Urban Survey for Meath. A motte (SMR 44:4) survives in the graveyard *c.* 70–80m to the south-east.

The monastic settlement of St Secundinius was founded to the north of the village. According to tradition, the church (SMR 44:3) was founded in the mid-5th century, and there are references to it in sources in the 9th century and later.

Monitoring was carried out on excavation of foundation trenches for the development, comprising a row of three two-storey retail units. Foundations of previous structures were exposed at the front corners of the site. A pit-like feature was exposed in the foundation trench for the back wall; it was interpreted as a soak hole for late 19th-century stables.

Otherwise nothing of archaeological interest was exposed.
*Rosanne Meenan, Roestown, Drumree, Co. Meath.*

### 685. FERGANSTOWN/BALLYMACKON
Cut features
288221 268351
98E602 ext.

Monitoring associated with the Navan Sewerage Augmentation Scheme was carried out in January 1999 in between the test-trenches associated with sites SMR 25:28 and 25:29 (Nos 699 and 686 below), along a short stretch of the Navan to Donore road.

Features identified were a series of cuts into the natural, filled with material that contained charcoal, ash and animal bone. These features extended over a distance of 12m and were directly opposite a previously unidentified archaeological site just inside the roadside field boundary to the north-west. This site was a low earthen bank, roughly square and *c.* 20m by 20m. SMR 25:28 was a Bronze Age cemetery recorded by Wilde in 1850, but it would appear that the newly identified site is not directly related to this. It is reasonable to assume that the archaeological deposits identified in the trench are related to the low earthen enclosure described above. A sample of charcoal from one of the features produced a radiocarbon date of AD 585–675 (95% probability).
*Clare Mullins, 31 Millford, Athgarvan, Co. Kildare.*

### 686. FERGANSTOWN/BALLYMACKON
Environs of 'Mound Site'
288803 268801
SMR 25:029
99E0011

A test-trench was excavated along the Navan to Donore road, just south of SMR 25:29, in January 1999, as part of the Navan Sewerage Augmentation Scheme. The site in question was a mound, destroyed in the 1970s, which contained a long cist and inhumation.

The test-trench was c. 150m long and was inserted along the route of a proposed sewerage pipe. Archaeological features had been recorded in the pipeline trench c. 200m to the west (see No. 685 above). No archaeological features were noted during the excavation of this trench.

*Clare Mullins, 31 Millford, Athgarvan, Co. Kildare.*

### 687. FERGANSTOWN AND BALLYMACKON
Souterrain
**99E0178**

On 30 January 1999 a souterrain passage was exposed at the south-west corner of a partially constructed sewerage treatment plant in the townland of Ferganstown and Ballymackon, south of the River Boyne, c. 3km north-east of Navan town. The souterrain was largely intact and consisted of a single drystone passage, leading roughly west into a simple beehive chamber. A limited excavation began in April 1999, with four trenches inserted across the site area. The aim of the excavation was to examine the areas of the site to be affected by the proposed development.

Trench A was across part of the souterrain passage. The passage walls were constructed from roughly shaped limestone rocks. The walls slanted inwards and were crowned by seven large lintels. The passageway was 3.3m long by 1m high and angled down towards the beehive chamber, which measured 2.65m (north–south) x 2.22m x 1.7m high. The chamber was constructed using both flat and rounded rocks and was sealed by a large capping stone. There was sufficient evidence to suggest that there may have been an entrance passage or drop-hole feature leading north from the exposed end of the existing passageway.

A faunal report (by M. McCarthy) indicated the presence of cow and pig bones in and around the souterrain passage, with evidence suggesting that slaughtering and primary butchery were carried out in the vicinity of the site.

Trench B flanked the existing hedgerow and revealed a substantial amount of activity, including a series of four (mostly linear) parallel cut features. Their nature and pattern were suggestive of agricultural (furrow) activity. Two shallow pits were also exposed. A curved, ditch-like feature and a circular structure were also identified. The shallow circular structure may have been a hut site; however, no associated stake- or post-holes were identified. This feature was outside the arc of the ditch-like trench.

Trenches C and D were to the south of Trenches A and B and failed to reveal any features of archaeological significance.

*Ken Hanley, 44 Eaton Heights, Cobh, Co. Cork, for Byrne, Mullins & Associates.*

### 688. GORTLONEY
Castle site (possible)
**5592 7383**
**SMR 15:68**
**99E0732**

An archaeological evaluation was undertaken at a proposed development site at Gortloney, Oldcastle,

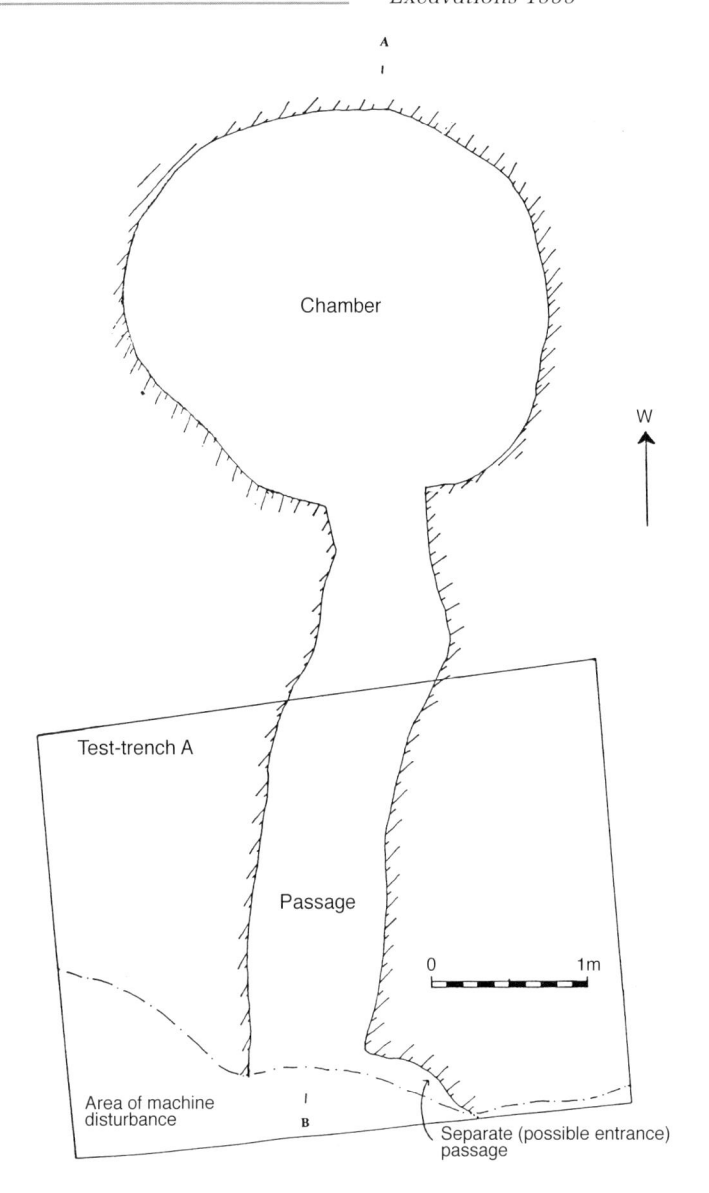

Plan of exposed souterrain at Ferganstown and Ballymackon (No. 687).

on 7 December 1999. The work was carried out in compliance with a request for additional information in respect of the proposed development of the site. Part of the development is within the constraints of a recorded monument known as Green Castle, described on the OS 6-inch maps as a castle 'in ruins'.

Eight trenches were excavated by machine in order to determine the nature and extent of any archaeological features within the development area. No features, deposits, structures or finds of archaeological interest, associated with the castle or any other possible archaeological site, were uncovered. Indeed, according to local information, part of the wall of the castle stood, until the late 19th/early 20th century, on a site to the north-west of the development site.

In addition to the testing, the extant buildings on the site were examined. One was constructed of concrete and did not warrant further attention. The other is the roofless and gutted remains of a former two-storey house. This building is constructed almost entirely of stone, with the walls up to 0.6m thick. A rear extension to the house was demolished in recent years. The walls of the house had been plastered both internally and externally in previous times, but parts of the stone wall are at present exposed. No fragments of reused cut stone were noted from this examination. This building will be reroofed and used as a garage/store.

It was recommended that no additional archaeological involvement was required in respect of the development.
*Martin E. Byrne, 31 Millford, Athgarvan, Co. Kildare.*

### 689. GRANGE/FIDORFE/KILRUE
No archaeological significance
O048475
99E0582

This work was part of the monitoring of pipe-laying for the Ashbourne/Ratoath/Kilbride Sewerage Scheme. Nothing of archaeological interest was recorded.
*Finola O'Carroll, Cultural Resource Development Services Ltd, Campus Innovation Centre, Roebuck, University College, Belfield, Dublin 4.*

### 690. PRIESTOWN, KILBRIDE
Possible medieval settlement
O010683
99E0208

The Ashbourne/Ratoath/Kilbride Sewerage Scheme comprises pipe-laying from Ratoath and Ashbourne to Kilbride, with a new pumping house at Kilbride. As there had been activity in the medieval period in the area of the village, it was recommended that the location of the new pump house be tested.

Three trenches tested the areas of greatest potential disturbance. The stratigraphy was nearly indentical in all, comprising ploughsoil 0.4–0.5m deep, overlying a grey, silty layer 0.9–1m deep. A stone drain was exposed in Trench 2, dug into the silty clay layer. The underlying material in the three trenches was a gravelly stone layer in a grey clay matrix.

Much of the land in this immediate area is badly drained and remains waterlogged after rain. This would account for the necessity of the stone drain encountered in Trench 2. There was no evidence to suggest that the drain was not post-medieval or modern in date.
*Rosanne Meenan, Roestown, Drumree, Co. Meath.*

### 691. PRIESTOWN, KILBRIDE
Adjacent to moat/ringfort
O065464
SMR 51:1
99E0580

This work was part of the ongoing monitoring of pipe-laying for the Ashbourne/Ratoath/Mulhuddart Sewerage Scheme. A short stretch of the grassy verge along the roadside but on the other side from that closest to the quarried-out 'moat' or ringfort was tested. Nothing of archaeological interest was uncovered. The route of the pipeline was through the road itself for the remainder of the distance through the village of Kilbride (Priest Town), so only monitoring was carried out. At this point the underlying shale was close to the surface, and nothing of archaeological interest was noted.
*Finola O'Carroll, Cultural Resource Development Services Ltd, Campus Innovation Centre, Roebuck, University College, Belfield, Dublin 4.*

### 692. KILLEEN CASTLE, KILLEEN
Tower-house and medieval church
N932548
96E0001

Following an application to Meath County Council for a revised layout of development in the vicinity of the castle and of the church and graveyard, further archaeological testing was requested by the National Monuments and Historic Properties Service. Testing in 1996 had revealed evidence for deposition of fill in the area to the north-west of the tower-house in order to create a terrace, presumably as a landscaping feature (*Excavations 1996*, 87). Testing to the south of the 19th-century extensions to the castle exposed evidence for disturbance caused by the construction of the castle and for further landscape features.

Two test-pits across the bank/edge of the graveyard on its south side exposed the presence of a low, crudely built stone wall along the edge of the bank. The date of the wall was not clear.

The further testing was requested in order to provide more information about the survival or otherwise of an enclosing element and/or burials around the graveyard and the nature of the fill in the terrace area to the north-east of the castle, with reference to the possibility of the survival of an earthen embankment associated with the tower-house or an earlier castle there.

Eight trenches tested the area to be affected by the more recent planning application. In the trenches that tested the vicinity of the graveyard, no enclosing feature was recognised other than a very crude stone wall exposed in Trench 5. No burials were exposed in any of the trenches. A stone wall probably associated with a 19th-century stone drain was exposed in Trench 7. The base batter of the tower-house was also exposed here. This was not observed in the 1996 test-trench in this area, as it had been robbed out when the 19th-century porch was added on to the east face of the castle.

Nothing of archaeological significance was observed in Trench 8.
*Rosanne Meenan, Roestown, Drumree, Co. Meath.*

### 693. KNOCKHARLEY
Holy well
99E0059

Geophysical survey and archaeological assessment were undertaken as part of a wider environmental impact statement on lands under consideration for a proposed landfill in Knockharley, Co. Meath. The site, 500m west of the N2 Dublin to Slane road and *c.* 1km north of Kentstown, is in a low-lying valley and consists of a large green-field area of 105 hectares. The site of the proposed landfill does not contain any recorded archaeological monuments; however, a possible holy well lies towards the centre of the site. Limited test-trenching in July 1997 by Hilary Opie (*Excavations 1997*, 141, 97E0190) did not reveal any archaeological features or deposits. A geophysical survey was undertaken at the site from September to October 1998. Seven test-trenches were excavated using a mechanical excavator.

The geophysical results provided a number of anomalous 'targets' for the test-trenching, although none appeared to be clearly archaeological. The site

of the well and the area immediately around it were tested. No archaeological stratigraphy was encountered, and no enclosing element for the possible well site was found. The testing did not prove or disprove that the feature described as a 'holy well' is such, or is indeed an archaeological feature. The test-trench strategy also tested a number of anomalous responses (mainly linear) found through the geophysical survey. In the tested areas where geophysical responses suggested linear features, all but one feature were found to be representative of removed field boundaries and natural geological variations within the subsoil. A wide cut feature revealed in Trench 2 was cut into the natural subsoil. No finds were recovered from the fill or the vicinity of this feature to confirm antiquity. The feature corresponded with a positive magnetic susceptibility response/zone, which faintly resembled a circular enclosure. No further soils, features or finds of archaeological significance were encountered.
*Malachy Conway for Margaret Gowen & Co. Ltd, 2 Killiney View, Albert Road Lower, Glenageary, Co. Dublin.*

### 694. KNOWTH
Multi-period
N995735
SMR 19:30
E000070

The excavation was exceedingly limited in area and consisted mainly of tidying up part of the north-west of the site. This work centered on the area of the 'curved trench' (Eogan 1984, 323–4). It appears that this trench surrounds a circular area *c.* 25m in diameter. In the area exposed, this averages 0.8m wide and 0.2m deep. No associated finds came to light.
*George Eogan, Knowth Project, University College, Earlsfort Terrace, Dublin 2.*

*Reference*
Eogan, G. 1984 *Excavations at Knowth 1*. Dublin.

### 695. NINCH, LAYTOWN
*Fulacht fiadh*
O162719
SMR 28:25
98E0501 ext.

The test excavations were positioned in order to assess the location and complexity of the site of a possible *fulacht fiadh*, noted during recent episodes of ploughing. The results showed that there was evidence that such a site existed in this area in the past. The remains, *in situ*, of the heat-cracked stone and black, charcoal-flecked soils attest to this. However, the fact that disturbed burnt mound material also survived in the furrows created by ploughing points to the probability that the site has been badly truncated by relatively recent agricultural improvements.

The area around the test site was field-walked, with numerous fragments of heat-cracked stone noted in the ploughsoil, adding strength to the above interpretation.
*Eoin Halpin, ADS Ltd, Unit 48, Westlink Enterprise Centre, 30–50 Distillery Street, Belfast BT12 5BJ.*

### 696. GUN HILL, LOBINSTOWN
Rectilinear earthwork
28941 28548
SMR 6:43
99E0725

Monitoring was conducted on the summit of Gun Hill, Lobinstown, Co. Meath, during the removal of a concrete base for a mobile phone mast and its associated cable network. The base measured 1.2m by 1.6m and was constructed within the confines of a rectilinear earthwork, recorded as 'Cromwell's Battery', consisting of a raised rectangular area defined by scarps and divided into two unequal parts by a north–south field fence and a double ditch.

The areas of excavation were confined to those that had already been disturbed by the insertion of the mast and the concrete base. The concrete base itself was only 0.2m thick and was laid on a thin layer of modern sand and gravel hardcore, which in turn lay above the natural subsoil and the redeposited fill of the cut for the timber mast. The mast itself was a timber telegraph pole and had already been cut down, leaving *c.* 2.5m of its base still to be removed. A small trench measuring 3m by 2m was excavated to the east of the pole to facilitate its extraction, exposing the natural, gravelly clay 0.3m below a thin layer of brown, sticky topsoil. The cut for the mast measured *c.* 1m by 2m and had been cut through the natural, gravelly clay to a depth of *c.* 2.5m and backfilled with fine, grey gravel. The ESB cables for the mast were to be laid within plastic ducting that had been laid in a trench 40m long by 1m, along the southern field boundary and partially through the bank of the earthwork. This trench was excavated to a depth of *c.* 0.3m to the top of the plastic ducting through a layer of redeposited natural and topsoil.

No finds were recovered, and no archaeological deposits or features were exposed. No further work is necessary on the site.
*Ian Russell, Archaeological Consultancy Services Ltd, 15 Trinity Street, Drogheda, Co. Louth.*

### 697. MONKNEWTOWN
No archaeological significance
3004 2751
SMR 19:15
98E0424

The development, the construction of chicken-rearing units, was 150m from a 'ritual pond'. An area measuring 120m by 26m was cleared to an average depth of 0.4m. No features, remains or deposits of archaeological significance were encountered.
*Christine Baker and Rónán Swan, Arch-Tech Ltd, 32 Fitzwilliam Place, Dublin 2.*

### 698. NAVAN SEWERAGE AUGMENTATION SCHEME
Canal bridge
98E0602

The Navan Sewerage Augmentation Scheme involved the insertion of sewerage pipes along several miles of road within a radius of *c.* 3 miles of Navan town. The project had been ongoing for some years and was nearing completion when an archaeological assessment was commissioned in September 1998. Monitoring commenced in January

1999, at which time there remained seven areas of operation.

Balreask Cross to Gainstown: no features of archaeological interest were identified.

Gainstown Road into Balreask Gardens (282m): no features of archaeological interest were identified.

Boyne Road (1320m): no features of archaeological interest were identified.

From the Balmoral Industrial Estate past the rear of Navan Carpets and looping back along the Kells road (1141m): no features of archaeological interest were identified.

Starting on the new Inner Relief Road and leading south around Navan town centre to the Commons Road (1570m). This route led diagonally across Circular Road and up to the County Council carpark. It then led onto Railway Street, Carriage Road and along the rear of McDermott Villas to the Commons Road. A buried canal bridge was identified on Circular Road, at the foot of Bridge Street. This dated roughly to the late 1790s and consisted of an arch *c.* 1.5m high and *c.* 7m wide. The canal itself, which was intended as a western extension to the Drogheda–Navan canal, was never completed.

Pumping station between Convent Road and the River Boyne: no features of archaeological interest were identified.

New sewerage treatment plant in the townland of Ferganstown and Ballymackon, *c.* 2 miles north-east of Navan, on the Boyne Road. Most of this site had already been developed. A souterrain passage was identified leading to a single beehive chamber. This monument was excavated under a separate licence (see No. 687 above).

*Ken Hanley, 44 Eaton Heights, Cobh, Co. Cork, for Byrne, Mullins & Associates.*

### 699. NAVAN SEWERAGE SCHEME, NAVAN
No archaeological significance
SMR 25:28 (adjacent to)
288137 268374
99E0010

Navan Sewerage Scheme commenced in the early 1990s. The most recent phase is in operation since November 1998. Clare Mullins completed an archaeological assessment of the route. The line of the sewerage trench close to a Bronze Age cemetery site was monitored. The trench was 1.2m wide and on average 2.8m deep. A sandy silt soil overlay layers of gravel and limestone bedrock.

No archaeological stratigraphy was recorded in the trench. No artefacts were recovered.

*Jacinta Kiely, Eachtra Archaeological Projects, Clover Hill, Mallow, Co. Cork.*

### 700. ATHLUMNEY, NAVAN
Monitoring
N884665
99E0479

Monitoring of topsoil clearance took place on the site of a new factory (Stage 1). The site lay 350m south-west of a souterrain complex recently excavated by Carleton Jones (see No. 701 below). The natural prominence of the site under discussion raised the possibility of an associated(?) settlement. The only features encountered during the stripping operation were associated with old field boundaries and land drains. No features or finds of an archaeological nature were uncovered.

*Mark Clinton for Margaret Gowen & Co. Ltd, 2 Killiney View, Albert Road Lower, Glenageary, Co. Dublin.*

### 701. IDA BUSINESS PARK, KILKARN, ATHLUMNEY, NAVAN
Souterrains
SMR 25:49
98E0596

The site is set on the high east bank of the River Boyne and consists of four souterrains, an overlying occupation layer and several large ditches. A disused sand quarry had removed the north-western portion of the site. Excavations were carried out between 12 January and 15 March 1999.

Souterrain 1 consisted of two portions truncated by the quarry, a short section of passage and a small portion of a circular chamber. The preserved portion of passage was very short, only 2.1m from the quarry edge to the end of the passage. The passage was 0.94m wide, ended abruptly and did not widen or constrict at its end. The abrupt south-east end of the passage may be a 'drop' entrance.

Souterrain 2 was almost completely intact. It had a ramped entrance, two right-angled left-hand turns in a gradually descending passage, a drop-creep, another short section of passage and then a T-junction with a passage that terminated at each end in a beehive-shaped chamber. The entrance to the souterrain was deliberately blocked with a fill of midden material and stones.

Only the very top stones of Souterrain 3 were exposed. It was planned and photographed and then covered again for preservation. The portion exposed was a 6.5m length of straight passage.

A possible fourth souterrain was encountered in a machine trench and subsequently reburied for preservation. The feature as exposed in the trench was a drystone wall, three courses high. It appeared to be the outside of a souterrain passage wall.

Where the site had not been disturbed by the quarry there was an occupation soil directly below the topsoil. Two hearths and a shallow ditch segment were associated with the occupation layer.

Several large ditches were also discovered. All of these ditches contained charcoal and/or domestic animal bones. The ditches do not form an integrated pattern that would suggest a single-phase enclosure. The ditches appear to be the result of several different phases of use of the site but may all be assumed to be roughly contemporary with the souterrains, as there was no evidence of significant activity on the site at other times.

Ditch A was 1.98m deep and 7.2m wide. Ditch B was 1.38m deep and 5m wide. Ditch C was very irregular in the section revealed, and this section may represent two ditches cut into each other. It was 1.5m deep at its deepest and 8.2m wide. Ditch D was 1.6m deep and 3.8m wide. Ditch E was 0.7m deep and 5.1m wide. Ditch F was at least 0.5m deep and 1.2m wide.

Finds were very scarce on the site. They are awaiting analysis, but a preliminary list includes two bone pins, a glass bead, fragments of lignite bracelets, a bone bead, a few lithic flakes and some

metal finds. Carbonised remains of both domestic and wild plants were recovered. The domestic plants were oats, barley, rye and wheat.
*Carleton Jones, 63 Cregaun, Tobarteascain, Ennis, Co. Clare.*

### 702. MOATHILL, NAVAN
Environs of motte and bailey
28598 26765
SMR 25:23
99E0653

The proposed development site is on the western edge of Navan town, immediately east of an Anglo-Norman motte and bailey in Moathill townland. The site is along the Athboy Road, close to a sharp, north-turning bend, with the motte and bailey dominating the site to the west and the playing fields of a local school to the north. On the south side of the road, directly across from the site, lies an open area of reduced ground level, the result of quarrying and dumping, while the precinct of a hospital lies immediately east of this. Two detached cottages with gardens front the site, and there are two large farm outbuildings and remains of several smaller sheds in the north-west area of the site, close to the base of the motte. All existing buildings on the site are derelict, and the west-lying cottage has been burnt out. The garden in front of the western cottage lies at least 1.3m above the road level, although there is a gradual fall-off to 0.5m in height of the garden area to the east, adjacent to the present access into the site.

On 25 November 1999 four trenches were excavated in the area of the proposed houses. Trench 1 was in the south-west corner of the site, in a garden area west of an existing dwelling. It was excavated in a north–south direction along the line of a series of proposed dwellings c. 20m east of the western perimeter of the site. The trench, 24m by 1m, was excavated to a maximum depth of 1.3m. Removal of sod (0.2m deep) revealed a homogeneous deposit of grey/brown, sandy clay up to 1.1m deep. Below this the clay deposit contained much natural limestone.

Trench 2 (22.5m by 1m) was in a former garden area immediately west of the access laneway and was excavated in a north–south direction along the line of a series of proposed dwellings. The trench was excavated to a maximum depth of 1.1m, revealing a homogeneous deposit of garden soil 0.4m deep over yellow/brown, sandy clay with occasional rounded stones up to 0.7m deep, lying over a natural deposit of compacted stone.

Trench 3 (24m by 1m) was in an area of very overgrown ground north-east of the existing sheds. The trench was excavated in an north-north-east/south-south-west direction from the north-east perimeter of the site, along the line of a series of proposed dwellings, to a maximum depth of 1.65m. Removal of brown topsoil (0.3m deep) containing occasional fragments of concrete and brick and stone rubble revealed two extensive dump deposits of black soil containing many early modern finds (bottles, drainage pipe, patterned ceramics, metal hooks, handles etc.). The two dump deposits, upper 0.2m deep and lower 0.9m deep, were interrupted by a layer of redeposited, coarse, grey, sandy gravel 0.2m deep, containing numerous fist-sized and smaller stones. The lower dump deposit overlay the natural, coarse, grey, gravelly clay at a depth of 1.4–1.65m.

Trench 4 (34m by 1m) was in very overgrown ground 15m from the north-east corner of the site and was excavated in an north-north-east/south-south-west direction from the north perimeter of the site along the line of a series of proposed dwellings to a depth of 1.9m. Removal of brown topsoil (0.5m deep) containing fragments of concrete, brick rubble and modern rubbish revealed a dump deposit of grey/brown loam including bottles and modern cans 0.14m deep over a tarmac surface 0.06m thick that extended for a distance of 3.2m from the northern end of the trench. Below the redeposited grey/brown loam and tarmac lay a fairly homogeneous deposit of grey/brown, sandy clay 0.7m deep over natural, grey gravel. An extensive dump deposit of early modern rubbish was found cut into the grey/brown, sandy clay 17m from the northern end of the trench and extending as far as the laneway to the south. This dump deposit, the same as that encountered in Trench 3, was at most 1m deep, capped by a layer of yellow/brown clay 0.35m thick extending east and west beyond the trench. The dump deposit contained numerous glass, ceramic, metal and plastic items.

No archaeological stratigraphy was encountered in any of the test-trenches. The presence of extensive early modern dump deposits over most of the north-eastern portion of the site points to ground reduction within this area. From the late 19th century extensive gravel quarrying has been undertaken in the immediate environs of this site, and even the motte itself has been quarried during the recent past.
*Malachy Conway, Archaeological Consultancy Services Ltd, 15 Trinity Street, Drogheda, Co. Louth.*

### 703. 22 TRIMGATE STREET, NAVAN
Urban medieval
N865676
SMR 25:25
99E0137

The development site is within the zone of archaeological potential in Navan as defined by the Urban Survey for County Meath. The Urban Survey suggests that the eastern wall of this property may be formed by, or include parts of, the medieval town wall, and it is possible that the rest of the property west of this wall may lie on top of the town ditch, if such existed. As Trimgate Street formed one of the main axes of the medieval town, there is also the possibility that houses along the street retain features of medieval fabric.

An archaeological assessment was requested by *Dúchas*, to include (1) a survey of the standing structures and (2) test excavations. A photographic survey was carried out before the test-trenching.

Four trenches tested the area to be developed. Three of them tested the foundation of the stone wall. These showed that the present stone wall along the east of the site had been inserted into a layer of dark grey silt loam that in places resembled garden soil. This material took a dip in Trench 1, but a corresponding dip was not observed in Trenches 2 and 3. A foundation trench for the wall was not observed. There were no finds other than two sherds of 19th-century pottery that came from the upper levels of the dark layer in Trench 3. The dip in boulder clay in Trench 1 was not substantial enough to suggest that it represented the remains of a town ditch.

Trench 4 tested the base of the back wall of the original house that fronted onto the street. Here, dark silt loam/garden soil was exposed under the concrete and overlying soft, brown, sandy clay, which in turn overlay a stony layer.

It would be expected that a medieval town wall would be founded on natural boulder clay or bedrock or that it would feature a base batter. This wall was found to be standing on material containing 19th-century material. There was no evidence to suggest that remnants of an earlier wall existed under the standing wall.

*Rosanne Meenan, Roestown, Drumree, Co. Meath.*

### 704. NAVAN–TRIM GAS PIPELINE
Monitoring
**99E0607**

Monitoring was conducted along the route of a four-bar, 250mm gas pipeline from Navan (Kilcarn Bridge, SMR 25:39) and, on the specific request of *Dúchas*, followed the construction of the line of the existing roadway to Trim for a distance of *c.* 16km.

Before the construction of the pipeline an archaeological appraisal of the proposed route was conducted, which identified only three known areas of archaeological potential: Kilcarn Bridge (SMR 25:39) south-east of Navan town, and a church and graveyard (SMR 36:14) and cropmark (SMR 36:15) in Kilcooly townland. The last two sites formed part of a complex on top of a hill adjacent to the western side of the roadway (the pipe was laid on the eastern side). The stretch of road in the vicinity of these monuments had also been straightened and upgraded recently. The report recommended that monitoring concentrate on the excavation of the trench across Kilcarn Bridge only after monitoring of trial-pits, before construction works, adjacent to SMR sites 36:14 and 36:15 led to the conclusion that 'given the location of the proposed pipeline within several metres of the road and in previously disturbed and built-up ground, the possibility of archaeological deposits surviving *in situ* is extremely limited'.

The required monitoring of this pipeline confirmed the recommendations made in the archaeological appraisal report (that monitoring should not have been required along the full length of the route) and proved that the additional inspections required were useful only in that they proved that the level of monitoring required was both wasteful and unproductive on this project. It should be pointed out that excavation for this pipe was generally no more than 0.4m deep and a maximum of 0.6m wide. It is almost impossible to view archaeological features successfully in such a narrow trench.

*Margaret Gowen, Margaret Gowen & Co. Ltd, 2 Killiney View, Albert Road Lower, Glenageary, Co. Dublin.*

### 705. NINCH/LAYTOWN
Bronze Age enclosure, *fulacht* trough
**SMR 28:25**
**98E0501**

Two test-trenches were excavated by Eoin Halpin through the site of a possible *fulacht fiadh*, and, although no archaeological features were uncovered, burnt stone was identified. Monitoring followed, and the licence was transferred to the writer.

A prehistoric ditched enclosure site was identified on the ridge. This enclosure was *c.* 33m in external diameter with a V-shaped ditch 1.4–1.8m wide and 0.9–1.2m deep. The lower fill contained flint, pottery and other stone artefacts. The pottery has been provisionally dated to the mid-Bronze Age. Monitoring also uncovered a number of pits filled with burnt stone. One of these pits was thought to be a *fulacht fiadh* trough pit.

Further clearances are to be undertaken in 2000 before extensions to the housing development, and these will be monitored for further archaeological features/materials.

*Martin Reid, 37 Errigal Road, Drimnagh, Dublin 12, for ADS Ltd.*

### 706. RIVER BOYNE, OLDBRIDGE
No archaeological significance
**30585 27545**
**99D013 and 99R034 (diver survey and detection device licences)**

Meath County Council commissioned an underwater inspection and metal-detector survey to be carried out along the southern shore of the River Boyne at the site of the proposed new bridge pylon for the Northern Motorway in Oldbridge, Co. Meath. The area surveyed extended from *c.* 15m upstream and downstream of the existing temporary works platform and associated access areas that continue east and west of the main platform. The linear area was *c.* 230m long. It reached out into the middle of the river channel, *c.* 30m from the natural shore and *c.* 15m from the toe of the working platform.

No archaeological features or finds were observed during the survey, which took place on 27 and 28 September.

*Niall Brady, 2 Vale Terrace, Lower Dargle Road, Bray, Co. Wicklow, for Valerie J. Keeley Ltd.*

### 707. PILLTOWN/PAINESTOWN/KILTROUGH/ BEY BEG/BEY MORE/PLATIN/CAULSTOWN/ CARRANSTOWN/COMMONS (DULEEK)/NEWTOWN/ LONGFORD/DOWNESTOWN/GILLINSTOWN/ GARBALLAGH/THOMASTOWN/SICILY/TUITERATH/ FLEMINGSTOWN/KENTSTOWN/KNOCKHARLEY/ CURRAGHTOWN/BROWNSTOWN/REALTOGE/ STAFFORDSTOWN/FOLLISTOWN/MOORETOWN/ ALEXANDER REID
Monitoring
**99E0356**

The laying of a new gas pipeline from south of Drogheda to the outskirts of Navan necessitated the stripping of a 15m-wide corridor and the subsequent digging of a trench that varied in width from 0.65m to 2.3m (at top) and 0.7m to 0.75m (at bottom); the average depth of the trench was 2m.

No features of a proven archaeological nature were uncovered during the operation. Indeed the corridor, when taken as random-sample survey, can be seen to have reaffirmed the perceived archaeological profile of the traversed terrain and its general environs. Of the 27 townlands crossed by the pipeline corridor, seventeen, to date, are totally bereft of archaeological remains of any description. A further eight townlands contain a mere one to three known sites. Only the early historic archaeological complex centred on Duleek indicates any proven significant activity in the general area. Evidence for a Neolithic presence is almost negligible. Similarly, the Bronze Age and Iron Age are poorly represented.

Given the size and land quality of the area under discussion, the sum total of remains does not help to establish the existence of intensive activity during practically all of the recognised epochs.
Mark Clinton for Margaret Gowen & Co. Ltd, Killiney View, Albert Road Lower, Glenageary, Co. Dublin.

### 708. RANDALSTOWN
*Fulachta fiadh*
SMR 25:1, 25:2, 25:3, 18:26
98E0352

An excavation was carried out in the townland of Randalstown, Co. Meath, on four *fulachta fiadh* discovered during monitoring of topsoil-stripping within the Northern Borrow Area, during construction of Stage 4a of the Tailings Dam Extension for Tara Mines Ltd. The excavation was carried out between 1 and 16 June 1999.

Topsoil extending to a depth of 0.4m was removed, revealing the yellow, natural glacial till beneath. A number of filled-in ditches of old field boundaries were exposed as areas of soft ground within the natural glacial till. Archaeological features were exposed at the southern end of one such boundary as spreads of burnt stone and dark soil highlighted against the natural clay, characteristic of levelled burnt mounds of *fulachta fiadh*. For the purposes of excavation these were divided into four archaeological areas.

Area 1 was revealed as a spread of burnt stone and charcoal-stained soil forming an approximate triangle measuring 8m by 5m. A rectangular trough 1.75m long, 1.65m wide and 0.58m deep was revealed at the eastern edge of the burnt mound spread. The top of the trough was sloped, with vertical sides towards the base, suggesting that it may have been lined with wooden planks. A squared recess 0.2m wide was cut into the natural clay in the south-east corner and may have secured a wooden upright. However, no post-holes were evident in the subsoil at the base of the trough. The spread of heat-shattered stones extended to the north-west from the trough and lay in an irregularly shaped hollow that was 0.25m deep. A large, subcircular pit measuring 1.7m by 1.3m was excavated to the north-west of the trough and was filled with burnt stones. This pit was 0.55m deep and had a broad U-shaped profile with sloping sides and a round base. Two further, subrectangular shallow pits were excavated to the east of the trough.

Area 2 was exposed as a large spread of burnt mound material consisting of a dense concentration of shattered stone and black silt measuring 12m north–south by 4m. This had a maximum thickness of 0.28m and lay within a hollow cut into the natural clay. The trough was exposed beneath the eastern edge of the burnt material and was an elongated subrectangular pit cut into the natural clay, measuring 2.5m by 1.1m and 0.44m deep. The fill

Section through trough of *fulacht fiadh* at Randalstown.

was a black, charcoal-flecked silt that was the same as the burnt mound material. The remains of a wooden plank lay lengthwise along the base of the trough and measured 1.4m by 0.32m. No trace of wood was observed on the sides of the trough, and no post-holes were visible in the base. A large pit 1.2m in diameter was exposed to the south-west of the burnt spread and contained a weathered, natural fill and occasional burnt stones.

Area 3 was a spread of black, sandy silt with burnt stone over an area measuring 13.5m by 5.5m. This had a maximum thickness of 0.38m and overlay a soft, wet, grey silt up to 0.15m thick containing charcoal flecks and burnt stones. This in turn lay above the natural, yellow glacial till. The trough was on the south side of the burnt stone spread and consisted of a flat-bottomed subcircular pit cut into the natural glacial till measuring 1.8m by 1.7m and 0.55m deep. A deposit of wet, black silt, 0.1m thick, was exposed at the base of the trough below a number of layers of natural silt. No evidence was observed for a wooden lining, which may have been considered unnecessary by the builders because of the impermeable clay sides. A bucket-shaped pit cut into the natural glacial till was exposed 0.5m north of the trough and was filled with a black, silty clay with charcoal and burnt stone. The pit measured 1.2m by 1m and was excavated to a depth of 0.56m.

Area 4 was a thin spread of burnt stone covering a small trough and two small pits. The burnt material was spread over an area measuring 15m by 10.5m. A dense concentration of shattered stone and black silt *c.* 2.5m in diameter marked the location of the trough. The trough measured 1.8m by 0.5–1m. A shallow U-shaped gully or hollow c. 0.25m wide and 50mm deep was exposed along the centre of the trough. This hollow may have held a wooden plank that was removed when the trough went out of use. Two possible stake-holes, c. 80mm in diameter, which may have secured a plank along the base, were exposed at the south end of the trough. A third stake-hole was exposed within a slot-like feature at the north-east of the trough. Two further possible stake-holes were also exposed at the surface. Two small pits were revealed 10m to the east of the trough. Both were subcircular in plan, measuring c. 0.6m in diameter and 0.26m deep, and were filled with wet, grey, silty clay containing charcoal and burnt stone.

At least four *fulachta fiadh* were excavated at Randalstown, along with a number of pits probably associated with their use. These conform to the general size range of other excavated troughs. There was surviving evidence for a wood lining in the trough in Area 2, with indirect evidence for a lining in the troughs in Areas 1 and 4. The fills of the trough in Areas 2 and 3 indicate a gradual silting-up over time, whereas the troughs in Areas 1 and 4 contained a homogeneous fill suggesting backfill in one operation. The presence of such a concentration of *fulachta fiadh* is a strong indication of significant Bronze Age activity in the immediate area and reinforces the evidence found at Simonstown for a densely populated prehistoric landscape.

*Donald Murphy, Archaeological Consultancy Services Ltd, 15 Trinity Street, Drogheda, Co. Louth.*

### 709. N4–N6 KINNEGAD LINK ROAD, ROSSAN
No archaeological significance
26014 24512
98E0481 ext.

Monitoring of the N4–N6 Kinnegad Link Road was originally undertaken by IAC Ltd for Valerie J. Keeley Ltd between 7 and 30 October 1998 (*Excavations 1998*, 166). This involved monitoring of all topsoil-stripping and below-ground construction activities associated with the 1km-long link road. Monitoring at that time failed to reveal the presence of either archaeological features or portable finds from within the development area.

An additional monitoring programme, over five days between 22 February and 5 March 1999, was carried out as a result of the construction of a road-over-river bridge that could not be undertaken at the time of the original groundworks.

Works associated with the bridge involved the excavation of a 150m-wide east–west river channel to the south of the existing Kinnegad River and the subsequent diversion of the river into this new channel. After the completion of the river diversion c. 0.5m of material was removed from the base of the river to accommodate a pre-cast concrete culvert that was placed on the riverbed to support the bridge construction above.

Monitoring of the excavation of the temporary river channel and the dredging of the base of the river failed to reveal the presence of archaeological features or finds. The Kinnegad River, which was excavated in 1936, was shown to have truncated *in situ* geologically deposited sand and gravels. Therefore dredging of the base of the river truncated *in situ* gravels. The previous course of the river was infilled by the material excavated from the construction works associated with the existing (i.e. 1936) Kinnegad River.

The temporary river channel excavated for this project truncated upcast also deposited at the time of the river diversion in 1936. This upcast was revealed in all areas of the development and sealed natural geology.

*Dermot Nelis, IAC Ltd, 8 Dungar Terrace, Dun Laoghaire, Co. Dublin.*

### 710. SARSFIELDSTOWN
Burials in a gravel mound
3147 2683
99E0688

The site was in Sarsfieldstown, Co. Meath, c. 7km north of Balbriggan, to the west of the N1. This previously unknown site was uncovered during land development of a gravel mound on a private farm. A machine trench excavated into the east of the mound revealed a number of human skeletons. The topsoil had been stripped surrounding the trench, revealing the presence of further human skeletons. A rescue excavation was carried out on behalf of *Dúchas* over five days in December, with a remit to retrieve the disturbed human remains from the machine spoil, to record the machine section stratigraphy and to excavate the skeletons truncated by the machine.

The sections revealed the remains of at least eight individuals including one infant, all buried in fairly shallow graves below the topsoil and all truncated by the machine. Many of these individuals had also been disturbed in the past by subsequent burials, ploughing and possibly also animal activity. Those in the north- and east-facing sections were cut through the natural gravel mound, whereas those in the south-facing section were cut through a deep layer of very stony, silty clay. No evidence of stone linings, coffins, shrouds or artefacts was recovered. The intact skeletons were orientated east–west with their heads to the west. It was not feasible to attempt to excavate all the human remains truncated by the machine without uncovering further skeletons, necessitating a large-scale excavation outside our remit. Two of the skeletons were excavated, and the rest were covered so that the trench could be backfilled and the mound restored.

Preliminary examination of the skeletons by Laureen Buckley suggested that they are very likely to be pre-medieval in date.

*Mary Deevy, ADS Ltd, Windsor House, 11 Fairview Strand, Fairview, Dublin 3.*

### 711. STAGRENNAN
Boyne dredging
99E0535

From September 1999 to February 2000 archaeological monitoring was carried out on the material dredged from the navigable channel of the River Boyne. This work was commissioned by Drogheda Port Company. The river was dredged from Tom Roe's Point to the sea using two methods. Cutter suction dredging was used for 2000m from Tom Roe's Point eastwards and was then replaced by the mechanical excavation of material into barges. In the

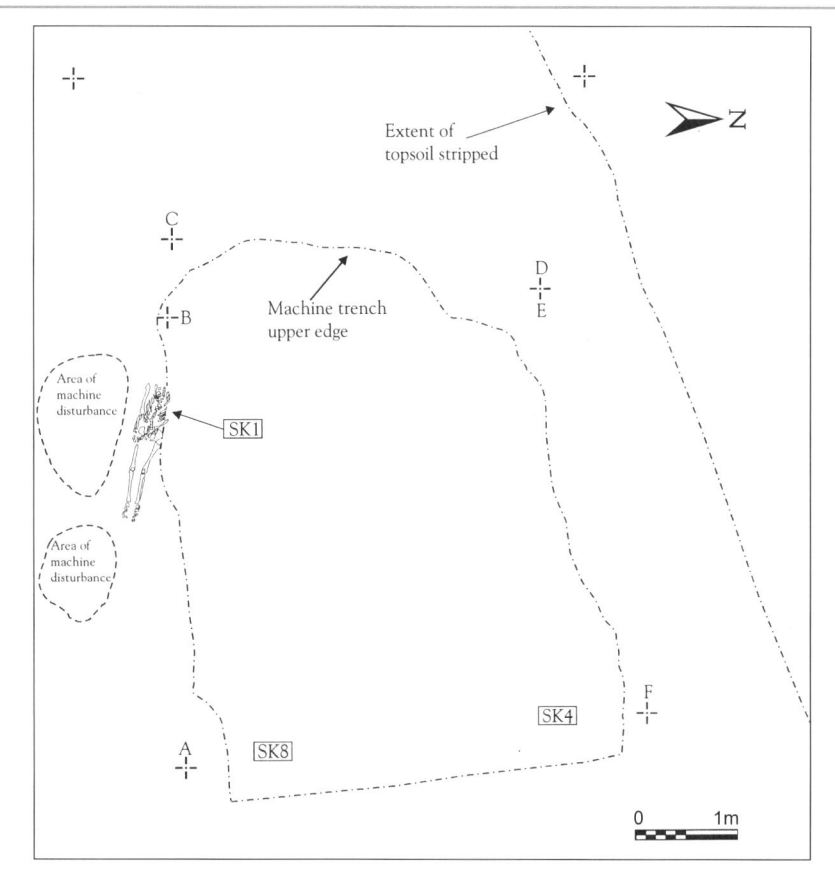

Plan of machine trench and truncated skeleton at Sarsfieldtown.

cutter suction method the sands and gravels were transported to a landfill site at Stagrennan Polder via a floating pipeline and pumped out in a 20–25% solids/75–80% water solution. The water was allowed to drain off and was released back into the river via a sluice-gate. The material retrieved by mechanical excavation was transported by barge to a purpose-dug surge pit close to Stagrennan Polder. It was then pumped out of this surge pit regularly, using the cutter suction dredger.

Monitoring was carried out on a seven-day-week basis during daylight hours. As the surface of the landfill was constantly changing, all surfaces were continually walked and metal-detected. The finds retrieved came from the following areas: the wash (water run-off area), the freshly bulldozed material and the existing bund material. The locations of the finds were recorded as they were retrieved from the landfill site. From an archaeological perspective, only the immediate finds, i.e. those from the freshly bulldozed material and from the wash, could have a potential original location given to them. The locations applied to this material were the daily dredger locations in the river. The material retrieved from the bund areas, as well as that pumped from the surge pit, is unfortunately lacking in context, owing to the procedure involved. The area close to the mouth of the outflow pipe could only be examined when pumping was not in progress. There were fairly frequent stoppages each day that allowed this inspection to take place.

The finds retrieved included over 3000 pieces of worked flint, large quantities of animal bone, an intact human skull, post-medieval and medieval pottery, tile and pipe, clay pipes, glass, leather off-cuts, 58 small wooden objects (mainly barrel bungs and pulley wheels) and some larger, possible ship timbers from various points along the river. Four interesting artefacts were retrieved—an antler hammer/macehead, a worked bone toggle-like item, a copper-alloy pin 0.21m long and a copper-alloy socketed and basal-looped spearhead.

*Jane Whitaker, ADS Ltd, Windsor House, 11 Fairview Strand, Fairview, Dublin 3.*

### 712. TANKARDSTOWN
Adjacent to ploughed-out ringfort
**O035508**
**99E0581**
**SMR 45:11**

This work was carried out as part of the ongoing monitoring of pipe-laying for the Ashbourne/Ratoath/Kilbride Sewerage Scheme. A 2m-wide ditching bucket was used to trench along the verge parallel to the area where the ploughed-out ringfort was sited. Telecom lines and a stone-filled ditch disturbed the area. Modern china and crock were recovered but nothing of archaeological significance. Subsoil was reached at a depth of 0.35m and was a pale beige/yellow clay.

*Finola O'Carroll, Cultural Resource Development Services Ltd, Campus Innovation Centre, Roebuck, University College, Belfield, Dublin 4.*

### 713. CASTLE STREET, TRIM
Environs of town wall
**279782 256495**
**SMR 36:28**
**99E0659**

Test-trenching was carried out in December 1999 at a site in Castle Street, Trim, in response to a condition of planning. Planning permission had been granted for the construction of a doctor's surgery and apartments on a site behind the rear garden of the southernmost of a row of two-storey cottages that front on to the western side of Castle Street, on a patch of land known locally as the 'nuns' garden'. Trim Castle is directly opposite this property, on the other side of the street, and the medieval town wall delineates the northern site boundary of the proposed development site. Three test-trenches were inserted over the proposed development site, positioned to examine the stratigraphy within the area of greatest impact from the development.

A layer of organic material was found to exist at a fairly constant level of c. 0.8–1m beneath the present ground surface, over the area of the proposed development site. Where tested, this organic horizon was found to continue for a further 0.7–1m in depth and appeared to rest upon the natural geological deposits, which occurred at 1.5–2m beneath the present ground surface. It is highly probable that some further variation in the absolute levels of these deposits exists in the untested areas of the site. This organic material was overlain in the main by a deep topsoil horizon that showed some evidence of modern disturbance.

This organic layer is considered to be of probable archaeological origin, and, while no evidence of structural features was discernible within it, it is thought highly likely that such structural information is contained within its depth. While there was a notable paucity of the usual inclusions found within medieval deposits and a total failure to recover datable artefacts such as pottery sherds, this situation is not without parallel in other medieval deposits.

The use of a piled foundation structure with specified restrictions was recommended in mitigation of the impact of the development on the archaeological potential of the site.
*Clare Mullins, 31 Millford, Athgarvan, Co. Kildare.*

### 714. DUBLIN ROAD (FRIARYLAND 3RD DIVISION), TRIM
Environs of castle
N997595
99E0071

As part of the ongoing Trim Sewerage Improvement Scheme a new pumping station was constructed beside the existing one, which was demolished. The hall was also to be demolished. The site is c. 100m east of the curtain wall of Trim Castle. This is well outside the line of the castle ditch, and the site is also outside the zone of archaeological potential for the town. It is likely that the area was disturbed in the past, both at the time of the construction of the existing pumping station and when the hall was built. The hall, a concrete block structure with a tin roof, served as a boxing club premises for some time, and the stretch of ground between the hall and the pumping station was surfaced.

When the hall was demolished it was found to have been built on ground that had been reduced by no more than 0.5m, with no foundation trenches for the walls. A thin layer of brown clay lay underneath, which came down onto a layer of grey gravel and sand. Combined, these two layers were c. 1.5m deep, and they overlay bedrock at that depth. The latter comprised a shaley limestone material.

An area c. 20m² and 5–6m deep was excavated by mechanical digger. The stratigraphy of brown clay overlying grey gravel/sand overlying bedrock was consistent over the area of the excavation. Bedrock was excavated out by machine.

It became clear that there was much disturbance when the existing pumphouse was constructed, as modern rubbish was found in the fill abutting the pumphouse. This extended to a depth of 6m. The upper levels west of the existing pumphouse had also been disturbed by the insertion of services etc. leading to the existing pumphouse.
*Rosanne Meenan, Roestown, Drumree, Co. Meath.*

### 715. HAGGARD STREET, TRIM
Urban medieval
280124 257012
SMR 36:28
99E0142

Archaeological excavation of a c. 90m length of pipeline trench was carried out along the western side of Haggard Street, Trim, during June and July 1999. Excavation took place before pipe-laying and following the identification during monitoring of the pipeline of what appeared to be a relatively complex archaeological stratigraphy at the southern end of the street. Throughout much of the monitoring project, which encompassed Mill Street, High Street and Haggard Street, a cobbled or metalled road surface was visible in the trench sections. This appeared as a relatively continuous layer, c. 0.2m deep, of a very stony and compact material, usually lying upon the natural and following a horizontal course at varying depths beneath the modern ground surface. Where this layer occurred at a deeper level it tended to be overlain by a silty, organic material and/or a dry, brown, clayey gravel, interpreted as representing a single episode of deliberate road-heightening. Occasionally a later episode of cobbling was identified closer to the modern road surface. Some sherds of medieval pottery were found in association with the earlier cobbled layer, but it was generally not associated with complex structural evidence (see No. 720 below).

At the southern end of Haggard Street the archaeological deposits became more complex. A large pit was transected by the pipeline, but it could not be established whether this pre-dated or post-dated the stony layer. North of the pit a linear stone feature that seemed to be too flimsy to represent a wall and that may be some form of kerbing was identified in section. Following the excavation of a manhole in the same area, a stratigraphy of c. 1.5m depth of archaeological deposits became visible on both sides of an area previously disturbed by a service pipe. At this point further trench excavations in the area were suspended pending excavation of what appeared to be an area of high archaeological sensitivity.

The excavation was divided into three sections, apportioned approximately evenly along the length of the trench; this strategy was designed to permit continued access to the carpark on Haggard Street on the western side of the line of the excavation. Excavation commenced in the central area and was completed before moving on to the area to the north. Finally, the southernmost stretch was excavated. A layer of cobbling (Road Surface 2), interpreted as representing a continuation of that identified in other areas of the town, proved to be a constant feature along the entire length of the excavation trench. The exposure of the surface of this layer provided an opportunity to examine its character as a road surface. It was somewhat denuded in places, but where best-preserved it appeared as a level surface of densely packed stones, placed to achieve as smooth a surface as possible. Though generally angular in form, the exposed, upper part of the stones was noticeably more rounded that the hidden underside. Throughout the excavation trench this layer was c. 0.2m deep and was usually overlain by 0.2–0.3m of a black, silty, organic deposit that produced medieval pottery and one fairly complete medieval leather shoe, as well as several fragments.

Towards the northern end of the excavation trench the eastern edge of a shallow gully that had been cut into the natural was identified beneath the cobbled surface. This ran parallel to the street line for several metres, widening eastwards as it travelled north, before descending to form a deep pit. A later gully cut through the earlier one at a right angle to the street line. Both gullies and the associated pit were sealed by the stony surface.

The most archaeologically sensitive area proved to be the southern end of the excavation trench, closest to the point at which the pipe-trench had originally been halted. Here the opportunity was provided to examine a short stretch of a later layer of cobbling (RS3) that pre-dated a modern layer (RS4). The cobble layers (RS2 and RS3) were separated by a depth of c. 0.4m of material consisting of a black, silty, organic deposit, generally lying directly over the cobbles, and an orange/light brown clay—a repetition of the stratigraphic pattern observed in the more northerly areas of the excavation trench, as well as in other parts of the town.

Not far from the southern end of the trench a mortared limestone wall was found that rested directly upon the earlier layer of cobbles (RS2). This wall was aligned in an east–west direction, at a right angle to the line of the street. It was 1m wide with facing-stones on its southern side and a rubble core. It seems likely that facing-stones originally lined the northern side of this wall, which would give it an original width of c. 1.3m. The wall survived to only one course in depth, and there was no foundation cut for it. This wall had clearly gone out of use at the same time as the cobbled surface upon which it rested, as the organic, black layer that overlay the cobbles also sealed the remaining course of the wall.

A foundation layer of silty sand containing a large volume of bone and wood underlay the cobbled layer (RS2) to a depth of c. 0.3m at the southern end of the trench. This layer may have been deposited to level up the area in preparation for the laying of RS2, as it diminished gradually in thickness moving north.

The vestigial remnants of what appeared to be another masonry wall were found at the extreme southern end of the trench, beneath this foundation layer of silty sand. This wall was aligned approximately north–south and was represented by a row of five possible facing-stones surviving to two courses. These stones rested upon a deeper cobbled surface composed of small stones (RS1), which was traced over a distance of at least 15m at the southern end of the trench. This wall was also constructed without a foundation trench. The layer of small cobbles was c. 0.1m deep and lay upon the natural.

It would appear that the cobbled layer, denoted as RS2, is the contemporary of the cobbled layer found in other parts of the town. It is certainly the same layer as that encountered immediately beyond the limits of the excavation to both the north and the south.

Finds from the excavation included a crutch-headed stick-pin, horseshoes and horseshoe nails, a copper-alloy chain and one fairly complete leather shoe.

*Clare Mullins, 31 Millford, Athgarvan, Co. Kildare.*

### 716. HAGGARD STREET, TRIM
No archaeological significance
99E0174

An extension to a shop in Haggard Street, Trim, required monitoring under Trim Urban District Council planning conditions. The site is within the area of archaeological potential of the town, immediately adjacent to St Patrick's Cathedral.

The topsoil was stripped to the rear of the existing shop for 23m. It was composed of black silt with rounded stones 0.05–0.1m across, and up to 1m in depth of it was removed. There were a few large, rectangular stones up to 0.3m long and three deposits of modern rubbish including animal bone, pottery and glass. Nothing of archaeological significance was noted.

The foundation trench was dug into the subsoil, 1m wide and 0.4m deep. The subsoil was yellow/brown and archaeologically sterile. The maximum depth of excavation was 1.5m.

*Carmel Duffy, The Mill Road, Umberstown Great, Summerhill, Co. Meath.*

### 717. KILDALKEY ROAD/ATHBOY ROAD/HAGGARD STREET, TRIM
Environs of town gate
280124 257012
SMR 36:28
99E0142

Test-trenching associated with the Trim Sewerage Scheme was carried out in the vicinity of the site of the Athboy Gate in May 1999. Test-trenches were opened along the Kildalkey Road and the Athboy Road/Haggard Street over a combined length of 50m. Intermittently, some remnants of cobbled road surfaces were encountered, but there was no associated dating evidence, and these may have been

Medieval wall resting on road surface, Haggard Street (No. 715).

quite modern. No evidence of either Athboy Gate or the town wall was found.
*Clare Mullins, 31 Millford, Athgarvan, Co. Kildare.*

### 718. LACKANASH, TRIM
Post-medieval
N829572
99E0246

An assessment was requested by Meath County Council as a requirement for further information following the lodging of a planning application for 199 houses. In addition the ESB intends to run underground cables across part of the site, coming in from the Lackanash road, where a pylon is to be constructed, and then running eastwards into the adjoining housing estate

There are no recorded monuments in the SMR for the townland. The site is between Trim and Newtown Trim, and it is likely that medieval remains survive at some point here, along with the possible survival of earlier monuments. Both fields retain evidence for ridge-and-furrow cultivation, possibly dating to the 18th century.

There is a tradition of an old road running along the southern boundary of the site, surviving in the portion of the field that runs parallel to the Lackanash road. The feature is represented by a flat area defined on the north side by a shallow ditch that slopes up to the area of the field to the north, which retains its evidence for ridge-and-furrow cultivation. The course of the ditch meanders slightly; it is *c.* 4m wide at the top. A small channel was cut through the north side of the ditch, which may represent a drainage feature.

The surface of the 'road' is level. If it was an old road it is not marked as such on the first edition of the OS 6-inch map and may therefore have been out of use by the 1830s. It has been built over by the houses that now front the Lackanash road to the west of the development.

The ridge and furrow respected the line of the feature, suggesting that it was in existence when the furrows were dug. Two of the fifteen trenches tested the area of the possible road, one of them in the location of the proposed pylon.

Cutting 1, a 19m-long trench, tested the possible old road, across its surface, through the ditch and through the higher ground on its north side. Ploughsoil 0.4m deep overlay yellow, sandier material 0.3m deep, overlying grey, very sandy gravel. The latter two layers were natural, and the interface between them was marked by an amount of decayed stone.

There was no evidence for a road surface underneath the sod. Both the ploughsoil and the underlying natural layers were featureless apart from the disturbance caused by the ditch along the south side of the 'road'. A stone shore was inserted at the bottom of the ditch, the top level of which was no more than 0.5m below the sod level. The shore comprised a layer of rough stones 0.5m wide. The maximum width of the ditch at the top was 2.2m. The fill of the cut of the ditch was the same material as the ploughsoil.

Cutting 7 tested the location of the proposed electricity pylon. It was within the area of the old roadway, but there appeared to have been some disturbance here caused by the piping of the ditch immediately to the west, which emerges into the ditch along the boundary of this site. Material may also have been dumped from the property immediately to the west.

The stratigraphy comprised grey ploughsoil 0.3m deep, overlying a layer of yellow clay 0.6m deep. These layers overlay a dark grey, natural, sandy gravel. The maximum depth of the trench was 1.5m.

At the south end of the trench a layer of stone immediately under the sod was exposed. These were small stones and did not have a consistent pattern, suggesting that the layer had been laid down during dumping of material in recent times.

Archaeological material was not exposed in this trench.

The other trenches revealed ploughsoil overlying mixed glacial layer deposits.

Some months later a trench for an ESB cable was excavated across the site. This was monitored. The same sequence of deposits was exposed here as in the test-trenches.
*Rosanne Meenan, Roestown, Drumree, Co. Meath.*

### 719. MAUDLIN/COMMONS, TRIM
Adjacent to medieval town
N805564
99E0512

Pre-development test-trenching was undertaken to provide additional information for the planning process. The site, currently an uncultivated garden 36m by 70m, is between Castle Street/New Dublin Road and Back Street, which leads into Patrick Street. It runs roughly north–south, although there is a kink in the long axis to the north-north-east. It is *c.* 260m south-east of and outside of the town walls of Trim and to the south of the River Boyne, the south bank of which is 50m away. The southern end of the site is level, and 30m north of the southern boundary the ground begins to slope downwards towards New Dublin Road/Castle Street and the river beyond. There is a difference of 7.5m between the upper and lower parts of the site.

Four trenches were excavated by mechanical digger using a 1.6m-wide ditching bucket. These spanned the area of the development site.

In Test-trench 1, subsoil was reached at about 0.4m along the level area of the cutting, then at less than 0.2m after the break of slope, which occurred 0.24m from the south end of the trench. Subsoil was a glacial till, generally yellow but variable in colour and composition, with sandy gravel patches that became the norm along the slope. The overlying topsoil contained bone, charcoal and occasional sherds of pottery, some of which were early medieval in date. The topsoil had clearly been cultivated, and the bases of a number of furrow systems were apparent in the subsoil in all trenches. Five features were noted in Trench 1, none on the slope.

F101 was an area of grey, silty clay containing lenses of ash, occasional angular stones, a small amount of animal bone, some of which was burnt, and six pieces of pottery ranging from 13th-century local wares to 14th–15th-century wares. The soil was dry and friable. The feature was 1.75m wide and ran diagonally across the trench from south-west to north-east into Trench 3. Both sides were demarcated by a sloping cut edge, but its length was not established.

F102 was a feature cut into subsoil, 0.9m wide, which ran across the trench in a roughly east–west direction at a point 9.6m from the southern end of the trench. The fill was a brown, stony silt containing charcoal flecks. Some sherds of pottery were recovered in its vicinity, but it was not clear whether they had come from the feature. None were recovered while cleaning it by hand.

F103 was similar in orientation and dimensions to F102, although it was wider, at 1.1m. It occurred at a point 13.3m from the south end of the trench. The cut sides were quite steep. The fill was a light brown clay over a dark brown clay with black, organic inclusions. It was considered that this may have been a field boundary, but it does not coincide with one shown crossing the site on a 19th-century map. Instead the boundary appears to coincide with the break of slope.

F104 and F105 are two parallel furrows that run north-north-west/south-south-east. F104 was picked up at the junction of the north side of F101 and the east side of the trench. It was traceable for a distance of 9.5m and was 0.3m wide on average. It was cut by F102 and could be traced as far as the west side of F103, which also apparently cut it. F105 extended from the west side of Trench 3, through into Trench 1, where it too was cut by both F102 and F103, and was traceable for some distance beyond F103, where it disappeared 16.5m from the south end of Trench 1. F105 was at its widest, 0.5m, in Trench 2. Both furrows had a fine, silty, brown fill.

The overlying topsoil deepened in Test-trench 2 to a maximum of 0.7m, although it averaged 0.6m deep. Again this soil contained occasional bone, modern and medieval/post-medieval pottery and charcoal. Features could only be discerned at or near subsoil level, and furrows were again visible. Six features (not including F105, which cuts through the west side of the trench) were recorded.

F201 was identified as the site of a test-pit dug by the owner to establish bedrock levels.

F202 was an irregular feature, possibly simply a dip in the underlying subsoil, with relatively undisturbed deposits surviving within it. It occurred at a point 4.2m from the west end of the trench. A possible furrow, F202a, ran through it on the west side, although this was not very certain, but its orientation was similar to furrows F104–5.

F203 was a possible second furrow that ran from immediately beside the north-east side of F202 south-west across the trench and was 0.2–0.3m wide.

F204 was a shallow dip that ran north–south across the trench at a point 7.8m from the west end. It was 0.4m wide, and the surface was blackened and contained some oyster shell.

F205 appeared to be another possible dip in the subsoil running north–south across the trench. It was revealed 8.7m from the west end of the trench and was 1m wide. Like F202 and F204, it had no definite cut edges, although it is quite regular and the base seems flat. The fill was a fine, silty, light brown clay c. 0.18m deep. One sherd of pottery, the slashed handle of jug, probably 13th-century ware, was recovered.

F206 was an area of in situ burning. It survived as a depression running parallel to F205 and 0.3m east of it. It had a maximum width of 0.7m and extended for 1.45m at a slight diagonal across the trench. A grey/brown, silty clay c. 70mm deep overlay a blackened surface. This covered subsoil that was oxidised to a bright red. The eastern edge of the feature was well-defined and may mark the edge of a flue. No finds were recovered from it.

Topsoil in Test-trench 3 was also on average 0.6m deep and contained inclusions of animal bone, charcoal and a mixture of modern and medieval pottery. Four features were recorded from it, although one was of recent date.

F301 was a pit that traversed the trench 3m from its west end. It was 2.4m wide and contained the skeleton of a calf. Sherds of modern china were found in direct association with the bones.

The east side of pit F301 was cut through a deposit of brown, silty clay with charcoal, F302. This was not the fill of a cut feature, and where the subsoil was naturally higher it did not survive.

F303 was a cut running north-west/south-east through the trench. It seemed to cut through F302, but the fill associated with the cut differed very slightly from F302. It contained charcoal, bone, one piece of flint and sherds of medieval pottery, both Leinster cooking ware and local 13th-century ware.

F304 was a cut 1m to the east of F303 and parallel to it with an associated fill extending east to the end of the trench. This c. 0.25m-deep, mid-brown silt contained some bone, charcoal and one sherd of medieval local ware.

The topsoil in Test-trench 4 was shallow, between 0.15m and 0.2m. A large sherd of medieval pottery had been recovered from topsoil in Trench 1 near to the junction with Trench 4, but no in situ features were noted in the underlying subsoil, which was principally glacial gravels. No finds were recovered from this trench.

Archaeological deposits were uncovered within the southern area of the site, probably of medieval date. Whilst evidence existed of the presence of substantial structures, there was clear evidence for in situ burning activity and for the presence of features dug into subsoil. There was no indication of prehistoric activity.

Finola O'Carroll, Cultural Resource Development Services Ltd, Campus Innovation Centre, Roebuck, University College, Belfield, Dublin 4.

### 720. MILL STREET/HIGH STREET/HAGGARD STREET, TRIM
Urban medieval
280124 257012
**SMR 36:28**
**99E0142**

Monitoring of a new ground-water pipe through Mill Street, High Street and Haggard Street, Trim, was carried out from April to August 1999. Along much of the route of the pipeline an old, roughly cobbled or metalled street surface could be traced, varying in depth from c. 0.2m to almost 1.5m beneath the present street surface. This layer varied in its precise composition but was generally characterised by angular stones lying in a compact matrix of red/brown, sandy clay with inclusions of animal bone and oyster shell. It was generally 0.1–0.2m thick and lay directly upon the natural, following a horizontal course wherever it occurred. On Mill Street and lower High Street this layer was sometimes underlain by a silty, grey/brown layer, which also followed a horizontal course and appeared to be closely and possibly functionally related to it. There was little doubt about the contemporanity of this layer where it occurred on Mill Street and High Street, although its continuity was occasionally broken by services.

This stony layer was sometimes overlain by a deep archaeological deposit that was in turn truncated by modern road construction. This deposit was a dark, silty, organic layer that tended to produce fragments of timber, straw and leather and occasionally sherds of medieval pottery. This dark, organic layer was in turn regularly overlain by a brown, clayey gravel. It is likely that these layers represent an episode of deliberate street-heightening.

At the junction of High Street and Haggard Street these layers became quite uniform in character. The stony layer interpreted as an old street surface occurred here at c. 1.4m beneath the present road surface and was generally overlain by 0.2–0.3m of silty, organic material. A short distance beyond the southern end of Haggard Street a substantial pit was cut through by the pipe-trench. This pit measured c. 3m in diameter and was not fully bottomed by the service trench, which extended to a depth of over 2m. It was unclear whether this pit post-dated or pre-dated the cobbled layer.

Immediately north of this pit a linear arrangement of roughly dressed stone, 2.15m long, was observed on the east side of the trench at a depth of 1.1m beneath the present ground surface. The cobbled layer was not clearly discernible in the vicinity of this stone arrangement, but the evidence indicates that it occurred at c. 1.7m below the present street surface in the general area. The cobbled layer continued northwards up Haggard Street, where it was associated with deeper archaeological deposits that became the subject of an excavation (see No. 715 above). These deposits comprised four separate and subsequent layers of a metalled or cobbled road surface interspersed with episodes of deliberate road-heightening, over a combined depth of almost 2m, as well as the remains of two masonry walls and a number of pre-road formation gullies. It is believed that the more widespread cobbled surface, as observed during monitoring in other parts of the town, is related to the second-earliest road surface examined during the archaeological excavation (Road Surface 2). Towards the northern end of Haggard Street, beyond the limit of the excavation, this layer could again be identified lying upon the natural and covered by a thin spread of black, silty material. These layers petered out just south of the junction of Haggard Street and Logan Street, but a layer of modern cobbles was intermittently visible for the remainder of the pipe-trench to the north, which continued a short distance out the Kildalkey, Athboy and Kells roads.

A well was encountered towards the northern end of High Street. This was post-medieval in date. Its cut clearly truncated the layers described above, and its upper courses were overlain directly by the modern road formation, suggesting that it may have been truncated during this event. Another well was encountered on Haggard Street, which again post-dated the archaeological layers.

At the western end of Mill Street the remains of two stone-and-mortar walls were tentatively identified. Both were aligned at a right angle to the line of the street, but they clearly post-dated any archaeological layers in the area. Neither wall appeared to have been very substantial.

Clare Mullins, 31 Millford, Athgarvan, Co. Kildare.

### 721. TRIM COURTHOUSE, MANORLAND, TRIM
19th-century courthouse and 13th-century Franciscan friary
**N802568**
**96E0247 ext.**

This excavation and associated monitoring were undertaken before and during the extensive refurbishment of and extension to the courthouse building during the summer of 1999. The courthouse was constructed in the early 19th century, and it is widely held that it was erected on or near the site of the early 13th-century Franciscan friary (Moore 1987, 147; NMI files).

An initial assessment was conducted on the site in 1997 by Dominic Delaney (*Excavations 1997*, 145–6). At this time two test-trenches were opened. Two burials, which appeared to be *in situ*, were revealed, one in each trench, with a possible third also revealed.

During excavation and monitoring undertaken in 1999, additional burials were uncovered, as well as finds, both of which suggested that 13th-century activity underlies the 19th-century courthouse building. Seven burials (most of which were incomplete owing to 19th-century disturbance) were revealed. Six of these appeared to be medieval in date and thus associated with the friary. One of the burials was later than the others and probably dates to the mid- or early 19th century. A significant amount of disarticulated bone, both human and animal, was revealed throughout the site during monitoring of general ground reduction. It is likely that a substantial number of burials were disturbed during the construction of the courthouse.

Finds from the site included sherds of medieval floor tiles, medieval pottery and a bronze stick-pin (the pin is probably a 'spatulate-headed' type A and thus dates to the late 12th to mid-13th century (O'Rahilly 1998, 29)).

Three small areas of walling were revealed. These were composed of one surviving course of small stones sitting in lime mortar. They appear to have been partially collapsed or robbed out but were probably medieval in date. Their full extent was not revealed as only very limited areas of the site were available for excavation. It is likely that these relate to medieval structural features, possibly even the friary itself, but given the limited area opened it was impossible to be certain.

A large, U-shaped cut feature was revealed; however, owing to the small area opened and extensive disturbance, it was not possible to determine the nature or extent of this feature.

*References*
Moore, M. 1987 *Archaeological inventory of Co. Meath*. Dublin.
O Rahilly, C. 1998 A classification of bronze stick-pins from the Dublin excavations 1962–72. In Conleth Manning (ed.), *Dublin and beyond the Pale*. Dublin.

*Avril Purcell, Margaret Gowen & Co. Ltd, 2 Killiney View, Albert Road Lower, Glenageary, Co. Dublin.*

**722. TOWNSPARK SOUTH, TRIM**
Urban medieval
28018 25693 (centred on)
SMR 36:48
99E0041

Test-trenching was carried along the route of two ESB duct-trenches between 20 and 23 January 1999. The proposed routes were within the zone of archaeological potential for Trim as identified in the Urban Survey of County Meath. Archaeological deposits discovered during the test-trenching led to further hand-excavation in selected areas and to intensive monitoring along the remainder of the duct trenches.

Duct-trench 1 ran for *c.* 90m in a south-east direction from Bridge Street, along the bank of the River Boyne, to the location of a proposed substation. Duct-trench 2 was in the north-west of the town. Its point of origin lay 35m from the north-west corner of the town wall. The trench then skirted the outside of the old town wall for a distance of *c.* 128m, to a point where it met Watergate Street.

*Test-trenching*
Five trial-trenches were opened along the route of the proposed development. Trenches 1–3 were along Duct-trench 1, and Trenches 4–5 were along Duct-trench 2.

Trench 1 was adjacent to the possible site of the Water Gate, which had been demolished at the turn of the century. It contained a number of archaeological features that could be divided into two phases. The first was the remains of three limestone-built walls. These were sealed by 1.1–1.2m of 19th–20th-century dumped deposits. These walls, while close to the approximate site of the Water Gate, are likely to have been later, perhaps dating to the 19th century. Local sources refer to a number of cattle pens in the area before the construction of the present carpark and swimming pool. It is therefore possible that the walls represent the remains of such a structure.

Trench 2 was roughly 35m west of Trench 1 and ran parallel to the projected line of the town wall. It revealed evidence of *in situ* archaeological deposits along this part of the proposed development. The first 0.5m of stratigraphy within Trench 2 consisted of episodes of relatively modern dumped material. This material sealed C14 and C17, which contained several sherds of 13th-century pottery, including part of a base of a cooking vessel.

Trenches 3–5 contained nothing of archaeological significance.

*Archaeological excavation*
The deposits exposed in Trench 2 were excavated between 1 and 5 February. A spread of over 16m of archaeological deposits was exposed extending eastward from the western end of Trench 2. The medieval stratigraphy was 0.5m deep at the base of the duct trench and was sealed by, on average, 0.5m of modern and 18th–19th-century dumped layers. The archaeology, as it survived, appeared to represent a series of medieval dumped deposits. The section face exposed during the excavation of Duct-trench 2 would suggest that these were dumped from west to east.

A shallow gully, C22, which was orientated north–south and was 1.6m wide and 0.61 deep, was recorded. It was filled by the medieval clays C24, C31 and C23 respectively. It is interesting to note that all the medieval deposits were confined to the east of C22, which suggested that it may have acted as some form of boundary defining a property/plot.

To the west of C22, stratigraphy consisted of 0.7m of modern and 18th–19th-century dumped layers overlying the natural clay.

Sixteen metres west of C22 lay another north–south-orientated gully, C27, which was 1.3m wide and 0.49m deep. It cut the natural gravel C28 and was filled by several episodes of silting. C25 was the only deposit that had any associated dating evidence, in the form of one sherd of modern china.

Interpretation of the excavation area toward the centre of Duct-trench 2 was made difficult by the narrowness of the area opened (0.5m) and the fact that, in places, the deposits were not bottomed out, leaving a number of stratigraphic relationships unresolved. Their proximity to the projected line of the old town wall to the south raises the possibility that they were dumped from there or perhaps from the Water Gate to the east.

*Monitoring*
The monitoring programme was carried out between 27 January and 5 February 1999. No features or deposits of archaeological significance were exposed along the length of Duct-trench 1. Natural geology was not reached within the trench, and the stratigraphy consisted of modern dumped deposits and rubble. No further features or deposits of archaeological significance were exposed along the length of Duct-trench 2 outside the area described above.

*Rob Lynch, IAC Ltd, 8 Dungar Terrace, Dun Laoghaire, Co. Dublin.*

## MONAGHAN

**723. CORNAPASTE**
Suspected brushwood surface
245731 318353
98E0408 ext.

A limited excavation was carried out at Cornapaste, Scotshouse, Co. Monaghan, in April 1999 of a possible brushwood surface uncovered during previous testing on the site by Eoghan Moore (*Excavations 1998*, 170). The proposed development consisted of an extension to an existing sawmills at Cornapaste. Sites in the vicinity include the Black

Pig's Dyke, an enclosure, a holy well and a possible ecclesiastical foundation associated with St Patrick.

An area measuring 12m east–west by 16m was excavated in the vicinity of the possible brushwood surface. A peaty layer averaging 0.4–0.6m deep overlay a grey, natural marl that contained the stumps of two trees. These had substantial roots penetrating into the marl and intertwining amongst themselves. They appeared to represent two trees along the edge of the marsh. No other features or finds were recovered from the area excavated.

*Donald Murphy, Archaeological Consultancy Services Ltd, 15 Trinity Street, Drogheda, Co. Louth.*

### 724. CORNAPASTE
Near Black Pig's Dyke
**246031 318353**
**99M0037**

Monitoring of topsoil-stripping for a proposed residential dwelling at Cornapaste, Scotshouse, Co. Monaghan, was carried out in April 1999. The site is to the east of the Black Pig's Dyke, or Worm Ditch, and lies close to the remains of an enclosure, a holy well and 'Roman Catholic Stations' where there is the tradition of a Patrician foundation.

Monitoring revealed that topsoil directly overlay natural boulder clay, and nothing of archaeological significance was noted.

*Donald Murphy, Archaeological Consultancy Services Ltd, 15 Trinity Street, Drogheda, Co. Louth.*

### 725. MANNAN CASTLE, DONAGHMOYNE
Anglo-Norman motte, baileys and stone castle remains
**SMR 28:118**
**99E0044**

The site of Mannan Castle is on the south-facing slope of a limestone drumlin ridge c. 2 miles to the north-east of the town of Carrickmacross and commands a panoramic view of the surrounding countryside. The site is composed of a motte and inner bailey connected by a causeway with an accompanying bank/ditch formation and an outer bailey without any bank/ditch. The stone ruins of a castle are on top of the motte, inner bailey and causeway.

The earliest archaeological survey of the site was carried out by Henry Morris and published in the *County Louth Archaeological and Historical Journal* in 1910. This survey was somewhat incomplete, and Morris stated in his report that 'the place is so overgrown with nettles, briars, and other kinds of brushwood that it is almost impossible to make perfectly accurate measurements, but the ones given in this article are as careful as I could make them' (Morris 1910, 263). There are brief descriptions of the site of Mannan Castle in Orpen 1908, 265; McKenna 1920, 398–400; and Brindley 1982, 90.

In March 1994 Donaghmoyne Community Development Committee, with the assistance of FÁS, initiated a Community Employment Scheme, the objective being to clear the excess shrubs etc. from the site of Mannan Castle in order that a full archaeological survey could be carried out. Permission was sought from the National Monuments and Historic Properties Division, then of the Office of Public Works, for this clearance work to be carried out under the supervision of a qualified archaeologist. Permission was granted, and in June 1994 this clearance work began. By June 1995 the site had been cleared. Kieran O'Conor carried out the first detailed archaeological survey of the site, while Kevin Barton, aided by Joseph Fenwick and Martina McCarthy, carried out topographical, magnetic susceptibility, magnetic gradiometry and resistivity surveys.

In conjunction with the archaeological and geophysical surveys, the early and medieval history of the parish of Donaghmoyne was researched. The results are contained in a report lodged with *Dúchas* The Heritage Service in August 1998 (Moore 1998).

During the 1190s the Pipard family had gained a foothold in the area of Donaghmoyne (Lawlor 1914–16, 314–23) and set about consolidating their position by constructing a motte and bailey(s) (described in the Annals of Loch Cé as a 'caisleán') in 1197, 'Caisslen Domnaigh Maighen' (Hennessy 1871, vol. 1, 186).

Why was Donaghmoyne chosen as the location for the Pipard motte and bailey(s)? Tom McNeill has argued that the locations of Anglo-Norman mottes, baileys and stone castles in Leinster were not part of defensive strategy against either external attack or internal revolt but rather for reasons of social status (McNeill 1989–90, 63). This would seem to be the case for the choice of the site of Mannan Castle. Within the townland of Donaghmoyne are the remains of the Early Christian foundation of Domnach Maigen (SMR 28:116), along with two ringforts or earthworks that surround the site of Mannan Castle (SMR 28:117 and 119), while another earthwork is recorded as having existed to the east of the site in the townland of Tullynacross (SMR 28:120). Also, two holy wells are close to the site of the castle—one dedicated to St Brigit in the townland of Donaghmoyne, and one dedicated to St Lasair in the adjacent townland of Aghavilla (SMR 28:121 and 124). Indeed the name Aghavilla is derived from the old Irish *Ached Bile* 'the field of the sacred tree' and would suggest that this place was of particular significance to the early inhabitants of Donaghmoyne. It can be concluded that the area within the vicinity of the early church site of Donaghmoyne was one of religious, social and political significance during the early historic period and that this was the reason why Roger Pipard constructed his *caisleán* there.

During the early decades of the 13th century the Pipard family experienced difficulty holding onto their lands in Donaghmoyne. In 1227 the Pipard lands were entrusted to Ralph Fitz Nicholas. He immediately set about rebuilding the motte and bailey(s). In 1228 Fitz Nicholas was granted the service of (the men of) Meath and Louth for forty days to help fortify the defences. Two years later the grant was repeated when the Irish burned the castle of Donaghmoyne. Fitz Nicholas then proposed to build a stone castle on the site (Smith 1999, 46). This plan eventually came to fruition in 1244, when the *caisleán*, or motte and bailey(s), at Donaghmoyne was encastellated in stone: 'Caislean Dhomnaigh Mhaighen do chumdach hoc anno' (Hennessy and MacCarthy 1887–1901, vol. 2, 302).

The remains of a small stone keep are still to be found on top of the motte at Mannan Castle, while the remains of stone walls still exist on top of the causeway and inner bailey.

At this stage it is necessary to ask what exactly was the nature of the *caislean* constructed in 1197. The fact that the annalist of the Annals of Loch Cé states that the *caislean* was covered in stone in 1244 would suggest that before this no stone construction was present on the site. It would be logical to assume, then, that only an earthen and timber construction was built in 1197. Moreover, from the archaeological remains it is clear that only the motte and inner bailey were encastellated in stone in 1244. It could be argued that the *caislean* constructed in 1197 was made up of only the motte and inner bailey and that in 1244, when the motte and inner bailey were encastellated in stone, the outer bailey was constructed to compensate for the loss of the area of the inner bailey. Of course it must be admitted that this argument is primarily based on the interpretation of the historical record and not on the evidence of the archaeology of the site. It could also be the case that a motte, inner bailey and outer bailey were all constructed in 1197 and that it was thought necessary or profitable only to fortify the motte and inner bailey in 1244.

In conclusion, two of the major questions about the site of Mannan Castle are, what was the nature and extent of the *caislean* constructed in 1197, and how did the encastellation of this *caislean* in 1244 affect the pre-existing configuration of the site. It was with these questions in mind that the present archaeological excavations at the site took place.

The objectives of the 1999 excavations at the site of Mannan Castle were to investigate that area at the southern extremity of the outer bailey highlighted in the geophysical surveys as the possible location for a perimeter ditch, to investigate the nature of ditch between the inner and outer baileys, and to investigate the area immediately to the south of the uppermost pond, to determine whether there was a palisade on top of the exterior bank at the north-west of the motte.

Eleven cuttings were excavated. Cuttings 1–6 were on the outer bailey, Cuttings 7–10 were within and on the sides of the ditch between the inner and outer baileys, and Cutting 11 was immediately to the south of the pond at the north-west extremity of the site.

*The outer bailey*
It is evident that the area of the outer bailey had been ploughed to a depth of *c*. 0.5m. On account of this, all of the uppermost layers in Cuttings 1–6 were disturbed. A total of 366 artefacts were uncovered during the excavation of Cuttings 1–6. All of these must be interpreted as having been uncovered in a disturbed environment. However, the huge amount of iron slag, pottery and iron nails/ironworking tools found would suggest that the southern part of the outer bailey was the location for intensive industrial/ironworking activity. In support of this is the fact that beneath the disturbed layers two working surfaces and a foundation trench for a small structure/workshop were also uncovered in Cutting 1. A ditch feature that formed the western boundary of one of these working surfaces was also revealed. Six sherds of medieval pottery were found in the fill of this boundary ditch.

The uncovering of a very shallow perimeter ditch (*c*. 0.3m deep) in Cutting 4 would suggest that the area of the outer bailey possessed a surrounding ditch/palisade trench. The presence of this shallow perimeter ditch feature had been indicated by the geophysical surveys.

*The ditch between the inner and outer baileys*
The excavation in the ditch area between the inner and outer baileys revealed that the ditch was U-shaped and made up of a shallow, homogeneous fill. This was a black, gritty silt and was *c*. 0.35m deep.

The most noteworthy feature uncovered in the area of ditch was a stone-and-earthen foundation on top of the north-western perimeter of the outer bailey. This was interpreted as the foundation for a wooden structure that crossed the ditch. The existence of a crude arrangement of stones on the berm-like structure in the ditch was also noteworthy, as it may constitute the remains of a stone foundation for the upright(s) for a wooden bridge connecting the inner and outer baileys.

The lack of any medieval finds in the area of the ditch would suggest that the north-western perimeter of the outer bailey was not an area associated with any industrial/ironworking activity.

*The area in the vicinity of the pond*
The limited excavation of Cutting 11 did not reveal the existence of any palisade on top of the outer ditch that surrounds the motte on its north-western extremity.

The excavation at Mannan Castle was funded by the National Monuments and Historic Properties Service, *Dúchas*, on the recommendation of the National Committee for Archaeology of the Royal Irish Academy.

*References*
Brindley, A. 1982 *Archaeological inventory of County Monaghan*. Dublin.
Hennessy, W.M. (ed. and trans.) 1871 *The Annals of Loch Cé* (2 vols). London.
Hennessy, W.M and MacCarthy B. (eds. and trans.) 1887–1901 *Annála Uladh: annals of Ulster* (4 vols). Dublin.
Lawlor, H.J. 1914–16 A Charter of Donatus, Prior of Louth. *Proceedings of the Royal Irish Academy* **32**, 313–23.
McKenna, J.E. 1920 *Parishes of Clogher* (2 vols). Enniskillen.
McNeill, T.E. 1989–90 Early castles in Leinster. *Journal of Irish Archaeology* **5**, 57–64.
Moore, E. 1998 Report on the historical background, archaeological survey, geophysical surveys and research design for proposed archaeological excavation at the site of Mannan Castle, Donaghmoyne, County Monaghan. Unpublished.
Morris, H. 1910 Mannan Castle. *Journal of the County Louth Archaeological and Historical Society* **2** (3), 263–71.
Orpen, G.H. 1908 Mottes and Norman castles in County Louth. *Journal of the Royal Society of*

Antiquities of Ireland **38**, 241–69.

Smith, B. 1999 *Colonisation and conquest in medieval Ireland: the English in Louth, 1170–1330*. Cambridge.

*Eoghan Moore, Prospect House, Dunsrim, Scotshouse, Co. Monaghan.*

### 726. ST PATRICK'S CHURCHYARD, DONAGHMOYNE
Site of Early Christian church foundation
**99E0697**

St Patrick's Churchyard is in the townland of Donaghmoyne, Carrickmacross, Co. Monaghan. It is on a limestone knoll that overlooks the surrounding countryside and is *c.* 750m to the south-east of the motte, baileys and stone castle remains known as Mannan Castle. It contains an early modern graveyard and the remains of an early 19th-century church.

In January 1993 Donaghmoyne Community Development Committee, with the assistance of FÁS, initiated a Community Employment Scheme to clear the excess shrubs, dead trees, nettles etc. from the site under archaeological supervision. During the work, the remains of what was thought to have been a series of walls were uncovered on a raised area near the centre of the churchyard. In February 1994 Joseph Fenwick carried out an archaeological and topographical survey of these church remains.

Two trenches were excavated at the site from 29 November to 10 December 1999. Trench 1 measured 4m (north–south) x 2m. The remains of the foundations of a church were uncovered *c.* 0.85m beneath the present ground surface. These were composed of two linear stone-and-mortar substructures that measured 2.2m x 0.4m. These substructures ran approximately on an east–west axis. A shallow groove, interpreted as a joist for a horizontal timber, was found on top of each of these substructure remains.

Trench 2 measured 4m (north–south) x 2m and was *c.* 13.6m to the north-east of Cutting 1. Two features were revealed. The first was a linear arrangement of large stones uncovered immediately beneath the top sod. This stone arrangement ran on a north–south axis and was interpreted as a boundary feature. Immediately to the east of the stone arrangement the remains of a possible stone surface were revealed. Two iron nails were uncovered at the interface between this possible stone feature and the top sod.

It is intended that a second season of excavation will take place here during 2000.
*Eoghan Moore, Prospect House, Dunsrim, Scotshouse, Co. Monaghan.*

### 727. LISGALL
Adjacent to rath
**H83800670**
**SMR 28:112**
**99E0270**

Assessment of a residential development adjacent to a rath included the excavation of six test-trenches in the area of the development. No archaeological remains were found.
*Cóilín Ó Drisceoil, 6 Riverview, Ardnore, Kilkenny.*

### 728. LISSARAW
Environs of ringfort
**H67532912**
**SMR 13:20**
**99E0736**

An assessment at the site of a proposed dwelling in Lissaraw townland, Co. Monaghan, was carried out on 21 December 1999. The site is 2km south of Monaghan town and 150m north of a ringfort.

Two assessment trenches were excavated across the front and rear foundation lines of the proposed dwelling, and a third was excavated across the proposed location of an associated septic tank north-west of the site of the proposed dwelling.

Trench 1, along the line of the proposed septic tank, was 12m long (north-west/south-east) by 1.2m. Dark brown topsoil, 0.3m deep, overlay mottled, orange/grey limestone boulder clay.

Trench 2, along the northern foundation line of the proposed dwelling, was 20m long (west–east) by 1.2m and was excavated to a total depth of 0.5m. Dark brown topsoil on average 0.25m deep overlay mottled, orange/grey limestone boulder clay. A single stone-filled field drain, 0.46m wide, ran diagonally (south-west/north-east) through the eastern section of the trench.

Trench 3, along the southern foundation line of the proposed dwelling, was 14m long (west–east) by 1.2m and was excavated to a total depth of 0.5m. Dark brown topsoil on average 0.25m deep overlay mottled, orange/grey limestone boulder clay.

The assessment did not reveal any soils, features or finds of archaeological significance.
*Malachy Conway, Archaeological Consultancy Services Ltd, 15 Trinity Street, Drogheda, Co. Louth.*

### 729. THE DIAMOND CENTRE, MONAGHAN
Urban
**99E0141**

Testing was carried out on a site of proposed development at the Diamond Centre, Monaghan, on 22–9 March 1999 on behalf of the North-Eastern Health Board.

One test-trench was mechanically excavated. It was *c.* 30m long on a north–south axis x 1.2m. A series of 19th-century walls was uncovered in the southernmost area of the test-trench. A large quantity of red brick fragments, modern pottery, plastic and metal pieces was also uncovered.
*Eoghan Moore for Arch-Tech, 32 Fitzwilliam Place, Dublin 2.*

### 730. THE DIAMOND, MONAGHAN
Near Franciscan friary
**26731 33380**
**99E0402**

An assessment of a proposed commercial development at the Diamond, Monaghan, was carried out in August 1999. The site is on the north side of the Diamond in the townland of Roosky and is not far from the Franciscan friary (SMR 9:39).

Testing was limited to two $1m^2$ test-pits, as the development is in the interior of a building. Evidence from both pits was very similar. Deposits below the concrete floor of the building exist to a depth of 0.5m and appear to be related to the construction of the present building on the site, which is most likely of late 18th- or early 19th-century date. Below this level a layer of roof slates covering a brown, peaty soil with animal bone was evident. This layer varied from 40mm to 80mm thick and overlay a hard surface composed of gravelly clay, stone and mortar. Both the peaty soil and the gravelly clay were interpreted as floors that relate to an earlier building phase on the site. The presence of roof slates in the overlying fill suggests that the floors belong to a building demolished before the erection of the present structure. A single sherd of brownware recovered from the hard surface would be consistent with a date in the late 17th or early 18th century. Thick clays exposed below these floors containing occasional charcoal flecks and animal bone may represent buried topsoil or garden soil pre-dating building on the site.

It was recommended that further archaeological work be carried out if the development is to proceed as planned.

*Deirdre Murphy, Archaeological Consultancy Services Ltd, 15 Trinity Street, Drogheda, Co. Louth.*

### 731. 57 DUBLIN STREET, MONAGHAN
Urban
99E0161

Testing was carried out at a site of proposed development at 57 Dublin Street, Monaghan, on 1–3 April 1999. One test-trench, measuring c. 5m x 1.4m, was excavated by hand. The remains of a (probable) 19th-century stone base/wall foundation, along with the remains of a stone wall and an associated stone-lined drain, were uncovered. No archaeological artefacts were found.

*Eoghan Moore, Prospect House, Dunsrim, Scotshouse, Co. Monaghan.*

## OFFALY

### 732. BUSHERSTOWN
Adjacent to earthwork
20552 18219
SMR 47:8
99E0593

The site is a private house development adjacent to a rectangular earthwork and overlooked by Moatquarter motte just over the county boundary in Tipperary.

The footprint of the house was tested, as were two trenches running parallel to the long axis of the house to front and rear. A series of features was noted that can best be interpreted as linear features running north-north-east/south-south-west across the four parallel trenches. The date and nature of the features are unclear, the only datable find being a sherd of internally glazed red earthenware of post-medieval date found to one side of one of the features. Several fragments of disarticulated animal bone were retrieved from deep within one of the features. The features run from east of the earthwork downhill towards the road across the front of the site.

The features seem to be restricted to the house area. Testing of the septic tank and percolation areas, further to the west, revealed no features, while two trenches at the very front of the site across the line of the new frontage wall also revealed no features.

*Brian Hodkinson, Annaholty, Birdhill, Co. Tipperary.*

### 733. CAPPANCUR
Church and graveyard (vicinity of)
23794 22509
SMR 17:8
99E0214

Test excavation was undertaken at the site of a proposed dwelling on 24 May 1999. The site (75m north–south by 45m) is adjacent to a church site and a graveyard. The *Archaeological inventory of County Offaly* describes 'a roughly rectangular graveyard within which Comerford (1883, 305) noted a small portion of a ruined structure possibly representing the remains of a church'. There are no visible remains of this structure at ground level, but a modern concrete enclosure, presumably representing the outline of the church, stands at the centre of the graveyard. The existing graveyard boundary is D-shaped (maximum dimensions 55m east–west by 35m), and, according to the SMR files, 'there is a strong possibility that the "D" is but the NNE half of an earlier circular enclosure'.

Four test-trenches were mechanically excavated at locations corresponding to the footprint of the proposed development. The topsoil was a grey/brown, silty sand, 0.25m thick, overlying a yellowish/brown, silty sand subsoil. Outcrops of shattered limestone bedrock and grey, silty sand and gravel were encountered at a depth of 0.45m. A flat/round-bottomed ditch, 2.9m wide and 0.75m deep, was encountered in three of the trenches, and this appears to represent portions of a continuous feature, possibly an enclosure associated with the nearby ecclesiastical site. The ditch fill was a light brown, clayey sand with infrequent inclusions of angular cobbles and boulders, animal bone and molluscs. No datable finds were recovered from the fill. In Trench 4 a deposit of orange, sandy clay, 0.4m thick, was present on the north lip of the ditch, and this may represent part of a levelled internal bank. Similar spreads of orange, sandy clay were encountered in Trenches 2 and 3, albeit at some distance from the ditch. It should be noted that the ditch encountered during testing is not aligned with the circular enclosing element that forms the north boundary of the existing graveyard.

A second, smaller ditch was encountered 6m south of the main ditch in Trench 4. It was 1.8m wide, narrowing to 0.8m at the limit of excavation, which was 0.4m below the top of the ditch. The fill was similar to that of the main ditch, and the two features are probably contemporary.

The proposed development would directly affect the archaeological features encountered during testing, and planning permission was refused for this reason.

*Dominic Delany, 31 Ashbrook, Oranmore, Co. Galway.*

### 734. CASTLETOWN BOG, CASTLEARMSTRONG
Brushwood trackway
217236 228818
99E0287

The following excavations (Nos 734–43 and 752–58 below) were carried out in the Lemanaghan area of

County Offaly as part of the Bord na Móna Archaeological Mitigation Project. They were undertaken to resolve known archaeological sites so that Bord na Móna could resume peat production in areas that had been cleared of archaeology. The fieldwork took place from June to September 1999.

The Lemanaghan complex of bogs is north of the River Brosna, between the towns of Ballycumber and Ferbane. This work concentrated in Castletown (99E0287–92), Tumbeagh (99E0377–8 and 99E0404–6) and Killaghintober bogs (99E0444–8), in which a total of eighteen excavations, comprising 35 individual cuttings, were completed. Areas of brushwood structures found close to each other were excavated in Castletown Bog (99E0287–91), as well as a linear plank trackway (99E0326). Three brushwood toghers (99E03778 and 99E0405), a brushwood platform (99E0404) and a linear plank trackway (99E406) were excavated in Tumbeagh Bog. Three linear plank trackways and a brushwood togher were excavated in Killaghintober Bog (99E0444–8).

*Castletown Bog, Castlearmstrong*
This site was a brushwood togher that extended on the Bord na Móna field surface for a distance of 31m. Excavation revealed a partially milled brushwood togher 0.75m wide and 0.23m deep. The site was composed of three layers of wood overlying each other. The upper layer was a substantial layer of longitudinal brushwood rods infilled with packing material and held in place with pegs. The upper longitudinals were ten to twelve rods wide and three to four rods deep at the best-preserved section of the togher. The longitudinals all ran in a north-west/south-east direction and measured 10–45mm in diameter. The spaces between the longitudinals were infilled with a packing material of twigs and small brushwood. This layer was the upper walking surface of the togher.

The brushwood associated with the second and third layers was less substantial than the upper longitudinals. The size of the wood ranged from tiny twigs to brushwood rods up to 42mm in diameter. The brushwood averaged 20mm in diameter. There were more twigs in this layer. Most of the brushwood and twigs ran longitudinally. The twigs along the western extent of the cutting had a more haphazard arrangement. Pegs were found along the outer edges of the trackway, preventing horizontal movement of the togher. The togher was traced for 25m. It is possible that it was constructed across a short stretch of particularly wet bog that could otherwise not have been crossed.
*Ellen O'Carroll, ADS Ltd, Windsor House, 11 Fairview Strand, Fairview, Dublin 3.*

### 735. CASTLETOWN BOG, CASTLEARMSTRONG
Brushwood togher
217238 228838
**99E0288**

This site was an area of degraded brushwood. A cutting 1m x 2m was placed over the site, and excavation revealed sixteen dispersed brushwoods with no particular arrangement. Three pieces of brushwood at the northern end of the cutting represented the remains of pegs. One of the pegs had a toolmarked end. The wood represents the substructural remains of a brushwood togher.
*Ellen O'Carroll, ADS Ltd, Windsor House, 11 Fairview Strand, Fairview, Dublin 3.*

### 736. CASTLETOWN BOG, CASTLEARMSTRONG
Brushwood togher
217246 228858
**99E0289**

This site was the remains of a brushwood togher on the surface of a Bord na Móna production field. Excavation revealed the remains of the upper elements of a linear brushwood togher and a lower layer of pegs. The togher was 1.32m wide, 60mm deep and 15m long. The wood was concentrated at the northern end of the cutting and was two layers deep. The upper layer was composed of some milled and broken longitudinals between 5mm and 47mm in diameter. The longitudinals were laid approximately north-west/south-east. There was also some transverse brushwood placed over and under the longitudinals. The transverses were slightly larger than the longitudinals, up to 50mm in diameter. This upper layer of wood represents the walking surface of the togher.

A second layer of wood was revealed underneath a thin peat layer. This context consisted mainly of pegs between 10mm and 40mm in diameter. The pegs were also clustered at the northern side of the cutting. Toolmarks were recorded and sampled from both of the wood layers. All were simple, multi-faceted, chisel-cut points.
*Ellen O'Carroll, ADS Ltd, Windsor House, 11 Fairview Strand, Fairview, Dublin 3.*

### 737. CASTLETOWN BOG, CASTLEARMSTRONG
Brushwood togher
217222 228811
**99E0290**

This site was a brushwood togher on the surface of a Bord na Móna production field. Excavation revealed the remains of a linear brushwood togher, two layers deep, secured into the peat with pegs. The togher was 0.95m wide and 0.13m deep. The first layer comprised both longitudinal and irregularly placed brushwood, five to seven rods wide and three rods deep. The togher was best preserved at its eastern end and quite disturbed at its western end from a combination of exposure to the elements and Bord na Móna milling. The brushwood rods ranged in diameter from 20mm to 50mm. There were several pegs noted around the edge of this togher, and some twig infill was recorded between the brushwood. The pegs were set into the peat at angles of 35–50°.

A second layer of wood was excavated underneath the upper brushwood, which consisted of an abundance of twigs, several pegs and some irregularly placed brushwood. These pegs averaged 20mm in diameter. Bark was present on over half the wood excavated. The site was traced along the Bord na Móna field surface for 20m.
*Ellen O'Carroll, ADS Ltd, Windsor House, 11 Fairview Strand, Fairview, Dublin 3.*

### 738. CASTLETOWN BOG, CASTLEARMSTRONG
Brushwood toghers
217268 228841
**99E0291**

This site was a 5m-by-5m cutting placed within a zone

of brushwood structures. The area previously could not be defined into individual, separate structures. The excavation revealed four wooden structures.

Site A was a small puddle togher, which was excavated in its entirety. It was constructed of layers of small brushwood and twigs to make a compact structure. The peat related to this site is indicative of a very wet environment. This togher was constructed to cover a very wet area of peatland to facilitate safe crossing. No pegs were associated with this togher, which suggests that the structure may not have been intended to be permanent.

Site B was a compactly constructed trackway composed of twigs, brushwood and pegs four layers deep. Bord na Móna milling had destroyed some of the upper elements of this site. The trackway was 0.16m deep and 32m long, and its maximum width was 0.9m. The site curved around an orange sphagnum area of *Sphagnum cuspidatum* peat, which probably represents a pool or area of open water at the time of its construction.

Site C was the milled remains of a brushwood togher constructed of two layers. The superstructure, which was the actual walking surface of the togher, was constructed using long, straight brushwood. The substructural layer was composed of lighter brushwood and some small twigs. The site was very disturbed in the central portion. Track C was traced for 1m to the north of the cutting and then petered out. This site was visible in the section of the drain face to the south of the cutting but could only be traced for another 1m after this. The total length of this togher was 8m.

Site D represented the remains of a sparsely constructed togher. This togher was only present at the north-western and south-eastern end, as milling had destroyed the middle portion. The track was 0.8m wide and 90mm deep. The superstructure was constructed of approximately ten longitudinally placed brushwood rods. The brushwood measured 15–40mm in diameter, and they were spaced *c.* 50mm apart.

A substructural layer was excavated underneath at the south-eastern end of the cutting. It was composed of six pieces of brushwood averaging 30mm in diameter. There was a bed of twigs also associated with the wood. This twig bed was 0.2m in diameter and was not as compact as the twig beds associated with Site B. There were two pegs associated with the togher, which were found at the south end of the cutting. Bark was present on 60% of the wood and twigs. Two toolmarked brushwoods were recorded from this layer. This track was visible on the field surface to the north of the cutting for *c.* 1.5m. It was also visible in the drain section to the south and was traced from there for another 1.2m. The total length of this togher was 8.5m.

All of the tracks described above were found very close together and appear to be running in the same general direction. They could only be traced for a maximum distance of 32m, and it is possible that they were laid down across a short stretch of particularly wet bog that could not otherwise have been crossed.

*Ellen O'Carroll, ADS Ltd, Windsor House, 11 Fairview Strand, Fairview, Dublin 3.*

### 739. CASTLETOWN BOG, CASTLEARMSTRONG
Remains of brushwood togher
**217289 228779**
**99E0292**

This site was an area of brushwood. Three clusters of brushwood survived in the cutting, the least damaged pieces at the southern end. They were placed longitudinally and measured 15–45mm in diameter. Some pegs and transversely laid twigs were also found at this end of the cutting. The twigs functioned as packing material in between the longitudinals. The remaining brushwood in the cutting was substructural in appearance and was more irregularly arranged, with several peg-like elements. The wood represented the remains of some superstructural and substructural elements of a brushwood togher. The site was traced for 11m.

*Ellen O'Carroll, ADS Ltd, Windsor House, 11 Fairview Strand, Fairview, Dublin 3.*

### 740. CASTLETOWN BOG, CASTLEARMSTRONG
Remains of brushwood togher
**218091 229157**
**99E0325**

Excavations revealed a large roundwood lying east–west 0.13m in maximum diameter, which narrowed gradually towards its western end. The roundwood was exposed for 1.27m in the cutting but could be traced outside the cutting to measure 1.65m in total length. The roundwood was orientated on an east–west axis, with several small fragments of wood at its eastern end. Several other milled and disturbed pieces of wood could be traced on the same field surface to the north. The track could be traced for 16.46m by the presence of disturbed pieces of wood on the Bord na Móna field surface.

The wood excavated in this cutting represented the remains of a linear brushwood togher. The roundwood may have been a transverse timber placed under the main track. The presence of the milled wood on the Bord na Móna field surface indicates the last remnants of this togher.

*Ellen O'Carroll, ADS Ltd, Windsor House, 11 Fairview Strand, Fairview, Dublin 3.*

### 741. CASTLETOWN BOG, CASTLEARMSTRONG
Linear plank togher
**Cutting 1: 218244 229372, Cutting 2: 218222 229280, Cutting 3: 218201 229168**
**99E0326**

The site was a linear plank trackway traced for 350m across the western extent of Castletown Bog. It has been dated to AD 684–9. Three cuttings measuring 10m x 2.5m were excavated, one at either end and one in the centre of the trackway.

Cutting 1 was opened at the northern end of the trackway to reveal the superstructural planks and roundwoods, which ran in a north-east/south-west direction. The superstructural layer in this cutting comprised three split planks and two roundwoods. The planks were laid end to end and were quite narrow, only 0.17m in maximum width. The planks were tangentially and radially split oak timbers, and their upper surfaces had been milled by Bord na Móna operations. The central portion of the cutting contained two roundwoods running parallel to the planks in a north-east/south-west direction. The planks ran under a peat pool at the southern end of the cutting. The upper plank was visible at the southernmost end of the cutting, where it emerged from the pool.

After the superstructural planks were lifted two substructural layers of wood were exposed. The first layer comprised five substructural transverses, the second a scattering of planks, wood chips, bark, brushwood and roundwoods. The five transverses (Layer 1) were exposed along the length of the cutting; they held the upper plank in place and prevented the walkway from sinking into the peat. Layer 2 was an irregular arrangement of densely compacted timbers found mainly in the middle and southern section of this cutting under the pool area. This second layer of wood was probably thrown down into the cutting, where it was exceptionally wet and where the upper plank walkway needed extra support. Hazelnut shells were found throughout the cutting.

Cutting 2 was placed at the central portion of the trackway c. 90m south of Cutting 1. The disturbed super- and substructural layers of the single plank walkway were revealed in this cutting. The superstructural layer, which was mainly confined to the southern half of the cutting, had been disturbed, possibly in antiquity. It was composed of a degraded roundwood and oak fragments at the northern end and a longitudinal plank and roundwood at the southern end. The plank and roundwood at the southern end of the cutting had slid off the substructural runners; they were lying to the west of the substructure, at an angle of 45°. The roundwood at the northern end of the cutting had also slipped away from the main body of the trackway.

The substructural layer of the trackway in this cutting was composed of approximately eight timbers with a lot of wood chips, parts of planks and brushwood rods. This array of wood was laid down in a haphazard fashion and probably functioned as infilling providing extra support to the superstructural walkway. The substructural timbers were closely spaced and were composed of planks, roundwoods and a single brushwood. The transverses were all found at the southern half of the cutting, alongside the eastern edge of the baulk. Five of the transverses extended beyond the eastern baulk. Four squared oak pegs were found in the central area of this cutting. These pegs would have also provided support to the superstructural walkway.

A leather ankle shoe was found beside the area of densely compacted wood in the central part of the cutting. It was front-laced, at the heel and the toe, and the sole was worn through, probably through walking. A 7th-century pedestrian who walked along the plank trackway may have lost this shoe.

Cutting 3 was c. 100m south of Cutting 2. The trackway lay c. 0.5m below the field surface. This cutting exposed the classic linear plank trackway composed of a superstructure of oak planks supported by a lower layer of two transverses. The superstructural layer was composed of two longitudinal planks laid end to end, converging at the northern transverse. A number of pegs were found on the western side of the cutting. These pegs did not provide any form of physical support to the togher as they were found c. 0.6m away from the main trackway elements. The pegs may have been laid down to mark out the routeway of the track before its construction.

This trackway will be studied in association with the adjacent dryland monuments, which include St Manchan's church and a number of ringforts and cashels.

*Ellen O'Carroll, ADS Ltd, Windsor House, 11 Fairview Strand, Fairview, Dublin 3.*

### 742. KILLAGHINTOBER BOG, CASTLEARMSTRONG
Remains of linear trackway
**Cutting 1: 217027 229440, Cutting 2: 216992 229320, Cutting 3: 216955 229240**
**99E0444**

This linear trackway was traced across the Bord na Móna field surface for a length of 225m. Three cuttings, 5m x 2.5m, were placed at both ends and in the centre of the site.

The wood from the northern cutting, which was exposed underneath the milled peat, consisted of two transverse roundwoods, three pegs and some wood chips. In general the wood associated with this cutting was in poor condition and had been milled on the upper surfaces. The oak wood chips exposed probably represent the superstructural plank, which would have rested on the transverses and would have functioned as the walkway. The roundwood found at the northern end of the cutting was orientated east–west and would have originally functioned as a transverse support to the upper plank. The second transverse, which was found c. 1.8m south of the northern transverse, was slightly displaced and had degraded. It was 70mm in maximum diameter and 1.86m long. This transverse would also have functioned as a support to the upper walkway planks. Two pegs found beside the northern transverse would have added support to the upper plank walkway.

The wood exposed in the central cutting was similar to that excavated in Cutting 1. The cutting contained elements of an upper plank walkway with associated transverses, displaced planks and pegs. Four displaced and milled planks, which probably belonged to the superstructural layer of the trackway, were revealed at the eastern and southern sides of the cutting. These planks were split from oak timbers. Also associated with this layer were four pegs. These pegs would have originally secured the superstructural planks into the peat to prevent the planks from moving. The substructure, which was revealed at the northern and southern ends of the cutting, consisted of three degraded transverse planks. These planks would have acted as substructural supports to the upper, longitudinal planks.

Some of the wood found in this cutting had been exposed on the field surface for some time, and milling had destroyed the upper layers of the trackway. After initial trowelling two roundwood timbers, four pegs and some wood chips were found at the north-eastern end of the cutting. One of the roundwoods represented the remains of a transverse timber that would have supported the upper walkway. The second roundwood ran longitudinally along the northern half of the cutting. This roundwood was worked with a metal tool at one end. It may have lain alongside the upper plank walkway, after which it sank into the peat.

The underlying peat associated with this cutting was yellow and brown and contained layers of *Calluna* (heather) and sedges.

Although the trackway was destroyed and milled along most of its length, the overall composition and constructional elements associated with this site can be fairly well understood from this excavation. The trackway was a fairly simple construction comprising a linear plank superstructure possibly laid end to end and then supported by plank and roundwood transverses. In places an occasional roundwood may have lain alongside the upper planks. These roundwoods would have provided extra support to the actual walkway. The substructural transverses supported the plank walkway and elevated it off the wet peat.

*Ellen O'Carroll, ADS Ltd, Windsor House, 11 Fairview Strand, Fairview, Dublin 3.*

### 743. KILLAGHINTOBER BOG, CASTLEARMSTRONG
Remains of linear trackway
Cutting 1: 216961 229306, Cutting 2: 217008 229431, Cutting 3: 216890 229143, Cutting 4: 216865 229083
99E0445

This linear plank trackway was traced across the Bord na Móna field surface for a length of 450m. Four large cuttings were placed along its length. Each cutting produced similar constructional evidence and preservation qualities.

The trackway was a substantial construction consisting of three layers of structural elements. The upper, walking surface was constructed of split oak planks laid end to end and pegged into the peat at each end through a mortice hole. These pegs were found beside the substructural transverse timbers and would have prevented the upper plank from slipping off the substructure. Owing to the weight of the overlying peat and the Bord na Móna milling machinery, the plank had sunk into the peat and was found at the same level as the substructural timbers. The planks were also broken in several places along their length and had fallen off the underlying transverses.

The upper plank walkway was supported at regular intervals by a two-layered substructure. This substructure was composed of roundwood transverse timbers underlain by longitudinal plank runners. These planks were radial split oaks *c.* 2m long.

A dressed rod was found on the north-western side of the trackway. It was driven vertically into the peat. It was 20mm in diameter and 1.2m long. The top end of the rod was slightly bent, while the bottom end was stepped and then pointed. There were areas of poorly decomposed sphagnum peat with inclusions of *Menyanthes trifoliata* (bog bean), which suggests that these were very wet areas, probably pools, at certain locations beside the track. There were also areas of *Eriophorum* (bog cotton) above and around the trackway, which suggest drier conditions.

The construction methods of this trackway can be clearly demonstrated from the excavations along its length. The substructural transverses; which consisted of a layer of roundwood and plank transverses underlain by longitudinal plank runners, supported the plank walkway and elevated it off the wet peat.

This trackway has been dendrochronologically dated by The Queen's University of Belfast to AD 596–7. The track can be traced from the dryland at Killaghintober to an island in the centre of the bog and appears to link up with a trackway of similar date and construction excavated by the IAWU in 1998 on the opposite side of the island (*Excavations 1998*, 176, 98E0464). The site then runs towards Lemanaghan Island, which houses the remains of St Mella's cell (a small Early Christian rectangular oratory), St Manchan's church and Early Christian grave slabs. Although this work is only at a preliminary stage, it is probably true to say that this trackway was associated with the construction of the monastery on the island, as it was founded sometime before St Manchan's death in AD 665.

*Ellen O'Carroll, ADS Ltd, Windsor House, 11 Fairview Strand, Fairview, Dublin 3.*

### 744. CLONMACNOISE
Ecclesiastical
201565 230580
99E0079

Testing of a proposed residential development was conducted on 22 February 1999. The area of development was 500m to the east of the major ecclesiastical site of St Ciarán (SMR 5:4–28) and 200m south of the Nuns' Church (SMR 5:27 (01)). The monastic site of St Ciarán lasted from the 6th to the end of the 17th century. It was anticipated that the site may be along the line of the ecclesiastical enclosure.

Test-trenches revealed a shallow cut into natural, grey sand, which appears to be a late feature, as well as post-medieval to modern pottery and a fragment of animal bone of indeterminate age. No features or artefacts of an archaeological nature were found.

*Donald Murphy, Archaeological Consultancy Services Ltd, 15 Trinity Street, Drogheda, Co. Louth.*

### 745. CLONMACNOISE
Early Christian ecclesiastical
20087 23047
SMR 5:4, 5:58 and beside 5:56 (hoard site)
99E0715

The site is within the ecclesiastical site of St Ciarán, close to the castle of Clonmacnoise and a recently discovered bridge. Midlands East Regional Tourist Authority Ltd proposes to develop a new tourist office on the site. A hoard of Hiberno-Norse coins (SMR 5:27 (1)) was found in 1979 less than 25m from the proposed development. An assessment entailing the digging of two trenches was carried out on 16 and 17 December 1999. Both trenches were excavated north–south along either side of the proposed building.

Trench 1 was excavated to the west of the site and measured 18m by 2m. A brown topsoil and sod overlay the natural, grey sand of the esker to a depth of 0.4–0.6m. Four furrows were exposed running

Trenches 1 and 2 at Clonmacnoise (No. 745), showing post-medieval furrows.

south-west/north-east through the trench. The furrows in the centre of the trench were cut through redeposited sand and bone, which may represent the backfill of a ditch. At the south end of the trench a deposit of brown clay containing iron slag was exposed below the sod and topsoil. Animal bone was recovered from this trench.

Trench 2 was excavated along the east side of the proposed building and measured 22m by 2m. The sod and topsoil were removed by machine. Sieving of this material yielded animal bone, two pieces of cut antler, some iron slag and an iron nail. The natural, grey sand of the esker was exposed at a depth of 0.4–0.6m. Six furrows were visible cut into the sand and ran south-west/north-east, as in Trench 1. A small pit was exposed to the north of the trench, which was filled with a brown loam containing charcoal. Ash and charcoal deposits were found at the south end of the pit. To the south of the trench a band of brown clay containing stone, bone and charcoal traversed the trench from east to west and may represent a backfilled ditch along the same line as that in Trench 1. A single sherd of medieval pottery was recovered from the top of the fill of one of the furrows.

It is clear that extensive tillage took place in this area at one time. The only dating evidence was a single sherd of late medieval pottery, but this cannot be seen as conclusive. Judging from the excavated trenches, it is likely that the proposed development area contains archaeological deposits cut into or resting directly on the natural sand of the esker. A full excavation is planned for early 2000.
*Donald Murphy, Archaeological Consultancy Services Ltd, 15 Trinity Street, Drogheda, Co. Louth.*

### 746. BALLYKILLEEN, EDENDERRY
Monitoring
26034 22690
99E0050

Monitoring of the site clearance for construction of a peat-fired electricity-generating station took place from late January until the end of April 1999. During monitoring, two unstructured burnt spreads were identified and excavated. No dating materials were recovered, and it is unlikely that either was archaeologically important. A chert hollowed arrowhead was found *c.* 30m south of the bank of the River Frigile; however, it was found in isolation from other identifiable deposits or materials.
*Martin Reid, 37 Errigal Road, Drimnagh, Dublin 12, for ADS Ltd.*

### 747. GLASSHOUSE
17th-century glasshouse
20420 19035
99E0191

An upstanding forest glass furnace near Shinrone became the focal point for investigating 17th-century glass manufacturing. Several families of French Huguenot glassmakers from Lorraine had been manufacturing glass in England in the late 16th and early 17th centuries. Members of two of these families, Bigos and Henseys (de Hennezels), are known to have held land in Offaly during this period. The Henseys are the most likely to have run the Shinrone glasshouse as they owned the townlands surrounding the upstanding furnace. In 1615 the manufacture of glass in wood-fired forest-glass furnaces was banned in England, though not in Ireland. However, in 1638–9 the exportation and manufacture of glass in Ireland was prohibited, and in 1641 another bill prohibited the felling of trees as a fuel supply for glass furnaces.

Before the excavation a magnetic gradiometry survey was conducted by Joe Fenwick (Centre for Archaeological Survey, Department of Archaeology, NUI Galway) over an area 40m x 40m centring on the upstanding furnace. It was hoped that magnetic anomalies, which can be caused by intensive heat, would give an indication of the position of subsidiary furnaces. Several anomalies were recorded, the highest reading from the upstanding furnace. The second-highest reading came from an area 17m south-west of the main furnace.

In order to investigate the high anomaly south-west of the furnace, a cutting 2m x 4m was opened. Upon excavation an iron band of relatively recent date was recovered that would have caused the high magnetic anomaly. A test-trench 1m x 4m was then excavated along the length of the cutting. Although no archaeological features were present, a thick layer of fine sand lay 0.5m below the sod. This may be the source for the sand used in the glass-making at this site.

A second cutting, 6m x 8m, was opened to the north, west and south of the upstanding furnace. Immediately beneath the sod was a large scatter of debris from the furnace, which included furnace fragments, crucible fragments and bricks. Below this were areas of internal flooring consisting of small stones in a mortared floor. In the north-west of the cutting an area of sand/ash was uncovered. Immediately north of the furnace's stoking trench was an area of fire-reddened clay, the result of intense heat. It was initially thought to be the result of direct, *in situ* burning; however, the results of archaeomagnetic dating of the deposit (by Gould and McCann, Clark Laboratory, Museum of London) revealed that it was not physically related to the primary heat source for the glasshouse. It was suggested that magnetisation of the deposit may have occurred via an intensely heated surface overlying this deposit or may have come directly from a lesser heat source. This fire-reddened clay produced a date range of AD 1620–50 at 68%

Plan of excavations at the glass furnace in Glasshouse.

confidence level and AD 1610–60 at 95% confidence level. This represents the last firing at the site. These dates verify that forest glass was produced in Ireland for several decades after this had ceased in England.

South-west of the furnace's southern stoking hole were two circular, shallow, flat-bottomed pits within a portion of the mortared floor. The pits, one with a diameter of 0.6m and maximum depth of 0.09m, the other measuring 0.93m x 1.3m with a maximum depth of 0.1m, have been interpreted as receptacles for vessels associated with the glass-making process. Immediately south of this a mortared trench for a stone wall was revealed. It was 0.7–0.9m wide and 0.15m deep and ran the width of the cutting in an east–west direction. This wall, from which most of the stones were robbed out, may be the southern boundary wall of the glasshouse itself. The remains of a compact clay floor were uncovered immediately south of the foundation trench.

Finds included sherds of light green window glass, typical of broad (Lorraine) glass, and waste glass including droplets and dribbles from within the stoking trench of the furnace, which are direct evidence of the glass-making process. Other glass found on the site may have been brought to the site to provide cullet, broken glass that was recycled to make a fresh batch of glass.

Large sherds of used crucible were recovered, though only two rimsherds and no bases. From the rims recovered it can be estimated that these vessels were 0.5m in diameter and 25mm thick. Crucibles are usually bucket-shaped with straight sides. The imprint of the base of one of the crucibles (diameter 0.4m) is still apparent on the seige platform within the upstanding furnace. Other finds included pottery sherds, slates, bricks and waste material.

This research excavation was grant-assisted by funding from *Dúchas* The Heritage Service, Department of Arts, Heritage, Gaeltacht and the Islands, on the recommendation of the National Committee for Archaeology of the Royal Irish Academy.

*Jean Farrelly, 'Sonas', Curraghscarteen, Moyglass, Co. Tipperary, and Caimin O'Brien, 'Illaun View', Glenbower, Coolbaun, Nenagh, Co. Tipperary.*

### 748. KILCORMAC OR FRANKFORD
Mound (in vicinity of)
21872 21415
SMR 31:13
99E0264

Monitoring of topsoil removal was undertaken before Phase 1 of a proposed residential development from 18 May to 4 June 1999. The site, a green-field area (*c.* 2 acres) on the east side of the town, is close to a recorded monument. The *Archaeological inventory of County Offaly* describes it as 'a low mound (diam. 13m N–S; H 1.5m) enclosed by a fosse (D 0.3m; Wth 1m) with an external bank visible from N-E-S'.

The stratigraphy was relatively uniform across the stripped area. A dark brown, clayey sand topsoil (0.45m deep) overlay a layer of mid-brown, sandy clay (0.2m deep), which contained post-medieval and modern pottery sherds, corroded iron nails, iron slag, coal, red brick, slate and animal bone. This overlay a compact, orange, silty sand subsoil that occurred in patches across the site. It had an average thickness of 0.2m and overlay a compact, light grey, natural boulder clay.

A random cluster of eight possible post-holes was exposed adjacent to the north baulk at the north-west end of the access road. One of these features was excavated. It was subcircular in plan (diameter 0.35m) and round-bottomed in profile (0.26m in diameter) and contained two sterile fills. The upper fill comprised a compact, orange, silty sand 0.12m thick, and this overlay a compact, mid-brown, clayey sand 0.14m thick. The excavation was inconclusive, but the features were covered with plastic sheeting and topsoil before the laying of hardcore for the access road. Further investigation will be undertaken should this area be exposed during the proposed second phase of the development.

*Dominic Delany, 31 Ashbrook, Oranmore, Co. Galway.*

### 749. KILLEIGH
Archaeological complex
23657 21830
SMR 25:17
99E0348

Test excavation was undertaken before an application for open planning permission for four detached dwellings from 19 to 22 July 1999. The site is within the area of archaeological potential around a recorded monument. An Early Christian monastery was reputedly founded at Killeigh by St Sincheall in the 5th century. An Augustinian priory and convent were established here in the 12th century, and a Franciscan friary was built in the 14th century. In a field on the south-west side of the village are the remains of an earthwork comprising two earthen banks with an intervening flat-bottomed fosse. This feature may be the remains of an Early Christian enclosure, possibly refortified in the post-medieval period. Aerial photography has revealed the outline of this enclosure encompassing the entire village of Killeigh. The present structural remains at the site comprise portions of a formerly extensive Franciscan friary, which may have been built on the site of an earlier Augustinian priory.

The proposed development site is 50–125m south-east of the extant structural remains. It comprises a relatively level football pitch and measures *c.* 110m north-west/south-east by 40m. A partially levelled earthen bank, 1m high and 5m wide, is visible 70m south-west of the proposed development site. The bank extends *c.* 30m north-east/south-west and is aligned with the earthwork and a curving field boundary in a field to the west. The bank may represent part of the enclosing element associated with the ecclesiastical site. There were no surface traces of this bank in the area comprising the site of the proposed development.

Two test-trenches, 65–90m long and 1.8m wide, were mechanically excavated at locations corresponding to the general footprint of the proposed development. A 5–7m-wide spread of compacted, silty sand was encountered at the south-east ends of the two trenches. This feature is orientated north-east/south-west and may represent levelled bank material and/or the upper fill of a large ditch. It is significant that this feature is aligned with the earthwork and the curving field boundary in the field to the west of the site. This strongly suggests that it is part of the enclosing element associated with the ecclesiastical remains at Killeigh. Two post-medieval features—a large, irregular spread of grey/brown, silty sand and an oval pit—were also encountered in Trench 2. The pit (2.5m north–south by 0.95m) contained a fill of light grey/brown, silty sand, and the finds included green glass wine bottle fragments, clay pipe stem fragments and several sherds of late/post-medieval pottery. A single sherd of Bellarmine pottery was recovered from the irregular spread. The other features encountered appear to be modern, but judgement must be reserved pending further investigation. The plans for the proposed development at this site have been revised, and a second phase of archaeological testing will be undertaken in 2000.

*Dominic Delany, 31 Ashbrook, Oranmore, Co. Galway.*

### 750. RATHCOBICAN
Various
25370 23233
SMR 11:17
99E0461

Test excavation was undertaken, from 30 August to 3 September 1999, before application for planning permission for four detached dwellings. The sites are within the area of constraint around a ringfort that consists of a raised circular platform (diameter 44.8m, height 1m), enclosed by a slight bank largely reduced to a scarp, and an external fosse (width 4m, depth 0.9m). The SMR file for this site also notes that a field system possibly associated with the ringfort exists in the area west and south-west of the monument. The ringfort is 25m from the eastern edge of the proposed development site, which measures 70m north–south by 125m.

Three test-trenches were mechanically excavated, 125m long and 1.5m wide, extending east–west across the site. The features encountered were three spreads of burnt material, probably levelled *fulachta fiadh*, and portion of a circular enclosure, possibly a ring-ditch. Several linear and curvilinear features were also encountered, but it was not clearly established whether these were of archaeological significance. The archaeological features were recorded as follows.

A large spread of burnt material (17m east–west) was encountered midway along Trench 1. The burnt material directly underlay the sod and had an average thickness of 0.35m, lensing out to 0.05m at the east and west. The eastern edge of the spread is clearly defined by a curvilinear feature, 1.7m wide, and a second curvilinear feature, 1.2m wide, was encountered 22m west of the burnt material. It is possible that the curvilinear features represent the east and west limits of a large circular enclosure (diameter *c.* 44m).

The south edge of a circular enclosure, possibly a ring-ditch, was encountered at the east end of Trench 2. The ditch is 1.2m wide, and the maximum external diameter of the exposed portion of the feature was 13m east–west. A spread of burnt material (9m east–west) was encountered at the west end of the trench.

A spread of burnt material (12.5m east–west) was

encountered close to the east end of Trench 3. The east edge of the spread is defined by a curvilinear feature, 2.4m wide, and a second curvilinear feature, 2m wide, was encountered 25m east of the burnt material. Again it is possible that these curvilinear features represent the east and west limits of a large circular enclosure (diameter c. 45m).

The cost of full archaeological excavation made the development unfeasible.

*Dominic Delany, 31 Ashbrook, Oranmore, Co. Galway.*

### 751. TULLAMORE/BALLYCOWAN
No archaeological significance
**23374 22529–23478 22462**
**99E0152**

An assessment was undertaken to define the potential adverse affects on the archaeological resource as a result of the Tullamore Water Supply Improvements, Contract No. 5. This involved the monitoring of excavations carried out during the site investigation contract. Twenty-five trial-pits and sixteen slit-trenches were monitored between 4 and 28 March 1999, both within the town centre and in outlying areas.

The walkover survey revealed that much of the proposed development runs along pre-existing road surfaces and through Tullamore town centre. The northern end of the pipeline runs through a forested area, while the southern end of the scheme, in the area of the Clonminch water tower, runs through green-field and wetland areas.

Nothing of archaeological significance was revealed during the site investigation programme.

*Rob Lynch, IAC Ltd, 8 Dungar Terrace, Dun Laoghaire, Co. Dublin.*

### 752. KILLAGHINTOBER BOG, TUMBEAGH
Linear plank trackway
**Cutting 1: 216740 229639, Cutting 2: 217008 229431, Cutting 3: 216890 229143, Cutting 4: 216865 229083, Cutting 5: 216582 229389, Cutting 6: 216563 229345, Cutting 7: 216645 229494, Cutting 8: 216591 229494**
**99E0446 and 99E0447**

These sites were recorded as two separate trackways during the reassessment survey in 1998. Excavations in 1999 revealed that they were actually both the same site, a linear plank trackway traced across the Bord na Móna fields for a length of 420m. This plank trackway has been dated by The Queen's University of Belfast Radiocarbon Laboratory to 940 BC.

The site varied slightly in composition along its length, as did the level of preservation. Eight cuttings were placed along the length of the site, which was a simple trackway construction composed of longitudinal oak planks laid end to end and underlain at the northern end by transverse planks. The average diameter of the superstructural walkway planks was 0.25m. The superstructural planks were quite substantial and would have acted as a flat walking surface to facilitate safe crossing over the bog. There were no evidence of pegs or mortices in these cuttings, and the impression one gets from its simple construction is that this site was not intended to have been in use for a long period of time.

This trackway appears to differ slightly at the southern and northern ends. The cuttings excavated on the southern side exposed a linear plank trackway constructed of split oak planks laid end to end. The trackway appeared to be quite disturbed at certain locations, and there was no evidence of mortices, pegs or supporting transverses. The cuttings excavated at the northern end of the trackway showed evidence of transverse supports underneath the plank walkway in the form of planks and roundwoods. The above evidence suggests that transverse supports were required at the southern end of the bog to prevent the plank walkway from sinking, as it may have been much wetter in this area.

*Ellen O'Carroll, ADS Ltd, Windsor House, 11 Fairview Strand, Fairview, Dublin 3.*

### 753. KILLAGHINTOBER BOG, TUMBEAGH
Remains of brushwood togher
**216644 229376**
**99E0448**

This site was the remains of a brushwood togher on the surface of a Bord na Móna production field. A cutting measuring 1.5m x 2m was established over the site. Excavation revealed the milled remains of the upper elements of a linear brushwood togher and two lower, substructural layers of brushwood, pegs and twigs.

The brushwood togher measured 1.7m in maximum width and was traced for a length of 14m. The site was composed of a milled superstructural brushwood and roundwood layer and a lower, substructural layer orientated east–west. The superstructural layer of the togher was badly milled. It was composed of two roundwoods and around eleven brushwoods, as well as several outlying fragments. Half of the elements run transversely, and half of them were placed longitudinally. There were also three pegs associated with this layer, one of which was worked to a simple chisel point.

Two lower, substructural layers were revealed underneath the milled upper surface. The lower layers were composed of brushwood averaging 15mm in diameter, pegs and some twig packing. The pegs were found along the edges of the togher. Some were worked to a point at one end.

The remains of a leather shoe were found on the Bord na Móna field surface c. 70m south of this togher. The shoe had been exposed on the field surface for some time and had been badly damaged. A cutting was placed around the shoe, and the area was trowelled, but there was no evidence of any wood. There was no indication of wood in the surrounding area. It is possible that this shoe was originally associated with the togher (99E0448) and became dislodged during Bord na Móna milling.

*Ellen O'Carroll, ADS Ltd, Windsor House, 11 Fairview Strand, Fairview, Dublin 3.*

### 754. TUMBEAGH BOG, TUMBEAGH
Dispersed brushwood togher
**215550 229183**
**99E0377**

This linear brushwood and roundwood structure varied slightly in composition along its length, as did the level of preservation. The site was a sparse arrangement of brushwood, roundwoods and twigs that lay in the centre of the bog and did not extend across to the dryland areas.

The wood comprised a roundwood, some brushwood and a small amount of twigs. The site was 0.8m wide and 60mm deep. The structure ran in an east–west direction, and the majority of the elements ran longitudinally. There was a low density of wood in the cutting. The twigs appear to have been used as packing between some of the brushwood. Bark was present on over 90% of the wood. There was some root found in the cutting, and it is possible that this root disturbed the site. The wood was not very well preserved, as it lay in fen peat. There was no evidence of pegs, but one of the roundwoods was cut to a chisel point at one end.

It was traced for 28m and was preserved to a greater degree at the eastern end of the site. This site probably did not function as a togher as the dispersed arrangement of wood could not have supported the average person's weight. The wood may have acted as a guide or routeway across an area where it was safe to walk.

*Ellen O'Carroll, ADS Ltd, Windsor House, 11 Fairview Strand, Fairview, Dublin 3.*

### 755. TUMBEAGH BOG, TUMBEAGH
Brushwood and hurdle togher
215550 229183
99E0378

This linear brushwood, roundwood, hurdle and plank togher varied in composition along its length. The site was a compact linear arrangement of wood five layers deep in places. The togher was orientated on an east–west axis. The wood extended to 1.9m wide, but the main body of the togher was tightly compacted and had a width of 0.55m and a depth of 0.01m.

The upper walking surface of the track was composed of five roundwoods and around ten brushwoods, with a small amount of interspersed twigs. Several of the roundwoods were broken along their length, possibly owing to pressure from the overlying peat. There were numerous brushwood outliers around the track. These outliers possibly fell away from the track in antiquity. The only evidence for pegs was a split brushwood, which had tooling at one end and may have functioned as a peg. There was very little bark present on the wood. After the upper layer of wood was removed a second layer was recorded underneath. This was a compact arrangement of roundwoods, brushwood, twigs and wood chips up to four brushwoods deep in places. This lower layer was composed of smaller elements, with only one roundwood recorded. The wood was densely packed together owing to the presence of small brushwood and twigs. There were a lot of acquatic-loving plants such as *Menyanthes trifoliata* (bog bean) recorded throughout this layer of wood.

A hurdle panel was laid down alongside the brushwood togher at its eastern end. At this point a Bord na Móna drain truncated the hurdle panel, so its true length could not be established. The panel comprised a moderately tight weave of single rods over single sails. The hurdle was 0.95m wide and 50mm deep. The hurdle structure was probably constructed on dry land and then transported onto the bog and laid down alongside the brushwood/roundwood trackway in an area where it was particularly wet.

This site was traced along the Bord na Móna field surface for a length of 32m and had been milled slightly along some of its length. This track could have supported a human's weight in an area that we know was very wet because of the presence of *Menyanthes trifoliata* (bog bean) in the peat. There were some substantial lenses of bog ore found in and around the trackway. Although there has been no evidence for the exploitation of these ores for industrial purposes, parallels for such activities can be seen in Holland. Middle Bronze Age trackways excavated by Casparie in Holland were constructed to provide access to areas of bog iron ore in the peat.

*Ellen O'Carroll, ADS Ltd, Windsor House, 11 Fairview Strand, Fairview, Dublin 3.*

### 756. TUMBEAGH BOG, TUMBEAGH AND KILLAGHINTOBER
Togher
215643 229960
99E0406

This site was excavated as part of the 1999 Bord na Móna Archaeological Mitigation Project. The site was a linear plank trackway that had been identified at the drain edges and across the field surfaces of Tumbeagh Bog at twenty sightings for a distance of over 350m. The site was dated to 949±9 BC (QUB-9524). Three cuttings were excavated, two at both ends of the site and one in the middle portion. Cutting 1 was in the townland of Tumbeagh, and Cuttings 2 and 3 were in the townland of Killaghintober.

The site ran across the bog in an east-north-east/west-south-west direction almost parallel to the small modern road from Cappanalosset crossroads to the village of Doon. Its depth below surface varied from 0m to 0.7m. Its construction remained fairly consistent: either single- or double-placed longitudinal planks supported by transverse planks and held in place with pegs. While the main line of the site ran in an east-north-east/west-south-west direction, it would appear that there were at least two junctions. One of the junctions was found at Cutting 2 and ran southwards from the line of the site for 13m. The second ran northwards from Cutting 3 and was traced for a distance of 20m.

The first of the three cuttings measured 2.5m x 5m and was on the western side of the bog. At this location the site was visible at the drain edge as a linear plank with the remains of a mortice 50mm below the field surface. The site appears to slope downwards from west to east at this point. The site was composed of a single radially split longitudinal supported by three transverse planks. One of the transverse planks had a damaged mortice with an *in situ* peg, 435mm long and 18mm in diameter. Another peg was found in the cutting, close to the eastern baulk. This was a squared oak peg 0.43m long and 50mm x 25mm in diameter.

The second cutting measured 2.5m x 6m and was placed at one of the central sightings of the togher. This sighting contained a north–south scattering of planks and roundwoods spread for a length of 11m along the field surface at the drain edge. This location was chosen for excavation to establish whether this spread of material reflected a change in the construction of the trackway or whether there was more than one site present at this location. Two disturbed plank toghers were exposed in this cutting, which represented the first of two possible junctions along the length of the site and had a similar construction to that of the site exposed in Cuttings 1 and 3. The main line of the plank togher was found in the northern end of this cutting, while the junction ran away from it in a south-east/north-west direction. The remains of two longitudinal planks and a transverse plank fragment were exposed. There were two squared oak pegs 37mm and 42mm in diameter set at 70° off vertical to the east of the transverse plank. These pegs were similar to the squared peg from Cutting 1.

The south-east/north-west-running togher was also quite disturbed and was composed of three longitudinal and two transverse planks. One of the transverse planks underlay and the other overlay the longitudinals. Two of the longitudinals had regular square-cut mortices.

The third cutting, 2.5m x 5m, was established at the best-preserved part of the site, at the eastern extent of the plank trackway close to the drain edge. This cutting contained two longitudinal planks, laid side by side, both of which had square-cut mortice holes at their eastern ends. One of the mortices contained a squared oak peg, with a smaller peg inserted alongside it to keep it in place. The eastern part of the cutting contained a scattering of plank fragments and four pegs along the line of the site, which represented the last remains of the site. The pegs were 39–40mm in diameter, and their lengths ranged from 0.62m to 0.97m. The absence of longitudinal planks in the eastern part of the cutting is not unusual as it is possible for wetland sites of this nature to become displaced in antiquity owing to the waterlogged conditions in the surrounding bog.

Milled longitudinal and transverse planks were found on the field surface 5m to the north of Cutting 3. These timbers represent the second of the two possible junctions mentioned above. These timbers ran in a north–south direction, from the nearby dry land towards the excavated site. This site was similar in composition to the excavated site. It was composed of two upper longitudinal planks supported by transverse and irregularly laid planks and was traced for a distance of 20m.
*Jane Whitaker, ADS Ltd, Windsor House, 11 Fairview Strand, Dublin 3.*

### 757. TUMBEAGH BOG
Brushwood platform
215450 229660
99E0404

Excavations were carried out in Tumbeagh Bog, Co. Offaly, as part of the 1999 Bord na Móna Archaeological Mitigation Project.

This site was initially recognised as an irregular grouping of brushwood rods and pegs visible on the field surface. It was composed of small rods and pegs with no discernible orientation or construction pattern. The wood was concentrated in an area measuring 2.5m x 2.8m. The site appeared to have a single construction phase and was 0.08–0.12m deep. It was composed of over 300 irregularly laid brushwood rods, approximately 50% of which were pegs. These were set into the peat at angles of 70° to 90°, and most were broken in several pieces. These elements varied from 0.04m to 0.46m long, none having diameters of more than 20mm. From the broken nature of the pegs, the site appears to have been disturbed by both the milling process and the weight of machinery passing over it.

From its small size, lack of orientation and the large quantity of pegs, it appears that the site may have been a small platform. The surrounding field surfaces were investigated, but it would appear that the whole site was contained within a 2.5m-by-2.8m area. A small gravel knoll *c.* 20m in diameter was found 30m to the east of the excavated site. This knoll is the highest point in the bog, rising *c.* 8m above the surrounding production fields. The underlying peat conditions would suggest alternating wet and dry conditions at the time of the platform's construction. It is hoped that further analysis will provide a more conclusive explanation for the construction of the site in this location.
*Jane Whitaker, ADS Ltd, Windsor House, 11 Fairview Strand, Dublin 3.*

### 758. TUMBEAGH BOG
Togher
215950 229340
99E0405

This excavation was carried out in Tumbeagh Bog, Co. Offaly, as part of the 1999 Bord na Móna Archaeological Mitigation Project.

The site was initially identified as a small brushwood togher on the surface of a Bord na Móna production field. A small cutting, 1m x 2m, was excavated and revealed the remains of a narrow, linear, brushwood togher. The site was composed of longitudinal brushwood and roundwoods placed side by side to provide a walking surface. This site was 0.33m in maximum width and three to four rods wide. The rods ranged from 20mm to 90mm in diameter, and their upper surfaces had been machine damaged. The substructure appears to have consisted of some irregularly placed brushwood underlying the upper longitudinals. Several of the elements had toolmarks that varied in type from pencil points to wedge and chisel points.

The surrounding field surfaces were investigated to establish the full extent of the site, which was traced for a length of 8m. The site did not appear on the adjoining field surfaces, although it is possible that it was originally longer and had been destroyed by peat production.
*Jane Whitaker, ADS Ltd, Windsor House, 11 Fairview Strand, Dublin 3.*

## ROSCOMMON

### 759. ARDANAFFRIN
No archaeological significance
99E0029

Following the preliminary archaeological assessment of this site, which is close to the Iron Age Doon of Drumsna, six trenches were opened using a mechanical digger, as part of pre-development testing.

Examination of the strata revealed no trace of any archaeological features, deposits or artefacts. The stratigraphy encountered was all natural. Trenching in the vicinity of the higher ground produced the same stratigraphy but with more rock. The natural deposits were less waterlogged and were undisturbed.

The site produced no evidence of man-made interference or archaeological deposits.

*Jim Higgins, 'St Gerard's', 18 College Road, Galway.*

### 760. ARDCARN
No archaeological significance
18668 30200
SMR 6:103
99E0139

Nineteen test-trenches were opened within the confines of an archaeological site, an ecclesiastical enclosure, that will be affected by the proposed realignment of part of the N4 at Ardcarn, Boyle. The results from the testing confirmed that the proposed realignment will have no direct impact on the site. In sixteen of the trenches the bedrock occurred very close to the surface. The remains of a field boundary wall were uncovered in one of the other three trenches, and the last two were sited on linear embankments to determine whether the embankments were of an archaeological nature. In the middle of both trenches, and underlying the topsoil, a drystone capping, two or three courses deep, was uncovered. The stone capping covered a linear embankment consisting of a bank of sterile, sandy clay. In one of the trenches a fragmented clay pipe was found beneath the stone capping. It would appear from the results of the testing that the linear features were the remnants of land clearance.

*Mary Henry, 24 Queen Street, Clonmel, Co. Tipperary.*

### 761. BALLYCONBOY
No archaeological significance
17840 28622
99E0123

The proposed development is in the centre of a rich archaeological landscape with Rathcroghan mound as the focal point. The site is c. 75–100m west of Rathmore, a raised rath constructed on top of a natural mound. The proposed development concerned an extension to the rear of the existing building, which is thought to have been built in the early 1920s.

In accordance with the planning condition, pre-development testing in the form of trial-trenches was carried out. Four trenches were mechanically excavated, revealing no evidence of features/deposits of archaeological significance. The layers present were a brown garden soil overlying the natural.

*Fiona Rooney, Arch. Consultancy Ltd, Ballydavid South, Athenry, Co. Galway.*

### 762. BALLYKILCLINE
Early 19th-century tenant village
M990860
98E0297 ext.

Field excavations were conducted at the early 19th-century townland of Ballykilcline in Kilglass parish, Co. Roscommon, from 5 July to 6 August. The excavation team consisted of seventeen undergraduate archaeology students enrolled in Illinois State University's regular summer field school in historical archaeology. Funds for the research derived from student fees generated as part of the course. The excavated portion of the village is owned by J.J. and Dolores Neary, who live in nearby Glebe House. The excavation was conducted with their complete support and encouragement.

During its final years the townland of Ballykilcline was a Crown estate. From the 1790s to 1834 the Mahon family, owners of Strokestown Park House about seven miles away, leased the townland from the Crown. In 1834, however, the townland reverted to the Crown. Before their eviction in 1847 and 1848 the tenants refused to pay their rents and were involved in a protracted and often violent strike.

Before the 1999 excavation Kevin Barton, of the Applied Geophysics Unit of the National University of Ireland, Galway, made a detailed subsurface survey of the site using ground-probing radar. The placement of the cuttings was based on the results of these tests combined with three other sources of information: the results of the 1998 excavation (*Excavations 1998*, 177–8), the results of earlier geophysical testing, and the house locations depicted on the Ordnance Survey map. A total of 38 1m-by-2m cuttings were excavated, and 1352 artefacts were collected.

All excavation was conducted with hand tools in natural soil layers, and all artefacts were collected regardless of size or temporal affiliation. All excavated earth was sifted through soil screens to facilitate the collection of small artefacts such as beads, straight pins and buttons. Accurate depth measurements (both below surface and below datum) were recorded for every artefact discovered.

With the exception of six isolated chert flakes, all of the artefacts date to the 1800–48 period. The artefact distribution breaks down into the following gross categories: ceramics (fine earthenware, coarse earthenware and porcelain) = 502 sherds (37.1% of the total sample); glass (curved and flat) = 610 sherds (45.1%); metal (iron, brass, lead and copper) = 166 pieces (12.3%); and 'other' (bone, charcoal, slate, animal teeth and bone, whitewash samples, turf samples) = 74 (5.5%). From a purely historical standpoint, perhaps the most interesting artefact discovered was a small, plain whiteware sherd with a hole drilled through it. This tangible evidence for use alteration confirms folkloric information about the repair and reuse of broken dishes in Irish homes.

Twenty-three contexts were identified in 1999. Three of these were layers identified in 1998, but the others were newly discovered. They included a cobble yard area or floor surface, the surface and curbing of a 19th-century roadway, and a pit feature possibly used for storage. Further evidence of the stone walls discovered in 1998 was not found.

The soil stratigraphy at the site was straightforward. It consisted of five layers: sod, topsoil, two horizons of dark yellowish/brown, loamy soil, and a deeper, dark yellowish/brown, culturally sterile clay. Most of the artefacts and the human-built features were found just below the topsoil, often in a zone mixed with medium-sized rocks.

Current thinking about the site, which was the 19th-century home of the Nary family, is that the archaeology reveals evidence of conscious site destruction. This is the second season of research at the old Nary home site, and a comparison of the 1998 results with those from 1999 indicates some horizontal movement of artefacts across the site from west to east. Although conclusions are now too preliminary to advance with confidence, it is possible that when the Nary cabin was razed after the evictions it was pushed to the right (towards the east) and that many of the stones from the wall footings and the yard areas were salvaged and used to built post-eviction buildings and walls. If this is the case, evidence for the evictions must lie all around the Kilglass area, much of it in plain sight.

The 1999 excavation was conducted as part of a larger archaeological effort to examine the material basis of rural life on the eve of the Great Hunger. Although Ballykilcline is the third site tested as part of this research project, it is clearly the most interesting and also the most promising for meeting the goals of this anthropological effort.

The ceramic sample continues to be especially interesting. The large amount of imported English fine earthenware in the sample implies that, instead of paying their annual rents to the Crown, the tenants used their meagre funds to improve their material condition. In addition, the collection of locally made coarse earthenwares further argues for the importance of this industry to the men and women of 19th-century rural Ireland. Ballykilcline is important from historical, anthropological and archaeological standpoints, and it is expected that further excavations will broaden our understanding of early 19th-century rural life in this part of the country.

*Charles E. Orser, Jr, Illinois State University and National University of Ireland, Galway.*

### 763. BALLYPHEASAN
No archaeological significance
1875 2639
SMR 39:55 (vicinity of)
98E0438 ext.

This development, for the construction of dwelling-houses and apartments, along with all roads and ancillary services, was in the townland of Ballypheasan, immediately east of Roscommon town. It encompassed 8.65 acres of undulating grassland. A field drain bordered the site to the east, with the land becoming marshy and waterlogged beyond the drain. Two parallel drainage channels run north–south through the field for a distance of 200m. The ground in the field is uneven, although, as suggested in the archaeological assessment (undertaken by Anne Connolly in July 1998), this may be the result of drainage in the area.

The development was c. 120m south of Roscommon Friary (SMR 39:55), founded for the Dominicans by Felim O'Connor in 1253 and consecrated in 1257. Originally the church would have consisted of one long aisle. Through the ages the building had many alterations and renovations, including the addition of the north transept in the 15th century. The remains of 15th-century tracery windows also survive in the east and west of the building and replaced the original lancet windows. One of the most interesting features in the building is the effigy of Felim O'Connor in a niche in the north wall. Carved between 1290 and 1300, it has been placed on a 15th-century tomb with eight warriors.

The initial assessment did not reveal any definite features of an archaeological nature within the site, but it did indicate an irregularity in the ground surface close to the north and west boundaries of the site. As a result it was recommended that pre-development test-trenching be carried out in that part of the site.

This was undertaken by Martin Fitzpatrick on 26 September 1998 (*Excavations 1998*, 178). Two trenches were mechanically excavated in the north-west corner of the site. Both were orientated east–west and measured 30m by 2m, and they were excavated 10m apart. They failed to reveal features or artefacts of archaeological significance. They both truncated the west drainage channel indicated in the preliminary archaeological assessment. The results of the test-trenching suggested that the land rises naturally from west to east, with the greatest depth of topsoil found at the west of the trenches.

While no features of archaeological significance were revealed in the excavation of the trial-trenches, the proximity of the development to the Dominican friary indicated the potential of archaeological deposits/features existing in the area. Therefore, monitoring of ground disturbance was recommended by *Dúchas* The Heritage Service.

Monitoring, carried out on 1 March 1999, was undertaken on twelve trenches excavated along the line of the land-take. It failed to reveal the presence of either archaeological features or portable antiquities on the site, with the only subsurface remains revealed being previously recorded drainage channels in the north-west corner of the site. All other excavation revealed topsoil directly sealing natural clays.

*Dermot Nelis, IAC Ltd, 8 Dungar Terrace, Dun Laoghaire, Co. Dublin, for ADS Ltd.*

### 764. DEERPARK, BOYLE
Burnt spread
98E0401

This project involves the monitoring of ground disturbance associated with the development of the Boyle Canal Project, Co. Roscommon. The works, which are being carried out by *Dúchas* Waterways, involve the mechanical excavation of a mooring and a navigable channel to facilitate the mooring of vessels closer to the town of Boyle.

During monitoring, a burnt spread 12.3m by 8.5m was encountered. The spread was bisected by a drain 4m wide, which resulted in burnt stone and charcoal fragments being revealed in the section face.

The excavation involved the cleaning and recording of the section faces before the manual excavation of the burnt spread. Removal of sod revealed the outline of a subcircular mound of burnt, angular stones. Concentrated areas of stones were evident in the centre of the mound and in the area to the south. Cleaning of the north-west-facing section face of the drain revealed a cut, 1.5m wide and 0.9m deep, the base of which was partly lined with timbers. A wattle screen, supported by two narrow wooden uprights, formed the sides of the cut. Very little of the wattle survived, but its presence was identified by the imprint on the sides of the cut. Where the wattle survived, it was found to consist of intertwined hazel rods.

No artefacts of archaeological significance were encountered during the excavations.

*Martin Fitzpatrick, Arch. Consultancy Ltd, Ballydavid South, Athenry, Co. Galway.*

### 765. CLOONGOWNAGH
Enclosure
190644 299970
99E0193

The excavation took place in Cloongownagh townland, 3 miles west of Carrick-on-Shannon, before construction of the Rockingham to Cortober Road Project. The enclosure was not recorded in the SMR but was uncovered during field-walking for route selection.

Only one half of the monument will be affected by road construction, and accordingly the excavation concentrated on the southern half of the site. The northern half will be preserved *in situ*.

The enclosure is 62m in diameter, with the area of the excavation measuring 62m by 34m. The enclosure was surrounded by an infilled ditch and a low earthen bank. The excavation comprised half of the enclosure and also the strip of road-take to the south of the archaeological site. The full dimensions of the overall excavation were 140m by 50m.

The southern half of the enclosure was very heavily disturbed by agricultural furrows. However, features did survive within the confines of the excavated enclosure. The ditch was completely excavated. It had an average width of 3m and a depth varying between 1m and 1.5m. All of the fills were manually excavated. The lower fills reflected silting of the ditch, and the later fills indicated that material had been tipped into the ditch much later to level up the site. The low internal bank had an average width of 3.5m and a very irregular thickness. Three entrances were uncovered and excavated. The main entrance was at the south side of the enclosure. It was 6m long and 4.7m wide. The second entrance, which was sited in the south-east quadrant of the enclosure, was 6.4m long and 3m wide. The third entrance was at the west side and was 4.4m long and 3.6m wide. All three entrances had cobbled surfaces. There was no trace of a causeway across the ditch for any of the entrances.

A long, linear feature, aligned east–west, was excavated within the confines of the enclosure. It was at least 10m long, 1.2m wide and 1.1m deep. Within the feature were three well-preserved wooden planks *c.* 1.5m long and four substantial uprights. The full extent of the linear feature was not uncovered during the excavation as it extended into the half of the site not affected by the proposed road. Its function remains undetermined. However, samples of wood have been submitted for dating. This linear feature appeared to be stratigraphically part of the latest phase of activity within the confines of the enclosure.

An oval cut, which contained a dark, organic fill and included occasional seeds, was uncovered towards the centre of the enclosure. This cut was one of the few features that contained organic remains. Many of the fills associated with the excavated cuts were very sparse in finds and had little or no organic content.

A circular house, 8m in diameter, was revealed in the southern part of the enclosure. The house was sited *c.* 2.5m north of the embankment surrounding the enclosure. Charcoal samples taken from a foundation cut for the house gave a date of AD 32. The house appeared to belong to the second phase of occupation within the confines of the enclosure. A series of arc features, of unknown purpose, contemporary with the house, was discovered under the embankment of the enclosure. These features appear to have been truncated by the ditch that extended outside the embankment. As well as the arc-shaped cuts, a series of ten circular and rectangular pits, also belonging to the second phase of occupation, was uncovered and excavated.

Several features were also discovered outside the southern perimeter of the enclosure. A possible Neolithic house was discovered to the west of the enclosure. This feature was a subrectangular foundation cut (10.2m east–west by 7m), with a compacted internal surface that contained a spread of ashes and burnt material, and a series of stakeholes.

A *fulacht fiadh* was discovered in a boggy area 45m to the south-east of the enclosure. This feature was 6m by 4m and consisted of a burnt mound, a trough cut and a series of pits that possibly pre-dated the *fulacht fiadh*.

Just outside the enclosure and to its south-east a new site was uncovered in late 1999. It was a subrectangular enclosure, part of which extended outside the land-take for the new road. This new site will be excavated in 2000.

*Mary Henry, 24 Queen Street, Clonmel, Co. Tipperary.*

### 766. DERRANE
Adjacent to earthwork
18704 26938
SMR 35:87
99E0561

Pre-development testing was carried out between 14 and 18 October 1999 at the site of a proposed development at Derrane townland, Co. Roscommon, which consisted of the realignment, by Roscommon County Council, of a 360m section of the N61, north of Roscommon town. The proposed development is adjacent to an earthwork.

Five trenches were excavated during the testing, positioned to cover that area of the proposed development nearest the monument. Four of them were to the west of the existing road and were excavated by machine. The fifth was to the east of the existing road, 0.5m east of the field boundary and in the same field as the earthwork, at 2–10m from the limit of the monument. It was excavated by hand (topsoil-stripped by machine). The five trenches were orientated north–south and were 13.5–20.5m long, 1–1.2m wide and 0.15–1.0m deep.

The stratigraphy was the same in the four trenches excavated to the west of the existing road: topsoil 0.1–0.2m thick, below which was a rubble backfill of stones 0.4–0.5m thick, below which was grey/brown, stony natural subsoil, visible to the base of the trench. The stratigraphy in the fifth trench was topsoil 0.15–0.3m thick, below which was natural subsoil, visible to the base of the trench.

No artefacts were in evidence in any of the four trenches excavated to the west of the existing road. A number of artefacts were recovered from the topsoil in the fifth trench. These were several fragments of modern glass, a clay pipe bowl fragment and five sherds of pottery (yet to be analysed).

The testing revealed undisturbed stratigraphy in the trench excavated to the east of the existing road. The remaining four trenches were opened in an area owned by the County Council and revealed evidence of backfilling in recent times. This is likely to have been carried out by the County Council when it last straightened this section of road.

*Richard Crumlish, Archaeological Services Unit Ltd, Purcell House, Oranmore, Co. Galway.*

### 767. DRUM HERITAGE CENTRE, DRUM
Adjacent to medieval site
172979 238700
SMR 51:06503
99E0511

This site is to the west of the Drum Church (SMR 51:65). Drum Heritage Ltd is extending the old national school (now the community centre) to house a visitor centre. The school had been built across the line of an enlcosure (SMR 51:06503), and thus the proposed extension is within the confines of the site.

A single trench was cut along the length of the proposed extension, 11m, and to a maximum depth of 0.8m. The only feature apparent was the line of a destroyed field fence, which was visible on the Ordnance Survey map.

*Rónán Swan, Arch-Tech Ltd, 32 Fitzwilliam Place, Dublin 2.*

### 768. HUGHESTOWN
*Fulacht fiadh*
18921 30085
99E0401

During the summer and autumn of 1999 Roscommon County Council undertook the realignment and widening of part of the National Primary Route (N4) between the towns of Boyle and Carrick-on-Shannon. During archaeological monitoring of groundworks for the road improvement scheme (see No. 774 below) a *fulacht fiadh* was uncovered and excavated. The newly discovered site was in the townland of Hughestown, c. 5km to the west of Carrick-on-Shannon. The *fulacht fiadh* was found in a low-lying and peaty area. The site was bordered on its north side by a narrow stream running in an east–west direction.

The site was divided into two areas. Area 1 was a *fulacht fiadh* with a burnt mound and a wooden trough. Area 2, to the west of Area 1, consisted of the remains of a number of different stone surfaces. Both areas were just to the north of the stream.

The entire area was very waterlogged, with a heavy and dense cover of rushes growing all over the site. At a depth of 1m and beneath a mid- to dark grey, sticky, silty clay were the first traces of an archaeological site consisting of a burnt mound, a well-preserved wooden trough and a series of post-holes. The trough was made of wattle, with interwoven rods supported by uprights. The mound consisted of two main deposits. One was a dark, sandy material that contained frequent small to medium-sized burnt stones, occasional pockets of sand and frequent flecks of charcoal. The deposit was quite thin (0.08–0.12m). The second deposit was quite similar to the first, except it was a lighter shade of grey; it contained similar inclusions. The full extent of the two deposits forming the burnt mound was 10m long and 7.6m wide (north–south). The burnt mound was deposited around the trough, and its western half was infilled with the burnt stone.

Following the excavation of the burnt mound feature, a wooden trough was uncovered. The trough was sited in the northern/north-eastern area of the excavated site, with the mound predominantly occurring to its south, south-west and west. The trough was in a good state of preservation, with the cut to accommodate it clearly visible. It was oval, 2.1m long (east–west) and 1.3m wide. The cut truncated a sticky, grey silt. The trough, revealed at the base of the oval cut, consisted of three main wooden planks. The planks were lying flat, orientated east–west, and were 1.3–1.72m long, 0.08–0.15m thick and 0.18–0.21m wide. The central plank was splayed, with its base wider than its upper surface. The planks were of ash, and toolmarkings were evident on all three. The planks used in the construction of the base of the wooden trough were sealed by a thin layer of light grey sand and a deposit of medium-sized stones. The sand and stone tended to be confined to the western half of the trough. It appeared that both deposits, the light grey sand and the stones, represented the final use of the trough. The residual from heating of the stones was dumped into the trough as it became defunct and there was no further use for it.

The wall of the trough was constructed from wattle, a series of 24 hazel uprights. Hazel provided flexibility, with each rod being malleable and easy to manipulate into the desired shape. The hazel uprights supported a dense series of rods. The rods, also of hazel, were interwoven in a figure of 8 around the uprights. The interlaced nature of the work gave a 'Moses' Basket'-like appearance to the walls of the trough. The external face of the wattle was partially packed with a peat-like material. The peat probably acted as a sealant to assist in retaining water within the trough. The hazel uprights had either wedge- or chisel-shaped points and hammered tops. There were no traces of any cuts for the uprights, and it appeared that they had been hammered directly into the soft peat and the natural, grey silt. A radiocarbon date from a collapsed piece of timber from the trough gave an age of 3783±56 BP.

A large number of post-holes were uncovered to the west of the trough. It is possible that the post-holes were related to the use of the occupation phase of the trough, as they truncated the same deposit. There were no traces of preserved wooden posts in the actual post-holes.

Area 2 occurred to the west of the mound and wooden trough. Two main stone pathways/surfaces were exposed during the excavation, one overlying the other. The surfaces consisted of frequent small to medium-sized, sub-angular and angular stones and sparse larger stones. The stones were of limestone and were packed quite close to each other. Both stone surfaces extended in an east–west direction. The surfaces were sealed by organic-type deposits. The deposits contained occasional animal remains with traces of butcher marks. The bones represented domesticated animals as well as hunted wild animals.

The remains of a thin burnt mound were uncovered. It was stratigraphically located between the two stone surfaces. It was very similar in composition to the burnt mound uncovered in Area 1. A series of five large stones, aligned north–south and set into one of the surfaces, was uncovered. The large, flat boulders extended into the nearby stream, which coincided with the northern edge of the site. The purpose of the large stones remains unknown, but they may represent a stone path running towards the north and across the stream.

*Mary Henry, 24 Queen Street, Clonmel, Co. Tipperary.*

### 769. KILTULLAGH HILL, KILTULLAGH
Late Iron Age/Early Christian cemetery
M530740
96E0179 ext.

In September 1999, excavations continued on the summit of Kiltullagh Hill, on the border of County Roscommon and County Mayo. It was anticipated that this season's excavations would define both the temporal and the spatial limits of the transitional pagan/Early Christian cemetery excavated during 1994 (by F. McCormick, *Excavations 1994*, 76, 94E0030), 1996 (by D.G. Coombs and K. Maude, *Excavations 1996*, 95) and 1998 (by M.E. Robinson and D.G. Coombs, *Excavations 1998*, 179).

A 10m-by-8m trench was placed on the Roscommon side of the border. This was positioned adjacent to a standing stone and small ring-barrow, which had been the focus of the previous seasons' excavations. The 1999 trench exposed natural deposits comprising a limestone rubble overlying a blue/grey pea gravel. Archaeological features cutting these natural deposits were infrequent. They included a small limestone quarry pit and, significantly, a grave. This grave was aligned east–west and contained a single articulated adult inhumation. No associated grave-goods were discovered. Examination in the field indicates that the skeletal remains were female, although this will be clarified when post-excavation analysis is completed. The character of the grave, the lack of grave-goods and its similarity to previously discovered inhumations at Kiltullagh indicate that it is probably the remains of an Early Christian burial. The date of the burial will be confirmed, however, by forthcoming radiocarbon dates.

A 7m-by-8m trench and four 1m-by-7m strip trenches were also excavated on the Mayo side of the border. These trenches were positioned close to an area that had been quarried in 1991 and in consequence had produced evidence of fragmentary human remains. Whilst two features were identified in the 1999 trenches, these, on excavation, were found to be modern in date. No burials or other remnants of ancient activity were discovered. This suggests that the earlier quarrying has destroyed any ancient features and that the limits of the cemetery have now been defined.

*R.A. Gregory, School of Geography, University of Manchester, and D.G. Coombs, Department of Art History and Archaeology, University of Manchester, Oxford Road, Manchester M13 9PL.*

### 770. KNOCKADOOBRUSNA
Environs of archaeological complex
18053 30032
SMR 6:118
99E0233

Testing was carried out in connection with the proposed development of a mobile phone antenna, associated container and access road c. 2km south of the town of Boyle, for Eircell Ltd.

Within the area are a number of barrows and enclosures, a mound, a linear feature and two large, subcircular enclosures. The two large enclosures are of the 'earthen embanked enclosure' or 'henge' type, i.e. the bank is composed of material scooped out from the interior of the site. Twenty test-trenches were excavated using a wide, toothless ditching bucket. These trenches were at intervals of 20–30m along the proposed roadway and at the site of the mast and container. They were an average of 3.5m long and 1.9m wide. Each trench was excavated to presumed natural boulder clay or bedrock. In general the topsoil and sod overlay a loose, gravelly, stony band intermixed with a grey, silty sand. This in turn overlay a compact, olive-brown to yellow, silty sand. Nothing of archaeological significance was uncovered during the work. However, given the proximity of the proposed site to a number of archaeological sites, it was proposed that a programme of archaeological monitoring be carried out.

*Declan Moore, 8 Yewland Green, Renmore, Galway, for Mary Henry & Associates, Clonmel, Co. Tipperary.*

### 771. KNOCKADOOBRUSNA
Archaeological complex
3005 1804
SMR 6:118
99E0366

Monitoring was undertaken at the above site on behalf of Eircell. This had been recommended as a result of the archaeological testing conducted by Declan Moore (see No. 770 above). The monitoring did not reveal any archaeological features or deposits, and in all cases the layers recovered were consistent with those identified during Moore's testing programme.

*Rónán Swan, Arch-Tech Ltd, 32 Fitzwilliam Place, Dublin 2.*

### 772. KNOCKMURRY
No archaeological significance
SMR 27:4
99E0190

Pre-development testing was undertaken on the site

of two proposed dwellings in Knockmurry, Castlerea, Co. Roscommon. The proposed development sites are within the designated archaeological area for SMR 27:4, an earthwork.

Six test-trenches, 8–18m long and 2m wide, were excavated by machine within both proposed development sites. No archaeological features or finds were recovered from any of the trenches.
*Gerry Walsh, Rathbawn Road, Castlebar, Co. Mayo.*

### 773. MONKSLAND SEWERAGE SCHEME
Monitoring
**99E0014**

Monitoring associated with the Monksland Sewerage Extension Scheme commenced in January 1999 and continued intermittently until mid-October. The work was undertaken in compliance with a request from the NMHPS, *Dúchas*, following the submission of an assessment report prepared by the writer.

The project area is to the immediate east and south-east of the urban boundary of Athlone, which also coincides with the county boundary between Roscommon and Westmeath, in the district of the Daneshill/Monksland/Old Tuam road and the Galway road. The scheme is, in general, a western extension to the Athlone Westside Main Drainage Scheme (see No. 856 below).

The work generally entailed the monitoring of specified pipe-trench excavations, mostly along existing roads, although a small portion of the scheme called for pipes to be laid in green-field areas. One such area was at Daneshill, where the ground conditions of peaty soils over an unstable, sandy subsoil caused the line to be abandoned and redesigned. It is expected that work will recommence in this area sometime during 2000.

To date, the only feature of interest was an area of burning *c*. 220m north of Millbrook Bridge on the Tuam road. This consisted of a layer of intermixed ash and charred wood. The layer extended for a length of *c*. 7m and lay up to 1.25m below the existing road surface. There was no evidence that the material lay in a cut. A sample has been submitted for $^{14}$C dating, and the material will also be submitted for environmental analysis. It is hoped that such analysis will aid in the interpretation of the feature.
*Martin E. Byrne, 31 Millford, Athgarvan, Co. Kildare.*

### 774. ROCKINGHAM TO CORTOBER
Monitoring
**99E0309**

During summer and autumn 1999 Roscommon County Council undertook the realignment and widening of part of the National Primary Route (N4) between the towns of Boyle and Carrick-on-Shannon. It was necessary to carry out licensed monitoring of topsoil-stripping that occurred along either side of the existing road. Substantial works remain to be completed, and the proposed Bypass section of part of the route has been deferred to summer 2000 or 2001. Advance archaeological investigations were undertaken in 1999 along the proposed Bypass section (see No. 765 above, Cloongownagh).

During monitoring of groundworks for the realignment of the existing road, archaeological sites were uncovered. In one townland, Hughestown, a substantial *fulacht fiadh* with a very well-preserved wooden tough was uncovered (see No. 768 above).

Elsewhere the remains of two *fulachta fiadh* along the route of the road scheme were uncovered and excavated. There were no traces of a wooden trough in either site. However, they were traces of the burnt mound in both sides. In other locations burnt spreads were uncovered. However, these appear to be little more than the remnants of hedge clearances.

Further monitoring works for the project will resume in 2000.
*Mary Henry, 24 Queen Street, Clonmel, Co. Tipperary.*

### 775. MAIN STREET, ROSCOMMON
Urban
**18769 26470**
**SMR 39:43**
**99E0294**

An assessment of an extension to an existing commercial premises at Main Street, Roscommon, was carried out in June 1999. The site is close to a former church site and to the west of the site of St Comman's Vat. It has also been reported that remains were unearthed on the present site during construction in the 1950s, and a headstone of early 18th-century date has been incorporated into the rear wall of the premises.

Three test-trenches were excavated in the area to be disturbed by the proposed extension at the rear of the existing premises. Below the surface an extensive and consistent spread of mortared stone was discovered lying directly on the natural boulder clay. This debris represented demolition, probably of a 19th-century building, and most likely destroyed any archaeological deposits that existed on the site.
*Donald Murphy, Archaeological Consultancy Services Ltd, 15 Trinity Street, Drogheda, Co. Louth.*

### 776. MAIN STREET, ROSCOMMON
Urban
**18769 26467**
**99E0372**

An assessment of a proposed commercial development was carried out at Main Street, Roscommon. The site is close to a former church site and to the west of St Comman's Vat. Previous testing on a site less than 100m to the north of the present development revealed nothing of archaeological significance (see No. 775 above).

Two test-trenches were excavated. The first was near the centre of the site, and boulder clay was exposed at a depth of 0.2m below a modern demolition rubble layer. The second trench was excavated further east to the rear of the site. For the most part, modern rubble overlay the boulder clay, which was exposed at a depth of 0.3m below the surface. Upon the removal of the rubble three pits were evident cut into the boulder clay. These were partially excavated and produced finds of 18th–19th-century date. They will not be affected to any significant degree by the proposed development.
*Donald Murphy, Archaeological Consultancy Services Ltd, 15 Trinity Street, Drogheda, Co. Louth.*

### 777. WARREN, OR DRUM
No archaeological significance
18185 30245
99E0180

Three trial-trenches were excavated to natural, undisturbed levels at the site of the proposed development at Warren, or Drum, Boyle. Nothing of archaeological significance was discovered.

*Anne Connolly, Archaeological Services Unit Ltd, Purcell House, Oranmore, Co. Galway.*

## SLIGO

### 778. GORTALOUGH, BALLINAFAD
Adjacent to Ballinafad Castle and the Red Earl's Road
1780 3088
SMR 40:189, 190
97E0339 ext.

Arrow Community Enterprises Ltd is developing a site for the National Field Study Centre in Gortalough, Co. Sligo, at the east end of the Ballinafad Valley between the Curlew and the Bricklieve Mountains.

The west half of the proposed development area is within the constraint areas of the medieval Red Earl's Road and the small, military Ballinafad Castle, 'The Castle of the Curlews', of 1590 or 1610 (Waterman 1961).

Testing had been carried out in October 1997 and 1998 (*Excavations 1997*, 155), and some flints, late pottery, clay pipes and metal slag were found. There were no features except for several drains and a very archaeological-looking ditch.

Development work and monitoring began on 2 December 1999, and by Christmas Eve over 75% of the area has been dug out, despite water coming from every possible direction. Two mountain streams flow from the south towards the land. In addition to the drains found in the test excavation in 1997, several more drains and modern water pipes were uncovered. These all indicate a long history of attempting to drain this land.

There is no indication so far of the 'great fortifications' referred to by Downing in 1684 (Ó Muraíle, forthcoming) nor of the early village of Ballinafad to the north of the site indicated on the Down Survey parish map.

Monitoring will continue sporadically well into 2000.

*References*
Ó Muraíle, N. (forthcoming) Downing's description of County Sligo, c. 1684, TCD MS 888/1 (formerly I.4.17). In M.A. Timoney (ed.), *A celebration of Sligo*.
Waterman, D.M. 1961 Descriptions of five 17th-century houses in Co. Sligo. In E.M. Jope (ed.), *Essays in building history*.

*Martin A. Timoney, Bóthar An Corran, Keash, Co. Sligo.*

### 779. BALLINCAR
No archaeological significance
1680 3384
99E0529

Monitoring of topsoil-stripping along a 340m stretch of roadway, part of the realignment of the R291, Sligo–Rosses Point road, was carried out on 23 and 24 September 1999. This section of the roadway was c. 3 miles east of Rosses Point, in the townland of Ballincar, Co. Sligo. The topsoil-stripping was confined to the north-east side of the existing roadway.

The area excavated was 340m long and 7–21.3m wide and included an earth-and-stone bank along the existing road boundary. A new junction was also constructed, with a smaller link road exiting from the north-east side of the R291. This involved the realignment of a short section of the link road, 60m long and 2.5–19.5m wide.

The stratigraphy encountered in the areas monitored was natural and undisturbed. No archaeological features or deposits were in evidence. The artefacts recovered from the topsoil were a number of pottery sherds of modern date, modern glass fragments, red brick fragments, two undecorated clay pipe stems, four blackware sherds, two brownware sherds, a glazed sherd dating to the 19th century and a body sherd of possible post-medieval date.

*Richard Crumlish, Archaeological Services Unit Ltd, Purcell House, Oranmore, Co. Galway.*

### 780. BALLINCAR
Adjacent to ringfort
1685 3382
SMR 14:14
99E0656

Pre-development testing was carried out on 24 November 1999 at this site at Ballincar townland, Co. Sligo. The development consisted of the realignment of the existing Sligo–Rosses Point road (R291). This involved the construction of a single-lane, undivided carriageway, 1.9km long and 5–88m wide. An enclosure is adjacent to the proposed development. The site was on a south-west- and west-facing slope in grassland, along the north shore of Sligo Bay.

Monitoring of topsoil-stripping along two separate sections of the R291 during realignment works in 1998 (*Excavations 1998*, 180, 98E0390) and 1999 (see No. 779 above) had already taken place, in accordance with the impact assessment recommendations. Four trial-trenches were excavated by machine to test that section of the proposed road realignment closest to the monument to the north-east. The four trenches were 19.1–19.5m long, 0.8–1.3m wide and 0.3–1.3m deep.

The testing revealed natural, undisturbed stratigraphy in three of the trenches. The testing in the trench closest to the monument revealed a dark brown subsoil, directly below the topsoil and above boulder clay, which contained occasional to moderate amounts of animal bone fragments and shell and a moderate amount of stones. This layer was up to 0.6m thick and 5.8m long and was revealed in the north-east half of the trench only, at the closest point of the trenching to the ringfort. Occasional to moderate animal bone fragments and cockle/mussel shells were visible within this subsoil. These would appear to be the remains of domestic refuse from the ringfort.

Further to the testing, it was recommended that

all topsoil-stripping before groundworks be monitored. All groundworks will be 1–2m further away from the monument than the trenches were.
*Richard Crumlish, Archaeological Services Unit Ltd, Purcell House, Oranmore, Co. Galway.*

### 781. CALTERAUN
Adjacent to souterrain
**SMR 44:17**
**99E0610**

Planning permission was sought for the conversion of a farm building to domestic use, with permission for a septic tank and percolation areas at Calteraun, Gurteen, Co. Sligo. Pre-construction testing was undertaken on 22–4 October 1999, as the proposed development occurs within the constrained area of a souterrain.

Four trenches were opened along the line of the percolation areas, septic tank and service trench. A depth of 0.15–0.2m of topsoil was removed from each trench; lying directly beneath was natural, light reddish/brown sand with small, rounded stone inclusions. This sand was tested to a depth of 2m to establish that it had not been redeposited.

No evidence of archaeology was uncovered in any of these trenches.
*Anne-Marie Lennon, 9 Buenos Aires Court, Strandhill, Co. Sligo.*

### 782. CALTRAGH, CUMMEEN
Enclosure
**G663363**
**98E0545 ext.**

The results of the site assessment revealed the possibility of an outer enclosing feature around Caltragh. However, it is not by any means certain that this second enclosure is contemporary with the monument. It appears to take the form of a shallow gully that, around the northern side of the enclosure, seems to run along the line of a natural break in slope. On the eastern side, where there are no visible remains of the break, the gully appears to survive. A re-examination of the 1950s aerial photographs of the monument would seem to suggest that the break in the slope/gully was visible, recording the northern and eastern sections of an ovoid enclosure. It is also possible that the same aerial photograph records the southern and western limits of the site surviving at that time. This would have meant an outer oval enclosure surrounding the circular Caltragh monument, measuring 230m east–west by 190m.

It is not possible, without further work, to say whether the large ditch noted to the south-east of the enclosure is archaeologically significant. The presence of a live sewer pipe may indicate that this feature is relatively recent; however, it may equally be an earlier ditch reused for convenience by those who laid the pipe.
*Eoin Halpin, ADS Ltd, Unit 48, Westlink Enterprise Centre, 30–50 Distillery Street, Belfast BT12 5BJ.*

### 783. CARROWHUBBUCK SOUTH
No archaeological significance
**12895 33039**
**SMR 16:15**
**99E0241**

Pre-development testing was carried out on 25 and 26 May 1999 in response to a condition of planning for a development consisting of the construction of seventeen houses and associated services at Carrowhubbuck South, Enniscrone, Co. Sligo. This condition was included because the proposed development was adjacent to a possible passage tomb. Three further development sites at this location had been tested by Suzanne Zajac in 1998 (*Excavations 1998*, 180, 98E0342). The site overlooks Killala Bay and is situated on a south-west-facing slope in an area of which 75% has been backfilled extensively in recent years. The remaining area of the site consists of fair grazing. A stream flows roughly east–west through the centre of the site. To the south-east is the possible megalithic tomb, visible on a rise.

Four trial-trenches were excavated by machine during the testing, positioned to best cover the area of the proposed development. The stratigraphy consisted of backfill and topsoil above a sterile marl subsoil and bedrock.

Three modern pottery sherds were found in the topsoil. The backfill contained modern inclusions and artefacts, e.g. plastic, tyres and red brick, and was obviously laid down in recent years. The testing revealed no archaeological evidence. The site had been levelled up over the last number of years, and below the backfill was natural, undisturbed stratigraphy.
*Richard Crumlish, Archaeological Services Unit Ltd, Purcell House, Oranmore, Co. Galway.*

### 784. INNISHFREE HOUSE, CARROWMORE
Within passage tomb complex
**SMR 14:209**
**99E0151**

Monitoring was carried out during the final phase of the garden landscaping of Innishfree House, just south of the recorded limit for the Carrowmore megalithic complex. The entire garden, which was tilled, was field-walked in search of archaeological finds or features. Nothing of archaeological signifance was recorded.

An area planned for a tennis court was soil-stripped, but nothing of archaeological significance was recorded.

At a newly constructed pond, an area of *c*. 100m$^2$ was levelled to a depth of *c*. 0.25m below the present topsoil. Two patches of black soil with soot and a few fire-cracked stones were discovered in this area. The patches measured *c*. 1m x 1m and had a depth of *c*. 0.3m. In the upper part of one of the features a flake of chert with signs of wear and retouching was found.
*Stefan Bergh, 47 Ferndale, Cairns Hill, Sligo.*

### 785. CARROWNANTY
No archaeological significance
**16605 31548**
**99E0100**

Three trial-trenches were excavated to natural, undisturbed levels at the site of the proposed development at Carrownanty, Ballymote, Co. Sligo. Nothing of archaeological significance was discovered.
*Anne Connolly, Archaeological Services Unit Ltd, Purcell House, Oranmore, Co. Galway.*

### 786. CLOONAGLEAVRAGH
No archaeological significance
13933 33551
**SMR 11:75**
**99E0195**

Pre-development testing was carried out on 4 May 1999 in response to a recommendation made by *Dúchas* The Heritage Service following the grant of planning permission by Sligo County Council for the construction of a potato store at Cloonagleavragh, Easky, Co. Sligo. It was undertaken because the proposed development was within the site of a recorded monument, a ringfort. No extant remains of the monument were in evidence during the excavator's initial site visit. The site was within a farmyard *c.* 2 miles south-east of Easky village, in relatively flat pastureland. An extant ringfort (SMR 11:73) was visible in the distance, to the west.

Two trial-trenches were excavated by machine during the testing, positioned to best cover the area of the proposed development. They were orientated north–south and were 20m long, 0.9–1.1m wide and 1.3–1.8m deep. The stratigraphy encountered was the same in both trenches: topsoil 0.1–0.3m thick, above an orange/brown, sandy subsoil 0.1–0.3m thick, above a dark grey, sandy subsoil 0.5–1m thick, above a compact, grey, stony boulder clay visible along the base of the trench.

The testing revealed no evidence of the ringfort sited here. What was in evidence was mostly natural, undisturbed stratigraphy. All four of the subsoils in the two trenches were sterile, containing only stones. Two sherds of modern pottery (whiteware) were recovered from the topsoil.

*Richard Crumlish, Archaeological Services Unit Ltd, Purcell House, Oranmore, Co. Galway.*

### 787. COLLOONEY
Infantry barrack, possible
1681 3264
**SMR 26:170**
**99E0652**

The site is in the village of Collooney, Co. Sligo, east of the carpark of Benson's Church of the Assumption and west of high ground on which the convent stands. A main road flanks the site to the north, with ground opening out to the south. High walls of 18th- or 19th-century appearance surround the site, and a further walled garden area lies to the south. The site measures 58.5m by 22m and is registered in the SMR as a 'Barrack-Infantry possible', although the site owner believes the site to be that of Coote's Castle. The castle, according to local tradition, was built by Sir Richard Coote in 1655, reputedly using the stones from the old McDonagh castle of 1408. This was near the confluence of the Owenmore and Unsion rivers, *c.* 1km to the north-east (SMR 20:207), and is not marked on any OS maps or included in the SMR. The enclosing stone wall is of varying height and level of preservation, with numerous wall scars and infills. No visible trace of any 17th-century masonry survives at this site or in the immediate environs. An archaeological survey and historical assessment of the site were carried out by Martin Timoney in 1999, leading to a recommendation from *Dúchas* The Heritage Service for an intrusive assessment to establish the archaeological potential of the site in the pre-planning stage.

Present ground level within the walled site lies at least 1.3m below the existing street level to the north, deepening to perhaps 2.2m towards the rear of the site. A garage adjacent to the walled garden in the north-west corner of the site overlies at least one cellar, with the tarmac surface surrounding the garage noticeably sagging or beginning to sink in areas.

Assessment was undertaken at this site on 26 November 1999. Three trenches were opened using a mechanical excavator.

Trench 1 was positioned north-west/south-east across the northern part of the walled garden area; it measured 36m by 1.4m and was excavated to a maximum depth of 1.1m. Dark brown topsoil 0.28m deep, containing modern finds, overlay medium-brown, loose clay loam up to 0.47m deep, containing roots, decayed stone, oyster shell and modern pottery. Natural gravel was encountered at a maximum depth of 0.75m from ground level.

Trench 2 was positioned north-west/south-east across the southern part of the walled garden area; it measured 26m by 1.4m and was excavated to a maximum depth of 1.2m, revealing sod and dark brown topsoil containing ash, cinder and modern finds, 0.3m deep. This overlay medium-brown, loose clay loam up to 0.35m deep, containing roots, decayed stone, shell fragments and modern pottery. Natural, grey, wet gravel was encountered at a maximum depth of 0.65m from ground level.

Trench 3 was positioned west–east, by the east wall, across the stone surface below the blocked window ope. It measured 2m by 1.8m and was excavated to a maximum depth of 1.4m, revealing sod and dark brown topsoil containing modern finds 0.34m deep, over a medium-brown, loose clay loam up to 0.56m deep, containing post-medieval pottery. Natural gravel was encountered at a maximum depth of 0.9m from ground level. A stone wall foundation, revealed 0.38m below the lower window ope, was 0.28–0.3m thick, sitting directly on the natural gravel deposit

The assessment did not reveal any soils, features or finds of archaeological significance.

*Malachy Conway, Archaeological Consultancy Services Ltd, 15 Trinity Street, Drogheda, Co. Louth.*

### 788. CREGG
Adjacent to rath
G664395
**SMR 14:128**
**99E0436**

The presence of a well-preserved rath so close to the development area made it very likely that something of significance would come to light during the testing. It appears that the line of a ditch, presumably associated with the enclosure, was uncovered, running around the north-east side. It is difficult to be precise, but it seems to be at least 1.6m deep and 8m wide, the lowest layers consisting of a dark grey, charcoal- and sea shell-flecked silt clay.

Nothing datable was recovered during the testing, but it seems likely that it is contemporaneous with the rath and therefore dates to the Early Christian period. The soils noted elsewhere on site are a product of relatively recent dumping from construction works on the adjacent hospital.

Subsequent alterations to the ground-plan of the proposed development meant that significant disturbance to the archaeological remains were avoided.

*Eoin Halpin, ADS Ltd, Unit 48, Westlink Enterprise Centre, 30–50 Distillery Street, Belfast BT12 5BJ.*

### 789. DRUMCLIFFE SOUTH/DRUMCLIFFE NORTH
No archaeological significance
16788 34207
**99E0347**

Monitoring was carried out on this development, which consisted of a traffic-calming and village enhancement project on the N15, at Drumcliff village in County Sligo, between 15 July and 7 October 1999. The works carried out were all along the main road, which passes through the constraint of two monuments, SMR 8:72 (bridge site) and 8:84 (ecclesiastical remains).

The traffic-calming works consisted of the installation of 50mm ducting (for electricity to supply proposed lighting columns) along two sections 407m and 263m long; the installation of 26 lighting columns; the laying of kerbing; the laying of surface drains along a 170m length; the installation of fifteen traffic signs; the construction of a coach park along the south-east side of the existing graveyard; the installation of telecom ducting between the bridge and the local post office; the installation of a sewerage pipe within the road just north of the Yeats Tavern premises; and the excavation of eleven trial holes to assess the subsurface deposits along a section of the route of the 50mm ducting. The village enhancement works consisted of the construction of three gateways and three new walls.

With all works being carried out alongside or within the existing road, the stratigraphy consisted of topsoil, the tarred road, redeposited subsoil, road-fill, existing concrete pipes and plastic ducting, backfill including hardcore/gravel, natural subsoil, boulder clay and bedrock. Most of this stratigraphy was disturbed and/or redeposited. Only modern artefacts were recovered.

*Richard Crumlish, Archaeological Services Unit Ltd, Purcell House, Oranmore, Co. Galway.*

### 790. MAIN STREET (CARROWHUBBUCK SOUTH), INISHCRONE
Adjacent to enclosure/barrow?
12881 32989
**SMR 16:21**
**99E0412**

Two commercial buildings are to be constructed on a small plot, 76m by 33m, on Main Street, Inishcrone, Co. Sligo. At the rear of the site is a small earthwork that should probably be classified as a barrow. Redundant fencing, abandoned window frames, wire and rubbish protruded through the long grass on the barrow. The foundations of recent housing remained at the front of the plot.

The earthwork consists of an oval, dished area surrounded by a bank of varying height. It measures 17m east–west by 14.7m. The internal, dished area measures 9.9m east–west by 11m. The bank is 2–2.7m wide and stands at most 1.5m above the ground outside and 1.15m above the interior; the bank is no more than 0.2m over the interior in places. These dimensions were recorded after monitored removal of the long grass and tidying of the barrow. The build-up of blown sea sand against the west side of the monument gives the illusion that the bank on that side is much more substantial than elsewhere.

The present condition of the barrow resembles that of the one at Deechomede, Co. Sligo, SMR 39:9, excavated by Farrelly and Keane in 1992 and 1993 (*Excavations 1992*, 56; *Excavations 1993*, 71, 92E0119) and dated to the Early Iron Age.

Monitoring revealed that beneath the sod of the area stripped for the building and the carpark was a layer of blown sea sand below which was a thin layer of soil over the brittle bedrock. Throughout the sod and sand were many discarded pieces of modern metal, china, glass, plastic and animal bones. Local information was that between 30 and 40 years ago there was a butcher shop at the front of the plot and the butcher used to bury surplus bones and offal within the centre of the earthwork and elsewhere throughout the plot. No archaeology was discovered in the monitoring.

*Martin A. Timoney, Bóthar An Corran, Keash, Co. Sligo.*

### 791. FEALL A'MHUILINN, INISHMURRAY
Horizontal mill
157390 353870
**SMR 30:1–30:2**
**99E0383**

The stone-lined undercroft of a horizontal watermill was identified by an archaeological survey of Inishmurray (1998). (The adjacent land parcel is called Feall a'Mhuilinn, and a horizontal millstone now lies within one of the churches in the cashel.) The remains of the mill are at the outfall of the island's only stream, where it breached a low sea cliff above a rubble beach. Like the other sites investigated in 1999 (Nos 792–4 below), the remains of the mill were suffering ongoing marine erosion. Limited investigation in 1999 aimed to recover samples for radiocarbon dating from the mill and from an adjacent wall remnant, thought to represent a kiln.

Well-stratified burnt sediments were found near the base of the mill wall. These abutted the rear of the wall within the cut of the undercroft pit and thus represent well-sealed contexts formed during the construction of the mill. Charcoals from these will be submitted for radiocarbon dating.

The adjacent wall remnant was not a kiln, as first suspected, but proved to be a low terrace revetment for a cultivation plot on the cliff edge. A single sherd of gravel-tempered ware provides a *terminus post quem* for this feature in the mid- to late 17th century.

This work was commissioned by *Dúchas* and undertaken by Glasgow University Archaeological Research Division. No further archaeological work by GUARD is proposed at this site. *Dúchas* may in due course attempt consolidation of the remains of the mill undercroft.

*Jerry O'Sullivan, 5 Bellevue Road, Edinburgh EH7 4DA.*

### 792. LAGHTA PATRICK, INISHMURRAY
Leacht
157390 353870
SMR 11:1
99E0382

An altar or *leacht* was recorded on a low point at the eastern extremity of the island by several authorities, including the Ordnance Survey (1837; 1912), William Wakeman (1886), Lord Mountbatten (unpublished, 1972) and Michael Herity (1989). Only John O'Donovan, in recording the site for the Ordnance Survey in 1836, made reference to an associated cross-slab. Sadly, the site appeared to have been entirely denuded by marine erosion when revisited by the present writer in 1998; no trace of the *leacht* was upstanding.

The aim of further investigation in 1999 was simply to establish whether the base of the *leacht* survived. The location of the monument itself was successfully identified from OS map evidence. Remains of the base were exposed by stripping topsoil over an area of *c.* 3m x 3m. A basic record of the monument was made (scale drawing and photography), but no further excavation was undertaken and the base remains *in situ*. The basal dimensions were found to be as previously described (*c.* 2.5m x 2.4m). The adjacent storm beach was inspected, but the lost cross-slab was not recovered. There were no other finds.

This work was commissioned by *Dúchas* and undertaken by Glasgow University Archaeological Research Division. No further work by GUARD is proposed at this site. *Dúchas* may in due course reconstruct the *leacht in situ*.
Jerry O'Sullivan, 5 Bellevue Road, Edinburgh EH7 4DA.

### 793. RELICKORAN, INISHMURRAY
Cemetery
157390 353870
SMR 4:1–4:8
99E0381

The cemetery enclosure at Relickoran is likely to be of medieval date. It contains two altars, or *leachta*—one within the main enclosure and one within an adjoining smaller enclosure—and associated cross-inscribed slabs. Like the neighbouring women's cemetery, it is on an eroding cliff edge. The southern sector of the enclosing wall has been destroyed, and both of the altars have been partly cast down by the sea. Excavation of the seaward half of the site commenced in August 1999; a further season of work is proposed in 2000.

The superstructure of the altar, or *leacht*, in the main enclosure contained many modern inclusions and had evidently been rebuilt within the last 100 years or so. The structure was gradually reduced to reveal a primary or basal level of erect, edge-set flags with a soil and rubble core (this was not fully excavated in 1999). Two small cross-slabs were found adjacent to the structure, one lying within a rubble spread where the altar had partly collapsed on its south side.

A well-laid pavement of rough flags made a circuit of the main enclosure at the inner wall face. A cross-pillar set within the paving was standing close to the eroding cliff edge and, consequently, was removed to the old schoolhouse, where other carved stones from the island are curated by *Dúchas*.

Small fragments of human skeletal remains were found throughout the main enclosure, and some grave fills were tentatively identified. None of these was excavated, however, and it is not clear whether the graves respect the pavement and altar or pre-date them. Further excavation in 2000 will aim to clarify this.

Within the smaller, adjoining enclosure the altar consisted of massive stone blocks. This structure appeared to be substantially intact (i.e. there was no evidence for rebuilding). Human skull fragments were found within the base, although it is not yet clear whether these represent a deliberate deposit or simply bones introduced by burrowing birds or small animals.

This work was commissioned by *Dúchas* and undertaken by Glasgow University Archaeological Research Division. It is likely that *Dúchas* will reconstruct the enclosing walls and altars *in situ* and attempt consolidation of the cliff face thereafter.
Jerry O'Sullivan, 5 Bellevue Road, Edinburgh EH7 4DA.

### 794. TEAMPULL NA MBAN, INISMURRAY
Women's cemetery
157390 353870
SMR 2:7
99E0380

The cemetery associated with the women's church—Teampull na mBan—is bordered on the south by a low cliff. Ongoing marine erosion has destroyed the enclosure wall on this side and is gradually encroaching on the cemetery. The exposed section in the cliff face was cleaned and recorded (drawn survey and photography) to assess whether any significant features were immediately threatened.

A shallow loam topsoil (*c.* 0.4m) was found to overlie compact, sandy till. The topsoil contained a few weathered human bone fragments and a single long bone, but no articulated human remains were exposed and no grave-cuts were identified. The bones were allowed to remain *in situ*; no other finds occurred, and no samples were taken.

This work was commissioned by *Dúchas* and undertaken by Glasgow University Archaeological Research Division No further investigation is proposed.

Consolidation of the cliff face may be undertaken by *Dúchas* at a future date.
Jerry O'Sullivan, 5 Bellevue Road, Edinburgh EH7 4DA.

### 795. KILBOGLASHY
Shell midden
1667 3293
99E0245

Pre-development testing was carried out on the proposed site of a sewerage treatment plant for Ballysadare at Kilboglashy townland, Co. Sligo, on 16 November 1999, owing to the location of a possible enclosure and a possible linear earthwork within the area of the proposed development.

The site was on a steep, east-facing slope in grassland on the north-west outskirts of Ballysadare, bounded on the east by the Ballysadare river and a mill-race, on the west by a tarred boreen, and on the south by a school playing area. A short distance to the north of the site was St Fechin's church and graveyard (SMR 20:109).

Four trial-trenches were excavated by machine during the testing, positioned to investigate the possible enclosure and the possible linear earthwork, identified in the initial assessment. Two trenches (A and B) were excavated across the enclosure, and two (C and D) were excavated across the earthwork. Trenches A and B were orientated north-east/south-west and were 10m long, 1–1.8m wide and 0.4–2.3m deep. Trenches C and D were orientated north-north-west/south-south-east and were 10–10.4m long, 0.9–1.2m wide and 0.1–1.1m deep.

The stratigraphy in Trench A consisted of topsoil, below which was a loose rubble backfill of stones and boulders. Because of the loose nature of this backfill the trench collapsed continually, which made close investigation impossible from a safety aspect. It also meant that the layer below the backfill was never visible. The stratigraphy in Trench B consisted of topsoil, below which was orange/brown, natural subsoil and redeposited material. At the north-east end of the trench was a shell midden 0.4m long, 0.3m wide and 0.1m thick. The stratigraphy in Trenches C and D was natural and undisturbed.

Occasional animal bone fragments were visible within the loose rubble backfill in Trench A and in the redeposited material in Trench B. No artefacts were in evidence in Trenches C and D.

Trenches A and B revealed evidence of backfilling, and, while no definite datable artefacts were recovered, the backfilled material in both trenches appeared recent. No bank was in evidence along the length of the possible enclosure but rather a scarp, which formed an arc. The backfilling appeared to end along the base of the scarp, which may indicate that this was the edge of a dump or a site backfilled for a purpose. The shell midden was at the bottom of the scarp in Trench B and therefore outside the limit of the backfilled material. The proximity of Ballysadare Bay could explain the isolated nature of its location.

Further to the testing, it was recommended that all topsoil-stripping before groundworks and all groundworks in the immediate vicinity of the possible enclosure be monitored by a licensed archaeologist.

*Richard Crumlish, Archaeological Services Unit Ltd, Purcell House, Oranmore, Co. Galway.*

## 796. KNOCKNAREA MOUNTAIN
Neolithic hut sites and bank
16251 33389
99E0483

The Knocknarea Archaeological Project is a two-year project (1999–2000) focusing on the characteristic mountain of Knocknarea, Co. Sligo. The main aim of the project is to expand our interpretation of the role of this mountain in the symbolic and physical world of Neolithic *Cúil Irra*.

The project involves extensive fieldwork, including a field-walking programme, field survey, trial excavations and geophysical survey, as well as digital survey of the prehistoric sites and the topography of the mountain. The main funding of the project comes from the Swedish Foundation for International Co-operation in Research and Higher Education. The geophysical and digital surveys have been funded by the Heritage Council, while the trial excavations have been funded by *Dúchas*.

On the southern part of the mountain a few hut-like features had been noted on aerial photographs. Some of these hut sites, which were recorded during field-walking, were in many ways identical to those excavated on the north-eastern side of the mountain. During the survey 21 hut sites or hut-like features were recorded in this area. Just east of this group of huts, at *c.* 240m above sea level, a substantial wall that followed the contour east of the huts and then cut diagonally down the hillside to the south, was noted. The occurrence of hut sites and a wall in the southern area made an obvious parallel to what had been noted in the northern area. As nothing was known about the date and context of this hitherto unrecorded complex, a limited excavation was considered highly important to the further analysis and interpretation of the mountain and its prehistory.

The main aim of the excavation in the southern area was to establish the cultural context of one of the hut sites. A second aim was to establish the relation between one of the hut sites and the wall. Two trenches of $3m^2$ were excavated. The first was in one of the huts, and the second covered the junction between a hut and the wall.

The hut had an overall diameter of *c.* 12m, and consists of a circular low wall of limestone slabs and smaller stones. There was an entrance at the north-east.

Finds from inside the hut consist of different chert and flint artefacts, as well as debris from tool production. The artefacts were dominated by different types of concave scrapers.

As the finds and construction recorded were identical to the excavated huts in the northern area, a Neolithic date also seems likely for this southern hut site.

The hut adjacent to the wall had an overall diameter of *c.* 12m and consisted of a low, semicircular wall, with both ends adjoining the long wall recorded.

Finds from inside the hut included different chert and flint artefacts (mainly concave scrapers), as well as debris from tool production. Stratigraphically, the finds were restricted to a single cultural layer in the hut and the uppermost part of the wall.

The finds were identical to those recorded in the nearby hut and in the hut sites in the northern area, again indicating a Neolithic date. The wall was *c.* 0.8m high and *c.* 4m wide and consisted mainly of different-sized stones. The upper part consisted of smaller stones, while the lower part consisted of larger, limestone slabs. No finds were made in the wall. The finds recorded in the uppermost layer of the wall give a *terminus ante quem* for the construction of the wall, indicating that it had been present during the use of Hut site B.

The preliminary interpretation is that the huts in the southern area represent an activity similar to that recorded in the northern area. The 21 hut sites or hut-like features recorded in the southern area may, however, indicate that this area was more

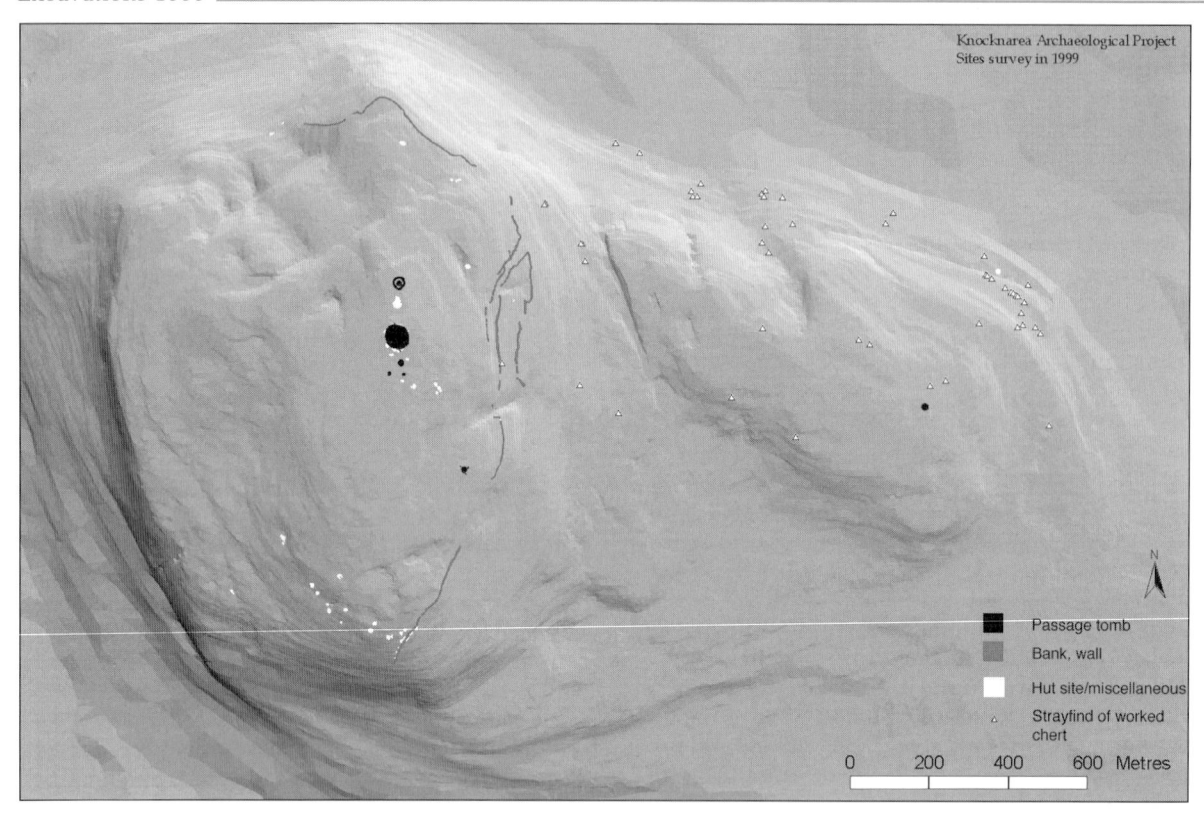

Knocknarea Archaeological Project, location of sites surveyed during 1999.

intensively used than the northern. The two areas are linked by the large wall/bank, and it should be noted that all the huts are on the uphill side of this large enclosure, cutting off the mountain to the east. The activity represented by the huts was clearly restricted to the upper part of the mountain, and it is reasonable to assume that this activity was in some respect linked to the ritual monuments on the very summit, dominated by the well-known cairn of *Miosgán Meadhbha*.
Stefan Bergh, 47 Ferndale, Cairns Hill, Co. Sligo.

### 797. KNOCKNAREA MOUNTAIN
Survey of prehistoric sites and stray finds
16283 33469
E000998

The Knocknarea Archaeological Project is a two-year project (1999–2000) focusing on the characteristic mountain of Knocknarea, Co. Sligo. The main aim of the project is to expand our interpretation of the role of this mountain in the symbolic and physical world of Neolithic *Cúil Irra*.

The project involves extensive fieldwork, including a field-walking programme, field survey, trial excavations and geophysical and digital surveys of the prehistoric sites and the topography of the mountain. The main funding of the project comes from the Swedish Foundation for International Co-operation in Research and Higher Education. The geophysical and digital surveys have been funded by the Heritage Council, while the trial excavations have been funded by *Dúchas*.

To understand the mountain and its prehistoric remains, a very detailed field-walking programme was undertaken. One of the main aims was to record Neolithic activity on the mountain, represented by the occurrence of worked lithics. Another aim was to achieve an updated record of the prehistoric sites on the mountain.

The survey falls spatially into two different areas: the lower, eastern ridge and the higher ground to the west, with the well-known group of passage tombs on the flat top. Unfortunately, the major part of the lower, eastern ridge is covered by very dense forestry. This has made field-walking in some areas impossible, which of course has had a negative effect on the result. Nevertheless, nearly forty locations with worked chert have been registered within this ridge, indicating that this hitherto neglected area was once the site of extensive activity during the Neolithic.

Besides the finds of lithics on the eastern ridge, a hut site was recorded on the lower part of its northern slope. The fact that only one previously unrecorded site was noted within the eastern ridge is a result of the very dense and insensitive forestation that has been allowed to develop here.

The field-walking and the survey carried out within the higher part of the mountain resulted in an unexpectedly high number of previously unrecorded sites. The survey has so far recorded 25 hut sites/hut features, four low cairns/stone spreads, four house? foundations, one kidney-shaped earthen mound and *c.* 2.3km of banks and walls forming an extensive system on the eastern side of the mountain. The well-known group of passage tombs on the flat summit remained, however, unaltered regarding number and location.
Stefan Bergh, 47 Ferndale, Cairns Hill, Sligo.

### 798. KNOCKNAREA MOUNTAIN
Complex of Neolithic banks
16283 33469
99E0227

The Knocknarea Archaeological Project is a two-year

project (1999–2000) focusing on the characteristic mountain of Knocknarea, Co. Sligo. The main aim of the project is to expand our interpretation of the role of this mountain in the symbolic and physical world of Neolithic *Cúil Irra*.

The project involves extensive fieldwork, including a field-walking programme, field survey, trial excavations and geophysical and digital surveys of the prehistoric sites and the topography of the mountain. The main funding of the project comes from the Swedish Foundation for International Co-operation in Research and Higher Education. The geophysical and digital surveys have been funded by the Heritage Council, while the trial excavations have been funded by *Dúchas*.

Within the Carrowmore Project in the early 1980s at least four hut sites were identified around the 275m contour on the north-eastern slopes of the mountain. During fieldwork in 1992 it was noted that some of these hut sites seemed to lie along a hitherto unnoticed bank-like feature, running diagonally down the hillside to an altitude of *c.* 240m. This bank seemed to have a length of *c.* 250m and constituted a major feature on the eastern side of the mountain. A possible interpretation was that it constituted a part of a route up to the summit, as it was placed at a point where the summit could be reached fairly easily in comparison to the modern path to the top. For the interpretation of the mountain's role in prehistory, it was important to understand the character of these features. A trial excavation was therefore carried out during 1999.

The main aim was to establish the nature and date of the bank and also to establish the relation between the bank and one of the recorded hut sites, seemingly lying immediately inside the bank.

An area of 51m$^2$ was excavated, divided into ten trenches. However, only a small part of this area was excavated down to undisturbed natural.

The preliminary results from the excavations can be summarised as follows. The substantial bank recorded along the hillside is a man-made feature. Where excavated, it had a core of stones and slabs, indicating an early phase in the form of an actual wall. This had been covered by gravel and smaller stones, creating a more smoothly shaped bank *c.* 1.2m high and *c.* 4m wide. The height and width, however, varied considerably along the bank. In some places the bank was clearly segmented by gaps.

Furthermore, probably the most important discovery was that the part recorded within the area of excavation proved to be just a portion of a very substantial system of walls enclosing the entire eastern side of Knocknarea Mountain.

There were no actual 'hut sites' (i.e. demarcated by circular banks) along the bank, as was originally assumed. Instead a number of horizontal 'floors' had been constructed along the bank on its uphill side. The 'floors' consisted of very fine limestone gravel, with a texture similar to marl. A large number of artefacts—flakes and splinters, mainly of chert—were recorded within these 'floors'. The most common artefact was the concave scraper. Flint was also present, both as artefacts and as flakes and splinters. The variation and the amount of debris implied highly intensive production of stone artefacts along the bank.

A few sherds of decorated Neolithic pottery and an amber bead were recorded in a low layer in one of the 'floors'.

The finds made within these 'floors' were identical to those made in the nearby hut sites excavated within the Carrowmore Project in 1980. As two of these hut sites were dated to *c.* 3000 BC, it is reasonable to assume a similar date for 'floors' along the bank.

As the 'floors' and the distribution of finds partly overlay the bank, and also formed an integral part of the bank, the dating of the 'floors' to the Neolithic gives a *terminus ante quem* for the bank. It is likely, however, that the bank and the 'floors' are contemporary. It should be stressed that no finds were made in the bank proper.

The excavation has revealed the presence of a large and relatively complex system of banks and walls along the eastern side of Knocknarea Mountain. The banks seem to have an early phase consisting of a stone wall with nearly vertical sides and a flat top. This wall has, in a second phase, been given a smoother profile by adding gravel and smaller stones, thereby creating a bank nearly 4m wide and *c.* 1m high. Just inside the bank, on the uphill side, several more-or-less levelled 'floors' have been created by adding limestone gravel.

Along these banks large amounts of debris from stone tool production, mainly in chert, indicate very intensive activity. The dominating artefact is the concave scraper, which occurs both in chert and flint. These implements seem to have been manufactured, used and disposed of along the bank.

The banks and huts are parts of a very large and complex system of features 240–270m above sea level, along the upper part of the eastern slope of Knocknarea. However, the nature of the activity represented by these feature is still not clear. It is obvious that this northern group of huts and banks has its southern counterpart, in regard to construction and activity, in the *c.* 21 huts recently discovered nearly 1km to the south. A central feature in the whole complex is the extensive enclosure on the eastern side of the mountain, linking the different areas and also cutting off the mountain to the east. The activity represented by the huts was clearly restricted to the upper part of the mountain, and it is reasonable to assume that this activity was in some respect linked to the ritual monuments on the very summit, dominated by the well-known cairn of *Miosgán Meadhbha*.

*Stefan Bergh, 47 Ferndale, Cairns Hill, Sligo.*

## 799. KNOXPARK
*Fulacht fiadh*
**G672282**
**99E0303**

A site assessment was carried out at a proposed landfill site in Knoxpark townland, south of Ballysadare, Co. Sligo. An environmental impact assessment had identified four features of archaeological potential—a kidney-shaped mound indicating a possible *fulacht fiadh,* a cairn, a standing stone and an old field system. Archaeological investigations at each of these features indicated that the mound was indeed a *fulacht fiadh,* the cairn was the result of field clearance and the 'standing stone' was part of the old field system that was dated to the post-medieval period.

The *fulacht fiadh* measured 13.2m east–west by 10.4m and had a maximum height of 0.54m. A small indentation was found midway along its southern edge, giving it a characteristic kidney shape.

A trench 9.6m long was cut east–west along the western edge of the mound and revealed that the bog had encroached over the lower limit of the mound along the western edge. Investigations indicate that the mound material consists of two distinct layers with varying quantities of burnt and heat-shattered stone and charcoal. This material directly overlay a fibrous, orange/brown peat.

Some timber was found running north–south within this peat, although on examination this would appear to be tree roots as opposed to part of a wooden trough. No features were uncovered cutting the subsoil within the limits of this test-trench.

*Cia McConway, ADS Ltd, Unit 48, Westlink Enterprise Centre, 30–50 Distillery Street, Belfast BT12 5BJ.*

### 800. RATHOSEY
No archaeological significance
SMR 25:15
99E0681

Pre-development testing was undertaken on the site of a proposed development in Rathosey, Coolaney, Co. Sligo. The site is immediately outside the zone of importance for an archaeological complex. Eleven test-trenches were excavated by machine within the proposed development. They varied between 14m and 20m long, and all were 2m wide. In all, the natural daub was found under the sod/peaty topsoil. A modern field drain was uncovered in the southern end of Trench 7. No archaeological features or finds were recovered from any of the test-trenches.

*Gerry Walsh, Rathbawn Road, Castlebar, Co. Mayo.*

### 801. ARDKEERIN, RIVERSTOWN
Adjacent to ringfort
SMR 27:120
99E0631

Pre-development testing was undertaken on the site of a proposed development in Ardkeerin, Riverstown, Co. Sligo, where a ringfort is situated. Five test-trenches were excavated by machine within the site.

In all trenches, which were 1.5m wide and varied between 14m and 25m long, a sod/topsoil layer directly overlay a natural, light brown/orange boulder clay, apart from in Trench 3. Here the stratigraphy was very disturbed. At the eastern end the sod, 0.12m thick, overlay a mix of white and brown mortar 0.24m thick Underlying the mortar was a mid-brown clay/topsoil 0.15m thick. This directly overlay the natural, brown/orange boulder clay. At the western end the sod, 0.1m thick, directly overlay a gravel and concrete rubble fill layer 0.4m thick. The upper stone of a rotary quern was recovered from this modern fill layer. The natural, brown/orange boulder clay directly underlay this.

Except for the quernstone, recovered from a disturbed modern fill layer, no archaeological features or finds were noted in any of the test-trenches.

*Gerry Walsh, Rathbawn Road, Castlebar, Co. Mayo.*

### 802. SLIGO AND ENVIRONS WATER SUPPLY SCHEME
No archaeological significance
1705 3343
SMR 14:133 (adjacent to)
98E0395

The monitoring report on the first two areas of Sligo and Environs Water Supply Scheme, those in Carns (Carbury barony) and Carns (Duke) townlands, is in *Excavations 1998*, 185–6.

The pipeline from the Water Treatment Plant Field in Carns (Duke) to the Break-Pressure Tank and the area for the tank itself in Tonaphubble townland required monitoring of the topsoil-stripping of an area 25m by 180m and was done in several short sections on various dates during 1999.

Nothing of an archaeological nature was found.

*Martin A. Timoney, Bóthar An Corran, Keash, Co. Sligo.*

### 803. SLIGO ENVIRONS WATER SUPPLY SCHEME
Urban
98E0533

Work has been continuing on this project since November 1998 (*Excavations 1998*, 186). After the completion of the Rosses Point section of the pipeline in April 1999, work was switched to Sligo town. Here *c.* 26km of pipe was laid, using three methods of pipe insertion: directional drilling, open cut and pipe bursting. Over 18km of pipe was inserted using the directional drilling method. As this was the first large-scale use of this method in Ireland, extensive archaeological testing was undertaken beforehand in both the zone of archaeological potential in Sligo town and the peripheral suburban area.

Very few archaeological strata were uncovered during testing or pipe-laying. Testing on the street in front of Sligo Abbey revealed the possibility of undisturbed burials at 1.4m. It was decided to excavate the line of this trench before pipe-laying. The trench was taken to a depth of 1m; large quantities of disarticulated human bone were uncovered between 0.6m and 1m. This bone had been disturbed in the 19th century by the construction of a large culvert that ran the length of the street.

The route of the pipeline crossed the 17th-century town fortifications in at least ten positions. No evidence for the fortifications was uncovered in archaeological testing or pipe-laying. Work is due for completion in early February 2000.

*Anne-Marie Lennon, 9 Buenos Aires Court, Strandhill, Co. Sligo.*

### 804. 6–7 ABBEY STREET, SLIGO
Urban medieval/post-medieval
16916 33593
99E0471

A rescue excavation was carried out for *Dúchas* between 13 September and 8 October 1999 on the site of a proposed new visitor centre at Sligo Abbey. The site is immediately to the west of the nave of the church belonging to Holy Cross Priory, which was founded in 1252 by Maurice Fitzgerald, second baron of Offaly, who was regarded as the founder of Sligo town. It is the burial place of O'Connor of Sligo and was occupied until 1698, when the site was granted to Sir William Taafe. Despite this, the friars continued to occupy a section of the abbey until 1760, when Fr Laurence Connellan decided to move elsewhere. Some repairs to the ruins were carried out by Lord Palmerston, who erected railings and removed several houses in 1849–50.

Excavation of the north-west corner of the site behind an existing 19th-century house revealed a loose, brown loam containing stones and rubble with some shell and animal bone extending to a depth of 1.5–2m, resting directly on natural boulder clay. This probably represents 18th/19th-century fill deposited in order to bring this area to the same level as Abbey Street. A ditch 2m wide by 1m deep was cut into the orange/brown boulder clay running east–west to the rear of the 19th-century house; no finds were recovered from the fill, but charcoal samples produced a date of 1165–1276 for the infilling of the ditch. As burials were discovered to the south on the opposite side of Abbey Street, this ditch may represent an enclosure for a cemetery. Three small furrows were visible to the north of the ditch, aligned west-north-west/east-south-east, varying from 0.8m to 0.4m wide and 0.09m to 0.3m deep.

Three pits were uncovered. One, 1.9m in diameter, cut into the natural boulder clay at the northern baulk and was filled with loose, dark brown soil to a depth of 0.94m. A pipe stem indicates a post-medieval date. A second, larger pit was filled with brown loam and rubble, along with disarticulated animal and human bone, and measured 10m east–west by 5m. Finds from the fill suggest that this pit may have been dug to accommodate the construction of the buildings to the north and supported a late 18th- to early 19th-century date. The third pit was found below the foundation of the north wall of the 19th-century house and was cut into natural boulder clay. It contained a grey/brown loam and disarticulated human bone.

Removal of the overburden over the eastern half of the site revealed an extensive cobbled surface at a depth of 0.6–0.7m, together with the substantial foundations of an earlier house in the south-east corner of the site adjacent to the 19th-century house along Abbey Street.

A narrow cobbled laneway was revealed between the two houses leading to what presumably had been cobbled backyards. Variation in the cobble size and orientation suggests that the western portion of the cobbled surface represents a roadway shown on Luttrell's town plan of 1689. The laneway between the houses may contain some fabric of this original road, as the alignment of the west wall of the earlier house follows the line of the 1689 plan. This house is shown on a 1791 illustration of the abbey by Grose. The north wall contained a doorway and an original sill, and a semicircular red brick fireplace was built into the south-west corner of the largest room of three.

The excavations revealed several phases of activity from the medieval period, represented by

17th-century house and cobbled yard at Sligo Abbey, Abbey Street.

the ditch cut into the natural boulder clay, to the post-medieval period, represented by the house and cobbled yard.

Analysis of the human bone revealed the presence of at least eight individuals identified as probably three female, three male and two indeterminate. One of the female skulls had a number of weapon wounds on the frontal bone made with a thin knife. Absence of healing indicates that they were fatal, possibly even a case of murder.

The greatest impact from the development will be in the western half of the site, where the proposed new building is to be constructed. This necessitated the excavation to natural boulder clay in this area. In contrast, there will be little or no impact on the eastern half of the site, and the features exposed here will be incorporated into the development.

*Donald Murphy, Archaeological Consultancy Services Ltd, 15 Trinity Street, Drogheda, Co. Louth.*

### 805. 8 ABBEY STREET LOWER, SLIGO
Medieval limekiln
**98E0216 ext.**

The medieval limekiln excavated in 1998 (*Excavations 1998*, 187) was dismantled to allow development to proceed. The work was undertaken in January 1999. All the stones of the kiln were numbered and placed in crates and are now in storage in the *Dúchas* depot in Sligo.

Detailed recordings of all the stonework were made. Many of the stones could not be removed intact because of heat damage.

*Alan Hayden, Archaeological Projects Ltd, 25A Eaton Square, Terenure, Dublin 6W.*

### 806. KEMPTON PARADE, BRIDGE STREET, SLIGO
Urban
**G694360**
**99E0487**

Nothing of archaeological significance is known from the site on Kempton Parade. However, the Urban Archaeological Survey for Sligo shows that the site is within the projected town walls of *c.* 1689. It is bounded to the north by the plots associated with the south side of Stephen's Street, and to the west by the line of Bridge Street. While it is impossible to be certain, it is likely that the area of the town now occupied by the site was in the intertidal zone of the River Garvoge.

Evidence from archaeological work on Rockwood Parade and Stephen's Street carpark suggested that both sides of the river had large intertidal zones before the walling of the river, presumably in the 18th century. Indeed, on the south side of the river the zone extended at least halfway up the present line of Watery Lane and Tobergal Lane. It is likely that a similar situation prevailed in the area of Kempton Promenade. Plots associated with the south side of Stephen's Street probably extended from the rear of the buildings down to the high-tide mark; thereafter the ground was subject to regular flooding and useful only for transitory activities.

Three trenches were opened to assess the nature, extent, complexity and date of any surviving archaeological deposits. The results revealed that there was on average over 1.8m of modern overburden on the site, beneath which were the remains of a relatively recent skeletal A-horizon, up to 0.3m deep. Below this was a further 1.7m of yellow/brown clay overlying a smooth, shaley bedrock (2.8m OD), which sloped quite steeply downwards from the north-west corner of the site.

It would appear that, like the areas tested on the south bank of the Garvoge River, this area was largely unoccupied in the past, presumably used simply as access to the river from the rear of the plots on The Mall. The archaeology uncovered would all appear to date from the later history of Sligo, when the area was used for industrial purposes.

*Eoin Halpin, ADS Ltd, Unit 48, Westlink Enterprise Centre, 30–50 Distillery Street, Belfast BT12 5BJ.*

### 807. MODEL ARTS CENTRE, THE MALL, SLIGO
Urban
**98E0006**
Trial-trenching before the refurbishment and renovation of the Model Arts Centre was carried out during 1999. Four trenches were excavated using a mechanical digger. Nothing of archaeological significance was uncovered during the excavation, and development was subsequently allowed to proceed.

*Eoin Halpin, ADS Ltd, Unit 48, Westlink Enterprise Centre, 30–50 Distillery Street, Belfast BT12 5BJ.*

### 808. TOWN HALL, SLIGO
No archaeological significance
**G691358**
**99E0016**
A phase of refurbishment led to an archaeological monitoring and assessment condition on the works in Sligo Town Hall. Sligo town, since its foundation in the 13th century by the Anglo-Normans, has been one of the most important towns in north-western Ireland. However, none of the many secular buildings known to have existed within the town during the medieval and post-medieval periods survives today. The only remnant of the town's extensive urban defences currently visible is the mid-17th-century earthwork known as the Green Fort, north-east of the town. The many archaeological investigations carried out in the town in recent years have not found any early building remains. It is thought that the town hall may be built on a site previously occupied by both the 13th-century castle and a 17th-century fort.

Construction work to the east and north of the town hall was monitored, with no evidence for an earlier castle coming to light. The insertion of column bases in the basement and ground-floor levels was also monitored, with no earlier deposits noted.

*Eoin Halpin, ADS Ltd, Unit 48, Westlink Enterprise Centre, 30–50 Distillery Street, Belfast BT12 5BJ.*

### 809. WEST GARDENS, SLIGO
No archaeological significance
**G692357**
**99E0054**
Four test-trenches were machine-excavated. Two were opened along the long axes of the front and rear of the new development, with a further two across the line of the building. Oil spillage in the area of the site, which was once used as a garage, badly contaminated the eastern end of the site. However, nothing of archaeological significance was noted.

*Eoin Halpin, ADS Ltd, Unit 48, Westlink Enterprise Centre, 30–50 Distillery Street, Belfast BT12 5BJ.*

### 810. METHODIST CHURCH HALL, WINE STREET, SLIGO
Urban
**3360 1689**
**SMR 14:65**
**99E0002**
The Methodist community of Sligo is replacing its church hall, one of a group of three Methodist buildings (manse, church and church hall) in Wine Street, Sligo.

According to Wood-Martin (1892, 148), the church was opened in 1832, but there is a date of 1830 in the inscription in an oriel feature high up in the north face. The church hall abuts the east side of the church, to which it was added sometime between 1830 and the time of the Griffith Valuation.

Test excavation, which began in October 1999, at the rear and the side of the replacement church hall site, revealed only 19th-century deposits associated with walls contemporary with the church. The test excavation cannot be completed until the area at the street front becomes available in mid-2000.

*Reference*
Wood-Martin, W.G. 1892 *The history of Sligo, County and Town, from the close of the Revolution of 1688 to the present time.* Dublin. Reprinted Sligo, 1990.

*Martin A. Timoney, Bóthar An Corran, Keash, Co. Sligo.*

### 811. SROOVE (LOUGH GARA)
Crannog
**SMR 46:29**
**97E0209**
The Crannog Research Programme has been working in Lough Gara since 1995. The work started with a survey and a mapping of areas around the shoreline. The project is interdisciplinary, involving quaternary geologists to investigate the lakebed of Lough Gara. The coring of lake sediments during the summer of 1996 was to give an understanding of former lake-level changes. With the financial support from the Heritage Council a large-scale sampling of wood and animal bones from other

island sites around the lake was carried out during summer 1999. The purpose of the sampling is to provide better knowledge of the settlement pattern in the lake over time. The samples have been radiocarbon dated by the isotope laboratories in Gronigen.

Crannog studies are to a large extent based on the findings from larger, royal sites such as Lagore, Ballinderry 1 and 2 and Moynagh Lough. In 1997 The Crannog Research Programme started the excavations in Lough Gara. Instead of focusing on a larger crannog site, the project has been involved in researching the archaeology of the small crannogs. With the excavation as a basis, the project aims at an understanding of the wider region of Lough Gara, incorporating an analysis also of the dryland monuments in Sligo, Roscommon and Mayo, as well as other features in the landscape. An article about the importance of islands in the cognitive and imaginative landscape mainly during the Early Christian period was published in 1998.

Information from previous seasons at this site, on the western shores of Lough Gara, have been published in *Excavations 1997* (156), *Excavations 1998* (185) and *Archaeology Ireland* (1998, vol. 12, no. 1). All the radiocarbon dates received to date show that the site belongs to the Early Christian period.

In 1999 the eastern half of the site, the side that is nearest to the water, was excavated. This involved continued work in the south-eastern trench. A new trench in the north-eastern area of the site was also opened. When the site was surveyed this area showed what was interpreted as a small harbour-arm. The stratigraphy largely followed that in the other excavated areas of the site. A layer of boulders lay above a layer of shattered, fire-cracked stones. Under the stone layers a floor/deck of horizontal timbers was exposed.

Among the finds this year were three bone pins and a piece of a lignite bracelet.

In general this small site shows a more modest material culture than the larger, contemporary crannog sites. These excavations should help to initiate discussion on the life on the lake shore of people that did not belong to the upper echelons of society.

The Crannog Research Programme thanks *Dúchas* The Heritage Service and the National Committee for Archaeology at the Royal Irish Academy for finances and support.
*Christina Fredengren, Department of Archaeology, Stockholm University, 106 91 Stockholm.*

## 812. STRANDHILL
No archaeological significance
G609361
99E0318

The test excavations took place on a proposed development to the north of Strandhill, Co. Sligo. The test-trenches were positioned in order to assess the location and complexity of the remains of any archaeological deposits on the site of the proposed development. The area consists of machair grassland and a thin turf line, less than 0.2m thick, lying directly on shell sand. The area is low and undulating, with a number of distinctive deflation hollows along the north-west portion of the site. A long linear depression, *c.* 10m by 25m, runs diagonally across the site from north-west to south-east, close to the line of the access road from the main road. The vegetation in the hollows and gully suggests that they regularly flood, presumably with the rising and falling seasonal water-table.

The only other pre-assessment features of note in the area were two mounds. The first, in the extreme south-east corner of the development, was rounded and steep-sided and stood *c.* 2.5m above the otherwise flat ground. The mound appeared to be the western end of a ridge, which extended in an easterly direction away from the site. As all development was to remain at least 10m from the edge of this feature, it was decided not to disturb it during the assessment. The second mound, *c.* 100m north-west of the first, was a much lower, more spread affair. However, it was clear from the geography of the adjoining field that it was also the western end of a long ridge that extended eastwards.

Nothing of archaeological significance was noted during the assessment. The thin turf cover, in all trenches, directly overlay natural, undisturbed shell sand. The linear striations noted in certain areas of the site indicate small-scale, short-term cultivation. The two mounds, one of which will not be affected by the proposal, are probably the natural remnants of a dune system, which have, over time, been covered in grass and stabilised. Such ancient dunes presumably gave the area its name.
*Eoin Halpin, ADS Ltd, Unit 48, Westlink Enterprise Centre, 30–50 Distillery Street, Belfast BT12 5BJ.*

## TIPPERARY

## 813. BALLYSHEEHAN STUD, BALLYSHEEHAN
Possible deserted medieval village
S093454
99E0419

During redevelopment of this stud farm a series of earthworks, which possibly represents the remains of a deserted medieval village, was being partially buried in topsoil to make the land safe for livestock. No topsoil-stripping was involved, and no archaeological features or finds were revealed.

In addition a small road was being constructed to provide local access to Ballysheehan Church. Again, no topsoil-stripping was undertaken, and no archaeological features or finds were revealed.
*Avril Purcell, Margaret Gowen & Co. Ltd, 2 Killiney View, Albert Road Lower, Glenageary, Co. Dublin.*

## 814. BALLYTARSNA CASTLE
Tower-house and bawn
SMR 53:66
99E0255

Extensive restoration of the tower and bawn is planned over the next few years. Eleven test-trenches were excavated by machine across the lines of the proposed new roadway and service trenches. No features or deposits of archaeological significance were revealed. Three of the trenches had a ditch-like feature running through them, which can be interpreted as part of an old boundary running from the castle to the road. At a low level in one of the trenches were several sherds of 18th-century wares.

The removal of topsoil along the new drive was monitored, as were the removal of a thick deposit of manure in the ground floor of the castle and the removal of hedgerows on either side of the tower. None of this work revealed features of interest. Planned clearance on the vaults within the tower did not take place this season.

*Brian Hodkinson, Annaholty, Birdhill, Co. Tipperary.*

### 815. KILLEMLY, CAHIR
Two enclosures
20668 12650
SMR 75:04301 and :04302
99E0047

Pre-construction testing was undertaken before selection of the final route for the proposed Cahir Eastern Relief Road to assess the nature and extent of two possible enclosures identified with the aid of aerial photographs. There were no traces above ground level of either possible enclosure, probably because the field has been tilled for several consecutive years. The testing followed a desk-based assessment and field study that looked at possible routes for the proposed Relief Road.

The enclosures are 40m apart. Eight trenches were manually opened across the enclosures. One trench was sited towards the centre of each enclosure, two were along the edges of each site, and one was outside each enclosure.

The predominant feature identified in the trenches opened along the northern edge, in the centre and on the periphery of the first enclosure was a ditch or drain-like feature. A modern sherd of pottery was recovered from the fill of this feature. It appeared that the drain had no association with the enclosure and was a more recent feature dug to improve drainage in an adjoining field. In addition to the drain, there was a series of furrows. The furrows had been truncated by the drain-like feature.

The drain and furrows appeared to have disturbed a number of potential archaeological features including a circular cut, possible post-holes and a fine stone/cobble surface. The surface was only partly picked up, as it extended beneath three sides of the trench. A wide, curved cut was picked up along the southern edge of the first site investigated. It was only partly exposed, as it extended beneath three sides of the trench. It had three different fills. No datable finds were recovered, but there was extensive charcoal-flecking in the fills. This feature may be the ditch surrounding the enclosure.

The second possible enclosure is 40m to the south of the first. A wide linear cut was uncovered in the trench opened in the centre of the enclosure. In addition a wide linear cut was picked up in the trench opened on the north-east edge of the site. It was 1.5m wide and 0.5m deep. This feature extended across the trench and disappeared beneath the north and south sides of the trench. Its fills were sterile except for charcoal inclusions. Two small circular features truncated the upper fill of the cut. The fills within the circular features contained large quantities of charcoal. A possible post-hole was identified to the north-west of the wide linear cut.

In the two trenches opened along the south edge and just outside the southern circumference of the enclosure, further features were uncovered. A curved cut, 0.75m wide and 0.35m deep, was identified along the south-east corner of the trench opened on the south edge of the enclosure. It had a pronounced curve. Its fill contained charcoal and small quantities of fragmented animal bone. By virtue of the location of this feature it was impossible to establish its extent or function. The final trench was just outside the confines of the enclosure. A deep cut, again of unknown width and length, was uncovered. There was a series of three fills, which sealed a wall. The drystone wall, 0.35m wide, extended across the length of the trench. The wall overlay two primary fills in the deep cut.

Non-identifiable archaeological remains were uncovered in all the trenches. Several linear and curved cuts and their associated fills, a possible stone wall and several post-holes were exposed. It was not possible to conclusively establish relationships between the important visible features uncovered during the testing and the two possible enclosures visible on the aerial photograph.

In only one instance were datable finds revealed. The fill in the relatively modern land drain uncovered and investigated in three of the trenches provided modern finds. This drain truncated most of the archaeology in these trenches. No artefacts were found within the other features or deposits, in context or *in situ*.

The testing works confirmed the presence of an archaeological site, although its date remained undetermined. The site was preserved *in situ*.

*Mary Henry, 24 Queen Street, Clonmel, Co. Tipperary.*

### 816. CARRICK-ON-SUIR
Urban
S215400
SMR 85:4
98E0259

The Carrick-on-Suir Main Drainage Scheme, Phase I, started in August 1998 and is currently ongoing (see *Excavations 1998*, 190, for the first stages). The scheme will see the laying of new storm and foul sewers in much of the town, including parts of the medieval town and its suburb of Carrickbeg on the south bank of the river. Pre-construction testing and monitoring of pipeline excavations are taking place. Work to date has been centred on the North Quays, the northern part of the town along the N24, and where the second and smaller of the detention tanks is being built in Carrickbeg.

The work on the Quay has revealed more of the late 18th/early 19th-century quay wall. Most of this is directly beneath the front walls of the buildings on the quayside, *c*. 5–8m behind the present quay wall. A propeller from one of the small tugs used on the Suir in the late 19th/early 20th century was found buried in the present quay.

Work along the N24 in the town revealed numerous 19th-century culverts. A concentration of dressed stone found amongst a large layer of fill on the Waterford road, 1.5km east of the town, also dates to the same period and was deposited when the road was realigned in the 1970s.

In Carrickbeg the only deposits found to date are natural subsoil or riverine deposits. A number of 19th-century culverts were also found.

Work on the project is continuing, with the core areas of the medieval town and suburb yet to be examined.

*Florence M. Hurley, 8 Marina Park, Victoria Road, Cork.*

### 817. MILL LANE, CARRICKBEG, CARRICK-ON-SUIR
Urban
2398 1214
SMR 85:4
99E0110

The development of a site at Mill Lane, Carrickbeg, Carrick-on-Suir, Co. Tipperary, required archaeological testing. The site is within the zone of archaeological potential for Carrick-on-Suir and is adjacent to the site of the medieval Franciscan friary.

Five trenches were dug. Two cut features and a cobbled surface were found. These all produced 19th-century pottery. A single sherd of possible 18th-century pottery was also found.

*Florence M. Hurley, 8 Marina Park, Victoria Road, Cork.*

### 818. BOHERMORE, CASHEL
Environs of medieval town
20758 1407
SMR 61:25
99E0687

Test-trenching before the grant of planning permission was requested for this site because of the proximity of the proposed development to the zone of archaeological potential for Cashel town.

Four trenches were excavated. Trench 1 measured 23m by 2m and was 1.5m deep. Stratigraphy consisted primarily of homogeneous garden soils. Towards the south end of the trench a large pit, 3.04m wide and 0.9m deep, was identified. The contents indicate its use as an 18th-century rubbish pit. Trench 2 measured 58.66m by 2m and was 0.8m deep. Trench 3 measured 20.8m by 2m and was 1m deep. Trench 4 measured 15.58m by 2m and was 0.8m deep. The stratigraphy exposed in Trenches 2–4 was quite similar, consisting of three basic layers—topsoil, garden soil and glacial deposits.

No artefacts or stratigraphy of an archaeological nature were identified during the trenching.

*Emer Dennehy, Eachtra Archaeological Projects, 3 Canal Place, Tralee, Co. Kerry.*

### 819. COLLIER'S LANE, CASHEL
Urban medieval/post-medieval
2075 1470
SMR 61:25
99E0159

The development of a site at Collier's Lane, Cashel, required an archaeological assessment. The site is close to the Dominican priory (founded in 1243) and is just outside the walled town. A number of small structures were shown along the lane frontage in the first edition OS map, but all of these have since been removed, and the site was covered by grass.

Eight trenches were opened. A brown, clayey silt, humic soil (a 'garden soil', the product of continuous cultivation over a long period) covered the site, varying in depth from 0.15m in the north-east corner to 1.2m along the southern side of the site. Twenty possible archaeological features were found. These were either cut into this material or covered by it. Four of these produced post-medieval or modern finds. Three produced medieval finds, and the remainder produced no finds. The majority were linear features aligned north–south. Most were 0.35–0.5m wide. Three were noticeably larger, although two of these, aligned north–south in Trenches 1 and 5, may be part of the same feature. The section in Trench 1 was excavated, revealing a V-shaped cut, 1m deep and 3.1m wide. This produced local medieval ware. The feature found in Trench 6 was similar in size but was aligned east–west.

In the south-west corner of the site a shallow pit was found beneath the garden soil. Where exposed, this measured *c.* 3.4m by 2m. It contained four fills, the latest a brown, clayey silt, producing seventeen sherds of medieval pottery and a hone stone. Underneath this lay two charcoal-rich deposits, the upper one containing a mixture of burnt soil and redeposited subsoil, and the lower one composed almost exclusively of charcoal. These lay over a spread of small and medium-sized sub-angular pieces of limestone.

Given that the Dominican priory is so close, that these lands most likely belonged to that order, and that they are known to have houses and gardens close to the abbey, it is most likely that these linear features are the drainage ditches that marked out these gardens and fields. It is noticeable that in all editions of the 6-inch Ordnance Survey map of the area the site is shown as being empty except for a series of small houses or sheds fronting part of Collier's Lane.

The large pit in the south-west corner of the site may also be connected to the priory. The unweathered and angular nature of the stone fill suggests that it may come from one of the periods of refurbishment of the abbey. The priory was substantially rebuilt after a fire in *c.* 1480. The layer of burning may be associated with that event, and the stone may be waste dumped out in the fields surrounding the abbey.

As a result of the work undertaken above, *Dúchas* recommended that monitoring of the removal of the topsoil and garden soil take place. During this a cobbled surface, a circular cut feature and a linear cut feature were uncovered at the southern edge of the site. Part of a post-medieval stoneware vessel and clay pipe fragments were found stratified above the cobbling. As these lay *c.* 0.7m beneath the proposed finished ground surface, they were left *in situ* after being recorded and covered in geotextile. These are likely to be associated with the six tenements in the priory precinct mentioned in the Dissolution account.

The areas where house foundations cut into archaeological features were monitored and hand-excavated. A total of 374 sherds of medieval pottery and 58 sherds of post-medieval pottery came from the garden soil.

*Florence M. Hurley, 8 Marina Park, Victoria Road, Cork.*

### 820. FRIAR'S STREET, CASHEL
Urban medieval
99E0588

Excavation of Cashel's medieval town wall and associated features was conducted before the construction of a library, adjacent to Friar Street. The site covered an area of 110m². The excavated area consisted of the north–south basal remains of the town wall, built *c.* 1265. The wall was built as two separate walls, running parallel to each other. They were constructed of mortar-bonded, dressed, inner and outer faces with a fill of small stone and mortar. Existing portions of the town wall throughout the town showed that this double wall would have been conjoined at parapet level. The footing of the outer wall on the excavation site was 0.4m below the inner portion. The outer wall also showed evidence of an external batter. A multi-phase external defensive ditch was revealed. Its maximum depth was 2.4m below the ground level, but it had a depth of 1.4m from the footing of the external wall. Subsequent disturbance of the ground had obliterated the external aspect of the ditch. However, it can be estimated that its full extent was *c.* 6m wide. Animal bone and 13th–14th-century pottery were recovered from the wall and ditch area, and 17th-century disturbance of the walled area divulged a cobbled path inside the walled area that would have traversed the wall itself. The town ditch had been allowed to silt up. Part of the silted area had been removed to create a stone-lined trough that had reused stone from the town wall. The fill of the trough's revetting structure was hard-packed, redeposited, natural soil, which had some scant evidence of being paved with limestone flagstones. The artefactual nature of the trough and cobbled path was consistent with a 17th-century date.

The inner portion of the town wall was built on the remains of a substantial backfilled ditch that extended beyond the excavation area. It was 1.8m deep. Part of a human burial was recovered from the base of this ditch. The backfill contained 13th–14th-century pottery. It is probable that the pottery entered here during the backfilling phase. The nature of the backfill is consistent with bank material. It is possible that this ditch and bank arrangement has some association with the nearby St John's Cathedral. St John's Cathedral is on the site of an earlier, medieval church. Feehan's Road immediately to the south of St John's Cathedral describes a curve, which may be the boundary of an ecclesiastical enclosure. If the orientation of the low ridge on which St John's Cathedral stands is considered with the curve of Feehan's Road, it is not implausible that the backfilled ditch forms part of an ecclesiastical enclosure. The partially excavated remains of the human burial would substantiate an ecclesiastical perspective.

*Niall Gregory, 25 Westpark, Blessington, Co. Wicklow, for Mary Henry & Associates Ltd.*

### 821. LOWER GATE STREET, CASHEL
Urban medieval/post-medieval
20758 14070
SMR 61:25
99E0428

The site of the development, a housing scheme, is just to the north-west of the centre of Cashel town. It is immediately outside the north-western stretch of the town wall, which extends for a length of 86m along the east side of the site and survives to a height of 5–6m above ground level. The development did not directly impinge on the town wall as it was 8m away from its line.

Nothing of major archaeological significance was uncovered during monitoring of the digging of strip foundations for the development. The findings confirmed that there was no medieval activity in this area of Cashel outside the walled town. It would appear that the area was a vacant lot abutting the town wall and was probably used as common ground, with no settlement or any other activity because of its closeness to the defensive medieval wall.

*Mary Henry, 24 Queen Street, Clonmel, Co. Tipperary.*

### 822. 100 MAIN STREET, CASHEL
Urban medieval
2075 1405
99E0096

Two small trenches were cut into the burgage plot behind 100 Main Street, to test ahead of a two-storeyed extension. A well was found *c.* 15m from the street front, probably inside a 16th/17th-century building, and contemporary ditches and platforms further back suggest domestic or industrial activity (rather than cultivation). There was little indication of earlier occupation, and the site appears to have been used as a garden in the late 17th/18th century, before being overbuilt in the late 18th/19th century.

The 17th/18th-century level was not disturbed during excavation for a raft foundation and drain.

*Dave Pollock, ArchaeoGrafix, Church Lane, Stradbally, Co. Waterford.*

### 823. LITTLE ISLAND, CLONMEL
Urban post-medieval
S20252220
98E0470

Monitoring was carried out at a development site at Hughes' Mill, Little Island, Clonmel, Co. Tipperary. Little Island is on the southern side of the River Suir, immediately outside the medieval town. There are numerous medieval and post-medieval references to milling on Little Island and at Hughes' Mill, where an extensive 18th- and 19th-century milling complex survives.

The monitoring of three engineering test-trenches revealed a complex of culverts running under the proposed development site. The engineering trenches were excavated to identify the location of these culverts and the surrounding ground conditions so that the foundations could be designed to avoid the culverts. The culverts are likely to date from the 18th century and appear to have been altered over the course of the use of the mill from this date. The arched entrance into one of the culverts at the head-race is constructed using wicker centring; this adjoins the site of the medieval bridge over the River Suir onto Little Island.

*Edmond O'Donovan, Margaret Gowen & Co. Ltd, 2 Killiney View, Albert Road Lower, Glenageary, Co. Dublin.*

### 824. 36–37 PARNELL STREET, CLONMEL
Urban medieval and post-medieval
1985 1236
99E0649

An archaeological impact assessment of the proposed development was requested ahead of granting planning permission to demolish the recent standing building on site and to construct a new, four-storey building in its place, within the existing boundary walls. A report was prepared on the standing building and walls, and three test-trenches were excavated.

The test excavations suggest that 17th-century (or older) buildings stood along the street front. A robbed wall trench had been backfilled with glazed ridge-tiles (17th-century?), pottery and bottle glass. Finds dating to the late 17th and 18th centuries were recovered from other contexts in Trench 1, but no medieval finds were recovered.

Excavation stopped at the level of the late 17th/18th-century features. An earlier, red/brown, silty soil overlying the gravelly subsoil was exposed but not excavated and is probably medieval.

Trench 2 cut through rubble 0.55m thick over a garden soil. The rubble (sandstone blocks, cobbles, slate and floor tiles) is likely to have derived from the walls of the 19th-century building previously on the site. The garden soil 0.4m deep overlay a red/brown soil (medieval cultivation?) over gravel. No finds were recovered.

Trench 3, on the street front, was excavated to a depth of 0.6m through compacted (recently), imported gravel.

*Jo Moran, ArchaeoGrafix, Church Lane, Stradbally, Co. Waterford.*

### 825. HEARN'S HOTEL, PARNELL STREET, CLONMEL
Urban medieval and post-medieval
1985 1233
99E0497

An archaeological assessment was required as a planning condition for an extension to the ballroom at the rear of Hearn's Hotel. The site is outside the medieval walled town, in the area of the 17th-century east suburbs. The hotel building has an integral carriageway that previously led to a courtyard where Bianconi established stables and workshops for his coaching enterprise.

A cobbled floor, drain and wall stump were uncovered, the remains of outbuildings around the yard. These overlay a deep garden soil (with no datable finds), over a thin, silty, red/brown soil over gravel. The red/brown soil is likely to be the remains of an earlier (medieval) cultivation soil, although no finds were recovered from the layer.

*Jo Moran, ArchaeoGrafix, Church Lane, Stradbally, Co. Waterford.*

### 826. SUIR ISLAND, CLONMEL
Urban
S204222
99E0606

This site is on an island in the River Suir and was the site of an early 19th-century mill, now demolished. Three test-trenches were opened on the site. In two of the trenches rubble was revealed sitting directly above river gravels. In the third trench a deposit of black, silty clay was revealed above the riverine deposits. This could not be examined in detail because of the depth of the trench but is probably 18th- or 19th-century in date, i.e. directly pre-dating the mill's construction. Further monitoring is to be undertaken on the site.

*Avril Purcell, Margaret Gowen & Co. Ltd, 2 Killiney View, Albert Road Lower, Glenageary, Co. Dublin.*

### 827. ROCKLOW ROAD, FETHARD
Urban medieval and post-medieval
22149 14325
99E0632

An archaeological impact assessment was sought for planning permission to renovate an existing building and to erect an extension to a property at Rocklow Road, Fethard. A report was prepared on the standing buildings, and a test-trench was excavated in the footprint of the proposed extension.

The test-trench identified a well-preserved cobbled surface 0.3–0.45m below present ground level, probably of 18th/19th-century date. The remains of a wall were identified on the street front, potentially the front wall of a building (with cobbled floor) recorded on an 1840s survey. Cobbles to the south would have surfaced an open yard.

A clay floor identified under the cobbles by the street front is likely to be the original floor of the building. A sherd of bottle glass recovered from the floor suggests a post-medieval date, but considerable root disturbance in the area undermines the reliability of the evidence. A small post-hole identified in a sondage under the floor suggests an earlier generation of buildings on the street.

*Jo Moran, ArchaeoGrafix, Church Lane, Stradbally, Co. Waterford.*

### 828. 26 KILLEENYARDA, HOLYCROSS
Ringfort
20777 15391
SMR 47:29
99E0224

Assessment took place before development adjacent to a ringfort. The site is 1 mile south of the 12th-century Cistercian Holycross Abbey (SMR 47:110). The ringfort has a shallow, overgrown outer ditch and bank visible, surviving to a height of 0.5m. The north-western corner of the property cuts into the bank of the monument. The proposed development sought to demolish the existing dwelling and build an extended house and septic tank on the site.

Three linear test-trenches were opened for the assessment, in the north-west corner of the site, and revealed the partially truncated enclosing ditch of the fort. This was a V-shaped enclosing ditch, 3.2m wide and 0.6m+ deep, giving an external diameter of 42.5m. A second V-shaped ditch was revealed, 6–8m from the inner ditch, 2.4m wide and 0.4m+ deep, with an external diameter of 57m. Several post-holes were noted between the two ditches but no trace of an outer bank.

Two unassociated features were also revealed, which represented a later boundary ditch and the terminus of a ditch or pit. The development plans were revised to avoid these ditches and move away from the monument. Monitoring of construction was recommended

*Paul Stevens, Farney Bridge, Holycross, Co. Tipperary.*

### 829. 26 KILLEENYARDA, HOLYCROSS
Monitoring adjacent to ringfort
20777 15391
SMR 47:29
99E0224

Assessment by Paul Stevens (No. 828 above) had revealed the presence of potential archaeological features within a trial-trench, c. 5m from the bank of the ringfort that lay to the east. Because of this the house plan was adjusted and moved a further 3m from the ringfort, making the closest point 8m from the bank.

Potential archaeological features were revealed during the monitoring of the excavation of the foundation trenches, which were to be preserved in situ. A sub-ovoid feature measuring 0.99m north-east/south-west by 0.41m had a maximum recorded depth of 0.44m and was revealed within the foundation trench closest to the ringfort. Three other features were also revealed within this trench, though not further investigated: a subcircular feature 0.74m by 0.5m, a vaguely linear feature up to 0.42m wide extending beyond both section edges, and a small, subrectangular feature 0.48m by 0.26m. All contained deposits of similar colour and nature. No datable material was recovered.

Apart from a former field boundary bisecting the site, no other features were revealed.
Stuart D. Elder, for Mary Henry & Associates, 24 Queen Street, Clonmel, Co. Tipperary.

### 830. KILFEAKLE
Medieval
R957373
SMR 59:127
99E0442

A proposed private development, to the west of the church and graveyard at Kilfeakle, Co. Tipperary, was tested in August 1999 as part of an archaeological impact statement.

Four 0.7m-wide trenches were inserted, two across each of the two proposed houses and access routes. They revealed a limited amount of medieval material in association with several undated (and therefore of potential archaeological interest) features. These were mostly furrow cuts and ploughmarks, with occasional large pits and larger, trench-like cuts. There was a higher concentration of features to the north of the site. The nature of the archaeology suggested agricultural or gardening usage. Based on the findings, some further archaeological examination was recommended, as was the repositioning of one (the northern) of the proposed houses.
Ken Hanley, 44 Eaton Heights, Cobh, Co. Cork.

### 831. GRANTSTOWN CASTLE, KILFEAKLE
Tower-house
R968397
SMR 59:08901
99E0563

Grantstown Castle is a fine tower-house of probable early 16th-century date, which is on a low bluff some distance north of the village of Kilfeakle, Co. Tipperary. The tower-house has been acquired and will undergo conservation, restoration and adaptation for use as a private dwelling.

The present, limited works involved the excavation of a service trench for a septic tank and pipe. The trench was opened by mechanical excavator using a grading bucket. No deposits of archaeological significance were noted.
Claire Walsh, Archaeological Projects Ltd, 25A Eaton Square, Terenure, Dublin 6W.

### 832. NEWTOWN
Vicinity of watermill
SMR 19:3
99E0030

Test-trenching of the footprint of a proposed house, septic tank and percolation area and two trenches across the line of the proposed entrance drive revealed no features of archaeological interest.
Brian Hodkinson, Annaholty, Birdhill, Co. Tipperary.

### 833. ABBEY STREET, ROSCREA
Adjacent to friary
SMR 12:10
99E0489

Trial-trenching on the site of a proposed development within the yard of Abbey Mills, just inside its boundary with the medieval Franciscan abbey, revealed no features or deposits of archaeological interest.
Brian Hodkinson, Annaholty, Birdhill, Co. Tipperary.

### 834. TERRYGLASS
Vicinity of castle
18583 20089
SMR 6:25
99E0534

Trial-trenching on a proposed private house development in a field to the south of Old Court Castle produced no material of archaeological interest. The footprints of the house, septic tank and percolation areas were all tested.
Brian Hodkinson, Annaholty, Birdhill, Co. Tipperary.

### 835. THE MUNSTER HOTEL, CATHEDRAL STREET, THURLES
Urban medieval
S130586
SMR 41:42
98E0598 ext.

Excavation was carried out between February and March 1999 at the site of the Munster Hotel redevelopment, Thurles. The site measures 53m north–south by 24–28m and is on the southern side of Cathedral Street, opposite the site of the Carmelite friary, built in 1291–1300 (Gwynn and Hadcock 1970, 29). Excavation was at the request of the developers, to facilitate the construction of a larger hotel building with basement on the same site.

The street-frontage area (Areas A and B) was found under 18th/19th-century and modern hotel buildings. It revealed archaeological features cutting natural, yellow boulder clay, 0.2m below the level of the present pavement, including the truncated beam-slots and post-holes of a square medieval structure, orientated south-east/north-west, over 7m long and 4.4m wide. A second, rectangular medieval structure was represented by a truncated informal hearth and measured over 11m east–west (continuing under the road outside the area of excavation to the north). In between these was a truncated medieval ironworking furnace. All three features were cut by a number of in-cutting east–west gullies and ditches, probably representing a formal widening and realignment of the main Dublin road.

Area C, 13–23m from the street frontage, contained an intense concentration of rubbish and cesspits dating to the medieval, later medieval, post-medieval and even early modern periods. Amongst them was a fine but undated stone-, cobble- and moss-lined square pit and an early modern limestone well. However, this area saw the most truncation by intrusive concrete foundations.

The southern portion of the site was represented by Areas D–F, between 23m and 52m from the street frontage. This southern area also revealed a high concentration of rubbish pits, including a pit lined with coppiced hazel and ash (identified by I. Stuijts), wickerwork, a rough limestone well and a stone wall footing. The last contained two sterling silver English pennies of Edward I, dated 1302–7 (identified by M. Kenny, NMI).

The southern half of the site was also cut by a number of north–south-running boundary ditches/gullies, dividing the site into four long, linear burgage plots, dating to the medieval period. These burgage plots were 5.5–6m wide to the east and 15m wide to the west. The western plots appeared far wider than the eastern two. However, there was also some evidence to suggest that the two westernmost plots had originally been one and were subdivided in the later medieval or early post-medieval period.

The rear 10m of the site (Area F) was sealed by 0.8m of garden topsoil and contained an unusual and undated multiple dog burial (two adults and a juvenile), within a north–south linear gully and marked by post-holes extending south into the baulk. This area also contained medieval pits and gullies continuing beyond the area of excavation. An extension to the east of Area F (Area G) revealed no further evidence of archaeological features east of the fourth north–south burgage plot gully.

The excavation produced a large assemblage of local and imported pottery from the medieval period onwards, as well as animal bone, glass, leather and rope (from early modern contexts), clay pipe and handmade brick. However, the best find from the site was a Class 3b (after Deevy 1998) gilt-edged silver ring brooch.

The results of this excavation show near-continuous, if heavily truncated, occupation on the site from at least the early 13th century, around the time of the foundation of the Carmelite friary opposite. It also indicates evidence for a relatively wealthy and semi-industrial eastern suburb to the medieval town, referred to as 'Brogmal' in the 17th century (Simington 1931, 385–8; Bradley 1985, 54; Carey and Farrelly 1985, 85), but it does not rule out the possibility of a twin town as suggested by Thomas (1992, 192–3).

*References*
Bradley, J. 1985 The medieval towns of Tipperary. In W. Nolan (ed.), *Tipperary: history and society*, 34–59. Dublin.
Carey, H. and Farrelly, J. 1985 *The Urban Archaeological Survey of County Tipperary North Riding, Parts 1 & 2*. Dublin.
Deevy, M. 1998 *Medieval ring brooches in Ireland*. Bray.
Gwynn, A. and Hadcock, R.N. 1970 *Medieval religious houses: Ireland*. Dublin.
Simington, R.C. (ed.) 1931–4 *The Civil Survey AD 1654–1656. County of Tipperary*, vol. 1.
Thomas, A. 1992 *The walled towns of Ireland*. Dublin.

*Paul Stevens for Margaret Gowen & Co. Ltd, 2 Killiney View, Albert Road Lower, Glenageary, Co. Dublin.*

### 836. CROTTY'S BAKERY, FRIAR STREET, THURLES
Urban
S124586
SMR 41:42/1
99E0678

Assessment was undertaken for a proposed development at Crotty's Bakery, Friar Street, Thurles. The site was in use as a bakery from the late 19th century and continued to be until recently. However, all buildings on the site post-date J. Rocque's Map of Thurles of 1755, and most are late 19th- and early 20th-century in date.

Two linear test-trenches were opened for this assessment, in the front courtyard area and the rear garden area. No archaeological soils or features were encountered.

*Paul Stevens for Margaret Gowen & Co. Ltd, 2 Killiney View, Albert Road Lower, Glenageary, Co. Dublin.*

### 837. KICKHAM STREET, THURLES
Urban
2238 1590
SMR 41:42
99E0488

The redevelopment of a site in Kickham Street, Thurles, required archaeological testing. The site is close to St Mary's Church, possibly the site of the medieval parish church. This area may have been a suburb of the medieval town.

Two trenches were opened, only one of which produced finds, all of which were 19th/20th-century in date.

*Florence M. Hurley, 8 Marina Park, Victoria Road, Cork.*

### 838. 1–2 PARNELL STREET, THURLES
Urban
S125586
SMR 41:42:1
98E0563

Monitoring was undertaken of a development at 1–2 Parnell Street, Thurles. The site is a mid-19th-century yellow brick townhouse and yard, backing onto the Black Castle, a 15th/16th-century tower-house and partial bawn, within the medieval walled town of Thurles.

Monitoring of a foundation trench, 11.5m by 8–9m and 0.5m deep, at the rear of the townhouse on 13 and 14 July 1999 revealed no archaeological features or deposits across the site. During construction, demolition of a lean-to exposed a portion of the Black Castle wall and revealed a blocked arrow-loop at ground-floor level. The loop was of cut and puckered-finished grey limestone and was splayed towards the base, with the opening recessed from the outside to allow greater cover. It measured 1.33m in height, 0.55m in sill width, 0.3m in lintel width and 0.12m in ope width and was blocked with yellow, handmade bricks. The arrow-loop and wall are outside the area to be developed.

*Paul Stevens for Margaret Gowen & Co. Ltd, 2 Killiney View, Albert Road Lower, Glenageary, Co. Dublin.*

### 839. TULLAHEDY
Burnt mound complex and ditches, multi-period
R842772
98E0540

Some of these sites were described in *Excavations 1998* (204–5). This fuller account describes all the archaeology found here.

Three burnt mounds (Sites A, B and C) were discovered in Tullahedy townland during monitoring of topsoil-stripping for the N7 Nenagh Bypass. Two further sites (Sites D and E) were found nearby this year. Excavations on all five were carried out and concluded in October 1999.

Tullahedy Site A was *c*. 35m south of Sites B and C and adjacent to the railway line. The burnt mound measured 23.5m east–west by 19m and was *c*. 0.7m in maximum depth. Three-quarters of the mound was fully excavated, the remainder is preserved. Excavations revealed up to seven clay-lined troughs, areas of cobbled surfaces and post and stake structures. One trough had a post at each of its corners and a cobbled surround. The north-east area of the site was distinct in having two separate clay surfaces; these produced worked chert, flint and a perforated stone bead, which came from the upper layer. The stone bead was similar to others found in the Neolithic site of Tullahedy, excavated by Cia McConway (*Excavations 1997*, 181, 97E0472; *Excavations 1998*, 203–4), to the west. The lower of these two clay layers produced two possible microliths. There was evidence for a hearth and structural evidence in the form of stake-holes. All of this activity was sealed by a succession of burnt stone layers that formed the mound. Within the later burnt mound strata, deposits of fine, yellow sand and a deposit of small iron objects mixed with burnt animal bones were found. Large amounts of iron slag were deposited in the mound surface when the site was abandoned.

Tullahedy Site B was the largest, roughly circular in plan. It measured *c*. 22m x *c*. 26m in diameter, with a 1.5m depth of burnt stones. Approximately half of the site was fully excavated down to natural to facilitate the road development, and the remainder is preserved. The excavation showed evidence for a multi-phase occupation of the site. Hundreds of stake-holes in an arc may have enclosed the original habitation, which in turn was sealed by a marl and peat deposit. The remains of a structure were found at the south-west of the site, consisting of a series of large, sand-filled post-holes. There was similar evidence at the north-east area for post-holes, as well as pits. It is hoped to use *in situ* wood remains from some of the posts for the dating of this period.

The primary burnt mound phase followed, and finds associated with this phase were wood, antler/horn, footpaths, cobbled surfaces, stone hearths, burnt spreads and a trough. A widespread deposit of distinct, grey, sandy clay, which may reflect long-term site abandonment or represent an archaeological stratum from a later phase, sealed this phase. Sealing this grey layer was the next burnt stone stratum. This phase may have been associated with an encircling ditch, which had at least two distinct, separate portions between which the ditch was formally terminated. Finds from the ditch included animal jawbones. The latest phase of this level had charcoal-rich, burnt stone deposits and also what appeared to be the ore-staining of burnt stones. Many metal and burnt bone fragments were recovered from this level, as was a ring-headed pin, a rotary quern fragment, hone stones, rubbing stones and worked bone.

The final phase of activity involved deliberate deposition of a sandstone kerb/revetment around the edge of the mound. The sandstone may have been placed for storage for use on the adjacent burnt mound, Site C. Associated with this phase was a deposit of iron fragments at the south-east of the mound.

Tullahedy Site C was the smallest burnt stone mound, a few metres east of Site B. It measured 12.5m east–west by 12m with a maximum depth of *c*. 0.3m. This site also had multi-phase activity. About three-quarters of this site was fully excavated, and the remainder is preserved. The primary phase involved a number of clay-lined pits and associated stake-holes. Bone and wood remains will help to date this phase. This in turn was sealed by a number of cobbled surfaces. A larger trough between Sites B and C produced a boar tusk. On the highest part of the site a four-post rectangular structure was revealed. There was much charcoal found along the base of the structure, and it was abandoned under a deposit of clay and stones. Two clay-lined troughs were revealed near this structure. All this activity was sealed by a low, charcoal-rich, burnt stone mound, which represented the final stage of activity.

Tullahedy Site D consisted of two ditches that were found in the exposed section of the road drain, *c*. 10m to the north-west of Site B. Although most of the ditches had been removed during the drain excavation, there was enough evidence to show that the ditches had a number of fills. Finds included butchered animal bones, slag, metal and charcoal. The ditches continued northward outside the development line.

Tullahedy Site E consisted of two to three ditches that were found in the exposed section of the road drain, *c*. 60m west of Site B. As the site only survived in section and produced no finds, little can be said about it. The ditches were filled with stone and pebble deposits, and the upper fills had sandstone deposits. The ditches were scaled by bog growth, which suggests an early date. The ditches survive beyond the road drain face and would be worthy of further investigation.

Owing to the complexity of the sites found here, the question of dates for the three burnt mounds and the ditches is very important. The latest phase on Site B is early medieval in date. However, the primary, pre-mound level may be prehistoric.

Similarly, the final-phase iron slag deposition on Site A may be Iron Age/early medieval in date, while the primary, pre-mound level may be prehistoric. It is hoped that the post-excavation work will help to clarify this.
*Richard O'Brien, ADS Ltd, Windsor House, 11 Fairview Strand, Fairview, Dublin 3.*

## TYRONE

### 840. LENDRUM'S BRIDGE
No archaeological significance
H435545

The site of Lendrum's Bridge Wind Farm covers an area 115m east–west by 60m and is in the Sperrin Mountains, generally above the 280m contour, equidistant from Fintona to the north and Fivemiletown to the south. The Glennamuck stream, a tributary of the Quiggery Water, cuts across the south-east area of the site, while tributaries of the Mary Burns River originate in the south and south-west.

Platforms for nine of the proposed twenty turbines and a substation were mechanically excavated under archaeological supervision during Phase 1. Each turbine platform measured *c.* 18m in diameter. The peat was excavated to subsoil and consisted of a homogeneous, light to mid-brown, soft peat, free of tree roots or timber. Subsoil was a firm, light brown, sandy/silty clay with rounded stone inclusions.

Nothing of archaeological significance was uncovered during this work.
*Cia McConway, ADS Ltd, Unit 48, Westlink Enterprise Centre, 30–50 Distillery Street, Belfast BT12 5BJ.*

### 841. NEWTOWNSTEWART CASTLE, NEWTOWNSTEWART
17th-century castle and bawn/Bronze Age segmented cist
H40208583
SMR 17:47

A research excavation was undertaken at Newtownstewart Castle to ascertain the level of survival of masonry remains before the opening of the castle to the public and in tandem with ongoing conservation work.

Newtownstewart is about halfway between Omagh and Strabane on the main road between Dublin and Derry. The Environment and Heritage Service acquired the castle, which is within the Newtownstewart Conservation Area, several years ago, and an adjacent grocery shop was subsequently demolished.

The castle was built by Sir Robert Newcomen in the early 17th century, on lands granted to him in the Ulster Plantation. The area had previously been controlled by the O'Neills, and the well-known 14th-century monument known as Harry Avery's Castle (after Henry Aimbreidh O'Neill) is three-quarters of a mile to the south-west of the town. Another early O'Neill castle, Turlough O'Neill's Castle, was reputed to have previously occupied the site of Newtownstewart Castle, but no evidence of any earlier fortification was uncovered.

By 1628 the castle passed into the hands of the Stewart family through marriage (which is how it got its name). It was attacked during the 1641 Rebellion but was later repaired and continued in use until 1689. In this year King James II stayed in the castle before and after the failed Siege of Derry. On his retreat back to Dublin he had both the castle and the town burnt. The town was rebuilt in the 1720s, but the castle was never repaired. In recent centuries the site of the castle was used as a market and store, and an internal, arched market wall has been retained to show this period of the castle's history.

Only the western, northern and fragments of the southern internal dividing walls of the castle survive to their full height above ground. The western gable is distinctive in having a triple crow-stepped gable, the middle one of which is surmounted by an eight-sided star-shaped red brick chimney, a mixture of Scottish and English Plantation architecture. The northern wall contains a projecting circular stair tower and, at the north-east corner, a square flanker with two gun-loops and a doorway with sandstone quoins. The castle originally consisted of three floors and a basement. It was at basement level that the excavation took place.

Seven trenches were opened around the castle, and approximately 70% of the area within the monument was excavated to subsoil levels (gravel and clay). As expected, the stratigraphy consisted mostly of dumped layers of rubble, brick and stone, post-dating the destruction of the castle. There was much evidence of masonry having been robbed out, possibly providing some of the stone used to rebuild Newtownstewart in the 18th century. At basement level there may have been a flagged floor, but the only parts discovered lay under a large fragment of collapsed masonry.

However, substantial sections of the castle survived intact below ground. The excavation uncovered the full extent of the south wall and much of the east wall, some of which had been completely robbed out earlier this century. A previously unknown doorway in the east wall was discovered, as well as a 7m stretch of the bawn wall, running southwards from the south-eastern corner of the castle.

Cut into the subsoil within the castle were internal slots and post-holes, which would have originally held wooden walls and beams. Pottery, clay pipes, roof and wall tiles, window leading and glass from the 17th and succeeding centuries were retrieved from the excavation. Most importantly, the excavation uncovered evidence of at least two phases of castle construction. It appears that in its earliest form the north wall simply had a centrally placed projecting stair tower and battered north-west corner wall. Excavation proved that at a later stage (after 1641?) a flanker was added to the north-west corner to improve defences.

Also uncovered during the excavation was an Early Bronze Age segmented long cist burial, contained in an oval grave pit cut into the subsoil. This was found *c.* 7m west of the junction of the southern and western walls of the castle, close to the current site entrance. The survival of the grave is remarkable, as it lay within the foundations of the now-demolished shop. Less than twenty of these

Bronze Age burials have been found to date in the whole of Ireland.

The cist comprised two chambers, each containing the cremated remains of a single individual and a highly decorated food vessel. Analysis of the cremated remains by Eileen Murphy revealed that they were of a juvenile of 12–15 years and a woman in her 40s or 50s. With the cremated remains of the juvenile was a burnt, hollow-base, flint arrowhead. Whether this was the cause of death or a treasured artefact buried with the individual is as yet unknown.

*Ruairí Ó Baoill, Archaeological Excavation Unit, EHS, 5–33 Hill Street, Belfast BT1 2LA.*

## WATERFORD

### 842. CROUGHATESKIN, BALLYMACARBRY
Adjacent to church and graveyard
S1912
99E0589

The proposed development was an extension to a house just south of Teampull na mBeinéad (SMR 5:26), a church site and graveyard (Annals of Inishfallen, 1361). The remains of the east wall of the church (7.3m long, 1m in maximum height) survive, within a rectangular graveyard containing an old school building. A pebble with incised crosses was found in the graveyard. Most of these graveyards were the sites of medieval parish churches. While the beginnings of the parish structure date to the 12th century, many of the extant remains of churches are of 15th- and 16th-century date (Moore 1999, 162).

Because of its proximity to a known monument, *Dúchas* recommended that an archaeologist monitor all ground disturbance associated with the development. This work was carried out on 19 October 1999.

The foundation trenches were 1m wide and were excavated to a depth of 1m. All trenches contained shallow topsoil above c. 0.2m of natural sandstone shingle and yellow/orange boulder clay.

*Reference*
Moore M. 1999 *Archaeological inventory of County Waterford*. Dublin.

*Joanna Wren, The Mile Post, Waterford.*

### 843. BUTTERY LANE, DUNGARVAN
Post-medieval cottages
2261 0928
SMR 31:4
99E0614

A site outside the walled town of Dungarvan but inside the zone of archaeological potential was assessed before a housing development. The two cottages standing at the roadside were probably built in the early 18th century, with low eaves, a steeply pitched roof, and distinctive chimney stacks. The buildings were refurbished in the late 18th/19th century (roof and openings raised, brick incorporated). A survey was made before demolition; no earlier buildings were found on site.

*Dave Pollock, ArchaeoGrafix, Church Lane, Stradbally, Co. Waterford.*

### 844. CARBERRYS LANE, DUNGARVAN
Urban medieval/post-medieval
2262 0930
SMR 31:4
99E0115

An open site between Carberrys Lane and Coxs Lane, at the edge of the walled town of Dungarvan, was assessed in April 1999, before redevelopment. Further investigation took place in July and August.

The town wall ran the length of the site, with its base down the side of a linear clay pit (floored with beach cobbles and used as a road to the shore) under Carberrys Lane. The wall could not be dated from finds, but the construction (drystone foundations with mortar poured in sporadically) was similar to that of lengths of wall elsewhere, and it was dated by pottery to the 17th century. A shallow and narrow cellar was cut against the wall and backfilled in the early 18th century (remains of the building overhead were removed in the late 18th or early 19th century), when the town wall was demolished and a long quay was built at the edge of the harbour. Although the entire site was truncated repeatedly, in the 18th and early 19th century, the pre-town wall ground level

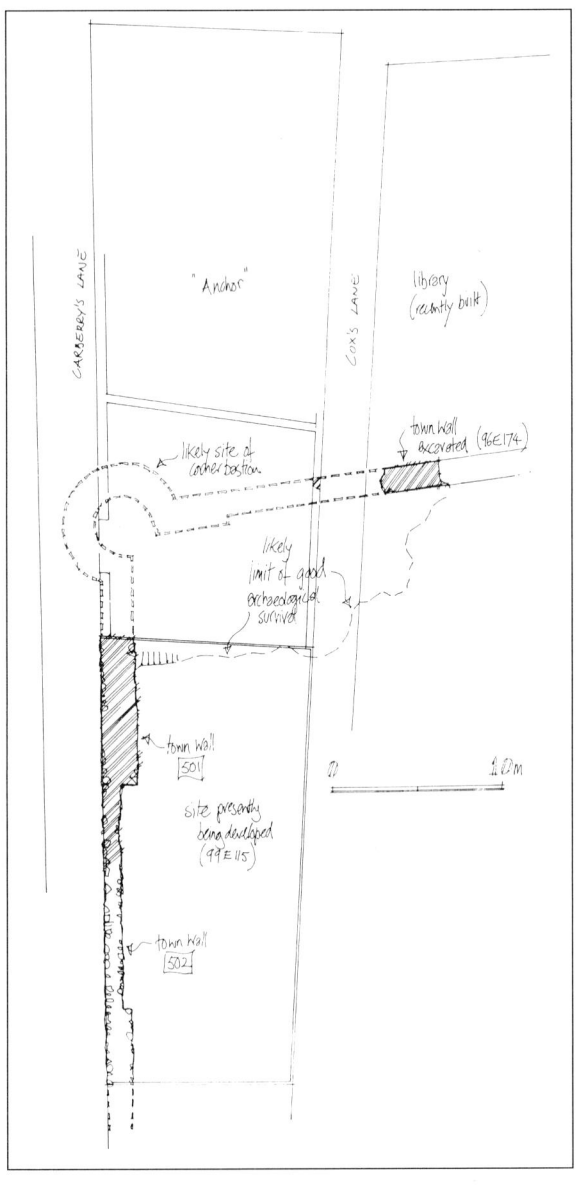

Likely site of north-west corner bastion at Carberrys Lane, Dungarvan.

has survived in a narrow strip at the north end of the site, where the ground falls suddenly onto the medieval beach. This implies good preservation for the corner bastion, 10m away under the adjoining site.

*Dave Pollock, ArchaeoGrafix, Church Lane, Stradbally, Co. Waterford.*

### 845. CHURCH STREET/PARNELL STREET, DUNGARVAN

Urban medieval/post-medieval
2262 0929
SMR 31:4
98E0591

The foundation cuts for four new townhouses close to the centre of medieval Dungarvan were inspected and monitored in November 1998. In April 1999 the stump of an old wall on site was investigated and the main service trench was monitored. Ground level at the north end of the site, towards the market place, had been raised during the construction of a number of 18th-century buildings (including Merry's restaurant). It is unclear how much of this area was damaged by earlier clay extraction, but some fragments of medieval levels should have survived (below the excavated foundation level).

At the south end of the site a long 18th-century building with outside stairs on the gable (hence the stump of wide wall) overlay a late 17th-century building with a revetted bank and ditch behind. The line of the bank and ditch survives as a boundary wall further south. Owing to recent disturbance (earlier service trenches), no early building remains or ground levels were observed closer to Church Street.

*Dave Pollock, ArchaeoGrafix, Church Lane, Stradbally, Co. Waterford.*

### 846. DAVITTS QUAY/OLD MARKET HOUSE, DUNGARVAN

Urban post-medieval
2263 0930
SMR 31:4
99E0666

Resurfacing of and relaying services below Davitts Quay, beside Dungarvan Castle, commenced in October 1999 without archaeological supervision. Shortly afterwards a monitor was appointed for further works, and cuts were made in the backfilled quay to assess the damage from recent groundworks.

Close to the shell keep an earlier quay was found 0.6m below the cobbled surface of Davitts Quay, and outcropping bedrock was found at the foot of the shell keep, close to an original door. The earlier quay was probably built in the 18th century, perhaps in the 17th century, but the bedrock shelf outside the shell keep was probably used as a quay from the beginning, in the late 12th/early 13th century.

Resurfacing the pavement outside the Old Market House, at the junction of Church Street and Parnell Street (formerly Market Place), was monitored at the start of December 1999. The building had been undergoing a conversion since August. Exposed fragments of the fabric suggested a construction date at the end of the 17th or early in the 18th century, when the structure was used as an arcaded market area with hall above.

Outside the building, construction waste overlay silt on a surface of beach gravel, close to present ground level but almost undamaged by the present pavement work. The surface is potentially late medieval/post-medieval (from pottery) and was generally trampled directly into the clay subsoil. A few earlier features were observed, cut by recent trenches, but no earlier surfaces. The old ground appeared to drop away to the south, into a hollow running under Quay Street and extending west under the Church Street/Parnell Street site investigated in November 1998 and April 1999 (see No. 845 above).

*Dave Pollock, ArchaeoGrafix, Church Lane, Stradbally, Co. Waterford.*

### 847. DUNGARVAN CASTLE, DUNGARVAN

Medieval and post-medieval castle
2263 0930
95E0080

Consolidation work at Dungarvan Castle in 2000 will include the restoration of the mid-18th-century (and *c.* 1700) barracks and the replacement of the concrete yard surface. From late October to late December 1999 test-pits were cut through the concrete surface of the yard and through the floors of the upstanding barracks at Dungarvan Castle. The outside elevations of the barracks were drawn (the render was recently stripped), and the foot of the walls was inspected.

Little of the original barracks has survived. Much of the *c.* 1700 building was taken down below ground-floor window level during the mid-18th-century reconstruction; only two window openings remain, both on the ground floor.

Most of the interior of the building (all but one room and a stair passage) was cut down in the mid-18th century to insert wooden floors; the later archaeological levels were truncated in the footprint of the building. On the south and west sides of the

Location of site of Dungarvan Castle.

barracks a mid-18th-century brick culvert destroyed the construction level of the original building.

This culvert, and a contemporary second culvert running from an underground water cistern, cut into a poorly mortared wall attached to the shell keep beside the drawbridge position. The wall was probably part of a later medieval fixed bridge or barbican.

Medieval surfaces of beach material (sand and gravel) were found below the south end of the barracks and below the middle of the yard, Elsewhere, to the north, the medieval ground level may have been cut away to extract clay subsoil for late defences overlooking the harbour.

The original road surface did not survive in the gateway; instead the lofty passage between the D-towers had been lowered in the late medieval period and resurfaced with beach gravel. A later fire in the passage is associated with considerable destruction (pre-dating the slighting at the end of the 17th century), recorded in the D-tower excavated in 1995 (*Excavations 1995*, 84–5).

*Dave Pollock, ArchaeoGrafix, Church Lane, Stradbally, Co. Waterford.*

### 848. KILMEADEN
No archaeological significance
S520108
99E0164

Testing was undertaken at the proposed site of two bungalows that was thought to be within the medieval rural borough of Kilmeaden. Five trenches were opened, but nothing of archaeological significance was discovered.

*Michael Moore, Archaeological Survey of Ireland, Dúchas, 51 St Stephen's Green, Dublin 2.*

### 849. WATERFORD MAIN DRAINAGE SCHEME, WATERFORD
Urban
99E0207

The drainage scheme commenced in May 1999 and will continue into summer 2000. The pipe-laying started in the grounds of the courthouse, crossed the carpark in Bolton Street, and reached the Mall via Lombard Street. For the most part, the pipes are being laid outside the city walls, along the length of the Quay. In the coming months the side streets at right angles to the Quay will be connected into the new system.

To date, monitoring has identified some early wooden timbers, which appear to form a trackway. These were uncovered in the grounds of the courthouse, the site of the medieval St Catherine's Abbey. Some stone walls were exposed at the town side of the trench along the Quay. These most probably signify the location of the earlier Quay wall, built using masonry from the city wall, permission for the demolition of which was granted by the Corporation in 1704–5.

Certain short sections of the pipeline were tunnelled rather than openly dug. Lombard Street was one such area. Here the pipe encountered the sunken wreck of a wooden boat. Key timbers were retrieved from the vessel, and it is hoped that a dendrochronological date can be obtained from them and from those of the trackway.

*Orla Scully, 7 Bayview, Tramore, Co. Waterford.*

### 850. BAILEY'S NEW STREET, WATERFORD
Urban medieval, post-medieval
S61051237
99E0103

A licence to monitor with a view to rescue excavation was granted in March 1999 for the site of the new housing office to be built in Bailey's New Street, Waterford City. The level of the site was to be reduced to a uniform 4m OD.

Clearance revealed that a large proportion of the site had been given over to cellars in the post-medieval period. The area west of these was excavated by hand (*c.* 10m x 4m), revealing several late house walls and one that was integrated into the foundations of the gable end of the Deanery. The date of construction of the present Deanery is believed to be mid-18th century. However, it is believed to be built on the site of an earlier Deanery. The wall unearthed in this part of the site may be part of a boundary or a garden wall pre-dating the street. The date attributed to the laying out of Bailey's New Street is 1542. This area of the site had quite a high yield of medieval and post-medieval pottery and roof and floor tiles.

Following a survey by the architects, the cellars were removed with permission from *Dúchas*. Because of the discovery that late cellars had largely truncated the site, it was decided to lower the interior finished floor level. As the writer was unable to undertake continued excavation of the site, Mary O'Donnell carried out the extension of the licence to facilitate the new design (see No. 851 below).

*Orla Scully, 7 Bayview, Tramore, Co. Waterford.*

### 851. BAILEY'S NEW STREET, WATERFORD
Urban
S61051237
99E0103 ext.

The site at Bailey's New Street, Waterford, is owned by Waterford Corporation, and before development of the site the removal of upstanding buildings was monitored by Orla Scully (see No. 850 above), under the same licence, in March 1999. This showed that the archaeological deposits in the area had been disturbed by the cellars of the 18th-century houses to a depth of *c.* 2.8m below street level. As the disturbance was so extensive, it was decided to determine whether it was feasible to provide the new building with a full basement, and to that end a test excavation was undertaken, in June 1999, by the writer. The results of the test excavation indicated that the basements were a feasible option but that further archaeological excavation was required to confirm this.

A more extensive excavation was carried out over four weeks from 5 to 30 July 1999. This revealed that the eastern side of the site contained the remains of two large ditches that had been filled in the late 12th/early 13th century. The remains of a probable 13th-century undercroft were uncovered on the eastern side of the site. It was then decided that the formation levels for the new building would be taken at existing ground level and the surviving archaeological deposits and structures would be preserved *in situ*.

The earliest feature was a large ditch (F207), which was *c.* 5.7m wide and 1.3m deep and extended for 15m north–south across the site. Two *c.* 2m-wide sections of the ditch were excavated. The finds from the fill of the ditch included 12th- and 13th-century pottery, two stick-pins and a ringed pin that may date to *c.* AD 950. Another ditch (F226), filled with material of similar date and extending parallel to, and east of, F207, lay mostly outside the area of the site. It was not possible to determine, within the constraints of the excavation, whether the ditches were contemporary or one was earlier than the other.

The ditches extended roughly north–south and would have been at right angles to the city wall, which lies immediately to the south, suggesting that they may have had a defensive function in association with the wall or an earlier defensive feature. The finds from the ditches indicate that they were filled in the late 12th/early 13th century.

Part of the east wall (F210) and of an internal mortared surface (F256) of a probable 13th-century undercroft were uncovered just west of the ditch F207. The area within the undercroft was not excavated. The foundation trench for the wall (F210) cut away the western edge of the ditch (F207), although the orientation of the undercroft wall along the line of the original edge of the ditch shows the continued importance of the line, this time as a property boundary, into the later period.

The discovery of the two ditches also has important implications for the understanding of the early history of Waterford City. Hiberno-Norse Waterford was situated on a triangular area of land bounded on the north-east by the River Suir and on the south-east by the marshy ground around St John's River, with Reginald's Tower at the apex. The original 10th-century Hiberno-Norse settlement in Waterford is assumed to have been centred on the eastern end of this promontory, around where the later Reginald's Tower now stands, in the area known as Dundory, before it expanded west in an extended period of development. The bulk of the extensive series of excavations in Waterford City in the 1980s and 1990s took place west of this area, so no evidence relating to the 10th-century settlement was uncovered.

Bailey's New Street, which extends north-east/south-west, is situated fairly centrally within the area suspected to be 'Dundory'. It is likely that the ditches (F207 and F226) uncovered in the excavation relate to the defences of the area immediately to the east, and they may mark the western limits of the area that later became known as 'Dundory'.
*Mary O'Donnell, Archaeological Services Unit, University College, Cork.*

### 852. 17–18 BROAD STREET, WATERFORD
Urban medieval and post-medieval
2605 1122
99E0004

An archaeological assessment of the site at 17 and 18 Broad Street, Waterford, was carried out ahead of a planning application to alter the existing buildings on site and to erect an extension at the rear. The eastern boundary of the site roughly corresponds with the north–south line of the city defences as depicted on Phillips's map of 1673 and found by Joanna Wren during her excavations at 9 Arundel Square (*Excavations 1998*, 207, 98E0091). The site therefore lies immediately outside the 12th/early 13th-century defences in the area of the clay bank (also recorded by Wren) and ditch.

A building survey, as part of the assessment, identified the standing buildings on site as early 18th-century, incorporating the walls of an earlier stone building and possible medieval timbers (to be tested by dendrochronology).

Remains of the 12th/early 13th-century clay bank and ditch of the city defences were found in three test-trenches at the rear of the site. Limited excavation was carried out to a depth of 9.59m OD. The excavated ditch fills included pottery dating to the 13th–14th century. Post-excavation work is in progress.
*Jo Moran, ArchaeoGrafix, Church Lane, Stradbally, Co. Waterford.*

### 853. 'OLYMPIA BALLROOM', PARNELL STREET, WATERFORD
Urban
F607125
SMR 9:5
99E0273

The site was tested on 5 June 1999. It is within the zone of archaeological potential of Waterford City but outside the medieval city wall of Waterford, in an area that was largely a marsh until the post-medieval period, when it was laid out in gardens. The earliest recorded buildings outside the walls in this area are of late 18th-century date, at a time when the wall was extended westwards to form Parnell Street. At that time the city wall was breached.

Three trial-trenches were excavated to a depth of 2.3m. All revealed a similar profile: mortar and red brick rubble *c.* 1m deep, overlying estuarine silt without any apparent internal stratification.

The earliest datable material apparent on the site was contained in the upper rubble fill and was of 19th-century date. Before this the entire area seems to have been an uninhabited marsh. The evidence for an absence of settlement in the area is in accordance with that of the historical maps.
*Maurice F. Hurley, 312 Bruach na Laoi, Union Quay, Cork.*

### 854. TANYARD ARCH, WATERFORD
No archaeological significance
2605 1115
99E0009

Four trenches were excavated within the Tanyard Arch carpark in Waterford City before the redevelopment of the area as a multi-storey carpark. The trenches were excavated to naturally occurring subsoil by mechanical digger. Some material of post-medieval and modern date was uncovered, in the form of walls and services associated with the previously existing buildings on this site. It was noted that, in a previous attempt to create a level surface across the site, which was on a hillside, the western portion of the area had been scarped, while the eastern portion had been deliberately raised.

Nothing of archaeological significance was found.
*Audrey Gahan for ADS Ltd, Windsor House, 11 Fairview Strand, Dublin 3.*

# WESTMEATH

### 855. ATHLONE WATER SUPPLY SCHEME
Culverts
99E0267

Monitoring associated with the Athlone Water Supply Scheme—Annagh Reservoir Project was undertaken from 26 April to 3 September 1999. The work was carried out as a result of archaeological mitigation procedures suggested in the archaeological assessment report prepared in relation to the scheme. There are a number of archaeological sites in the general environs of the project area, which is to the north-east of Athlone. Furthermore, much of the pipeline was laid in areas of peatland, an environment that considerably aids the preservation of artefacts and features of archaeological and historical interest. Most of the monitoring was undertaken by Teresa Bolger and Agnes Kerrigan, under the supervision of the writer.

An initial programme of engineering trial-pits aided in the final decision on what areas required full-time monitoring. The project consisted of a reservoir area and pipelines, the total length of the latter being c. 8459m. Topsoil-stripping at the reservoir area and topsoil/trench excavations of all but c. 1500m of the pipeline were monitored.

The only features of note were two stone-built culverts in Annaghgortagh td. These culverts crossed under the road, and it is likely that both were associated with a former mill that stood near the road.
*Martin E. Byrne, 31 Millford, Athgarvan, Co. Kildare.*

### 856. ATHLONE WESTSIDE MAIN DRAINAGE SCHEME
19th-century fortifications
99E0109

The Athlone Westside Main Drainage Scheme was situated on the western periphery of Athlone town. The project area was bounded to the east by a canal, part of which forms the western extent of the zone of archaeological potential associated with the town. The only known site of archaeological/historical interest within the project area is part of a 'fortifications site' in Athlone South td, SMR 29:11. This was part of an extensive *tête-de-point* defence system of eight gun emplacements, behind moats and ramparts linked by sunken pathways, constructed in 1803 to c. 1817. Six of the gun emplacement sites and their associated magazines, guardrooms etc. were within the project area. By 1912 these had been incorporated into a golf-course, and they were largely demolished by 1952. 'The Batteries' now contains a number of housing estates, schools etc. One section of wall is the only extant remains of the former fortifications.

Monitoring commenced in early February and consisted, initially, of the inspection of engineering trial-pit excavations, which aided in the formulation of the overall monitoring policy for the scheme.

Parts of the scheme were along existing roads, many of which proved to have the basal remains of a peat layer under the road formation material, with the greater part in a green-field area. This area consisted of marshy ground, some of which was prone to flooding, as a consequence of which the pipes were routed along a piled superstructure.

The only feature of note was the remains of a wall foundation uncovered in the 'Batteries' area. This was 0.8m wide and stood up to 0.6m high. The location and line of the wall would indicate that it was associated with the fortifications mentioned above. No other features or structures were identified within the area of the project, and a number of post-medieval sherds of pottery were recovered.
*Martin E. Byrne, 31 Millford, Athgarvan, Co. Kildare.*

### 857. NORTHGATE STREET, ATHLONE
Town wall
203790 241445
98E0210 ext.

Archaeological testing at the site of a proposed residential, hotel and leisure complex undertaken in April 1998 (*Excavations 1998*, 208–9) uncovered a section of the 17th-century town wall. However, the exact extent and line of the wall on the western area of the site could not be determined because of the presence of 20th-century factory buildings. These were demolished in mid-1999, and additional testing was undertaken in October.

This revealed that the foundation remains of the town wall had been truncated and entirely removed by construction of riverside industrial buildings in both the 19th and mid-20th centuries. No additional features or finds of archaeological interest were recovered during this phase of testing.

In addition an extant gasworks building was subjected to an industrial archaeological assessment and survey by Colin Rynne before its demolition.
*Martin E. Byrne, 31 Millford, Athgarvan, Co. Kildare.*

### 858. SEÁN COSTELLO STREET, ATHLONE
Urban
24138 204320
99E0125

Monitoring of the excavation of foundations for an extension to a shop within a zone of archaeological importance uncovered no archaeological materials.
*Cóilín Ó Drisceoil, 6 Riverview, Ardnore, Kilkenny, for Dominic Delany.*

### 859. CARRICK
Close to site of castle and house
24144 24620
99E0370

The site is on the eastern shore of Lough Ennel, on the former estate of Tudenham Park in an area that was once below the present water level. It is close to recorded monuments 26:05201 'house' and 26:05202 'Castle Site', on a promontory called Inchacrone. The proposed development entails the building of an office, toilets and a pond as additions to an existing caravan park. Trial-trenching was carried out on 22 July 1999. A trench was excavated on the site of the proposed buildings, which measured 5m by 2m and exposed stony, white marl under 0.1–0.15m of topsoil.

As the development is to be carried out on what was once open water as shown on the OS 1837 map, it is unlikely to have any impact on possible archaeological remains. It was recommended that no work be allowed on the former island of Inchacrone.
*Deirdre Murphy, Archaeological Consultancy Services Ltd, 15 Trinity Street, Drogheda, Co. Louth.*

### 860. CASTLETOWN GEOGHEGAN
Medieval borough
24122 24400
99E0394

An archaeological assessment of a proposed residential dwelling at Castletown Geoghegan, Mullingar, was carried out in August 1999. The site is on the west side of the main street and close to the Anglo-Norman motte and bailey and the site of two castles.

Three trenches were excavated. These exposed natural gravel close to present ground level, and there was no evidence of previous disturbance of the site. No finds of archaeological interest were recovered, and no further excavation was necessary.
*Deirdre Murphy, Archaeological Consultancy Services Ltd, 15 Trinity Street, Drogheda, Co. Louth.*

### 861. BALLYHEALY ROAD, DELVIN
Souterrain
26040 26232

An archaeological survey of a souterrain discovered during the construction of a housing development at Ballyhealy Road, Delvin, was carried out in May 1999. The souterrain is *c.* 400m south-east of the Anglo-Norman motte in Delvin village.

The souterrain consisted of a passage with two levels that terminated in a beehive-shaped chamber. The entrance to the passage has been interfered with in recent years, probably during the time of construction of houses that lie to the west of the souterrain. The passage extends in a roughly north–south direction; the chamber is to the north, and the entrance is to the south. The floor of the passage rises gradually, and there is a drop in the roof level towards the entrance, which suggests that originally there was a creep in this area of the passage. However, there is a large amount of spoil in this area, and without excavation it is impossible to determine the exact type of entrance or its dimensions.

The walls of the passage were constructed of reasonably regular, roughly cut, greywacke blocks. Large, subrectangular stones measuring 0.5m by 0.3–0.5m rested on the floor of the passage, above which smaller stones were placed. These averaged 0.3m by 0.2m, and the roof of the passage rested on these. The roof consisted of large, flat lintels almost 1m long and 0.7m wide. Only six lintels spanned the roof of the upper passage (excluding the area over the drop-hole), while the lower passage was roofed with three large lintels. The drop-hole was open when discovered, and there was no evidence for a capstone or lintel that would have covered the floor area of Level 1 and hence blocked access to Level 2. The beehive chamber was constructed of drystone with a corbelled roof; it measured 2.8m north–south by 2.82m. Spreads of charcoal were concentrated in the chamber, which may suggest that it was temporarily occupied. However, the absence of an air vent suggests that the souterrain could only have been occupied for short periods of time. No domestic artefacts or occupation material were evident on the surface of the souterrain, but it is possible that excavation would yield some examples.
*Deirdre Murphy, Archaeological Consultancy Services Ltd, 15 Trinity Street, Drogheda, Co. Louth.*

### 862. FARRANCALLIN
No archaeological significance
N465616
99E0579

Monitoring of all earth removal associated with the building of a house was carried out. The site was adjacent to SMR 12:59.

The entire footprint of the house and driveway was stripped of topsoil, which was on average 0.3m–0.4m deep. The topsoil was a mid-brown,

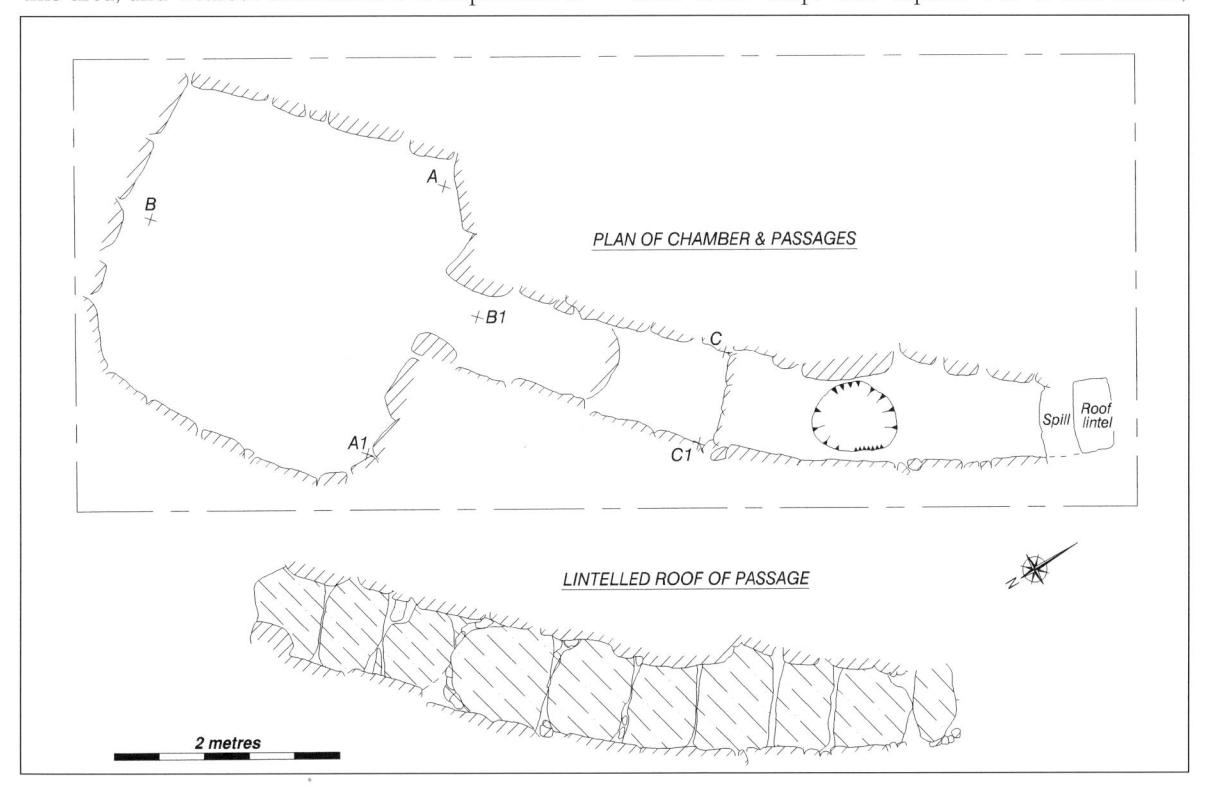

Chamber and passage at Ballyhealy Road, Delvin.

sandy clay loam. It was homogeneous, and ploughing had clearly been carried out in the past. A piece of cut animal bone was recovered, but this was undatable. A fragment of post-medieval/modern pottery was also recovered. Subsoil was a mottled clay with gravel and sand inclusions. No cut features were evident. Foundation trenches were dug to c. 0.6m, and the septic tank was placed at the rear of the house. Nothing of archaeological interest was uncovered.

*Finola O'Carroll, Cultural Resource Development Services Ltd, Campus Innovation Centre, Roebuck, University College, Belfield, Dublin 4.*

### 863. GLASSON
No archaeological significance
**99E0237**

A pre-development test excavation was conducted on 24 May 1999 before the construction of a domestic dwelling. Seven 1m-wide test-trenches were dug to determine the nature and extent of archaeology, if any. No historical or archaeological structures or artefacts were uncovered. The trenches contained 1m of topsoil before the natural subsoil was encountered.

*Niall Gregory, 25 Westpark, Blessington, Co. Wicklow, for Archaeological Consultancy Services Ltd.*

### 864. TULLAMORE ROAD, KILBEGGAN
Town
**23336 23537**
**SMR 38:17**
**99E0062**

Test excavation was undertaken before the construction of two proposed dwellings at Tullamore Road, Kilbeggan, Co. Westmeath, on 6 February 1999. The site is adjacent to a recorded monument. Five test-trenches (average length 40m) were excavated, and two stone-lined drains, a pit and a circular, stone-lined well, all modern, were encountered. No archaeological deposits or features were found.

*Dominic Delany, 31 Ashbrook, Oranmore, Co. Galway.*

### 865. RATTIN, KINNEGAD
No archaeological significance
**25531 24389**
**99E0626**

An assessment was undertaken at a proposed residential development at Rattin, Kinnegad, Co. Westmeath, on 3 November 1999. The site is c. 1500m north-west of SMR 34:8, a substantial 16th-century tower-house called Rattin Castle. The site is also close to the possible path of the *Slí Aisiul*, or Royal Road, which ran west from Tara, crossing the barony of Moygashel in County Westmeath. An Ordnance Survey memo by George Wynne from 1837 records that traces of an old roadway were visible at that time in the field across the road (north) from the castle.

Six test-trenches were excavated across the areas to be disturbed by the proposed development of two single-storey houses, in a field of fairly low-lying pasture without any noticeable topographic expressions.

Trenches 1 and 2 were positioned west–east along the proposed north and south foundation line of the dwelling in Site B (west). Both trenches measured 19m by 0.8m. Brown topsoil 0.4–0.5m deep, which overlay natural, grey, gravelly clay with a high stone component, was found in both trenches.

Trench 3 was positioned north-west to south-east along the line of the proposed septic tank and drain to percolation area from the proposed dwelling in Site B (west). It measured 15m by 0.8m. Brown topsoil up to 0.6m deep overlay natural, grey, gravelly clay with a high stone boulder component.

Trenches 4 and 5 were positioned west–east along the proposed north and south foundation line of the dwelling in Site A (east); both trenches measured 20m by 0.8m. Brown topsoil 0.4–0.5m deep overlay natural, grey, gravelly clay with a high stone boulder component. A north–south, linear, U-shaped gully was found c. 6m from the west end of Trench 4, cut into subsoil, and represents the remains of a field drain that continued into Trench 5, c. 6m from the western end.

Trench 6 was positioned north-west to south-east along the line of the proposed septic tank and drain to percolation area from the proposed dwelling in Site A (east); the trench measured 15m by 0.8m. Brown topsoil up to 0.5m deep overlay natural, grey, gravelly clay with a high stone component.

The assessment did not uncover any soils, features or finds of archaeological significance.

*Malachy Conway, Archaeological Consultancy Services Ltd, 15 Trinity Street, Drogheda, Co. Louth.*

### 866. AUSTIN FRIARS STREET, MULLINGAR
No archaeological significance
**243937 253091**
**98E0039 ext.**

Testing was carried out at Austin Friars Street, Mullingar, in fulfilment of conditions attached to planning permission for a commercial and residential development. The site is within the bounds of the medieval town and close to the position of the Augustinian monastery where a significant number of inhumations were excavated to the south-east of the present site. Previous testing by Deirdre Murphy in 1998 (*Excavations 1998*, 210) revealed no features of archaeological significance.

Two trenches were excavated running north–south down the length of the site. Both were almost 17m long and 1m wide. Deposits containing 19th-century material were excavated in both trenches to a depth 0.42m and 0.72m below existing ground level. A layer of grey/brown, stony gravel was encountered under these deposits and was completely sterile. This layer was excavated to 1.44m below existing ground level to ensure that it was not redeposited. No archaeological material was recovered.

*Matthew Seaver for Archaeological Consultancy Services Ltd, 15 Trinity Street, Drogheda, Co. Louth.*

### 867. EMPLOYMENT EXCHANGE, BLACKHALL STREET, MULLINGAR
Urban medieval
**243619 252888**
**98E0138 ext.**

Testing undertaken at the site by Clare Mullins in 1998 (*Excavations 1998*, 211–12) resulted in a recommendation that groundworks associated with the construction project be monitored. Much of this monitoring was undertaken in 1998. However, because of structural problems it was necessary to construct three columns to underpin existing wall and roof structures. The monitoring of the pit excavations associated with this work was carried out from 29 March to 1 April 1999.

The monitoring revealed that a buried soil layer, covered in rubble, lay 1.9–2.15m below the existing floor surface; it was damp and organic in nature. Similar layers produced animal bone and sherds of pottery during the 1998 investigation. It is probable that this layer is an original 'topsoil' layer buried whilst levelling up the site in the more recent past.
*Martin E. Byrne, 31 Millford, Athgarvan, Co. Kildare.*

### 868. CHURCH AVENUE, MULLINGAR
Urban medieval
243771 252820
SMR 19:89
99E0127

Testing was carried out at the site of a proposed extension to All Saints National School, Church Avenue, Mullingar, on 26 April 1999. The extension was to consist of the addition of a room to each end of the existing building.

The site is to the south of All Saints Church, immediately beyond the area of the present-day perimeter of the church grounds. The site was formerly part of the garden of the rectory associated with the church. The ground surface within the development area was *c.* 1m lower than that of the graveyard to its immediate north, suggesting some interference with natural ground levels, possibly during the construction of the school.

Two test-trenches were inserted, to coincide approximately with the front gable walls of the proposed extension. Stratigraphy within Trench 1 consisted of a sod layer to a depth of 0.2m, lying directly upon the natural. It was clear from this trench that the ground had been truncated in this particular area, probably during the construction phase associated with the building of the school.

Stratigraphy within Trench 2 consisted of a deep layer of topsoil that lay upon the natural at a depth of 1.4m. At the western end of this trench what was interpreted as a stone-filled sump was found between the layer of topsoil and natural. It is difficult to explain the considerable depth of the topsoil in the area of Trench 2, but it may represent an attempt to level up the area. Several fragments of bone were found within the topsoil here but were all of animal origin.
*Clare Mullins, 31 Millford, Athgarvan, Co. Kildare.*

### 869. COLLEGE STREET, MULLINGAR
Urban
N434532

The developer was required by his planning permission to have excavation of his development site monitored by an archaeologist. The development is a two-storey building with a shop at the ground floor and a flat above.

Nothing of archaeological interest was exposed during excavations.
*Rosanne Meenan, Roestown, Drumree, Co. Meath.*

### 870. FRIARS MILL ROAD, MULLINGAR
Urban post-medieval
243850 253189
99E0069

Testing was carried out at Friars Mill Road, Mullingar, before a proposed commercial development. Part of the site is within the medieval walls and lay on the road between Castle Street and the Dominican priory, where the mill was situated. It is east of a small Presbyterian church first opened in 1825.

Five trenches were excavated across the site. Trench 1 was 9.9m by 1.2m and ran east–west. Concrete and modern soil containing brick, plastic and pottery up to 0.8m deep overlay a light brown layer of humic soil containing red brick fragments, ash lenses and 18th-century pottery up to 0.43m deep. This overlay a layer of compact, sticky, grey marl containing frequent small stones. Below this was sterile, grey, natural gravel, which was dug to 1.5m below ground level to ensure that it was not redeposited.

Trench 2 was 20.2m south of the modern boundary wall of the cemetery and ran east–west. It contained an identical stratigraphical sequence to that in Trench 1. Trench 3 was 5m from the southern boundary wall and ran east–west. It contained an identical stratigraphical sequence to that in Trenches 1 and 2.

Trench 4 ran north–south along almost the entire length of the site. It contained concrete, dark brown, modern soil and light brown, 19th/18th-century pottery. The last deposit overlay a single extended inhumation orientated north–south in a shallow grave-cut that contained 18th- and 19th-century pottery in the fill. The skeleton was examined by Laureen Buckley and was thought to be a young adult male between 18 and 25 years of age with an estimated height of 1.79m. He appeared to have been involved in heavy manual labour from an early age. The cause of death was not detectable.

Another trench excavated to the east revealed no further burials. A comparison of the graveyard boundaries on the 1854 town plan and the modern 1:1000 map shows that the original church property incorporated this site. A parliamentary act of the early 19th century required enclosure of cemeteries, and this may have resulted in contraction of the property. Later trial excavations to the south in the grounds of the Manse house found a number of further inhumations, some of which were covered in lime. These burials appeared to have been the result of a cholera epidemic in the mid-19th century, during which the Manse house was used as a hospital (D. Murphy, pers. comm., and see No. 871 below). This may explain the early death of the individual uncovered to the north.
*Matthew Seaver for Archaeological Consultancy Services Ltd, 15 Trinity Street, Drogheda, Co. Louth.*

### 871. FRIARS MILL ROAD, MULLINGAR
19th-century graveyard
243850 253189
99E0069 ext.

An assessment carried out by Matthew Seaver in February to March 1999 at Friars Mill Road, Mullingar, before a commercial development revealed the presence of an extended inhumation of an adult male (No. 870 above). Further work was recommended, and the excavation of foundation trenches was monitored by the writer in May 1999 under an extension to the existing licence.

The site is close to the medieval town wall and is partially within a 19th-century graveyard. Monitoring exposed the remains of three further individuals close to that of the previously discovered inhumation. The burials were in shallow graves, covered with lime, and were accompanied by sherds of 19th-century pottery. A coffin handle was recovered from the fill of the third burial. All were found at the south end of the site in a foundation trench, and it was only the lower part of the burials (i.e. the leg bones) that were exposed. The upper parts of the skeletal remains lie outside the development site and were not disturbed.
*Donald Murphy, Archaeological Consultancy Services Ltd, 15 Trinity Street, Drogheda, Co. Louth.*

### 872. LACKAN, MULTYFARNHAM
Ringfort with souterrain
23758 26438
SMR 6:70
99E0036

Eleven test-trenches were excavated by machine, during January 1999, on the site of a souterrain. It was proposed to erect two houses within the general area of this monument, the exact location of which was not known before the test excavations.

Five trenches for House 1, which varied from 10m to 20m long and were all 1.5m wide, were excavated by machine down to natural boulder clay, which was revealed at 0.3m below the sod. These trenches, in the southern portion of the site, revealed no archaeological remains.

A further six trenches, including a small cut for a sewage tank, ranging from 10m to 20m long and 1.5m wide, were excavated in the northern portion of the site for House 2. All of these trenches revealed charcoal flecking and archaeological features. The trenches revealed that the souterrain lay within the central area of the proposed location for this house. The souterrain passage ran completely across the width of the site for House 2 in an east–west direction. It was traced for a length of 25m, and it was obvious that it extended out under the present Multyfarnham road. The souterrain lay only 0.2m under the topsoil and consisted of large stones, 0.3m x 0.2m, laid flat. These stones appeared to form the roof of the souterrain, which was 1m wide.

Several other features were revealed within the trenches. Trench 1 revealed a linear feature cut into the natural boulder clay, 3.5m wide and 0.4m deep. Trench 2 revealed two linear features. Both were up to 3m wide with a maximum depth of 0.7m. The fill of these features contained a considerable amount of charcoal and bone. Although the features appeared as linear cuts, they may have been portions of pits, filled with occupation debris. Trench 2, within which the souterrain passage was clearly defined, also revealed areas of paving and deposits of charcoal. The souterrain passage was also clearly revealed in Trench 9 and again was associated with linear cuts and disturbed soil.

It was apparent that this large souterrain passage was within a substantial ringfort. The southern bank and ditch are well defined, but the western portion was very difficult to ascertain, as was the northern portion. The remains of the bank and ditch were investigated on the southern portion of the ringfort. The ditch was just under 1m wide and 0.6m deep, and the bank remained to a height of 0.6m, with a width of 2m. Observations on the ground indicate that the northern portion of the ringfort may have extended into the grounds of an extant cottage and that the ringfort may also have extended across the road. An approximate estimation of the ringfort within the area outlined for the houses is 38m north–south by 30m.

A small quantity of animal bone, together with some sherds of post-medieval pottery, was retrieved from the trenches.
*Sylvia Desmond, 25 Rowan Hall, Millbrook Court, Milltown, Dublin 6, for Judith Carroll & Co. Ltd, Pine Forest Art Centre, Pine Forest Road, Glencullen, Co. Dublin.*

### 873. NEWDOWN
Adjacent to earthworks
SMR 27:1 and 27:4
99E0359

An environmental impact statement was undertaken of the area of the proposed widening and realignment of the N4 to the east of Mullingar. Two levelled earthwork sites are to the immediate north and south of the construction corridor. Four test-trenches were excavated in the area of the construction corridor between the levelled archaeological sites. No archaeological stratigraphy was recorded, and no artefacts were recovered in any of the trenches.
*Jacinta Kiely, Eachtra Archaeological Projects, Clover Hill, Mallow, Co. Cork.*

## WEXFORD

### 874. BROWNSWOOD
Vicinity of *fulacht fiadh*
99E0371

Monitoring was carried out at Brownswood, Enniscorthy, Co. Wexford, as part of the expansion of a quarry at the site. The area of development was a grass-covered field, in an area of agricultural land, on the brow of the slope overlooking the Slaney River. The development area is north of a *fulacht fiadh* (SMR 26:21), no trace of which is visible. Nothing of archaeological significance was noted.
*Cara Murray, IAC Ltd, 8 Dungar Terrace, Dun Laoghaire, Co. Dublin.*

### 875. FERNS SEWERAGE SCHEME
Multi-period
30210 14973
98E0132

Monitoring of the pipe-trench revealed three ditches, one pit, a shallow trench associated with a medieval layer of occupation, and a culvert. A small Iron Age ring-ditch (see No. 877 below) and an adjacent pit were also uncovered and were fully excavated.

Phase 1 of the Sewerage Scheme was carried out in three stages, comprising topsoil removal, pipe-laying and reed bed preparation. Monitoring of topsoil removal recorded no finds.

Monitoring of pipe-laying revealed three areas of interest.

Between OF6 and OF8, two ditches that were 45m apart may belong to the same field monument.

A ditch and ditch terminal (or a pit that was truncated by the pipe-trench) were found between the F24 and F23 manholes within 10m of each other. Eighty metres further west, between F22 and F21, a shallow medieval layer of occupation contained a narrow trench at its east end.

A culvert made of limestone was found at the F25 manhole.

Archaeological work relating to these finds was confined to identifying the characteristics of the features (size, depth below surface, soil layers, location).

Monitoring of the reed bed area exposed two features—a pit *c.* 3m in diameter and 1m deep and a ring-ditch of Iron Age date *c.* 5m in diameter. These lay in the north corner of the field within 20m of each other. The pit was fully excavated and forms the last section of this report.

The ring-ditch was excavated under licence no. 99E0450 and so is discussed in a separate report (No. 877 below).

*Location of features within pipe-laying trenches F28–F21*
A stone culvert with a slate base and flat limestone slab capstones was cut diagonally by the pipe-trench south and west of manhole F25. The profile consists of 0.15m of tar at road-surface level overlying 0.2–0.25m of hardcore fill above a 0.8m-deep layer of subsoil and 0.2–0.25m of soft rock.

At F24, to a depth of 2.2m, the profile is unchanged.

At 25m west of F24 a V-shaped ditch was intersected diagonally by the pipe-trench. It was 3m wide at road level. The ditch was 1.7m deep below the road hardcore and contained an upper layer of charcoal-rich, crumby, brown soil with small stones above a horizontal band of charcoal-rich, brown soil. Another charcoal-rich layer contained slag and a furnace bottom. A sample of this charcoal layer was taken for dating purposes.

At 30m west of F24 a pit or ditch terminal was truncated by the pipe-trench, the full profile of which was visible only on the south side of the trench, as it terminated in a semicircle within the trench fill before reaching the north side of the trench. It was 1.4m wide and 1.6m deep with a fairly flat base and almost vertical sides. The fill was not horizontally laid down but contained a brown, sticky, soft layer of soil at the base, some evidence of burnt clay and a core of light brown, silty, sticky soil containing shell remains. The bottom 0.4m was excavated by hand. The manner in which the deposits were exposed would indicate that the feature was probably a pit rather than a truncated trench terminal.

At F22–F21 a shallow spread of medieval occupation comprising 0.15m depth of mid-brown, crumby soil containing a shallow trench-like feature at its south end, 0.35m deep x 0.9m wide, was cut diagonally by the pipe-trench. The fill of this feature contained fragmentary remains of glazed medieval ware and an iron nail fragment. The trench-like feature formed the eastern boundary to the medieval layer, which extended for 4.2m.

*Pipe-laying trenches from OF1 to OF8*
Six metres north-west of OF7 a 0.6–0.75m-deep upper layer of redeposited gravel with a silty soil mix overlay a charcoal-rich lens of silty soil for a distance of 6m as far as OF7. The north face of the pipe-trench showed a ditch-like feature that was not in evidence on the south face of the pipe-trench. The profile of the feature consisted of sloping sides and a curved base. It was 0.8m deep and 1.7m wide at the top. The 'ditch' fill contained a homogeneous layer of silty, brown, crumby soil with some gravel and stones.

The appropriate south face contained a concentration of charcoal-rich soil in a horizontal band at a depth of 0.6m below the topsoil level. A sample of charcoal was extracted for dating purposes. This lens could be traced as far as OF7.

A second ditch feature was clearly defined on the north face of the pipe-trench, 6m north-west of OF8. It was 5m wide at the top with sloping sides and was 1.8m deep. The base was curved. The feature contained three layers of fill. The upper layer was of light brown, silty soil (containing some roots) to a depth of 1.1m. It contained a charcoal-rich lens that extended 2m south-east of the ditch on the surface below the topsoil. A layer of gravel up to 0.5m thick formed the middle fill of the ditch, with a layer of light brown, silty soil at the base.

These two ditch features are *c.* 45m apart and may form the outer limit of the ringfort, SMR 15:4.

The ground level falls away to the south-east, where gravelly, sandy subsoil gives way to marl 3m south-east of OF8. The ground remains marly between OF8 and the river for a distance of 60m.

*Monitoring of reed beds*
A 200m-by-120m area was scarped by a bulldozer to make it flat in order to facilitate the growth of reeds for the purification of outflow water for the sewerage septic tanks.

Two adjacent features in the north corner of the reed bed area were found.

The ring-ditch was immediately visible by its circle of charcoal-rich soil, 5m in diameter, which contained evidence of scorched earth and cremated bone (No. 877 below).

The pit was visible initially as a linear charcoal feature 0.5m long and, when excavated, revealed a pit *c.* 3m in diameter and *c.* 1m deep containing evidence of several layers of *in situ* burning.

The pit had been backfilled for half of its diameter. The remaining 'half-pit' contained four distinct layers of burning evidence. A thin surface of scorched earth forming the base was covered by a layer of sterile subsoil. This supported a layer of charcoal that was covered by a second subsoil layer, the surface of which contained evidence of scorching. This in turn had been covered by another layer of subsoil, the surface of which also contained evidence of scorching due to *in situ* burning.

It was apparent that the pit was completely emptied after each burning and backfilled with

### 876. CASTLELANDS, FERNS
Pits
**T022499**
**99E0527**

Preliminary archaeological assessment was undertaken on a large development site on the outskirts of Ferns, Co. Wexford, on 5 October 1999. The site is a large green field, which slopes gently from north to south. It is *c.* 60m south-west of the early 13th-century castle of Ferns.

Test excavation was undertaken in tandem with geophysical ground investigation, carried out by GSB Prospection, Bradford. Anomalies noted through geophysical detection were investigated by opening a trench using a mechanical excavator with a grading bucket.

Visibility of features varied, depending on the nature of the fill, but in general the underlying pale boulder clay facilitated the identification of negative features.

Archaeological features were noted in Trenches 1 and 2. All were sealed by topsoil. While no datable artefacts were recovered from either area, the absence of medieval or later pottery from the features, and in any significant quantity from the overlying soils, suggests that they are probably of earlier date.

An extensive grouping of shallow pits, containing burnt material, soil and stones, is indicated on the southern end of the site. Further work is required to determine the nature, date and extent of this group of features.

Unusually for a well-drained area close to a medieval town, there were very few sherds of medieval pottery in the topsoil, while post-medieval wares were noted in all trenches except Trench 4. There is scant evidence of continuous cultivation of this field, and there appear to be no features of medieval date in this area of the town.

*Claire Walsh, Archaeological Projects Ltd, 25A Eaton Square, Terenure, Dublin 6W.*

### 877. FERNS LOWER, FERNS
Ring-ditch
**99E0450**

A small ring-ditch was revealed in the north-west corner of the reed bed area following bulldozing of the field. The site, which comprised a circle of charcoal-rich soil *c.* 5m in diameter and 0.5m wide, contained surface evidence of burnt bone and scorched earth. It contained the charred remains of large oak timbers, which underlay the cremated remains of five individuals, three of which were accompanied by grave-goods.

Excavation revealed five areas within the ditch fill that contained cremated bone; three of these also contained grave-goods. The cremated remains appear to have been burnt elsewhere and then transferred to the ring-ditch. The charred remains of timber planking underlay one of the cremated deposits, indicating the use of a wooden stretcher for interment.

Evidence of substantial oak beams was found in the ditch fill below the cremated remains. These were extensively burnt before the interment of the cremations and contained a series of small iron nails that were attached to the upper surface.

The lowest level of the trench, which was up to 0.4m deep, contained a layer of redeposited subsoil within which some stake-holes were found.

At least fifty glass beads, some of which were fused together, a stone pendant, fragmentary bronze and a single sherd of unglazed coarseware pottery were found with the cremated remains. A minimum of thirty small iron nails and about a dozen fragments of iron were associated with the underlying charred oak. The finds are awaiting conservation.

The cremated remains and soil sample have been sent for analysis. Following wood species identification, suitable samples will be submitted for radiocarbon dating.

*Frank Ryan, Mary Henry & Associates, 1 Jervis Place, Clonmel, Co. Tipperary.*

### 878. FERNS UPPER, FERNS
Proximity to Early Christian town
**T018499**
**99E0538**

Six test-trenches were excavated on the site. Furrows were apparent, cutting into subsoil; no other features were revealed. The site was of no archaeological significance.

*Avril Purcell, Margaret Gowen & Co. Ltd, 2 Killiney View, Albert Road Lower, Glenageary, Co. Dublin.*

### 879. GRANGE, FETHARD
Urban medieval
**99E0092**

Twenty-five test-trenches were excavated in Grange townland before a housing estate development, to comply with a planning condition. The southern section of the site is within the zone of archaeological potential for the historic town of Fethard.

No archaeological stratigraphy was recorded in any of the trenches, and no artefacts were recovered.
*Jacinta Kiely, Eachtra Archaeological Projects, Clover Hill, Mallow, Co. Cork.*

### 880. GLASCARRIG NORTH
Adjacent to monastery
**321550 149320**
**SMR 17:10**
**99E0107**

An archaeological assessment of a residential development adjacent to Glascarrig Priory included the excavation of test-trenches in the area of the development.

Monks from the order of St Tiron founded St Mary's Priory at Glascarrig in *c.* 1190. Glascarrig was the only Irish priory of the monks of St Tiron, although little is known about the history of the Priory. It is known that it held many lands and benefices in County Wexford. The Priory was suppressed in 1543, and in 1560 the remains are described as comprising a cell, a church, a hall, two rooms, a chantry and a small yard. The south wall of the church survives, and some of the foundations of the Priory church can be traced in the ground, forming a rectangular building. The east and part of the north wall are built into a residential house, and the western part of this building is shown on the first edition OS map.

The development site was 20m south of the church, in a ploughed field. Eight test-trenches were excavated mechanically. Nothing of archaeological interest was found in Trenches 1–6.

Trench 7 was excavated along the north of the site. The topsoil here was 0.5–0.6m deep and overlay light brown marl throughout most of the trench. Near the west end of the trench a subcircular refuse pit of medieval date was uncovered. The pit measured 1.4m x 1.1m and was cut into the marl. The fill was a compact, sticky, light grey, silty clay of moderate stoniness with frequent inclusions of charcoal and animal bone. Four sherds of late 12th–13th-century pottery were recovered from the surface of the fill.

Trench 8 was parallel to Trench 7. The topsoil was 0.1–0.5m deep and overlay a sterile sand that was 0.5m deep and overlay the light brown marl. Near the west end of the trench a cobbled surface was found sealing a large, 19th-century refuse pit. The pit cut through marl and was subcircular with vertical sides. It was 1.3m deep and 4.05m wide. It was exposed for 2m, but its full length north–south was not ascertained. The fill of the pit was a wet, soft, grey/black, silty sand with frequent large, angular stones. There were frequent inclusions of red brick, leather off-cuts and 19th-century pottery. The fill also contained a large amount of animal bone, including the incomplete skeleton of a horse.

The development had no impact on either refuse pit, and no further archaeological work was recommended.

*Cóilín Ó Drisceoil, 6 Riverview, Ardnore, Kilkenny.*

### 881. MILL LANDS, GOREY
No archaeological significance
T157592
99E0086

Monitoring of the construction of a small development of twenty houses was undertaken in February and May. Nothing of archaeological interest was noted.

*Alan Hayden, Archaeological Projects Ltd, 25A Eaton Square, Terenure, Dublin 6W.*

### 882. HOOK LIGHTHOUSE, HOOK HEAD
Medieval lighthouse
2733974
99E0020 and ext.

Eight trenches were opened by mechanical excavator at Hook Lighthouse, Hook Head, Churchtown, Co. Wexford, in April 1999 before the development of the modern lighthouse keepers' houses into a heritage centre. They revealed the survival of a stone-walled enclosure around the lighthouse as depicted on 17th-century drawings. A thin deposit of brown clay overlay subsoil within the enclosure. It contained medieval pottery. A shallow pit containing sherds of Ham Green ware and a piece of Dundrystone was also uncovered within the enclosure.

Work was undertaken in conjunction with Ben Murtagh, who carried out an architectural survey of the fabric of the medieval lighthouse.

Monitoring of the construction of the development was undertaken in September. None of the foundation trenches was deep enough to encounter medieval deposits, and only a few sherds of North Devon gravel-tempered ware vessels were uncovered.

*Alan Hayden, Archaeological Projects Ltd, 25A Eaton Square, Terenure, Dublin 6W.*

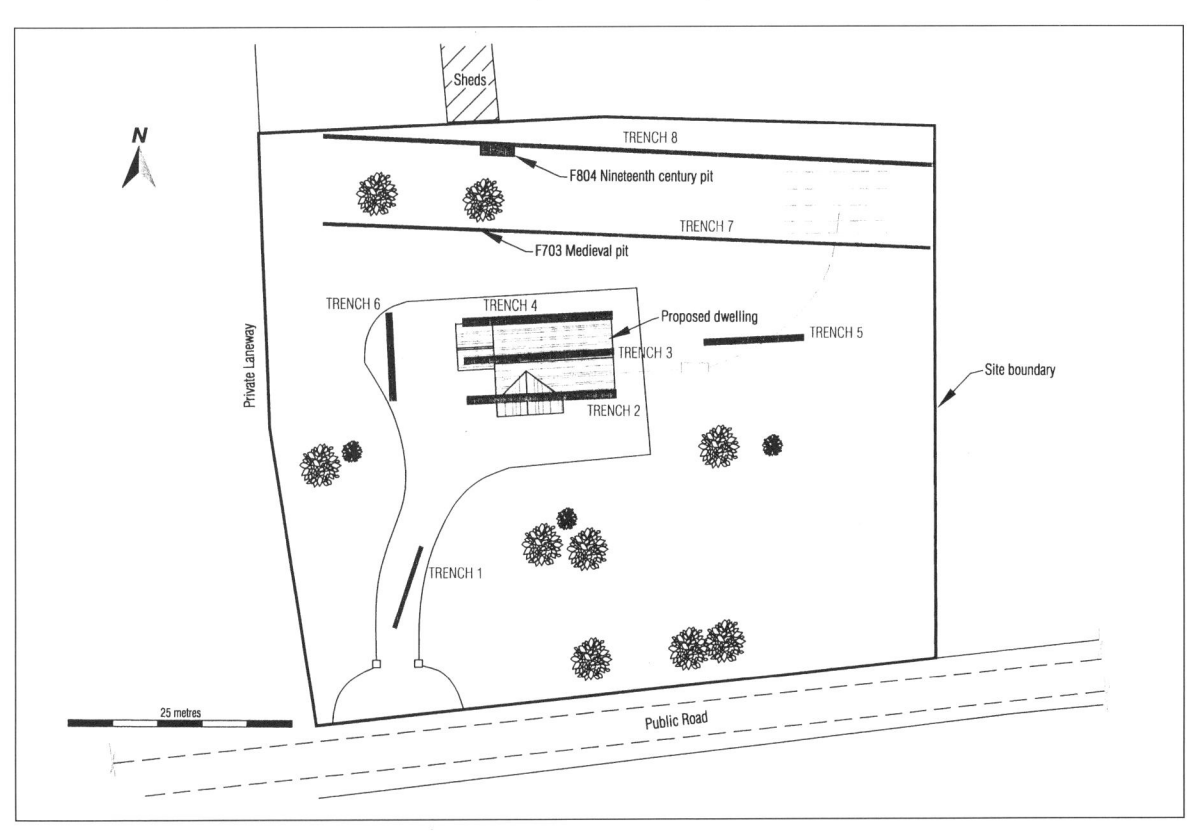

Location of test-trenches at Glascarrig North.

### 883. MAYGLASS
Post-medieval house
T0312
98E0587

A clay-walled vernacular farmstead at Pollwitch, Mayglass, Co. Wexford, is being conserved under funding from the Heritage Council. Most of the buildings on the site pre-date the 1840 Ordnance Survey maps, and the main dwelling-house dates to c. 1700 (O'Reilly et al. 1997). In late 1998 a temporary protective structure was erected over the building. The work was monitored by Cathy Sheehan (Excavations 1998, 217).

The licence was transferred to the writer, to cover excavation beside the north-east gable of the house. It was believed that the house was originally longer at this side. The excavation uncovered evidence of a clay foundation on the line of the south-east wall and a clay-and-post foundation parallel to the existing north-east wall. These were interpreted as the remains of the original walls of the house and served to extend it to the north-east by a maximum of 4m.

*Reference*
O'Reilly, B., Mac Cárthaigh, C. and Ní Fhloinn, B. 1997 *Preliminary report on the survey of an important vernacular farmyard at Pollwitch, Mayglass, Co. Wexford.*

*Joanna Wren, The Mile Post, Waterford.*

### 884. IRISHTOWN, NEW ROSS
Pits
98E0565

Archaeological monitoring of the housing development is now complete (see *Excavations 1998*, 225, for summary of 1998 season). The site borders the zone of archaeological potential for New Ross as identified in the Urban Archaeological Survey. It is adjacent to St Stephen's Cemetery, which may be an early ecclesiastical enclosure.

Monitoring of access roadways, services, topsoil removal and the excavation of the foundations for the townhouses took place.

Two burnt pits below the level of the topsoil were identified during the excavation of the foundation trenches. The first pit, at the south-western quadrant of the site, was subrectangular and measured 1.1m (east–west) by 1.5m. The second pit, at the northern side of the site, was partially removed by the mechanical excavation of the foundation trench. The remaining portion was 0.65m long (east–west). No archaeological strata were associated with either of these isolated pits.

The archaeological monitoring at this site is now complete.
*E. Eoin Sullivan, 39 Trees Road, Mount Merrion, Co. Dublin.*

### 885. MARSHMEADOWS, NEW ROSS
Possible standing stone
27100 12590
99E0276

An assessment of a possible standing stone at Marshmeadows, New Ross, was carried out following the identification of three possible stones during a survey in connection with the proposed River Barrow Training and Dredging Works. Because only one of the stones was to be affected by the stripping of the area before the deposition of dredging material, a single cutting was opened in the vicinity of the third standing stone.

An area measuring 5m by 3.5m was opened, and a compacted layer of mortar and red brick was evident directly below the topsoil. The natural, sterile marl was uncovered below this at a depth of 0.3m, cut by the standing stone. The backfill was found to contain sherds of white-glazed earthenware, glass bottles, mortar and red brick fragments. It was clear, therefore, that the stone was probably inserted sometime in the 19th or 20th century, as a scratching post for cattle, and is not of archaeological significance.
*Donald Murphy, Archaeological Consultancy Services Ltd, 15 Trinity Street, Drogheda, Co. Louth.*

### 886. MILLBANKS, ROSBERCON, NEW ROSS
Adjacent to medieval suburb
268580 127700
99E0209

Assessment of a 38-house residential development at Millbanks included the excavation of eighteen test-trenches in the area of the development. No archaeological materials were found.
*Cóilín Ó Drisceoil, 6 Riverview, Ardnore, Kilkenny, for Mary Henry & Associates.*

### 887. ROSSLARE HARBOUR INTERIM DRAINAGE SCHEME
Monitoring/testing
99E0429

Assessment took place along the proposed route of the upgraded sewer network. A total of 61 trial-pits, 30 slit-trenches and 10 boreholes were dug by the contracting geotechnical engineers at various points along the proposed route.

Nothing of archaeological significance was found in any of these areas, and subsequent archaeological test-trenching was undertaken, both at the site of the proposed treatment works and at a low mound in the same field that had already produced waste flint/chert in the initial walk-over assessment. Four test-trenches were opened in all, with one at the treatment works site producing a single struck flint flake, and the one on the mound producing a single sherd of medieval green-glazed pottery. During reinstatement a damaged stone axe was recovered from the topsoil adjacent to the trench on the mound.

Further investigation and/or excavation was therefore recommended.
*Stuart D. Elder for Eachtra Archaeological Projects, Clover Hill, Mallow, Co. Cork.*

### 888. TAGHMON
Ditch features
291857 119649
98E0483 ext.

Archaeological excavation and monitoring were conducted at a site in Taghmon, Co. Wexford, intermittently between December 1998 and December 1999. Testing had previously revealed the presence of archaeological features, at least one of which appeared to represent a ditch (*Excavations*

*1998*, 217–18*)*. As a result, a monitoring requirement was incorporated within the grant of planning. Groundworks commenced in December 1998, and shortly afterwards a pattern emerged that indicated the presence of two large, parallel ditch features running from north-west to south-east through the northern end of the site (Ditches 1 and 2). Other linear features, which did not appear to form part of any comprehensible pattern, were found in the area of these two large ditches.

Continued monitoring in early 1999 revealed further ditch features along the western side of the site (Ditches 4 and 5). These were smaller than Ditches 1 and 2, and Ditch 4 formed a clear-cut arc of *c.* 10m diameter, curving from north-east to south-east. Further south on the western side of the site another, smaller ditch (Ditch 5) ran from the north-west to the south-east. Along the southern side of the site the ditch features that had been characteristic of other parts of the site were virtually absent, and instead the evidence indicated a cluster of more discrete features, mainly pits.

All evidence appeared to suggest that the most sensitive areas of the site were in the north and north-west. Accordingly, an agreement was reached with the developer that the north-west corner would be reserved for open-plan excavation before development. Open-plan excavation of an area measuring 27m north to south by 16m was carried out in August 1999. This revealed another large ditch feature (Ditch 3) running from north-west to south-east. This ditch ran parallel to Ditches 1 and 2 and was of similar proportions; all three were of approximately equal distance apart. A length of this ditch measuring 26m was uncovered, and a slight curve to its line could be discerned over this distance. This ditch lay amidst several smaller and separate ditches, and there were three well-defined points of convergence between Ditch 3 and the other ditches, where it could be unequivocally demonstrated that Ditch 3 was the latest feature.

The branching network of ditches uncovered in the open-plan excavation helped to place in context the more incongruous linear features identified in and around Ditches 1 and 2. Although the three large ditches were originally interpreted as contemporary and related features, the radiocarbon and pottery results indicate a 1st–5th century date for Ditch 1 and a 12th–15th century date for Ditch 3 and possibly Ditch 2.

Further large ditches were transected by service trenches to the south of Ditches 1 and 2. It is likely that some of these represent continuations of Ditches 1 and 2, although this could not be demonstrated. Most of these are aligned in the opposite direction to Ditches 1 and 2 and thus argue strongly in favour of a south-west return to the previously noted south-east line of these ditches. No evidence of the continuation of these ditches was found along the western side of the site, precluding the possibility of a full circular enclosure.

Only one apparent linear feature was recorded along the southern side of the site, and the principal archaeological feature here was of the discrete variety. Many of these features produced ceramic evidence consistent with the medieval date of the large ditches. One feature found in this part of the site was prominent by virtue of its size and associated features; this was a large pit, over 3m in diameter and *c.* 0.6m deep, with sides that were almost perfectly vertical and a flat, sloping base. This pit produced considerable quantities of charcoal, many pieces identifiable as small twigs and branches of hazel, as well as significant quantities of cremated bone. The concentration of charcoal and burnt bone from this pit was considerably greater than found anywhere else on the site. A small, funnel-shaped channel led from the western side of this feature, and a row of three stakeholes was identified a short distance from the pit's edge, on the same side. This may suggest some form of superstructure associated with this pit. This pit has been radiocarbon dated to AD 660 to 795 (95% probability).

There was much evidence of surface truncation of the archaeology on this site, while evidence of modern disturbance in the upper levels of the archaeology in the area of the open-plan excavation was also noted. The site had been partially developed in the 1970s, and this doubtlessly resulted in a considerable degree of disturbance. The entire eastern side of the site had been heavily disturbed well below the level of the natural, and it is impossible to determine whether the archaeological site originally extended into this area, but, given the distribution of archaeology within the site, it seems likely that at least some outlying activity occurred here.

The site at Taghmon seems to contain two distinct phases of activity. Evidence suggests that some of the smaller ditches in the north-west corner of the site, and possibly Ditch 1, date to the Iron Age/Early Christian period, while there is a 12th–15th-century date for Ditch 3, Ditch 2 and several of the discrete features. The later phase of activity seems to be the more predominant on the site, but the 7th/8th-century date for the large pit on the south side suggests that the earlier phase of use may also extend some distance. This chronology is borne out by the stratigraphic evidence where some of the smaller ditches of earlier date are cut by Ditch 3. While the occurrence of archaeological material of two distinct phases can only be viewed as coincidental, the parallel alignment and similarity of dimensions and fills between the large ditches, especially between Ditches 1 and 2, are very surprising in view of their disparate dates.

*Clare Mullins, 31 Millford, Athgarvan, Co. Kildare.*

### 889. THE SHAMBLES, CHURCH LANE, WEXFORD
Urban
305070 122200
99E0411

Archaeological assessment of alterations and an extension to a public house at the Shambles included the excavation of two test-trenches. No archaeological materials were found.
*Cóilín Ó Drisceoil, 6 Riverview, Ardnore, Kilkenny.*

### 890. THE FAYTHE, WEXFORD
No archaeological significance
SMR 37:32
96E0013

The proposed development was a continuation of

site works that commenced in January of 1996 at No. 13 The Faythe, in the townland of Townparks, Wexford. As The Faythe is within the zone of archaeological importance for the town of Wexford, the site was tested under licence in accordance with the planning directive. In 1996 a total of sixteen pits were opened, which revealed no indications of archaeological material within the area designated for the new buildings.

The street frontage was unavailable for testing in 1996 because of the presence of standing buildings. Consequently, in January 1999, an extension to the licence was obtained to monitor the excavation of service trenches. In addition to the service trenches, the excavation of foundation trenches for a boundary wall constructed at the western extent of the site was monitored.

Monitoring of the service and construction trenches revealed a naturally deposited sand horizon overlain by modern infill. There were no indications of archaeologically significant material.
*Cathy Sheehan, Hillview, Aglish, Carrigeen, Kilkenny.*

### 891. PAUL QUAY/CRESCENT QUAY, WEXFORD
Urban
P051218
99E0621

Monitoring of five shell and auger boreholes and of the excavation of four engineering test-pits took place on a site at Paul Quay/Crescent Quay, Wexford. The site is subject to a planning application for development to Wexford Corporation.

No archaeological deposits were recorded during this monitoring; however, it became evident that there was a high water-table and a high degree of oil/fuel contamination of the site. It was recommended that any future archaeological investigations on the site take into account the problems that the high water-table and the heavy oil contamination will pose in the identification and recording of archaeological deposits and features.
*Tim Coughlan, Margaret Gowen & Co. Ltd, 2 Killiney View, Albert Road Lower, Glenageary, Co. Dublin.*

## WICKLOW

### 892. BALLYMAGHROE
Adjacent to ecclesiastical enclosure
32175 19784
SMR 25:01/4
99E0302

Test-trenching was undertaken at a house site as part of the requirements of Wicklow County Council for granting planning permission for construction of a dwelling. The site is beside an ecclesiastical enclosure that contains the ruins of a church and 18th-century graveyard at Ballymaghroe, Ashford, Co. Wicklow.

The ground slopes gradually down to the southern end of the site, where the proposed house is to be built. A tracking machine with a 2m-wide flat bucket was used to strip the soil to a depth of 0.2m for half the width and for the full length of the driveway, west of the graveyard. A new entrance driveway to an existing house north of the graveyard

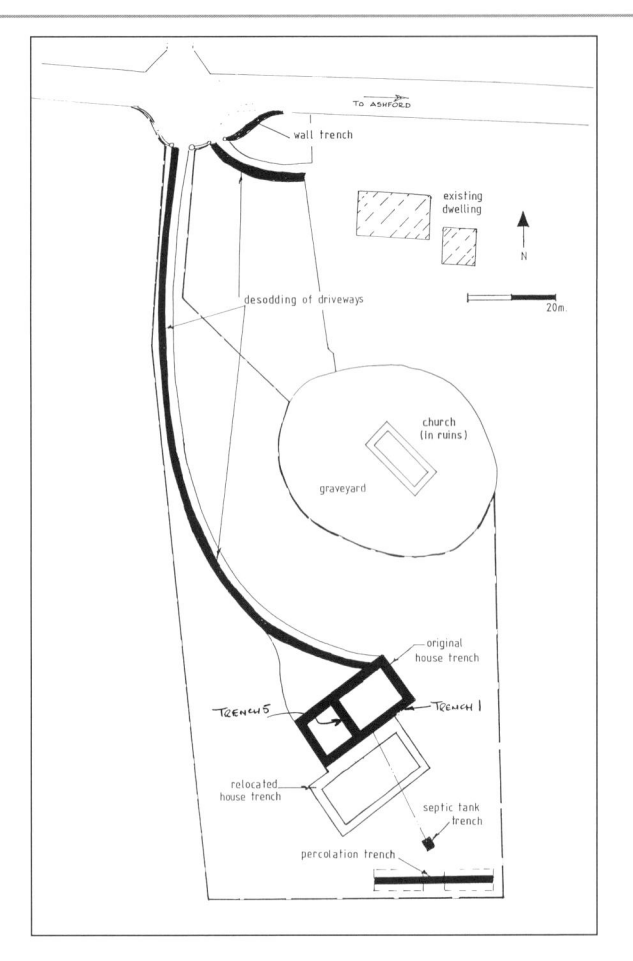

Site plan of Ballymaghroe.

was similarly de-sodded, and a wall trench was dug to accommodate a wider entrance.

Test-trenching was carried out around the original location of the proposed house, in the percolation area and on the site of the septic tank. Trenches were dug to the depth of the undistributed subsoil where the outside-wall trenches were to be dug. The south-east trench (1) revealed a 4m-long, 0.2m-deep layer of charcoal-rich soil below the topsoil, which contained evidence of ironworking. The feature extended northward (Trench 5) to cover an area of at least 4m diameter. A second, similar feature was exposed to the north of this area.

It was agreed with the owner that a parallel set of house trenches be tested 15m south of the original position in order to avoid the necessity to excavate the feature.

No other archaeological features were recorded.
*Frank Ryan for Mary Henry & Associates, 1 Jervis Place, Clonmel, Co. Tipperary.*

### 893. MILL STREET, BALTINGLASS
Estate town
290178 188932
SMR 27:24
99E0319

An archaeological evaluation was undertaken at a proposed development site at Mill Street, Baltinglass, Co. Wicklow, on 3 July 1999. The work was carried out in compliance with a request from *Dúchas* The Heritage Service. The site is within the boundaries of the area of archaeological potential for Baltinglass, a 17th-century estate town that was made a borough in 1663, and to the immediate east of the site of a medieval parish church.

Five trial-trenches were mechanically excavated. No features, structures or finds of archaeological interest were uncovered.
*Martin E. Byrne, 31 Millford, Athgarvan, Co. Kildare.*

### 894. BURGAGE MORE
Environs of earthwork site
29734 21321
SMR 5:46
99E0301

Monitoring of ground reductions associated with a link road between two phases of a housing development and related partial field boundary clearance was undertaken on 26 June 1999. The monitoring was carried out in the environs of a possible archaeological site described as an 'earthwork (site)' in the *Register of Recorded Monuments and Places for County Wicklow*. The site had originally been the subject of an assessment by Valerie Keeley Ltd and was subsequently evaluated by Carmel Duffy (*Excavations 1996*, 115, 96E0122).

The results of the monitoring were similar to those of the evaluation in that no features, deposits or finds of archaeological interest were uncovered during the work.
*Martin E. Byrne, 31 Millford, Athgarvan, Co. Kildare.*

### 895. WICKLOW ARMS PUBLIC HOUSE, DELGANY
Adjacent to medieval graveyard
3277 2108
SMR 13:004001
99E0231

Testing was undertaken on the above site on behalf of Mandalay Services Ltd, who propose to extend and refurbish the existing premises. The objective was to determine whether there were any surviving features or deposits associated with the adjacent graveyard.

This site has undergone several periods of renovation and reconstruction with the demolition of previous buildings. This was further reflected in the stratigraphy, with disturbed layers evident in each cutting. As no archaeological deposits or features were recovered within the areas tested, the site may therefore be considered as being archaeologically resolved.
*Rónán Swan, Arch-Tech Ltd, 32 Fitzwilliam Place, Dublin 2.*

### 896. DUNBUR LOWER
Monitoring
T333927
99E0748

Monitoring before construction of a housing scheme commenced in November 1999. The development will result in the construction of 32 houses with services, access roadways and associated landscaping.

The site is *c.* 2km south of Wicklow town and *c.* 1km west from the coast. Before development the site consisted of a green field comprising a series of raised, shale bedrock outcrops linked by a number of reasonably level terraces. This field had an area of 4.5ha.

Little is known about the townland of Dunbur Lower. Price cites a reference to 'Dunborr' from 1627 and to 'Dunbar' from a coastal chart of *c.* 1700. In relation to the placename, O'Donovan considered '*Dún báirr*, fort of the top' as a likely basis for the modern placename 'Dunbur' (Price 1967, 434).

Where the soil was stripped, stratigraphy was found to consist of a sod layer underlain by 0.3–0.4m of reddish-brown topsoil containing occasional angular pieces of shale. Natural subsoil was found to be made up of a loosely compact, reddish-brown, sandy clay with shale fragments. Natural shale bedrock outcropped through this subsoil. In approximately 40–50% of the area stripped for the access roads, natural bedrock occurred directly under the sod.

Features revealed during monitoring included a field drain in the north of the site, traces of a levelled field boundary in the centre of the site and a small, undated hearth toward the east. A disused road surface serving an adjoining property was uncovered in the east of the site. This had been used within living memory.

Further monitoring of topsoil removal in 2000 is envisaged.

*Reference*
Price, L. 1967 *Place-names of Co. Wicklow. VII—the baronies of Newcastle and Arklow*. Dublin.

*Ian W. Doyle, Margaret Gowen & Co. Ltd, 2 Killiney View, Albert Road Lower, Glenageary, Co. Dublin.*

### 897. MARKET SQUARE, DUNLAVIN
Urban medieval
28777138 201662
98E0547 ext.

The development of additional holiday homes at the site required that archaeological testing be carried out. This was undertaken by Clare Mullins (*Excavations 1998*, 221*)*, who recommended the monitoring of foundation excavations. This was carried out by the writer in December 1998 (*Excavations 1998*, 221) and January 1999. One additional feature was identified during the latter period of monitoring. This was the remains of a 19th-century wall foundation, associated with the return of an extant wall that forms part of the southern boundary of the site. This feature had previously been identified during initial testing. No further features or finds of interest were revealed.
*Martin E. Byrne, 31 Millford, Athgarvan, Co. Kildare.*

### 898. KILMACURRAGH
No archaeological significance
T323176
99E0211

Testing consisted of the machine-excavation of four test-trenches at this site. There had been a suggestion that the house was built on the site of an early burial-ground or church; however, no evidence was found for either.
*Martin Reid, 37 Errigal Road, Drimnagh, Dublin 12, for ADS Ltd.*

### 899. CARYSFORT, MACREDDIN
Historic town
SMR: 34:9
99E0150

The site is in Macreddin West townland, 3km north

of Aughrim village, and is within the southern precinct of the historic town of Carysfort, established as a borough by Charles II in 1628 as part of the wider Plantation of Wicklow and developed as a garrison town. The townland name appears to comprise two elements, the first derived from *Magh* meaning 'the plain', reflecting local topography, followed by a personal name, possibly Cridan (or Credan), found associated with several holy men.

The proposed development area is within a green-field site bounded to the south by a stream and Macreddin Bridge, with the Aughrim Road (east), pasture (west) and an enclosed graveyard (north-west) surrounding the site. The north-east area of the site is occupied by a series of farm buildings, which will ultimately form part of the proposed development. The site lies on ground that slopes gently from north-east to south-west, with a marked hollow towards the south-west corner.

Monitoring of four engineering test-pits was undertaken at the site on 12 March 1999 before the archaeological assessment. No archaeological deposits, features or artefacts were uncovered.

The excavation of four assessment trenches did not reveal any soils, features or finds of archaeological significance. Trench 1 was positioned towards the south-east corner of the proposed development area; Trench 2 was excavated perpendicular to the north end of the Trench 1; Trench 3 was excavated further north-west; and Trench 4 was excavated towards the southern end of the development area.

Trench 1 (2m by 60m), aligned north-east/south-west and excavated within the south-east corner of the site, revealed dark brown topsoil 0.2–0.4m deep over orange/brown, sandy clay containing some stone, 0.4m deep, with interrupted spreads of grey, sandy clay, blue/grey clay and yellow boulder clay. A linear feature comprising a deposit of blue/grey clay 0.5m wide was noted in the basal orange/brown clay at a depth of 0.4m. The feature lies almost exactly on the line of a field boundary depicted on the second edition OS map of 1886 and is possibly the remains of an associated field drain.

Trench 2 (2m by 30m), aligned north-west/south-east and lying perpendicular to the northern end of Trench 1, revealed dark brown topsoil 0.4m deep, containing occasional fragments of natural quartz. This overlay orange/brown, sandy clay containing occasional stones.

Trench 3 (2m by 15m), aligned north-west/south-east, was excavated 20m to the north-west of Trench 2. Dark brown topsoil 0.4m deep overlay orange/brown, sandy clay containing occasional stones.

Trench 4 (2m by 30m), aligned west–east, was excavated close to the southern end of the proposed development site, 13m south-west of Trench 1. Dark brown topsoil 0.3m deep overlay a deposit of blue/grey, sandy clay containing occasional stones.

The excavation of the test-trenches to an average depth of 0.5m did not reveal features or deposits of archaeological significance. The feature recorded in Trench 1 represents the remains of a now-removed field boundary depicted on the 1886 OS map. Several fragments of unworked quartz were discovered in Trench 2.

Monitoring of topsoil removal from the field on the eastern side of the Aughrim road in connection with the proposed development did not reveal any features or deposits of archaeological potential; however, a scatter of 18th-century ceramics was uncovered, possibly deposited during manuring.
*Malachy Conway for Margaret Gowen & Co. Ltd, 2 Killiney View, Albert Road Lower, Glenageary, Co. Dublin.*

### 900. N11 NEWTOWNMOUNTKENNEDY/ BALLYNABARNEY ROAD IMPROVEMENT SCHEME
Flint scatters
**99E0684**

It is proposed to partially align the existing N11 and to construct a new road from Newtownmountkennedy (south of Killadreen td—OS 19) to Ballynabarney (OS 25). The area is characterised by the hilly ground of the foothills of the Wicklow Mountains on the western side and more gently rolling ground declining towards the sea to the east. The environmental impact statement prepared in relation to the proposed scheme identified a number of sites of archaeological interest within and in the immediate environs of the proposed route. It is suggested that many of these sites are possible *fulachta fiadh*. One of the recommended mitigation strategies in relation to the scheme was the archaeological monitoring of the excavation of trial-pits for engineering/geotechnical purposes. This work commenced on 1 November 1999.

Up to 220 trial-pit excavations, six of which revealed material of archaeological potential, mostly in the form of burnt material, were inspected up to 14 December 1999. In addition 27 flint pieces were recovered from fifteen additional trial-pits. Analysis of the flint by Nyree Finlay (pers. comm.) revealed that almost half of these pieces were considered to be natural pebbles or chunks. However, a number were identified as struck or potentially struck artefacts, as a result of either human or natural processes. Flint scatters have previously been identified in County Wicklow, in the *Archaeological inventory of County Wicklow* (Grogan, E. and Kilfeather, A. 1997). In addition an extensive lithic assemblage was recovered at Johnstown South by Martin Fitzpatrick (*Excavations 1996*, 116, 96E0156) during archaeological investigations undertaken as part of the Arklow Bypass.

Additional monitoring will be undertaken in January 2000, following which appropriate additional mitigation strategies will be suggested.
*Martin E. Byrne, 31 Millford, Athgarvan, Co. Kildare.*

### 901. 'THE CHESTNUTS', CHURCH HILL, WICKLOW
Adjacent to medieval church
**331344 194029**
**99E0425**

The site is on the summit of Church Hill and adjacent to St Thomas's Church of Ireland parish church, which stands on the site of the medieval parish church. It is south of the 'Round Mount'; this monument may be an Anglo-Norman motte or a Hiberno-Norse or earlier burial mound. It is within the zone of archaeological potential of Wicklow town. The site is currently a garden. This excavation took place in response to a condition in the grant of planning permission for a dormer bungalow.

Excavations of three trenches by mechanical digger revealed no archaeological features or remains. In each of the trenches sod and topsoil were found to overlie undisturbed, natural subsoil at an average depth of 0.35m. No further archaeological work is required on this site before development.
*James Eogan, ADS Ltd, Windsor House, 11 Fairview Strand, Dublin 3.*

### 902. 1 CHURCH STREET, WICKLOW
Urban
**T313940**
**99E0365**

Two test-trenches were excavated at the rear of 1 Church Street, Wicklow, before the construction of an extension. Several fragments of medieval pottery were recovered in a deposit that also contained 18th-century wares; however, there was no evidence for *in situ* archaeological deposits.
*Martin Reid, 37 Errigal Road, Drimnagh, Dublin 12, for ADS Ltd.*

### 903. CHURCH STREET/WENTWORTH PLACE, WICKLOW
Urban
**98E0431**

The development site is at the corner of Church Street and Wentworth Place, Wicklow, and within the zone of archaeological potential of the town. Recent excavations in an adjoining property by James Eogan (*Excavations 1997*, 202, 97E0118) identified a series of medieval pits and two shallow ditches.

Trenching was carried out by Una Cosgrave and involved the mechanical excavation of two trenches (*Excavations 1998*, 223). Limited archaeological deposits consisting of light brown, fine, sandy clay with occasional charcoal flecking were recorded. No datable material was recovered from this layer.

*Dúchas* The Heritage Service recommended archaeological monitoring of all further subsurface works. This was carried out on 15 and 16 January 1999 and revealed the same formation processes of modern rubble and gravels sealing rubble layers containing red brick as identified in the test-trenching programme. The light brown, fine, sandy clay with occasional charcoal flecking was revealed in the north-eastern corner of the site. However, as excavation for foundation trenches proceeded only to a depth of *c.* 0.65m in this area, only the top 50mm of this layer was exposed. As this layer was only revealed in a 1m-long east–west foundation trench, it was not possible to define fully its extent, character and condition. There would be no further disturbance caused to this layer by the development. No datable material was recovered from this layer. No further archaeological features or finds were revealed.
*Dermot Nelis, IAC Ltd, 8 Dungar Terrace, Dun Laoghaire, Co. Dublin, for ADS Ltd.*

# ADDENDA

## LOUTH

### AD1. DUNDALK STREET, CARLINGFORD
No archaeological significance
31885 31163
99E0066

Archaeological assessment of an extension to a shop situated within a zone of archaeological importance included the mechanical excavation of test-trenches in the area of the development. No archaeological materials were found.

*Cóilín Ó Drisceoil, 6 Riverview, Ardnore, Kilkenny, for Archaeological Consultancy Services Ltd.*

### AD2. NEWTOWNBALREGAN, CASTLETOWN
No archaeological significance
30294 30785
99E0015

Archaeological assessment of a housing development adjacent to two recorded monuments, Dun Dealgan motte (SMR 7:28) and a souterrain (SMR 7:25), included the mechanical excavation of eighteen test-trenches in the area of the development. No archaeological materials were found.

*Cóilín Ó Drisceoil, 6 Riverview, Ardnore, Kilkenny, for Archaeological Consultancy Services Ltd.*

### AD3. 74 TRINITY STREET, DROGHEDA
No archaeological significance
30837 27537
99E0007

Archaeological assessment of a residential development within a zone of archaeological importance included the mechanical excavation of test-trenches in the area of the development. No archaeological materials were found.

*Cóilín Ó Drisceoil, 6 Riverview, Ardnore, Kilkenny, for Archaeological Consultancy Services Ltd.*

## WEXFORD

### AD4. KILCARBRY, ENNISCORTHY
No archaeological significance
29719 13638
99E0707

Archaeological assessment of a residential development adjacent to a church site included the mechanical excavation of ten test-trenches in the area of the development. No archaeological materials were found.

*Cóilín Ó Drisceoil, 6 Riverview, Ardnore, Kilkenny.*

# APPENDIX 1

## FIELDWALKING AT ROBSWALLS, MALAHIDE, CO. DUBLIN
O244454

Fieldwalking was requested on this site before its redevelopment as premises for a local football club. It is within 200m of a large flint scatter at Paddy's Hill previously excavated by Keeling and Keeley (D. Keeling and V. Keeley, 1994 'Excavation of a flint scatter on Paddy's Hill, Malahide, County Dublin', *PRIA* 94C (1994)).

The development site has been ploughed for some years and was ploughed several weeks before fieldwalking began. It was then systematically fieldwalked, and worked flint was retrieved. A total of 55 pieces of worked flint were collected from the ploughsoil. Of these, 27 were modified tools including nineteen scrapers, six modified flakes and two blades. The remaining objects recovered included unmodified flakes and debitage. Many of the objects retrieved were heavily patinated and weathered.

The find spot of each object was plotted on a distribution map to see whether concentrations of objects were apparent. The results showed that the objects were scattered over the entire area. On the lower ground to the north of the development there was a slightly denser spread of objects than on the upper ground to the south. However, this pattern may relate to the direction of ploughing and the fall of ground. Although a considerable volume of objects was recovered, no particular area of intensive activity could be pinpointed on the basis of the fieldwalking. Further work is to be undertaken in tandem with development.

*Avril Purcell, Margaret Gowen & Co. Ltd, 2 Killiney View, Albert Road Lower, Glenageary, Co. Dublin.*

# APPENDIX 2

## THE LOUGH MASK REGIONAL WATER SUPPLY SCHEME, STAGE II, CONTRACT 6, BALLINROBE–CLAREMORRIS–BALLINDINE
Prehistoric
94E0017 ext.

Archaeological monitoring and excavation on the Lough Mask Regional Water Supply Scheme, Stage II, Contract 6, commenced in December 1994 and were completed in September 1995. Following monitoring of topsoil removal, six areas produced features and/or small finds of archaeological importance.

The archaeological licence issued for this scheme, 94E017, was an extension to that issued for the Ballinrobe Sewerage and Sewage Disposal Scheme (*Excavations 1994*, 66–8).

*Site No. 40—fulacht fiadh, Friarsquarter East*
Following topsoil removal, an area of charcoal-enriched soil and fragments of heat-shattered sandstones was exposed in Friarsquarter East townland. The burnt material was very shallow, only c. 0.05m thick. No features or small finds were recovered from the site.

*Site No. 41—fulacht fiadh, Cloonnagashel*
Following topsoil removal, an area of charcoal-enriched soil and fragments of heat-shattered sandstones measuring 1m x 1.5m was exposed in Cloonnagashel townland. The burnt material was very shallow, only 0.03m thick. No features or small finds were recovered from the site.

*Site No. 42—fulacht fiadh, Clareen*
Following topsoil removal, an area of charcoal-enriched soil and fragments of heat-shattered sandstones measuring 5m x 4m was exposed on the northern side of the wayleave in the townland of Clareen. The burnt material, which was only 0.05m thick, produced 150 fragments of animal bone, all of which were cattle. One long bone fragment, a femur, had been cut, and this provided the only example of butchery from the site. Seven of the eleven epiphyses were fused, suggesting an animal older than 2½ years.

*Site No. 43—fulacht fiadh, Pollaweela*
Following topsoil removal, an area of charcoal-enriched soil and fragments of heat-shattered sandstones measuring 2m x 1.5m was exposed in Pollaweela townland. The burnt material was only 0.04m thick. No features or small finds of archaeological importance were recovered from the site.

*Site No. 44—stone scatter, Clare*
During topsoil removal a small number of chert flakes were recovered in the townland of Clare.

*Site No. 45—Bronze Age settlement site, Leedaun*
Two areas, c. 30m apart, produced evidence of Bronze Age activity.

The earliest evidence for human activity in Area I was represented by five ditches that cut into the natural subsoil. While these may be isolated features, it is likely that they represent a number of parallel ditches that ran north-west/south-east across the site.

Overlying these ditches was a layer of redeposited natural soil. The main occupation levels were recorded overlying this redeposited natural and consisted of a general spread of grey, charcoal-enriched soil.

A radiocarbon date of 2121–1750 BC was received from this occupation layer. The occupation layer was bounded on one side by a wide, shallow, curved trench. A concentration of stake-holes, a hearth and a number of horizontal charcoal stains were found immediately to the south-west of this trench.

A total of 263 lithic artefacts were recovered from Area I. These were made predominantly from chert but also from black limestone, flint and quartz. They consisted of 110 flakes, six cores, five blades and nineteen retouched tools. Eleven of the retouched tools were scrapers. Seventy-nine animal bones were recovered. The collection was dominated by cattle bones, with pig and sheep poorly represented. Butchery was noted on cattle humerii only.

Area II, 30m north-east of Area I, also revealed some important archaeological features and small finds. The wayleave here partly truncated a levelled *fulacht fiadh*. This area was dominated by a series of criss-cross cultivation furrows. Some of these were of recent date, while the remainder were of unknown date. A radiocarbon date of 1606–1400 BC was obtained for a charcoal sample from this area.

A total of 267 lithic artefacts were recovered from Area II. The assemblage mirrored that from Area I, except that the retouched artefacts were somewhat different in that there were less scrapers and more robust flakes.

Ninety-six chert flakes, six cores, five blades and twelve retouched tools were recovered. The finding of a large flint flake and a polished mudstone axe, which are more reminiscent of a Neolithic tradition, was of note. Two single cattle teeth and two very fragmentary prehistoric pottery sherds were also recovered.

*Gerry Walsh, Mayo County Council, Castlebar, Co. Mayo.*

**Editor's note:** This report had not been published in the relevant *Excavations* bulletin, and Mr Walsh requested that this error now be put right.